D0505058

AS Level and A Level
Sociology

Andy Barnard, Terry Burgess
and Mike Kirby

CAMBRIDGE
UNIVERSITY PRESS

PUBLISHED BY THE PRESS SYNDICATE OF THE UNIVERSITY OF CAMBRIDGE
The Pitt Building, Trumpington Street, Cambridge, United Kingdom

CAMBRIDGE UNIVERSITY PRESS
The Edinburgh Building, Cambridge CB2 2RU, UK
40 West 20th Street, New York, NY 10011-4211, USA
477 Williamstown Road, Port Melbourne, VIC 3207, Australia
Ruiz de Alarcón 13, 28014 Madrid, Spain
Dock House, The Waterfront, Cape Town 8001, South Africa

http://www.cambridge.org

First published 2004

Printed in the United Kingdom at the University Press, Cambridge

Typefaces Meridien and Dax   *System* QuarkXPress®

A catalogue record for this book is available from the British Library

ISBN 0 521 53214 0 paperback

ANDY BARNARD

Midway through the writing of the first edition of this book, Andy was admitted to hospital. He died after a short illness in November 1993.

This book is for Linda, Natalie, Erika, Stefan and Daniel.

ACKNOWLEDGEMENTS

Terry Burgess would like to thank all those who have helped in the production of this book, particularly the staff at Cambridge University Press, and Christine, to whom he owes everything, including a few holidays.

The publishers are grateful to the following for permission to reproduce photographs:

AFP/CORBIS pp. 175, 225; Art Directors/Trip pp. 68, 228; Gerry Ball pp. 15, 17, 21; Bettman/CORBIS p. 36; Said Belloumi/CORBIS p. 52; Hulton Archive/GETTY IMAGES pp. 139, 164; Rob Lewine/CORBIS p. 167; PA Photos p. 197; Polak Matthew/CORBIS p. 276; Popperfoto.com p. 27; Vittoriano Rastelli/CORBIS p. 185; Reuters Popperfoto.com p. 246; Torleif Svensson/CORBIS p. 135; Nabeel Turner/GETTY IMAGES p. 173; Peter Turnley/CORBIS p. 26; Janine Wiedel p. 45.

Cover image by Digital Vision Ltd

We would like to thank the following for permission to use their material:

ANIMAL FARM by George Orwell (Copyright c George Orwell, 1945) by permission of Bill Hamilton as the Literary Executor of the Estate of the Late Sonia Brownell Orwell and Secker & Warburg Ltd p 17.

Figure 9.5 by permission of the University of Chicago Press; Table 8.1 reprinted with the permission of The Free Press, a Division of Simon & Schuster Adult Publishing Group, from *Social Theory and Social Structure* by Robert K. Merton, copyright 1949, 1957 by The Free Press, copyright renewed 1977, 1985 by Robert K. Merton, all rights reserved; Table 3.4 by permission of HarperCollins; Table 3.3 is reproduced by permission of Oxford University Press; Tables 3.6, 9.1, 9.2, 9.3, 9.5, 10.1, 11.1, 11.2 and Figure 9.7 by permission of Palgrave Macmillan; Table 11.5 by permission of Pearson Education; Tables 7.2, 9.6, 9.7, 9.8 by permission of the Policy Studies Institute; Table 5.1 by permission of Routledge.

All tables and figures from *Social Trends*, as well as tables 4.4., 5.3 and 9.12 and Figure 9.2, are Crown copyright and are reproduced with the permission of the Controller of HMSO and the Queen's Printer for Scotland.

Past examination questions are reproduced by permission of the University of Cambridge Local Examinations Syndicate.

Contents

4   Health, welfare and poverty

5   The family

6   Education

10 Mass media

11 Politics and power

1 The sociological perspective

Introduction

This chapter begins with a discussion of the origins of sociology, its key concepts and theories and its differences from and similarities with other social science subjects. The relationship between sociology and social policy is examined and this is followed by a discussion of whether sociology can and should be based on the methods of the natural sciences. The chapter continues with a review of the main sociological theories, including the functionalist, Marxist, interactionist, feminist and post-modernist perspectives. This is followed by a discussion of the concept of socialisation and the processes involved in the construction of social identities. The concepts of social order and social control are examined and the chapter concludes by considering what is meant by culture and subcultures.

The study of society

Sociology has been studied as an academic discipline for around 150 years. The factors that brought about industrialisation, **urbanisation** and the growth of the **nation-state** in the nineteenth century also provided the context in which the idea of studying society in a detailed and systematic way first gained acceptance. Auguste Comte (1798–1857) is credited with formulating the word 'sociology'. He derived it from 'socius' – a society (Latin) and 'logos' – knowledge, or word (Greek). Comte believed that sociology was to be the crowning glory of human studies – the 'Queen of the Sciences'. Although modern sociologists are rather more modest in their claims, there is still a sense that sociology is something special and quite different from other subjects.

A basic definition of sociology is: 'The systematic study of human society, dedicated to the understanding of social interaction as people form groups, communities and societies'. To say that sociology is a 'systematic study' implies that it is not 'just common sense', and is more than statements of the obvious. There is a great difference between being an observer of social life as it happens – everyone does that – and undertaking a systematic study based on sociological theories and methods. Sociology is an academic discipline, and as such it is bound by certain rules of evidence. Moreover, the sociologist tries to be **objective** and not let personal opinions and

prejudices influence his or her work. Sociologists seek to define terms precisely and to use appropriate methods of investigation. Most importantly, they are committed to looking beyond commonsense explanations and beyond 'the official view' in an effort to explain why things are as they are in a society and why they change.

Concepts and theories

Like the other social sciences – economics, politics, psychology and anthropology – sociology has its own theories, concepts and methods of investigating social behaviour. Sociologists do not simply collect 'facts' about social behaviour – crime rates, patterns of divorce, voting habits and so on. By themselves such items of information tell us little about how a society operates. They need to be interpreted to be of interest to the sociologist and this is where theory comes in. Theory provides a framework for fitting together the miscellany of facts with which sociologists are bombarded.

It is important to understand the nature of theories. Let's begin with concepts: these are general ideas such as **'authority'**, **'ethnicity'**, 'social **class'**, etc. Theories are concepts brought together in order to explain something. They set out to explain the relationship between one set of concepts or facts and another, e.g. theories have been put forward to explain the high rate of certain types of crime associated with young

working-class males. Much sociological research involves taking theoretical concepts and operationalising them or exposing them in such a way as to make them measurable.

Perspectives

When a number of similar theories are drawn together into a single approach, we term this a '**perspective**'. The main perspectives in sociology – **functionalist**, **Marxist**, **feminist**, interactionist, and **post-modernist** – are outlined later in the chapter. Quite simply a perspective is a way of looking at things that helps us to understand what is going on. We can liken a perspective to a pair of glasses: when we put them on, we see things more clearly. So we can put on our functionalist glasses (the perspective made up of various functionalist theories) to help us understand the **consensus** and harmony that we find in society. Alternatively, we can put on the conflict perspective to understand disharmony or strife. The interactionist perspective acts like a magnifying glass, enabling us to understand small-scale human interactions. Each perspective enables us to view society in a slightly different way. Likewise, the competing perspectives all have their relative strengths and weaknesses.

Methods of investigation

Sociologists employ a range of techniques to collect data. Data are necessary to verify theory. Sociology is **empirical** – it seeks to make statements about social behaviour that can be corroborated by evidence from the real world. It is the data which sociologists collect that provide such evidence.

As you will discover in the next chapter, different techniques of investigation produce different types of data. Generally speaking there are two types of data: **quantitative** and **qualitative**. Quantitative data are statistical in form and are generated by the survey technique. **Social surveys** are normally large-scale studies that obtain data by either structured **interviews** or **questionnaires**. Qualitative data are generated by a range of non-statistical techniques including open interviews and **participant observation**.

Sociological explanation

There are basically two branches of theory within sociology – *macro* and *micro*. Macro theories focus on society as a whole and aim at establishing the general characteristics of societies. The aim of **macro-**sociological theory** is to answer three basic questions about the nature of society:

→ How do societies hold together, or what is the basis of *order* in society?
→ What are the sources of *conflict* in society?
→ How do societies *change*?

There are two broad schools of macro theory: consensus and conflict, distinguishable by the different answers they give to these questions. In contemporary sociology **functionalism** is the main representative of the consensus school and **Marxism** of the conflict school.

Micro theories focus on the individuals who make up a society, rather than on the society itself. There are two main forms of **micro theory**: **symbolic interactionism** and **ethnomethodology**. Symbolic interactionism is concerned with the principles of face-to-face interaction. Unlike macro theory, which tends to view the individual as a product of his or her society and tries to show the various ways in which the behaviour of individuals is determined by the social structure of which they are a part, micro theory regards the social structure as something created by individuals as they interact in socially meaningful ways. Ethnomethodology is the study of how individuals experience and make sense of the society in which they live.

Sociology and the social sciences

The boundary line between sociology and the other social sciences is not a clear or permanent one. There is a substantial overlap in subject matter between many of the social sciences and several of them use similar methods. To help identify the points of similarity and difference with sociology, we will take a brief look at the other major social sciences – anthropology, psychology, political science and economics.

Social anthropology

Social anthropology and sociology can be said to have almost identical theoretical interests, since they both investigate social and cultural aspects of group behaviour. Additionally, social anthropologists believe human beings are fundamentally alike and share the same basic interests. They therefore study systems of beliefs, and examine the relations between beliefs, customs and institutions and actions.

However, there are two important differences between sociology and social anthropology. Sociologists concentrate more on social relationships than on **culture**, whereas the social anthropologist is very interested in ideas and beliefs (religious and symbolic) as well as social relationships. The other difference is that social anthropologists typically work in communities that are small scale, simpler technologically and less familiar socially and culturally. They have thus pursued an interest in total social systems, in which all of the members know each other, which is difficult to parallel in complex, large-scale societies.

Psychology

Some psychologists focus on biological processes in explaining human behaviour, while others place greater emphasis on environmental factors. This latter group clearly overlaps with sociologists in terms of fields of interest. Stanley Milgram (1992), for example, in his studies of **conformity** and obedience to authority, has developed many ideas of interest to sociologists, and it is at this point that the divide between the two disciplines becomes somewhat artificial.

Psychology has, however, adhered to a more scientific approach, seeing the laboratory experiment as the most effective means of investigation. By contrast, most sociologists see the laboratory as too isolated from reality to give an adequate description, explanation and prediction of everyday behaviour. Another difference between the two subjects arises from the fact that sociology is the study of the attitudes and behaviour of people as a result of the influences of groups and of the whole society. This emphasis on the communal dimension contrasts sharply with psychology, which is more concerned with studying individual characteristics and which tends to assume the important role of internal factors such as personality and **intelligence** that may be inherited from parents.

Political science

Political scientists are interested in the study of **power**, of authority, and of how we decide whether power is **legitimate** or illegitimate. Sometimes, therefore, they focus on the political institutions of national and local government and sometimes on other behaviour which indicates how political ideology affects what we do, for example the relationship between voting and social class. Questions on the origin and nature of power, explanations of voting behaviour and so on are clearly of interest to both political scientists and sociologists. Moreover, political scientists use many of the same methods of research – questionnaires, interviews, participant observation – that are available to

sociologists. In many ways, therefore, there is very little to separate the two disciplines. Indeed, political science could be seen as a branch of sociology, though the distinctive nature of its subject matter usually means that it is taught as a separate subject in universities. This emphasises the rather arbitrary divisions that are made between the social sciences.

Economics

Economics has been defined as the study of the twin factors of scarcity and choice in the satisfaction of human wants. It differs from sociology in its area of interest, the perspective through which the subject matter is viewed, and in its methodology. Economics is solely interested in one sphere of society, only taking into account others such as the political domain and education insofar as they affect economic activity. Sociology is much more widespread in its interests, examining the inter-relationships between all aspects of society.

This leads to the two disciplines having a different focus on a particular social phenomenon, e.g. a strike. Economists will be interested in the effects the strike might have on levels of demand and supply, unemployment and so on, while sociologists may also be concerned with the personal interactions leading up to the strike situation, its significance for family life, and its possible implications for the power structure of society. Economics has also developed more in the direction of being a science, with one whole body of theory, and the use and accumulation of statistics are seen as important. Sociology has less agreement on methodology, and many sociologists treat the use of statistics with a great deal of suspicion.

In a number of ways, however, these differences should not be exaggerated. There is an increasing realisation of the value of studies combining several techniques and approaches. The development of econometrics (the collection of evidence about economic trends) within economics has meant a greater emphasis on the empirical collection of information, a practice firmly embedded in the sociological tradition.

Sociology and social policy

Social policy refers to the actions that are taken by the government to maintain and improve the welfare of its citizens. It includes social security, health and welfare services, **State** pensions, housing, education, and crime and its treatment. Social policy aims to deal with what are defined as potential or actual social problems. Poverty and crime are both examples of social problems that have far-reaching consequences for the individuals concerned and for the society as a whole.

It is sometimes wrongly assumed that sociology is the study of social problems. This misconception arises from the idea that all sociologists are motivated in their work by a concern to find solutions to the various dilemmas and ills that beset society. It is true that social problems are part of what sociologists study. It is also the case that there are some sociologists who want to use sociology as a vehicle for changing society.

However, it is important to recognise that there is a distinction between sociological problems and social problems. A social problem is some aspect of social behaviour that gives rise to conflict in society and/or misery for particular individuals. Unemployment is a clear example of a social problem. However, sociologists do not confine their studies just to social problems. Rather, they are interested in studying any pattern of relationships in society that calls for an explanation. Any social phenomenon, be it 'nice' or 'nasty', that requires explanation is a sociological problem. Social problems (i.e. something identified as harmful to society and needing something doing about it) are merely one type of sociological problem. Thus, divorce is both a social problem and a sociological problem, whereas marriage (which sociologists also study) is a sociological problem only.

It is questionable whether there is a general consensus about what are the most important social problems, but the important questions for sociologists to consider are:

→ What is considered a social problem?
→ Why is it a social problem?
→ Who says it is a social problem?
→ Why is this issue being considered to the exclusion of others?
→ What are the policies proposed and who will benefit from them?

Subjective and objective elements

Social problems tend to have a subjective and an objective element, with interactionists emphasising the former while structuralists emphasise the latter. During the nineteenth and early twentieth centuries the origin of social problems was located in individuals. To some extent this perspective re-emerged in the 1980s. Individuals may experience a problem subjectively – it is their problem and they are suffering from it. It may cause anxiety, tension, stress or depression. Such subjective feelings may be caused by poverty or unemployment, for example. At the same time unemployment is an 'objective' reality in that it transcends the individual and has structural causes. Its solution lies in collective action and relatively large amounts of investment and spending.

The concept of a social problem is relative. What constitutes a social problem in one society may not be regarded as such in another. Poverty is an example of this. Even within a particular society social problems can be and often are viewed differently. For example, some groups in our society may regard immigration as a problem while others may regard **racism** as a problem.

Voluntary and involuntary problems

Some social problems are 'voluntary', for example divorce and vandalism. Other social problems are 'involuntary' such as being elderly or being a member of a minority group. This distinction between the voluntary and the involuntary may be criticised as many social problems are a mixture of the two. Behaviour is patterned, follows social trends and is influenced by structural forces. To what extent therefore is divorce or unemployment voluntary? Equally it is not so much the involuntary growing old or being a member of a minority group that matters so much as society's 'voluntary' attitudes and response to these phenomena.

Power

It is important to discover where the power lies in the process of identifying and dealing with social problems. This emphasis on power is made largely by Marxists but is accepted by interactionists. The role of the media in developing our 'awareness' of certain social problems to the exclusion of others should not be underestimated and has been highlighted in the work of the Glasgow Media Group, Stan Cohen's work on mods and rockers (1972) and others (see chapter 8).

The poorest in our society and those **marginalised** within it have great difficulty in getting their definitions of the situation accepted by the wider society and the **agenda setters**. This could be due to lack of economic resources or to ideological subjugation and exclusion from the media and seats of power.

Social policies

The existence of social problems suggests that not all members of society are equal beneficiaries of its wealth and institutions. Some may be regarded as victims of society or trouble-makers within it. What may be at stake is a conflict of **ideologies** and interests. In the formulation of social policy there are many possible means to achieve a given end. The means chosen depend largely on the ideology of those with the power to determine social policy. In order to reduce poverty, some policies (particularly those on the left) advocate a redistribution of **wealth**, a minimum wage and a minimum income. Others argue that in order to reduce poverty we must encourage economic growth; this may lead to increasing inequality but the wealth will trickle down and everyone will benefit. Social policies may have unintended side effects: some right-wingers argue that a minimum wage will have the unintended effect of increasing unemployment and poverty by increasing industry's costs. On the other hand, increasing wealth and income at the top may result in lower productivity due to a lack of incentive to work. It may also result in the creation of an **underclass** with no vested interest in the social and economic system and which therefore poses a threat to social stability.

The list of questions and policy options is endless. Consider the following:

→ Is crime best reduced by 'short sharp shocks' or by the creation of more alternatives to custody schemes?

→ Do we need more police in patrol cars or more police walking the street?

→ Are the interests of the elderly or mentally ill best served by the process of deinstitutionalisation? There is much evidence, for example, that such a process places a great burden on the family and particularly women in the family. This may be regarded as an unintentional consequence or it may be regarded as the result of **patriarchal** attitudes by those in positions to make decisions. It is also necessary to note that the process of deinstitutionalisation – community care – arose due to economic pressure on the **Welfare State** and the problems associated with institutions.

→ Should welfare be provided by the State or by the private sector?

→ Should welfare benefits be universal or should they be targeted at those who most need them?

Historical development

The relationship between sociology and social policy is not particularly clear from a reading of the writers who laid the foundations of sociological thought. For Auguste Comte, sociology was the new religion, the scientific humanism that would unravel the laws of human society and lead to rational social planning. Yet Comte's sociology was profoundly **conservative** in nature and advocated a 'wise resignation to the facts'. Such social facts were not open to reason. Comte's sociology was therefore unlikely to give rise to a social policy that played a radical or reforming role, despite his wish that sociology should influence rational social planning.

Some sociologists of the late nineteenth century and early twentieth century, such as Rowntree and Booth, adopted a much more empirical approach in their sociological investigation of a particular social problem. Even here, though, the relationship between sociology and social policy is quite crude – the main method employed by these sociologists in their demonstration of poverty at the turn of the century in England was that of the exposé.

Importantly, the period 1930–1960 is marked by the increasing attempt by sociology to be accepted as a discipline into the academic world. As part of this (largely successful) process the scientific nature of the discipline was stressed. This included a need to detach the subject from its perceived link with the identification of social problems and consequent social reform.

There is a great deal of controversy within sociology as to whether sociologists should have any direct input into the study of particular social problems or should be involved in espousing particular social policies. This is due to the desire on the part of some sociologists to produce value-free sociology and themselves remain neutral. Such a desire is linked to conceptions of what constitutes science and indeed what constitutes social science or sociology. It is also linked to a desire to be accepted into the academic establishment, to secure adequate funding and to get one's research actually used.

Weber

Writing in the early part of this century, Max Weber (1904–5) was at pains to clarify the role of sociology in social research. He makes a clear distinction between research and researcher when he states that 'To apply the results of [sociological] analysis in the making of decisions … is not a task which science can undertake; it is rather the task of the acting, willing person: he weighs and chooses from among the values involved according to his own conscience and his personal view of the world. Science can make him realise that all action and naturally, according to the circumstances, inaction imply in their consequences the espousal of certain values and … the rejection of certain others.'

Weber accepted that it is within the role of a sociologist to choose the social problems they wish to consider but emphasised that the actual research must be strictly objective. He also wished to distinguish sharply between sociology and social policy which he saw as two different 'worlds', both of which are valuable but whose distinctions and ways of working should be made clear. In discussing Weber on this subject, James Coleman (1979) draws on the analogy of the two worlds of discipline and action, with sociology being in the world of discipline and social policy being in the world of action. The term 'discipline' in this context means an area of academic study. The world of discipline is pure and value-free; the world of action is impure, laden with conflicting interest groups, may be secretive and is not value-free. The sociologist treads a wary line between the two worlds.

Weber's conception of the relationship between sociology and social policy is that sociology provides the technical information from which policy makers decide social policy. In this respect Weber is a technician. Much of American empirical sociology since the Second World War has been of this technical nature. Clearly not all sociologists take this view. Marx said that 'Philosophers have interpreted the world. The point is to change it.' So Marx himself did not share the same concern about being value-free and on the contrary wished to join in the world of action.

Other sociologists see a place for **values** in sociology and a place for the sociologist in the making of social policy. Robert S. Lynd (1939) does not quite go this far but he does argue that values are relevant in the choosing of an important social problem and in the guiding of policy makers on the likely outcome of their decisions. C. Wright Mills (1959), too, against the trend of contemporary American sociologists, took an anti-technician stance and argued for the place of values in sociological research. Howard Becker, the interactionist (1967), argues not only for the place of values in sociology but for a particular set of values which promote a favourable outcome in social policy terms for disadvantaged members of society. This position is one shared by many European left-wing sociologists such as Peter Townsend, Stuart Hall and Jeremy Seabrook.

Undertaking research

Of course the underdogs in society are not in much of a position to initiate social policy research themselves. Indeed much social policy research is carried out for various interested parties. These include:

→ government – both national and local, who may want to try out ideas on a small scale before applying new social policies;

→ government – both national and local, who wish to assess the impact of existing social policy;

→ business interests – wishing to develop market research into present and future lifestyles;

→ business interests – wishing to develop raw data which support a particular lobbying position that promotes their interests, e.g. Adam Smith Institute;

→ promotional interest groups – wishing to influence government, public opinion, or gain media time, e.g. Friends of the Earth;

→ sectional interest groups – establishing the effects of current or future social policy on a particular social group, e.g. trade union support of the Low Pay Unit or Child Poverty Action Group;

→ independent researchers – rarely.

Results

One argument that seems to present itself here is that social policy research does not necessarily reduce conflict between interested parties and produce social laws as Comte might have hoped, but such research may make the conflicting interest groups better informed – if the information is freely available.

Social policy and power

On the relationship between social policy research and power there are of course different positions. Some sociologists have argued that the increased knowledge gained will enable those with power to strengthen their hold by manipulating their subjects. The increased information may help those in power to respond to public wishes and remain in power. Alternatively policy research may undermine those in authority by revealing the gap between their claims and the actual outcome of their policies. However, in order for this to be the case such policy results would have to be placed in a context where they could be published and utilised by alternative decision makers.

Social policy has different and competing goals. There are also different means of achieving the same policy goal. Sociology has had an uneasy relationship with social policy. This was seen in Comte's conservatism, the attempt to disassociate sociology from social problems and the controversy over values. Conflicting interests sponsor research. The effects of research on those in authority are uncertain, as are the uses to which research is put.

Questions

1 What is meant by the term 'social policy'?
2 What are the differences between sociology and social policy?
3 Is there likely to be a link between the findings and recommendations of a piece of research and the agency funding it?

Sociology and science

In the early nineteenth century the French mathematician, Auguste Comte (1798–1857), impressed by the achievements being made in natural sciences such as physics, chemistry and geology, argued that there were three discernible stages in the evolution of human thought. The first stage, which he called the 'theological' or 'fictitious' stage, explained events as God's work, for example thunder occurring when God is angry, or famines being the result of not worshipping him enough. The second stage was characteristic of the middle ages with explanations involving subtle emissions from the divine and mystic influences. He called this the 'metaphysical' stage. The third stage was based on the evidence of the previous two hundred years which appeared to demonstrate that the natural world is subject to the rule of definite laws that can be observed through experiment and the collection of 'positive facts'.

His boldest assertion was to take this one stage further and state that the systematic collection of facts and the search for laws should not be limited to the natural world. Everything, even human society, obeys laws of behaviour. He foresaw a new science of society which would discover these laws and become the 'queen' of all science. In anticipation he called this as yet unresearched science 'sociology'. When all human thought was based on science then the positive stage would be complete.

Many sociologists are unhappy with the idea that the work of writers such as Marx and Durkheim can be called positivist in any meaningful way. They point to studies such as Durkheim's *Suicide* (1897), which argues that the real cause of suicide is not religion, the family or the contemporary political situation but something

unmeasurable – the extent of integration and moral regulation in society. Strictly speaking, then, **positivism** in sociology corresponds to the narrow definition of science as quantifiable, generalisable and concerned to identify clearly observable causes and correlations. Theorists such as Marx and Durkheim were working towards a broader view of this scientific project.

Positivist and structural sociology

Positivism is one of the key concepts in social science. Unhelpfully, it is used differently in subjects such as law ('positive' law), economics ('positive' economics) and sociology. In sociology, positivist sociology and structural (or 'realist') sociology are often thought of as the same thing.

Positivist sociology is similar to the concept of **empiricism**. It is mainly interested in pursuing a research programme that is parallel to that of the natural sciences, seeking to discover patterned and regular events in the social world whose occurrence is either caused by another event, or strongly correlated with that event. A social mechanism may be clearly identified and measured, for example the relation between attendance at parents' evenings and the educational attainment of the children.

Structural sociology is thought to be concerned with the cause of events at such a deep level that they may not be observable in a simple way so that it is not possible to say that one event causes another to happen. Causes exist in the structure of power and social relations. Society is not made up of a simple series of mechanisms as a complex machine is. Empirical research therefore becomes much more difficult.

However, the idea of formulating a science of society was attractive to many, and by the mid-nineteenth century writers were beginning to claim this status for their social theories. Marx, for example, in outlining **historical materialism**, describes 'the material transformation of the economic conditions of production which can be determined with the precision of natural science'. He contrasted his own view of how socialism would emerge from capitalism with that of others, claiming that his view was scientific and theirs merely utopian. They might wish it to happen, but he could identify how it was written into the laws of historical development. By the turn of the century Durkheim could show that suicide in society could be understood through the collection of '**social facts**' and the identification of external variables determining human behaviour. His contemporary, Weber, though, had profound reservations about the search for general social laws, believing each society to be a unique formation. He also wrestled with the problem of **determinism**, suggesting instead that humans have some control over their lives.

Although a 'positivist' sociology clearly now exists, scepticism exists both inside and outside sociology as to how successful and valid it is. Social science has not achieved anything like the degree of unanimity, certainty or ability to predict of the natural sciences. Its methods are nothing like as rigorous. It cannot, for example, use laboratory experiments in the same way to derive its data. Aside from the ethical problems of placing people in artificial situations, it only makes sense to study people's behaviour in an existing social setting. The closest sociologists can get to orthodox scientific methods is to use field experiments – for example gauging reactions by posing as old when you're young, or black when you're white – or by making comparisons between different groups, societies and cultures (the comparative method). These, of course, are difficult to repeat or have other researchers verify. With these limitations, social scientists have far greater difficulty in establishing the cause or causes of events. At best, all that can be established are strong **correlations**. It lacks the precision of natural science.

Sociologists have responded to these criticisms in a number of ways. From a positivist point of view, while many of the above criticisms are accepted, the argument remains that what most sociologists do is, nevertheless, scientific in that sociology constitutes a body of organised knowledge developed through systematic enquiry, using techniques that approximate to those of natural science, yielding data of similar **reliability** and **validity**.

The hypothetico-deductive method

Many scientists would argue that good science is based on the **hypothetico-deductive method**, which proceeds through the following stages:

→ *Observation*: All scientific activity depends on systematic observation, recording and description of its subject matter.
→ *Conjecture*: In order to explain any given observation scientists must think up a plausible reason for its occurrence.
→ *Hypothesis formation*: The conjecture must be 'operationalised', in other words it must be put in a form that will allow the scientist to determine how well it explains the occurrence of the observation.

At this stage, an attempt is made to predict the result of a test.

→ *Testing*: The **hypothesis** must be rigorously tested under controlled conditions through an experiment to show whether it can be proved wrong or not.
→ *Generalisation*: If the hypothesis has not been proved wrong by the test, it shows that the conjecture explains the occurrence of the observation. It can then be generalised, either into a law-like statement (for example, light rays bend at an angle dependent on the density of the medium they enter) or a probabilistic statement (for example, there is a 70 per cent probability that x will occur when y is also present under conditions z).
→ *Theory formation*: A number of generalisations are ordered into a coherent model or theory, which explains a given range of phenomena.

The hypothetico-deductive method further requires that the researcher be totally neutral at all times, and in no way allow their own views or prejudices to colour any aspect of the research programme. If they don't remain objective but become **subjective**, then their work ceases to be scientific and becomes corrupted and distorted.

The realist approach

An altogether different view of science has emerged from what has been termed the 'realist' school. This argues that it is misleading to typify science as being based on experiment and that, outside the laboratory, scientists are faced with as many uncontrollable variables as social scientists. Although men have landed on the moon with great scientific precision, meteorologists, with banks of technical equipment, cannot tell you with certainty whether it will rain or not in a month or even a day's time, or for how long. Nor is it the case that scientists work solely on the basis of observation. They cannot see viruses spreading from human to human or continents drifting apart, but they are able to surmise these facts from the evidence of epidemics striking people down, or from earthquakes and volcanic eruptions. The real causes are often knowable only by their effects. This, the realists claim, allows social scientists to claim that they, too, are engaged in the same scientific project where many and complex variables are at work.

The phenomenological approach

Phenomenologists regard the question of the relationship between sociology and science with great scepticism. Whatever the claims of natural science, there is a crucial difference between people and inanimate objects in that humans think for themselves and have reasons for their behaviour. This, in turn, enables them to make active sense of their world. Sociologists should be concerned with interpreting this view. Whether social causation exists or not is irrelevant.

Scientists themselves, from the phenomenological point of view, are as involved in interpreting reality as any other group in society. All knowledge is simply the product of interaction between human beings. It is more valid – as well as more interesting – to analyse science as a set of subjectively held meanings. Events are not passively observed. To understand anything, whether tribal life in the South Pacific or the messages across VDUs sent by radio telescopes, a theoretical framework has to be imposed on what is observed. Forming this framework is a creative process, derived from ideas of what is thought to be already there. All knowledge is socially constructed.

There are at least three positions, then, on the debate about the scientific status of science. Positivist sociologists claim that the methods they use, while not identical to those of the natural sciences, approximate closely enough to them. Social science can be like natural science. The realists claim that in both branches of science, similar problems are faced in postulating the influence of unseeable structures and forces. For phenomenologists, the search for causes and laws is dismissed and science itself is studied as a social construct.

Questions

1 What differences are there between natural and social science?
2 What is the realist view of science?
3 What does it mean to say that knowledge is socially constructed?

Is science scientific?

While there has been considerable pressure on sociologists to consider what they mean by their use of the word 'science', the use of this word by natural scientists has also come under the microscope. What does it mean to call their work scientific? Are they any more objective, rigorous or closer to 'the truth' than social scientists? Even if objectivity is possible, should these scientists want to claim detachment from the objects they study?

At first sight, it seems easy enough to assume that what natural scientists do is to systematically record observations of the patterns of behaviour and movement of matter, without preconceptions of what they might find. As many philosophers of science have pointed out though, the process is more complex – and less objective – than it first appears.

Popper

The very idea of deriving conclusions from the process of making observations is itself problematic. Although 999 white swans may have been observed floating past a point on a river, it is a logical mistake to assume that the next swan to swim past will also be white. This is what Karl Popper (1963) identifies as the problem of **induction**. It cannot be assumed that what has always happened in the past will always happen in the future. It follows, for Popper, that collecting more and more data about an event will not prove a proposition to be true, as there is no reason why past events should predict the future. The black swan of scientific data may well be around the corner, waiting to drift into view.

Instead, Popper argues that scientists should proceed by looking, not for the proof of their hypotheses, but for their disproof. Although it cannot be proved that something is true – only that something has always happened that way in the past – the best evidence will be that it has not yet been disproved or 'falsified'. Science must abandon the inductive method of attempting to make theories fit facts and adopt a deductive method where facts are only admitted into a theory through the process of falsification.

Kuhn

In one of the most important books on this subject, Thomas Kuhn (1962) asks whether scientists do indeed allow the possibility of their theories being falsified, and examines how new scientific theories emerge. According to Kuhn, scientists work not as individuals but as part of a community. Within this scientific community a consensus exists about the nature of the world they are investigating. Kuhn calls the theoretical framework that results from this consensus a **paradigm**. For long periods of time the scientific community engages in activity designed to bear out the validity of this paradigm. Kuhn calls this a time of 'normal science'. Eventually, though, individuals or groups working outside the dominant paradigm will put forward alternative theories that can be supported by equally valid evidence. They will have to be outside of the dominant paradigm to do this. There then follows a period of revolutionary or 'multi-paradigmatic' science where the rival paradigms struggle for supremacy, and advocates of alternative theoretical frameworks are overthrown or beaten off.

An example of what Kuhn had in mind would be the challenge mounted against Newtonian physics by Albert Einstein in the early part of the twentieth century, where intense battles were unsuccessfully waged by the 'normal' scientists to maintain scientific orthodoxy. If long-standing paradigms can be overthrown, then the defeated scientists have to admit that the theories they were working with were not so much 'true' as merely 'very useful' in helping them make sense of the data they had gathered.

It is not the case, then, that those who are working within paradigms of normal science approach what they examine with open minds, or are prepared to look anew each time at what they are observing. Some commentators have argued that the problem is more deep-set than this, in that all scientists, by definition, start off with the unfalsifiable assumption that every event has a cause. Furthermore, from the realist point of view, not every event – or every possible cause – is observable or knowable. The study of plate tectonics and earthquakes by geologists, for example, requires a series of guesses to be made about what is probably happening in the earth's structure. The problem of causation, of identifying specific causes, is as much of a problem for natural scientists as it is for social scientists.

In the same vein, it is no less true to say that, although the subject of natural scientific study may be inanimate or non-human, scientists themselves are human beings who have to impose a structure on what they see in order to make sense of it and they have to select some facts from others to put a theory together. In this way, scientists are as prone to imposing their own subjective views of the world as any other humans. That they need to choose to prioritise some data means that they are making value judgements about which data is most helpful to test their hypothesis. When they start making choices about the status of facts, then they have, strictly speaking, ceased to be objective. Facts have become values.

Questions have been asked not only about the methodology of the natural sciences but also their ethics. Radical and feminist critics have brought into the debate not only the methodology of science but

the knowledge that the application of this methodology produces.

Medawar

Medawar (1985) has argued that the real sequence of scientific research is inspiration then observation *not* observation then inspiration as implied by the hypothetico-deductive method. Normal science consists of problem solving with the results anticipated because they will fit into the existing jigsaw. As the data is collected it impinges on a mind already anticipating it.

What Medawar is suggesting is that the actual process of research may follow no logical pattern but this reality is hidden from the public, because scientific papers omit false starts, changes in direction and dead ends.

Some scientific evidence has been found to be fallacious. Lynch (1993) studied the work of scientists who were carrying out laboratory investigations into the brain functioning of rats. He found that the types of feature they were looking for and expected to find influenced many of their conclusions. In other words, they were using the data they collected to confirm their theories, rather than keeping an open mind and seeking to test their ideas objectively.

'Big' science

Sociologists have argued that scientific knowledge in the natural world arises from an objective and independent search for truth and also from the priorities and values of those who have funded the research. For Leslie Sklair (1973), what most people think of as scientific knowledge is better thought of as 'big' science – research undertaken to further the control and interests of the military-industrial state over its people. Examples of this would include research into space and weapons technology, or business-led research into systems whose sole aim is profit-maximisation. The resulting popular image is of scientists as men in white coats, developing large-scale and impersonal structures on multi-billion pound projects without regard for how their creations will be used. Their technology is thought to be part of an objective science because of the power and prestige of those who fund them. Their concerns are thought to be our concerns.

Science and ideology

Feyerabend (1998) argues that scientists have no special method and that they frequently change what they are doing and the approach used. He suggests that science is basically an ideology completely shaped at any moment in time by its historical and cultural context. Despite scientists' claims to the contrary, the rule in science is that anything goes.

Support for this view comes from Gomm's study of Darwin's theory of evolution. Roger Gomm (1982) argues that Darwin's views about evolution and natural selection were poorly supported by the available evidence and in some respects were clearly not true. Nevertheless, Darwin's ideas gained widespread support in the nineteenth century because they fitted closely with the ideologies of dominant social groups in Britain. For example, the idea of 'survival of the fittest' and 'natural selection' could be used to justify the free-market capitalist system and the harsh treatment of the poor.

Feminism

For feminists, science is a male world from which women have always been excluded. Scientific achievements and scientific knowledge reveal only male priorities in which nature, always characterised as female, has to be brought under control. Areas of traditionally female knowledge of previous centuries such as healing and midwifery have become the brutal male domains of medicine and obstetrics. For Hilary Rose (1982), it is male science that has brought about 'the mechanisation of childbirth through routine induction, massive pollution of the environment and the ultimate terror of nuclear holocaust', as well as forms of contraception based on controlling women's – rather than men's – fertility.

Male science is not objective if objectivity is thought only to concern how scientific research is done, and not the reason why that research came into existence, or what the social consequences are. Sandra Harding (1987) states that 'Defining what is in need of scientific explanation only from the perspective of bourgeois, white men's experiences leads to partial and even perverse understandings ... an androcentric [male-centred] picture of nature and social life emerges from the testing by men of hypotheses generated by what men find problematic in the world around them.' It was, after all, this very same male-centred science that claimed to have 'proved' that women were biologically and socially inferior to men. Furthermore, it is men alone who have produced the technology to make chemical and nuclear weapons.

If women are to enter the exclusive world of male science then, feminists have argued, science must be reconceptualised and made more humane. Scientists themselves have to become accountable for their actions. Technology will be seen not as 'value-free' but assessed in terms of the impact it has in bringing about meaningful change in social relations. Men, as well as women, would be seen as capable of reproduction. Given that scientific advance has relied as much on inspired guesses as its own methodology, a feminist perspective would reintroduce and relegitimise the intuitive approach. In this way science will become a means of enhancing human freedom rather than being a threat to survival as at present. What has been a defensive and conservative discipline will become healthy and liberatory.

It can be argued, then, that there are a number of ways in which the supposed objectivity of science can be questioned, to such an extent that belief in objectivity in science – within and without the scientific world – is now crumbling. If this is the case, then it begs the question of the status of sociology as a social science, conceived specifically to emulate the achievements and aspirations of natural science.

Questions

1 What does Kuhn mean by 'paradigms' in science?
2 How do feminists view science?
3 What is the 'inductive method'?

Values and sociologists

One of Max Weber's main aims in setting up the German Society for Sociology was to establish sociology as a discipline free from value judgements. What he meant by this was clear from the society's statute, which demanded the advancement of sociology as a science, giving equal space to all directions and methods in sociology, without at the same time advancing any specific religious, political or ethical goals.

Weber

In this aim he has been frequently misunderstood and misinterpreted. He did not mean that sociologists could not be politically active, that they should not hold opinions about the worth or relevance of their work or that they should not be interested in the values and opinions of the people they studied. What he really wanted was for sociologists to recognise that facts and values are separate phenomena. 'These two things are logically different and to deal with them as though they were the same represents a confusion of entirely heterogeneous problems.' Weber believed that sociologists should propagate facts, not values, although he knew it was not easy to recognise where the line between the two should be drawn.

Nevertheless, Weber argued that values in sociology are important in that they help guide sociologists towards relevant areas of research. These will be decided by what are seen as the dominant cultural problems of the age, and will change over time. In this, he anticipates the possibility of paradigmatic change in all forms of science. Value freedom, however, is not the same as objectivity. Values concern the choice of subjects studied; objectivity refers to the collection of data without bias or prejudice. Yet objectivity is only possible within a framework of values.

Sociologists need to recognise that the choice of studying ethnic minorities in education rather than girls in education; working-class rather than middle-class **deviance**; or dependence on the Welfare State rather than the distribution of wealth is an evaluative one. Clearly, some choices are affected by the researcher's own values. What Weber was concerned with was that these values should be recognised and clearly stated. Only then can data be gathered and conclusions reached in an objective way. If values still influence the process then the researcher is guilty of making 'value judgements' and the status of the resulting research must be called into question. Often the 'facts' which a sociologist unearths are picked out because they suit his or her values, while other, perhaps equally relevant, 'facts' are ignored. Facts are often established because they fit in with an underpinning theory.

Functionalism

For Alvin Gouldner (1970), the functionalism of Parsons and Merton is a good example of misunderstanding Weber. What these writers have done is claim a value-free status for their work, projecting an image of political and ideological neutrality. They saw their work as above politics and non-partisan and, to that extent, as value-free. This can be construed as a form of intellectual dishonesty: the truth is that it is a conservative ideology presented as social science, believing in the inherent harmony and stability of the status quo. Hiding this confuses objectivity with value freedom.

At the other extreme are the openly partisan sociologists, for example Howard Becker and many Marxists and feminists. In Becker's work (1967 and 1973), values dominate the choice of which social

phenomena are studied. Scientific and moral questions are inseparable. Some people may want to disguise their morals as science, because it gives their moral stance greater weight. Instead he suggests that those opposed to the status quo 'whose sympathies I share, should attack injustice and oppression directly and openly, rather than pretend that the judgement that such things are evil is somehow deducible from sociological first principles, or warranted by empirical findings alone … we sometimes begin with the actions we want to take and the people we want to help, as a basis for choosing problems and methods'. This does not necessarily mean to say that how something is studied is lacking in objectivity, even if values determine which social phenomena are studied.

An example given by Becker is the disproportionate amount of research into juvenile behaviour and crime which is conducted. According to Becker, most researchers begin by asking 'what is wrong with the kids of today?' This shows an immediate bias towards the status quo, reflecting the views of the police, parents and social workers. Resulting explanations, if allowed to masquerade as value-free science, take on the status of 'truth'. This could be to the detriment of those involved, particularly the young. Openly partisan, Becker sympathises with the underdog, suggesting that it would be equally valid to ask the question 'what is wrong with the parents of today?'

Marxism

A similar campaigning thrust exists among Marxists, taking their cue from Karl Marx's statement (1845): 'The philosophers have only interpreted the world in different ways; the point is to change it.' Marxism is openly value-laden in its examination of social dynamics, being anti-capitalist and pro-communist, although Marxists nevertheless believe that their depiction of reality is objective and scientific: the progression from **capitalism** to **communism** is inevitable.

Feminism

Likewise with feminism, which criticises existing sociology for reflecting male values and male methods. Explicitly feminist knowledge, it has been claimed (Harding, 1987), 'emerges for the oppressed only through the struggles they wage against their oppressors. It is through feminist struggles against male domination that women's experience can be made to yield up a truer (or less false) image of a social reality than that available only from the perspective of the social experience of the ruling class races. Thus a feminist standpoint is not something anyone can have by claiming it, but an achievement. (A standpoint differs in this respect from a perspective).'

Ann Oakley (1981) argues that feminism demands a particular rationale of research, which breaks down patriarchal approaches by seeing respondents as equals, to whom information is divulged by the researcher as willingly as it is given by the respondent. Feminist theory therefore has a built-in inclination towards qualitative methods.

The problem of objectivity and value freedom is unlikely to be easily solved. Because sociology is the study of humans by other humans, the problem of consciousness and selective perception will always be present. Whether this jeopardises the possibility of a 'scientific' status for sociology depends on how both sociology and science are defined.

Post-modernism

Post-modernist theorists argue that language is value laden, and social phenomena cannot really be defined in a value-free way. For example, knowing what to include in a study of the sociology of art depends on a value judgement as to what constitutes, or does not constitute, art. A similar problem is encountered in the study of poverty. Shipman (1981) argues that values are implicit in the selection and use of established evidence, a body of work which constitutes what he terms 'the mythology of the subject'. Some studies are frequently mentioned yet the evidence on which they are based is frail. Shipman gives the example of the Hawthorne experiments of the 1930s, which examined the importance of human relations in the workplace. He argues that the superiority of good human relations in the workplace over good material conditions and financial regard does not seem justified by the results of the experiment, but it was a 'comfortable' conclusion to draw. This is ultimately because of the support that it gave to other values in our culture.

Questions

1 You have read the section on sociology and values. Now try to define the following terms:
   (a) objectivity   (b) subjectivity
   (c) value freedom   (d) ideology
   (e) patriarchy
2 Are sociological perspectives value free or should they be viewed as ideologies?

Sociological perspectives

Most sociology textbooks, this one included, present sociology as a divided discipline, with a marked cleavage between two philosophical traditions. Figure 1.1 reflects the commonly accepted structure of sociological perspectives.

Figure 1.1

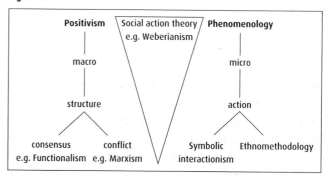

Positivism and phenomenology

Positivism and **phenomenology** are the philosophical roots or traditions from which the main perspectives in sociology have evolved. Positivism, a term first brought into use by Auguste Comte (1798–1857), holds that all knowledge can be based on science and scientific thought, and that all behaviour, whether of objects or of people, is subject to general laws. The possibility of identifying these laws inspired a generation of mid-to-late nineteenth-century theorists in many areas of knowledge, although the extent of its influence on writers such as Marx and Durkheim remains under dispute.

The term phenomenology is most closely associated with Edmund Husserl (1859–1938), and in sociology with Alfred Schutz (1899–1959). In this tradition the belief is that positivism's search for social causes is illusory, falling into the trap of determinism. Phenomenology denies that social behaviour, like the movement of atoms and molecules, is determined by external forces which are beyond human control. All that can realistically be achieved is an understanding of how people, individually and collectively, interpret, understand and place meaning on their social reality. Phenomenologists assert that people possess a greater degree of **free will** than positivist sociologists are willing to admit.

Structure and action

The debate between the two camps of sociology can also be seen as one between the concepts of structure and action. For the structuralists, sociology should be the study of the effects of the structure of society on social life – the macro or large-scale view. Patterns created by structures such as religion, the family, organisations or, for Marxists, capitalist relations of production, are seen to be the starting point in explaining anything in society. The analysis begins at a structural level. Hence some may argue that an increase in unemployment can lead to an increase in the crime rate, or that social disintegration is the cause of suicide. 'Social facts' exist as definite realities.

Other sociologists, taking the micro or small-scale view, doubt the validity of this position. The idea of a social structure is an abstract one, assuming a world 'out there' for us to investigate. The truth is that we are already in that world, with each of us having very different assumptions of what it looks like. They argue that the search for structural clues to social causes and effects should be abandoned in favour of piecing together the way individuals and groups make sense of the world they live in. This involves the analysis of social action, not the intangible structures they are thought to inhabit. 'Social facts' do not exist but are created and constructed in the process of social interaction.

These two approaches can be compared to a telescope. One end will show everything in enlarged form and in great detail (the microview), the other will display a world that is small and distant (the macroview). Both are 'true' pictures of the same thing. In sociology, there is no agreement about which approach is best or how the two can be made compatible.

Marxism and functionalism

Marxism and functionalism are seen as two perspectives both of which look at how the structure of society determines behaviour.

Symbolic interactionism and ethnomethodology

Symbolic interactionism and ethnomethodology are presented as perspectives emphasising small-scale understanding of how groups and individuals structure their perception of action and meaning in society. These perspectives are often referred to collectively as **interpretive sociology**. Somewhere in between the two is the tradition emanating from Max Weber, which explores the possibility of uniting theories of structure and action in society.

This view of sociology is certainly common. A typical exam question, implicitly or explicitly, amounts to 'Compare and contrast Marxist and interactionist views of sociology', and most textbooks are written to cater for this demand.

Whether intended or not, the end result is an intellectual condition known as 'perspectivitis', whose main symptoms are the obsessive need to label a piece of sociological research positivist or phenomenological, Marxist, functionalist or Weberian, interactionist or ethnomethodological. The truth is, however, that such simplistic labelling can be misleading.

'Good' sociology

While it is certainly true to say that clearly discernible sociological traditions of thought do exist, very few writers begin their sociological research solely in order to contribute to the body of knowledge of a given perspective. What they are principally trying to create is 'good' sociology, attempting to answer the question: 'How much can we reliably and validly know about human societies?' If they find that the best way to do this is by drawing on the theoretical assumptions and methodological techniques of the dominant sociological traditions, then so be it. There is no reason, as Paul Willis (1977) found, why someone using observation techniques, typical of the interactionist perspective, should not come to conclusions informed by Marxism. Similarly, feminism draws from all perspectives, while at the same time being both critical and sceptical of the inherent male bias in sociological theory and research to date.

Questions

1 You have looked at a discussion of sociological perspectives. Now try to define the following terms:
   (a) a sociological perspective
   (b) positivism
   (c) phenomenology
2 What is meant by 'structure' and 'action' in sociology?

Functionalism

No one has ever seen a society. All they can ever see is small parts at work at different times in different places. The nearest anyone could come would be to observe a small community, preferably with what seems to be a simple way of going about their everyday life. It should then be possible to work out what the importance of the things these people do is to the way their community works. Some anthropologists, who themselves come from industrial societies, have undertaken studies of pre-industrial societies still in existence. Among the best known is A. R. Radcliffe-Brown (1881–1955). A central part of the way he observed these pre-industrial societies was his belief that social activity, if it was recurrent, must be functional to the working of that community. In other words, an observable pattern of group activity must help maintain the life of that community: it must have a function. If, for example, a group of people are regularly observed sitting around smoking pipes communally, this activity may function to bind together or integrate the group as a community and reinforce the values of friendliness and co-operation. If the men taking part in this activity are elderly then it may be one way of maintaining their social power, and a respect for age.

In this way, a wider picture of how society works can be built up. Like many sociologists before him, Radcliffe-Brown made great use of what is called the organic analogy in his examination of the way societies work, though this idea really comes from Herbert Spencer (1820–1903) and was also used by Emile Durkheim.

EMILE DURKHEIM (1858–1917)

French sociologist who did much to establish sociology as a discipline, particularly with works such as *Suicide* (1897). He emphasised the importance of examining society as a whole and the role of the 'collective conscience'. He strongly influenced the work of Talcott Parsons and the development of American structural functionalism.

The organic analogy

The idea behind the organic analogy is that societies can be compared to the way a biological organism works. Someone who had no idea how the body works might find, from slicing a human apart, that there were various organs inside that make humans work. The heart functions to pump blood around the veins and arteries, the kidneys clean the blood, the intestines are involved in digestion and so on. Each organ has a function which contributes to the working of the greater whole. So too with society, where the organs might be the family, education, the system of religion, work, etc. Any examination of these institutions should begin by asking the question: 'What does it do to help the wider society function?' Homeostasis is the term applied to the way in which an organism regulates itself to cope with changes in internal and external conditions. For example, after exercise, the heated-up body sweats to help the body temperature to stay stable. When this concept is used to understand how equilibrium is maintained in society, then the organic analogy becomes more effective.

The analogy also has many limits, however. It is difficult, for example, to compare the way organisms grow to the way societies grow and change. Is there a social equivalent to DNA, the genetic programme present in every species? Does a society really have a series of complementary institutions which work together to make the whole function smoothly to the mutual benefit of all? In the same way that the skin holds a human body together, so too do **norms** and values bind society together. But does this help us understand who determines the norms and values by which we live and how the wider society is organised?

Another way of looking at society is to compare it to a mechanism in the way it works, where all the small parts, such as in a clockwork watch, function together to achieve the aim of demonstrating the time of day. Similarly, when people pull together in society, they can achieve collectively held goals such as improvement in the overall standard of living.

Parsonian functionalism

This is close to Talcott Parsons' (1902–79) view of the way society functions, and in the 1950s and 1960s Parsonian functionalism was virtually the dominant paradigm in sociology. The model of society he put forward has been subsequently heavily criticised, but it is important to understand how his model of society worked in order to understand the criticisms.

Parsons argues that any society has four functional needs or prerequisites that need to be met for it to survive: these are adaptation, goal attainment, integration and latency (AGIL). It is hard to believe now that sociologists were excited by the bland and fruitless way that Parsons went about examining society, but many US college students went into their exams with the four letters AGIL stuck in their heads (or on the palms of their hands).

TALCOTT PARSONS (1902–79)

American sociological theorist and leader of the functionalist school that dominated American sociology from the 1940s to the 1960s. In his famous work *The Social System* (1951) Parsons tried to show how consensus based on shared values is essential to social order. The stratification system is crucial in maintaining consensus in society.

They then would have given Parsons' view that, firstly, all societies must have ways of adapting to change, whatever that change might be (A); they must have social aims that everyone wants which help the society determine the direction it's going in (G); they must have ways of binding their members together to identify with and realise these collective goals whether through religion or newspapers or marriage or whatever (I); and there must be a way in which a society's way of living can survive through generations of people (L). This scheme can be found detailed in works of his such as *The Social System* (1951). People born within this system are socialised into it and come to take on the roles the system demands: the whole is greater than the sum of its parts.

Manifest and latent functions

One of the key additions to Parsons' structural-functionalism has been made by his American contemporary, Robert Merton (born 1910). This is the distinction between manifest and latent functions. A **manifest function** is evident when an institution achieves the goal it clearly intended, for example the way a family socialises its young. A **latent function** would be an unintended consequence of an aspect in society. No one commits a crime with the deliberate intention of revealing the boundaries of normative behaviour to the rest of society! Nevertheless, a latent function of their criminal behaviour is to demonstrate the limits of socially acceptable behaviour.

Criticisms of functionalism

One of the most frequent criticisms of the functionalist perspective is of a logical problem it embraces: if something in society is recurrent, functionalists say that it must be meeting a need. But how do we know that this need exists? Because of the phenomenon that we observe! It exists because it exists; it is because it is. In philosophy, this type of going-nowhere argument is known as a tautology.

Secondly, because it focuses on the way in which different members of society integrate and work in harmony around a value consensus, functionalism lacks any real power to explain social change. One concept that attempts to overcome this is Merton's use of the concept of dysfunction: the way in which some aspects of society work against its overall harmony and consensus. Functionalism leans heavily towards describing society in a stable condition, and seems to emphasise the status quo: inequality is inevitable; poverty is inevitable; the media reflect all views; women are domestically orientated; marriages are happy. Functionalists such as Parsons and Merton appear to be using their own middle-class, middle-American view of the world and saying this is what society is like.

Functionalism should not be dismissed too quickly, however. Functionalists argue that advanced industrial societies are stable: people do seem to have faith in their political system in a democracy; industrial conflict is diminishing; and the major political parties are competing for the same middle ground. It is not difficult even now to make a strong case for arguing that a value consensus exists in advanced societies.

Question

You have now looked at an introduction to functionalism. Try to define the following terms:
(a) the organic analogy
(b) functional needs
(c) the mechanical analogy
(d) a manifest function
(e) dysfunction

Marxism

At first sight, Marxism seems difficult to understand. It seems to use more new words and phrases than any other perspective in sociology. This is not because Marx was being awkward, but because of the richly creative nature of his thought. He needed a number of new terms to describe his ideas.

Marx's historical materialism

Marx did not want to simply analyse the world; he wanted to play a part in changing it. His life's work was devoted to understanding the way in which modern industrial societies change. Marx's theory is sometimes described as 'historical materialism'. The

KARL MARX (1818–83)

German-born economist, sociologist, philosopher and revolutionary. Spent most of his life in poverty in London, financed by his friend, Friedrich Engels. Developed the theory of historical progression to communism through class struggle (historical materialism). His best-known works are *The Communist Manifesto* (1848) and *Capital* (1867).

term materialism is often used to describe the acquisition of consumer goods (consumerism) but in Marx's time materialism meant the opposite of idealism, the belief that the physical world is created by ideas, particularly religious ideas. Marx argued instead that ideas themselves are products of the material struggle for existence in the economic base of society. Historical materialism sees change in society emerging from this struggle.

There are, according to Marx, three main periods of change that have occurred in the way human societies are organised. These periods he calls epochs, which are characterised by the way in which production happens – the **mode of production**. The three main epochs are the classical societies of ancient Rome and Greece, the feudal societies of the Middle Ages, and the one in which he lived (and which interested him most) – capitalist society.

What distinguishes each epoch are the different **relations of production**, determined by who owns the **means of production** – the method of producing the things we need to survive. In a classical society, the relations of production were between slave owner and slave; in **feudal** times they were between the landowner and his serf. In the development from land-based production to factory production, the key relationship became the one between the **bourgeoisie**, who owned the means of production (usually in the form of a factory), and the people

hired by the (bourgeois) capitalists – the new landless **working class** or **proletariat**. According to Marx, it is conflict about ownership of the means of production, that is the class struggle, that causes change in society. In his various writings, Marx projected that this cause of conflict would only come to an end when there was no separate ownership of the means of production. He believed that the new industrial working class would be the class that brought about this change, taking over the means of production from the bourgeoisie. No new classes would be formed in their wake, so the result would eventually be a classless (or communist) society.

The labour theory of value

The bulk of Marx's work in the period from writing *The Communist Manifesto* (1848) to his death was devoted to showing how this transition to communism would come about. The bourgeoisie, he says, is an immensely dynamic and creative class. They were the driving force behind the Industrial Revolution, it was with their capital that mines were dug, roads were built, canals constructed, ships riveted together and steel foundries opened. But the bourgeoisie were only part of the story. Who actually hammered the rivets into the ships, took the pickaxe to the coal-face and shovelled out the earth to make the road? Not the bourgeoisie, but the people who have only their ability to work – labour power – which they sell to the bourgeoisie to make a living – the proletariat. And, Marx asks, what do they get in return? George Orwell put this point very well in his novel *Animal Farm* (1945). Orwell uses the example of the suffering experienced by farm animals as a metaphor for the exploitation and degradation of the proletariat.

'Now, comrades, what is the nature of this life of ours? Let us face it: our lives are miserable, laborious, and short. We are born, we are given just so much food as will keep the breath in our bodies, and those of us who are capable of it are forced to work to the last atom of our strength; and the very instant that our usefulness has come to an end we are slaughtered with hideous cruelty. No animal in England knows the meaning of happiness or leisure after he is a year old. No animal in England is free. The life of an animal is misery and slavery: that is the plain truth.

'But is this simply part of the order of nature? Is it because this land of ours is so poor that it cannot afford a decent life to those who dwell upon it? No, comrades, a thousand times no! The soil of England is fertile, its climate is good, it is capable of affording food in abundance to an enormously greater number of animals than now inhabit it. This single farm of ours would

support a dozen horses, twenty cows, hundreds of sheep – and all of them living in a comfort and a dignity that are now almost beyond our imagining. Why then do we continue in this miserable condition? Because nearly the whole of the produce of our labour is stolen from us by human beings. There, comrades, is the answer to all our problems. It is summed up in a single word – Man. Man is the only real enemy we have. Remove Man from the scene, and the root cause of hunger and overwork is abolished for ever.

'Man is the only creature that consumes without producing. He does not give milk, he does not lay eggs, he is too weak to pull the plough, he cannot run fast enough to catch rabbits. Yet he is lord of all the animals. He sets them to work, he gives back to them the bare minimum that will prevent them from starving, and the rest he keeps for himself. Our labour tills the soil, our dung fertilizes it, and yet there is not one of us that owns more than his bare skin. You cows that I see before me, how many thousands of gallons of milk have you given during the last year? And what has happened to that milk which should have been breeding up sturdy calves? Every drop of it has gone down the throats of our enemies. And you hens, how many eggs have you laid this year, and how many of those eggs ever hatched into chickens?'

Major's speech from Animal Farm by George Orwell.

Profit and surplus value

The owner of capital wants to invest this money in order to make more capital. This is done by first buying the raw materials, machines and tools necessary for the manufacture of goods. Let us say that the capitalist believes that wooden chairs will be a good source of potential profit. They therefore buy the necessary wood, lathe machines, chisels etc. for their chair factory. Labour is taken on for the production of the commodity (anything which is bought and sold), in this case chairs. Once the chairs are sold the capitalist has a lot of money but now needs to pay for the machinery, raw materials and any other overheads, principally wages. How much should the proletariat be paid? The capitalist is only in business for one reason – to make as much profit (which Marx calls **surplus value**) as possible. The workers will therefore be paid as little as the capitalist can get away with. But who actually turned the raw materials into saleable commodities? The labour of the proletariat is added to the raw material to turn it into a marketable commodity; in return they receive as little payment as possible. It is this difference that Marx calls exploitation. When the true nature of this exploitation becomes realised – when they achieve

Figure 1.2 The cycle of capital

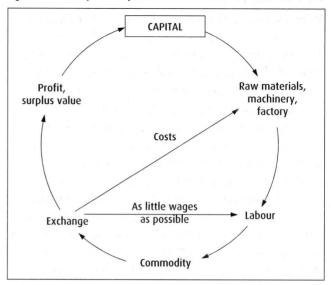

class consciousness – the proletariat will become revolutionary and overthrow the exploitative bourgeoisie. Another way of understanding the Marxist concept of exploitation is to consider the situation of builders who spend their lives building houses but may never be able to own one themselves.

Although the meaning of the terms 'profit' and 'surplus value' is close, Marx does not use them interchangeably. When workers add value to things and turn them into commodities, what they are adding is their labour-time. The amount of labour-time – 'necessary labour' – put in to earn their wages is not the same as their total output. The labour-time remaining is called 'surplus labour', in which time the worker will create 'surplus value'. It is in this time that the worker will be reproducing capital for the capitalist. 'What appears as surplus value on capital's side appears identically on the workers' side as surplus labour in excess of his requirements as a worker, hence in excess of his immediate requirements for keeping himself alive' (Karl Marx, *Outlines of Political Economy*, 1857/8, more commonly known as the *Grundrisse*). Without surplus value produced in this way by extra unpaid labour-time there can be no profit. The rate of profit is not the same as the rate of surplus value, because the concept of profit involves variables such as the total amount of all possible capital used, or the amount of raw materials. The rate of profit is always lower than the narrower concept of the rate of surplus value. This difference was an important element in Marx's view of the labour process in relation to work, automation and unemployment.

Class consciousness

Why the proletariat never achieves revolutionary class consciousness is the central question asked of Marxism, though its supporters point to the closing years of the First and Second World Wars, and the British General Strike of 1926 as examples of heightened class awareness. One answer is because the structure of bourgeois society works continuously in favour of the bourgeoisie. Because they control the most important aspect of society – the means of production – they are able to decisively influence the structure of everything else. This is what is meant by the **economic base** determining the superstructure, which is composed of the other vital aspects of society – the family, religion and the political, educational and judicial systems. As we describe in later chapters, for Marxists all of these institutions serve, in a capitalist society, to maintain bourgeois control.

Marxism after Marx

In the twentieth century, particularly from the 1950s on (when Marxist sociology began to witness a revival in the West), many people have argued that, given the obvious failings of the former Soviet Union, 'Marxism doesn't work.' This point of view was considerably strengthened by the spectacular collapse of communist regimes in Eastern Europe at the end of the 1980s and the break-up of the Soviet Union in 1991. So is Marxism dead?

Stalinism and the Soviet bloc

There are a number of points to be made here. Firstly, Marx would not have identified the Eastern Bloc countries of 1917–91 as lying beyond capitalism. These societies were, from 1930 on, Stalinist, not Marxist, and many non-Soviet Marxist studies have highlighted this crucial difference.

Although Stalin's Soviet Union claimed to be Marxist, Stalin's own ideas and the unique historical and political situation were much more influential than the political and economic theories of Marx. Marx had envisaged a socialist revolution based on class struggle between a rising proletariat and a decadent bourgeoisie in advanced capitalist countries, particularly Germany. This was definitely not the situation in pre-revolutionary Russia, which was a largely peasant-based society, not dissimilar to some of today's **Third World** countries. The perceived need to ruthlessly accelerate the economies of what became the Eastern Bloc in order to catch up with and

overtake the more developed West meant that Stalinism superseded Marxism. After the Soviet invasion of Hungary in 1956, many Western Marxists finally broke with what they then saw as a grotesque misrepresentation of Marx's ideas in the Soviet Union. This led to the emergence of the 'New Left' and eventually 'Eurocommunism'.

One of the main criticisms levelled at Marxists since the death of Marx is that it has become a complex and sophisticated excuse for the lack of socialist revolution in advanced industrial nations, as Marx had predicted. Most revolutions carried out in his name have occurred in countries with mainly agricultural economies, such as China, Cuba, Nicaragua and even Ethiopia.

Neo-Marxism is concerned with explaining the reasons for this non-revolution, and concentrates on analysing the use of ideological means of control by the ruling class. Working-class consciousness has been prevented from crystallising in any decisive way by **ideological State apparatuses** such as the media, politics and education.

Marxism has been used by sociologists as a tool of analysis of capitalist societies in the post-war period and has produced remarkably fruitful studies. For these Marxists, nothing has essentially changed the nature of Western capitalism to make these societies less amenable to Marxist analysis; the class structure may have changed slightly, but capital and the bourgeoisie are as much in control as ever (see chapter 3).

The Frankfurt School

Critical theory is an approach to the analysis of society that developed in Germany during the inter-war years and later found a home in the USA. It began as an attempt by Western Marxists to reappraise Marxist theory in the light of contemporary developments such as the rise of fascism and Stalinism, the growth of monopoly capital and the power of the **mass media**. It was centred around the Frankfurt School of critical theory whose members included Max Horkheimer, Erich Fromm, Herbert Marcuse and T. W. Adorno. The Frankfurt School exercised a major influence on radical thinking in the period 1923 to the late 1960s, and it has since enjoyed a revival through the work of the contemporary German sociologist, Jürgen Habermas.

A key feature of critical theory was the emphasis on adopting an interdisciplinary approach combining Marxism with Freudian concepts, philosophy with psychoanalysis, economic research with historical and cultural analyses across a wide range of fields from the family to the media, the economy to the State. The underlying aim was to liberate the individual in modern society by critically analysing all forms of domination. Critical theory was, thus, in the same tradition as Marx's concept of **alienation** and Durkheim's concept of **anomie**, a cry for the freedom of the individual amid the all-pervasive and stifling forces of **bureaucracy**, technology, the media and the State.

The Frankfurt School identified ideology as a major source of domination in modern societies and sought to show how it conceals and legitimates the power of the ruling class. This was an extension of Marxist analysis, although members of the school were careful to distinguish themselves from traditional Marxism, which they denounced as another ideological force that was undermining the freedom of the individual. They also rejected the crude economic determinism of many earlier Marxist writers and regarded the cultural and ideological aspects of society as having a relative autonomy from the influence of the underlying economic forces.

Habermas

Habermas (1976) argues against the Marxist idea that economic crises will inevitably lead to the overthrow of capitalism. He suggests that in advanced capitalist societies the State has developed mechanisms for coping with economic crises. It has also found means of incorporating the working class in the capitalist system so that at present there is little class consciousness or will to bring about revolutionary change.

Insofar as there is a crisis in advanced capitalist societies, Habermas sees it as a crisis within the realm of ideas and the State rather than within the economy. The State justifies its intervention in the economy on the principles of justice, equality and freedom. It is a **democratic** State that must strive to serve the interests of everyone in society. However, the capitalist economy, which is based on inherently unequal relations between owners and workers, places limits on the extent to which the State can fulfil its commitment to act on behalf of the community as a whole. For example, the principles of justice and equality demand that the State intervene in the economy to combat the problem of unemployment, but as the causes of unemployment are largely beyond the control of the State its policies will inevitably fail or prove less successful than people hoped for. If people's expectations of the State are constantly disappointed, a legitimation crisis may

result whereby the State finds it difficult to maintain the popular support it requires for it to survive in its present democratic form.

Habermas' analysis of advanced capitalism reflects his general belief that non-material factors such as ideas and language make a fundamental contribution to the structure of society and need to be analysed in their own right rather than reduced to a mere reflection of material forces.

Questions

1 You will now be aware of the basic principles of the Marxist perspective. Now try to define the following terms:
  (a) mode of production
  (b) forces of production
  (c) relations of production
  (d) capitalism
  (e) class consciousness
2 How does a Marxist explanation of the way a society works differ from the functionalist explanation?

Weberianism

Max Weber (1864–1920) is one of the most difficult, but also one of the most important, theorists to come to terms with in sociology. In attempts to 'pigeon-hole' him, no one quite knows where to put him. He was aware that social structures exist and are important, but he was also aware that these structures are, at the same time, made up of individuals, with their own understanding of the meaning of their actions.

Weber and Marx

One of the standard sociological clichés is to say that Weber's work amounts to a 'debate with the ghost of Marx'. This is a phrase which is meant to highlight the similarities as well as differences between the two. Weber was, in part of his work, pointing out an alternative theory to Marx's materialism, but much of his output was concerned with completely different areas of sociology.

One reason for this was that, while Marx was concerned to develop a revolutionary theory for the proletariat and their allies, Weber, as a co-founder of the German Sociological Association, was more interested in establishing sociology as an academic discipline. If Weber's ideas seem hard to grasp it is because Weber was a complex and profound thinker –

MAX WEBER (1864–1920)

Highly influential German sociologist and founder of the German Sociological Association. He made important contributions to most areas of sociology including religion (e.g. in *The Protestant Ethic and the Spirit of Capitalism*, 1904–5), organisations and theory. His criticisms of the limitations of social science are particularly important.

because his ideas *are* difficult and, sometimes, even contradictory and the subject of continuing debate. Weber's analysis of Marx's ideas is an important aspect of his work but, rather than being involved in a debate with Marx, he actually took account of Marx's economic theories and to a certain extent encompassed them within his own larger argument. He agreed with much of the economic theory which Marx put forward, but he attempted to describe a more complex system of stratified inequality in capitalist societies. Weber saw his version of the social structure as running alongside that of Marx and believed that there was a need for as many alternative explanations as possible in order to arrive at some sort of understanding. He stressed that the researcher should consider as many aspects of each social structure as possible, and not focus on the economic level alone.

To study each society, the sociologist must study its history, its economy, and its culture, and attempt to understand that culture. According to Weber, each society is unique. History was important to Weber but he did not see it as just the history of class struggle. Like Marx, Weber saw that conflict is of great consequence in the analysis of human actions. Economic class, he believed, is often a source of conflict, particularly in capitalism, but economic relations are not the only source of conflict in society.

Rationalisation

Weber considered that the growth of **rational thinking** – a scientific way of understanding – was taking over from previous, supernatural, sacred ways of looking at the world. The concept of rationalisation of thought plays an important part in his theories. The industrialisation of societies and the growth of complex social structures required a cultural outlook which could cope with rapid change. It was no longer enough to put it all down to God or the devil; humans needed more satisfying explanations to help them take control of their lives.

This is clear from what is perhaps Weber's best-known work, *The Protestant Ethic and the Spirit of Capitalism* (see also chapter 7). Here, Weber also outlines his views on social change. He is concerned with the simultaneous emergence of a particular type of Protestantism (Calvinism) and the capitalist mode of production, though he is quick to point out that there is not a causal relationship. One did not cause or invent the other, rather they happened to arise at the same time and complemented each other. He calls this an 'elective affinity'. It is a good example of the need to understand all the aspects of a culture that make society work. Calvinism preached that only a chosen few could get to heaven. Its followers did not know who was among the chosen, so the best bet was to be honest, hard working, thrifty and live decent, sober lifestyles. These attributes happened to fit in well with the 'spirit' of capitalism, being a more rational approach to economic organisation. Looking to the East and discerning slow or non-existent industrial growth, he wondered if the nature of eastern religions was incompatible with the sort of organisation that makes capitalism possible. His later religious studies centred on this.

However, Weber also saw the growth of rationalisation as the downfall of industrial societies. With the State ruling through what he called 'rational-legal' authority, an overwhelming system of bureaucracy would arise. Although he saw bureaucracies as the most rational and efficient way of pursuing organisational goals, red tape would proliferate and bureaucratic regulations would begin to function purely for their own sake. The **white-collar** class would expand to become the largest group in society, a group to deal with and create more rules. The individual would eventually be swamped and life in these societies would become stifled by an 'iron cage' of bureaucracy. Life would become aimless and purposeless unless strong political control was exercised over the bureaucrats by politicians. His predictions of the future, then, took a very different path from those of Marx. Where one saw a vision of true communism and people leading fulfilled lives, the other envisaged a bureaucratic nightmare.

Ideal types

A major concept that Weber introduced is that of the **ideal type** – a model idea which is used to help the researcher when studying an area of society. This 'ideal' can never be a reality but it is used as a perfect hypothetical example against which reality – such as the organisation of the church, market competition or bureaucracies – can be compared. For Weber, any theory in society was an ideal type.

As well as making important contributions to the sociology of organisations, religion and stratification – in fact most areas of sociological theory – Weber also initiated and developed some of the central methodological debates that persist today, particularly the issues of value freedom (discussed later in this chapter) and the importance of interpretation.

It is another of the clichés of sociology to say that Weber is 'the father of interpretive sociology', though this perhaps overstates the case. In a number of texts Weber highlighted the need for sociology and social science to move away from seeing human behaviour as a response to external stimuli and, instead, to develop an understanding of what he called **social action**. By this he meant human activity in a social context that is conscious, meaningful and purposive, not reactive. It is necessary to understand human action both as being rational and as existing in a social context. Weber used the German word *verstehen* to convey this. This takes sociology away from its positivistic roots and in a new direction where human values and beliefs matter.

However, in saying this, Weber remained unwilling to depart from a structural analysis of social causes, as the phenomenologists were later to do, though the extent that he wanted sociology to move in this direction continues to be debated. Weber has a foot in both camps. He is widely seen as having opened the door to interpretive sociology, although he did not describe in detail what lay beyond that door.

Weber, then, was more concerned with the practical and theoretical considerations of sociological research than Marx, and he was as concerned to debate methodology with the positivists as he was to take issue with Marx's economics. His overall contribution

to sociology is massive, and only now are the effects becoming apparent. With his method of using structure and interpretation in the study of society, he opened up the possibility of a sociology which takes account of history, social structure and the richness and complexity of everyday life.

Questions

1 Try to define the following terms associated with the sociology of Max Weber:
   (a) ideal type
   (b) social action
   (c) bureaucracy
   (d) rational-legal authority
2 How does the sociology of Max Weber differ from that of Marx?

Symbolic interactionism

The founder of symbolic interactionism, George Herbert Mead (1863–1931), was more interested in psychology than sociology, and some critics say his theory reflects this. Symbolic interactionism is essentially a theory of **socialisation**. Becoming a human is not just a matter of being born. It's all about becoming a social being, which happens through interactions between the child and those around it.

Language and socialisation

According to Mead the inner 'I' has to be converted into the social 'me' – an individual with a social identity and understanding of the world based upon the shared experiences of interacting with others. Mead goes into great detail on how this comes about, comparing the evolution of the species with the creation of the social self. Humans have evolved beyond other animals, due to the complexity of human consciousness linked to the intricate system of symbols which we use to communicate with each other. This symbolic system is called language, and it is through using these shared meanings to communicate that humans come to be aware of themselves. Self-conscious beings learn to understand that if they wish to take part in social interactions, they will have to recognise that they have a role to play, and the way they play this role will affect other people. They must learn to try and gauge the effect they are having on other people – to see themselves as others see them. Mead calls this 'taking on the attitude of the other'.

Primary socialisation

The human infant learns that far from being 'at one' with its mother, as it had been up to birth, it is a separate being, an individual. Psychologists use the rouge test to prove this. At about eight months the child begins to recognise a mirror image as itself, and will, for example, remove a smudge of red make-up from its nose. This is a crucial stage in the development of a **social self**. The child will then go on to see its own actions in terms of the effects they have on specific others in its life – parents or caregivers. Writing on the wallpaper, for example, produces anger. The child also 'tries on' the role of others by dressing up in parents' clothes, wearing lipstick or giving the teddy bears and dolls a hard time for being naughty. To see yourself and the consequences of your behaviour as others might see them is the first step on the road to becoming a social being.

Secondary socialisation

The next stage is to move beyond the world of the family and primary socialisation into the wider society and secondary socialisation. This is called the 'game stage' by Mead, who compares it to playing as a team member. To do this successfully it is not enough to judge the effects of your performance on the reactions of a specific other; the individual must gauge the response of a whole group of people. When you learn to operate as a member of a wider group you are taking the attitude of the **generalised other** in Mead's terms. Your behaviour will be noted not just by those nearest to you but by the rest of your social group. What you have done is to develop an inner moral conscience, making you the guardian of your own behaviour. Talcott Parsons calls it internalisation of norms and values. Marx calls it taking on the ideology of the **ruling class**. Mead's contribution is to provide an in-depth interactionist account of how this actually happens.

Labelling and self-fulfilling prophecies

The taking on of the attitudes of others has a clear relationship to a central premise of interactionist theory – **labelling**. By accepting the judgements of others in this way, we are socialised into accepting the prophecies which others make about us. This is why they become **self-fulfilling** (see also chapters 6 and 8). However, Mead points out that the process is not just one way. There is conflict, and the inner 'I' is never totally blotted out. The individual is capable of

acting upon these social situations, of influencing interactions. Therefore, the social world is never entirely taken for granted, but is the result of social constructions through symbolic interactions. Ethnomethodology takes the construction of social reality a lot further.

Questions

1 Define the following in terms that are associated with symbolic interactionism:
   (a) the social self
   (b) socialisation
   (c) the 'I' and the 'me'
2 When does a human being become a social being?
3 What is meant by 'self-fulfilling prophecy'?

Ethnomethodology

Harold Garfinkel

The theory which stands at the opposite end of sociology to the most extreme forms of positivist, so-called scientific research, is ethnomethodology. This is about the way all people try to make sense of what other people do and say. It is usually associated with Harold Garfinkel, an American who studied sociology under the leading functionalist of the 1950s, Talcott Parsons. Garfinkel's perspective could be seen as a reaction to Parsons' middle-class, right-wing theories. The essence of Garfinkel's approach is that there is no such thing as society, so there is no point in arguing about which theory you use to investigate social behaviour. We all attempt to make sense of social experiences by formulating theories in our everyday lives to interpret and explain what is happening to us. Sociological explanations may be more precisely stated, but that does not make them any better than individual theories of social behaviour.

Ethnomethodology and social reality

Positivists claim that social reality exists in the form of social facts, for example crime rates and suicide rates. The symbolic interactionists see social reality in the shared use of symbols in the process of social interactions. However, according to ethnomethodology, it is something which is never actually there. Small-scale analyses of social situations reveal that the best we can do is to arrive at some sort of shared reality during the course of one encounter with another human being. This shared reality breaks down quite easily under certain types of pressure. Conversational analysis shows the fragility of interactions such as these:

'Hello, how are you?'
'Hello, I'm fine. How are you?'
'Very well, thank you.'

All very well on the surface, but does it actually mean anything? Garfinkel's method of studying such social encounters would be to get an experimenter to work at undermining this shared reality:

'Hello, how are you?'
'How am I what?'
'Well, how are you doing?'
'How am I doing what?'

This would continue until the interaction breaks down in embarrassment or anger. The other participant would usually attempt to ignore these inconsistencies, trying desperately to retrieve some sense of social reality from the situation. Eventually, however, they would break off blaming you for the failure of communication.

Garfinkel's students were encouraged to undermine social reality at every opportunity. When family and friends realised that their strange behaviour was associated with sociological studies, this was grasped at with relief as an explanation. What they were investigating was the nature of social reality, and how it depends upon each individual attempting to make sense of the situations they become involved in.

There is no guarantee that all of the people in any one situation will hold the same interpretation as to what is going on. For example, the police often find eye-witness accounts of the same event vary widely. When people discuss a film or television programme they have seen they may find they have different explanations of the plot, motive or outcome. Look around at people in a lecture or a lesson. Some are listening, some are daydreaming, others are just asleep. When they all leave that room, do they carry the same social reality, the same experience? Or, as the positivists would argue, does the register – the official statistical record of who attended that class on that day – hold the only reality?

Atkinson (1978) worked in coroner's courts and examined the interpretative processes by which suicide verdicts were arrived at. He concluded that the ways in which coroners work, their concepts and interpretations, lead to the 'official' suicide rates. He said that there is no 'real' suicide rate because the official statistics are produced after the process of interpretation.

If you have been sitting in your sociology class planning what to do at the weekend, that has been your reality. The official story has it that you were studying sociology for a specified amount of time on a certain day in a particular room.

Is ethnomethodology a social science? The positivists and structuralists would say that ethnomethodological investigations tell us little of sociological significance. Garfinkel encourages people to pick up the phone when it rings and say nothing. The caller is supposedly confused, because they have no cues for the interaction. Undoubtedly true, but what does it reveal? Ethnomethodology ignores the impact of the social structure upon these situations. Class, culture, socio-economic status can all provide explanations which could help us to understand everyday interactions. Ethnomethodology is more like social psychology than sociology, but it does play an important role in the debate between micro and macro perspectives, and highlights the problems of accepting 'social facts' as reality.

Questions

1 How does ethnomethodology undermine belief in 'social facts'?

2 How do ethnomethodologists interpret the phrase 'social reality'?

Feminism

In the past few decades, a new approach has emerged which challenges the way that sociologists have looked at the society they study. Feminism criticises sociology for uncritically adopting a male perspective and marginalising the roles of females in society. Feminists believe that this failure both reflects and contributes to the undervaluing of women. Why has sociology had so little to say about women's lives and experiences?

'Malestream' sociology

Prior to the 1960s, there was undoubtedly a strong case for arguing that sociology could be seen as male ideology. Women did not figure in studies of **social mobility**; little was written about women and deviance; their 'natural' domestic role went largely unquestioned; studies of work were largely about men. Feminists argue that the consequence of this 'malestream' research is that women have been ignored, distorted and marginalised in sociology.

Feminist responses

Following the realisation that sociology has looked at society only from a male perspective, feminists have responded by trying to create a sociology that explores and attempts to explain women's subordination and places women at the centre of the sociological study. It has not been a unified response, but one which has taken three directions: integrationalist, separatist and reconceptualist. The integrationalist approach argues that **sexism** in sociology can be overcome by making every attempt to take the role of women into account when looking at work, leisure, crime, education and so on, grafting them on to the existing body of knowledge. The separatist approach argues that women should be studied separately from men, on the grounds that all women's experience is qualitatively different from men's. The most important division in society, separatist feminists argue, is based on gender. (This point of view is examined further in chapter 3.) The reconceptualist approach argues that it is not possible to make up for the imbalance in sociology by simply including women in existing research, or by constructing a sociology of women only. Instead, sociology and sociological priorities must be reconceptualised: sociological theory must be rethought and rewritten, and the basic assumptions of malestream sociology fundamentally challenged. This third view implies a revolution in the way sociology is practised, breaking down the traditional categories of sociology and emphasising new priorities, especially the private sphere of the home and domestic relationships.

Feminism: a new perspective?

Are we then entitled to add feminism to the list of existing perspectives in sociology (functionalism, Marxism, Weberianism, ethnomethodology and symbolic interactionism)? Abbott and Wallace (1990) argue that the answer is no 'because there are a number of distinct feminist perspectives, not just one'. Feminist sociologists may embrace other perspectives: 'what they have in common is a commitment to looking at the world through the female prism'.

The debate regarding the status of feminism within sociology continues, and is a necessary part of the development of sociological theory. The impact of feminism upon sociology is undisputed, and has broadened and deepened the analysis of society. Why 'malestream' sociology emerged in the first place is now the subject of much feminist analysis, and is a good example of the way sociology continually examines and criticises itself.

Questions

1 What are the main issues that concern feminist sociologists?
2 Why has it been necessary to develop a feminist viewpoint in an attempt to understand society?

Post-modernism

It has been increasingly argued in recent decades that fundamental changes have taken place in the way that Western societies are organised, and that these changes are clearly visible in all spheres – economic, cultural, political, social and intellectual. The 'modern' era, with its origins in the seventeenth and eighteenth centuries, has come to an end and has been superseded by a 'post-modern' age. This argument has profound implications for the future of the study of sociology.

Traditional and modern

The modern era can itself be said to have superseded the 'traditional' when the rural and **agrarian** gave way to an urban and industrial society. This is described by W.W. Rostow. At the heart of this transition to modernity was the founding of an intellectual tradition that sought to reject old ways of understanding the world based on religious knowledge, and replace it with knowledge based not on faith but on reason. It was out of this movement – usually known as the Enlightenment – that the embryo of sociology was formed, and it is the claims of the Enlightenment project that its new critics – the theorists of **post-modernism** – are most concerned to contest.

The Enlightenment

Although it was a broad-based movement, the Enlightenment can be described as the collective writings of eighteenth-century French thinkers such as Rousseau (1712–78), Voltaire (1694–1788), Diderot (1713–84) and Montesquieu (1689–1755), who are sometimes collectively known as the *philosophes*, and Scottish writers such as Hume (1711–76) and Adam Smith (1723–90). In a theological age, these writers argued the case for raising the status of science, for a more rational understanding of the world, based on belief in the possibility of the use of reason to increase human understanding of the world in which they lived. At the same time, they sought also to contest the claims of what they believed to be ignorance, prejudice and superstition. Through the use of reason, and their commitment to test all ideas against what their senses told them, they believed that they could come up with a scientific knowledge whereby truths that applied in any situation – universals – could be found to exist.

Underlying this aspiration was the belief that part of this knowledge would lead to improvements in the way society was organised and the way people led their lives. As a secular intelligentsia, they were progressive in their thinking, making claims for the individual as the centre of their analysis, an individual who would be free and allowed to think whatever they dared, without fear of religious or political persecution. In doing so, they opened the door to the possibility of a science of society, to the extent that some have claimed that in the eighteenth century 'sociology' would have been translated as the work that the *philosophes* were doing, before it was further developed by Saint-Simon (1760–1825) and Comte (1798–1857). During the nineteenth and early twentieth centuries these ideas became professionalised and institutionalised by the 'founding fathers' – Marx, Durkheim, Tönnies, Simmel and Weber – and it is their intellectual inheritance, in the form of social science, that has been largely described and discussed in this book.

Post-modernist criticism

The theorists of post-modernism attack the Enlightenment inheritance at its foundations. A project committed to the pursuit of truth, reason, certainty, progress, secularism and control over nature has produced a world which in the twentieth century has witnessed two world wars, continued famine, global pollution, 'ethnic cleansing', the sustained rise of religious **fundamentalism** and the collapse of the Soviet bloc. It is therefore difficult to conclude that there is an inner logic of history leading to the perfection of the human condition. As Zygmunt Bauman remarks, 'the two-centuries-old philosophical voyage to certainty and universal criteria of perfection and a "good life" seems to be a wasted effort' (Bauman, 1988). This sense of disillusionment is what has been described by one of the most prominent post-modernist writers, Jean-François Lyotard (1984), as 'the post-modern condition'.

This new condition is present in all aspects of life. In philosophy, it is marked by the claims of relativism – there are no universals, and there is no objective or scientific truth. Sociology, which is strongly linked to philosophy, also exhibits the post-modern condition in that in all of sociology's subject areas post-modern thinking is making a significant and subversive

The failure of social science? Ethnic cleansing in the Balkans at the end of the twentieth century.

contribution. It is no longer possible (if it ever was) to scientifically analyse an increasingly secular and industrial world as if the class structure of an isolated nation-state were the key to understanding behaviour, explaining how people vote, their consumption of 'high' or 'low' culture, or their propensity to criminal acts. Men are no longer the sole breadwinners, living in nuclear families with the same job and a wife for life, with a limited choice of programmes to watch on television. The projections of modernist sociology have been examined and found wanting.

Post-industrialism

The growth of service industries and the absolute decline of manufacturing industries, the spread of flexible working, part-time working, temporary contracts, niche production and so on mean that the industrial world has become post-industrial, and Fordist production has become **post-Fordist** (see chapter 9). In the analysis of **stratification** the dimensions of age, gender and ethnicity are now seen to be at least as important as the concept of class, which in turn has ceased to be defined simply by the relationship people have to the means of production. Patterns of consumption of goods and services are now thought to be equally as important as an increasing number of people own property and contribute to pension schemes and private health care plans. If there is an overall pattern to be perceived, it is one of diversity and differentiation at all levels.

The boundaries of the nation-state have been breached as capitalism has become a global economic system, marshalled by a stateless, transnational capitalist class. New technologies have also brought about the possibility of a global media village. The main distinction to be drawn in the post-modern era is that between what is global and what is local. New social movements are evident in the way people behave politically, contesting not traditional battles drawn on class lines but uniting to take on planners and supermarket owners in the interest of environmental and neighbourhood protection. The

'green' movement is becoming a force in all areas of life as more and more people attack the equation that 'big' science equals progress. The idea that humans are the most superior life form – anthropocentricity – is being radically attacked. The dominance of traditional religious organisations within Christianity is being challenged not by full-blooded atheism but by the emergence of **sects** and an interest in new age religions emphasising individually attained spiritual awareness and fulfilment. New age travellers have challenged modernist notions of community. As family forms diversify into **nuclear**, single parent and reconstituted families, and as more and more people choose to live alone, the 'post-modern family' has been identified. There is now a great variety of routes by which educational qualifications can be attained, in an education system that has become increasingly localised in its control and administration. Decades of criminological research have resulted in a crisis of **aetiology** where the causes of criminal behaviour in a welfare society are now thought to be highly complex, if they can be understood at all.

Disneyland: fantasy, reality or hyperreality?

The ubiquity of mass media technologies has broken down the distinction between high and low culture and even the distinction between culture and society. All have become equally indistinguishable from the economy as we become defined as consumers with needs, and cultural artefacts are either used to sell commodities, or have become the commodities themselves. 'Pop' art appears in art galleries, and classic art appears on T-shirts, compact disc covers, and is now commonly used in all areas of advertising. Style and surface have superseded content. Because the world of media signs, symbols and images is central to our discourse, the nature of reality has also been transformed. For Baudrillard, people do not visit Disneyland to escape America, but because it is America in its 'hyperreal' form. 'Disneyland is presented as imaginary in order to make us believe that the rest is real, when in fact all of Los Angeles and the America surrounding it are no longer real, but of the order of the hyperreal and of simulation. It is no longer a question of a false representation of reality (ideology), but of concealing the fact that the real is no longer real' (Baudrillard, 1988).

Metanarratives

Yet it is at the level of the overarching theories – or **metanarratives** – in sociology that the most powerful body blows are being aimed. This is encapsulated in Lyotard's now famous and frequently quoted declaration that post-modernism can be described as 'incredulity towards metanarratives', where a metanarrative is a grand-scale attempt to show how empirical and rational methods can be used to demonstrate how society as a whole works, revealing its inner logic and dynamic. In sociology, theories such as Marxism, functionalism (particularly Parsons' *Social System*) and feminism, can be described as examples of these 'totalising' theories, seeking to cover an impossibly large subject area, making ridiculously vast generalisations, and in the end only telling stories like any other fiction.

If the progress to truth and absolute knowledge has not been achieved, then what has been created can be better described as stories (narratives) or even 'mythologies' that can never be verified. Positivism, Marxism, and objective science are no more than modern mythologies, comforting people with the pretence that attempts are being made to answer the great questions of existence. The post-modernists (though very few of them accept this title) reject what they see as the pretensions and pomposity of science, particularly social science, claiming that at best it should be seen as 'language games' and 'rhetorical jousting'.

Identity

Even the way we think about ourselves is in transition. Here, the Enlightenment view differs from the sociological, in that, from Descartes on (1596–1650), people were seen primarily as individuals, particularly in the formulation of law, economics and the Protestant religion. An individual's identity was seen as something that stayed the same throughout their lives. In this sense, their identities were 'centred'. Sociology, particularly through the contributions of writers such as Cooley and Mead, sees people not as isolated, free-standing individuals but as **socially constructed** in the process of interaction between the 'self' and society, taking on the roles and identities of the world we live in and are socialised into.

Post-modernism sees identity as fluid, arguing instead that the processes of fragmentation and differentiation mean that identities are continuously changing and even contradictory. We have no fixed, essential or permanent identity. If we nevertheless believe that we have maintained the same identity throughout our lives, constructing what Stuart Hall (1990) calls a 'narrative of the self', it is only to comfort ourselves, in the same way that other narratives and metanarratives (or mythologies) have been constructed to solve other existential problems.

Traditional identities such as class, family and neighbourhood membership are being eroded away. New identities, however, are not being formed to replace these. For some writers, the mass media and popular culture now provide the sole but nevertheless inadequate frame of reference for the construction of identities. Yet: 'No new forms or institutions, no new ideas or beliefs can now serve to give people a secure and coherent sense of themselves, their place and time, nor are there any longer legitimate and acceptable ways by which they can define themselves to themselves and to others' (Strinati, 1992).

Post-feminism

Writers describing themselves as post-feminists or feminist post-modernists have entered this debate by questioning the feminist assumption that all women can be assumed to live similar lives and share similar experiences. Women's lives are cross-cut by other dimensions such as class, age, ethnicity, 'colour', sexual orientation and able-bodiedness. The way that these identities are perceived (not least by the individual) can change many times in a person's life. As Elizabeth Spelman (1988) argues, metanarratives about 'woman's oppression' therefore become highly problematic, when it is so unclear which woman feminists have in mind.

Resistance post-modernism

In its denial of the claims of the modernist project, two directions have been discerned in post-modern analysis. Lather (1991), for example, contrasts her own 'postmodernism of resistance' against the nihilism and cynicism of a 'postmodernism of reaction', where the latter takes a pessimistic view of the possibility of human emancipation. Such a pessimistic view can be found in the writings of Jean Baudrillard (echoing Nietzsche) who states that 'The mass is dumb like beasts, and its silence is equal to the silence of beasts … it says neither whether the truth is to the left or to the right, nor whether it prefers revolution to repression. It is without truth and without reason' (Baudrillard, 1983). Elsewhere he argues that post-modernism is 'more a survival among the remnants than anything else' and that 'All that remains to be done is to play with the pieces. Playing with the pieces – that is postmodernism.'

Resistance post-modernism (sometimes called oppositional post-modernism), however, sees possibilities in the diversity and multi-centredness of the post-modern condition. Traditional forms of resistance have broken down but have been replaced by a multiplicity of localised, participatory and non-hierarchical forms, for example within the multi-voiced post-feminist movements.

Criticisms of post-modernism

Many writers have been unwilling to dismiss the Enlightenment project as easily as the post-modernists (such as Lyotard) have done, seeing instead serious flaws in the post-modernist case. A frequently made point is that it contradicts itself in the claim that there are no universal truths – facts that everyone agrees are true. The statement 'all things are relative' sounds very much as though it is itself claiming the status of absolute truth. For sociologists, although no two cultures are the same, comparing cultures can be fruitful even if we conclude that these cultures have different ways of interpreting their worlds.

The Marxist reply

Marxists and neo-Marxists have been particularly active in refuting the post-modernist position, especially because they are one of this group's main targets. Alex Callinicos (1990) is dismissive of post-modernism as a theory, seeing it in Marxist terms, as 'the product of a socially mobile intelligentsia in a climate dominated by the retreat of the Western labour movement and the "overconsumptionist dynamic of capitalism in the Reagan–Thatcher era"'. The implications of this are clear: the class struggle is not over yet and never will be until **post-industrialism** also means post-capitalism. Furthermore, it is not even the case that Fordism as a form of work organisation has yet run its course.

Modernity is really only a poor synonym for capitalism. Marx made it clear as early as 1848 that this is a highly dynamic system: 'The bourgeoisie cannot exist without constantly revolutionising the instruments of production, and thereby the relations of production, and with them the whole relations of society … Constant revolutionising of production, uninterrupted disturbance of all social conditions, everlasting uncertainty and agitation distinguish the bourgeois epoch from all earlier ones. All fixed, fast frozen relations … are swept away, all new-formed ones become antiquated before they can ossify. All that is solid melts into air' (Marx, 1848).

According to Callinicos, Marxist theory continues to be the best living example of 'Radical Enlightenment'. All that has really happened is that some former socialist intellectuals have turned to defeatist posturing as a way of earning a living. Socialist feminists have also made it clear that post-feminism makes little sense until a post-patriarchal society is attained.

Jameson

Less fundamentalist Marxist theorists have been willing to concede some of the post-modernist arguments. Frederic Jameson (1991) agrees that post-modernist analysis is possible at a cultural level, but sees it as 'the cultural logic of late capitalism', where late capitalism has superseded market and monopoly capitalism, even turning culture (as aesthetic production) into something to be bought and sold. While it is true to say that class politics are in abatement, and 'new social movements' are mounting the most successful resistance to global capitalism, it is in the logic of Marxist theory that a transnational proletariat will eventually unite to wage a global class struggle. To date, however, there is scant evidence of this occurring.

Harvey

In a similar vein, David Harvey (1989) agrees that in many respects the way people live their lives has changed rapidly and substantially in recent decades. 'Time-compression', by which he means the way that countries and markets can be reached in hours rather than weeks, or instantly through communication networks, encourages people to think that they live in a fast-moving world. The way work and employment practices are regulated has also changed very quickly. Yet it is also possible to find much continuity present through a period of change, and to find cultural conflicts similar to those described as the post-modern condition in earlier periods of modernity. Unable to choose between modernity and post-modernity as the most useful way of describing the age in which we live, Harvey argues that 'Whatever else we do with the concept, we should not read postmodernism as some autonomous artistic current. Its rootedness in daily life is one of its most patently transparent features.'

Giddens

From a non-Marxist position, Anthony Giddens (1990) also concedes some of the post-modernist argument, particularly their criticism of the view that there is a continuous progression in history, and their view that the 'indubitable foundations' of knowledge that the Enlightenment thinkers sought do not exist: 'no knowledge can rest upon an unquestioned foundation, because even the most firmly held notions can only be recognised as valid "in principle" or "until further notice". Otherwise they would relapse into dogma and become separate from the very sphere of reason which determines what validity is in the first place.' Yet to accept these points does not at all mean that all of post-modernist theory has to be accepted. As with other writers, Giddens argues that the post-modernist position is contradictory, recycling older arguments and mistaking them for something new.

It is contradictory, for example, to argue that, on the one hand, we have moved from modernity to post-modernity, and on the other to say that history has no shape or direction. It is equally paradoxical to write books that say that no knowledge is possible, when the books themselves constitute knowledge. What has been described as post-modernism is better seen as the engagement of critical reason in

'radicalised modernity', in an age where more and more people in the Western world – not simply intellectuals – are becoming more self-aware and inquisitive about the roles that they play. What is happening is that modernity has become more reflexive, looking inwards on itself, which may reflect the overall decline of the West's privileged and **hegemonic** position in the world, as the process of **globalisation** gains in intensity. We cannot therefore describe a new post-modern world.

Interactionism

What is perhaps most curious in the debate about sociology raised by the post-modernists is that it is only directed at part of sociology, the scientific or positivistic tradition to which Marxism, functionalism and (to a lesser extent) Weberianism have been the main contributors. Doubts about their scientific status are not new to sociology. Since at least the 1920s interactionist sociologists have raised questions of cultural relativism and have sought to examine the nature of small-scale interactions in the generation of meaning, and the plastic and changing nature of identity. It is at least debatable whether these theorists would recognise much that is new or that they would wish to take issue with in the post-modernist argument.

Questions

1 In what ways can post-modernism be defined?
2 Why do classical Marxists reject post-modernism?
3 How could modernity be distinguished from post-modernity?
4 Can the economic be distinguished from the cultural?

Values, norms, roles and status

Values

A value is a belief that something is good or valuable. It defines what is important, worthwhile, and worth striving for. For example, in modern Britain the value of individual achievement is highly regarded, while in many smaller-scale societies the importance of group solidarity is emphasised. Values imply that there are certain appropriate forms of actions that ought to be taken; for example, life is precious, therefore it is wrong to kill anybody.

Values change as times and circumstances alter. Child labour, for example, was considered quite acceptable in Britain until the mid-nineteenth century when opponents began to express their opinions publicly. Today, the thought of young children working in the mines and factories would be abhorrent to the population.

Norms

The word norm may cover many types of rules, including customs, conventions, social etiquette, morals and laws. The factor common to all of these is that social pressure in some form is exerted to increase the chances of conformity to the norm. Some norms appear trivial, such as those about appropriate dress at the theatre, or the correct use of cutlery at formal dinners. Others may be deeply felt, and serve as a basis for the moral order, such as those that forbid incest, treason, or murder. The common link between them is that a person who fails to obey them in the appropriate situation will meet with punishment, disapproval or even exclusion from the group.

Roles

The values of the culture in which we live define the roles that we play and the pattern of behaviour that goes with those roles. Roles can be defined as a set of normative expectations. We all play many roles in the course of our life, sometimes even in the same day. Other people see us not as the unique individuals we perceive ourselves to be but by the particular roles we are playing at that time. The relationships we form as a direct result of having a role are called a role set. Unhappiness with or consciousness of playing this role is described as role distance. Social order is only possible because we understand that others are playing certain roles. Some roles are replicated throughout institutions, for example teacher and student. On occasion, individuals may find themselves playing two contradictory roles at the same time, such as employee and mother, or they may define their role differently to the way others expect them to. Such situations involve role conflict.

Status

The term **status** refers to the level of social honour or prestige given to someone by others, either as a result of the formal role they are playing in their social position, or for the individual skills and talents they display. Different occupations are associated with different levels of status, although differences of status also exist within an occupation – a status hierarchy. Some statuses are given to us or ascribed, such as mother, father, daughter or son. Others may be chosen, or achieved, such as employment roles –

being a firefighter or a judge. The status accorded a role is defined by the culture in which you live. The elderly as a status group, for example, carry a lower status in Western than other societies. Taking on a new role that carries higher status than the previous role may lead to status dissonance if individuals find it difficult to play that role.

In industrial societies, the primary stage of socialisation is further extended when children enter the education system. This is called secondary socialisation. At school they learn wider values of society outside their experience of the family, and are treated not as particular individuals but as members of a larger community. When they leave school socialisation continues as they prepare to enter adulthood and when they become parents the cycle begins all over again. Socialisation is a continuous, never-ending process.

Criticisms

This somewhat mechanical picture becomes far more complicated when attempts are made to operationalise these concepts, that is, to make them work in a meaningful way in the process of research. Over time, these terms have come to be hotly contested in such a way that the simple and one-dimensional definitions given above are no longer agreed upon by sociologists.

The link between norms and values, for example, may not be as strong as first supposed. Some people may share a cultural desire to become close to God, and this may be their sole reason for attending a place of worship. Others may go to please their family and friends, or to maintain their social status. Just because people behave in the same way it does not mean that their motives are the same. This may mean that it is not possible for sociologists to make generalisations about the motives behind behaviour.

Further questions have to be asked: do people have a choice in playing their various roles? Exactly how does socialisation happen? Can it be resisted? What are sociologists referring to when they describe the culture of a society? Does everyone really share the same values of the culture they live within? It may be the case, if we look carefully, that there is as much evidence of conflict around these values, as there is consensus.

The clear implication of these questions is that there can be no one single view of culture and socialisation; rather there are many. Taken to its extreme, there could be as many views as to what constitutes a culture as there are individuals living in that culture, as we cannot assume that everyone perceives the world around them in the same way. Sociologists can choose to don many different pairs of spectacles in their efforts to 'see' something as complex as a society. As with other academic disciplines, as we have seen, there are many perspectives in sociology.

Questions

1 Define the following terms which were discussed in the previous section:
   (a) norms
   (b) values
   (c) role set
   (d) status
2 Describe the values of schools or colleges with which you are familiar.
3 What are the norms involved in classroom behaviour?
4 What are the differences between the roles played by teachers and the roles played by students?
5 List the roles that you may play in any one day of your life.

Socialisation

Sociologists agree that sociology is about understanding what humans do, not through studying the biological or individual psychological make-up of individuals, but by examining the way that the society in which they live influences and shapes what they do. In the debate about whether humans behave 'naturally' or are 'nurtured', sociologists are firmly on the side of nurture. This is the central argument of sociology.

Societies work or function because each individual member of that society plays particular roles and each role carries a status and norms which are informed by the values and beliefs of the culture of that society. The process of learning these roles and the norms and values appropriate to them from those around us is called socialisation. It takes place because people learn that social sanctions exist to encourage behaviour appropriate to their roles and to discourage inappropriate behaviour. These sanctions may be negative or positive. Negative sanctions operate at a number of levels. **Gender** roles, for example, can be maintained informally by calling people names, such as 'tomboy' for girls and 'sissy' for boys. Persistent offenders may be ridiculed or even excluded by those around them. Positive sanctions can include praise for what is considered appropriate behaviour, remarking on a girl's pretty dress or a boy's toughness and

determination. The most intensive period of socialisation occurs within the family and is called primary socialisation. It is in the family that, by imitation, babies learn to walk and talk, to act like mummy and daddy, and in the process take on the gender roles of those they identify with. In this way, we learn to be human.

Different conceptions of what is meant by the term socialisation, and of how this process takes place, tell us much about the wider philosophical positions taken in sociology already outlined. In particular this debate concerns the question of whether a social identity is something that can be chosen and interpreted by individual actors or whether an individual's identity is in reality more analogous to an actor playing a role in a stage play where their lives and lines have already been written for them.

Durkheim

From one point of view, socialisation is seen as a one-way process in which society, through agencies such as the family, the education system and peer groups, inculcates individuals into the roles already prescribed for them by those agencies. This view is strongly put by one of the 'founding fathers' of sociology, Emile Durkheim: 'Certainly society is greater than, and goes beyond, us, for it is infinitely more vast than our individual being; but at the same time it enters into every part of us. It is outside us and envelopes us, but it is in us and is everywhere an aspect of our nature. We are fused with it. Just as our physical organism gets nourishment outside itself, so our mental organism feeds on ideas, sentiments, and practices that come to us from society' (Durkheim, 1902–6). Society can be seen as a system of moral norms in which individuals are essentially passive, responding without choice to imposed rewards and punishments. Socialisation then comes to mean virtually the same as training, or even taming, where each individual becomes a microcosm of a society's values. As the emphasis is on the lack of choice open to an individual in taking on their social roles, this is also sometimes described as the 'totalitarian' view of socialisation.

Parsons

This view is less stridently present in the systems theory of Talcott Parsons. Here, the focus is on how society as a social system maintains order, where a system is defined as 'two or more interacting units which are at the same time actors and social objects to each other' (Parsons, 1951). Social order is maintained by individuals learning to desire what the culture of a society provides, and in doing so their personalities become structured by the social roles they internalise, i.e. these social roles become part of them. The end result is conformity. Deviant behaviour – behaviour that goes against social norms – can therefore be explained as the consequence of inadequate socialisation. The consequences of this particular argument and much of what follows below are explored in much greater detail in the sociology of crime and deviance (see chapter 8).

Mead

From another perspective, built on the theories of G. H. Mead outlined earlier in the section on symbolic interactionism, the focus is on how an individual passes through a series of stages in taking on their social identity. From birth, children are confronted with a number of ready-made roles which, as they pass through the various stages of socialisation, they consult in the same way that a map can be read. In doing so, they become socially competent, taking on the social skills and knowledge necessary to interact with others. Individuals are portrayed as active in the acquisition and negotiation of their social identities or selfhood. This is a continuous process throughout their lives, sometimes referred to as a 'biography'.

It is through the family that the child's identity is formed, a process identified by C. H. Cooley as primary socialisation. Even here there is opportunity for reciprocity and negotiation in that parents learn their roles as parents (defined with the birth of the first child) at the same time as the child learns its role. A child may be said to have become self-conscious when it realises that it can not only talk to others but can be reflexive and talk to itself. It can objectify itself when it realises that it exists as an independent entity. It becomes a self-conscious individual only through interaction with others: its 'I' becomes the socialised 'me', where the socialised part of the self is seen as its identity, and socialisation is equated with the acquisition of language.

G. H. MEAD (1868–1931)

American social psychologist and a founder of symbolic interactionism. Mead's social psychology revolved around the theory of the way the mind worked, the concept of 'self', the origin of communication and the social act. In sociology his ideas were built upon by Blumer as a basis for symbolic interactionism.

C. H. COOLEY (1864–1929)

Early American sociologist. Trained as an engineer, he moved away from science and turned to sociology. He advocated that sociologists should try to use the sociological imagination to imagine the imagination of actors. He came up with some major concepts: the looking-glass self and the idea that there is a distinction between primary groups, characterised by face-to-face interaction and co-operation, and secondary groups.

Secondary socialisation

Later in life, at the stage of secondary socialisation, it will choose from the roles of the generalised other – which at its widest is society. By taking on the role of the generalised other, the self becomes fully social. Primary socialisation may not be a lasting or determining influence on this stage. Does the school, for example, simply take over from the family? Some symbolic interactionists employ the concept of a career here, though they stress that in these careers, there is no necessary, laid-down path for people to follow in their identity transformations. This is particularly true in the notion of 'deviant careers', for example becoming a drug user or an alcoholic. At this stage, in responding to 'situations', there are a great many opportunities for the negotiation and interpretation of identities. H. Blumer emphasises the choices facing individuals: 'the acting unit necessarily has to identify the things that it has to take into account – tasks, opportunities, obstacles, means, demands, discomforts, dangers, and the like; it has to assess them in some fashion and it has to make decisions on the basis of the assessment' (Blumer, 1969).

H. BLUMER (1900–86)

American sociologist. He is credited with developing the term symbolic interactionism. He advocated the small-scale study of social interaction against the claims of large-scale, abstract theorising.

Goffman

For Erving Goffman, roles are best seen as played, performed or dramatised within the rules surrounding social rituals (for example, getting dressed up to 'go out'), where what we do in private is seen as backstage activities, and possessions are seen as props. Of particular interest to Goffman is what happens when these props are removed, for example on entering an asylum, when 'existence is cut to the bone' and the individual undergoes what Goffman calls 'mortification of the self'. In the asylum studied by Goffman, patients' personal possessions were taken away from them, the patients were cleaned and issued with clothing by the asylum. All this entails a loss of their former sense of self. An individual's sense of self is recovered by a range of modes of adjustment, for example bending the rules of the institutions: 'Our status is backed by the solid buildings of the world, while our sense of personal identity often resides in the cracks.' He therefore moves beyond Mead's view of the self as a constant entity by distinguishing 'person' from self: 'Person and self are portraits of the same individual, the first encoded in the actions of others, the second in the actions of the subject himself' (Goffman, 1971).

Although two different perspectives on socialisation are being presented here, one emphasising the action of society on individuals, the other emphasising the individual's interpretation of social roles, neither are uncritically accepted, either inside or outside sociology. Other sociologists have been critical of the lack of attention paid to economic and political forces, arguing that being born into a rich or poor family, for example, influences the form taken by primary socialisation. Psychologists, following Freud, question whether sociologists, in denying the importance of nature, limit their view of a process as complex as the acquisition of a human social identity.

> ### ERVING GOFFMAN (1922–82)
>
> American sociologist and major contributor to the interactionist perspective, particularly in works such as *Asylums* (1961) and *The Presentation of Self in Everyday Life* (1959). The study of small encounters and interaction in everyday life is of particular interest to Goffman.

Wrong and oversocialisation

In what has become an important and influential essay, Dennis Wrong (1961) takes issue with what he believes has become the 'oversocialised concept of man in modern sociology'. In using the term 'oversocialisation' Wrong is highlighting what he believes is sociology's inability to take into account the emotional or affective aspect of people's lives. Socialised individuals cannot be seen simply as 'roles in system'. The internalisation of norms is not analogous to the programming of a computer, with humans dehumanised into an input/output model. There is no necessary reason to

suppose that individuals will automatically play the roles assigned to them, or will internalise them to the same degree. They can become overburdened by the weight of role prescriptions. Wrong holds that psychology, Freudian psychology in particular, has important lessons for sociology.

Freud

Psychology has been much concerned with the problems of innate behaviour in its debates about the relative importance of 'nature' and 'nurture'. Freud was less concerned with innate behaviour, but he did aim to analyse forms of unconscious conditioning. Freud chose to use the German word 'Trieb' rather than 'Instinkt' to denote what he saw as psychological drives and desires rather than biological instincts. Freud saw an individual's psyche as being in a state of conflict between their ego (the conscious reality-testing self), their id (instincts and unconscious, perhaps repressed life) and their super-ego (the values internalised from parents and the wider society). What we know of someone is only their ego. Internalisation of values is not synonymous with conformity. Hence, as Wrong states, 'To Freud, it is precisely the man with the strictest superego, he who has most thoroughly internalised and conformed to the norms of his society, who is most wracked with guilt and anxiety.' Such a person, rather than being the 'best' socialised, may suffer psychological illnesses and be unable at times to function well in society.

> ### SIGMUND FREUD (1856–1939)
>
> Practising physician, specialist in the treatment of nervous diseases, and founder of psychoanalysis. Freud developed the concept of the unconscious. According to this, motives and ideas, unavailable to the conscious mind, originating in childhood, play a major part in the life of the adult.

It would also be a mistake to believe that because an individual has taken on a role they have therefore been socialised into it – that they have internalised the role. It is important to distinguish between socialisation and social control, where the latter refers to situations where individuals have no choice but to play their role. The ethnomethodologist Harold Garfinkel criticises ways of looking at people as 'cultural dopes', as if they simply play roles given to them. The interactive process of socialisation is missing, as is the possibility of people individually or collectively rejecting their roles. As Blumer argues,

HAROLD GARFINKEL (1917–)

He is most strongly associated with ethnomethodology, examining how people make sense of everyday life. His work was of most interest in the 1970s; there is less enthusiasm for it now.

'The common repetitive behaviour of people in such situations should not mislead the student into believing that no process of interpretation is in play.' Furthermore, this type of sociological thought 'rarely recognises or treats human societies as composed of individuals who have selves … These typical conceptions ignore or blot out a view of group life or of group action as consisting of the collective or concerted actions of individuals seeking to meet their life situations' (Blumer, 1969). This moves the emphasis away from seeing people as harmoniously socialised into the world.

Both Mead and Parsons were aware of the implications of Freud's work for their own theories and chose to reject or incorporate parts of his work. Parsons, for example, admits that there are many aspects of personality that cannot be explained by 'role obligation' and he describes these aspects as an individual's 'autonomy'. Indeed, he says, without this autonomy, creativity and personal morality would not be possible (Parsons and Shils (eds.), 1951). In order to understand how individuals come to develop the 'need dispositions' that enable the social system to function, Parsons employed Freud's concept of the super-ego. This concept, he argues, is equivalent to Durkheim's notion of the constraining role of moral norms. The similarity between these two ideas, he says, 'from two quite distinct and independent starting points, deserves to be ranked as one of the truly fundamental landmarks of the development of modern social science' (Parsons, 1952), although the problem of conflict within an individual's psyche is left unresolved.

Gerth and Mills

Problems with Mead's account of secondary socialisation and the 'generalised other' were taken up by Hans Gerth and C. Wright Mills (1954). For Mead, 'generalised other' refers to the general values and moral rules of the culture in which a child develops. But does this culture mean the whole society or only part of it? Mead gives no clear definition of what he means by the term 'society' – 'the great co-operative community process', seeing it in places as synonymous with 'the generalised other'. For Gerth and Mills, the generalised other of any given person or persons, however, does not necessarily represent the 'entire community' or 'the society', but only those who have been or who are significant to them. From this point of view, it is difficult to know what Mead means by the term society in any detail if all individuals one comes into contact with are significant others, representatives of the generalised other.

Gerth and Mills' own attempts to integrate Freud's theories with Mead's are only partially achieved. They reject any notion of instinct and choose instead to employ neo-Freudian notions of the self as plastic or malleable. Freud's 'drives' or unconscious motives are seen simply as 'unverbalised areas of feeling and conduct' which may be obstacles to self-realisation. In doing so, they claim that 'Various philosophical assumptions that had crept into Freud's theory have been torn out with little or no damage to what remains as usable heritage.'

On the central question of socialisation, some writers have argued that a synthesis of Parsons' and Mead's positions can be achieved if it is accepted that Parsons starts with society and ends with the individual and Mead simply does the opposite. This conclusion has been vigorously resisted by Mead's defenders, particularly Herbert Blumer, who argues that, in reality, there is no opportunity for individual choice in Parsons' theory, and therefore he is incompatible with Mead: 'The gap between Mead and Parsons is profound' (Blumer, 1975). Moreover, 'Structural features such as "culture", "social systems", "social stratification" or "social roles", set conditions for … action but do not determine action.' Attempts to fully incorporate Freud's model of the self have also largely been resisted although Marxist sociologists such as Marcuse, Habermas and Althusser and non-Marxists such as Parsons and Philip Rieff have used other aspects of his theories. What we are left with is an unresolved debate concerning the problem of the self, identity, socialisation and oversocialisation. This debate reproduces itself in all other areas of sociology.

Questions

1 What is the difference between primary and secondary socialisation?
2 What is meant by oversocialisation? Have sociologists successfully countered its implications?
3 How important is language in socialisation?

Socialisation in childhood

Evidence for the importance of socialisation

The importance of socialisation is demonstrated if we look at what happens when children are deprived of human contact. The cases we shall examine illustrate different degrees of exclusion from culture and include examples where children have been partially deprived of what a culture has to offer as well as those extreme cases of children who reputedly have been reared in the wild by animals.

In the United States in the 1940s two girls, Anna and Isabella, were separately discovered who had been living in almost total isolation from human contact. In both cases the girls were illegitimate and had been hidden away because the parents and grandparents were ashamed. The girls were discovered at around the same age of development (six years). Neither girl could walk, talk or feed herself. Both had great difficulty understanding anything that was explained to them or done for them. After being taken into care and looked after, Anna and Isabella made good progress, learning to feed themselves and to speak a few sentences. This would seem to demonstrate the essential role played by the environment and education in the stages of child development.

There are also several cases of children who, reputedly, had been raised by animals. One of the best documented concerns the so-called 'wolf-children' of Midnapore. Two females, aged two and eight, were reportedly found in a wolf den in Bengal in 1920. They walked on all fours, preferred a diet of raw meat, and lacked any form of speech. Whether these children had been raised by wolves or simply abandoned and left to their own devices in the forest is unclear.

In 1978 another well-known case came to light when a boy of about five was discovered playing with wolf cubs in the Musafirkhana forest in India. He hid from people and would only play with dogs. At night Shamdev, as the boy was later named, grew restless and it was necessary to tie him up to stop him going out to follow the jackals that prowled around the village at night. If people cut themselves, he would smell the blood and rush across to it. His favourite food was chicken. He caught them, killed them and ate them raw.

Such examples indicate that socialisation involving prolonged interaction with adults is essential not only for fitting new members into society but also to the process of actually becoming human. However, they may also lend support to the idea that the capacity to be socialised and to be human has a genetic basis. The

Nature and nurture: will the courses of identical twins' lives be more influenced by their biology or socialisation?

cases of Anna and Isabella in particular would seem to suggest that most human characteristics are virtually resistant to obliteration by even the most deprived early environments. The girls made good progress in developing human characteristics and skills once they were exposed to an intensive socialisation process. It is difficult to see how this could have been achieved were environmental factors the only influence on behaviour. In some way, the capacity to learn language and to interact successfully with others would seem to be part of what we inherit from our parents; in other words, it has a basis in nature, though of course it also requires nurturing in an appropriate environment to bring these potentials to fruition.

The construction of social identities

The cases of children brought up with little human contact illustrate the importance of socialisation in acquiring general human characteristics such as the ability to communicate using language. However, socialisation is also important in shaping the particular identities that each person acquires during his or her lifetime. These identities are linked to the performance of particular roles, such as male/female, child/adult, member of a cultural or occupational group, etc. A conventional assumption is that social identities reflect natural differences between people. Thus it may be assumed that playing with toys and seeking the attention of adults are forms of behaviour that infants are naturally predisposed towards. The process of growing out of childhood and maturing into an adult is also often seen as something that happens automatically to people once they reach a certain age. Yet these commonsense assumptions run up against the problem that there is considerable cultural diversity in the behaviour patterns of infants. Similarly, the age at which people are considered adults varies between societies. These cultural differences suggest that, far from being natural, the identities associated with the roles 'child' and 'adult' are shaped to a large extent by social factors.

Similar issues arise in discussing gender identity. A commonsense view is that merely by being born male or female we are in some way 'pre-programmed' to know how to behave appropriately as a 'boy' or a 'girl', a 'man' or a 'woman'. But again we find that the rules regarding sex-appropriate tasks vary enormously from one culture to another. Without being part of a particular culture and *learning* its norms and values, it would seem impossible to know how to behave as a 'man' or a 'woman' in that society. In this view it is nurture (what we learn from others) rather than nature that is the key to understanding gender differences. It is worth considering this debate in more detail as it has played a central part in attempts by sociologists to demonstrate the importance of socialisation.

Gender identity

The terms sex and gender broadly correlate with the distinction between nature and nurture. Sex refers to the biological differences between the sexes. These physiological features determine whether a person is male or female. All differences which are psychological or cultural are gender differences. These are social constructions and depend upon the individual being socially identified and having an identity as a man or a woman. So sex differences determine that women shall bear children but it is a gender difference that results in more girls following examination courses in home economics.

The biology case

Tiger and Fox (1972) take the view that for the greater part of human history, women were involved in the highly specialised task of bearing and rearing children, whilst men hunted the game, fought the enemies and made the decisions. They argue that through 99 per cent of history men have been hunters and that the aggression, power and leadership qualities required for this pursuit have been built into their genes by a process of 'biogramming'. Women and their children are the essential social unit, and women are programmed for softness, affection and non-aggression. To go against this biogrammar was to go against nature. Tiger and Fox believe biogrammar overrides the influence of culture, and is even stronger than instinct. Thus the roles of men and women complement each other; they are biologically shaped and socially functional.

There are others who take a similar position, believing a woman's biological constitution predetermines her for household and child-rearing tasks. Talcott Parsons (1959a) argues that the two main functions of the modern family are socialisation and stabilisation. He sees women as naturally in command of the socialisation process and as the 'expressive' partner of the marital relationship. Parsons sees the expressive role of a woman as necessary both for the security of her children and for relieving the tensions of her working husband.

Murdock (1949) argues that man's greater strength and woman's ability to bear children make men better equipped to do the heavier jobs and women more suited to doing the lighter and less essential jobs. Therefore, the sexual **division of labour** is an efficient means of dividing socially necessary tasks among the members of a population. In his study of 250 societies, Murdock found that men hunted, mined and lumbered, while women gathered food, cooked, carried water and made and mended clothes. As women were hampered by child-bearing and children it was better that they took the less essential tasks that were nearer to home and were better suited to their weaker constitution and physique. According to Murdock the division of labour by sex arises from differences in strength (for males) and the demands of pregnancy and motherhood (for females).

Critique of the biology case

Feminist sociologists reject the suggestion that biology makes women into better mothers and housewives than men. They argue that sexual differences are socially, not biologically, determined. The term used to describe the socially acquired characteristics associated with a particular sex is gender. Ann Oakley (1972, 1981) argues that although a division of labour exists, men do not always perform the same jobs. She took Murdock's 250 societies and found 14 societies where lumbering is female or shared; 36 where clearing the forests is female work and 38 where cooking is shared. She draws our attention to the Mbuti pygmies, who have no division of labour by sex at all, and to the Aborigines, for whom fishing and seal hunting is women's work. In the former USSR and Eastern bloc countries and in Israel, women are not discouraged from 'male work' on the roads or in the steel mills. In India, 12 per cent of the workers on building sites are women. Oakley concludes that biological theories are based on the benefits and values of Western culture so are biased and not scientifically well founded.

The study by Margaret Mead (1928) of the Arapesh, Tchambuli and Murduganor tribes highlights the variation in culturally imposed roles. In Murduganor society both sexes are assertive and are fully involved in all aspects of social life. Among the Arapesh, both men and women are what we would call 'feminine' – gentle, passive, caring. Child-rearing is a shared activity. After a few days the wife will start hunting again, leaving the children with her husband or her parents, and she could be as long as 14 days away from home. The Tchambuli role organisation is

completely the opposite of what we take for granted as normal. Males are regarded as the emotional ones. They adorn themselves, gossip and dance. The women run the society and are the more assertive sex.

The importance of Mead's study is that these three tribes are biologically identical but they differ markedly in the social roles they assign to male and female. This suggests that, to a large extent, the patterns of behaviour associated with men or women in a particular society are learnt.

Sherry B. Ortner (1974) puts forward the view that women are devalued in society because they are associated with 'natural' activities, e.g. pregnancy and birth. Such natural activities are accorded a lower status than politics, religion and top business posts that are largely undertaken by men. Feminists argue that these inequalities of status between men and women in wider society spill over into inequalities within the family.

Feminist sociologists use the term 'patriarchy', the domination of women by men, to argue that women are exploited in the home, at work, and in education. This exploitation is not 'natural': it does not rest on biology, but is cultural and ideological. Men's power over women is built into the social structure, even within sociology itself. Feminists believe this must be attacked and changed.

Gender socialisation

Gender roles are socialised into children in the family and reinforced at school. Gender role socialisation refers to the various ways in which a child learns to act in a manner which society regards as being appropriate to his or her sex. Role modelling and role expectations play an important part in this process. Parents expect their children to behave in certain ways according to their sex. Even apparently innocent observations such as: 'He's going to be a big strong boy' and 'Isn't she a pretty little girl?' imply that males should be active and females passive. As children grow older they are increasingly typecast into what sociologists term masculine and feminine gender roles. To play a social role is simply to act a given part.

Books and comics may also influence the process of gender socialisation. Children's story-books, for example, present traditional **stereotypes**. Princes rescue princesses. The heroes are males. The boys indulge in danger and the girls stay out of trouble, 'scared'. Children's book-reading schemes such as the 'Ladybird' series show Peter with his trucks, Jane with her doll and Peter up the trees retrieving the ball while Jane watches. Girls are presented as passive, caring and dependent; boys as aggressive, adventurous and independent.

Similar points can be made about the choice of children's toys. Many regard 'Lego' as a sexually neutral toy, but look at the choice of sets bought by parents and other relatives:

→ 95 per cent of model cars/planes and train sets go to boys
→ 85 per cent of dolls' furniture goes to girls
→ 95 per cent of fire station sets go to boys.

The children themselves buy only 7 per cent of the sets that are sold; parents and grandparents buy the vast majority. Thus even a simple playbrick can reinforce differences between masculine and feminine behaviour. This process continues in schools, as you will see in a later chapter. When girls leave school at 16 or 18 they often get jobs that are as well paid as those held by boys of a similar age, but opportunities for career advancement and salary increase are considerably fewer.

Subtle processing of females into gender roles takes place through activities in the media and advertising. The cosmetics industry uses unvarying, all-pervasive images of female beauty in its advertisements in order to exploit women's insecurities about looking beautiful and being desirable in order to catch a man. Television dramas present stereotypes such as the nagging wife or the dumb blonde. Some newspapers and magazines feature photographs of naked or semi-naked young women, thereby portraying women as the passive objects of male fantasy.

Are there any fixed differences between males and females?

The feminist sociologists we have considered so far have attempted to show that social influences are more important than biological factors in determining the behaviour of the sexes. Other writers have gone beyond this level of debate to question the very basis of what are seen as the biological ('fixed') differences between men and women.

Kessler and McKenna (1978) are ethnomethodologists who have investigated the way that scientists categorise the differences between males and females. They argue that there is no clear-cut way of differentiating between men and women on the basis of biological 'facts'. Chromosome counts can be misleading because it is possible for an individual to have male chromosomes yet appear female, and vice versa. Nor can genitals be regarded as a clear indicator

of sex. Hermaphroditism is a condition where a person has both male and female genitals. There is also the evidence of transsexuals who have the genitals associated with one sex but feel themselves to be members of the 'opposite' sex.

Birke (1986) has argued that there are no 'pure' biological differences between men and women. Rather, these differences are the product of a complex interaction between biological and cultural interpretations. She points out that the belief that hormonal differences are crucial in shaping the behaviour of men and women is held despite the fact that there is no one hormone, or even class of hormone, that belongs uniquely to one gender or the other.

The social construction of age

In the same way that we are happy to use terms such as 'working class', 'middle class', 'masculine' and 'feminine' without ever defining precisely what we mean, so we also use terms describing age without putting an exact figure against them. When does infancy end and childhood begin? When do you cease to be an adolescent and become an adult? When do the middle-aged become old? Are all 'old' people the same or are there groups among them, such as the 'young elderly' and the 'elderly elderly'? If you are 70, are you 'old' or simply 'as old as you feel'?

Age and the law

These questions can lead to a number of enquiries about past and present perceptions of age, yet what is important here is to recognise that age is a significant way of defining status within society, and one way that society is stratified. (There is a more detailed discussion of stratification in chapter 3.) The most obvious forms of stratification or inequality exist at either ends of the age scale. If you are 'young', a number of legal rights are denied to you throughout your youth, and are gradually gained with increasing age, ending in Britain with the right to stand for Parliament at 21 years. (You can vote from the age of 18 years.) At the age of 65 (for most men and now women) you are obliged to retire from your employment, and make do with whatever savings and pensions you have for the rest of your life. At 70 you will have to reapply for your driving licence. Although it is not always the case, power in industrial societies tends to be concentrated among those who are middle-aged – approximately 40 to 60, though when middle-age begins and ends is as hotly contested as any other age-band.

> ## CHILDREN: RIGHTS AND RESPONSIBILITIES
>
> Growing up is marked by a continuous succession of years in which new rights and responsibilities are gained. In the UK:
>
> → **At five** children can drink alcohol in private although they must also receive full-time education.
>
> → **At ten** they can be convicted of a criminal offence if it can be shown that they know the difference between right and wrong.
>
> → **At twelve** they can buy a pet without a parent being present.
>
> → **At fourteen** they must pay full fare on public transport, and can be held fully responsible for a crime. If convicted, boys can be sent to a detention centre, and convicted of rape.
>
> → **At sixteen** they can leave school, whereupon they become eligible to pay prescription charges and for some dental treatment. They can also buy fireworks, premium bonds and enter a brothel legally.

The main ages that sociologists have been interested in studying are childhood, youth and old age. All three, it is argued, are phases of life that came to take on distinct identities in industrial societies in the twentieth century. If the parameters of these phases vary from time to time and place to place, then they cannot be absolute or fixed stages of life, but products of the society that they inhabit; these concepts of age are socially constructed.

Childhood

As a result of historical research, Philippe Ariès (1962) concluded that the idea that children should be treated separately from adults, and that childhood is a separate and distinct phase of life, dates back only a few centuries in Western Europe. Before 1600, he claims, 'the idea of childhood did not exist … as soon as the child could live without the constant solicitude of his mother, his nanny or his cradle rocker he belonged to adult society'. The separation of childhood from adulthood is a product of later centuries, particularly, in Britain, the Victorian era of child legislation, reforms in child labour, and the imposition of compulsory education.

Up to 1750 more infants died than lived. The infant mortality rate was high, as was the incidence of childhood illness and disease. There was a general indifference to children until they reached five or six years. Life for most people was harsh. Towards the end of the sixteenth century, dead children began to be represented on their parents' tombs, the sign of a new era. Children were becoming more valued by their parents, but there was still no separate world of childhood.

Many people slept in the same room. The home was not, as we now think of it, a private place reserved for the family. Children grew up and worked and played alongside a range of kinfolk, acquaintances and friends; socialisation was a by-product of community life.

In the nineteenth century, children of the lower classes still went out to work at an early age in the mines, climbing chimneys and labouring in factories. Gradually laws were passed restricting the hours they were permitted to work. Attendance at school finally became compulsory in the 1880s and the school-leaving age was gradually raised. This has had the effect of prolonging the age of dependence of children.

Changing relationships within the family and the decline in family size further contributed to the new position of the child. Families today are better off and if they have financial problems the State will help them. Higher standards of living have benefited children, and today, with reduced working hours, parents have more time to devote to them. Children are seen as the means by which the family can progress. As a result of these changes, Ariès argues that young people have experienced very protected lives and this has given them high and idealistic expectations of society.

Perspectives on childhood

Although the historical accuracy of Ariès' view has been disputed – by, for example, Linda Pollock (1983) – the emergence of childhood as a distinct phase has been variously explained by sociologists. Thus for functionalists, the growing complexity of industrial societies and the increasing division of labour lead to the need for an extended period of primary and secondary socialisation. For Marxists, it is clear that the emergence of childhood results from the transition from feudalism to capitalism and the growth of wage labour. As with female labour, the costs of reproducing labour become the responsibility – and burden – of the wage earner. Labour power is reproduced without cost as the worker pays for children's upbringing, not the employer. In the same vein, feminists such as Shulamith Firestone (1970) see this same process intensifying the patriarchal position of the male breadwinner over his wife and children, as economic and political power is appropriated to him.

The role played by children in the family is, according to J. Hood-Williams (1990), better described as 'age patriarchy'. Contrary to the functionalist view he argues, with clear echoes of David Cooper (1972; see chapter 5), that the study of childhood should presume 'the existence of antagonistic relations within families' and should focus attention on 'the differential distributions of power, work, violence and rewards. All this is at some distance from analyses which study children through concerns around play, pedagogy, development or even mass media and markets.'

All these views reflect the observation that, in the same way that concepts of childhood have differed from time to time and from place to place, so also there is nothing fixed about the status of children: their role is socially constructed and is not a consequence of the 'nature' of children. A clear example of this is the difference between the roles of children in the developed and less developed worlds, with child labour prevalent in the latter. Childhood is a central fact of age stratification in particular and stratification in general.

In the light of this perception, childhood has become of increasing interest to sociologists. It throws doubt on any studies (such as those of Jean Piaget (1954)) that view childhood behaviour as biologically determined, with generalisable and universal phases of development. For interactionists, there is also clearly a need to examine not only the passive aspects of children's lives – undergoing socialisation – but also how they are active in creating their own child-centred view of the world, and their own distinct culture. (Discovering this world has obvious problems for the participant observer!)

Childhood in transition

Iona and Peter Opie (1967) claimed to have identified a 'self-contained community in which children's basic lore and language seem scarcely to alter from generation to generation'. This view of childhood as separate and unchanging is now open to doubt. In industrial societies, Neil Postman (1985) argues that children are becoming increasingly empowered, speaking more for themselves, conscious of their own rights, becoming sports and media stars, and, increasingly, watching the same programmes and enjoying the same music as their parents. Children are no longer seen as 'economically worthless but

emotionally priceless'. With children becoming increasingly expensive to raise, and work becoming more and more home-centred, V. Zelizer (1985) argues that, in a newly democratised domestic setting, the phenomenon of 'housechildren' could emerge along with that of 'househusbands'.

Critical perspectives

However, others have argued against any attempt to reach general conclusions about the nature of childhood. Such conclusions downplay the importance of factors that separate different groups of children, such as social class, ethnicity and gender. J. and E. Newson (1974) identify differences between children of middle- and working-class parents, for example. They argue that middle-class children tend to be future-orientated; they are more likely to be brought up to expect the future to be better than the present as the family standard of living rises and as the parents move up through the pay scales of their occupations. In contrast, children of working-class parents tend to go for immediate satisfaction, as their family future prospects are less secure. Newson goes on to argue that middle-class children (particularly boys) tend to be more sheltered and protected by their families than children of working-class parents.

Another distinction identified by Newson is the encouragement that middle-class children have to become good communicators (spoken and written). Working-class children receive less support to assist communication skills. Differences have been detected in the play style, with middle-class children playing more imaginative, role-taking games. Interactionists, following G. H. Mead, stress that children's play is crucial to the creation of the self by social interaction.

Ariès' argument that children today lead sheltered, confined lives separated from the harsher realities of the adult world may also be questioned for failing to give enough consideration to differences between different groups of children. While many children, particularly those in the middle class, are largely removed from adult experiences, there are still many young people from socially deprived backgrounds who lead lives of cruelty, exploitation and abuse. Their experience of childhood will inevitably be very different from that of children from more advantaged backgrounds.

Social order and control

Order and predictability are important if society is to exist. There must be rules and regulations that guide human behaviour if people are to engage in any form of social life. How could people cooperate in any joint venture if they lacked a common understanding of how they are expected to behave and what they aim to achieve? Without this mutual understanding social encounters would be chaotic and demoralising. Indeed, it is unlikely under such circumstances that the evolution of humankind as a species set apart from other animals would have been possible.

Social rules and regulations are only very general guides to action, however, and there is much scope for them to be interpreted in different ways depending on the individuals and groups involved. This can sometimes lead to conflict over how rules are to be applied and what standards of behaviour should be followed. Indeed, there are few, if any, societies that are completely orderly. Nearly all the modern industrial nations have experienced severe conflict in recent history, both with other nations and internally. Extreme examples of conflict include wars and civil unrest. Thankfully for most countries these forms of conflict are infrequent. But there are many other forms of conflict and disorder that occur as a routine part of most societies. Examples include industrial disputes, crime, disruptive behaviour by pupils in the classroom, disagreements between family members, etc.

In many instances, order and conflict exist side by side: two teams in a hockey match, for example, are able to play against each other successfully only on the basis that they have the same commitment to the rules of the game, and yet they may also fall out during the match over, say, a contested penalty decision. Where people are interacting together there is always the possibility that a misunderstanding or disagreement may occur that will transform an orderly process into a conflict-laden encounter. Likewise, many conflicts can be seen as an attempt by the parties involved to resolve disputes and establish or restore 'order' by putting right something that each perceives in different ways to have gone wrong. Victory in the Second World War, for example, allowed the Allied powers to bring about 'a new world order' that included the United Nations Charter and other mechanisms for defining how nations should behave towards each other and treat their own citizens. Similarly, conflict may occur in a marriage where the partners have different ideas about how they should behave within the relationship. Each partner would be putting forward his or her own view of the norms and values that should be followed (the 'social order') if they are to have a harmonious, conflict-free marriage.

Conflict may also lead to changes in the values and beliefs that govern behaviour in a society. In the UK, for example, the suffragette movement organised demonstrations and other forms of protest as part of a campaign to win voting rights for women in the early years of the twentieth century. Though they faced considerable opposition, the suffragettes were eventually successful in their campaign and the law was changed so that women were enfranchised on the same basis as men.

Social control

In order to persuade people to follow the normal ways of behaving, societies have developed two methods of ensuring conformity: informal and formal social control. The most common form of social control is informal and is based upon the socialisation process. Socialisation and social control are mixed together, so it is difficult to distinguish one clearly from the other. After all, it is through the socialisation process that people learn about the values of society and if this process has been successful conformity will follow automatically. In this case, social order is produced through a form of moral agreement or what functionalists refer to as 'value consensus'. Marx fully recognised that this process occurs, but he argued that the poor and exploited are often socialised to accept a social order that is against their true interests. He described this as a form of ideological control that the rich and powerful exercise through the influence they are able to bring to bear on institutions that play a key part in the socialisation process, e.g. education, religion, the State, etc.

Informal social control refers to the mechanisms that are used to reinforce socialisation. It is based on rewards and encouragement for correct behaviour and sanctions such as ridicule, gossip and comment for incorrect behaviour. Threats of punishment in the after-life, for example, have been used in many societies over the centuries to discourage people from behaving badly. Likewise, the promise of heaven has been put forward as a reward to encourage conformity to the moral codes that people are taught through socialisation.

Since the end of the nineteenth century, however, the power of religion has declined in modern industrial societies and that of the education system and the mass media has increased. The mass media exercise informal social control in a variety of ways. They may discourage people from behaving 'abnormally', for example, by portraying such behaviour as deviant and unacceptable to the majority of the population. Likewise, schools exercise a social control function through teaching the core values of society and punishing pupils who fail to conform to the rules and regulations.

Informal social control may also be exercised within small-group settings. Tactics such as ridicule and ostracism may be used, for example, to punish people who contravene the group's expectations about what is acceptable behaviour. They may act as a powerful deterrent to people who might otherwise reject the group's norms and values. In some cases, however, it can have the opposite effect. For instance, it may trigger a rebellious non-conformity by people who find the group norms too restricting and inappropriate for the way they want to live.

Formal control refers to the public, legal forms of controlling the population. Certain activities are regarded as dangerous to society, by those who hold power, and are therefore forbidden. Special agencies appointed for the purposes of social control include the police, the courts and the prisons. They catch, judge and punish anyone who breaks the law, and in the process they attempt to deter others from doing the same thing. The armed forces are also a means of formal social control, though in general they are only used as a last resort to prevent order breaking down or when it has already broken down.

Social order

There are different views about how social order is created. Thomas Hobbes, a seventeenth-century philosopher who was writing during and after the civil war in England, believed that humans are naturally selfish and competitive. He argued that without strictly enforced rules and order, the degree of competitiveness between people was such that they would constantly be locked in a relentless and chaotic struggle against each other. The only way of avoiding anarchy, or what Hobbes termed 'the war of all against all', was through the security derived from strong government. Hobbes considered that people are rational and that therefore they would accept the need for strong government in order to restrain their selfish desires and avoid chaos in society.

A different approach to the problem of social order can be found in the work of Emile Durkheim (1893,

1912). He agreed that humans naturally have unlimited desires; no matter how much we have, we will always want more. This means that if desires are to be satisfied, some way must be found to limit them. But for Durkheim, it is society (not the rational individual) that acts to limit our desires through establishing a set of moral codes that the individual learns to accept as the appropriate way of behaving in relationships with others. The individual not only accepts these moral standards, but he or she also *internalises* them. That is, the individual comes to want that which the society deems it proper for him or her to want. The rules of society become incorporated in our personalities so that they shape our thoughts, feelings and desires. Durkheim referred to this phenomenon as the *collective conscience*.

For Durkheim, society is *in essence* its moral codes, the rules of which govern the relations between its members. He claimed that two types of bond that help to cement human relationships underpin these codes. He called them the mechanical and organic principles of solidarity. Mechanical solidarity is characteristic of small-scale and simple societies, where there is little division of labour, and little differentiation of institutions. People use similar skills and perform similar tasks; and their bonds arise from this sense of shared experience. In contrast, organic solidarity is characteristic of modern complex societies, in which there is a high degree of division of labour. In such circumstances, people lead very different lives, and receive very different rewards for what they do. But in spite of such pressures to instability, we are aware of the interdependence that is a result of the division of labour and which makes it impossible for any of us to survive without the support of others. This discourages any individual or group from acting alone and disregarding the feelings, interests and views of others. There is an impetus to accept rules and standards that are good for others, and not just for our self.

Durkheim's description of the two types of social bond highlights the importance he places on moral codes in a complex society. If we were only motivated by calculations of self-interest, as Hobbes claimed, such a complex interdependence would be too unreliable, and would surely break down. For modern society to exist, Durkheim argued, there has to be a basic agreement on values. We mentioned above that functionalists refer to this as 'value consensus' and that Marxists are sceptical about how far such moral codes reflect the interests of society as a whole, as opposed to serving only the selfish ambitions of the rich and powerful. It is interesting to contrast Hobbes' and Durkheim's views of how social order is achieved with those of Marx.

The Marxist view of social order

For Marx, social order is achieved through the domination by the few over the many, and that domination is possible because it reflects the economic circumstances of the groups. In capitalist societies, for example, order arises from the economic pressures that force the working class to accept the conditions of employment and way of life imposed on them by the privileged few (the bourgeoisie) who own the means of production. It is only sustained by the domination of non-owners by the owners, which the latter achieve by maintaining a monopoly of power, by being the creators of the dominant ideas of each era, and by their continuing economic control. But this order is constantly unstable precisely because it is based on inequality, and it leads in turn to an inevitable and continuing conflict of interest between those who own the means of production and those who don't.

Because the Marxists are seeking explanations of order in power relationships, they criticise the functionalist assumption of value consensus. They use the word 'value' to mean the same thing, but do not accept that there is only one set of values in a society. Instead, for Marxists, values are the reflection of social relationships. Our consciousness of the options available to us may largely arise out of our experiences and the generally accepted views in our society, but it is a dynamic and changing consciousness, and it is likely to differ from the consciousness of others in different positions in the social structure. Thus Marx believed that although people in the working class may be influenced by the dominant ideology of the ruling class so that they have a degree of 'false consciousness' about the extent of their exploitation and where their true interests lie, this did not rule out the possibility that a different consciousness would develop among members of that class – a socialist consciousness, for example, that would challenge the status quo and inspire the fight for equality and the redistribution of wealth. History suggests that Marx was right, at least in the sense that socialist labour movements developed among the working class in various industrialised countries during the late nineteenth century and went on to gain considerable popular support in the following century.

The interactionist view of order

The interactionists, in contrast to the functionalists and Marxists, emphasise that members of society are not just constrained in their everyday lives by moral codes or by economic relationships which come from 'society outside', but that as actors in each situation they negotiate about which moral standards are to be taken as relevant in that particular situation. Additionally, interactionists argue that our way of making sense of our everyday world is, in a sense, a moral process. Because of the nature of language, it may be difficult to distinguish fact ('A man has just pushed in front of me in the queue for the bus') from my evaluative response to it ('A man has just pushed in front of me in the queue for the bus. I think that is a very rude thing to do, and it makes me angry.').

In practice, we put a moral value on many facts, and often feel morally obliged to accept as real what other people believe to be facts. Yet what is 'real' to one person may not seem equally objectively true to another. A successful young American lawyer may genuinely believe that there is equality of opportunity in America based on her own experience, and that of a proportion of the people she knows. A homeless, unemployed person of the same age and colour, and of the same original social class, may believe equally genuinely that there is not equality of opportunity in America, because she now meets and mixes with a different group of people, whose experiences contradict that assumption. Their differing experiences will colour their expectations, and their expectations will influence the interpretations they make of the succeeding experiences they have. For interactionists, it is important to notice that people are not just passively doing as they are told, and not just cogs in the wheel of economic pressure. They are bringing their own existing expectations to a situation, and these expectations will influence the outcome of the interaction.

Questions

1 What is meant by the phrase 'age is a social construct'?
2 Distinguish between formal and informal social control.
3 How is social order enforced in modern industrial societies?

Do mass cultures still exist?

Culture

The term culture has frequently been used by sociologists to denote the way of life of a society. This concept has itself been adapted from social anthropology, where in the late nineteenth century E. B. Tylor used it to describe 'that complex whole which includes knowledge, belief, arts, morals, law, customs and any other capabilities acquired by man as a member of society' (Tylor, 1871). If society is composed of social institutions and activities, then culture defines the values and beliefs that underlie those institutions, activities and the form that they take, whether they are the family, education, religion, or even what is acceptable to eat and the way it is eaten. The focus is on shared meanings. This way of looking at culture is sometimes described as the culturalist view, where the stress is on interpreting the meanings of a culture that is lived.

The investigation of the nature and dynamic of these shared meanings has come to be a central concern for sociology. However, a second definition of 'culture' has also been used by sociologists, and this originates in social anthropology and the work of Claude Lévi-Strauss. This sees culture as a social practice where communication is the central activity. This communication can take many forms, for example verbally in the form of language, but principally takes the form of the signs and symbols which create shared meanings. From this point of view, culture is a set of signifying practices – an example of which could be the way that authority is symbolised. All of these produce meaning, according to the structure by which they are arranged. These symbolic forms, which can be any cultural artefact, are described as texts. As such, they can be read or 'decoded' by sociologists. This approach is often described as a structuralist approach, where the focus is on the analysis of the production of meaning, although the term structuralism is also used to emphasise the influence of society as a whole.

CLAUDE LÉVI-STRAUSS (1908–)

An anthropologist and the founder of structural analysis in this discipline. This looks at how the analysis of concepts can reveal the working of the human mind by reference to myths, totems and language. His work has strongly influenced writers such as Barthes, Foucault and Lacan.

It is a short step from Lévi-Strauss's concept of structuralism to the more modern discipline of **semiotics** (see also chapter 2). Here, the emphasis is on the communication between signifier, signified and sign. The sign can be anything – the clothes you wear, the commodities you buy, the newspapers you read. These signs are said to denote in representing particular cultural values, they also connote by engendering particular feelings. It is this interpretation of culture that has been of particular value in the study of youth cultures (see also chapter 3).

In attempting to answer the question of whose meanings are being shared, and where they have originated from, many writers have distinguished not one culture within the structure of Western societies but many. Most are agreed that something that could be described as a separate culture exists among a minority at the apex of society, though opinion is divided as to how to describe this minority, whether as an élite or as a ruling class.

High culture

This culture, usually described as 'high culture', is frequently mistaken as constituting the sole culture of a society, to the extent that high culture and high society have been read as *the* culture and *the* society. This stems partly from claims it makes for itself, as Q. D. Leavis (1932) made clear: there exists 'a select, cultured element of the community that sets the standards of behaviour and judgement, in direct opposition to the common people'. For her, and many other members of a disparate group described as the 'élite' or 'mass society' school, this culture is clearly superior to any other form of culture, being the location of virtue, reason and human excellence – 'the best that has been thought and said in the world', in Matthew Arnold's phrase. Those outside of this culture are seen as the folk, the people or, following the growth of mass education, universal suffrage and the mass media at the end of the nineteenth century, the masses.

Edward Shils (1971) has described not two but three distinct levels of culture in industrial societies: the highbrow (superior and refined), middlebrow (mediocre) and lowbrow (brutal), where, in the latter, 'the depth of penetration is almost always negligible, subtlety is almost entirely lacking, and a general grossness of sensitivity and perception is a common feature'.

Elite theory

As the pre-industrial folk culture of the people gave way to mass culture and 'mass man', many writers, such as Vilfredo Pareto, Friedrich Nietzsche, Dwight Macdonald, T. S. Eliot and F. R. Leavis (with differing emphases), gave great attention to the question of how high culture could be kept separate and preserved. Little good could be found in the culture of the masses, who, as Giner remarks, were 'seen as powerless when well ruled, and ephemerally powerful when its riotous crowds are allowed to get out of control … This mass is basically amoral, superstitious and ignorant … mass man … is not really a member of civil society: he is manipulated, unfree and alienated' (Giner, 1976). In the view of mass society theorists what lay beyond high culture was moral disorder, the disintegration of traditional society ties that bound individuals to the community, and anarchy.

One of the main forces in the creation of this mass culture was the mass media, originally the press and cinema, which substituted a 'pulp' culture for folk culture. 'Mass' man ceased to be directed by inner feelings and traditions and instead became 'other directed' – easy to manipulate by those who control the mass media. The implications of this argument are explored further in chapter 10.

Criticisms of élite theory

Most of the claims of the **élite** or mass society theorists have been contested. Doubts have been raised about their romanticisation of folk culture; the argument that high culture is superior to, rather than different from, other cultures; and the simple division of society into an élite and the mass. Edward Shils, for example, argues against 'the utterly erroneous idea that the twentieth century is a period of severe intellectual deterioration and that this alleged deterioration is a product of a mass culture … Indeed, it would be far more correct to assert that mass culture is now less damaging to the lower classes than the dismal and harsh existence of earlier centuries had ever been.' Other writers have argued that the high/mass culture distinction is better described as bourgeois and working-class or popular culture. Finally, the idea of a single mass culture has been queried.

The Frankfurt School

Some of the élite theorists' fears about mass culture were shared – albeit for different reasons – by the writers of the Frankfurt School. They were concerned to explain the failure of the Russian Revolution of 1917 to spread across the industrial world as Marxists expected it would. Class conflict appeared to be dying out. For these writers, particularly Theodor Adorno, Max Horkheimer and Herbert Marcuse, the emergence of mass culture did not promise social improvement but rather the opposite and could substantially help explain the apparent absence of class conflict, and even the rise of fascism in the inter-war period. For these writers, who came to be called critical theorists, 'all mass culture is identical'. Mass culture produced not anarchy but uniformity, standardisation, conformity and predictability and was a major prop to maintaining the status quo. Mass culture was directed and controlled by a capitalist culture industry, served up like any other commodity. Consciousness of the need for, and possibility of, social change was being eliminated by cultural practices that contained and defused conflict between social classes. The working classes were being depoliticised. At the same time, the suffocating spread of bureaucracy and 'technical reason' (the unfeeling logic of a technologically based society) had also carried into the intellectual world in the form of rationalism, positivism and value-neutrality.

Marcuse

For Marcuse, capitalism would always deliver the goods, which had become ends in themselves, symbolising all that was good in capitalism: 'The products indoctrinate and manipulate; they promote a false consciousness … it becomes a way of life. It is a good way of life – much better than before – and as a good way of life it militates against qualitative change. Thus emerges a pattern of one-dimensional thought and behaviour' (Marcuse, 1964). Knowledge of any other possibility of social and cultural organisation becomes impossible as society falls under the hypnotic spell of a capitalist mass culture. The massification of high culture removes its key quality – its separateness and its critical quality, even its capacity to subvert the existing status quo – and it ceases to be two-dimensional. It loses its 'authenticity'. Marcuse and others of the Frankfurt School aimed to develop critical theory, which could 'transform the will itself, so that people no longer want what they now want'.

Criticisms of the Frankfurt School

Although the Frankfurt School theorists have been influential critics within cultural studies, they have been criticised by other Marxists for being

HERBERT MARCUSE (1895–1979)

An important member of the Frankfurt School, influenced by Marx, Freud and phenomenology, he attempted to explain how capitalism produces false consciousness in the working class.

insufficiently orthodox in their Marxism. In particular, it has been argued that they overemphasised the importance of the 'superstructure' of society and downplayed the social 'base'. In Marxism the base refers to the economic conditions of production, and the **superstructure** refers to the social and political forms. This is made clear by Marx in one of his most-quoted passages: 'The mode of production of material life determines the general character of the social, political and spiritual processes of life. It is not the consciousness of men that determines their being, but, on the contrary, their social being determines their consciousness' (Marx, 1859). In this reading, what we have been calling 'culture' cannot be studied in isolation but has to be understood as the product of the specific mode of production and social relationships in operation at the time. Capitalism is an economic system in which a small social class, the bourgeoisie, owns the capital and a large social class, the working class, has only its labour to sell. The culture of a capitalist society is everywhere affected by these basic social relationships.

Marxism and ideology

For Marxists, the concept of culture overlaps, although not exactly, with the concept of ideology. As Stuart Hall remarked: 'Something is left over when one says "ideology", and something is not present when one says "culture". "Culture" … operates along certain dimensions which "ideology" does not, while "ideology", in its turn, brings into play a set of meanings which are not present in the concept of "culture"' (Hall, 1978). The concept of ideology adds a political dimension to the concept of culture. Marx himself had no doubt where the leading ideas in society originate: 'The ideas of the ruling class are in every epoch the ruling ideas, that is, the class which is the ruling material force of the society is at the same time its ruling intellectual force' (Marx, 1845–6). This formulation explicitly relates economics, politics and culture in a way which cultural theory does not.

Many Marxists, however, have tried to develop a more subtle understanding of the relationship between the base of society and the superstructure, arguing that Marx can also be read in such a way as to show a two-way interaction between the two.

Althusser

This interpretation is present in the writings of the French Marxist, Louis Althusser, although his style of writing was itself far from straightforward and is itself the subject of many competing interpretations. This is particularly true of the way he uses the term 'ideology'. In one formulation he uses it to describe how ideology blinds people to the real nature of their social relationships, making them see imaginary relationships, not real ones. Ideology is 'profoundly unconscious'. Furthermore, it is through ideology that social relations are reproduced through what he calls 'ideological State apparatuses', for example the family, education, religion, politics and the culture industry. These are not neutral institutions but are filled throughout with ideological assumptions (for example, the way 'knowledge' is presented in a school – see chapter 6).

In turn, however, Althusser has been criticised for seeing ideology as all-pervasive, and capitalism as all-powerful. There seem to be no chinks in the armoury of capitalist ideology. If it cannot be resisted or challenged then the dominance of the bourgeoisie is permanent. It is for this reason that the concept of hegemony, developed by the Italian Marxist Antonio Gramsci, has in recent decades been built into the way ideology is understood.

LOUIS ALTHUSSER (1918–89)

A French communist intellectual and Marxist philosopher. He argued that social formations consist of distinct areas – economic, political and ideological – each of which has a level of independence from the others. The economic area determines the shape of a society, in the last instance, but not without the influence of the other areas.

Hegemony

Hegemony refers not to ideological dominance but to ideological leadership, and does not presuppose that the ruling class will be the leading intellectual or moral force, or that the subordinate class or 'masses' are passive and quiescent. The hegemony of one group over another is never total but has to be continually won, maintained and reproduced in the form of consent. This was, after all, how the bourgeoisie came to be the leading class as it won social and political power from the aristocracy in the formation of the capitalist mode of production. Importantly, if hegemony can be won then it can also be lost. In the resulting 'crisis of hegemony', when consent is being lost, order can only be maintained through the coercive power of 'repressive state apparatuses', such as the army, the police and the prisons. This fact was of particular relevance to Gramsci, who spent much of his adult life in prison under Mussolini's fascist government.

ANTONIO GRAMSCI (1891–1937)

Italian Marxist imprisoned for ten years by Mussolini. Best known for the concept of hegemony, he argued that ideas are not produced in the economic base alone. He also identified the importance of civil society as an arena for struggle.

Hegemony is never fully achieved as it ultimately always relies on consent. Gramsci describes this as a 'moving equilibrium'. It is the possibility of punching holes in the canopy of hegemony that has allowed many writers to argue that what has traditionally been seen as 'mass culture' is better described as 'popular culture', where cultural activity that has traditionally been seen as being imposed from above becomes seen as working-class people gaining 'cultural space' for themselves, and transforming ideas and artefacts for their own purposes. This has also been construed as the beginnings of proletarian resistance.

Popular culture

As with all of the terms we have discussed in this section, 'popular culture' has been variously defined. In this case, what matters is what it is being contrasted with. In some usages it describes everything that is left over when high culture has been taken into consideration, or it is used as a synonym for 'mass culture'. In these usages, popular culture is compared unfavourably with a pre-industrial folk culture and, as we have seen, is thought to have little intrinsic value or worth.

The concept of hegemony, however, allows for a different interpretation, in that popular culture can be seen as the cultural activity that emerges from 'the people', in all their various guises, including resisting their position as a subordinate group or challenging their consensual role as recipients of an imposed culture. It is in this light that many writers (particularly those at the Centre for Contemporary

Cultural Studies at the University of Birmingham) have examined a wide variety of groups such as youth, ethnic minorities, women's groups and many aspects of working-class culture.

Mods, skinheads and punks, for example, have been examined, not simply as examples of popular culture but as groups taking everyday items provided for them (such as boots, scooters and bin liners) and reappropriating them in their attempts to gain 'cultural space'. This challenge is seen not ahistorically but in the context of a break-down in hegemony. How successful they are in achieving this, and how they are reincorporated, is of great importance to the usefulness of hegemony as an analytical concept. The authenticity of groups such as rastafarians or punks has to be questioned if the oppositional content can be defused, for this is what defines them as 'popular culture' in this definition, and they can be easily incorporated and become a source of profit for record companies and merchandisers and, in the process, it seems, become part of mass culture. It is for this reason that popular culture in general is seen not simply as the culture of resistance, but as an area of negotiation and transaction, of exchange, between a culture imposed from above and its active consumption by popular forces. This process of resistance, challenge and incorporation recurs throughout in the study of sociology.

Consumer culture

In modern popular culture the individual is regarded primarily as a consumer whose pursuit of a materialistic lifestyle is focused on the acquisition of standardised products and entertainments, such as cars, clothes, Hollywood films, and meals from fast-food restaurants. The media reflect and thereby reinforce the image of the individual as a consumer. This is obviously the case with advertisements, which are designed to inform and persuade an audience whose members are seen as potential customers for the product or service on offer. But the same point can also be seen in the way that the media place such an emphasis on providing entertainment for the consumer. Consider the content of the popular newspapers, for example, which is based mainly on stories which are intended to take the reader away from the reality of his or her everyday life; for example, stories about serious crimes, disasters, celebrities, and professional sport.

The media pay very little attention to covering the concerns of people as workers rather than as

consumers. Despite the fact that **work** occupies such a large proportion of our time, the media provide us with very few details of what the process of wealth creation involves and its effects on people.

Much of the political debate conducted in the media also assumes that the reader or viewer is a consumer. For example, journalists frequently question politicians about how their policies will affect the standard of living of the 'ordinary person in the street', and what actions they intend to take to provide better services – hospitals, education, roads, etc. – for the taxpayer. The connection is rarely made in the media that many of the people who benefit from lower taxes and improved services will also be producers (workers and owners of businesses) whose interests might suffer as a consequence of the very policies that bring benefits to them in their other role as consumers.

Questions

1 How can high culture be distinguished from mass or popular culture?
2 Is it true to say that high culture is superior to mass or popular culture?
3 How does culture differ from ideology?
4 In what ways can popular culture be seen as a culture of resistance?

Culture and subculture

When sociologists use the term culture, they mean the whole way of life of a particular society characterised by generally accepted standards of behaviour, beliefs, conduct and morals. A **subculture** is a distinctive way of life within the wider culture in society.

When examining the relationship between a subculture and the culture of which it is a part, the latter is referred to as the 'parent' culture. The subculture, though differing in important ways from the culture from which it derives, will also share some things in common with that 'parent' culture. If it did not, it would constitute a separate culture.

Subcultures must, however, by the same token exhibit a distinctive enough shape and structure to make them identifiable from the parent culture. They must be focused around certain activities, values, certain uses of material artefacts, territorial spaces, etc., which significantly differentiate them from the wider culture.

Male and female subcultures

Paul Willis (1977) studied a group of working-class boys in their last two years at school and their first six months at work. He identified two working-class male subcultures: 'the lads' – the anti-school culture; and 'the earoles' – the conformist, academic culture. Willis found that 'the lads' expressed an aggressive macho pride in their practical physical skills. They rejected academic work as effeminate and sissy, and were destined for traditional male working-class occupations. What was important to them was 'having a laff' and 'knowing a bit about the world'. They set limits on their own learning. They emphasised immediate gratification and were quite prepared to engage in illegal activities.

Griffin (1985) studied a group of 16-year-old girls in Birmingham and their first two years in the labour market. She found that it was not possible to apply Willis' model. Unlike the boys, who went around in gangs, the girls either had one extremely close 'best' friend or spent their time in a small group. The definition of conformity and deviance in school was different for boys and girls. Deviance for the boys centred around verbal and physical aggression; for girls it was usually defined in relation to their sexuality. 'Being a troublemaker can be associated with being too feminine and too heterosexual.'

There were pressures to get a boyfriend that overlay pressures to get a job, and academic success was seen as unfeminine. Some of the girls wanted to do office work, as it was clean and would allow them to 'dress nice'. Factory work was seen as boring, insecure and unpleasant. In practice, office work seldom lived up to the image. Others favoured factory work, seeing it as being more friendly. But Griffin found it was not possible to distinguish clearly in terms of the girls' aspirations. There was some evidence of female pro- and anti-school groups, 'the swots' and 'troublemakers', and a link with office work and factory work respectively, but there was no clear cultural connection. Griffin concludes that the Willis 'gang of lads' model is inappropriate for understanding girls' experience of school, and that cultural resistance in working-class girls is quite different from that in working-class boys.

Ethnic minority subcultures

Many of the parents of non-white youths in Britain left their country of origin in order to get away from poverty. On arrival in Britain they expected hardship, but their children, often born in Britain, expected equal treatment. Instead they have encountered considerable problems in the form of social deprivation, prejudice and discrimination. In the light of these problems, it has been suggested by Brake (1985) that black working-class youth has a consciousness of **subordination**. There develops, he suggests, a 'colony culture', an Afro-Caribbean community against white society. Brake identifies three subcultural reactions to subordination:

→ *Hustler*: Instead of working in the white labour market the hustler prefers to earn his living through petty crime. Hustlers are men on the street with style.
→ *Rudie*: These groups are heavily involved in drug pushing, gambling and violence. This particular subcultural reaction was strong in the 1960s. Rudies wore 'stringy brim' hats and dark glasses and listened to blue beat, ska and reggae music.
→ *Rastafarian*: The Rastafarian is perhaps the main figure in the Afro-Caribbean youth culture, drawing on the deep religious feeling of African people. Rastafarians believe that the trials and tribulations of life in Babylon (white society) will end after their exodus back to Africa. They believe in the black Messiah, Haile Selassie, former King of Ethiopia. (His name before being crowned was Ras Tafari.)

Rastafarians frown on property, alcohol and gambling but they see marijuana or ganja as sacred. With the drug, thought is transformed into feeling, and belief becomes knowledge. The Rasta is identified by uncut, long 'dreadlocks', beard and woollen cap (Ethiopian colours of red, green and gold). Reggae is the music, with the rhythms of the 'burra', drumming and lyrics that preach black brotherhood and revolution in Babylon.

Rastafarianism, according to Marxists, can be viewed as an attempt to establish a cultural identity, a resistance against the dominant values of white capitalist society. Whether Rastafarians would articulate their response as resisting capitalism is debatable. Brake's analysis could perhaps also be criticised for focusing on what are seen by many as deviant responses. A study by Pryce (1979) of subcultural groups found a much wider variety of responses than these oppositional ones.

Asian parents generally exercise great control over their children and most adolescents expect to marry a partner chosen and approved by their parents. Girls are guarded against any secret relationship with boys. Asian youth are not encouraged to get involved in multi-racial youth organisations, as parents fear that the contacts thus arising may undermine their own religion and culture. In fact, Asian communities have, until recently, lacked distinct youth subcultures.

The situation with Asian youth may be changing due to a number of factors. Berry (1978) has argued that Asian youth today experiences alienation in two respects: they no longer identify so closely with the culture and values of their parents and grandparents, yet they also feel frustrated in their attempts to gain acceptance within the mainstream Western culture. As a response, some young Asians are forming their own youth groups with a distinctive subculture that encourages a more assertive approach to promoting the interests and rights of Asian people in British society.

Youth subcultures

Youth is present only when its presence is a problem, or is regarded as a problem

Dick Hebdige, Subculture, *1979*

As Geoffrey Pearson (1983) shows, adolescents have continually been seen as a social problem since at least the mid-nineteenth century. Groups such as the 'Peaky Blinders' emerged in the 1880s, and anti-Nazi youth cultures even existed in wartime Germany (the Edelweiss Pirates). As a distinct social group, however, youth only became an important sociological concern in the 1950s.

The main focus has been on the concept of 'subculture' – a group with its own norms, values, leisure pursuits, and sometimes even a uniform, coexisting within mainstream culture. The supposed disrespect for authority and conventional morality and the sometimes illegal and organised activities of these groups have also led to intense media attention and the labelling as modern-day 'folk devils' of groupings such as teds, mods, rockers, skinheads and punks in Britain, and hell's angels in America (see chapter 10).

Youth subcultures take shape around the distinctive activities and 'focal concerns' of particular youth groups. They can be loosely or tightly bound. Some subcultures are merely loosely defined strands of 'milieu' within the parent culture: they possess no distinctive 'world' of their own. Others develop a clear, coherent identity and structure. Some youth subcultures are regular and persistent features of the 'parent' class culture; the 'culture of delinquency' of the working-class adolescent male, for example. But others appear only at particular historical moments; they become visible, are identified and labelled (either by themselves or by others): they command the stage of public attention for a time; then they fade, disappear or are so widely diffused that they lose their distinctiveness.

Distinctive though they are, however, it is important to realise that youth subcultures continue to coexist with the more inclusive culture of the class from which they originate. Members of a subculture may act and look different from their parents and from some of their peers, but they belong to the same families, went to the same schools, do similar jobs, and live down the same streets as their peers and parents. As Mungham and Pearson observe (1976): 'Behind all the talk of generation and generation gap there is the forgotten question of the class structure of society. It is as if when youth are discussed that social class goes on holiday. But youth is not a classless tribe.'

Explanations for youth subcultures

Explanations for youth behaviour and lifestyles encompass many areas: from peer group formation to **pluralism**, from increasing social mobility to changing class structure, from the extension of the school-leaving age to the emergence of a distinct youth labour market, and from new patterns of consumerism to the very fact of age itself.

This latter approach is the one taken by S. N. Eisenstadt (1956) who, looking at youth from a functionalist point of view, argues that a distinct phase of life is necessary in society to allow the transition from the **particularistic values** of the home to the **universalistic values** of the rest of society. The phenomenon of youth and youth cultures is society's solution to this problem of transition. If conflict exists, it is essentially emotional, and results from young people's sense of marginalisation and powerlessness while developing the values and relationships that allow them to stand on their own two feet. The main point is that youth cultures are functional to society and in fact help maintain social order.

The obvious point that not all young people experience the transition to adulthood in the same way and that some people are more marginalised and powerless than others was made by American subcultural theorists from Albert Cohen onwards (see chapter 8). As youth and youth cultures were further investigated, dimensions of class, ethnicity and gender, as well as of age, were also developed.

In the mid-1970s the Birmingham-based Centre for Contemporary Cultural Studies examined the links between youth, class, pop culture and social life – for example, Hall and Jefferson (1976). Focusing mainly on working-class youth, they argued that youth cultures were attempts to solve problems, not necessarily of age, but which affected the working class as a whole. Simply put, the old values of hard work and pride in the job were being challenged by the new consumer affluence. As old traditional communities disappeared, young people tried to re-establish working-class values in their own way. The search for a uniform style and the links with certain types of music were all interwoven in a complex way. These are not 'real' solutions to the social problems but 'magical' ways to deal with them. Strange clothes – teddy boy's Edwardian dress, skinhead's braces and boots, mod's suits and parkas and stripey trousers and Doc Martens of the grunge generation of the early 1990s – and conflict with parents are seen as ways of coming to terms with the problems of forming an identity against a rapidly changing class and cultural backdrop.

A central question asked by these writers concerns the extent to which youth cultures can be seen as a form of resistance to the dominant culture, gaining 'cultural space' to call their own. The concept of hegemony, which was discussed earlier in this chapter, most closely associated with the Italian Marxist Antonio Gramsci, is central here. Youth subcultures, by the fact of their very existence and the symbolic messages they transmit, threaten the dominant ideology, punching holes in the hegemony. The most distinctive youth cultures take over and claim symbols for themselves, whether it is a Lambretta scooter (an old man's vehicle before the mods got hold of it), skinheads in workmen's boots or punks with safety pins through their noses.

Other writers have not seen youth cultures in the same romantic way. What appears as resistance can equally well be seen as an elaborate way of acquiescing to the dominant ideology. Resistance through ritualistic leisure pursuits does not really solve the problems of poor education and unemployment. The ability of youth cultures to resist dominant values is severely limited, and their artefacts are soon taken over by commercial interests and turned into mass-market consumer items. Any political ideology can effectively use youth groups to further their ends, as with the extreme right and the harnessing of skinheads across Europe. Furthermore,

Youth culture: an attempt to gain 'cultural space'?

by focusing on the most identifiable youth cultures, the ordinariness of growing up for most young people remains unexamined.

McRobbie and Garber (1976) ask whether girls do not appear in subcultural studies because of the sexism of 'malestream' sociology or because there are no female youth subcultures. Their answer is the latter. The culture of femininity which places a high value on passivity, and allows girls less free time, marginalises them into the position of onlookers, reading romantic magazines and thinking about boys. Girls escape into fantasy rather than rebel. If they do resist, it is by acting in a male way or by getting pregnant. Later research by Sue Lees (1986) confirms most of this argument, showing how the behaviour and attitudes of adolescent girls continue to be seen in terms of male opinion. For example, their behaviour is controlled by the use of pejorative labels like 'slag'.

Black youth is a largely under-researched area of the sociology of youth, yet, whether it is as 'rude boys' in the 1960s (whose style was partly copied by mods and the earliest skinheads) or as Rastas in the 1970s and 1980s, they have made crucial contributions to the definition of youth subcultures. Rastafarianism, with its view of white civilisation as 'Babylon', is closer to a counter-culture than it is to a subculture.

Berger (1966) argues that youth culture has little to do with youth. He puts forward the hypothesis that what we are in the habit of calling 'youth culture' is a creation of the not-so-young. He suggests that the kind of behaviour associated with this phrase is in fact more typical of certain occupations – bohemian business, show business and some working-class occupations – than of adolescence. Certainly there appear to be in people's minds very clear stereotypes of what pop singers are like, and the assumption is frequently made that if pop singers engage in deviant behaviour, their followers will copy them. So behaviour seen to be typical of certain groups in the population comes to be associated with that of some adolescents.

The stereotype is characterised by irresponsibility. But adolescence is related less to the irresponsible nature of adolescent roles and more to lack of appropriate roles. Adolescents are seen as being irresponsible in the negative sense that they do not play adult roles, rather than because they play roles that are specifically irresponsible. Yet they are legally and socially prevented from adopting many responsible adult roles. The stereotyping process has important implications for changes in patterns of adolescent behaviour.

How adults regard adolescents will influence their interpretation of what adolescents are doing and therefore the way in which they interact with them. If it is believed that adolescents are irresponsible, people tend to highlight that part of their behaviour that has an irresponsible element. In this way, labelling procedures are brought to bear upon adolescents in situations of contact. Associations between the stereotypes of adolescence in general and stereotypes relating to various deviant adolescent groups may result in adults attaching deviant labels to adolescents in general. Consequently, the young may find themselves increasingly being pressed into deviant roles. In a sense then the 'youth culture' is artificially created.

Little has been said about youth culture in recent years, partly because of scarce funding but also, as many sociologists have argued, because there is perhaps little more to say. 'The spectacular sub-cultures of the 1950s and 1960s are now impossible' (Willis, 1990). Wider groups than working-class young people have appropriated subcultural styles, particularly for marketing purposes, while the declining numbers of young people in the West, youth unemployment and homelessness, and increasing numbers of adolescents in full-time education have removed the social basis for distinctive youth cultures. Could it be, as Mark Abrams argued as early as 1959, that a 'teenager' is now little more than a marketing category?

Questions

1 What youth cultures exist today?
2 How distinctive are the norms and values surrounding their behaviour?
3 What social conditions have been identified behind the emergence of post-war youth cultures?

2 Sociological methods

Introduction

This chapter examines the different methods sociologists use to obtain information about the societies in which we live. It examines different sources of data such as primary and secondary and different types such as quantitative and qualitative. The various methods used by sociologists are discussed in detail, as is the process of research. The role of ethics and other key concepts in research are also investigated, as is the relationship between theory and methods. The chapter concludes by discussing the extent to which different types of method can be combined.

Types of data

Primary and secondary data

Sociologists have two sources of data available to them: information they have generated themselves for their own specific research purposes (primary data); and already existing data which has not specifically been created for sociological purposes (secondary data). Primary data can result from, for example, the employment of **questionnaires**; structured, semi-structured and unstructured **interviews**; and observation techniques. Secondary data can be more or less anything else: statistics produced by the **State** (for example, census data) and by private companies, and also letters, diaries, newspapers, books, television (where the study of the **mass media** is called content analysis) and so on. Secondary data have the great advantage of being cheaply, quickly and easily obtained, but have the serious disadvantage of not having been produced by sociologists. They are therefore unlikely to match sociologists' requirements exactly. Sociologists are wary, for example, of using uncritically statistics produced by civil servants. Both primary and secondary data can be **quantitative** or **qualitative** in form.

Quantitative and qualitative data

Any data or information used for sociological purposes, whether derived from primary or secondary sources, can also be described as quantitative or qualitative in form. Quantitative data is usually presented in numeric form and derives from large-scale survey methods. Data from various **social mobility** studies (see chapter 3), showing how many people have or have not changed their class in their lifetime (but not what it is like to experience this change), are a good example of quantitative data. One object of using quantitative data is to achieve precision.

Qualitative data deals directly with people's experiences, as well as their feelings about, and interpretations of, the situations they find themselves in. This data is generated through in-depth contact with sociologists, whether by in-depth (or unstructured) interviews or through observation, and will normally appear in prose form or in the form of transcripts of conversations. The term **ethnography** is often used to refer to studies that generate an in-depth understanding of the way of life of an individual or group. Sociologists working from within the positivist tradition often use quantitative data because of its numeric form, allowing trends, patterns and correlations to be identified, whereas sociologists working within the interactionist tradition may be wary of such claims, and in any case see greater validity in qualitative data, allowing them a more detailed understanding of the small groups and individuals they study.

Questions

1 How does quantitative data differ from qualitative data?
2 Why might one form of data be preferred to the other?

Research methods

Questionnaires

Questionnaires are a set of written questions that are either given to respondents to complete or are posted to them. These questions may be open ended or closed ended, where a closed-ended question is designed to give a specific and definite answer (such as 'Yes' or 'No'). Open-ended questions are designed to allow respondents to give their own answers to questions. Closed-ended questions are often preferred for this method in that they will help the researcher achieve what they principally want from questionnaires: clear, definite answers that can be quickly obtained and easily quantified and then presented in numeric form.

Questionnaires may well result from an attempt to operationalise a concept, the process by which an abstract idea is broken down into subheadings that are more easily understood. A good example here would be Robert Blauner's (1964) operationalising of the concept of **alienation** at work into the subheadings of isolation, meaninglessness, powerlessness and self-estrangement (see also chapter 9). These subheadings were then broken down again in order to gain quantifiable indicators about each of these concepts in each industry studied.

These questionnaires can be distributed in a number of ways, including by hand and by post. Postal questionnaires are most likely to reach the largest group, although they have the lowest response rate. Those who return them may well do so because they have an interest in the subject under research.

Questionnaires are widely used because they allow a large number of questions to be asked to a wide group in a short space of time. An example is John Goldthorpe and David Lockwood's *Affluent Worker* studies (1968, 1969). Questionnaire results are easily quantified and presented numerically, especially if devices such as optical character readers are used. Their data are reliable and generalisable. Trends and relationships can be identified, hypotheses tested, and causal relationships identified. Unlike structured interviews, which they closely resemble, they avoid the problem of interviewer bias, where the physical presence of the interviewer can discourage respondents from giving the answers they may give anonymously. An enquiry in this format may well be the only way of gathering large amounts of data across a wide range of people.

Researchers may be unwilling to use questionnaires, however, given that they rely on the goodwill of respondents for their completion, give them no opportunity to clarify the questions they ask, and expect a certain level of literacy and numeracy for their completion. They also delimit the range of responses, particularly in the case of closed-ended questionnaires. There is also the assumption that the respondent really means what they say in the answers they give.

From an interactionist perspective, the main problem with questionnaires is that they lack **validity**. Although respondents may answer a question in the same way, the meaning they give to that answer may vary from individual to individual, according to the way they have understood and interpreted the question. What may matter to a researcher, and be seen as significant, may not be of the same importance to the respondent. A very small part of the respondent's view of the world is revealed, and the researcher gains little or no first-hand experience of the world view of others, or how they interact with those around them. Finally, completing a questionnaire does little to involve or empower the respondent in the research process.

Interviews

Interviews can be of three main types – structured, semi-structured and unstructured. Although they are all types of interview, this should not mask very significant differences between them.

Structured interviews

Structured interviews, as used, for example, by Marshall *et al.* in their study of social mobility (1988), are in many ways the same as questionnaires, in that they contain pre-set questions that are asked in the same order every time. The only real difference is that a structured interview consists of a spoken question-and-answer session between interviewer and interviewee, whereas a questionnaire will be given to a respondent to complete privately.

The presence of the interviewer in this process creates many advantages and disadvantages when compared to questionnaires. Among the advantages are the fact that questions can be clarified for the respondent, and that an interview is guaranteed to be satisfactorily completed and returned, where a questionnaire may not. Where interviews are conducted by telephone, a potentially wide-ranging sample can be reached. The presence of the interviewer can also be a major disadvantage in that the respondent may feel more restricted in their answers, particularly if their own social characteristics are markedly different to that of the interviewer. Interviewing is also a far more time-consuming process than administering questionnaires.

Semi-structured interviews

A semi-structured interview is a mixture of structured and unstructured interviewing methods, where a number of questions may be predetermined, but the interviewer may feel free to deviate from these questions to explore issues raised by the answers. It is likely that this approach is more frequently used than is acknowledged, and is seen as simply more natural. The proportion of predetermined questions in the interview will vary according to the purpose of the research and the type of data it is designed to yield. This technique was also used by Goldthorpe and Lockwood in the *Affluent Worker* studies.

Unstructured interviews

Unstructured interviews more resemble conversations than the tightly structured interview schedules of a structured interview. The purpose of unstructured interviews is to gain an in-depth understanding of an interviewee's perception of particular subjects or issues. Usually, the interviewer will allow conversation to develop freely around these subjects, and they will be non-directive and non-judgemental in their own contributions. They usually take place between two people, though group interviews can also be used to gain insight into the collective view, where members of the group can act as prompts for each other. The interview session can be several hours long or, as with Barker's study of Moonies (1984), constitute several sessions over the course of a week. Notes may be taken of the interview, or it may be taped and subsequently transcribed by the interviewer.

Unstructured interviews are designed to produce qualitative data, and as such are likely to be favoured by sociologists from an interactionist perspective. They have the advantage that they can be used flexibly to explore issues at a range of levels. They allow respondents to feel empowered and have some influence on the research process, allowing them time for thought and reflection. An in-depth interview can give valuable and unique insights into the way the interviewees understand the world, particularly in situations where a relationship of trust has been established with the interviewer.

Unstructured interviews also carry many disadvantages. They generate large amounts of material that can be time-consuming to originate and then transcribe. Much of this may be of little use, and the selection of usable material is itself a subjective process. There is no reason to believe that interviewees are telling the truth, particularly where the subject may concern deviant behaviour. As with questionnaires, what people may say in response to a question may not then accord with what they do in everyday life. They may yield qualitative data, but this is nevertheless artificially generated and not as valid as observing people living their lives. As with structured interviews, the presence of the interviewer, as well as their social characteristics, may well influence the respondent's contribution. As **ethnomethodologists** have observed, the researcher becomes a part of the process being studied.

Observation

Observational methods, where the aim is to observe the behaviour of a group, usually for an extended period of time, do not commence from a formal hypothesis but from a set of preliminary aims, which can be modified, retained or rejected as research proceeds and unexpected and interesting material presents itself. Observation ranges from mere eavesdropping to participating in the activities of the people involved. As such, the holistic approach taken by observers, particularly participant observers, allows this method to make an important contribution to ethnography, the study of a way of life.

This research may be covert or overt, participant or non-participant. Overt **participant observation** means that those being studied are aware of the true reason for the researcher's presence. This has the considerable disadvantage of ensuring that the subjects do not behave as they normally would, leading to behavioural changes such as factory workers increasing productivity as a response to increased interest in their work, and **deviant** gangs putting on extravagant displays to impress their willing audience. In covert observation, the researcher's true identity is unknown to the group throughout the research period. In participant observation the researcher engages in the group's activities, while in non-participant observation they merely observe, aiming to play as little a part in the group's activities as possible.

Covert participant observation (such as that undertaken by 'James Patrick' (1973)) therefore involves a researcher secretly becoming part of a group and taking a full part in their lives. This has the advantage of being as close as possible to the 'natural' behaviour of the group in their own environment, placing the researcher inside the group's value system and being part of their everyday behaviour. Where deviant groups are being observed, particularly those engaging in illegal activities, the covert presence of the observer is less likely to alter their behaviour than if the group knew they were being observed, although it may nevertheless be the case that this new member, no matter how hidden their identity may be, may nevertheless influence the group's behaviour. This can happen, for example, if the researcher is older, giving validity to a teenage group's behaviour. Lengthy engagement with a group (over a period of months or years, for example) can also create the possibility that the observer over-identifies with the group, and loses their objective approach to their research.

Overt participant observation (for example, David Morley and Roger Silverstone, 1990) involves a researcher being known to the group and engaging in their activities. For many researchers, this approach is more ethically acceptable than covert observation because there is no deception over their identity and purpose. It is also less dangerous in that there is no chance of their hidden identity being discovered, and there is no expectation for them to engage in illegal behaviour. It also allows them, in their role as overt researchers, to ask questions concerning the group's activities. Declaring your identity and purpose, however, will immediately mean that the group will become conscious that an outsider has joined the group, and may modify their behaviour accordingly. This immediately reduces the chance of observing the 'natural' behaviour of the group.

In covert non-participant observation the researcher secretly observes the group without taking part in any of its activities, allowing them to achieve a certain detachment from the group, and to remain objective towards them, though this form of research is close to spying. Overt non-participant observation (such as the well-known Hawthorne studies undertaken by Elton Mayo (1933); see also chapter 9) involves a researcher being known to the group without taking part in their activities, removing the possibility of becoming engaged in criminal offences as well as not requiring the researcher to have the same social characteristics as the group. It is also the form of observation furthest removed from placing the researcher inside the group's value system, where it is very likely that they

will be highly conscious of the person watching them.

Observation in general is seen by those in favour of qualitative methods as being high in validity in that the relatively small size of the group, or on occasion individuals, as well as the long periods of time spent with them, means that a considerable amount of highly detailed first-hand data can be gained about a small number of people, usually in an environment of their own choosing. For **phenomenologists**, the purpose of research is to get as close as possible to the realities underlying human interaction.

However, there are nevertheless many reasons why this approach might not be adopted. Along with the amount of time taken on such research, there is a danger that the researcher may come to identify too closely with the group and cease to view their behaviour objectively. It can also be dangerous, especially for covert researchers if their deception is uncovered, as well as risking disapproval of such methods from the wider public. There are also many ethical questions to be asked, particularly concerning the adoption of false identities.

For those in favour of a quantitative approach, the disadvantages are obvious: results are unlikely to be quantitative; it is difficult to compare one piece of research with another; it relies on the researcher to record what they find and then choose certain events from the totality they experience; the ultimate report may appear to have more in common with journalism than the rigorous, scientific methods they advocate.

Experiments

An experiment is used typically to test a hypothesis by controlling a variable in order to discover which factor or factors are important in bringing about an effect, as with Albert Bandura's well-known (1961) study of children and media violence. Often, to isolate other, external, factors, these take place in a laboratory. Experimental results are usually highly **reliable** and are usually presented in numeric, quantifiable form. Correlations and causation can be readily identified.

The use of a laboratory is immediately problematic for sociologists, because it involves removing people from their social environments and placing them in artificial surroundings. For this reason they have been little used in sociology, unless the whole of society is seen as one giant laboratory.

One half-way house between the social whole and a laboratory has been the field experiment. These have taken place in smaller settings such as street corners, classrooms, offices or shop floors. These then effectively become social laboratories. Such experiments have been used to determine responses to different behaviours such as how people might interact with people of different classes or different conditions of work. Much of what is called 'sociological' research in this area is also very close to the work undertaken by some social psychologists.

The value of such research has been questioned in terms of its validity. People will behave differently if they know they are part of an experiment. They will also respond differently to different experimenters, bringing factors such as class, ethnicity, gender and age into account – 'experimenter bias'. Important questions concerning the ethics of such research have also been asked, for example whether subjects should know that they are taking part in an experiment. With, for example, Jane Elliott's work with primary school age children, discrimination was encouraged between the children according to the colour of their eyes, where blue-eyed and brown-eyed children were encouraged to treat each other as inferior. Although this research yielded interesting results about the effect of discrimination on school behaviour and performance, ethical problems exist around encouraging such behaviour in school children, as well as the role of the teacher in lying to them about the importance of eye colour. (This work is recorded in the video *The Eye of the Storm*.)

Longitudinal studies

Longitudinal studies take place over time, often over intervals of many years, with the purpose of exploring long-term trends. Usually, the same sample is used to monitor phenomena such as changing social attitudes, with the resulting data usually taking a quantitative form. Such samples can be determined by characteristics such as age, as with The Child and Health Education Survey, or by family and school, as in the case of J. W. B. Douglas's *The Home and the School* (1964). Some **longitudinal research** can yield qualitative data as with some participant observation studies which have looked at groups over several years, examining, for example, the effects of ageing on delinquent youth behaviour (as with Parker, 1974).

Longitudinal studies have many advantages for research: in this way change over time within the same group can be explored, avoiding the view of research as a 'snapshot' in time. They also allow a larger number of variables to be considered. They are also seen as valid in that they overcome the need for respondents to rely on their own fallible memories.

However, they can be problematic in that they make demands of the group researched to be available over long periods of time, during which the group's willingness to take part in the project may change (as happened with the television series *Seven Up*), or, as with Douglas's research, which began with 5,362 children, significant numbers may become difficult to trace in later years. There is also a strong risk that their attitude to the research may change as the group become more aware of how the research is being used, and how they themselves appear in it.

Case studies

Case studies examine one phenomenon only, investigating it in depth. This could be a locality, an institution, a social group or even an individual. The aim is to gain as detailed and comprehensive an understanding of that single phenomenon as possible. Findings can be used in a number of ways – to present examples that may verify or falsify hypotheses, to generate typologies that allow categorisations to be made or to show the world from a group's perspective.

As with many methods in sociology, its strengths are also its weaknesses. Despite the often rich insights provided by case studies, they are difficult to generalise from, as they only concern one subject at one time in one place. Where attempts have been made to undertake case studies of a number of similar institutions, the resultant data is more likely to be seen as valid if it is collected in the same way by the same researchers in a brief period of time. Paul Willis's (1977) study of twelve youths in 'Hammertown' (see chapter 6) is a good example of this technique, demonstrating all the reasons why some researchers are attracted to case-study research, as well as the disadvantages others have found in such an approach.

Content analysis

The method of content analysis is almost exclusively confined to the study of the mass media (see also chapter 10), where it has become one of the most successful methods in use. This can include analyses which take specific types of media (such as television or newspapers) and examine how a particular group such as women or ethnic minorities are represented. This could be as simple as counting how many times a group or type is referred to. It can also investigate specific themes, such as a strike or war, looking to see what messages are encoded within these representations. The language used in the mass media has been of particular interest in content analysis ('textual analysis') particularly by the Glasgow University Media Group, from their first publication, *Bad News*, to the present.

Such approaches have been frequently criticised for the subjective and selective way in which parts of the mass media have been used to show a perceived bias or partial representation. Any analysis of media presentations will reveal some form of bias, which can nevertheless be interpreted differently by different researchers. It is unlikely that a uniform view of such messages will emerge. In this way, it has been argued (for example, by Martin Harrison, 1985) that the final research can reveal as much about the values of the research group as the mass media they are investigating. Equally, little or no attempt is made to discover how these messages are received or decoded by their intended audience.

With audience analysis, a form of content analysis, some attempt is made to overcome these problems. In David Morley's now classic study (1980) of the 1970s television news magazine *Nationwide*, different social groups (students, businessmen, trade unionists) were shown the same episode of a television news magazine, and questioned about their perception of the programme. However, this is still a long way from gauging audience interpretation of the mass media in their own, more natural setting, such as the home, where they may respond differently.

Semiology

Semiology is usually associated with a structuralist approach to sociology and the contributions of Ferdinand de Saussure (1857–1913) and later Claude Lévi-Strauss (1908–). It is concerned with examining the science of signs, particularly those contained within language. According to Saussure, any sign consists of two parts: the signified and the signifier, where the signified is the concept which is being indicated (sometimes referred to as a 'text') and the signifier is the way the object is thought of when it is mentally recited (the meaning we give to that object). Signifiers are defined in terms of other signifiers, and beneath these signifiers lie linguistic rules concerning their usage in relation to each other. These rules constitute the structure of a language, which Saussure refers to as its 'langue'.

Language in use is referred to as 'parole'. These are the words that are passed between people in their interaction/discourse, whether verbally or in writing. In using these words as signifiers, Saussure argues that they refer not to the world of objects and things,

but to other related signifiers. Signs therefore become more 'real' than the objects behind them and together can be seen as part of a socialised code. Our ability to understand the world is limited to the words we have available to describe it, and the scope and variety of the words used to describe the signified will vary from culture to culture, each carrying differences of meaning within them.

Language, and the rules underlying its use, therefore becomes the object of sociological interest in that they will reveal much about the culture of a society and the shared meanings that exist within it, as phenomenologists have urged. It informs work on areas such as conversational analysis and the concept of labelling in deviance and education (see chapters 8 and 6).

More recently, semiological analysis has extended beyond language to other areas, such as clothing in, for example, the study of youth subcultures (see, for example, Dick Hebdige, 1979; also discussed in chapter 1) or the role of television, film or advertising in the mass media (for example, Robert Hodge and David Tripp, 1985). The semiological method can be extended beyond language and linguistics to all of human experience, which can be read as a text in the same way. Reading these texts therefore involves a process of decoding or deconstruction.

Semiological analysis is a relatively new approach in sociology, and has contributed much to the analysis of the mass media in particular. It is not without its critics, however, particularly the view that an encoded sign can be universally decoded to reveal the same meaning to all actors – wearing jeans may still signify a fashionable and rebellious stance to some people over the age of 50, while to younger people they may just indicate comfortable middle age. Not all encoded messages are read in the way their encoders may have intended – messages are polysemic, having many meanings.

Documents

The range and type of documents that sociologists may access are enormous, and can include historical documents such as church records (for example, Peter Laslett, 1972) and early censuses, which allow a longitudinal and quantitative view to be taken, as well as life documents such as diaries, letters and even suicide notes, where detailed qualitative information about the subjective side of people's lives can be gathered. As historical and life documents represent secondary data for sociologists, not generated for specific research purposes, they are particularly open to selective interpretation. The usefulness of life documents can depend on the audience they were written for. Where sociologists have asked for research subjects to keep diaries, for example, they are more likely to contain relevant material than privately kept diaries, which are only made public several years later. The latter may reveal more about the subject's own introspective state than events in the world around them.

Official statistics

Official statistics are data gathered by government bodies for a wide variety of purposes, such as recording demographic details in censuses, unemployment and crime rates, records of births, marriages and deaths, and educational performance through the collection of statistics such as examination results. As they have not been gathered for explicitly sociological purposes, they represent secondary data for the sociologist. They represent an important source of quantitative data that is readily available and cheap to obtain, covering very large samples, sometimes detailing trends over many decades or even centuries. They appear to be objective and representative, gathered for neutral purposes.

They are also a source of data that sociologists have learnt to be wary of. This is not only because their use can at best be indirect but because a number of important questions have been raised concerning their validity, particularly by interactionist sociologists, who see them not as hard 'social facts' but as having been socially constructed, the end result of a series of common-sense assumptions.

The problems surrounding the use of official statistics in sociology can be seen most clearly in the field of crime and **deviance** (and are further explored in chapter 8). For many years around the turn of the twentieth century, crime statistics (including those for suicide) were taken at face value by sociologists, and uncritically incorporated into their research. In the second half of the century, sociologists began to view them more sceptically, raising fundamental questions about the validity of such data, and whether the richness and variety of human experience could ever be represented by numeric tables and data sets.

At the heart of the problem lies the concern that all information – 'official' or not – has at some point been created from human experience. What is presented as a 'fact' is really the choice of some people to see some activities as significant enough to try to represent that activity quantitatively. These facts are really the end product of a series of choices. Crime statistics, which rely on a chain of individuals (the public, police and other officials) deciding on the nature of such behaviour, will therefore always be vulnerable to changes in public priorities concerning what is significant, and what is not. This is illustrated very clearly by Cicourel's work (1976) on the problems of accurately recording rates of juvenile delinquency in California.

Attempts have been made by official statisticians to address some of these criticisms, for example through self-report crime studies (such as the various British Crime Surveys) which attempt to capture crimes unreported to the police. In this way, it is argued, the validity of crime statistics can be increased, and the true extent of crime discovered. However, critics argue, because of the way these surveys are conducted, all of the problems associated with methods such as questionnaires and structured interviews remain, particularly the expectation that respondents can and will give an honest and accurate account of what they know.

For conflict sociologists, official statistics are immediately problematic in that they have been produced for the State, which they regard as an instrument of the **ruling class** or **élite**. Official statistics are therefore far from neutral, and exist to sustain the power of the dominant, as Ian Miles and John Irvine (1979) argue. The statistics are not lies or fabrications, but will be collected for ideological purposes, to create or support a particular view of the world that favours the interests of the ruling group. Data that may be embarrassing, such as high unemployment rates or long hospital waiting lists, will be distorted in such a way as not to reflect the underlying realities. In some instances, the data may cease being collected, as with the decision in the early 1980s in the UK to abolish the Royal Commission on the Distribution of Income and Wealth.

The frameworks within which statistics are created also reveal much about the values of those who create them. The Registrar-General's standard occupational classification is a good example for conflict sociologists here (see also chapter 3), where, for this group, the classification presents a view of stratification that ignores the **class** conflict in society between those who rule, and those who are ruled.

This view of official statistics, however, is less persuasive in view of the fact that a great number of statistics resulting from the use of this classification show strong correlation between social class and poor health, education and welfare, as they have since it was first introduced in 1911 to examine whether infant mortality was related to social class.

Questions

1 Which of the methods described above are quantitative and which are qualitative?

2 How do structured interviews differ from unstructured interviews?

3 Which of the above methods use primary data and which use secondary?

The stages of research design

Any sociological research project takes on a series of clear stages, all of which need to be carefully considered in advance. Deciding what to research is not in itself a value-free exercise. What is examined, and the way it is examined, may make a statement about the researcher's **values**, or of the research organisation that has agreed to fund the project.

Having decided on an area of subject for research, a typical project would need to:

→ decide on research strategy;

→ formulate research problems and hypotheses;

→ decide on how and whether to use sampling techniques and pilot studies;

→ conduct the research;

→ interpret the results;

→ report the findings.

Deciding on research strategy

The extent to which a topic or issue can be studied will depend on a number of factors, including: time available, human and physical resources available, accessibility of data, as well as considerations of what kind of data will need to be generated – whether primary or secondary and quantitative or qualitative. The theoretical standpoint of the researcher will also be important, particularly their views on the importance of a scientific approach, and the role of **positivism** and **phenomenology** in sociology. The methods to be used to generate data may be chosen at this stage.

Formulating research problems and hypotheses

How the area of research is framed as a research project will force the issue of what type of data is required. Studies that are based on **hypotheses** (statements that demand to be tested) will usually take the researcher in the direction of a search for 'hard' quantitative data, where the emphasis is on 'proof' and reliability, echoing the methods of the natural sciences, with the object of generalising results across the overall population in consideration. Questions of validity may be secondary.

Studies set in the form of problematic statements or more general research aims may lend themselves more to 'soft' data and a greater emphasis on validity. Decisions also need to be made about the relative importance of primary and secondary sources of data, taking into account the relative merits and demerits of each.

Deciding on how or whether to use sampling techniques and pilot studies

On most occasions it is necessary to test the viability and appropriateness of a research project before beginning the research project itself. A questionnaire or structured interview can be tested on a few people to see if the questions are clear and intelligible. A few hours of participant observation can be done before engaging in the full project, a process that may last much longer. Amendments can then be made to the project from the lessons learnt. This stage of any research, where the project is trialled in microcosm, is known as a pilot study.

With data designed to generate quantitative data, for reasons of time and resources, it is unlikely that the entire field can be surveyed. Generalisations will therefore have to be made from a smaller group, or sample. The overall group from whom the sample is drawn (which may be as large as the population of a nation) is called the **sampling** frame. Considerations concerning who is to be studied are less important to qualitative research, but the final group selected will nevertheless need to be representative of the wider phenomenon under consideration.

There are many types of sampling.

Random sampling

This is any form of selection where any individual has the same chance of being selected as another from the sampling frame – probability sampling. The social characteristics of the individual are not seen to be as significant as overall membership of the sampling frame itself.

Stratified random sampling

A stratified random sample would endeavour to represent as exactly as possible one or many of the social characteristics of members of the sampling frame. Thus, if the sampling frame was all the pupils of a school sixth form where 30 per cent were male and aged 18, then the sample would contain 30 per cent of 18-year-old males among its respondents, selected at random with each individual having an equal chance of being selected. Age and sex then become key variables in interpreting the resulting data. Other factors that may also be included in stratified sampling include ethnicity and social class. A random stratified sample is therefore as exact a cross-section of the particular features of a group or community as possible.

Quota sampling

This carries many of the features of stratified sampling in that the aim of both is to show a cross-section of a group or community. The key difference is that in quota sampling individuals will be selected until a particular quota of types or classifications has been met, without any effort being made to ensure that there is an equal chance of any individual from the sampling frame being selected.

Multi-stage sampling

This involves taking a sample of a sample, and is most often used where the sampling frame is large and complex. The first stage of this process is to find sub-sets of the sampling frame that are representative, and then take samples from that subset. For example, the population of a country may contain a town with a demographic profile that is representative of the wider population. Within that town there may also be a district which is demographically representative. A random stratified sample taken from this district would therefore be representative of the wider sampling frame.

Snowballing

This is a rarely used technique which enables the researcher to build up a sample through a chain of personally referred contacts, that is, where one person will refer the interviewer to another as a means of building a wider picture, for example from a criminal group, as with Polsky's (1969) study.

Conducting the research

Once considerations concerning the size, shape and practicality of any research have been made, methods chosen and trialled, then the research project can now be conducted. In doing so, due regard will have to be given to the important concept of **objectivity**, as well as practical considerations concerning time and resources, and the ethical issues described below.

Interpreting the results

Once the research has been conducted, data will have been amassed. This data can take a very large variety of forms – statistics that may need to be processed through a computer database, tape recordings that need to be transcribed (turned into verbatim paper accounts), contemporaneous notes that need to be written up into a coherent account. As it is very unlikely that all data collected will ultimately be used, decisions will need to be made about what to include and what to leave out, and why. At this point, the concept of objectivity becomes very important.

Reporting the findings

Research reports need to be as full an account of the project as possible, comprehensively detailing all the stages listed above. In doing so, consideration needs to be given to existing and comparable research in that field. The researchers also need to evaluate the project in two ways – first, to consider how successful it has been in achieving its stated outcomes, and second, to consider what the research has revealed in relation to its initial aims and hypotheses. Finally, there should be a discussion of how these findings may contribute to existing theory and research.

Questions

1 Why might choice of a particular research subject reveal the researcher's values?
2 Is sampling always a necessary stage of research?

Theory and methods

The link between theory and research methods is considered to be at the heart of the understanding of sociology. Sociologists emphasise the importance of this link, a concern which can be really frustrating for students who want to get to grips with some actual explanations for the things which happen in society. The whole point about this so-called 'science' of society is that the arguments about the explanations are as important (if not more so) as the explanations themselves.

Sociology is a set of disagreements, firstly about the type of explanatory framework to use – theoretical disagreements – and secondly about the actual explanations which you provide. So if you're a Marxist you look for conflict, if you're a functionalist you look for consensus, and interactionists just look! A theory is a frame through which we can look at society and see a particular view. Once you have chosen your frame you find out that along with the set of ideas which link together to provide an explanation of society – theoretical concepts – comes a set of ways in which to apply these concepts in research – research methods.

Positivist and interactionist methods

The relationship between theory and methods is actually quite straightforward. If you take the positivist viewpoint, that the structure of society is the place where explanations for social behaviour can be found, you will not be concerned with the feelings, emotions and experiences of human individuals. To the positivists these are not important – they are simply a product of the workings of the larger society. To study society means to study the social structure in order to understand what makes it work. The logical, scientific analysis of numerical data, gathered using such sources as official statistics, questionnaires and structured interviews, provides the raw material which can then be examined and explained by the scientific sociologist. However, from the interactionist viewpoint the reality of social behaviour is to be found when human individuals interact and create their own social experiences. To understand these, the sociologist must attempt to probe into the meanings and beliefs of individuals acting together in groups. Numerical data is itself a product of human interactions, and therefore not to be taken at face value. Instead of researching in the files and statistical tables the interactionists would actually observe these figures being constructed. They would not consult the statistics on bullying in the playground, but rather take on a job as a play supervisor and watch it happening. This data deals with the 'quality' of human experience, not in the 'quantities' which record some aspects of it.

Quantitative and qualitative methods

If you are a structural, positivist sociologist, you believe that individuals are determined, shaped and moulded by the larger society, and to understand that moulding process, you must analyse the 'quantitative data'. Large-scale 'macro' analysis will provide a knowledge which is on a par with natural science. If you are an interpretive, interactionist sociologist, you believe that individuals create society through their joint activities. To explain social behaviour, you need to understand individual interpretations, the meanings which individuals themselves give to that behaviour. This data, supposedly rich in 'quality' and depth of meaning, is 'qualitative data'. These two very different types of data, qualitative and quantitative, are related to the type of sociological theory you use. They are collected using completely different methods. In the minds of the sociologists who use them, their own methods and data are the only approach to the study of society. It is obvious, then, that the 'two sociologies' are in complete disagreement. Each one thinks that the theory and methods of the opposing side are worthless. Are they both right?

The positivist view

From the positivist view, the starting point of interactionism is wrong. To provide explanations based only upon the in-depth analysis of individual meanings or processes uncovered by observing group interactions is just a descriptive exercise. The quality of data is equal to that given by a journalist or novelist, interesting to read but telling us nothing about the causes of behaviour. These 'causal relationships' can only be discovered by analysing the social structure in which behaviour takes place. The scientific method which positivists are so keen on is all about discerning patterns in the data collected, and locating the reasons for these patterns within the wider framework of society. Positivists wish to rise above the merely subjective, descriptive data which interactionist sociology provides, to identify patterns and their underlying senses and therefore establish general laws which can be used to predict (and perhaps manipulate!) future behaviour. Positivists look for 'structural switches' which turn the lights of society on and off. They claim that they deal in 'hard facts', whereas interactionists produce publications closer to fiction than hard science. Objective, social facts are taken as evidence to back up theoretical assumptions. Subjective reports of experience and meaning are discarded as interesting but irrelevant. Positivists believe that it is pointless to rely on reported experiences, because the people involved are not aware of the extent to which their lives and actions are influenced by constraining factors within the social structure.

The interactionist view

On the other hand, the interactionists are critical of the positivist stress upon 'social facts'. To base all of your explanations upon official statistics or questionnaires, the interactionists say, is to ignore the ways in which this type of data is constructed, that is by human beings who bring their interpretations and meaning systems to bear upon the very construction of the so-called facts. If this 'hard evidence' is created by humans who use their own experiences and feelings in the process, then the starting point for analysis has to be in that process. To ignore the human factor is to provide false explanations. The classic example here is inevitably suicide. Durkheim's (1897) analysis of the official statistics is regarded by positivists as a masterpiece of sociological enquiry (see also chapter 8). Durkheim argues that rigorous analysis and comparison of the official suicide statistics provide 'social facts'. But according to interactionism they are **social facts** compiled by humans – doctors, coroners, the police and the families and friends of the dead person – who all have an axe to grind. Taking these official statistics at face value, they argue, is to ignore the interactive processes which contribute to their creation.

Positivists claim that examining human interactions in 'micro' detail is not 'proof' in the scientific sense. Each study is merely descriptive because the sample is small and unrepresentative; no generalisations can be made and therefore no laws established. According to interactionists, positivist methods, which attempt to apply science to the study of society, are inappropriate because people do not react like substances in the natural sciences. People react, reflect on their own behaviour, have awareness and consciousness of their existence, and therefore explanations for the patterns of their lives can never be found using the cold objective approach of the scientists.

Questions

1 What are the main criticisms that positivists make of the interactionist approach?
2 What are the main criticisms that interactionists make of the positivist approach?
3 How are theoretical approaches linked to sociological research methods?

Research methods and ethical responsibility

In the same way that it is difficult to find a research method that can meet all the requirements of **reliability** and validity, so too is it unlikely that a

research method can be used that meets the ethical approval of all sociologists, regardless of how successful that method is in meeting its stated aim.

Two key issues here concern **power** and truth. Quantitative methods have been criticised by many, particularly critical theorists, for placing all control in the hands of the researcher, and rendering powerless those who are being researched. This is clearly the case with experiments. But similar claims have been made for questionnaires and structured interviews. The latter have been characterised by some feminists as representing a masculine 'rape' model of research in that it is carried out anonymously and quickly, the respondent is relatively powerless, is forced into certain options and has no control over any outcomes.

Equally, observation techniques, particularly covert ones, have been highlighted for the deception involved in hiding an identity and giving those observed no knowledge of the uses to which that research has been put, until they discover detailed accounts of their lives appearing in print, written by someone who, until only recently, had been masquerading as a friend. This can also be seen as a power issue when it is considered that most observation studies are of relatively powerless deviant groups. Conversely, very few attempts have been made to undertake covert participant observation of corruption and fraud within ruling groups, for example a multinational company board, or the upper reaches of élite groups or the judiciary.

Ultimately, these questions can only be satisfactorily answered by considering whether the ends of the research are justified by the means employed, the issue raised in particular by critical social theorists who are concerned that sociology itself does not become another tool of social control.

Question

Should ethical considerations influence research?

Key concepts in research

Validity

Validity concerns whether a research method gives a true picture of what it claims to have recorded, and shows social realities as they really are. No matter how reliable data may be, it will always be limited in its validity if the researcher cannot show that it gives a true account of what is being studied. For example, suicide statistics may enable comparative research to be undertaken across European countries, and a number of numeric correlations made, but until the problem of knowing the dead person's intention is solved, there will always be questions concerning their validity (see the discussion of the sociology of suicide in chapter 8). The issue of validity is particularly problematic for quantitative methods, where the general aim is to gather large amounts of numeric data quickly, without attempting to examine a subject in the detail demanded by qualitative methods.

Reliability

If the findings of one piece of work can be replicated by another research group, or by the same research group at a later occasion, and it produces the same result, then it is deemed to be reliable. Total reliability is difficult to achieve in any social research, although quantitative methods are most likely to aspire to it. It is almost impossible in any qualitative research, given that this research may typically take the form of a single individual observing a group over several years, though this kind of research may in any case wish to emphasise the validity of its data over its objectivity.

Objectivity

Research is objective if it uncovers facts that are undoubtedly there – objective truths which, regardless of their prejudices, values and opinions, anyone would have to acknowledge. It ceases to be objective when researchers choose to ignore discoveries which may contradict what they expected to find, or refuse to admit detail which may falsify their hypothesis.

As Popper (1963) has argued, the most useful research therefore sets out not to prove its hypothesis through testing, but attempts to falsify it. The implication of this position is that all we can ever say about any theoretical position is not that it is right or correct, but that it has not yet been found to be wrong. It is objectively true, whether we want it to be or not, as far as we know.

Post-modern theory, however, in rejecting the possibility of objective knowledge, also rejects the possibility of objective research. All apparent objective truths, whether derived from research or not, then, in this view, become matters of mere opinion.

Representativeness

Representativeness is close to the concept of generalisation. It concerns the extent to which any research may be said to have successfully shown in microcosm the trends, patterns and behaviours that exist in the wider society it claims to be representative of. The decisions made in constructing the sample will be very important in any claims of representativeness. Some projects do not aspire to representativeness, for example those qualitative case studies that examine specific phenomena in detail, with the emphasis on validity.

Questions

1 How important are the concepts of validity, reliability, objectivity and representativeness to the research process?
2 Which kinds of research might emphasise validity, and which reliability?

Methodological pluralism and methodological purism

So far in this book we have suggested that there is a strong relationship between positivism and quantitative methods on the one hand and interactionism and qualitative methods on the other. This division is real in sociology, marking a real debate, as Martyn Hammersley acknowledges: 'While positivist social scientists have themselves varied somewhat in their interpretations of science, in general they have taken quantitative measurement and the experimental or statistical manipulation of variables as its key elements. And it is against this conception of scientific methods that anti-positivists in the social sciences have rebelled most strongly, often advocating instead the use of qualitative methods' (Hammersley, 1993).

Behind this statement lies the argument that the use of a particular method or methods aligns the researcher with a particular view of what the world is like, and how the study of society should be carried out, given the researcher's real aim of generating theory.

Triangulation

Increasingly, as we have argued at the beginning of this chapter, sociologists are prepared to drop this division in favour of simply 'doing' sociology, using whatever methods are appropriate, whether quantitative or qualitative. At the same time, they do not seek to call themselves positivists or interactionists but simply sociologists. This approach is called **methodological pluralism** or sometimes, using Norman Denzin's (1970) term, **triangulation**. Thus sociologists are willing to use a range of methods while at the same time refusing to have themselves simplistically pigeon-holed as belonging to one or other of the perspectives in sociology.

As early as 1957, Trow argued that we should 'be done with the arguments of participant observation versus interviewing … and get on with the business of attacking our problems with the widest array of conceptual and methodological tools that we possess and they demand'.

A good example of a response to such a challenge of methodological pluralism was provided by Howard Gans in *The Levittowners* (1967), where his main method was participant observation achieved by buying a house in Levittown, USA. He also, however, sent out 3,100 questionnaires to people about to move to Levittown, and conducted structured interviews with a smaller sample of Levittown residents, repeated after two years. Gans was thus prepared to use a range of methods in order to discover what it was like to move to, and live in, Levittown.

Disciplinary ethnocentrism

Researchers such as Gans had few qualms about combining quantitative and qualitative data, believing that there would be no corresponding loss of theoretical rigour and coherence. For this to continue, what Warwick (1983) calls 'disciplinary ethnocentrism' will have to come to an end. 'Many quantitative social scientists,' he argues, 'fancy themselves as "hard heads" – true scientists whose propensity for numbers betokens a deep and undying commitment to truth. Those who do not share this faith are "soft heads" who do not deserve the name of science. For their part social scientists of a qualitative persuasion often portray their approach as humane, sensitive, intuitive and comprehensive … Quantitative researchers, by contrast, are methodologically gross, insensitive to contexts and more often than not wrong in their assessment of community dynamics.'

At the heart of this debate concerning the reliability and validity of types of data in sociology is the question of the status of the sociology produced through the employment of these methods. 'Purist' sociologists at either end of the spectrum will remain convinced that their unadulterated perspective will produce either the most reliable or valid information about the nature of human organisation. Positivists will continue to see their work as a contribution to scientific knowledge. Given Durkheim's aim of developing a science of society, it is hard, for example, to see him using anything other than quantitative methods in his study of suicide (see chapter 8). Phenomenologists will continue to raise fundamental objections to the way such data seems to fail to describe people and the societies they live in. The danger of methodological pluralism may well be the creation of a generation of sociologists who are competent in everything and proficient in nothing.

Questions

1 What are the strengths and weaknesses of 'methodological pluralism'?
2 In what ways would Durkheim's study of suicide have changed if he had gathered qualitative data?
3 Is disciplinary ethnocentrism simply a form of arrogance?

3

Social stratification and differentiation

Introduction

This chapter begins by looking at what is meant by stratification. It examines functionalist, Marxist and Weberian conceptions of social stratification. The chapter goes on to look at the difficulties encountered by sociologists in measuring levels of social mobility in society. Later there is a discussion of the idea that the working class are adopting middle-class norms and values and this is contrasted to the opposite theory of proletarianisation. There is then a discussion of the notion of the underclass. The chapter closes with a discussion of different forms of stratification: gender, ethnicity and age.

Dimensions of inequality

Sociologists have noted that in most societies people are divided into a number of broad groupings between which there are marked differences in **wealth**, **power** and prestige. They refer to this 'layering' of society as social **stratification**. The lines of four important social divisions are clearly identifiable to most sociologists: those of **class**, **gender**, **ethnicity** and age. These are the four keys that are used to unlock any social analysis. Together and separately they can be used to define and measure the strata that exist within society. As with most terminology used by sociologists, however, there is no precise agreement on what these terms mean, or how they should be used.

Elements of social stratification

The concept of social stratification can actually be broken down into a number of elements. The first element is *inequality*; some people are better placed in society than others in terms of income, wealth, power, etc. But this inequality is not randomly distributed between individuals, rather it is a feature of the social groups to which people belong. There are unequal groups that are defined by their relationship to each other in a hierarchy. So, for example, in a system of stratification based on social class we can talk about there being a lower class, a **middle class** and an **upper class**.

Sociologists often describe social stratification as a *structured pattern* of inequality. Structure refers to the idea that there is a definite shape to the stratification system with the different groupings fixed in a particular relationship to each other. The reference to 'pattern' simply means that the structure tends to persist or repeat itself over time. Thus, as an example, in a system based on extremes of wealth and poverty, the rich and poor groups are likely to remain in their respective positions for at least several generations.

Of course, social structures do not remain unchanged for ever. There are many cases of societies which have experienced significant changes in stratification. In Britain, for example, there was the transformation from **feudalism** to the modern class system. However, these changes tend to occur gradually and history suggests that attempts to abolish a particular system of stratification through radical means such as revolution are rarely successful – either the revolution is defeated or, if it is successful, elements of the old system of stratification nevertheless continue to survive under the new regime.

Another element of social stratification is that the members of a particular group or stratum will have many *common characteristics*. These characteristics include:
→ a shared culture and identity
→ common interests
→ similar life chances.

Life chances are the choices a person has of obtaining those things defined as desirable and avoiding those things defined as undesirable in his or her society.

Many people, when discovering the way that sociology operates, are unwilling to accept the validity of these concepts of stratification in the first place. From their point of view, structured inequalities only exist because sociologists perceive them to exist – they are simply an invention of sociologists. There are no class divisions, nor is there a systematic bar in operation against women or ethnic minorities. Age does not matter. Society is made up of unique individuals who fail or succeed, are powerful or weak, not as a consequence of stratification but because of their individual biographies.

Class

Against this, there is a wealth of evidence which strongly suggests that social divisions are real and tangible. Figures demonstrating the distribution of wealth and income quickly show that substantial financial resources are held by very few in most societies. For the UK, if the Standard Occupational Classification is used (formerly the Registrar-General's Scale), the statistics show that the higher the class a person is in, then the more likely they are to survive the first year of their life, to do well in school examinations, to get into higher education, to live longer, and even have their natural teeth into old age. As we shall see, many sociologists have argued that different classes display different **norms** and **values**, have different lifestyles and perceptions of society, in short that distinct class **cultures** exist. For them, the real debate is about where the line between these classes should be drawn, a consideration that occupied much of sociology's time and thought in the twentieth century.

Gender

It is only in recent decades that gender has been considered as a dimension of stratification, yet this inequality is evident in all walks of life. Although there are more women than men in the United Kingdom, they have much less social, economic, political and domestic power than men. Occupationally, they are under-represented in the boardrooms and senior management positions of the largest companies. On average, they earn less than men. They are vastly outnumbered in the House of Commons, where men make decisions on the availability of contraception, abortion, pornography and divorce. When a woman becomes a cabinet minister it is still a rare enough event for it to provoke great interest. This inequality in power between women and men is evident in most societies.

Class and stratification: extremes of wealth and poverty are often side by side.

Ethnicity

It is a similar picture for members of ethnic minorities, though here it is important to be specific about which ethnic minority is being considered. Careful study has revealed distinct differences in the social and economic position and experience of groups classed as either 'West Indian' or 'Indian', for example, reflecting their different cultural histories. Different patterns of integration are evident, and sociologists have had to learn to be careful to make these distinctions.

Age

The need for careful distinctions is generally true of all studies of stratification. The fact of age stratification is obvious, with the young and old being the least powerful, in a society where age determines many life events, whether it is starting school, finishing school or retiring from employment. The problems begin when age is seen to be the only important or determinant aspect of a group or individual's existence. The experiences of middle-class teenagers may be very different from those of working-class teenagers. The financial situation, health and social integration of retired middle-class men tend to be much more favourable than for retired working-class men. The life experiences of black working-class people and white working-class people may be very different. Although age stratification is very important and helps us to explain and understand a great deal about people's experiences, other ways of stratifying may cut across those based on age.

Sociologists of stratification attempt to explore and explain the reasons for divisions in society and also to analyse how society holds together under such strains. The models constructed by sociologists are, in Weber's terms, **ideal types** which need refining on the evidence of research. What sociologists have found is that class, ethnicity, gender and age are all complexly interrelated dimensions of stratification. How much weight should be given to each remains debatable. Marxists assert that class is most important. Some feminists see gender divisions as being more significant. Youth cultures may be viewed as expressions of age, gender, class or ethnic identities – or all of them.

Social versus natural inequality

The inequality that sociologists refer to when considering social stratification is the inequality of social position, not personal attributes. The differences were pointed out by the eighteenth-century French philosopher Jean-Jacques Rousseau. He argued that natural or physical inequality is established by biology and consists in differences of age, health, bodily strength and the qualities of the mind. By contrast, what Rousseau called moral or political inequality depends on 'a kind of convention' and is established, or at least authorised, by 'the consent of men'. This type of inequality consists of the different privileges which some people enjoy to the prejudice of others; such as that of being 'more rich, more honoured, more powerful, or even in a position to exact obedience'.

Rousseau believed that inequalities between people based on personal attributes were small and relatively unimportant, whereas socially created inequalities provide the major basis for systems of social stratification. Most sociologists would agree with this view.

The opposite view is that wherever stratification exists it basically reflects the natural inequalities between people, such as differences in their genetic make-up or innate **intelligence**. An example of this view is the idea that some people are richer than others because they are more intelligent or naturally more competitive. The view that social stratification is biologically based is often developed in the form of beliefs that are used to justify a particular system of stratification. For example, some men might claim biological superiority over women and see this as the basis of their dominance in systems of sexual inequality.

However, the idea that stratification is biologically based is hard to sustain. A social group or stratum will invariably contain people with a wide range of personal qualities, so that no particular pattern of natural characteristics is apparent. For example, the argument that male dominance is based on men being more aggressive than women runs up against the problem that while some men may show aggressive qualities, others do not. Moreover, if any specific personal quality is isolated for analysis from people of one group, it is likely that examples of people having this quality can also be found in other groups. It could not therefore be claimed that such a quality is unique to a particular group and forms the basis for the position it occupies in the stratification system. There is also the point that in some systems of stratification, such as that found in feudal society, people inherit the **status** of their parents. Their position in society is determined automatically at birth, regardless of their biological make-up.

Systems of stratification

In most societies throughout history there has been some form of social differentiation between people. The basis of this social differentiation has varied. The types can be distinguished according to the rigidity of the differentiation and the possibility of mobility between the strata.

Ancient societies

Most notable among these were Greece and Rome. The basic distinction in these societies was between the free and the unfree. The free were the members of the family, which was a central institution in both societies. The unfree were the slaves who were regarded as the property of the head of the family.

Another type of ancient society can be distinguished, known as *hydraulic societies*. These included the following societies at some time in their history: Ancient Egypt, Mesopotamia, China and Ottoman Turkey. All these societies needed an efficient system of water collection, conservation and control if they were to survive because of the arid nature of the local climatic conditions. To maintain an efficient system, a **bureaucracy** sprang up that had absolute power. The major division in the society was between a **ruling class**, who comprised a hierarchy of officials and enjoyed high prestige, and the mass of the ruled who performed whatever tasks were asked of them in connection with the system of irrigation and agriculture.

Indian caste society

The **caste system** is by definition a form of differentiation that is hereditary and extremely rigid. The system is usually maintained by religion. It is synonymous with traditional Indian society. According to Hindu religious doctrine, there were five distinguishable groups in Indian society. In order of importance these were:

→ Brahmans – the priest caste, who had been born from the mouth of the Hindu god;
→ Kshatriyas – the military caste, created from the arms of the god;
→ Vaishyas – the merchant caste, formed from the thighs of the god;
→ Sudras – artisans, born from the feet of the god;
→ Untouchables – outcasts employed only in the most menial tasks.

There were strict rules about eating habits and to touch a lower-caste individual or anything touched by one brought the necessity for ritual cleansing. A caste was a social group, membership of which was hereditary and fixed for life (except for the possibility of becoming an outcast) and whose members were constrained to marry within the major caste but outside their own clan. Each major caste was subdivided; each subdivision was frequently subdivided; and so on, almost ad infinitum, each subdivision being treated as a caste with its own strict rules concerning food preparation, eating, drinking, smoking, bodily contact, spatial proximity to members of other castes, the wearing of ornaments, language and occupation.

Life for the majority of people was made palatable by the doctrine of karma, i.e. caste membership in this life is the result of good or bad conduct in a previous life, and rebirth into a higher caste could be achieved by those who behaved well in the caste into which they had been born.

Feudal society

Here we have a type of social differentiation found in many European countries in various forms over several hundred years. (It was only in the nineteenth century that it died out in Japan.) In the English version, the pattern of stratification was as follows:

→ royalty – nobility – ecclesiasts
→ lesser gentry
→ free tenants
→ villeins
→ cottars
→ slaves

The system developed because fighting men were required to defend territory, both nationally and locally. Nobles offered a fief or feud (an area of land) in return for military service. The system gradually became hereditary; the eldest son received the rights of land on the death of his father. In return for providing armies for the king, the feudal lords obtained immunities from taxation, and power in their own locality. Positions of local power were originally personal but later became hereditary and a class of nobility with its sense of family tradition, privilege and knightly conduct emerged as a powerful and inward-looking élite. The church also gained power. Later, as Britain became more involved in trading, the social system became more fluid.

Social class systems

The class systems of modern societies do not rest on law or religion and there are no rigid or legal restrictions to prevent individuals or groups moving from one class to another, although that is not to say that such movement is necessarily easy. Sociologists agree that social class rankings are about differences in wealth, power and prestige, but there is no general agreement on definitions and models of class.

However, most sociologists are agreed on the importance of class because it affects the life chances and opportunities of people in modern societies. In studying sociology it is important to understand social class because it cuts across so many other areas of society – education, family culture, and so on.

Theories of social class

In sociology, three main theories exist which attempt to explain the nature and prevalence of stratification. These derive from Marx, Weber and **functionalism**. The contrast between **Marxism** and functionalism is noticeably at its sharpest in this area, exposing the weakest area in functionalist theory, and the strongest area in Marxism.

Functionalist theories of stratification

Functionalism is weak on the concept of stratification partly because so little has been written from this perspective. Stratification is certainly discussed by early functionalists such as Herbert Spencer and Emile Durkheim, but neither saw it as the focus of their study. Durkheim evidently saw social inequality as a necessary and universal feature of society because functionally more important roles should have higher status and rewards. Unlike Marx, he did not see social inequality as a key source of social conflict, and in any case believed that inequality could be mitigated by the prevalence of **social mobility** – movement of people from one stratum to another.

Davis and Moore

These points were taken up and enlarged upon by the authors of what has become one of the main statements of the functionalist view of stratification. Davis and Moore's (1945) view is that some positions in society become more functionally important than others, because of the organisational demands necessary for any society to function. Some roles can only be taken by certain individuals. Only they possess the necessary scarce skills and initiative. In order to entice them into these positions, they have to be rewarded with greater status and rewards than others. Systems of stratification exist to ensure that the most appropriate

people are selected for these roles. Moreover, because stratification is functional, it follows that it must be a permanent, inevitable and necessary fact of the way any society is constructed. Attempts to alter or do away with social inequality are at best misguided. Similar points are made by Talcott Parsons (1953).

Parsons

Parsons (1951) lays emphasis on the way in which social stratification, while clearly a potential source of conflict and instability in society, actually serves to integrate and order society. For Parsons, stratification involves the distribution and allocation of social prestige. Industrial societies are not split into two classes, as Marx suggested; rather there is a series of strata ranked one above the other in terms of the amount of prestige they are accorded by members of the society. Parsons' scheme is clearly derived from Weber's concept of status.

Parsons believes that people evaluate the behaviour of others in accordance with values that they hold in common and on which they agree. Members of a society will, says Parsons, agree on their estimation of good and bad. Thus there will be general agreement (consensus) on the status of different social strata.

Criticisms of the functionalist view

In putting this view forward, these post-war American functionalists have been heavily criticised for the assumptions they have made about the existence of a **meritocratic** society, i.e. a society where everyone has an equal chance of achieving high social status and reward. Such a benign view of the role and effects of stratification only works if many other features of society are ignored or even distorted. Firstly, as Melvin Tumin (1953) asks, why are some social positions assumed to be functionally more important than others? Who decides and how? Is it functionally more important to be the director of a company making products that are not necessary than to nurse people, dig coal or clean streets?

The concept of 'functional importance' is value laden. Deciding which positions are functionally more important than others cannot be done objectively. If a journalist earns five times as much as a clerical worker in an office, does this mean he or she is five times more important? Are the best-paid jobs the most important? Top soccer stars in the UK are currently earning in excess of one million pounds a year – six times more than the Prime Minister.

It is doubtful that material rewards are the only means by which societies can induce their members to fill positions, as the theory suggests. People may be motivated by the prospect of job satisfaction, or out of a sense of duty, or by the opportunity to wield power. The functionalists argue that high rewards are justified as a compensation for the sacrifices of loss of earning power and the cost of training during the period of preparation for functionally important jobs. Examples would be doctors and lawyers. It would be possible to argue that the salaries they receive allow them quickly to recoup losses. It is also true to say that the costs of training usually fall on the parents, and far from the period of study being a depriving experience for students, it is a stimulating and relatively leisured experience not available to their peers. Most students who attend university enjoy their time there.

The inequality justified by the theory may be dysfunctional and damaging. It may generate conflict and antagonism between social strata rather than furthering social integration. Stratification may well inhibit the full development of talent (as a result of inequality of opportunity) and lead to bitterness and frustration amongst individuals with ability and potential.

The functionalist account of inequality naively assumes 'functional importance' as the determining factor in unequal rewards at the expense of other crucial influences. But access to privilege and wealth may be by accident of birth. Rewards may accrue to certain groups in our society, not because they are more functionally important than others in respect of job and social position but because they are well organised into **trade unions** or **professional** associations and have well-developed strategies which further their claims for differential rewards. It is interesting to note the market philosophy which has been applied in pay bargaining in the last few years. The better pay increases are found where there is a shortage of skilled labour.

Tumin (1953) argues that the functionalist theory is an apology for the status quo, a justification for existing social arrangements and inequality. Even if unequal rewards are desirable, then we are faced with the difficult problem of deciding how unequal the rewards need to be. He questions exactly what inequalities are required for the so-called functional well-being of society, such that the so-called functionally important jobs continue to be satisfactorily filled.

Frank Parkin (1971) is critical of the use functionalists make of evidence which appears to indicate agreement about the prestige ranking of occupations. Although people seem to agree on the hierarchy of rewards, this apparent consensus is not the sum of people's personal evaluations regarding the relative importance of different jobs, but a reproduction of what they have been socialised into accepting, which, when asked, they reproduce as a matter of fact. This apparent **consensus** is an expression of the particular value system that operates. It reflects the capacity of those in dominant positions to persuade the rest of society that the attributes they consider admirable, and their evaluations of worth, are somehow the 'right' ones. He goes even farther and argues that the functionalist theory is itself an expression of the same value system.

Finally, the whole question of power is problematic in functionalist theory. The emphasis on consensus over inequality leads to a neglect of the possible, or actual, use of power for exploitation and the pursuit of self-interest. It is wrongly assumed that power is always used benevolently simply to ensure the smooth running of the system.

Meritocracy

The functionalist view also assumes the existence of a meritocratic society, where everyone has an equal opportunity to rise to the top. It can be equally forcibly argued that the system of stratification prevents as many people – if not more – from rising to the top as it allows through. From this latter perspective, at best a genuinely meritocratic society lies far into the future, at worst it is a naive view. In a deeply unequal society such as that in Britain, the existence of private schools, for example, allows social status to be bought, regardless of any innate talent.

The functionalist view of how power and status are gained and maintained is also a serious weakness in the theory. Does the wealthiest man in Britain, Gerald Grosvenor, Duke of Westminster, own thousands of acres of the world's most expensive land because he possesses the scarce skills needed to perform a functionally important role in society, for which he should be rewarded with high status and privilege? Perhaps a more realistic view is that the Grosvenor family wealth exists because, many centuries ago, a distant ancestor of his received Mayfair as a wedding dowry when it was still farmland. His status was not achieved by him but was rather ascribed to him at birth.

Class power

This opens up a wider consideration of class power. Writing from a Marxist perspective, John Westergaard and Henrietta Resler (1976) point out that the more property an owner has, the more immune he or she is from the need to render any service of social substance at all. The wealthier you become, the less socially significant your contribution. Little research of any real value has ensued from the functionalist view of stratification, and it is difficult to square the perception of the nature of stratification put forward by writers such as Davis and Moore with any empirically based study. Too much contradictory data exists surrounding studies of social mobility, education and wealth and income for it to have any real currency. Instead, some writers, for example Frank Parkin (1971), have suggested that the functionalist view is little more than an ideological justification of inequality in society that is intended to make inequality acceptable. More searching explanations and insights are required.

The Marxist view

Class is the most important concept in Marxism. As Marx (1848) wrote: 'The history of all hitherto existing societies is the history of class struggles.' His view was that when these struggles come to an end, with the emergence of a classless society, then the first stage of history – what will be seen as prehistory – will be over. Humans will at last be able to live in a world where they are not prevented from realising their full potential by the constraints of class societies.

The collapse of capitalism

What excited Marx was that he believed that, in his age – the nineteenth century – it was possible to witness the emergence of the preconditions necessary for the transition to a classless, or communist society. Two great classes – the **bourgeoisie** and the **proletariat** (see chapter 1) – were assuming formations that would lead to the disappearance of one and the victory of the other. For Marx, the bourgeoisie was doomed, unable to control socio-economic forces beyond its grasp, prone to greater and greater crises in profitability, **accumulation** and production. The details of this emerging crisis were elaborated in his book, *Capital* (1867).

Since the publication of *Capital*, Marxists have sought to identify signs of this historical dynamic in motion, most clearly in connection with the First World War (1914–18) but also at several other junctures in the twentieth century, for example the

General Strike of 1926 in Britain, or the events in France in May 1968 when the Gaullist government came close to being overthrown by sections of the **working class**. The central idea that modern Western societies are composed of two antagonistic classes, one of which benefits at the direct expense of the other, has led to rich fields of research in all areas of sociology, particularly the family, education, stratification, power, work and poverty. It is when attempts are made to operationalise the key concepts in Marxist theory that disputes have emerged.

What did Marx mean by class?

The concept of class itself is highly problematic in Marxism. At first sight it is clear what Marx meant by this term – the bourgeoisie rule by virtue of their ownership of the **means of production** and therefore constitute a class. In the mid-nineteenth century, when Marx was writing, only those with titles or property were able to participate in political activity. This political power was manifestly derived from economic power. Those who had only their labour to sell were the proletariat, the source of the bourgeoisie's wealth. They too constituted a class. The difference between the two classes lay in the level of self-realisation. The bourgeoisie were conscious of their own existence as a class, both in itself and for itself. The proletariat had yet to realise their existence as a powerful and ultimately victorious class. This, future Marxists were to decide, was the task of Marxist socialists, leaders of the working class.

Leaving aside the important question of whether there remains a clear link between economic and political power (see chapter 11), a further question to face is whether anything as tangible as a working class, in Marx's sense of being potentially class-conscious and revolutionary, any longer exists. In recent decades there has been little real evidence (apart from in Eastern Europe) to suggest this development is still possible.

The proletariat

In Britain the people whom Marxists describe as 'the proletariat' rarely act as one. They do not vote uniformly for the largest working-class party – the Labour Party – nor are they interested in the many neo-Marxist parties in existence. Trade-union membership is in long-term decline, and the traditional working class, built on the Victorian staple industries of iron and steel, coal, shipbuilding, textiles and engineering, underwent a major transformation in the 1980s. The industries themselves shrank rapidly, while many of those people still in work, far from having nothing to lose, found their houses, cars, foreign holidays and videos threatened by loss of employment. In the Western world (and increasingly in Eastern Europe) the power of capital has never looked stronger, and proletarian revolution less likely.

While Marxism has not been abandoned as a tool of analysis, and though it is still very easy to demonstrate, objectively, that capitalist societies are highly divided on class lines, the paradigm Marxism puts forward of a polarised class society looks implausible at a subjective level. A more fruitful analysis has, therefore, been sought by sociologists to accommodate the shortfalls of Marxist analysis.

Developments of Marxist theory

Marxists in the twentieth century sought to update Marx's theory in the light of changes in capitalist society. Louis Althusser (1969, 1971) rejected the idea that social relations are determined in a simple way by economic forces. Rather, he argued that class societies consist of three levels: the economic, political and ideological combining differently in different societies.

The economic dimension does not always govern the other levels. For example, there is no reason to assume that the contradictions inherent in capitalism will inevitably be expressed in antagonistic relations between the proletariat and the ruling class. Wage-labour relationships may be mediated by institutional arrangements like collective bargaining and the powerful trade unions which have come into existence since Marx wrote down his theories. Althusser also recognised that historical events and other developments such as wars could influence the relationship between the two classes.

Nicos Poulantzas (1969) has argued that Marx's theory needs to be refined in order to take account of changes in the occupational structure in modern society. He suggests that not all workers today can be seen as part of the proletariat. What is important is whether labour produces surplus value. Productive labour (producing commodities) is that which produces **surplus value**, whereas unproductive labour (performing services) is that which does not. Thus most **white-collar workers**, though wage earners and not property owners (not bourgeoisie), are involved in performing services and circulating commodities and are thus not part of the proletariat. The proletariat consists only of workers engaged in the production of surplus value.

Poulantzas proposes that, politically and ideologically, the white-collar workers are in a different class position from manual workers, often opposed to unions and with an outlook of individualism. But he also recognises that within each group there are divisions within classes, which he calls 'fractions', preventing these groups acting together as a single class. The effect of such a conception of class is to make the domination of classes and their relationship with one another extremely complex compared to Marx's model.

Questions

1 Why do functionalists think stratification is inevitable and necessary?
2 What is meritocracy from the functionalist perspective?
3 Can functionalism be accused of being an ideological justification for inequality?
4 From the Marxist perspective, what is the relationship between class struggle and history?
5 Why don't the proletariat act as a class?
6 How did Marx see the downfall of capitalism coming about?
7 What criticisms would a functionalist make of the Marxist concept of class?

The Weberian view

Although Marx recognised the existence of other classes – the petty bourgeoisie (or small-scale owners, for example shopowners) and the lumpenproletariat (the unemployed, vagrants etc.) – the underlying dynamic at work in his view of class conflict means that economic forces – primarily the centralisation of capital – would bring the two great classes in history into direct conflict.

Aware of this view, and provoked by it, Max Weber produced his own conflict-based theory of stratification. While owing something to Marx, it made considerable and important refinements, playing down the importance of class, adding a further dimension to its meaning, and introducing other, separate factors that he believed contributed to stratification in societies. Weber's theory has opened up new areas of insight within sociology, and comes closest to explaining the dynamics of stratification in modern societies. Like Marx, he recognised the importance of ownership of property, and the existence of conflict between owners and workers. Unlike Marx, he anticipated a greater proliferation of classes, with a new class of white-collar employees, administrators, technicians and civil servants, growing in number and importance. He highlights the importance not of property relations but market position and marketability as decisive in determining an individual's class position. He rejected Marx's view that workers (or employees) have nothing but their labour to sell to the highest bidder. What they possessed, in greater or lesser quantity, were skills, the distribution of which could be controlled to be kept scarce and increase their marketability. This was particularly true of white-collar workers – those who are involved in non-manual work.

Status and party

For Weber, class was not the only factor determining social status. It could be mitigated by two other aspects of individual or group positions, neither of which necessarily depended on class. These he called **party** – access to political power – and 'status' – the amount of honour or prestige accorded to someone (Weber, 1922–3). By separating politics from class he was clearly distinguishing himself from Marx in his belief that political power and activity were not simply expressions of the economic base. Many groups could possess effective political power without direct economic leverage, for example the military or trade unions through political parties. Social inequality could exist because some were more politically powerful than others.

So too with status, one of Weber's most slippery concepts. He recognised, and believed to be important, the observation that people could be of the same class but have different social statuses. Equally, they could have the same status but occupy different class positions. The use of the concept of status is Weber's recognition that life chances are determined by more than class. The concept of status has a wide meaning, embracing all the ways that individuals and groups are regarded by others in recognising your social standing. If you are newly rich, you may find it harder to be accepted – to gain status – by the established rich, even though objectively you are of the same class. If you are born an untouchable in India, no matter how wealthy you become abroad, you will remain an untouchable within the Indian caste system. Weber was aware of this example of ascribed status. In his concept of status, Weber used terms of reference other than property qualifications or market position. This definition has been used in recent decades by neo-Weberians to understand the position in stratification systems of many groups, for

example ethnic minorities. They may occupy the same class position as some white groups in Britain, but they do not command the same political or social status. The life chances of a black doctor or manual worker are different to those of white ones.

Marx and Weber

Because Marx and Weber contested the same terrain, it is worth contrasting the differences in their approach to stratification in society. Where Marx believed that relationship to the means of production was all-important, Weber focused more on the market position of those in employment. Where Marx saw a progression towards increasing polarity between classes and revolution, Weber saw the growth of a large white-collar class that would mitigate against the collapse of capitalism. Where Marx believed that class was an all-embracing fact of life, Weber allowed for separate political and status factors to come into play. We can therefore say that, despite similarities in the natures of the societies they perceived, they came to different understandings of other, more important, forces they saw at work in capitalist societies.

Developments of Weber's theory

The American sociologist, Lloyd-Warner (1953), used Weber's notion of status as his starting point. He argued that social status was a far more appropriate measure of stratification for a modern society than class. Lloyd-Warner felt that class was an outmoded concept.

Lloyd-Warner argued that there were two dimensions of status in a modern society: first, 'who mixed with whom' socially. People who mixed socially (e.g. invited or were invited to parties or went on holidays together) constituted a status group. Second, status groups could be placed in a hierarchy by virtue of the type and location of the houses in which they lived.

Lloyd-Warner realised there would be odd anomalies, such as the lottery winner who lived in an expensive house but was not socially acceptable to his neighbours, or the person who had come down in the world and did not fit in with neighbours in a lower housing area. However, in general, he felt his categories reflected reality. *Figure 3.1* illustrates Lloyd-Warner's model.

Like Lloyd-Warner, Ronald Frankenberg (1957) saw status groups as an appropriate form of social stratification. However, Frankenberg used a wider measure of social status; he saw the consumption of

Figure 3.1   Lloyd-Warner's model of status

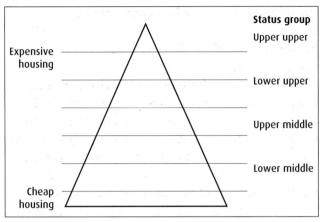

goods and the lifestyle as characteristics of a status group. People relate to other status groups as reference groups. Later sociologists have developed the notion of reference groups as follows. People relate to groups of which they may or may not be members. These groups are used by the individual to locate him/herself in the order of things. Reference groups provide a reference point. It is possible to analyse the concept of reference groups as follows:

→ *Comparative reference groups*: a group whose situation a person contrasts with his or her own. This is very evident in wage negotiations, as for example when car workers contrast their pay with that of other car workers in another company.

→ *Normative reference group*: a group from which an individual takes his or her standards. An example would be when a pop personality's style of dress is copied by others.

The number of reference groups a person has will be limited by the extent of his or her knowledge and experience. Frankenberg (1957) was interested in how people moved up to higher status groups. He adopted the term 'spiralists' for people who rose through a series of positions, often moving about the country to achieve promotion and higher living standards.

Measuring social class

As we have seen, social class is only one form of social stratification, and there are different theoretical views. Indeed, there is a good deal of discussion in the sociological literature about the nature and meaning of social class. In order, however, to conduct empirical research, some objective measuring device was needed and occupation seemed the most easily

accessible. Many sociologists regard occupation as the most reliable indicator of social class because an occupation reflects income, prestige and 'popularity' (many people may wish that they were in that occupation).

Despite the complexity of classifying occupations, some British sociologists make use of the Registrar-General's five socio-economic classes model, illustrated below:

Socio-economic class	Description
I	Professional
II	Managerial and technical
III (non-manual)	Clerical and minor supervisory
III (manual)	Skilled manual
IV	Semi-skilled
V	Unskilled

The basis for assigning particular jobs to particular classes is 'the general standing within the community of the occupations concerned'. In other words, the status or prestige of occupations is the basis for assigning people to classes. However, the Registrar-General points out that the value ascribed to particular occupations is linked to a number of other social inequalities including education and economic reward. The Registrar-General regrades occupations after each census.

For most of the twentieth century, this method of measuring class has been used to yield data on almost every aspect of life, from infant mortality to life expectancy, from educational achievement and dietary habits to how many hours of television each group watches, and the data produced have become a useful source of secondary data for some sociologists. The use of a scale can be justified on the grounds that it allows class to be standardised and thus enables comparisons to be made both between studies and over time. It is also economical in that it gives an accessible measuring device for minimum expenditure.

There are, however, problems with models of class based on an occupational scale. They tell us little about those who are without occupations, such as the unemployed, students, or 'housewives' and 'househusbands'. The scale shows class as static, without any notion of class as a dynamic power relationship. It ignores the question of ownership of property – are professionals really in the same class as the large-scale owners of the means of production who have the power to hire and fire them? There is also some confusion between the social class of unskilled non-manual and skilled manual workers in the

Registrar-General's scale and how the dividing line is drawn. Self-assigned class (how people feel and see themselves) is also very important in determining people's behaviour, e.g. voting behaviour. The classification scale overlooks the point that the same job title can mean very different things in different circumstances. For example, a solicitor can mean a senior partner in a very successful law firm with offices in the City of London, or a newly qualified solicitor working in a community law centre in a poor inner-city area and earning a comparatively low salary.

There are other scales in everyday use, e.g. those used by market researchers, but they still rely on occupational measures.

Subjective measures

There is another way of looking at social class, which involves asking people how they perceive it. This is a **subjective** measure, but some would argue that it is more meaningful to let respondents give their views on social class than thrust categories upon them. For instance, in *The Affluent Worker*, a study by Goldthorpe *et al.* (1969), the researchers attempted to gain a view of their respondents' image of class with a number of open-ended questions. From the replies, the researchers drew three basic images of social class:

→ a power model with two classes;
→ a prestige model based on three or more classes, determined by lifestyle and social background;
→ a money model with one large, central class and one or more small ones, based on wealth, income and consumption.

This approach has become more popular with the interactionist school but it makes comparison between studies difficult and the studies of social mobility which we consider later in the chapter would be impossible with such measuring devices.

For operational purposes then, occupation is used but it is recognised that this is imprecise. People replying to questions about class tend to have different ideas about what the term really means and attach varying degrees of importance to their class identity.

Social mobility

'Social mobility' is a term used by sociologists to refer to the movement of individuals or groups between the different levels or categories making up the system of social stratification. The 'feudal' and 'caste' systems, as we noticed, were characterised by a great deal of rigidity in respect of the possibilities for individuals to move within a lifetime to any other level of the stratification system. These systems can be characterised as closed, an individual's status for life being fixed at birth. Sociologists refer to this as 'ascribed status'.

Birth is only one form of ascribed (fixed) status. Other systems of stratification exist that are based on ascriptive criteria, but which do not fix an individual for life in a low or high position, e.g. the age-grade or age-set systems of the Maasai or Aborigine peoples. (Here the social development of an individual is identical with that of his age-mates and although elders hold decisive authority, each male in his time becomes an elder.)

It is generally agreed that modern industrial societies are considerably more open or fluid than the caste or feudal systems in that movement between different levels of the system of social stratification is much more common. These societies are characterised by what is known as 'achieved status'. An achieved status is one where individuals take up a social position according to their own talent and ability. It should therefore follow that any systematic investigation into the amount of movement by individuals up or down the class structure – social mobility – should reveal high rates of mobility as a feature of industrial societies. You should bear this hypothesis in mind when reading about the findings from mobility studies below.

Social mobility may be upward or downward and may be achieved or forced. In industrialised societies, when sociologists have studied social mobility, they have usually focused on the movement of individuals between occupations, either **intergenerational** (comparing father's job with son's – at a similar stage of the life cycle) or, less frequently, **intragenerational mobility** (focusing on job changes in the careers of individuals).

Social mobility may be short or long range – in modern industrial societies most movement is usually over short distances. Long-range mobility does occur occasionally, but it is a quite restricted phenomenon. There are many factors that may affect the extent of social mobility. Changes in the occupational structure can be particularly important; for example, the expansion of skilled positions in professional, managerial and technical occupations in recent years has created many new opportunities for white-collar employment. The extent of social mobility is also affected by the extent to which the education system provides for equality of opportunity and thus some kind of meritocratic placement thereafter. In this respect the issue of relative class chances in access to further and higher education is of some importance. The number of suitable people available to fill positions is another influence on levels of social mobility; for example, if there is a fall in the number of young people available for employment without a corresponding fall in the numbers of jobs available, the opportunities for upward mobility will be increased.

Reasons for studying mobility

Social mobility studies may be able to tell us something about the extent of movement taking place but they are often less able to tell us why such movement has taken place, or what the real implications of such movement are. There are a number of reasons why sociologists are interested in social mobility. First, the structural question of class formation: it has often been thought that low rates of social mobility may contribute to class solidarity, since common life experience over generations may be perpetuated and perhaps more collectivist solutions to perceived inequalities are likely to be a consequence. Second, from the point of view of an individual's group membership, such studies can reveal perspectives on life chances, i.e. the influence of origins on likely destinations. Third, mobility studies can reveal the consequences of upward and downward social mobility for the attitudes and behaviour of those who experience it. For example, does the experience of upward mobility act to legitimise the social structure in a person's eyes and does the possibility of limited forms of social mobility act as a safety valve for the conflicts inherent in unequal societies by syphoning off talented and highly motivated members of the **underclass** – at the same time weakening class solidarity? Such questions have made the area of social mobility studies of considerable interest to sociologists.

David Glass

There have been two major studies of social mobility in Great Britain. The first was carried out by David Glass's research team in 1949 (published 1954). In order to analyse both the system of stratification in Britain and movement within it, Glass used a more sophisticated version of the Registrar-General's scale – the Hall–Jones scale. This has seven levels.

The Hall–Jones scale

1 Professional and high administrative
2 Managerial and executive

Table 3.1   Social mobility (%) – Glass

Father's STATUS CATEGORY	Son's STATUS CATEGORY						
	1	2	3	4	5	6	7
1	39	15	20	6	14	5	2
2	11	27	23	12	21	5	2
3	4	10	19	19	36	7	6
4	2	4	11	21	43	12	6
5	1	2	8	12	47	17	13
6	0	1	4	9	39	31	16
7	0	1	4	8	36	24	27

3 Inspectional, supervisory and other non-manual (higher grade)
4 Inspectional, supervisory and other non-manual (lower grade)
5 Skilled manual and routine grades of non-manual
6 Semi-skilled manual
7 Unskilled manual

Glass obtained his results by comparing the occupational position of 3,497 men with that of their fathers (*see Table 3.1*). Reading the table from left to right, it shows that, for example, 39 per cent of sons whose fathers were in status category 1 are themselves in status category 1, while only 2 per cent of them are in status category 7. Similarly, 27 per cent of those whose fathers were in status category 7 have remained in that category, while none of them has moved to status category 1. The main finding of Glass's study is that although social mobility exists – a third experienced upward mobility and a third downward mobility – most of it was short range, or across only one or two bands. There was very little long-range mobility, where individuals have moved from one end of the scale to the other. For example, only 13 per cent of the sample had moved from category 7 to above category 5, and no one from this band had moved into the top band. This pattern is almost identical in category 6. Most mobility for the working class was therefore within the working class itself.

The Oxford Mobility Study

In a similar but more widely based study of 8,575 men, a research team of sociologists at Nuffield College, Oxford University, undertook a second intergenerational study with 1972 as the base year. This is frequently referred to as the Oxford Mobility Study, whose findings were written up by John Goldthorpe (1980). The stated intention of this study was not only to update Glass's work, but to examine the reality of three theories of social mobility and class formation. These were that there is social closure at the top of the class structure; that there is a buffer zone around the manual/non-manual boundary beyond which it is difficult to progress; and that education is the main means of social mobility. The Oxford study used a seven-point scale which was similar but not identical to the Hall–Jones model (see Table 3.2).

The scale used here is not directly comparable to that used by Glass, but is as follows:

1 Higher professionals, higher-grade administrators, managers in large industrial concerns and large proprietors
2 Lower professionals, higher-grade technicians, lower-grade administrators, managers in small businesses and supervisors of non-manual employees
3 Routine non-manual workers
4 Small proprietors and self-employed artisans
5 Lower-grade technicians and supervisors of manual workers
6 Skilled manual workers
7 Semi-skilled and unskilled manual workers

The chief difference between the two scales is that, where the Hall–Jones scale used by Glass emphasises occupational prestige, the Oxford scale emphasises concepts of market rewards. In the first table, the manual working class embrace three bands; in the second only two.

The Oxford Mobility Study clearly identifies greater long-range mobility than that discovered by Glass. More, for example, have moved intergenerationally from the top to the bottom and vice-versa. As many as 7 per cent of those whose fathers were in class 7 have moved to class 1, and 6 per cent of those born in class 1 have now moved to class 7. Those who experience this long-range downward mobility are sometimes called 'skidders'. But, on the other hand, 46 per cent of those who began life in class 1 have managed to remain in it. This is called 'élite self-recruitment'.

Service, intermediate and working class

To make their data manageable, and give greater meaning to the figures, the Oxford team grouped their first two social categories together and called this 'the service class' (a term borrowed from the Austrian Marxist Karl Renner). They termed social categories 3, 4 and 5 'the intermediate class' and 6 and 7 were called 'the working class'. In general, and unlike Glass, the Nuffield team found that there had been net upward mobility – more people moved up than moved down. This meant that, with few people entering the working class from above, it remained a homogeneous or uniformly constituted class. But with fewer people leaving the service class, and more entering it from below, it became more mixed or heterogeneous, what Goldthorpe termed 'a class of low classlessness' (Bourne, 1979), meaning that its class consciousness and solidarity are low.

As with any statistics in sociology, these tables need to be interpreted carefully.

The changing occupational structure

What has happened in the twentieth century in the advanced industrial countries is that the amount of manual work has declined, while service and intermediate occupations have correspondingly increased (see Table 3.3). Where manual work made up three-quarters of all occupations in 1911, it was only three-fifths in 1971. At the same time, where roughly only one in 14 jobs was in the service class in 1911, by 1971 one in five jobs were classed in this category. Compounded by the fact that the working class has the highest number of children per family, this means that upward mobility is inevitable, regardless of the degree of openness of the class structure. This makes social mobility studies complex, as they are only directly comparable over time if the class structure and fertility rates remain constant. This is reflected in Table 3.4, which synthesises data from both Glass and the Oxford Mobility Study.

The level of mobility has been constant, at just below 50 per cent of all men, though there has been a

Table 3.2 Social mobility (%) – The Oxford Mobility Study

FATHER'S CLASS	SON'S CLASS						
	1	2	3	4	5	6	7
1	46	19	12	7	5	5	6
2	29	23	12	6	10	11	9
3	19	16	13	7	13	16	16
4	14	14	9	21	10	15	16
5	14	14	10	8	16	21	17
6	8	9	8	6	12	31	26
7	7	9	9	6	13	25	32

Table 3.3 Male occupations, 1911–71 (%)

OCCUPATION	1911	1951	1971
Managerial and Professional	6.9	12.6	21.5
Intermediate	11.9	13.3	14.5
Manual	73.6	68.4	58.8

Source: Goldthorpe, *Social Mobility and Class Structure in Modern Britain*, 1980.

Table 3.4   Social mobility rates of men (%)

Birth date	Pre-1890	1890–9	1900–9	1908–17	1918–27	1928–37
Upwardly mobile	16.5	23.3	23.2	19.9	24.5	30.5
Downwardly mobile	33.0	25.9	24.6	25.3	23.2	20.4
Total mobile	49.5	49.2	47.8	45.2	47.7	50.9

Source: Heath, *Social Mobility*, 1981.

steady increase in upward mobility, and a steady decrease in downward mobility.

Problems of mobility studies

Mobility studies may fascinate statisticians and give number-crunching opportunities to the positivists but how much do they tell us of the realities of the system of stratification as well as people's own experience of class and social mobility? The Oxford Mobility Study has been the target of a number of criticisms, both ideological and methodological.

Rosemary Crompton (1980) has argued that occupations may not be comparable over time because the status of those occupations change, as the debate between writers such as Harry Braverman (1974) and David Lockwood (1958) demonstrates. Being born to a clerical worker at the turn of the century gave you a different status to being born to a clerical worker in the 1960s. The same could be said of printers, with the growth of electronic technology and desktop publishing. Against this, Goldthorpe argues that it is common for work and market conditions to change, but this does not imply changes in class position. In his classification, he did not look at occupational labels, but at a full description of what each occupation entailed.

A second criticism is that Goldthorpe's class 1 – those at the top – is too broad to tell us anything about the chances of reaching the very top, the highest echelons of the ruling class. A narrower band is required. As long as there is homogeneity in the ruling class, where real and effective power resides, as long as the exclusive **élite** networks are in effective operation, then mobility rates at other levels in the class system are less meaningful. Goldthorpe's class 1 contains roughly 12 per cent of all men in work. Other studies of those at the very top – those in élite positions such as company chairmen, chief executives and managing directors – have shown that élite self-recruitment is very high, and entry into this group highly restricted and exclusive.

Marxists see mobility studies as an illusion. They argue that the limited mobility that does occur is merely a means of creaming off the ablest of the working class to help run the capitalist system, so leaving the rest of the proletariat leaderless and divided. The outcome of studies showing mobility to be possible helps legitimise capitalism by making the system seem fair, however limited the numbers involved.

Women and social mobility

A third, and most damaging, criticism is that the mobility studies exclude women. As such, they should be retitled 'The social mobility of men'. The argument is that women are not permanently in the labour market, therefore any valid measurement is impossible. If this view is accepted, then the role of women in the stratification system goes unresearched.

It is certainly difficult to include all women in a stratification model based on occupation because many women either do not work, work part-time or leave the labour market temporarily to have children. Moreover, many women find themselves pushed into one area of work, particularly secretarial and clerical work, making differentiation difficult. Yet women do play a key role in stratification systems. How can their experience be measured?

There have been a number of attempts. Glass collected information on women in his survey but never used it. Chapman (1984) and Abbott and Sapsford (1987) produced empirically based studies that examine this area. Abbott and Sapsford (using the Social Grading Scale, a similar scale to the Registrar-General's) found that the daughters of professional and managerial workers were much more likely to be downwardly mobile than their sons, and that the daughters of manual workers were less likely to be upwardly mobile than their sons. There is a strong tendency for those at either extreme to gravitate to the centre of the stratification system. In Chapman's survey, only 12 per cent of the daughters of men in the top class managed to remain in that class. They are less likely to be counter-mobile, that is to move up the scale again after an initial decline in their status in commencing employment.

Marshall *et al.* (1988) collected data on social mobility in the late 1980s and found that the results for men were fairly similar to those in Goldthorpe's Oxford study. However, the results for women show different patterns of social mobility. In particular, they noted that women's mobility patterns are affected a great deal by the concentration of women in routine non-manual jobs. Large numbers of women were both upwardly and downwardly mobile into class 3. However, they also found that class background influences women's mobility as much as it does men's.

Questions

1 What are the differences in the findings of the Nuffield and Glass studies on social mobility?
2 What are the main problems with measuring the social mobility of women?

Dimensions of class
The ruling class

Central to Marxist theory is the concept that there is a ruling class in society, whose power is based on ownership of the means of production – the bourgeoisie. This has been analysed from a number of angles, raising the following problems:

→ Is the term 'ruling class' too simplistic?
→ In Marxist terms, do those who own the means of production also rule society?
→ Are the few in power better described as an élite? (See chapter 11.)
→ Does the group in power still own the means of production, or has it passed into the hands of others?
→ Is there a difference between ownership and control?

Wealth

If we look at ownership as being related to wealth, then it is clear that this remains in the hands of the few. In the UK, despite the abolition of the Royal Commission on the Distribution of Wealth and Income in the early 1980s, it is still possible, through the Inland Revenue, to picture the distribution of wealth in the last quarter of the twentieth century (*see Table 3.5*).

In 2000, a quarter of the population owned 74 per cent of all marketable wealth, and half the population owned 94 per cent. Alternatively, 75 per cent of the

Table 3.5   Marketable wealth, United Kingdom, 1976–2000

Percentage of total wealth							Owned by percentage of population
1976	1981	1986	1989	1993	1996	2000	
21	18	18	18	17	20	22	most wealthy 1%
38	36	36	38	36	40	42	most wealthy 5%
50	50	50	53	48	52	54	most wealthy 10%
71	73	73	75	72	74	74	most wealthy 25%
92	92	90	94	92	93	94	most wealthy 50%

Source: Social Trends 33, 2003

population owned 26 per cent of the wealth and 50 per cent owned only 7 per cent. The sustained ownership of the majority of wealth by a minority of the population is not enough, though, to show the existence of a capitalist class or ruling class. Further examination is needed of how this wealth is owned, and how it is used.

Managerialism

The idea that the owners of the means of production are individuals or families belongs to the nineteenth century. From the 1870s the growth of the joint-stock company or corporation, characterised by many shareholders, saw what some writers have argued was the transfer of effective power from the owners to the directors of enterprises. This is what Berle and Means (1932) described as 'the managerial revolution'. Where share ownership is so widespread that shareholders are unable to act as a unified group, management control prevails, allowing those in senior management positions to run the enterprise as they wish, free from interference by shareholders. Berle and Means's figures showed that 44 per cent of the top 200 non-financial organisations in the USA were subject to management control in 1932. According to Larner, by 1963 the number had increased to 83.5% (Larner, 1966). Power therefore lay with the controllers, not the owners of capital.

Daniel Bell (1961) distinguishes between industrial and **post-industrial** society. In an industrial society the main economic activity involves the production of goods through labour-intensive industries. This was the type of society that Marx wrote about in developing his ideas on capitalism. Bell suggests that industrial society has been superseded by post-industrial society where the provision of services is central to the economy. Evidence of this comes from the decline in these societies of the goods-producing sector. The number of people employed in manual occupations has fallen, while there has been a massive expansion in white-collar jobs associated with the service sector.

Information and knowledge are the most important resources in a post-industrial society. From this, Bell concludes that knowledge has replaced the ownership of capital as the main source of power, and people in the management, professional and technical occupations have replaced the owner-managers of industry as the dominant group in society. These expert élites are the people who are equipped by their education and training to provide the kind of skills that are increasingly demanded in the post-industrial society.

Post-industrial society?

The assumptions of the post-industrial society thesis have been challenged primarily by Marxist writers. They argue that knowledge may be increasingly important in the process of production, but knowledge is produced through capital investment to serve the interests of capitalist-run businesses. They also suggest that there has been no significant separation of ownership and control of companies. Many companies are still run by owner-operators. Moreover, top managers are often shareholders in the companies that employ them. As such, they have an interest in the maximisation of profit. Even if top managers wanted to eschew profit maximisation and pursue other goals for their companies, they would not be able to do so. This is because profit is essential for a company to stay in business in a competitive capitalist system.

John Scott (1979) argues that while a case can be made for a managerialist stage in the development of US and Japanese capitalism, it is more difficult to apply to other advanced capitalist economies and more recent periods of history. He writes that it is more appropriate to see control as being exercised by a 'constellation of interests' where 'no single majority shareholder has sufficient shares to exercise minority control on their own and any temporary coalition is likely to be countered by another. There is no community of interest among the large shareholders over and above their common interests as shareholders.' Although individual share ownership has increased – from 7 per cent of individuals in 1979 to 26 per cent in 2001 – the proportion of shares they own has fallen.

The group that has become dominant is the financial sector, composed of institutions or impersonal structures such as banks, insurance companies and pension funds. These have become increasingly influential throughout the advanced capitalist economies.

Citing evidence from the USA, Britain, Australia, Canada, France and Japan, Scott is able to conclude that 'the managerial revolution is a myth: salaried managers have not usurped the powers of capitalist shareholders. The joint stock company has not led to the demise of the capitalist class … but it has produced an important transformation in the structure of property ownership' (Scott, 1986). This view is echoed by Maurice Zeitlin (1989). In America, he says, it is still the case that propertied families retain economic control.

Both Scott and Zeitlin agree that a capitalist class remains in control of modern capitalism, though their hold is now through financial institutions. For Scott, there are four groups visible within this class: the **entrepreneurial** capitalists, actively involved in their personal property; rentier capitalists with personal investments in many different companies; executive capitalists with an official post in a joint-stock company; and finance capitalists holding many directorships in several companies.

That this capitalist class exists does not mean that they are necessarily the ruling class. For those, like Scott, who are close to Marxism, this immediately draws them into the debate between Ralph Miliband and Nicos Poulantzas (see chapter 11). Scott's own analysis (1991) uses Gramsci's concept of a power bloc, emphasising the use made by the capitalist class of the machinery of the State.

Questions

1 How has the distribution of wealth and income changed since the 1970s?
2 Can it be argued that there is a unified ruling class, whose power is based on ownership of the means of production?

The working class

From his vantage point in the middle of the nineteenth century, Marx argued that it was in the laws of capitalist development that the class structure of capitalism would eventually polarise into two distinct classes – an increasingly small and increasingly wealthy bourgeoisie, and an increasingly large and increasingly impoverished proletariat, joined by those members of the petty bourgeoisie who had been pushed down into the proletariat by the process of the centralisation of capital.

Proletarian consciousness

Eventually, as the proletariat became poorer and poorer – increasingly immiserated – they would make two key realisations. Firstly, the nature of their exploitation would become clear as they understood that they had a common identity and common cause. A class *in* itself would become a class *for* itself as it achieved **class consciousness**. Elements of this process were emerging in Marx's own lifetime, for example with the formation of the International Working Men's Association, with Marx as its first General Secretary. Secondly, as the system fell into stagnation and decay, the proletariat would realise that the bourgeoisie had become a decadent class, morally unfit to rule and unable to develop the forces of production any further. The only choice left was for the proletariat to take control of the means of production for themselves. This socialist revolution would be the first stage towards a **communist**, classless society.

A century and two world wars later, many sociologists were arguing that elements of a classless society had indeed emerged, though not in the way that Marx had foreseen. Industrialisation had run its course and polarisation had not taken place. On the contrary, the middle class had grown in number, and the working class had become relatively more, and not less, affluent. Consuming goods had become as much part of their lives as producing them. The traditional working class depicted by writers such as Dennis, Henriques and Slaughter (1956) was fragmenting. Important sections of the working class had become better off, gaining a stake in capitalism. Class conflict was disappearing as workers had come to share the same goals as their employers. They had undergone a process of **embourgeoisement**, whereby they were taking on the norms and values of the middle class. Working-class culture was disappearing. There was no longer any real difference between the lifestyle and attitudes of the middle class and the affluent working class.

This was the argument put forward in the 1950s and early 1960s by a series of writers (Abrams *et al.*, 1960; Butler and Rose, 1960; Mogey, 1956; Young and Wilmott, 1957 and Zweig, 1952) echoing similar arguments in the USA. Some **psephologists**, for example, used this argument to explain the victory of the Conservative Party in Britain in the elections of 1951, 1955 and 1959. Other sociologists, though, were far from happy with the idea of abandoning one of the key concepts in sociology. In the early 1960s a research team was set up to investigate the truth of the embourgeoisement theorists' claims.

The Affluent Worker

In what has become one of the best-known and important studies of the British working class, Goldthorpe, Lockwood, Bechhofer and Platt (1969) chose to study selected working-class groups in Luton, where they thought the conditions for embourgeoisement would be most clearly present. At three industrial sites (Vauxhall Motors, Skefco Ball Bearings, and Laporte Chemicals) and in their homes,

they conducted a detailed examination of the norms, values, attitudes, economic circumstances and lifestyles of 229 blue-collar and 54 white-collar workers.

Their findings are presented under three headings: economic, political and relational. Under the first they found that although manual workers might, on occasion, earn the same amount as the non-manual workers and possess similar consumer durables, their wages were not earned in the same way. The manual workers had to work longer hours, in shifts, frequently taking on overtime. They had less job security, less opportunities for promotion, and fewer of the fringe benefits enjoyed by the non-manual workers such as sick pay and pension rights. Moreover, they were distinguished by their instrumental attitude to work. Work was not a means to finding satisfaction or fulfilment; it was simply a means to an end, and that end was found in their pay packet.

The term 'relational' referred to who the workers spent their free time with. Here they found scant evidence that the manual workers associated with white-collar workers, from inside or outside the workplace. Most of the time was spent with family or friends drawn from the same class. Unlike the non-manual workers, their time was spent in informal, unstructured activities.

At a political level, the team found little evidence to suggest that these workers were not aligned to either trade unions or the Labour Party. Of their sample, 80 per cent had voted Labour in 1959, and 87 per cent were members of trade unions, though in both cases they found that these decisions were made, again, largely on the basis of instrumentalism. It was the workers' belief that Labour and the trade unions could preserve their status as affluent workers.

Privatisation

What was a new trend, though, was the increasing number from both classes who were becoming more home-centred or privatised, with the men spending more time at home with the children and doing mending-and-making jobs around the home. This was not a result of one class adopting the norms of another, but of a process of convergence between the two.

What *The Affluent Worker* showed was that there was no evidence for the original **hypothesis**. The working class had not undergone a process of embourgeoisement. New trends, though, were discernible. Male workers spent more time at home and they saw work as a way of earning the money necessary to buy consumer goods. Trade unions and the Labour Party were supported to help them become more affluent. The workers they had studied were therefore 'privatised instrumental collectivists'.

Criticisms of *The Affluent Worker*

As well as creating a great deal of interest, and becoming the model for further research, *The Affluent Worker* has also provoked a great deal of criticism. Some of this is aimed at the research methods used. Although they felt unable to say that their study was generalisable for all affluent workers, they claimed at the time that the Luton group were 'prototypical', containing the seeds of future trends in the working class. As T. H. Marshall argued at the time (1970), this is an ambitious claim, as the aim of their study had been to test the embourgeoisement thesis, not detect future trends in the working class. A different research design would have been necessary to do this. Doubts have also been raised about the composition of the research group, in that many of the workers who had moved to Luton in the 1950s had come from the depressed areas of the north-east and Scotland: 'Far from being the vanguard of the working class, a significant section of the work force has to be understood as labour peripherally recruited and therefore untypical. Prototypicality, given this finding, would be an even more unsubstantiated claim' (Grieco, 1987).

The workers in the sample were said to have an instrumental attitude, i.e. be willing to accept deprivations at work because of the compensation of high and relatively secure wages. In this sense they were **alienated** and happy at the same time. The picture of harmony may have been overdrawn as there was a bitter strike in 1966 at the car plant where many of the sample worked, and industrial relations in the 1970s were poor, judging by the number of strike days lost.

Marshall *et al.* (1988) questioned the extent to which sectionalism and instrumental attitudes among the British working class were a recent development. Historical evidence suggests that there were artisans who gave primary emphasis to their home life, and who had an instrumental attitude to work, in the nineteenth century. The study also found that among contemporary workers many regard work as at least as important as non-work activity, and they do not follow completely privatised lifestyles.

Lockwood and Goldthorpe's study may point to a possible reduction in the potential for class consciousness and conflict, privatisation replacing the collective spirit found in traditional working-class communities. However, if high wages are not met then the workers could easily revert to collective class action. The depth of the attachment to privatisation is thus uncertain.

While Lockwood and Goldthorpe's study is generally taken as the test of embourgeoisement, it may be prudent to bear in mind the methodological criticisms and remember it was but one study in one part of Britain at one point in time.

In the 1990s, Fiona Devine (1992) undertook a second study of the Vauxhall car plant at Luton, by now shrunk in size from the 22,000 workers of the 1960s to 6,000 under the impact of a global recession. Her aim was to reinvestigate the concept of privatised instrumental collectivism. Having interviewed 62 men and women at the Vauxhall plant, she argues that the portrait painted by *The Affluent Worker* team was too simplistic. Her respondents had moved to Luton to escape redundancy and job insecurity and to find cheaper housing. Many had done this while at the same time maintaining strong **kinship** and friendship links. Their lives were not exclusively family- or home-centred, yet neither were they wholly public or communal. 'Bettering' themselves and their families was a dominant aspiration of all the interviewees. Their individualism was tempered by an awareness of how others in their class also had to work for a living and of the unequal distribution of wealth and income. They still looked to trade unions and the Labour Party to improve not only their own lives but the lives of others like them, although they were critical of, and disappointed by, the shortcomings of both unions and the party.

Devine argues in her research that the connections between individualism, privatism and instrumentalism are not as strong as *The Affluent Worker* proposed, and that working-class lifestyles and values have not changed as much as they had suggested. Workers accept that they have to earn a living under capitalism, although they do not necessarily accept the social order determined by capitalism, nor are they necessarily committed to this system. Their class consciousness is evident from a sense of solidarity with others in a similar financial position to themselves.

The issue of the class position of the skilled working class remains a live issue today. Although the term 'embourgeoisement' is now rarely used, it is frequently argued that the working class has fragmented into at least two different layers, definable in terms of hopes, aspirations and patterns of consumption: the 'new' and 'traditional' working class.

Questions

1 Can you see any evidence that embourgeoisement is occurring today?

2 What are the main strengths and limitations of *The Affluent Worker* study?

3 What is Weberian about the approach of *The Affluent Worker* authors to the question of embourgeoisement?

The middle class

In the same way that we have identified differences amongst the working class, there is a need to question whether non-manual occupations can any longer be grouped together. A number of changes in modern industrial societies over the last fifty years have, perhaps, fragmented the middle class. For example, there has been a decline in small businesses (the petit bourgeoisie in Marxist terms). In 1951, 5 per cent of the working population in the UK were employers and proprietors; by 2001, the proportion was only 2.6 per cent. At the same time, there has been an increase in the number of managers and administrators. In 1951, 5.5 per cent of the working population were managers and administrators; by 2001, it was 11.6 per cent. This reflects the growth in professional management as ownership and control of companies have become separated. The joint stock company, owned by a relatively large number of shareholders, has become the typical form of capitalist enterprise. The scale of industry and government has increased. This has, in turn, increased the need for professional administrators. Within this group there are differences in pay and conditions between the private and public sectors, the product of various government pay strategies. In addition, the work of C. Wright Mills (1956) draws attention to the split of the middle class into those wielding considerable power and those who are relatively powerless office workers.

Is the middle class fragmented?

These changes have broadened the middle class. We now find at one end of the spectrum lower professionals and **white-collar** workers turning increasingly to trade unions and finding it difficult to maintain the real value of their standard of living, whilst at the other end professionals negotiate directly with employers, and managers have accrued many more fringe benefits as attempts have been made to circumvent government pay policies.

The key **empirical** findings which question the cohesion of the middle class are those produced by Roberts *et al.* (1977) who studied the class images of 243 male white-collar workers. They found a number of different images, the most common being as follows. Some 27 per cent saw themselves in the middle mass of a class structure with a small, rich upper class and a relatively deprived lower class. The second largest group (19 per cent) saw themselves as squeezed between two increasingly powerful groups: the working class and small upper class. Small businessmen typically held this view.

Goldthorpe *et al.* (1969), in a study of 398 small shopkeepers and their spouses, employ the term 'marginality', suggesting that shopkeepers were in, but not of, the middle class. The authors conclude that small traders do deserve to be treated as a separate stratum from both the so-called 'lower middle class' and 'independent' working class. They are indeed petit bourgeois with three key elements affecting their economic vision – belief in 'independence', distaste for the 'rational legal' elements of our society (bureaucracy mistrusted) and dislike of change.

The third group in Roberts' sample were the white-collar group who saw society in terms of a four-step graded ladder. They tended to be well educated and relatively well paid. They often rejected the whole principle of social class and had no apparent class loyalty. The smallest group in the white-collar sample held a proletarian image of society, seeing themselves as working class. They were typically employed in routine white-collar work with few promotion prospects and relatively low wages. The research led Roberts *et al.* to conclude that there had been a 'fragmentation of the middle class into distinguishable strata'.

Proletarianisation

As we have seen, part of Marx's projection about the development of the class system under capitalism concerned the argument that sections of the middle class would become depressed into the proletariat. In the process, they would adopt working-class norms and values. In other words, they would undergo a process of proletarianisation. As with the concept of embourgeoisement, this idea continues to be keenly debated. In many ways, the proletarianisation debate is the mirror image of the embourgeoisement debate, with sociologists taking similar theoretical positions and employing similar analytical tools. It is mainly a debate between Marxists and Weberians. Specifically it is a debate about the class position of clerical workers.

Lockwood

In *The Black-Coated Worker*, David Lockwood (1958) presents us with evidence that suggests that clerical workers have undergone a process of proletarianisation since the nineteenth century. At that time, holding the position of a clerk implied the high wages and status accorded to those possessing the skills of numeracy and literacy. This situation has changed as the proportion of clerks in the workforce has increased – from 0.8 per cent in 1851 to 13 per cent by the 1950s. Wages have also dropped to a point where they are roughly equivalent to those of the better-paid manual workers. What was once a high-wage, high-status occupation for men has become comparatively low-paid, low-status work dominated by women.

The task Lockwood set himself was to determine whether these changes were enough to indicate that a process of proletarianisation had taken place. He argued that clerks' position could be best understood by reference to three criteria: work situation, market situation and status situation. The first refers to how much they earned, how secure they were in their jobs and what their chances of promotion were. The second refers to the labour process and social relations at work of the clerical workers. The third defines the amount of prestige these workers had in the wider society.

Although Lockwood found that it was now the case that some clerical workers earned less than some of the manual workers on the same site, he found that their conditions of service were preferable in that they were less likely to be made redundant, worked shorter hours, had greater access to fringe benefits and had greater opportunities of promotion.

The labour process of clerical work did not resemble manual work. It did not take place on factory floors, their work still involved the acquisition of skills and specialisations. Their work had not been routinised, nor was it as easy to replace a clerical worker as it was a manual worker.

Status ambiguity

Their status situation, though, had changed. This was because there was both a greater supply of clerical workers and a greater demand for clerical work, and because clerical workers were predominantly female. Although this amounts to a decline in status for these

workers, this is not enough to say that they are now proletarian. Nor are they middle class – this is what Lockwood calls a situation of 'status ambiguity'.

Lockwood has been criticised for failing to take into account the increasing size and militancy of white-collar unions, which some sociologists see as evidence that a proletarian consciousness is spreading amongst non-manual workers. Nor does Lockwood examine the specific disadvantages experienced by women in white-collar jobs. Heath and Britten (1984) have argued that there are many women in routine non-manual jobs who cannot be differentiated from women in manual work in terms of pay, career prospects, decision-making powers, etc., and so have to be seen as being in basically a proletarian market situation.

Braverman

Writing sixteen years later, and from an explicitly Marxist perspective, Harry Braverman (1974) will have none of Lockwood's Weberianism. Clerical workers, he clearly states, are now proletarian. As with manual work, non-manual work has suffered at the hands of Taylorism (see chapter 9). It has been standardised and routinised in the era of **monopoly capitalism**. He dates the earliest attempts to apply Taylorist principles to office work from the publication of W. H. Leffingwell's *Scientific Office Management* in 1917.

The proletarianisation of clerical work has advanced relentlessly. By 1960, the Systems and Procedures Association of America had produced a manual entitled *A Guide to Office Time Standards: A Compilation of Standard Data Used By Large American Companies*. In true positivist tradition, everything that could be measured, was:

Open and close	Minutes
File drawer, open and close, no selection	.04
Folder, open and close flaps	.04
Desk drawer	.014
Open center drawer	.026
Close side	.015
Close center	.027
Chair activity	
Get up from chair	.033
Sit down in chair	.033
Turn in swivel chair	.009
Move in chair to adjoining desk or file	
(4ft max.)	.050

Source: Braverman, *Labor and Monopoly Capitalism*, 1974

According to Braverman, the widespread application of these timings shows clear evidence that there is no longer any difference between the labour process of manual and non-manual workers.

The continued attempt by some sociologists to maintain this distinction is itself ideological as far as Braverman is concerned: 'This terminology is … considered serviceable by those who are alarmed by the results of a more realistic terminology – those, for instance, whose "sociology" pursues apologetic purposes. For them, such terms as "white collar employees" conveniently lump into a single category the well-paid, authoritative and desirable positions at the top of the hierarchy and the mass of proletarianised inferiors in a way that makes possible a rosier picture: higher "average pay" scales etc.'

Attempts to operationalise the concept of class stratification frequently founder on the issue of how routine non-manual workers should be classified. John Goldthorpe (1980) has conceded that in his study of social mobility (see above) some of those he classed as routine non-manual – the personal service workers (Class 3) – would be better reclassified as working class, although he continues to see secretaries as part of the middle class.

While sympathetic to some of his ideas, later studies have claimed that Braverman has exaggerated the extent of **deskilling** and overlooked the importance of other means through which the owners and managers are able to control their workforce. Crompton and Jones (1984) point out that there is not a homogeneous mass of workers in the clerical sector all subject to the same deskilling process. They are affected in different ways by changes in technology with some being better placed than others.

Wright

Erik Wright's (1985) first attempt to construct a Marxist class model centred on the concept of exploitation through relationship to the means of production foundered on the problem of where to place routine, non-manual workers. Sometimes he placed them in a category of semi-autonomous workers, who have some control over their work, at other times he placed them in the same category as workers taking it as understood that they had been proletarianised. This was the key difference between his model and that constructed by Goldthorpe. Later he decided to place this group in either the working class or the new middle class according to the qualifications they possessed, their job title, and how much control – or autonomy – they had over what they did at work. In doing so he found himself moving closer to a Weberian model of class.

As with so many debates in sociology, part of the disagreement here stems from different uses of the same terms. Proletarianisation can be used to describe different social changes. It can refer to the changing nature of work, for example through deskilling, where technological changes mean that the same job now requires less skill to carry it out. It can refer to changing political consciousness, for example white-collar workers becoming active trade unionists. It can also refer to the experience of downward mobility. In one of the most recent studies of social class, Gordon Marshall *et al.* (1988) argue that, however it is defined, there is no contemporary evidence for proletarianisation.

Proletarianisation refuted

In a study drawn from a national random sample of 1,315 male and female workers in 1984, Marshall *et al.* found that it was mainly manual workers who claimed that their work had been deskilled. Over 90 per cent of routine non-manual workers did not believe that their jobs had been deskilled. Nor did they report that they experienced less autonomy over the labour process than manual workers. The research team did not find any evidence of significant downward mobility for either male or female routine non-manual workers, at any stage in their working lives. They were as likely to identify themselves as middle class as working class, and more likely to vote Conservative than Labour. Marshall *et al.*'s unequivocal answer to this question is that proletarianisation is not taking place.

As we can see, the most heavily researched area in the sociology of class concerns the question of where to draw the line between the working and middle classes. How this is done depends, as ever, on the perspective used to conceptualise class.

Questions
1 How can non-manual workers be described as proletarian?
2 What is the best way of describing the class position of clerical workers?

The underclass

The notion of an underclass was first developed in the USA to refer to those who seemed permanently trapped in poverty and unemployment. These tended to be people living in black ghettos. The term is highly controversial. Its very use is seen by some to be derogatory and discriminatory. It derives in part from the Marxian idea of the lumpenproletariat. The lumpenproletariat were the 'rotting mass' thrown off by the lowest layers of the old society. They were seen as too disorganised to take any part in any coming revolution.

Where the term 'underclass' is used by sociologists today it generally means a substratum of society somewhere below the working class, economically and socially distinct from the rest of society. Characteristically, they live in inner-city areas, are dependent on State benefits, are likely to be caught up in crime, are perhaps drug addicts, were conceived when their mothers were in their teenage years, or become teenage parents themselves, have children who frequently miss school, or missed school themselves.

There is disagreement amongst sociologists, however, over why an underclass exists – is it a structural or a behavioural phenomenon – and who belongs to it? There is also doubt expressed about whether the concept of an underclass is a useful one or not. Many of the arguments are similar to those surrounding poverty (see chapter 4). In this section we look at the argument that a black underclass can be distinguished.

A black underclass?

To many writers, in Britain and America, there seems to be a disproportionate number of people from ethnic minorities in this class. This is the group studied by Rex and Tomlinson (1979) and in the USA by W. J. Wilson (1987). Thus, for Wilson, 'today's ghetto neighbourhoods are populated almost exclusively by the most disadvantaged segments of the black urban community', some of whom are 'engaged in street crime and other forms of aberrant behaviour as well as families that experience long-term spells of poverty and/or welfare dependency. These are the populations to which I refer when I speak of the "underclass".' It is partly for historical reasons that black people have accumulated in inner cities, especially in the northern USA, many of whom have been left high and dry as jobs have moved out, along with some of the more affluent black and white working class. What remains are poor blacks.

This type of structural explanation for the emergence of a black underclass is echoed by neo-Weberian views that emphasise the status inequality that results from racial discrimination leading to, for example, black workers being confined to the secondary labour market which is characterised by low pay, poor promotion prospects and little job security.

Conflict theory

A number of sociologists doubt the usefulness and appropriateness of the concept of an underclass. Marxists see no ethnically differentiated substratum of the working class but the common disabilities of class being experienced by people who happen to be black. R. Miles (1982), looking at migrant labour, argues that 'migrants occupy a structurally distinct position in the economic, political and ideological relations of British capitalism, but within the boundary of the working class. They therefore constitute a fraction of the working class.'

Rather than engage in a sterile debate about whether ethnic minorities are part of the underclass or a fraction of the working class, it is perhaps more helpful to see the similarities between the Marxist and Weberian positions. Both agree that racial discrimination has a socio-economic basis and this racism is widespread and affects all blacks in Britain and the USA. They further agree that the only jobs available to some blacks are those that whites are unwilling to undertake, particularly manual labour (making them a replacement population) and that they have an experience of life and a consciousness different to the white working class.

Yet there are also important difficulties attached to any attempt to equate ethnicity with membership of an underclass. The underclass is far from exclusively black. Both Peter Townsend (1979) and Frank Field (1989) describe an underclass without specific reference to ethnicity. Field's underclass is simply composed of elderly pensioners, lone parents and the long-term unemployed (see chapter 4).

It is also important to disaggregate the groups so often described as the 'ethnic minorities'. The experience of West Indians, Asians, Indians, Pakistanis, Bangladeshis and African Asians of life in Britain is not uniform. African Asians and Indians in particular have a class profile similar to that of whites. Largely for this reason a shared colour-consciousness has not emerged.

The underclass concept refuted

In the same way that the idea of a black underclass is problematic, so is any concept of a homogeneous group that can be described as an 'underclass'. In the same way that not all of those so categorised are necessarily criminals, or teenage parents, or black, so too are they not necessarily a static group. If it does exist, it is a class that people – except perhaps the long-term unemployed – move into and out of. Nor, according to Bradshaw and Holmes (1989) are even the long-term unemployed part of a separate group. 'In no sense', they argue, are they 'a detached and isolated group cut off from the rest of society. They are just the same people as the rest of our population, with the same culture and aspirations but with simply too little money to be able to share in the activities and possessions of everyday life with the rest of the population.'

It therefore seems to be the case that, while social divisions and inequality in society have become more pronounced in recent decades, few sociologists are willing to unreservedly describe the emergence of a new underclass, black or otherwise. The term has been criticised for being a stereotype of a heterogeneous group, inadequately describing the experience of all black people, all lone parents, all women, or even all of the long-term unemployed. At worst, it has been seen as a dangerous concept, used by some as a euphemism for race while playing down the existence of discrimination. It has been used as an umbrella term to attempt to link social problems such as the rise in lone parents, ethnic discrimination, relative poverty and increasing criminality that, as Jencks and Peterson (1991) argue, are in reality only tenuously linked. The case for the emergence of a distinct and separate underclass remains problematic.

A black underclass in the USA?

Douglas Glasgow (1981) discusses the underclass thesis in terms of characteristics in the USA. He sees the underclass as characterised by a lack of social mobility of both an **intra-** and **intergenerational** variety. (The lower class does have long-range social mobility.) The lack of effective connections with educational institutions and unions reduces their job chances, and the opportunities that do exist for work carry no promotional prospects. They are offered, or are in, dead-end jobs. This position is unlikely to change, argues Glasgow, as long as racism exists. He sees the racism of today in the USA as probably worse than when it was more visible: 'The exclusion is carried out now by computers, which ostensibly reject people on the basis not of "race" but of "social profile"; the institutions of the country are more completely saturated with covert expressions of racism than ever.'

QUESTIONS
1 Does an underclass exist?
2 Given the evidence presented, who may belong to it?

New directions in class analysis

In viewing class as an aspect of stratification, the Registrar-General, Hall and Jones, Marxists, and to some extent Weberians, all accept the importance of viewing social divisions principally as based on the way people live their lives as providers of goods and services. The focus is on what people do in their working lives. This view has caused increasing problems for sociologists in recent decades.

By focusing on production, occupation and employment, only a particular sector comes into view. We learn little about those who are not part of the formal economy, for whatever reason, whether they are in education, retired, unemployed, housewives, sick and disabled, or institutionalised.

Excluding these groups has caused many problems. New directions have had to be taken to discover the importance of unpaid domestic labour, the 'informal' economy or what it is like to be unemployed or never intending to work again. Very little has been written concerning the sociology of disability. These areas slipped out of focus because of the centrality of paid work in sociological analysis. Now sociologists are discovering and uncovering whole new areas to study.

Not only does measuring stratification by formal **work** role hide as much as it reveals, but it no longer tells us very much about how people behave. This argument is at the heart of current thinking in the sociology of politics – for example in the **partisan alignment** debate which examines the relationships between class and voting behaviour. It is also important in the focus on consumption in the sociology of the community.

The rise of consumerism

Steven Lukes (1991) has examined the two perspectives of embourgeoisement and proletarianisation in the light of recent changes in the spheres of production and consumption. He argues that class conflict has been restructured as a result of developments such as: the increased participation of women in the labour market; State intervention in economic processes; and the shift from manufacturing to service industries. Lukes suggests that the distinction between manual and non-manual labour has become irrelevant. The rise of mass production and consumption (the focus on ownership of material possessions, housing, etc.) means that work has become less central to the identity and consciousness of workers. Lukes claims that the UK is now a society divided against itself in a number of ways that criss-cross traditional class divisions. These new divisions include:

→ those who own private property and those who do not;
→ the waged and the unwaged;
→ those in economically buoyant areas and those in areas which are in decline;
→ those economically secure and those on the margins of poverty.

New sectional interests have emerged based on instrumental, pecuniary and egoistic values and attitudes. The result is that sectional conflicts are conducted in the workplace whilst the home and environment are a haven from this, where individuals seek their private satisfactions in leisure and home life. This new sectionalism and self-interest help to break down class politics and the electorate becomes fragmented along unfamiliar political lines. The structural shifts in the nature of stratification, it is held, serve to undermine traditional social class solidarity.

An investigation of 'sectionalism' based on consumption and income was undertaken by Marshall *et al.* (1988). They looked in particular at voting intention and housing tenure, since many commentators have suggested that the home-ownership movement has helped to break down class voting. They found that whilst class voting was mediated by housing tenure, the familiar class link was still important. Marshall *et al.* concluded that class is a common source of collective identity. They did not suggest that there was a growing class consciousness in a Marxist sense but rather that class is still important in providing identity.

Self-provisioning and consumerism

The view that formal work roles may not be as significant as previously supposed has been taken up by Marxists such as Manuel Castells (1977) as well as non-Marxists such as Ray Pahl (1984). Pahl's argument is that a fundamental change has taken place in the nature of work. Full-time work has come to play less of a part in people's lives as the domestic sphere has taken over. With people mending their own cars, building extensions, doing their own decorating,

growing their own food ('domestic self-provisioning'), the home, not the workplace, is now the centre of most people's lives. Yet he claims the people who engage in self-provisioning are not the unemployed, with time on their hands, but those in work – those with money who choose to make time. As many of the working, domestic self-provisioners are also home-owners (or mortgage-owners), there now exists a marked and visible social division between the 'middle mass' and those without their own homes and the opportunity to work, formally or informally.

Public and private divisions

For Pahl, this division is now more important than that between manual and non-manual workers. Two distinct sectors exist: the public world of council housing, State pensions, public transport and the National Health Service, and the private world of home ownership, private pensions, the motor car and, increasingly, private health insurance (*see Table 3.6*).

Your life chances are increasingly being determined by whether your consumption pattern is private or public, what Patrick Dunleavy (1979) has termed 'consumption sector location'. This could, for example, be the key to understanding why the Conservative Party won four consecutive elections between 1979 and 1992. It also means that sociologists now need to move away from the study of the workplace, and move into other people's homes, the privatised world of millions of individuals.

This is not a new debate in sociology. Changes in lifestyles and consumption were at the heart of the post-war assertions – when there was also a sustained period of Conservative government – that sections of the working class were undergoing a process of embourgeoisement. As we know, the 'Affluent worker' studies found this hypothesis to be unproven, and class and occupation remain key sociological terms.

Table 3.6   Household tenure in Great Britain (%)

Form of tenure	1914	1945	1951	1961	1971	1981	1987	1998	2002
Owner-occupation	10	26	29	43	53	54	64	69	72
Local authority rental	0	12	18	27	31	34	26	17	13
Private rental	90	62	53	31	16	12	10	14	15

Source: A. H. Halsey (ed.), *British Social Trends Since 1900*, Macmillan, 1988 and *Social Trends* 33, 2003

The death of class?

For Lukes and Pahl, contemporary class analysis must embrace the study of a wider range of social relationships than just those located within the sphere of work and production. Patterns of consumption and the lifestyles and opportunities that they facilitate have become particularly important in understanding the divisions and inequality on which the system of stratification is based in modern industrial societies.

Some post-modern theorists have gone even further by questioning whether class still exists. Jan Pakulski and Malcolm Waters (1996) argue that classes exist only if there is a 'minimum level of clustering, or groupness', and such clusterings or groupness are no longer evident. People no longer feel that they belong to class groupings, and members of supposed classes include a wide variety of very different people.

Pakulski and Waters believe that class can be seen as just one, not very important, division in society along with ethnicity, gender, age, disability, etc. They offer a number of explanations for the death of class. The development of welfare states and the institutionalisation of class conflict have reduced the direct impact of class relationships. Property has increasingly moved from private hands to being owned by organisations and the **division of labour** has become more complex.

Moreover, increasing affluence for the majority has meant that most people are able to exercise choice in what they consume and therefore in how they create their identities. Class background no longer restricts people's opportunities, confining them to a particular pattern of life and range of experiences. Consumerism makes it possible for people to create different identities and associations, and to relate to each other in ways that are more flexible and fluid than used to be the case when relationships were dominated by social class and economic status.

Consumption, according to Pakulski and Waters, is becoming the standard by which individuals judge others and themselves. Consumer goods become signs of association and lifestyle. They are consumed for the images they convey, rather than because of utility or aesthetics, much less out of necessity. However, by claiming that consumption patterns and differences in lifestyle have become more significant than class differences, Pakulski and Waters neglect the point that class differences influence the types of lifestyle that different groups can afford. People with few resources – those in the 'underclass' for example – are inevitably excluded from the many choices about lifestyle and consumption that are only available to those with sufficient income or wealth.

Westergaard (1996) has argued that far from dying, class differences became stronger in the late twentieth century, particularly in the UK. He supports his claim with reference to a range of statistics. For example, between 1980 and 1990, the earnings of the highest-paid tenth of white-collar workers rose by approximately 40 per cent in real terms, while the poorest-paid tenth of blue-collar workers saw virtually no rise in their real incomes. Private ownership of property has also become more concentrated. Thus the share of marketable wealth owned by the richest 5 per cent of the British population rose from 36 per cent at the start of the 1980s to 38 per cent at the end of that decade.

Westergaard argues that the power of the highest social classes and of big business has also been growing. He says that the power of private business has grown, as free-market government policies intended. To take just one instance, business representation in the governance of public education and health has been consistently stepped up; and, more generally, business-style prescriptions for 'cost-efficiency' have spread widely in the conduct of public-sector affairs. In the UK, the policy of denationalising has resulted in the return of large parts of the economy to private ownership.

As with many issues in sociology, therefore, the issue of whether or not class is 'dead' is hotly debated and subject to many different interpretations. From here the debate can go in two directions – one, to greatly emphasise the importance of consumption (in its widest definition). The other is to recognise that before there can be consumption there must first be production. If this is the case, the concept of 'relationship to the means of production' must be redefined in such a way as to include not only those in paid employment, but all members of the population, working or not.

QUESTIONS

1 Is occupation the most important indicator of people's class?
2 What are the problems of this indicator?

Sex and gender

The models of class presented so far have seen class in terms of occupation and have been geared to the measurement of the experiences of men. In recent decades it has become clear that this bequest of the 'founding fathers' creates a sociology in which it seems that women are bolted on as an afterthought. Classical Marxism, for example, argues that all forms of stratification are subordinate to that of class. Marx's economics are constructed on the assumption that surplus value is generated by paid labour at the point of production. He has little to say about unpaid labour. It was left to Marx's friend and collaborator, Engels (1884), to explain how women's exploitation was caused by capitalism, and specifically the link between the State, private property and the family.

'Malestream' sociology

This is generally true of most 'malestream' sociology to date, and since the 1970s a series of books and articles have exposed sociology's intrinsic sexism. Women have only been assumed to exist as appendages of men. Furthermore, the models of class we have looked at so far assume that they are married, live in families, and if they work they earn less than their husbands. The Oxford Mobility Study, for example, was conducted on the assumption that families, not individuals, are the fundamental units of society. As individuals, women are therefore thought not to have an independent experience of class, but are classified according to the occupations of their partners.

Limitations

The limitations of studies based on this assumption are obvious, as Acker (1973) has pointed out. Not all women are married or live with men. Some households may contain couples where the woman is the higher or only earner. Not all women work in paid labour. Most single-parent families are headed by women. Finally, it is not necessarily the case with working couples that they have the same type of occupation and therefore the same class position in their hours of work, regardless of their domestic situation. Seeing class in this way obscures any understanding of the position of women in society.

In defending what has come to be seen as the 'traditional' view, John Goldthorpe (1983, 1986) has countered these claims by stating that, statistically, it is reasonable to say that most people do live in families, and that the head of that household is usually a man.

Women are intermittent, limited and conditional members of the labour market. It is not patronising or sexist to devise a model of class that acknowledges that women are socially subordinate to men, because this is a known and measured reality. Indeed it is the starting point for feminist analysis. In situations where there are dual-career households they can be analysed according to who has the salient or most prominent occupation, measured by wages and the amount of qualifications needed to get that job.

It is nevertheless maintained by many theorists that the relationship between women, class and gender is more complex than this traditional view claims. Many writers have argued that there is sufficient empirical evidence to show that men occupy their class position *because* women occupy an inferior one: class structures are gendered. Marshall *et al.* (1988) state that their research shows that men have higher absolute rates of mobility than women, receive higher rewards, and are more highly paid for their qualifications. Only 2 per cent of highly qualified men are in routine non-manual jobs compared with 32 per cent of equally qualified women. Crompton and Jones (1984) found that only 12 per cent of female clerical workers had reached supervisory positions compared with 36 per cent of their male counterparts, and only 1 per cent of women got to management, compared to 34 per cent of men. The effect of women's employment is to privilege men.

Within sociology there is a lack of agreement about what is the basic unit of analysis in society. Where some maintain that it is the family others argue that married women in full-time employment should also be included. This would reveal what Britten and Heath (1983) call the 'cross-class family'. Marshall *et al.* see men and women as individuals in families, while Stanworth (1984) and Giddens (1973) argue that women and men have to be accounted separately in any account of stratification. Delphy (1981) takes the argument further than this when she claims that married women constitute a class separate to men because, whether in paid labour or not, they all engage in the same unpaid labour at home, and many are solely dependent on men for access to money. This is what she calls the 'domestic mode of production'.

The idea of women as a homogeneous class has itself been seen as problematic. Among feminists, there has been little agreement about what it is that pushes women into their shared oppression, with radical feminists emphasising men and marriage, and Marxist feminists highlighting the issue of women and class. Anne Phillips (1987) has suggested that the most effective way of understanding the complex position of women is to recognise the equal importance of gender and class as parallel oppressions.

Explaining gender divisions

The simplest and most widely accepted explanation (outside academic circles) of divisions and inequalities between men and women is the biological one. This emphasises the biologically given fact of 'sex'. Men are stronger, superior in intelligence and physically adapted for an outgoing role. Women are soft, caring, and built mainly for childbearing. Different male and female behaviour can be attributed to differences in sex. This type of explanation is known as biological determinism, although some notable sociologists (for example Talcott Parsons, 1959a) have also leaned in this direction. Thus men play 'instrumental' and women 'expressive' roles within the family.

The great majority of other social scientists have, for a long time, been highly sceptical of this argument. As Oakley (1972) and others have argued, the roles of men and women change from society to society and from time to time within the same societies. There is nothing inevitable about male or female behaviour. How they act in society is a consequence of that society's conception of gender roles – the culturally accepted definitions of masculinity and femininity. Differences between men and women are as much socially produced as they are biological. Sociologists are interested in gender, not sex.

Gender role socialisation

From this point of view, how men and women behave is a result of a process of gender role **socialisation**. Individuals internalise social roles. The traditional ideologies about men being 'masculine' and women being feminine are not difficult to reconstruct. You are probably doing it now, in your mind. We live with it in the media and have been brought up with it. The traditional associations with male and female gender roles are so strongly internalised that it shocks us when they are transgressed – when a female plumber, surgeon, engineer, or a male nanny, au pair or beautician is mentioned. In Western industrial societies, males performing social tasks traditionally associated with females are so few that they are seen as the leaders of a change in social values and are termed 'new men'. They are seen as oddities by the media and regarded with suspicion by some feminists. This highlights the social acceptance of the traditional, normative behaviour according to gender roles and people's dismay when a man takes on a role considered appropriate for the 'inferior' sex.

Liberal feminism

There are different strands of feminist sociology, each with its own way of explaining the inequalities experienced by women in modern industrial societies. Liberal feminists draw heavily on the concept of gender role socialisation that we have just discussed. In this perspective the explanation for gender divisions rests not so much on the structures and institutions of society, but in its culture and the attitudes of individuals. Traditional expectations of female and male roles, and discrimination are the key obstacles which need to be overcome in order to liberate females.

The creation of equal opportunities, particularly in education and work, is the main aim of liberal feminists. They believe that it is possible to achieve this aim without a major upheaval in society. To this end, they support the introduction of laws to promote equality (e.g. the Sex Discrimination Act, which was introduced in the UK in 1975) and attempting to change attitudes.

Marxist feminism

Marxist feminists regard the economic position of women as crucial to their oppression. This oppression starts in the family, where women are seen as unpaid home-makers, dependent on their husbands, and continues in the employment market, where they are given poorly paid, low-status, part-time jobs.

The argument in relation to jobs is developed by Breugel (1979), who sees married women's economic dependency on their husbands as making them a useful industrial reserve army that can be moved in and out of the economy as needed. They are regarded as marginal workers and are advantageous to capitalism. Marxist feminists believe the interests of women lie with the liberation of the working class and the overthrow of capitalism.

Feminist Marxists

While agreeing with some of the points made by liberal and Marxist feminists, feminist Marxists believe more emphasis should be given to the role of **ideology** in maintaining women's oppression and male power. According to Michelle Barrett and Mary McIntosh (1985), ideology explains why women continue to get married and live in conventional families when these are the very things that oppress them. The **nuclear family** is seen as natural and inevitable and women are not encouraged to look for alternative ways of living. This family ideology makes them dependent on men and limits their activities and achievements. To achieve liberation, women will not only need economic freedom but masculine and feminine **stereotypes** will have to be transformed.

Radical feminists

Radical feminists focus on **patriarchy** and the role of men in oppressing women. Their main concern is with 'sexual politics'. This refers to the ways in which men individually and as a group dominate women, both in the family and in sexual and personal relationships. Radical feminists view men and women as opposing groups. Women are linked together in the same class position.

Max Weber utilised the concept of patriarchy to describe a household organisation in which the father was dominant. Patriarchy enables us to distinguish women's subordination as a sex from other forms of inequality. Some writers go so far as to see it as transcending all other social divisions. Kate Millett (1970) argues that there remains one ancient and universal scheme for the domination of one birth group by another – the scheme that prevails in the area of sex. She says that this is evident in the fact that every avenue of power within the society – the military, industry, technology, universities, science, political office and finance – is controlled primarily by men. Millett suggests that women have fewer permanent class associations than men. They tend to be economically dependent and rarely rise above working class in personal prestige and economic power.

Patriarchy penetrates class divisions, different societies and different historical epochs. Its roots are in the family, where the male dominates women's reproductive capacities. Shulamith Firestone (1970) argues that this is because women throughout history, and before the advent of birth control, were at the continual mercy of their biology (menstruation, menopause, female 'ills', childbirth, care of infants, etc.) which made them dependent on males. The natural reproductive difference between the sexes led directly to the first division of labour, and this is partly because human infants have a long period of dependency. Moreover, a basic mother/child relationship has existed in some form in every society and has shaped female psychology. Biologically, men and women are not created equally. Biology necessitates male domination. In order to free

themselves, Firestone argues that women need to control their own fertility.

A different account of patriarchal exploitation has been presented by those writers who have looked at labour carried out by women in the family home. Christine Delphy (1981) sees the unpaid labour of women within the home – producing and rearing children, feeding and servicing their husbands – as the basis of their **subordination**. For all this work they receive no wage but only get maintenance in return. She argues that this is analogous with slavery. The domestic situation is the main enemy for women. It enables men to dominate and control them.

A woman's position *vis-à-vis* her husband's parallels the relationship of the proletariat to the bourgeoisie. For a woman it matters not whether her husband is a capitalist or a worker. She still has the same 'class' relationship to her husband. A woman's standard of living does not depend on her relationship to the means of production 'but her serf relations with her husband'.

Criticisms of feminism

There are problems with the patriarchy explanations. For instance, the relationship between men and women varies in different societies, suggesting that the social organisation of the society is more significant than the fact that women have babies and men do not. Delphy's account suggests that gender is far more important than class in understanding subordination. Yet it is hard to reconcile the lot of the upper-middle-class woman with the aid of a household help/nanny and that of the working-class woman with no help.

The concept of patriarchy may also obscure the political, social and economic differences between women. The wife of an aristocratic lord would have a different position from that of a labourer's wife, as would the female chief executive of a multinational company from that of a factory worker. The concept of patriarchy all too easily presents a static model of a male-dominated society when, plainly, social relationships are subject to change.

The Marxist feminist view too has its problems. In particular, it does not explain why there has emerged a demand for female labour in certain sectors of the workforce. Some writers have suggested that women's employment reflects an extension of their domestic tasks. This may be an adequate explanation with nursing or teaching but clerical work and electronics prove a little more difficult to reconcile with this view.

Black women and gender

Black feminists such as Bell Hooks (1990) and Rose Brewer (1993) have argued that other feminists, as well as male anti-racists, have not addressed the particular problems faced by black women. Hooks notes that although black women played an important part in the fight for **civil rights** in the USA, women's issues received little consideration as the organisations were male dominated. Brewer suggests that the distinctive contribution of black feminist theory is to focus attention on the way that race, class and gender act as simultaneous forces, with each inequality reinforcing and extending each of the other inequalities.

Post-modern feminism

Post-modern feminism has some similarities with black feminist theory. Both are sceptical about the claim that there is a single theory that can explain the position of women in society. Post-modern feminism, in particular, tends to focus on the differences between women (for example, black women, lesbian women, young women, white working-class women) and rejects the idea that there is a single, all-embracing solution to the inequalities that women and girls experience. Whereas some feminists see differences between groups of women and between individual women as obstacles to women's liberation, post-modernists view this diversity in a positive light. The idea that there is a single, unitary essence to the concept of 'woman' is part of a dangerous metanarrative that downplays the significance of differences between women in order to promote a particular theory and agenda for 'liberating' women. Post-modern feminism encourages the acceptance of many different points of view as equally valid. Women as individuals and within groups should draw on their own experiences in seeking to understand the causes and forms of their oppression. In this way they may see through the limitations of any general, overarching theory that regards all women as having essentially the same characteristics.

Post-modernists encourage women to explore language as a deep, underlying source of their oppression. Helen Haste (1993) suggests that language is structured in a way that reflects male domination. She argues that male metaphors, such as the idea of 'man the hunter', have been used to reinforce such divisions as public and private. Men are encouraged to enter the public sphere and do the literal or metaphorical hunting, while women should be focused on the private sphere of home life and the family.

Race and ethnicity

Ethnicity and inequality

Distinctions based on ethnicity are a basis for social inequality and sociologists have for some time applied their perspectives to understanding the complex relationships between different ethnic groups in society. A distinction is often drawn between 'prejudice' and 'discrimination' as two mechanisms through which one ethnic group may maintain a dominant position over another. Where a cultural group holds rigid beliefs about its social superiority to another group, this is known as prejudice. Regularly behaving towards a group in a way that denies them equal access to scarce resources such as jobs, houses, transport and social facilities, thus limiting their life chances, is discrimination.

There are many studies that have documented the relative deprivation of ethnic minorities living in the UK in terms of their worse jobs, higher rates of unemployment and poorer housing. We will look at some of the comparisons.

Housing

When new Commonwealth immigrants arrived in the UK in the late 1950s and early 1960s they were unable to obtain council housing and were forced into poor and often expensive private rented housing or equally poor-quality owner-occupation. In 1961 nearly half of the immigrants of Afro-Caribbean and Asian background were living in shared dwellings. By 2001 the proportion was only 3 per cent. Among Asians there has been a move to owner-occupation, while among Afro-Caribbeans there has been an increase in the proportion of households renting from the council.

However, real inequality in the quality of housing still exists. Only 6 per cent of ethnic minority households live in detached houses or bungalows compared with 21 per cent of white households, and five times as many Afro-Caribbeans as whites live in high-rise flats. There is also evidence of racial discrimination in the allocation of council homes, with Asians and Afro-Caribbeans tending to be housed in the oldest dwellings.

Jane Lakey (1997) found that for a number of reasons ethnic minorities tended to live in more disadvantaged neighbourhoods. The extent of disadvantage was greater for some ethnic minority groups than others, and the forms of disadvantage also varied between ethnic groups.

Employment

The research findings on those in employment suggest that since the 1970s there has been an increase in those Asian men and women entering managerial and professional jobs in the UK, but at the other end of the socio-economic spectrum there has been an increase in the proportion of both Asian and Afro-Caribbean men in the unskilled manual jobs. These jobs continue to be more at risk of redundancy in a time of recession. Within the ethnic groups there are, however, wide variations in employment opportunities. Bangladeshis, for instance, are the most disadvantaged group in the labour market with over 66 per cent employed in semi-skilled and unskilled work. At the other extreme African Asians are spread throughout the socio-economic categories in roughly the same proportions as whites. In all occupations though, there is a tendency for Asians and Afro-Caribbeans to be located on the bottom rungs of the career ladder and they have lower chances of promotion. It is also the case that they are more likely to be found doing overtime and shift work than whites.

The earnings of full-time ethnic minority male workers were 14 per cent less than whites in 2000, although this inequality does not compare with the position of black workers in the USA, who earn 35 per cent less on average. The explanation in part lies in the fact that ethnic minority workers are likely to be found in the lower socio-economic categories. While 40 per cent of Asian men and 35 per cent of Afro-Caribbean men are employed in semi-skilled and unskilled jobs, the comparative figure for white men is 16 per cent.

Tests have been conducted by various sociologists to measure the frequency of racial discrimination in the process of getting a job. Michael Banton (1987) has reviewed the findings and estimates that at least 10,000 cases of direct discrimination in recruitment or employment occur each year. Around 1,000 cases per year of alleged racial discrimination at work are reported to industrial tribunals.

Figures produced by Modood and Berthoud (1997) suggest that there has been some reduction in inequalities in job status between ethnic minorities and whites. He argues that while ethnic minorities were initially downwardly mobile after emigrating to Britain, they are now beginning to regain the occupational statuses they had in their country of origin. Nevertheless, Asian and Afro-Caribbean ethnic minorities still face considerable disadvantages, and these are particularly acute at the top of the occupational structure.

Unemployment

In the mid-1970s the unemployment rates of ethnic minorities and whites were about the same, but by 1982 the rate for ethnic minorities was much higher. The 'shake-out' in industry brought redundancies in many unskilled, low-status jobs in which Afro-Caribbeans and Asians were concentrated. The decline in the fortunes of the British textile industry had a particular effect on the employment opportunities of Asian women. The trend for ethnic minorities to suffer a higher rate of unemployment than whites continued during the 1980s and 1990s. By 2003 the gap had narrowed, though the highest rates of long-term unemployment were still found among Asian and Afro-Caribbean groups. Youth unemployment (of 16–20-year-olds) amongst the ethnic minorities is twice that of their white counterparts. When vacancies are few, the evidence suggests that racial discrimination by employers will adversely affect Asians and Afro-Caribbeans.

Earlier in the chapter we noted that many sociologists believe that people from Asian and Afro-Caribbean backgrounds in the UK form an underclass; that is, a group of people denied access to the better jobs who are forced into poorly paid employment, or unemployment, and who have very much worse life chances than the rest of the population.

Ethnic minorities and stratification

Sociologists have different views about how ethnic minorities should be perceived as a stratified group. From a Marxist perspective, ethnic conflict is seen in terms of political and economic power relationships. Ethnic inequality is viewed ultimately as a consequence of historical domination of one society, i.e. the subject society, by another (the metropolitan power). The argument is that when one ethnic group succeeds in conquering another, those colonised come to be looked upon and treated as inferiors. The obvious signs of their presumed cultural inferiority (if they are accredited with having a culture at all) are the physical characteristics they have in common which differentiate them from their masters.

The extension of the master principle is the status of slave, who has often been forced from their native country to the conquering country (slave trade). From a Marxist viewpoint, it is more than just subordination in the workplace; it is treating the whole person as a commodity to be bought and sold – slaves subsequently being seen as a lesser breed of humans. Since slaves were in fact mostly black Africans, the 'inferior' attributes of slaves became attached to the race from which they were drawn and gradually this view of human types and the perception of slave-like qualities became attached to colonial oppressed people. Slavery did, of course, disappear but it has left a legacy. The categories of racial difference and perception of these differences persist and assume a power of their own, long after the conditions which produced such ways of thinking disappeared. The descendants of slaves bear the mark of a history characterised by poverty, a low level of education, poor living conditions and low-status, low-pay occupations.

The economies of their own countries of origin are still dominated by the economies of the richer sections of the world and their welfare (in the form of aid) is outside their own control. So it is possible to view the dominated people as a class exploited by the richer countries of the world, i.e. they are an external proletariat whose existence raises the aspirations and standard of living of the working class in metropolitan countries and thereby dampens their own tendency to revolt. Similarly, it is argued, blacks in metropolitan countries find their life chances restricted in terms of having to make do with inferior housing, jobs and social conditions, thus relegating them to a second-class citizenship.

Castles and Kosack (1973) adopt a Marxist perspective in seeing black immigrants as part of the working class, on the basis that they do not own the means of production and have to sell their labour to survive. They suggest, however, that the working class is divided in economic, social and political terms as a result of manipulation by the capitalists, which helps to foster a false consciousness of superiority amongst the white working class. They believe this will eventually disappear when it is supplanted not merely by a correct understanding of the position of immigrant workers but by a class consciousness which reflects the true position of all workers in society.

Assessing the Marxist view

The Marxist view appears to explain so much with a handful of assumptions. It has had much appeal, not only to sociologists, but also to the exponents of black power movements, since it offers a theory to account for their circumstances as well as a potential ideology to mobilise support and to change those circumstances.

There are certainly many parallels between the circumstances of racial discrimination and aspects of social class. Members of ethnic groups that view themselves as 'superior' often do not regard 'inferior'

groups as deserving of full political rights, e.g. South Africa during the period of apartheid and white rule. This was true in earlier periods of European history when the upper class had rights the working class did not have. Members of 'superior' groups have often considered, and still do consider, their 'inferiors' to be lacking in intellectual and mental skills. The same again was true in the past, the upper class regarding the lower orders as stupid and incapable. Members of upper classes, as with those of dominant ethnic groups, rarely marry downwards. The lower classes, as with 'inferior' ethnic groups, have often been considered by their superiors to have undesirable habits.

However, some sociologists would argue that reducing the phenomenon of ethnicity to social stratification does not answer all the questions that we might want to raise, or account for all the features of relations between ethnic groups. If an exploited social group constitutes a social class, then why is it also necessary for that 'class' to be additionally treated as an inferior social group? Some Marxists might reply to this that ruling classes in Western societies have an interest in promoting ethnic divisions, since by doing so the black and white working class can be divided and set against each other and as long as they regard their interests as 'opposed', the unity of the working class against their real oppressors will be weakened.

A factor that cannot be explained away so easily is the major inconsistencies between the different dimensions of inequality that occur in multicultural societies. Ethnic ranking is not necessarily always in alignment with class (i.e. economic and occupational position). The negative social status attaching to black minorities in the UK and the USA, or Jews in Europe, cannot simply be explained in class terms. These factors are a product of a complex set of historical circumstances.

Marxist analysis argues that the true long-term interests of exploited minorities (ethnic/racial) should be in collaboration with other members of the proletariat. However, some political movements, such as the 'Black Power' movement of the 1960s, have argued that 'integration' of such a kind is a mirage and they have aimed to encourage 'colour consciousness' rather than class consciousness. (Hence the slogan 'Black is Beautiful' can be seen as an attempt by blacks to redefine their own social worth.) Few sociologists would hold to the view that blacks in the USA constitute a class (or indeed, for that matter, Asian and Afro-Caribbean immigrants in the UK). In the USA it is certainly true that blacks now cut across class barriers, although the problems of poor blacks often get most attention.

In the UK, according to Westergaard and Resler (1976), Asian and Afro-Caribbean immigrants do not constitute a stratum within the working class or a separate 'underclass' beneath the indigenous working class since that would ignore the heterogeneity of circumstances amongst these cultural groups (i.e. there are differences of race, religion, culture, reasons for emigrating, differences in skills, etc.). Westergaard and Resler observe that being Asian or Afro-Caribbean in British society carries disadvantages, but such disadvantages are also common to other groups: women, the poor, the unemployed, etc. They conclude, therefore, that stratification by ethnicity in no way replaces stratification by class.

To say this, however, is quite different from saying that there is no relationship between the two. Some would argue that the more closely stratification by ethnicity overlaps with stratification by class, such that racial and cultural differences overlap, or coincide with differences in power and access to wealth, then the more the factor of power differences will itself emphasise ethnic differences and conflicts of interest are more likely to be perceived and acted upon. The best example is South Africa during the apartheid era, where class relationships and ethnic divisions coincided almost exactly.

Paul Gilroy (1987) agrees with some aspects of the Marxist perspective, but moves away from it in other respects. He accepts that ethnic conflicts have been influenced by the development of capitalism, but he rejects the idea that the exploitation of Asian and Afro-Caribbean groups can be understood solely as a form of class exploitation. The factors that lead to discrimination and prejudice against ethnic minorities are, in many ways, separate and distinct from the processes of class formation. Indeed, Gilroy argues that class conflict is becoming less important in modern capitalist societies. Conflicts based on other factors, such as ethnicity, are acquiring increasing significance.

The Marxist perspective tends to assume that exploited ethnic minorities exist as fixed, readily identifiable groups. Other sociologists have drawn attention to the importance of studying how ethnic identities are produced and the ways in which they may change over time. Stuart Hall (1990) argues that defining people in terms of broad racial categories, such as blacks and whites, risks ignoring the important diversity of social experiences and cultural identities within each group. He suggests that

differences within ethnic groups provide the basis for a wide range of ethnic identities. Out of this 'melting pot' of diverse cultural influences, new hybrid ethnicities are developing that weaken the importance of the divisions between black and white. Hall argues that it is a feature of modern societies that many people have a number of identities and may act and think in terms of belonging to a whole variety of groups. He sees this as generally a positive trend, helping to liberate people from the old racial prejudices and conflicts that divided society.

It is true that ethnic identities have been exposed to significant cultural changes in countries such as the UK in recent years. However, Hall has been criticised for overlooking the possible negative consequences of this development. Intolerant and fundamentalist beliefs may develop in minorities because they feel threatened by the sorts of cultural changes that Hall describes.

Ethnicity and gender

In the same way that black women have argued that they have a different experience of sexism to that of white women, so too have they laid claim to a different experience of ethnic inequality to that of black men. Although they are generally located further down the class system than white women, the type of work they do and the pay they earn is more comparable with this group than with black men. Cook and Watt (1987) note that both black and white women tend to be concentrated in low-level, white-collar work and semi-skilled manual work. This adds yet another dimension to the sociology of stratification, and further emphasises the interplay between class, gender and ethnicity.

Stratification and age

Studies of traditional societies show clearly that age is a form of stratification. Humans move from one age grade to another as they grow older, making transitions from child to young man or woman, from unmarried to married and eventually to elder. Often these transitions are marked by rituals which signify movement from one age 'set' to another, each age set being responsible for certain duties in the society.

Youth

In Western societies, age is not dominant as a means of stratification. As Shelton (1992) notes, the social system based on age is not clearly and consistently developed, and it is possible for relatively young people to gain access to positions of economic and political power, and to the associated rewards. Nevertheless, there have been some sociological studies that have looked at age as a source of division in modern societies. The focus of the literature has been on youth. Nevertheless, it can be argued that youth is exploited by older people through a manipulated consumer market and that through the extension of education young people are as a group 'dependent'. Some sections of youth found political expression in student protest movements of the late 1960s in many industrialised countries, but this protest tended to be confined to middle-class youth.

It can be concluded from this that although youth cultures and temporary youth class groups exist, socio-economic classes cut across youth groups. Exploited youth will become exploited adults and the impoverished old. Therefore, as a permanent feature in stratification, youth must be rejected.

However, other sociologists have a different view. Berger and Berger (1983) see youth culture as cutting across class lines. They suggest that youth culture has created symbols and patterns of behaviour that are capable of bestowing status upon individuals coming from quite different class backgrounds, and youth culture has a strong egalitarian ethos.

The phenomenon of youth unemployment should also be considered as a factor which adds to divisions in society based on age. In 1999 the average unemployment rate among those under 24 in the UK was 7 per cent compared with 5 per cent for the population as a whole. These figures largely exclude 16–17-year-olds. However, there is evidence to suggest that unemployment is more likely to be a long-term problem for older members of the workforce.

Old age

The 'rising tide'

The number of elderly people has been steadily increasing in Western societies throughout the twentieth century, with the proportion of people of retirement age becoming politically significant. At the turn of the century a little over 6 per cent of the population of Great Britain was over 65 years old. By 1931 this had risen to nearly 10 per cent, going up to 15 per cent by 1951 and almost 25 per cent by 1991. It is projected to rise to around 27 per cent by 2021. The age at which people actually retire is also falling, as the idea of 'natural wastage' – encouraging people to take early retirement – gains popularity. This proportionate growth is sometimes referred to as the 'greying' or 'rising tide' of the population (*see Figure 3.2*).

Figure 3.2 Population of pensionable age in the UK

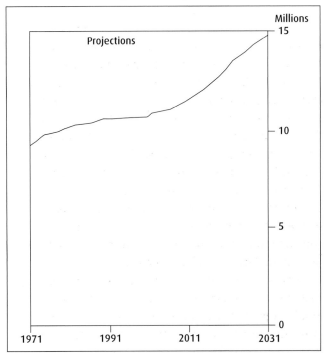

Source: *Social Trends* 21, 1991

The main reason for the increase in the number of the elderly is not necessarily that people are living longer, but that less people die in their early life. A much higher proportion of young people reach old age. It is not the case that people are now expected to live longer once they reach old age. The consequence, however, is that there are proportionately less people paying taxes to pay for those not engaged in waged labour, and a larger section of the population that is relatively powerless.

Another possible implication of the growth in the proportion of elderly people in the population of industrial societies is the extra strain for women, who are usually expected to take the burden for the care of the elderly. In some families the woman's income is essential, so to care for an elderly person could have financial costs. If there are no relatives then responsibility for care will lie with the local authority. The working population will have to contribute more in taxes and this will affect family income. As the cost of State care is expensive, there is likely to be pressure to keep the emphasis on family care.

The elderly and the family

It has been suggested that while better provided for in a material sense, old people are more isolated from their families and hence neglected in modern industrial societies today. Townsend (1985) documented the way that old people in the Bethnal

Green area in London in the 1950s became increasingly dependent upon their family for help and support as age and infirmity weakened their independence. He also emphasised the aid that the old people gave in return, whenever they were able, especially in the rearing of the grandchildren. He found that often the **extended family** was the dominant interest of old people, and that this interest kept them out of homes and hospitals.

In another study, Townsend (1979) looked at several institutions and homes for old people in England and Wales. These studies and others highlighted the key problems facing old people in modern industrial societies:

→ Compulsory retirement ages: many old people have stressed that they would like to continue working at least part-time if they enjoy good health.
→ The lack of preparation for retirement: not knowing what to do with their free time when they stop working.
→ Inadequacy of financial provisions: many old people are on the verge of poverty.
→ The problems of loneliness and isolation, together with the problems of 'fitting into' family life (having low status, being a burden on others).

Ageism

A number of theories have been advanced to try and explain why it is that the elderly come to be devalued and poorly treated in advanced industrial societies. Robert Butler (1975) argues that:

Our attitudes towards the old are contradictory. We pay lip service to the idealised images of beloved and tranquil grandparents, wise elders, white-haired patriarchs and matriarchs. But the opposite image disparages the elderly, seeing age as decay, decrepitude, a disgusting and undignified dependency. Childhood is romanticised, youth is idolised, middle age does the work, wields the power and pays the bills, and old age, its days empty of purpose, gets little or nothing for what it has already done. The old are in the way.

From a functionalist perspective, the elderly need to be progressively disengaged from socially important roles in order for others to take over, and for society to function without disruption. Happiness comes from the recognition that more competent people are taking their places. Age-based ascribed status has been replaced by the greater importance of achieved status. Retirement is essential to make way for others.

Others have argued that this view of ageing is insufficient, and that the elderly, like other groups suffering social discrimination, are the victims of the ideology of **ageism**, which is as powerful and harmful

as **sexism** and **racism**. There is no necessary reason to suppose that, as people age, they become any more miserable, inflexible, unproductive or isolated than anyone else. These forms of behaviour result from cultural and social expectations, **labelling** and **self-fulfilling prophecies**. By obliging people to retire, we create a distinct subculture, based on age. This **subculture** either accepts their new role passively, or resists it, as the 'Grey Panthers' of the USA have.

The elderly and class

With the growth in the numbers of the elderly, and the increasing phenomenon of early retirement (which may simply be another term for unemployment), the class position of the elderly is a growing question in sociology. This is part of the general move away from viewing stratification purely in terms of paid employment. Two views have been put forward. Proletarianisation theory sees the elderly as a **homogeneous group**, pushed towards poverty by the fact of age, and constituting an underclass. Labour-market continuity theory sees social inequalities persisting into old age as a result of previous market position. Thus, the age at which people retire is determined by class, as is the amount of income they will receive after retirement. Those in higher classes will receive higher occupational pensions and payments from unearned income such as shares. Income differentials are narrower than among those still in work, but are sufficiently wide for the experience of old age to continue to be structured by class.

As the elderly become a more significant social group then, as with gender and ethnicity, sociology too will have to change its focus away from conventional class-based views of stratification to take on the growing realisation that age is an important and significant form of stratification. This is beginning – but only beginning – to be reflected in the available literature.

Today, analysis recognises that the terms 'old' and 'elderly' are too imprecise and it has become necessary to distinguish between the 'young old' and the 'old old' and to recognise the enormous differences between individuals. The phenomena of social class, ethnicity and gender also give rise to important differences between groups in the elderly population.

Questions

1 How can the class position of the elderly retired be measured?
2 In what ways are the elderly a significant group in society?

4

Health, welfare and poverty

This chapter develops some of the themes covered in the previous chapter on social stratification. It begins by examining the relationships between health and social class, geographical location, gender and ethnicity, and the various explanations that have been put forward for these relationships. The social factors that affect health and illness are discussed and we also consider the role and power of the medical profession. The chapter continues with a discussion of poverty and the development of the Welfare State in Britain. We will examine some of the sociological research into poverty and consider the problems with the measurement of poverty. This is followed by an examination of the explanation for poverty, looking at functionalist, culture of poverty, structural determinants and situational constraints explanations. Gender and ethnicity and their relationship to poverty are also examined. The chapter concludes with an assessment of the Welfare State from different theoretical perspectives.

The social construction of health

Measuring health

In order to assess the health of an individual, group or society, forms of measurement have first to be found. This immediately causes problems. There are two main indicators: **mortality** and **morbidity**, where mortality refers to death and morbidity to sickness. Of these two, mortality is the easiest to measure, although the causes of death, both in the long and short term, may be more difficult to ascertain. In the short term – the direct cause of death – the debate around suicide can be cited (see chapter 8). In the long term, the question 'why did someone die when they did, and of that particular cause?' is one that produces a variety of answers.

At first sight, the biological explanation that an individual can die of 'natural causes', that there is a biological time clock that simply expires at a certain point, is persuasive. Alternatively, someone may be 'unlucky' and develop the symptoms of a terminal illness – it could just as easily have happened to someone else. Sociologists dispute both ideas: that health and illness are simply biological processes or merely matters of chance.

Social causes

Against these explanations, the sociological view points to the fact that life expectancy varies from time to time, and from place to place. It is higher in an **urbanised** society than a rural one, and increases as that industrial society develops. Even in an industrial society there are clear differences in life expectancy between social **classes**, within the occupations constituting each social class, between men and women, between **ethnic** groups, and between regions. For most sociologists, the existence of these statistical regularities points to social, economic and environmental causes of mortality, rather than causes based on biology or chance.

The role of medicine and the medical profession

A number of reasons have been put forward to explain why life expectancy has increased, including improved diet, declining fertility, sanitation, the decline of infective diseases, and improved medical care. Of these, the role of medicine and medical care is disputed. The evidence available suggests that conditions such as tuberculosis were beginning to disappear long before effective vaccines and medical treatment emerged. McKeown (1976) claims that hospitals in the nineteenth century were as likely to kill, for example through the spread of disease, as they were to cure. In the first third of the twentieth century, infant mortality fell most sharply during the First World War (1914–18), when 60 per cent of doctors had joined the armed forces, suggesting that the real cause of decline was temporarily improved living standards (rations, full employment) for the very poorest during wartime.

Health care in the United Kingdom is geared towards curing people when they are ill, not preventing them becoming ill in the first place. As some have cynically suggested, the NHS could be renamed a 'National Illness Service'. Doctors have a vested interest in people being ill, as have drug companies. Yet if illness and disease are socially and environmentally caused and produced, why do we turn to the medical solution in times of illness? This is explored further in the next section.

Question

Are health and illness medical or social issues? Can they be both?

Inequalities in health

Health and social class

The Black Report

In 1977, the Labour government set up a Royal Commission, under the chairmanship of Sir Douglas Black, the Department of Health and Social Security chief scientist, to investigate how successful the NHS had been in meeting its aims in the immediate post-war period, implicit in which was the idea of meeting everyone's health-care needs equally, regardless of age, class, ethnicity, region or **gender**. The main aim of the commission was to discover whether inequalities in health had lessened since 1948.

The answer was that they had not. The commission found, using mortality rates and the Registrar-General's table, that whatever way mortality was tabulated, people in social class I (see chapter 3) were less likely to die than those in social class V, and the classes in between had rates in accordance with their position between I and V. Whether using the mortality figures for stillbirths, for infants (up to the age of 12 months), for children up to the age of 14 years, or for adults of working age (15–64), the occupational mortality statistics for 1970–72 show that your chances of living, or living longer, are greater the higher your social class. There is a particularly pronounced increase in the jump from the semi-skilled workers of social class IV to the unskilled workers of social class V. The picture is still roughly the same if the statistics are disaggregated into causes

of death, with the clearest **correlations** between social class and illness being shown in diseases of the respiratory system, in both males and females, and accidents, poisoning and violence, among men in adulthood, and the least clear correlations being shown in tumours and congenital anomalies in childhood and malignant tumours in adult women. As the report, which was eventually published in 1982 as *Inequalities in Health, the Black Report* edited by Townsend and Davidson, argues: 'if the mortality rates for Social Class I had applied to Classes IV and V during 1970–72, 74,000 lives of people aged under 75 would not have been lost.' The report discusses four possible ways of explaining why these apparent inequalities in health exist:

1 The artefact explanation

From this point of view, the form of measurement used in *The Black Report* is suspect. Although the mortality ratios are standardised to take into account the proportion of people nationally in each social class, they are nevertheless unrepresentative and inaccurate. Social class V, for example, is unrepresentative in terms of age. Workers in this class are generally older than those in other classes, as younger and better trained recruits to the labour force will enter the increasing number of skilled occupations. Older people are more likely to feature in mortality statistics, therefore social class V has the highest mortality ratio. The statistics used by *The Black Report* are therefore artefactual, or made up – invented.

2 Theories of natural and social selection

Put simply, this group of theories argues that people are not ill because they are in social class V, but in social class V because they are ill. Illsley (1955) found, by looking principally at maternity, that upwardly mobile women were likely to be the most healthy. Building on this, Stern (1983) argues that upward and downward mobility are the effects, not causes, of good or bad health. If you are wealthy but in poor health, you are vulnerable to downward mobility. If you are poor but in good health, upward mobility is more likely than for those in the same and adjacent classes in worse health. **Social mobility** becomes a genetic, not a social phenomenon. The only accurate way of measuring the relationship between health and class is to use an individual's class of origin, not their class of destination. As the statistics are recorded, it is no surprise that social class V, into which the unhealthy have sunk, records the highest mortality rates.

3 Theories of material deprivation and structural explanations

Neither of the first two theories discussed are based on sociological factors. The theorists of material deprivation locate the causes of premature mortality and ill-health in the material or physical circumstances of people's lives. In particular, they point to whether people are employed or not, what income they receive, what their conditions of work and security of tenure are, how happy they are in their work, and their possession of wealth and property. This position is closest to that of **Marxism** in explaining inequalities in health.

There is certainly a strong correlation between mortality statistics and measures of relative material deprivation. What is more difficult to establish is **causation** – does one circumstance (in this case their class position) cause another event (in this case a mortality rate) to occur? Is it enough to say that because one thing happens at the same time as another that one, therefore, causes the other? It is because of this problem that some people have pointed to the need for the following explanation.

4 Theories of cultural deprivation and behavioural explanations

One of the reasons that it is difficult to argue that ill-health and premature death are caused by material deprivation is that the main causes of death are no longer directly related to want. The diseases most typical of poverty and malnutrition are infective diseases. These are the illnesses Beveridge had in mind when he located 'disease' as one of the five evils. These infective diseases have largely been stamped out in developed countries. The main killers today are degenerative diseases associated with smoking, a rich diet and inactivity: diseases of the respiratory and circulatory system, as well as cancer. This points away from the problem of not having enough to looking at how people use what they do have.

As in theories of educational under-achievement and poverty, it is the culture of groups – their **norms** and **values** – that is highlighted here. Health care is the responsibility of individuals. Only they can properly make choices about how to look after their own bodies. Everyone, for example, is now aware that there is a strong correlation between smoking and lung cancer, and government health warnings state unequivocally that 'smoking causes cancer'. Yet there is also a strong correlation between cigarette consumption and social class. Smoking is a cultural habit most prevalent among manual workers, particularly the unskilled. If premature death in this social class is to be reduced then this cultural practice has to change, or be 'recoded'. Young people have to find other ways of marking the transitions from childhood to adolescence to adulthood. Women need to find symbols other than cigarette smoking as a means of asserting personal independence.

It is more difficult, however, to assert that manual workers smoke more because of cultural rather than material deprivation. Why did they start smoking? Why do they continue? Stress at work would be a material factor. 'Being sociable', expressing group solidarity, a sense of fatalism, or an inability to defer gratification are cultural factors.

Reactions to *The Black Report*

The publication of *The Black Report* during the first Thatcher government caused immediate controversy. Attempts were made to suppress and limit its publication. New and further research, however, was commissioned and undertaken to determine whether health inequalities were statistical mirages, the result of the struggle of the fittest to survive, or the consequences of material or cultural deprivation.

The Health Divide

In 1987, the Health Education Council (now the Health Education Authority) published *The Health Divide: Inequalities in Health in the 1980s*, a review prepared by Margaret Whitehead. Using data collected up to the mid 1980s, and thus updating the base years of 1970–72 used in *The Black Report*, she finds 'convincing evidence of a widening of health inequalities between social groups in recent decades, especially in adults. In general, death rates have declined more rapidly in the higher than in the lower occupational classes, contributing to the widening gap. Indeed, in some respects the health of the lower occupational classes has actually deteriorated against a background of general improvement in the population. There was also a widening gap between manual and non-manual groups in their rates of chronic sickness from 1974 to 1984, and during the late 1970s the gap widened for acute sickness too. The exception to the widening trend was in relation to deaths in babies under one year.'

Having collated this evidence, she then reviews new research on the four explanations offered in *The Black Report*:

1 The artefact explanation

She rejects the arguments of those such as Illsley (1986) and Jones and Cameron (1984) that the Registrar-General's classification artificially inflates the size and importance of mortality and morbidity differentials, and renders comparisons meaningless. While agreeing that this classification could be bettered, 'the recent evidence continues to point to the very real differences in health between social groups which cannot convincingly be explained away as artefact. On the contrary [new evidence suggests] the Registrar-General's classification may under-estimate the size of the social class gradient in health.'

2 Theories of natural and social selection

New data have emerged principally from Illsley's finding that taller women tend to move up the social classes at marriage, whilst shorter women tended to move down at marriage, and Wadsworth's evidence (1986) that seriously ill boys were more likely than others to experience a fall in occupational class by the time they were 26. Yet, she remarks, in both studies the size of the selection effect suggests that it accounts for only a small proportion of the overall differentiation between the social classes.

3 and 4 Materialist/structuralist and cultural/behavioural theories

Whitehead notes a trend towards arguing that the distinction between the two explanations is becoming increasingly artificial, as one explanation frequently cannot be separated from the other, and that they are strongly interrelated.

As *Table 4.1* shows, nearly all groups are smoking less, but the rate of reduction is still determined by class. Similar gradients exist for alcohol consumption, food and nutrition (such as consumption of white and brown bread, fresh fruit and vegetables, and fats) and exercise in leisure, particularly swimming and walking.

New evidence, however, points away from cultural and behavioural explanations for these patterns. Calnan and Johnson (1985), for example, compared the health beliefs of women from social class I and social class V and found no difference in beliefs about concepts of health and the perception of vulnerability to disease: 'The importance of the "culture of poverty" model as an explanation of poor service use and health-damaging behaviour may have been over-estimated in the past, and new appraisals of health behaviour are needed.'

Table 4.1 Prevalence of cigarette smoking by sex and socio-economic group (%)

| | | SOCIO-ECONOMIC GROUP | | | | | | all over |
		A	B	C1	C2	D	E	16 years
Men	1972	33	44	45	57	57	64	52
	1984	17	29	30	40	45	49	36
	1990	16	24	25	36	39	48	31
	2000	17	23	27	33	36	39	30
Women	1972	33	38	38	47	42	42	42
	1984	15	29	28	37	37	36	32
	1990	16	23	27	32	36	36	29
	2000	14	20	26	26	32	35	25

Source: *Social Trends* 33, 2003

There is now a wealth of information that socio-economic or material factors, specifically housing conditions and income, strongly influence **cultural** behaviour. Hilary Graham (1984) argues that low use of preventive health services by poor families may be the result of an economic decision: 'for poor families in particular, a rational decision may be one which rejects professional care. The mother may choose instead to invest her limited resources of time, money and energy in other areas of family health – in food for the family for example, or in keeping her children warm.' Some actions, such as smoking, may be the only way that mothers can stay sane and act responsibly towards their family, as it helps relieve tension, without having to leave the room. Socio-economic factors, Whitehead concludes, play an important part in determining class-based forms of behaviour concerning health.

Health and region

In the same way that mortality and morbidity rates vary from country to country, and by class, age, ethnic group and gender, there are also distinct regional differences (see *Table 4.2*). *The Black Report* found that mortality rates were lowest in the South and South East of Britain, and highest in the North and North West. These differences have persisted into the 1980s. The pattern remains the same if examined by class and gender. Social class I men and women have lower standardised mortality ratios in the South than in the North.

The obvious explanation for these regional differences is material deprivation which, as Whitehead suggests, 'may be the key to the North/South gradient', yet there is a similar pattern between regional differences and smoking (see *Table 4.3*).

It was also, notoriously, people in the North to whom the then Under-Secretary of State for Health,

Table 4.2 Mortality of men and women in different regions of Britain, 2000 (per thousand population)

	Males	Females
Wales	10.9	11.7
England	9.7	10.4
North East	10.8	11.3
North West	10.4	11.2
Yorkshire and the Humber	10.0	10.7
East Midlands	10.0	10.3
West Midlands	10.1	10.4
East	9.5	10.0
London	7.8	8.3
South East	9.3	10.5
South West	10.7	11.6

Source: Mortality Statistics, general (series DH1 no. 33)

Table 4.3 Prevalence of cigarette smoking by region – persons aged 16 or over Great Britain, 2001

Region	% smoking cigarettes
Scotland	36
Wales	33
England: North	32
North West	30
South East	27
South West	27

Source: *Social Trends 31*, 2001

Edwina Currie, was referring when she claimed that their failure to look after themselves produced their poor health profiles.

Health and gender

Women have lower mortality rates than men, as shown in *Table 4.4* from *The Black Report*.

In 1984, the life expectancy of men was 71 years and it was 77 years for women. On the other hand, women seem to suffer more sickness in their lifetime than men, as *Table 4.5* suggests.

Table 4.4 Death rates by sex and social class

	Males	Females	Ratio male to female
I	3.98	2.15	1.85
II	5.54	2.85	1.94
III (non-manual)	5.80	2.76	1.96
III (manual)	6.08	3.41	1.78
IV	7.96	4.27	1.87
V	9.88	5.31	1.86

Adapted from *Occupational Mortality 1970–72*, death rates per 1,000 population, published by HMSO and compiled by the Registrar-General

Table 4.5 Use of health services by gender and age, 1998–9, United Kingdom (%)

	16–24	25–34	35–44	45–54	55–64	65–74	75 and over	All aged 16 and over
Males								
Consultation with GP	7	9	10	12	16	17	21	12
Outpatient visit	12	14	13	15	20	25	29	17
Casualty visit	7	7	5	4	3	3	3	5
Females								
Consultation with GP	15	18	16	19	17	19	21	18
Outpatient visit	13	13	12	17	19	21	26	17
Casualty visit	6	4	3	3	3	3	3	4

Source: General Household Survey, Office for National Statistics; Continuous Household Survey, Northern Ireland Statistics and Research Agency (from *Social Trends* 31, 2001)

Interpreting the statistics

Interpreting these statistics highlights many of the methodological problems involved in the sociology of health. The artefact explanation would argue that women may visit their doctors more often than men because they often do so on behalf of others, especially children, and that if they live longer than men there are therefore more elderly women than elderly men visiting the doctor. A further problem is that the official statistics used for mortality in *Table 4.4* measure married women according to their husband's occupation, further distorting the figures. (This problem is discussed further in chapter 3.) Leeson and Gray (1978) point out that if maternity and disorders of the breast and reproductive tract are excluded, then more men than women are hospitalised.

Female longevity

Other reasons for women's longevity have been put forward although any generalisations are inevitably prone to stereotypical portrayals. In their first twelve months, boys have a higher infant mortality rate suggesting that, genetically, it is boys who are the weaker sex. Through their **socialisation** as men they try to ignore minor illnesses and do not care for themselves properly. Men are more aggressive, take more risks, form the majority of car drivers and motor-cyclists, and generally lead more hazardous lives than women. They manage stress differently as they are not socialised into showing their emotions in the same way as women. At work, more men work full time than women, and they tend to work longer and more unsociable hours, working in areas of higher risk and hazard, and taking on greater responsibility than women. They are more prone to industrial accidents and diseases, and at home they will want to be the ones who climb up ladders and crawl over the roof. Finally, until the 1990s they retired at a later age than women.

For theorists of social selection, the fact that women live longer than men (and records show this to be true as far back as 1838) is evidence of their superior genes, suggesting that women have a greater aptitude to survive than men. However, other evidence suggests that women have not always, on average, outlived men and their life expectancy can be lower, as it is, for example, in Nepal and Bangladesh. Similarly, the gap in life expectancy has changed over time, particularly in the mid-twentieth century.

The materialist explanation argues that gender differentials in mortality rates are based on occupation. This would explain why female rates were at their relative lowest at the point of their greatest exclusion from the labour market. Overall, the fact of work and occupation causes premature death.

From a cultural/behavioural point of view, there is clear evidence that male and female behaviour is different: men smoke more and drink more than women. Although there is still very little **empirical** research on this question in Britain, Waldron (1976) argues that in the USA men die at twice the rate of women from seven of the major causes of death: coronary heart disease, lung cancer, emphysema, motor-vehicle and other accidents, cirrhosis of the liver and suicide. Given that these account for 75 per cent of the sex differential in mortality, Waldron concludes that gender differences in behaviour are more important than genetic factors.

Questions

1 Do the findings of the Black Report differ from those of *The Health Divide*?
2 Using the four possible explanations cited in the Black Report, decide which you find the most useful in explaining inequalities of health by:
   (a) social class
   (b) gender
   (c) region
3 Which of the Black Report's four explanations are sociological? How does material deprivation differ from cultural deprivation?
4 Are official statistics on mortality and morbidity reliable?

Health and ethnicity

The relationship between health profiles and ethnicity is problematic. In the first place, it is far from clear what the concept of ethnicity means and how it should be used in understanding the experience of health by different ethnic groups. In the UK, death certificates, for example, record country of origin but do not show ethnic group membership for the increasing proportion of second-generation black British. The same is true for white Britons born outside the United Kingdom. Furthermore, how should people of mixed parentage be categorised?

Mortality

From the studies that have been undertaken to date, for example Whitehead (1987) and Mares *et al.* (1987), the evidence is that members of ethnic minorities die from mainly the same causes as the rest of the community, that is from cancer and circulatory problems. However, people of Afro-Caribbean and Indian, Pakistani and Bangladeshi descent are more likely to die from cancer of the liver, diabetes and tuberculosis. Asians suffer from a higher than average incidence of heart disease and osteomalacia (softening of the bones) and there is a greater possibility of infant mortality for mothers who were themselves born in the Indian subcontinent. Afro-Caribbeans are more likely to die from strokes and hypertension (high blood pressure), to be diagnosed as mentally ill and to receive electro-convulsive therapy (ECT). All ethnic minorities are more likely to die from accidents, poisoning and violence.

Explanations

As with social class, attempts to explain the patterns of health differences experienced by different ethnic groups have focused on genetic, cultural and material factors. In the earliest explanations it was thought that there was likely to be a higher incidence of mortality from sub-tropical diseases. There is, however, very little evidence for this. While it is true to say that one in every 300–400 people of Afro-Caribbean descent develops sickle-cell anaemia, and people from the Mediterranean, Middle East and Asia inherit thalassaemia (a blood disorder), they are not exclusive to these groups and have been found among members of the white population of Britain. There is therefore thought to be little – or no – link between 'race' (defined biologically) and mortality.

Greater emphasis is given to other factors. The cultural argument has tried to explain high perinatal mortality among Asian mothers by their low attendance at antenatal classes and high rates of coronary heart disease for Asians in general by the use of ghee in cooking. Similarly, diabetes has been blamed on a high carbohydrate diet. Against this it has been argued that equivalent groups in the Indian subcontinent suffer lower rates of heart disease (Coronary Prevention Group, 1986).

The 'material' argument sees physical factors as overriding these other arguments. From this point of view what matters most are the consequences of **racism** and the low class position occupied by most members of ethnic minorities in the United Kingdom (see also chapter 3). Their poor health profiles can be best explained by bad housing, unemployment, low pay and the greater likelihood of working in hazardous or unhealthy jobs such as textiles and footwear. High rates of long-term unemployment, low job security, too much shift work and working nights lead to stress which in turn leads to high blood pressure. As Mares *et al.* found, deaths from hypertension are four times as common in men living in the UK who were born in the Caribbean than they are among their white counterparts and six times as common in women.

Among others, McNaught (1987) has argued that racism is a factor in both type of housing and employment that people from ethnic minorities get, as well as in their relationship with organisations such as the National Health Service, which has been slow to adapt to the demands of a multicultural society. Racism in the NHS can be seen in the employment of large numbers of black people in ancillary work (such as catering or cleaning) and in the less prestigious aspects of nursing or medical work. It can also be seen in the organisation of the NHS which needs to be adapted to accommodate the different cultural and religious beliefs of different ethnic groups. Language, hygiene (for example, the importance of washing in running water to Moslems) and death rites are all important factors which should be taken into account if the NHS is to be truly accessible to all British citizens regardless of ethnic origin.

Questions

1 How important are material and cultural factors in explaining the health profiles of ethnic minorities?
2 How important is social class to an understanding of the health profiles of ethnic minorities in the United Kingdom?
3 How important is it that the NHS adapts itself to a multicultural society? How much of a bearing might this have on the health of ethnic minorities?

Doctors and patients

The sick role

Sociologists have contributed a number of theories to explain the **power** of the medical profession in Western societies. For Talcott Parsons (1951), doctors are necessary because, by identifying people as sick, they enable people to adopt a 'sick role' whereby they can escape their social obligations for a short period of time. Doctors regulate and control behaviour to the extent that they decide when people should and should not go to work. This is 'motivated deviance', in which doctors co-operate. The patient is socially allowed to be ill and exempt from some social duties as long as they take reasonable steps to get better and use the available medical services. The function of doctors is to facilitate the sick role for patients.

In this argument Parsons is assuming that illness is a temporary phenomenon. This falls down when chronic or long-term illness is considered as it both allows a more explicit and threatening form of deviance to challenge the social system, and also questions the competence of the medical profession, as they are unable to find a cure for the illness. As someone who studied psychology before moving on to sociology, Parsons regarded most illness as psychosomatic – only in the patient's imagination – and simply another opportunity for role-playing.

Marxism and the medical profession

For Marxists, the existence of a curative rather than preventative model of health care is a consequence of capitalism. As Navarro (1976) argues, the dominance of the medical profession in health care helps obscure the social and economic causes of illness, the resolution of which demands political, not medical, action and initiatives. While health care may be free at the point of delivery (though this is increasingly less true), there are also vast profits to be made, firstly by companies selling drugs and high-tech equipment to hospitals, and secondly through the ability of industry to ignore and bypass health and safety legislation where prosecutions are rare and fines negligible and which permits activities such as cigarette smoking. Health care is still primarily about profit and the relative powerlessness of consumers.

Weber

The power of the medical **profession** itself is the focus of the Weberian view. This is best illustrated by Friedson (1975) who emphasises the way in which the medical profession monopolises the practice of health care, through legal–rational means (see also chapter 9). As such, it is a highly secretive, autonomous organisation, successfully preventing outside intervention in its practice even on behalf of the ruling class. (The medical profession was also the group that the then Minister for Health had most trouble with in setting up the NHS in 1948 until he 'stuffed their mouths with gold'.) The medical profession, according to Friedson, has successfully brought about the untested belief that it knows best, as industrial societies have come to place a high status on 'scientific' knowledge, partly due to the successes of the medical profession in eliminating some diseases. Primarily, the profession exists to serve its own interests, not those of the **ruling class**, and certainly not the interests of the consumers of medical care.

Iatrogenesis

Ivan Illich (1975) provides a radical critique of the way health care has evolved, focusing on the concept of iatrogenesis or doctor-originated illness. This happens in three ways. Clinical iatrogenesis results from the actual practice of medical health care, for example through the use of humans as 'guinea pigs', because of the side-effects of drugs (treatments where the cure is worse than the illness), and through addiction to prescribed drugs. Social iatrogenesis can be characterised by the way that, for example, birth and death have become medicalised. Here he is thinking of the way that the birth process has come under the control of doctors, not mothers, and is geared to doctors' demands. In reaction to this clinical control campaigning organisations were formed, such as the National Childbirth Trust, which aims to help mothers regain some control over childbirth. It also led to attempts to minimise the medical side of childbirth which causes anxiety to mothers. The French obstetrician Leboyer encouraged women to give birth in a warm bath in low lighting which

greatly reduced the stress. Thirdly, Illich claims that cultural iatrogenesis has resulted in individuals abdicating responsibility for their own health to a self-regarding medical profession and alienating technology. As with education, a return to smaller-scale and more democratic structures is required.

The interactionist approach

This approach has focused attention on the importance of the meaning of the social situation to participants in a medical consultation and the interpretation of the social interaction. Thus in some studies sociologists have recorded their own experiences with health professionals, while other studies have involved observational study of interaction between patients and health-care professionals.

Much American research in this field has attempted to discuss why people in minority groups do not make more use of the services of doctors. The answer has usually been couched in terms of the 'culture of poverty' rather than the high cost of private medicine, or the repressive characteristics of the charity sector. A criticism of this approach is that these researchers tend to portray hospitals and doctors' surgeries as though they existed in a vacuum, with doctors and patients acting out their predetermined roles, unaffected by the material and social world in which they are living and dying. Consider for a moment what happens when you enter a doctor's surgery. Is there a pattern to the interaction? What is the nature of the doctor/patient relationship? Who holds the power? Can the interview be seen as a process of negotiation? These are the kinds of question the interactionist approach considers.

A number of interactionists have used their own illnesses and time spent in hospital to conduct participant observation studies of the social interaction between patients and medical staff. J. Roth (1979) fell ill with tuberculosis and studied a sanatorium from the inside. His role as a patient gave him insights that a sociologist studying from the outside would miss. Likewise, Goffman (1961) provides insights into life in a mental home.

Doctors' power over women

Similar points have been made by **feminists**. Ann Oakley (1981) finds little evidence to suggest that technological intervention in childbirth is beneficial for mother or child. Generally, doctors have a great deal of control over women's fertility, through controlling access to some types of contraception and to abortion. The contraceptive pill in particular, a form of birth control targeted at women, not men, has come under strong criticism for its side effects, such as depression, excessive weight gain, headaches, nausea and even loss of sex drive.

Questions

1 What is the 'sick role'? How is it functional for the individual and society? How might it be dysfunctional?
2 What is meant by the term iatrogenesis? Think of other examples of what Illich means by this term.
3 What have some sociologists said are the effects of the power of the medical profession?
4 In what sense could medicine be said to be a part of the capitalist mode of production?

Mental health

One of the most controversial areas of medical sociology is the debate about mental health. Critics of psychiatry, both within sociology and outside of it, have analysed the diagnosis and treatment of mental illness as value-laden social constructions.

The 'medical' model has, until recently, dominated concepts of mental illness. Society and the individual are seen as manifesting the symptoms of the ill or diseased body; social illness becomes equated with physical illness. Thus some social behaviour is defined as unhealthy in the same way as doctors view the body, and to recognised illnesses such as fevers or fractures have been added such conditions as neuroses, or depressions; even homosexuality and divorce may be seen as 'illnesses' in some countries because they offend certain kinds of social norms. Thus mental illness is thought to be a condition of the individual, residing within him or her.

However, while it is relatively easy to define a state of bodily health, there is no general agreement about what constitutes the social health of individuals or societies. The limitation of this approach is that it locates the source of illness in the individual and so ignores response to, and interpretation of, individual actions. An alternative approach ignores, for the sake of analysis, individual manifestations of mental illness, and concentrates instead on the social situation in which mental 'illness' becomes defined and the process by which role and status positions are created and proffered to those considered mentally ill.

Scheff

Scheff (1982) argues that there is no such thing as 'mental illness'; it is simply a category used for people whose behaviour does not make sense to society. All of us, he claims, act oddly at times, but usually our depression or strange behaviour is excused. If, however, it comes to the attention of the medical profession, it can end up with us being **labelled**. The medical profession is trained to see abnormal behaviour as a symptom and to treat it in culturally prescribed ways. Thereafter, even marginally abnormal behaviour is likely to be treated as mental illness. Primary deviance is followed as an inevitable consequence by secondary deviance.

Scheff has described what he terms the 'social institution of insanity'. Attitudes to, and images of, mental illness are built up in the individual during and after childhood; people learn from an early age to regard certain situations, or people, as 'crazy'. These **stereotypes** receive support in adult life through social interaction and through channels such as the mass media. Thus people use such phrases as: 'Are you crazy?' and 'running like mad' in everyday conversation, so building up certain ideas of how 'mad' people act. These ideas are supported by **mass-media** reports of violence or murder in which it is suggested that the assailant has a 'history' of mental illness. All this serves to establish that mentally ill people are 'different' from the general population and draws a dividing line between the two groups.

Szasz

Thomas Szasz (1992) has argued persuasively that there is no such thing as mental illness. Mental illnesses, he suggests, are normal reactions to the problems of living. Mental illness is the label placed upon certain 'deviant' behaviour. Such behaviour is taken as evidence of mental illness, and then this mental illness is cited as the cause of the behaviour.

In mental problems, what happens is that behaviour, much of which may be the person's verbal communication about his or her problems, is measured by the psychiatrist's reference to norms related to what one expects from 'normal' people. The norms are not medical but psycho-social. Yet medical remedies are sought. The disorder is defined by one set of terms and its remedy is sought in others.

Note that Szasz is not arguing that there are not emotionally troubled people. Instead, he insists that the problems of living in modern society prove to be troublesome and disturbing for many people. But they are not 'ill' in some medically objective sense; instead, they have problems of living that may be much more disturbing to them than they usually are to other people.

The problem of mental illness, then, is partly a problem of those so defined. It is also a problem of definition; that is, a problem of how definitions of normality and reality are made in society and used as judgements of what is conventional and what is deviant behaviour.

Goffman

Erving Goffman (1961), in a study of mental institutions, tried to answer the question why some people are labelled as mentally ill and others not. He suggests the concept of a 'career' offers the answer. This is the process of a person being defined as mentally ill. During this process the individual learns to see him or herself in a different way.

Goffman emphasises that it is the social reaction to behaviour that is more important than the behaviour itself. He suggests that a person attracts a label usually because it is in someone's interest that they do. In the feature film, *Family Life*, directed by Ken Loach, a young girl is admitted to a mental hospital and is duly processed by the system as mentally ill. In fact the film suggests the problem is not hers but a problem of the family and she is in effect being blamed. Once labelled, the girl was caught up in a situation where her protests at the treatment she received and her behaviour were seen as further evidence of her illness.

Goffman highlights the range of adaptations made by individuals to cope with institutional life. In terms of mental illness he noted situational withdrawal (where the patient withdraws into himself); non-cooperation, which often leads to the patient being treated with sedative drugs; colonisation, where the individual finds support in the institution and becomes dependent; conversion, where the patient co-operates and is given simple tasks; and **conformity**, where the patient acts according to the rules.

Benedict

The anthropologist, Ruth Benedict (1982), pointed out that behaviour that would be considered symptomatic of mental ill-health in one society is seen as normal or even admirable in another society. Benedict tells us that the behaviour of Kwakiutl Indians would be seen as typical of mental illness in our society, expressing, for example, delusions of grandeur, seeing visions, etc. Yet in Kwakiutl society, this behaviour is seen as normal.

Rosenhan

Rosenhan (1994) conducted an experiment in which a range of people of different ages, from doctors to students, were admitted to mental hospitals in the USA with false medical records which suggested that they were suffering from schizophrenia. The subjects in the experiment were asked to write down what happened to them and behave normally. In a number of cases their 'cover' was exposed, not by doctors or nurses, but by other patients who saw them as normal and not in need of treatment. Some of the patients even guessed it was an experiment. Doctors and nurses, on the other hand, saw the subjects' 'writing' as confirming their illness and when the pseudo-patients spoke to staff they were frequently ignored.

Mental illness and gender/race

Research has emerged on mental illness and gender/race in recent years, paralleling research elsewhere. Women have a higher recorded rate of mental illness, as do black people and Asians in modern Western societies. The attitude of a predominantly male medical profession to the treatment of women's emotional problems may help explain why women experience a higher recorded rate of mental illness. Likewise, it has been suggested that black and Asian groups experience discrimination by doctors (predominantly white) who may perceive the health problems of these other ethnic groups in a biased way. Proportionately there is also a greater number of ethnic minority groups in the lower social classes. Material deprivation is greater in the lower social classes and this is often linked to stress. Hence, social inequality may help explain why black and Asian groups have a higher recorded rate of mental illness in modern Western societies.

Questions

1 Is mental illness a myth?
2 Why do women and some ethnic minority groups have higher rates of mental illness?

Poverty and the Welfare State

Laissez-faire

The guiding principle of politics in the nineteenth century in Britain was that of *laissez-faire* (let it happen). The dominant ideology held that industrial capitalism would best develop with minimum **State** interference and that inequalities in wealth would be evened out as economic development progressed and then everyone's standard of living would improve. Economic opportunities were there for all to take, and those who missed out failed to take them because of their own fecklessness and idleness. If you were poor, then it was probably your own fault, and your problem.

Poor Laws

The options open to anyone who fell on hard times were few. The Elizabethan Poor Laws of 1597 and 1601 became highly punitive following the amendment of 1834. The central principles were that no 'relief' (from poverty) would be given to the able-bodied except through the workhouse, and that this relief should bring a worse standard of life than that of the worst-off labourer – the principle of 'less eligibility'. This system was to survive until well into the twentieth century. The alternative was to turn to the charitable institutions of private philanthropists.

As the nineteenth century progressed, the principle of minimal State interference began to be gradually eroded through, for example, public health legislation and the Factory Acts. By 1891 the State was providing free and compulsory education for all children up to the age of ten partly as a consequence of the realisation that British industry was beginning to lose ground to its main competitors. By the turn of the century, considerable evidence was available to show that there had been little or no 'trickle down' of wealth to the poor and Marx's concept of capitalist development 'immiserating' or 'pauperising' those at the bottom was gaining credence.

Studies on poverty: Booth and Rowntree

Two key studies emerged from English philanthropists to confound those who continued to believe that poverty was a small-scale and individual problem: Charles Booth's *Life and Labour of the People of London*, published in seventeen volumes between 1889 and 1903, and Seebohm Rowntree's *Poverty: A Study of*

CHARLES BOOTH (1840–1916)

A shipowner who became famous for his work on poverty. Booth started his research on poverty in London to disprove claims made in the *Pall Mall Gazette* that a quarter of Londoners lived in poverty. Booth found that the figure was far worse.

Town Life (1901) which investigated poverty in York where Rowntree's family were one of the main employers in the chocolate industry. These two works represent the first real systematic studies of the nature and extent of poverty.

Both studies used similar measurements for their definition of poverty, based on the needs of a family of two adults with three children. Rowntree, in his study of poverty in York, took advice from medical scientists as to what exactly were the minimum requirements in terms of food and clothing in order for an individual to simply subsist. He then gave these a financial value. To be above his poverty line a family of five needed an income of 21s. 8d. a week (about 108p). He found that if this amount was used correctly, without any spending on 'luxuries' or waste, 7,230 people or 9.91 per cent of the population of York were in 'primary' poverty.

Rowntree described the lives of those living in primary poverty. They must, he said, 'never spend a

SEEBOHM ROWNTREE (1871–1954)

An industrialist with a major interest in unemployment and social welfare which led him to undertake a number of population surveys to measure the extent of poverty in York.

penny on a railway fare or omnibus. They must never purchase a half-penny newspaper or spend a penny to buy a ticket for a popular concert. They must write no letters. They must never contribute to church or chapel or give help to a neighbour. They cannot save, nor can they join a sick club or a trade union. The children must have no pocket money. The father must smoke no tobacco and must drink no beer. The mother must never buy any pretty clothes. Should a child fall ill it must be attended by the parish doctor; should it die it must be buried by the parish. The wage earner must never be absent from work for a single day.'

When those who were extravagant, or spent their money 'unwisely' (secondary poverty), were added, he calculated that 28 per cent of the population of York were in poverty. If this was worrying to a factory owner, then the main cause of their poverty was even more so: 51.96 per cent were in poverty due to low pay.

Charles Booth's study indicated that 30.7 per cent of the population of London were in poverty. The evidence from both sources showed that, at the heart of the vast British Empire, at the height of its power, and after more than a century of industrial advance, more than a quarter of its population did not have enough to live on from one week to the next. The Boer War fought against Afrikaner farmers in South Africa (1899–1902) provided further evidence when 60 per cent of recruits were found to be physically unfit for service.

Poor Law reforms

In the best British tradition, the Conservative Party, on its last day in government in 1905, formed a Royal Commission to investigate the Poor Law and consider its reform. This took until 1909, when the Commission, which included Charles Booth, issued its 47-volume report. This actually consisted of two reports, a majority report and a dissenting minority report, produced by the left-wing members of the Commission.

Liberal government reforms

Although the recommendations of both reports were largely ignored, the Liberal government, inspired by Lloyd George, did make some important inroads into the principle of non-intervention by the State. In 1908, old age pensions were introduced at 5s. (25p) per week for those over 70, and in 1911 compulsory health and unemployment insurance was introduced for workers in selected industries. Even then, however, the health insurance covered only the worker, not their family. Three years later Britain was at war, with 282,000 people still living in workhouses. By 1916, when Lloyd George became Prime Minister, the principle of non-intervention was completely abandoned when the Liberal government conscripted all men between 18 and 40 into military service. Of every nine conscripts examined, four were totally unfit for service and another two were fit only for supporting service.

In the inter-war period, despite two periods of Labour government, there was no return to the reforming zeal of the years immediately prior to the First World War. In 1921, 2,038,000 insured workers were unemployed. In 1922, two million people received Poor Relief. Unemployment never fell below one million throughout this decade, and began to rise steeply as the decade ended. By 1932, 23 per cent of all workers were out of work, with as many as 60 per cent of shipbuilders unemployed. Throughout this inter-war period, those not eligible for **unemployment benefit** had only the ministrations of the Poor Law between them and starvation.

It would be a mistake, however, to see the inter-war years as being entirely characterised by depression. For those still in work, real wages rose by 50 per cent between 1918 and 1938, and increasingly affluent lifestyles developed. This is reflected in Rowntree's second poverty survey in York in 1936, where he found, using similar standards as before, that only 18 per cent of the population were now in poverty, although low pay still accounted for 42 per cent of these cases. Three years later Britain was at war again.

Wars produce fundamental social and economic changes. The State takes an ever-increasing role in directing the economy. Women are brought into the workforce as unemployment falls, and children may be evacuated into non-urban areas. Politicians and citizens unite around a common cause. The welfare of the people once again becomes a central political issue.

In the Second World War there was a widespread determination not to return to the socio-economic conditions prevalent after the First World War. To this end, the coalition government commissioned a report into how the welfare of the people could be improved, in the advent of peace. Written by a civil servant, William Beveridge, the 1942 *Report on Social Insurance and Allied Services* is the most important document in twentieth-century British social policy. In it, Beveridge identified five 'giants' or 'evils' to be eradicated: disease, ignorance, squalor, want, and idleness.

The Beveridge Report, as it became known, was immediately popular, and the belief that the Labour Party was the party most intent on implementing its recommendations was largely responsible for its winning of 393 seats compared with the Conservatives' 212 seats in the election of summer 1945. Before this, in 1944, Butler passed the Education Act that provided free secondary education for all (see chapter 6). Following the landslide Labour victory, there was an intense flurry of legislation that comprehensively established the **Welfare State**, with the aim of caring for its citizens 'from the cradle to the grave'. This legislation was put through against a background of post-war economic adversity that found the Labour government being forced to consider introducing prescription charges in 1949, and then charges for false teeth and spectacles. The free provision of such items was undoubtedly necessary and popular, with 187,000,000 prescriptions written, 8,500,000 dental patients treated and 5,250,000 pairs of glasses prescribed in the first year 1948–49, yet the rapid introduction of charges for some of these caused the chief architect of the NHS, Aneurin Bevan, to resign.

Ignorance: to be defeated by free secondary education for all, following the 1944 Education Act.

Squalor: to be defeated by the New Towns Act 1946, creating a ring of new towns (e.g. Stevenage and Harlow) around London. Also the Town and Country Planning Act (1947).

Idleness: to be defeated by a commitment to maintaining 'full employment', through following the economic policies of J. M. Keynes – 'Keynesianism'. In 1944 a White Paper on employment was followed by Beveridge's book *Full Employment in a Free Society*.

Disease: to be defeated by the setting up of the National Health Service, following the 1946 National Health Act. From 5 July 1948, all health care and treatment was free to all at the point of delivery.

Want: to be defeated by a universal National Insurance Scheme (following the 1946 Act) and a National Assistance Act (1948) whose opening words were: 'the existing Poor Law [of 1601 and 1834] shall cease to have effect'. Also, family allowances were initiated from 1943.

The end of poverty?

Nevertheless, it was widely believed that the newly founded Welfare State was improving the standards of living for all. In his third, and final, survey of poverty in York, in 1950, Rowntree found that only 1.5 per cent of people lived in poverty. The battle, he was able to conclude, was over – at least in his lifetime.

Questions

1 What were the main factors that led to the creation of the Welfare State?
2 What does the term Welfare State mean?
3 What influence has ideology had on the development of the Welfare State?
4 What is the difference between primary and secondary poverty?

The sociology of poverty

In the 1950s, anxieties concerning poverty in the UK were largely dispelled, as politicians were able to claim that the British people had 'never had it so good', and the idea of the **embourgeoisement** of the **working class** gained ground (see chapter 3). In many ways, it was believed that the social problems of the first half of the century had been overcome, and that a new consensus existed.

The rediscovery of poverty

This new mood did not satisfy some sociologists, who argued that poverty still existed, though a new perception of its nature was needed to identify it. It was argued by, for example, Wootton (1959), Abel-Smith and Townsend (1965), Coates and Silburn (1970) and Kincaid (1973) that the problem of poverty had far from disappeared. In the work of these sociologists, poverty in Britain was 'rediscovered'.

Abel-Smith and Townsend argued that the State's poverty line – the National Assistance level (later Supplementary Benefit, and now Income Support) – was set too low to reflect a normative standard of poverty. If the poverty line was set 40 per cent higher than the National Assistance level (i.e. 140 per cent of National Assistance, a figure chosen by the two researchers to reflect their concept of what was needed to be out of poverty) then a different picture emerged. According to information supplied to them by the Ministry of Labour, the official number in poverty in 1953 of 1.1 per cent increased to 7.8 per cent when recalculated by the authors, and the official figure of 3.8 per cent in 1960 should be revised upwards to 14.2 per cent. From these new statistics, poverty ceased to be mainly a problem for the elderly (who represented 68.1 per cent of those in poverty according to Rowntree in 1950) and principally a problem of low pay (40 per cent of those in poverty in 1960, according to Abel-Smith and Townsend, were low-paid). Low pay was also the chief cause of poverty in Rowntree's surveys of 1899 – 52 per cent – and 1936 – 42 per cent. Statistically, there was no reason why low pay should have disappeared as a problem, as the earnings of the lowest-paid 10 per cent of income earners had remained constant at just above two-thirds of the average wage through the century, reflecting an unchanging wage structure, despite the Welfare State.

Poverty in the United Kingdom

In a later, and more widespread, study undertaken between 1968 and 1969, Townsend (1979) enlarged on the principles established in his earlier works, this time basing his research on three forms of measurement. The first was the State or

Supplementary Benefit standard, showing 6.1 per cent of households, and 9.1 per cent of income units (or individuals), in poverty. According to the relative income standard (those with incomes of less than 50 per cent of the average for households of their type), 9.2 per cent of households and 19.6 per cent of income units were living on the margins of poverty. By the deprivation index (see p. 115) 22.9 per cent of households and 25.9 per cent of income units were in poverty. This meant that 12.5 per cent of the population were in poverty. In particular, Townsend pointed out that 'Elderly people who had been unskilled manual workers and children in the families of young unskilled manual workers, especially those with substantial experience of unemployment, sickness or disablement and in one-parent families, were most likely to be poor.'

The new underclass

The publication of Townsend's book revived controversies around the concept of poverty not witnessed since Rowntree. New evidence has continued to be amassed. Frank Field (1989) details how he believes a new **underclass** has emerged in Britain since the optimistic decades of the 1950s and 1960s. As evidence, he cites the number of those receiving National Assistance/ Supplementary Benefit/Income Support as increasing from an initial 963,000 in 1948 to 2.8 million in 1979, and 4.9 million by 1988. In 1949, 1.5 million were dependent on Supplementary Benefit alone. This figure increased to 4.4 million in 1979 and 8.2 million in 1988.

Field observes that the type of group most vulnerable to poverty has changed in the course of the twentieth century. Booth and Rowntree found that a vast majority of those in poverty were on low wages, or were wage-earners with large families of five or more children. Between the wars, poverty was increasingly associated with unemployment, as well as low wages. In the immediate post-war period the concern was with old age. From the 1980s, the focus has returned to low incomes. The underclass now, Field says, consists of the long-term unemployed, particularly school leavers who have never had a job, and those older workers who have been without work for very long periods; single-parent families, whose number doubled between 1979 and 1988, particularly those dependent on welfare for long periods of time, and elderly pensioners who are entirely dependent on old age pensions and Income Support. These people belong to 'an underclass that sits uncomfortably below

that group which is referred to as living on a low income' (see chapter 3).

In 1985 the Conservative government introduced a new series of official data called 'Households Below Average Income'. This measure led to the production of a consistent set of statistics over a number of decades. Despite the intervention of the Welfare State, figures released by the Office for National Statistics show that the gap between the rich and poor increased over a period of twenty-five years. Where the poorest tenth of the population earned one-third of the richest tenth in 1971, by 1997 it was less than a quarter. The main reasons for this were tax and benefit changes, which benefited the highest earners significantly more than the lowest paid.

Recent studies, for example Howarth et al. (2000), have tried to address the problems of poverty statistics by focusing on 'income dynamics', using three indicators: long-term dependency on income support and job-seeker's allowance (which showed three million people claiming for more than two years in 1997); length of time on low income (which showed that between 1992 and 1994 20 million people in the UK experienced at least one spell of low income) and 'self-reported difficulty managing financially'. While people above pensionable age are most likely to be represented under the first two headings, people below pensionable age are most likely to be found in the third. As with Field's work, the most vulnerable groups remain lone parents and pensioners. Ethnic minorities are over-represented, particularly Bangladeshi and Pakistani households. The most important causes of poverty are related to employment status (full-time, part-time, unemployed, retired, sick, parent, disabled), with, as Hills (1998) notes, one-third of those living in poverty in Britain at the end of the twentieth century being in employment – the working poor.

Questions

1 What does the term poverty mean to you? How would you define it?
2 According to Field, who are the new underclass?
3 How was poverty rediscovered?

The measurement of poverty

There is now no agreed measure of the extent of poverty in the United Kingdom. Most people would agree that it exists, but how much there is and why it exists depend on how it is defined and measured. The amount of poverty perceived depends on where the line is drawn.

Absolute poverty

Rowntree, in 1899, drew his line according to what has become known as an **absolute** standard. After consulting nutritionists, he then estimated the average nutritional needs of adults and children, translating these needs into quantities of different foods and then into their cash equivalent. He then added minimum sums for clothing, fuel and household sundries according to the size of family. Families were in poverty, he said, if their 'total earnings are insufficient to obtain the minimum necessaries for the maintenance of merely physical efficiency'. Even this absolute standard changed in 1936 (eventually becoming the basis of Beveridge's figures for the amount of National Assistance) when additional necessities were added, and as John Veit-Wilson (1986) observed, even Rowntree's conception of poverty was relative, not absolute. The State's measure of poverty – the Income Support level – is an absolute measure in that it attempts to meet basic physical, and not cultural, needs.

Relative poverty

Most conceptions of poverty are **relative**. Peter Townsend (1979) is in no doubt about how he conceives poverty: 'Individuals, families and groups in the population can be said to be in poverty when they lack the resources to obtain the types of diet, participate in the activities and have the living conditions and amenities which are customary or are at least widely encouraged or approved, in the societies in which they belong.' Here, the emphasis moves away from what humans need to exist to what the society they live in expects in terms of living standards. The poverty line is always moving. So how can it be fixed at any one time?

Deprivation index

Townsend's own answer was to compile a 'deprivation index' comprised ultimately of twelve items the lack of which, he argued, pointed to poverty. This included things such as not having a week's holiday away from home in the last twelve months, children not having a party at their last birthday and households not having a fridge. Built into this index is the realisation that poverty is both material and social. In a later work (1987) he makes a distinction between deprivation and poverty, where the former implies unmet need

and the inability to participate in activities, and the latter describes the lack of material resources that causes this deprivation.

The main problem with this type of index is that it is **subjective**: it is based on what Townsend and his research team believed constituted poverty. Yet the index includes items such as 'does not have fresh meat ... as many as four days a week' (number 4), 'has not had a cooked breakfast most days of the week' (number 9) and 'household does not usually have a Sunday joint (3 in 4 times)' (number 11). In Townsend's carnivorous world, poverty clearly exists when meat is not eaten on most days.

Feminist views

Feminist theory has contributed a number of important reflections on the way that poverty is defined and assessed. It points out the drawbacks in using the income of the head of the household or main breadwinner, as a measurement of where a family is placed in relation to the poverty scale. The standard of living enjoyed by the husband or male partner in the family may in practice be very different from that enjoyed by his female partner and any children. For example, a family with a husband who is earning a good wage may not be classed as 'in poverty' using conventional measures. However, the reality may be that the husband controls (and spends) the family income in such a way that his wife and any children are denied the benefits of a good standard of living, effectively placing them in a position of poverty.

Women may also be unequally disadvantaged by the experience of being in poverty. Payne (1990) notes that the strain of managing on a low income can impose an emotional burden, much of which falls to women. The responsibility for managing the household budget generally falls on women and this exacts a price in terms of stress, anxiety and sheer hard work: 'the worry of finding goods, entertaining children with no toys, keeping their minds off their hunger, taking them with you to the shops, and feeling guilty about everything'.

Subjective definitions

Neither Rowntree nor Townsend seem concerned with what people themselves believe is poverty – what subjective ideas of poverty are. To correct this, in 1983, Mack and Lansley (1985) asked 1,174 people what were necessities in contemporary Britain. Where more than 50 per cent of the respondents agreed on the necessity of items, then the authors decided that it meant that those without them lived in poverty. This gave them 22 items on their list, ranging from heating living areas of the home if it's cold (agreed by 97 per cent) to 'two hot meals a day for adults' (64 per cent) and 'presents for friends or family once a year' (63 per cent). This index revealed that 7.5 million people, or 13.8 per cent of the population of Britain lived in poverty, as defined by its population.

Since the election of the Labour government in 1997 in particular, the concept of social exclusion has become closely linked to that of poverty, with the creation of a Social Exclusion unit within the Cabinet Office. The concept is also widely in use across the European Union, though it is not without criticism. Room (1995) and Abrahamson (1998), in particular, see the use of this term as an attempt to move away from looking directly at the issue of poverty. Duffy (1995) has defined it as follows: 'Social exclusion is a broader concept than poverty, encompassing not only low material means but the inability to participate effectively in economic, social, political and cultural life, and, in some characterisations, alienation and distance from the mainstream society.' While parts of this definition are very similar to Townsend's definition of relative poverty (lack of economic integration), there is also an increased emphasis on the concepts of citizenship and social rights (lack of social integration). The European Union's emphasis on measures to overcome social exclusion may nevertheless result in a diminution of economic poverty in the United Kingdom.

Questions

1 How can absolute and relative poverty be distinguished?
2 What was Townsend's purpose in developing a deprivation index? What problems are associated with using this index?
3 How might the concept of subjective poverty be criticised? What are its merits?
4 Do definitions of absolute, relative and subjective poverty remain constant over time?
5 Why are women and ethnic groups vulnerable to poverty?

Why does poverty exist?

No one really argues that poverty does not persist in Great Britain. The debates around poverty concern its nature, extent and causes. A number of theories have been developed to explain its persistence.

The functions of poverty

From the **functionalist** point of view, if poverty is a prevalent feature of society, then it must in some way be functional, although it is clearly dysfunctional to those in poverty. Poverty must serve a social function. This argument has been elaborated by Howard Gans (1973). He delineates fifteen ways in which poverty can be functional, for example:

→ Poverty helps to ensure that dirty, dangerous, menial and undignified work gets done.
→ The poor help to uphold the legitimacy of dominant norms by providing examples of deviance (e.g. the lazy, spendthrift, dishonest, promiscuous).
→ The poor help to provide emotional satisfaction, evoking compassion, pity and charity, so that the affluent may feel righteous.
→ Poverty helps to guarantee the status of the non-poor.
→ The poor add to the social viability of non-economic groups (e.g. fund-raising, running settlements, other philanthropic activities).

'A functional analysis', he says, 'must conclude that poverty persists not only because it satisfies a number of functions but also because many of the functional alternatives to poverty would be quite dysfunctional for the more affluent members of society.' 'Phenomena like poverty', he concludes, 'can be eliminated only when they either become sufficiently dysfunctional for the affluent or when the poor can obtain enough power to change the system of social stratification.' The poor, he suggests, will always be with us.

The culture of poverty

Other analyses focus on the norms and values of those in poverty, rather than the society that requires poverty. This group of theories argues that a distinct **subculture** of poverty is identifiable. For Oscar Lewis (1961), 'poverty in modern nations is not only a state of economic deprivation, of disorganisation, or of the absence of something. It is also something positive in the sense that it has a structure, a rationale, and defence mechanisms without which the poor could hardly carry on. In short, it is a way of life, remarkably stable and persistent, passed down from generation to generation along family lines.' These subcultural features can be found in any major city, whether in London, Glasgow, Paris, New York or Mexico City. In another study (1958), he argues that 'by the time slum children are aged six or seven they have usually absorbed the basic values and attitudes of their subculture and are not psychologically geared to take full advantage of changing conditions or increased opportunities which may occur in their lifetime.'

Despite the clearly value-laden concepts underlying this theory, it has been discussed at governmental level, both in the United States in the 1960s – at the time of the battle against 'cultural deprivation' and 'Operation Headstart' – and in Britain, in particular by Sir Keith Joseph, the former Cabinet minister and intellectual mentor to Margaret Thatcher.

It is also a theory that has come under sustained fire. Lewis, in particular, is seen as looking only at *some* people in poverty, and abstracting their characteristics. Lewis himself was aware of this: 'my rough guess would be that only about 20 per cent of the population below the poverty line in the US have characteristics that would justify classifying their way of life as that of a culture of poverty'. Many other people are poor, but do not necessarily behave in the way Lewis describes, as Rossi and Blum (1968) conclude: 'our review of the literature concerning poverty does not support the idea of a culture of poverty in which the poor are distinctively different from other layers of society'. A research programme set up by Sir Keith Joseph failed to identify a cycle of deprivation. Rutter and Madge (1976) found that 'At least half of the children born into a disadvantaged home do not repeat the pattern of disadvantage in the next generation. Over half of all forms of disadvantage arise anew each generation.'

The structural determinants of poverty

Other criticisms are that, firstly, the theory concentrates on those in poverty, without examining the possibility that the cause of their poverty may originate from the society in which they live. In other words, poverty may be structurally determined. By concentrating on the individuals – or more particularly the families – involved, the theory of a subculture of poverty, Townsend (1979) says, encourages 'the recurrent prejudice that poverty is the fault of individuals and family or community groups rather than of society itself'.

As we know, to become part of a subculture you must be socialised into its norms and values. This theory suggests that poverty is something you learn from your parents, as an attitude and a way of life. From this perspective the solution to your poverty is that you must be socialised out of it, hence the wide range of schemes launched to this end, for example the Department of Social Security's 'Restart' programme.

Situational constraints

The idea of 'situational constraints' takes issue with the culture of poverty argument and claims instead that the behaviour of the poor is simply a consequence of the constraints of the situation in which they find themselves, with little money and few opportunities to get hold of any more. If their situation was to change then – contrary to Lewis's claim – so too would their behaviour. There is no fixed culture of poverty, and the poor are only detached from everyone else because of their financial position.

This is the central argument of Elliot Liebow's *Tally's Corner* (1967), where the behaviour of a group of black men on low incomes was explained by him as a response to their awareness of their likely future. He makes it clear that they share the aspirations and values of mainstream society, from a stable family life to well-paid, full-time employment. However, an overstated and temporary culture of manliness among the men developed to compensate for their poverty, their sense of failure and their inability to support a family. This cultural response is not seen as an important or permanent aspect of their lives.

Marxism – the problem of wealth

Other views of poverty point to the structure of society as its cause, not those in poverty themselves.

POVERTY DESCRIBED

Oscar Lewis, *The Children of Sanchez* (1961), gives the following descriptions of the lifestyles of the poor. They are characterised by 'a miscellany of unskilled occupations, child labour, the absence of savings, a chronic shortage of cash, the absence of food reserves in the home, the pattern of frequent buying of small quantities of food many times a day as the need arises, the pawning of personal goods, borrowing from local money lenders at usurious rates of interest, spontaneous informal credit devices organised by neighbours, and the use of second-hand clothing and furniture'.

The poor live in 'crowded quarters, [with] a lack of privacy, gregariousness, a high incidence of alcoholism, frequent resort to violence in the settlement of quarrels, frequent use of physical violence in the training of children, wife-beating, early initiation into sex, free unions or consensual marriages, a relatively high incidence of the abandonment of mother and children ... little ability to defer gratification and plan for the future ... a belief in male superiority [and] a corresponding martyr complex among women'.

For Marxists, poverty is a consequence of the ownership of capital by a few people, at the expense of the rest of society. When most of a society's wealth is in the possession of a handful of people, then we are all in a sense relatively poor. Inequality is essential to **capitalism**, and a consequence of its exploitative dynamic. The problem of poverty is not the poor themselves but the rich, as R. H. Tawney (though not himself a Marxist) observed in his well-known statement: 'what thoughtful rich people call the problem of poverty, thoughtful poor people call with equal justice the problem of riches'. If you are poor, it is because someone rich has got the wealth that is, by rights, yours. Their wealth, not your poverty, is the problem.

Weber and market position

The Weberian view stresses the weak market position of the poor – their poverty is the consequence of a lack of bargaining power. This is a common feature of those who are most vulnerable, particularly the unemployed, low-paid, single parents and the elderly. Recognising this, and adopting a position close to neo-Weberianism, Peter Townsend makes a number of recommendations in order to eliminate poverty, including payment of incomes to dependants, a legally enforceable right to work, and restricting the grip of professional organisations.

Gender and poverty

Feminists have stressed the feminisation of poverty, pointing out that those who suffer most from poverty are women. Women have always been particularly vulnerable to poverty. In 1908, three out of five Poor Law recipients were women, in 1983, three in five Supplementary Benefit recipients were women and in 1992 62 per cent of those in receipt of Income Support were female. As Millar and Glendinning (1989) argue: 'the conditions under which women obtain access to resources, the levels of those resources, women's control over resources and their degree of responsibility for the welfare of others in deploying material resources – all these are factors which make women more vulnerable to poverty, and which shape women's experience of the impact of poverty'. There is a hidden poverty within the family that means that women experience poverty more intensely than men in that, for example, they are more likely to feed others before themselves when little food is available. It also falls largely to women to manage poverty, and they consequently have a disproportionate amount of their time caught up in this activity.

Ethnicity and poverty

It is also argued that poverty disproportionately affects ethnic minorities in Britain. Despite the paucity of statistics specific to ethnic groups, Leech and Amin (1988) argue that 'there has been an increased racialisation of poverty: blackness and poverty are more correlated now than they were some years ago … the condition of the black poor is deteriorating'.

Immigration policy

A number of reasons have been put forward for this. Immigration policy has made it difficult for some groups to approach welfare services. The 1971 Immigration Act specified that wives and children could only enter the United Kingdom if those who were going to finance them were able to do so without using public funds. This was defined in 1985 as meaning Income Support, Housing Benefit and Family Credit. This emphasis discourages eligible groups from taking up benefits although it does not prevent the portrayal of some ethnic groups as 'scroungers'. This is compounded by the weak market position of many ethnic minorities who are either unemployed or in low-paid work and the fact that, proportionately, there are more young people in ethnic minorities than there are in the population as a whole. While there are proportionately less pensioners than among white groups, the younger age profile of ethnic minorities means that they are more vulnerable to changes in **child benefit**, **family credit** and Income Support. Afro-Caribbean – though not Asian – families are more likely than white families to be headed by lone parents.

Perspectives on the Welfare State

Since 1945 there has been considerable expansion in the range and scope of welfare services in the UK. The cost of these services as a proportion of public spending has increased accordingly. Although the Welfare State enjoyed widespread support from all the major political parties during the 1950s and 1960s, the situation began to change as the British economy declined during the 1970s. Right-wing critics became more vociferous, denouncing existing welfare provision as too generous and unrealistic. Successive Conservative governments since 1979 pursued the aim of reforming welfare services in order to achieve what they saw as a more cost-efficient and effective system. This involved reductions in services, changes in eligibility rules for claiming various benefits, and the withdrawal of certain provisions such as free dental care and eye tests.

Although the Labour Party, which came to power in the UK in 1997, is opposed in principle to the reduction of welfare services, it too is concerned about how to pay for a system that consumes an increasingly large proportion of government revenue – for example, social security expenditure in 2001 accounted for one-third of all public expenditure at just over £80 billion and nearly eleven million people now receive benefits.

New Right theories of welfare

The basic idea of the Welfare State, as well as whether in reality it has actually achieved its goals, has been attacked by a number of right-wing politicians and academics who, because of their views, have become known as the New Right. From this perspective David Marsland (1989) has argued that the Welfare State creates a 'culture of dependency' where those who rely on State benefits become so used to them that they lose all motivation to seek other means of looking after themselves, such as paid employment. He suggests that a pattern of living develops among those dependent on State benefits whereby they lose their sense of social responsibility and self-reliance and that it is this problem of 'attitudes' that serves to keep them in a state of poverty. Rather than eliminating poverty, therefore, the Welfare State exacerbates the situation. Marsland's views have some links with the 'culture of poverty' explanation of social inequality that was outlined earlier in the chapter.

Further criticisms from the New Right stem from the belief that the public expenditure necessary to pay for welfare services is a waste of the profits made by industry, and that the finance would be better reinvested in industry and/or given back to the 'taxpayer' so that he or she could spend it according to individual choice.

The New Right is not totally against government provision of welfare services. However, it does believe that the scope and number of services should be reduced so that there is minimal provision, i.e. support is available only for the most needy. In this view, eligibility for benefits in all cases should be selective and so involve means-testing – in general, only people with a very low income would qualify for benefits.

Responses to the New Right

A number of sociologists and left-of-centre (social democratic) politicians have challenged the arguments of the New Right. For example, Le Grand (1982) has pointed out that it is the middle class rather than the poor who have benefited most from the Welfare State, and this is one of the main reasons why the Welfare State has failed to eliminate poverty. In health care, the middle class have the knowledge, power and money to make sure they get proper treatment. In housing, the middle class benefit from tax relief on mortgage interest payments to a much greater extent than the poor benefit from housing benefits.

Alan Walker (1990) has challenged the idea that benefits present a disincentive to work. For most, the move on to benefit leads to a drop in income and a sharp drop in the standard of living. In a study of Income Support claimants, it was found that four out of five unemployed respondents said that their situation had deteriorated since living on benefit. Three out of five lone parents and a similar proportion of sick or disabled respondents, and just over two-thirds of those over retirement age, also felt they were worse off.

Jordan (1989) has argued against the New Right idea that benefits should be available only on a selective basis. He points out that societies such as the USA, which rely upon means-tested benefits, tend to develop a large underclass that has little chance of escaping from poverty. If members of the underclass accept low-paid jobs, they lose benefits and the right to free services, and they may end up worse off. Insofar as there is a disincentive to work, therefore, it is not because the welfare system is too generous but rather the opposite – the system is too mean.

Other writers on the left have been critical of means-testing and the stigma that it involves. They point out that the stigma is socially divisive and may discourage many people who are in genuine need from applying for benefits they are rightly entitled to.

The New Right perspective is based on an individualistic view of human nature and society. From this perspective, people are motivated by self-interest and the search for personal reward. Only by encouraging self-reliance and individual initiative can society make progress. Critics of this view warn against the dangers of promoting individualism at the expense of social unity and collective provision. Many on the left see the Welfare State as part of a caring society that encourages people to develop the altruistic side of their nature and to help and support each other. From this perspective, the idea that each person should be left to his or her own devices in making a success or failure of life is abhorrent and is denounced as part of a philosophy of greed and selfishness.

A Marxist view of the Welfare State

As we noted earlier, Marxist sociologists believe that it is impossible for the Welfare State to eliminate poverty because of the wider structural inequalities in society. For example, John Kincaid (1973) argues that because poverty is caused by the grossly unequal distribution of income and wealth in capitalist society, only the overthrow of capitalism and the institution of a fair and just society can eliminate poverty. Therefore, from a Marxist perspective, poverty – like wealth – is an inevitable consequence of the capitalist system. It can only be abolished in a socialist society, in which human needs and not profits determine the allocation of resources.

John Westergaard and Henrietta Resler (1976) see the provision of welfare services as a concession offered to the masses by the ruling class in order to alleviate the worst excesses of poverty and thereby discourage a revolutionary uprising. They argue that the existence of the Welfare State has helped to contain the demands of the working class within the existing system.

Poverty survives in part because it is useful to a number of rich and powerful groups. The existence of poverty ensures that a pool of low-wage labour is always available and willing to perform dead-end, dirty and dangerous jobs. By helping to get these jobs done cheaply, the poor are subsidising the better-off sections of the community, who are more likely to buy the goods and services. Poverty also provides employment and financial security for people in a range of 'caring' professions who serve the poor, or help to control their activities. These include the police, probation officers, social workers, psychiatrists, doctors and administrators of the Welfare State.

Questions

1 Has the Welfare State succeeded?
2 Has the gap between the rich and the poor been closed since the end of the Second World War?
3 How is the Welfare State criticised by:
   (a) Marxists
   (b) the New Right?

---

5 The family

The discussion on the family begins by examining the functionalist perspective and then goes on to look at the ideas of Marxism and feminism. Then there is a discussion on the disadvantages of the nuclear family. The next section looks at the effect of industrialisation on the family. The discussion then moves on to look at power and labour within the family. This is followed by a review of the relationship between the family and the State, and the chapter finishes with an account of the social significance of the rising divorce rate in modern industrial societies.

Sociology and the family

Trying to explain society entails arriving at conclusions about the reasons for social behaviour. Themes like nature or nurture, **free will** and **determinism** and the relationship between the individual and the culture of society are central issues. Is **intelligence**, however we define it, passed on genetically, or is it a product of nurture, of **socialisation**? How is **culture**, with its restrictive **norms** and **values**, forced into children, so that they may become 'social beings'? The first contact which a child has with culture is through whoever is providing nurture – caregivers. In most societies, this role is taken by the biological or adoptive parents of the child, in a family situation.

Functionalists claim that the family exists in all societies, that it is the 'natural' way to live and reproduce. The family is important in society, and society is important in the family. Societies ritualise and reinforce family life through celebrating the various stages in the individual's experience of the family – births, deaths and weddings, religious celebrations, holidays, parties and visits. The family dominates the media in sitcoms, soaps, ads and serials.

Sociologists have devoted a lot of time and effort to studying, analysing and arguing about the family. It is the place where society is shaped and passed on to be reproduced generation after generation. The answers to questions about nature and nurture, culture and the individual, free will and determinism are never found, but arguments arise, as usual, about theories. A lot of the ground work on the family, and particularly the family in Britain before and since industrialisation, was carried out by sociologists who were 'pro-family', and they raised anxieties about its possible decline. Throughout the 1960s and 1970s radical perspectives within **Marxism**, **feminism** and **interactionism** also pointed to the apparent break-up of the traditional family form, but they did so gleefully, seeing the family as the breeding ground for the justification of inequalities in society – between men and women, capitalists and workers, and parents and children in families.

What is the family then? According to your point of view, it's a place of love and security which produces and trains future members of society and sustains adults in their daily lives; it's an emotional, repressive 'rat's nest' which twists and distorts the personality; it's a **patriarchal** structure which ensures the domination of women by men or it's an offshoot of the **mode of production** and provides 'factory fodder' for the **ruling classes**.

Household and family types

The term *household* refers to an individual or a group defined by the fact that they reside in a particular property. A *family* can be defined as a distinct group in society whose members are related to one another by ties of either blood or marriage, and who support each other economically and emotionally.

If everyone resided in a family group there would be no need to distinguish between families and households. The two would overlap completely. Not all households are based on family units, however. Household types that are not families include, for example, people living alone, friends who are sharing accommodation, and various communal arrangements such as women living in a refuge for victims of domestic violence and monks in a monastery.

The image of a typical family in modern industrial societies is that of a wife and husband plus a young child or children. This is known as the **nuclear family**. In some cases the two adults in the family may not be married, i.e. they cohabit. Sociologists disagree about whether or not a cohabiting couple with children can be included within the definition of a nuclear family. The nuclear family is also sometimes referred to as the conjugal family. Less than 50 per cent of families in the UK are nuclear units.

The **extended family** (sometimes called the consanguine family) consists of the basic nuclear family unit together with other relatives, such as grandparents, aunts and uncles, and cousins. All the members of the group do not have to live in the same residence for the group to be regarded as an extended family. The key requirement is that they form a close-knit unit for religious, social and economic purposes.

Where there are young children who are looked after primarily or solely by one parent this is known as a *single-parent family*. In most single-parent families the one parent is female. The term matrifocal family has been used to refer to female-headed families.

With the increase in the divorce rate and the tendency for people to remarry, another type of family unit has been identified. This is where parents who have had children with different partners may live together with their children, i.e. the family is composed of step-parents and step-children. The term *reconstituted family* has been used to characterise this type of family. Many sociologists regard the reconstituted family as a modified version of the nuclear family.

Functionalism and the family

Functions of the family

The theory which looks for a function in every aspect of social life has spent a lot of time listing and explaining the many functions of the family. Society has certain basic needs which must be provided if the structure is to continue to be stable. It needs a steady supply of new members, to continue its existence. These new members have to be initiated into the rights and wrongs, taboos and laws, norms and values – the culture – of their society. Whilst undergoing this long period of initiation, the would-be social beings need food, clothing and shelter. The family provides all

these things, and therefore it is seen as the 'natural' way to organise human life. The functionalists examine the ways in which family forms and structures meet the needs of society, and they go on to look at the relationship of the family 'organ' to the other organs in the organism of society. They find that the family way is the best possible way of meeting the basic needs of society, and that the relationship between the family and society is on the whole smooth and harmonious. The family 'feeds' the education system which provides workers who look after families. Relations between family members are also mainly positive, and the family form is said to provide well-balanced, socialised human beings who are in full agreement with the aims and goals of their society, and fully equipped to take their place within it. Functionalism has always been a 'pro-family' theory then, and the debate between the functionalists and the so-called 'anti-family' theories – Marxism, feminism and interactionism – is still going on.

Parsons' two basic functions of the family

Talcott Parsons' ideas about the role of the family in the socialisation process have been influential in the analysis of the family. His work, which mainly appeared in the 1950s, reflects the importance of the family in the functionalist view of society, the leading view at that time. He concentrates on what he calls the two 'basic, irreducible functions' of the family:

1 to reproduce and socialise children;
2 to maintain and stabilise adult personalities.

Parsons himself reflects the popular psychological thinking of the time in using a watered-down version of Freud's ideas to explain how the biological needs and desires of the individual must be formed and controlled to fit in with the moral requirements of society. Sex was central in Freud's theory of individual development, and functionalists acknowledge its importance – where would society be without it? However, the sex drive is powerful and needs to be controlled, social approval is given only to expressions of sexuality between the 'right' people (male and female) in the 'right' place (bedroom) and at the 'right' time. Society makes rules first and foremost about sexuality, and parents have to instil these rules into the personalities of the children they reproduce.

Socialisation

The values of society have to be internalised, and Parsons uses his 'do it yourself' psychoanalysis to explain the process of 'internalisation'. Socialisation is a process – a sequence of stages which have to be passed through. Primary socialisation takes place within the family, and is therefore of great importance. Parsons uses a ladder metaphor to explain the progress of the individual through the stages of socialisation. When you climb a ladder, you always keep one foot on the rung below as you progress to the next rung. Each stage of socialisation is linked, and the connections lead you all the way up to society. Parsons sees society as a set of systems and subsystems. The family exists as a subsystem of society. Relationships within the family such as mother/child, father/child, mother/father are also subsystems. All these subsystems lock together, and make it possible for the culture of society to enter into the family through the adult roles, and, from the adults acting out their roles, into the children. Parsons' sociological works are littered with boxes which are split up into four smaller boxes, with smaller boxes being further divided. His family box considers the roles of men, women and children in society and in the family.

Gender role development

The family can be divided in terms of roles, the leading/following roles which always emerge in small groups, and the instrumental/expressive roles (see *Figure 5.1*). The instrumental role is active, it is concerned with ideas and goal attainment which are external activities taking place in the outside world. The expressive role is one of custodian and caregiver, and it is concerned with internally directed activities. The adult male is instrumental and leads his male offspring in this arena, for example teaching him to hunt, taking him to football matches or teaching him to drive. The adult female is expressive and leads her daughter in this field, teaching her to give care, cook and clean, gather berries or go to the supermarket. The family system, then, functions for society, and gender roles are reproduced within the family.

Figure 5.1 Parsons' model of family roles

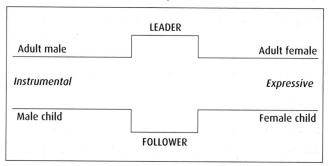

Internalisation

Internal voices of moral authority are a product of culture. Freud claimed that psychological and sexual development were one and the same. Parsons himself spends time analysing the psycho-sexual development of the individual. He sees socialisation as a two-sided process, on one side the individual, and on the other side the culture of society. Culture must get into the individual in some way, but it is not something which just sits on top of what is already there. It must actually become the personality of the individual, it must inform and shape that person. Moral judgements, senses of right and wrong, must become the framework on which the individual is constructed. The individual grows up to look at the world and to deal with other members of society on the basis of these moral roles. If he or she goes against this morality then it feels wrong, they feel uncomfortable, aware of a sense of wrong-doing. They feel guilty. In order to experience this guilt, the morals of society must be so deeply ingrained that the person does not know they are there. They are simply part of that person. How does this internalisation of the voice of society take place?

Development of adult personalities

The Freudian model, which Parsons borrows from selectively, sees this process of socialisation as a set of stages in which conflict must be resolved; for example, the conflict between the base and instinctive desires of the individual (the urge to rape and/or kill others) and the social and moral requirements of society. For Freud the conflicts are never resolved, just more or less successfully repressed. Parsons, however, makes little mention of any conflict in this process and has been criticised for giving us a picture of passive, conformist and 'over-socialised' individuals. The parental voice is successfully internalised when the child comes to recognise the authority and leadership of the 'instrumental' father figure. Any actions which the individual is then tempted to perform will be considered in terms of consequence – what would the father say if I did such and such? The voice of reprimand and discipline, which used to be external when the child was small, has been internalised and the child becomes the regulator of its own behaviour. Therefore, well-balanced adult personalities emerge from the 'child factory' and take up their places in society. However, the problem does not always run as smoothly as this.

Parsons acknowledges that there may be difficulties. Deviant parenting could lead to conflict. If the socialising agents do not balance out their role they could overdo the nurturing, expressive role, ultimately leading to incest. The taboo against incest functions to prevent this though, and on the whole there is little conflict. Strain may be experienced whilst undergoing socialisation, but the male child has more problems than the female as he has first to struggle free of the mother/child subsystem, then to get out of the whole family system itself (escaping into another family). He then becomes the instrumental leader in his own family, having internalised the moral structure of society. The analysis of adult sex roles in Parsons' theories of the family has received a lot of criticism.

Maintenance of adult personalities

Family roles are enshrined outside the individual, within society. These duties and obligations have been internalised, and anyone who goes against them will feel the vengeance of moral conscience, through guilt. Adult roles, then, entail working through one's daily duties and responding to the pressures of the world. This activity is a strain, and possible conflict is avoided because the family performs the second of Parsons' basic functions – the maintenance and stabilisation of adult personalities. The family home is a haven where the pressures of the outside can be escaped. The parents can indulge in childish behaviour through the children, for example, by playing with their toys. They can recharge their batteries and relax in a harmonious environment, free from the strains and stresses of everyday life. This appears to be a function which services males, for the female rarely escapes her place of work to 'recharge'. There is also a naive ignorance of family strain and conflict. Parsons is also criticised because he seems to have based most of his ideas upon middle-class American families, taking no account of culture, class or other factors. Many of his ideas are based upon the research of a fellow functionalist, George Murdock.

The family defined

George Murdock is famous in sociology because he gave a definition of the family which has been memorised by sociology students for exam purposes ever since. According to Murdock, the family is 'a social group characterised by common residence, economic co-operation and reproduction. It includes adults of both sexes, at least two of whom maintain a socially approved sexual relationship, and one or more children, own or adopted, of the sexually co-habiting adults.' Murdock is also famous for the piece of research upon which he bases this definition, as he claims to have found this family in one form or another, in every society he looked at – over 250 in all. This study – *Social Structure* (1949) – gives functionalists a good basis for their claim that the family is a 'universal' form, in other words it exists all over this planet. The societies that Murdock studied range from the simplest to the most complex. Some cultural groups still live in nomadic hunter–gatherer bands, and these give Murdock his historical ideas about sex roles: men hunt, women gather.

The hunter–gatherer bands move from place to place, building temporary shelters (a man's job requiring physical strength) and clearing trees and planting crops (women's work requiring small fingers). The men then go out to hunt (an aggressive, fast, brutal business) whilst the women stay at home making curtains out of bamboo leaves and looking after the children. They need to be at home with the young babies, and therefore they provide the caring, 'expressive', emotional role. These roles have survived into the larger, more complex industrial societies which Murdock looks at, noting that men are involved in economic production, politics and fighting wars, and women are still putting up curtains. The nuclear unit is still the dominant way of organising family life – why?

Sex and reproduction

According to Murdock, the nuclear unit is the best way of getting what you need. Sex needs are provided for. Note the definition of the family – 'at least two of whom maintain a socially approved sexual relationship'. The socially approved bit depends upon the norms and values of the society in question. The family provides an outlet for sexual needs. Reproduction is another necessity for which the family provides. The human infant relies upon its parents for a longer period than any other animal – there are no cultures (as yet) where you have to go off and build your own house as soon as you have learned to walk. The child needs a safe place to grow, and the family is there.

Economic and educational functions

Economic co-operation means working together to produce the materials of life – food, shelter, etc. If you have a 'common residence' someone has to pay the rent. So families work together. The last family function outlined by Murdock is what he calls 'education', i.e. socialisation of children. As these functions – sexual, reproductive, economic and educational – are performed so well in the nuclear family form described by Murdock, it would seem to be the best possible form. It 'fits' the needs of society and of individuals. He identifies this structure in all societies, sometimes surrounded by an outer ring of extended family, and sometimes isolated – the nucleus itself. According to this view, male and female roles are dictated by biology, and again their apparent 'universality' proves that they are 'natural'. Although Parsons and others have based their views of the family and sex roles on Murdock's study, ever since the voices of Marxism and feminism began to be heard in sociological circles, they have been severely criticised.

Criticisms of Murdock

The main criticism of Murdock is that of bias. Murdock is a Western male, and as such has been socialised into a culture which only admits the existence of the 'one man, one woman, two children, good sex and lots of happiness family model'. He sees what he has been taught to see, and this is because he applies his male, Western eyes to the groups he is 'studying'. Critics point out that his definition is too narrow and limiting, and many 'family' structures cannot be included. The gender role argument is challenged, as critics offer up examples of women who build, hunt and fight, and men who shop, gossip and bicker over vegetables. Even some of the groups studied by Murdock show a lack of traditional gender roles. This debate has developed into a sociological analysis of the family from perspectives which are in opposition to most of the functionalist ideas. This sociology, far from seeing the family as a positive and valuable institution, sees it as confining, restrictive and harmful to the individual and society.

In particular, it is claimed that the family is not always the warm, loving institution painted by functionalists. The nuclear family is so small that it turns members in on themselves. If the family is functional, it is more functional for men than it is for women. Moreover, socialisation within the family is sometimes crippling for the personality of the child. The set of roles that make up the family can be the arena for conflict rather than harmony.

The New Right

The New Right is a rather loose term that is used to characterise the views of a number of contemporary right-wing politicians and critics. Although it is not a sociological perspective as such, the New Right shares many of the assumptions about the family that are characteristic of functionalist theory. In particular, it sees the nuclear family as a key institution that carries out vital functions for the individual and society.

However, New Right thinkers are concerned by what they see as a recent demise in the influence and role of the family in modern industrial societies. They cite as evidence of this decline the increase in the divorce rate and the number of single-parent families, and they link these trends to what they believe is a general decrease in parental guidance and control of children.

For the New Right, the so-called 'breakdown' in family life is identified as contributing to the increase in such social problems as crime, homelessness, poverty, and lack of respect for authority. Lack of parental control and guidance is seen in this perspective to lie behind many contemporary social problems, such as drug abuse and juvenile delinquency. It is also claimed that more people – mothers and children – have become dependent on **State** benefits due to the increase in the divorce rate and declining respect for the values of family life based on monogamous marriage between a man and a woman.

The New Right has supported a number of policies designed to support the nuclear family structure and halt what they see as the decline in moral values associated with the family and marriage. In the UK the controversial Child Support Agency (CSA) was introduced by the Conservative government in the 1980s with the aim of ensuring that so-called 'absent parents' contribute an appropriate amount financially to the upkeep of their children. Many New Right thinkers have expressed support for the CSA, seeing it as a way of reducing the costs to the State of supporting single-parent families and encouraging a more responsible attitude to parenting.

Questions

1 What are the 'functions of the family'?
2 What are 'expressive' and 'instrumental' roles?
3 How does the family develop and maintain balanced adult personalities?
4 What is Murdock's view of the family and what criticisms have been made of it?

Alternatives to the family

Functionalists assumed that the nuclear family was a universal institution, i.e. one that could be found in all societies, because it fulfilled indispensable functions. However, there are alternatives to the nuclear family, and we shall now look at a few of these.

The Oneida community

John Noyes founded this community in Vermont in 1846. At its height it had 300 members. Noyes preached perfectionism in life on earth and saw **monogamous** marriage and private property as barriers to the unselfishness required for fulfilment of the perfectionist doctrine. He introduced a system of 'complex marriage' based on the assumption that all men should love all women. Only persons approved by a central committee were entitled to become parents. Children were reared apart from 'parents' in a separate part of the community.

The community prospered financially but encountered resistance from the wider society. Outsiders ridiculed children of the community and there were rumours of impending legal prosecution of the adults. Some of the children failed to accept completely the teachings of the community. By 1880 the community had broken up.

The Nayar

Kathleen Gough (1959) provided a detailed description of the Nayar tribespeople of India. She showed that they have little concept of marriage, as we know it. Although most girls go through a ritual marriage to signify social maturity, the bridegroom is not required to have contact with his wife after the ceremony. Sexuality is free among the people and when a girl falls pregnant, she is the responsibility of the menfolk of her own people – her father and brothers. The 'bond' then is between mother and child and brother or nearest male relative as protector. This arrangement developed out of the fact that all Nayar males were soldiers and were thus frequently away from home and could not be active husbands.

The Ashanti of Ghana, whilst they have marriage and 'permanent' wives, do not cohabit. A family of some kind exists but not a nuclear family.

In terms of Murdock's definition of the family, no family exists in Nayar society or among the Ashanti, since those who maintained 'a sexually approved adult relationship' did not live together and co-operate economically. This means that either Murdock's definition of the family is too narrow, or the family is not universal.

Matrifocal families

Murdock's definition of the family includes at least one adult of each sex. However, both today and in the past, some children have been raised in households that do not contain adults of both sexes. In the majority of cases women have headed these families. Families that consisted of mother and dependent children were widely found in the slave plantation areas of the southern states of the USA. There is some dispute about their origins but it has been suggested that marital unions of slaves were not of long duration and women had full responsibility for bringing up children. When slavery was abolished the pattern remained and black families in other parts of the USA retain similar characteristics. The percentage of matrifocal families is also high in parts of Central America and the Caribbean. Some sociologists view matrifocal families as resulting from desertion by the husband because he has insufficient funds to play the role of father and breadwinner. Others accept that poverty is the basic cause of female-headed families, but add that to some extent they have become an expected and accepted alternative to the nuclear family in the subculture of the poor.

The Israeli kibbutz

A kibbutz is an agricultural collective in Israel, the main features of which include collective ownership of all property, equality between the sexes and communal child-rearing. There are several hundred kibbutz settlements and they range in size from 200 to 2,000 in each community. All adults work and no form of work is supposed to be better than any other. Children are usually brought up communally in the 'children's house' by child minders known as metapelets. The parents visit their children perhaps once a week for what is called the 'hour of love'. The children are seen as belonging to the kibbutz as a whole. The individual couple work for the commune rather than to retain their integrity as a nuclear family.

Marxism, feminism and the family

The main statement of the Marxist position on the family comes not from Marx but from his lifelong friend Friedrich Engels (1884). Engels' study of the family was written to contribute to a contemporary debate on the social position of women in the late nineteenth century, and to enlarge on Marx's theory of **historical materialism** (see chapter 1).

Women and children as private property

On publication, it immediately caused controversy across Europe and the debate about whether Engels was working along the right lines or not has yet to die down. Engels traced the history of the family as a social unit back to when he believed it emerged, at approximately the point where hunters and gatherers became farmers, when concepts of private property became distinct. Without saying why it applied exclusively to men, Engels argued that at this point in history men needed ways of knowing what was theirs; they made women and children part of their private property through the institution of the family, and secured for their own children the right of inheritance of their property.

Abolition of the family

It follows for Engels that if private property and the family emerged at the same time, then there will be no place in a society without private property for the traditional family structure which, Engels argued, exploits women in the **capitalist** era. 'Within the family', Engels wrote, the man 'is the bourgeois, and the wife represents the proletariat.' In other words, the set-up of the family, with the man having all the economic and legal power, is effectively a trap for women. But Engels believed that this is not necessarily a fixed position for women, and that 'the first condition for the liberation of the wife is to bring the whole female sex back into public industry … this in turn demands that the characteristic of the monogamous family as the economic unit of society be abolished.' For women to be truly free, they must have a way of securing their own livelihood, and the implication of this is that the family as we know it must disappear.

In the hundred years since it was written, Engels' text has been continuously influential, particularly in what was known as the 'communist bloc', where his ideas became part of State policy. In the Soviet Union in the 1920s, for example, serious attempts were made by the infant Soviet government to abolish the family as a **bourgeois** institution, and bring domestic work into social production. For the Russian revolutionary Alexandra Kollontai (1872–1952) this would come about by making all labour paid labour, replacing domestic work with communal kitchens, canteens and laundries. As Kollontai (1977) claimed,

'The individual household is dying. It is giving way in our society to collective housekeeping. Instead of the working woman cleaning her flat, the communist society can arrange for men and women whose job it is to go round in the morning cleaning rooms.' At the same time, married women were given the right not to live with their husbands if they chose not to, or not to move with them if they changed jobs. Marriage was secularised and children born to single women were given the same rights as those of married women. These reforms were reversed under the Stalinist dictatorship of the 1930s.

For feminists, Engels has been equally influential, and many feminists, for example Rosalind Delmar (1976), have found it worthwhile to consider his ideas and recognise that, in the first place, he 'asserted women's oppression as a problem of history, rather than of biology'.

> **FRIEDRICH ENGELS (1820–95)**
>
> A journalist, social historian and businessman, he is best known as the friend and financial supporter of Marx. He wrote on the condition of the working class and the family, as well as editing the third volume of *Capital* after the death of Marx in 1883.

The origins of patriarchy

But there are also serious flaws which feminists see in Engels' work. As with many other male writers, his view that women's situation will improve by becoming waged workers is seen as simplistic. He naively suggests that all the familiar aspects of a **patriarchal** society, such as the unequal distribution of power and wages within the world of work (see chapter 3) and men's attitude to women, would automatically improve if the nuclear family was replaced by a different form of economic organisation. It could be argued that patriarchy originates from men's sexuality instead. Then the problem facing women would not be the family itself but men.

Meeting the needs of capitalism

From a Marxist-feminist point of view, the exploitation of women in the family serves the interests of a capitalist economy. After all, they point out, women reproduce and service the next labour force (their children) for free, they also service the existing labour force (their husbands) without any extra cost to the bourgeoisie, and when they themselves go out into the world of paid work, they do it for less than men! It follows that it would require a different economic system to liberate women. As well as examining how the family under capitalism benefits the capitalist class, Michele Barrett and Mary McIntosh (1982) also point out that the way in which the family excludes non-family members at the same time as maintaining the conviction that life within the family is the most correct and appropriate way to live leads to other forms being seen as abnormal or even **deviant**. The consequence of this **ideological** belief, they argue, is that many people are misguided in their belief that the family is the only appropriate structure in which to live.

Non-Marxist feminists do not believe that women would necessarily be free in a different economic system. It is not capitalism as such, and the way that the family is structured under capitalism that oppresses women, but men and patriarchy.

Alternatives to the housewife-mother role

From this perspective, it is a mistake to see the problem for women originating in capitalism, and to wait for a post-revolutionary solution. The problem of women's built-in subordination in the family has to be tackled now. This realisation leads to a number of feminist positions on the family, all attempting to challenge women's housewife-mother role fundamentally. There have been many suggestions about how to abolish the housewife-mother role and thus the family as it currently stands, and the belief is that this would lead to the end of **gender**-role socialisation in the family. One idea is to move towards gay-parenting where parents would be either homosexual or lesbian. Other ideas include: conceiving and gestating babies outside the womb; collective child-rearing on the lines of communes and kibbutzim; and professional parenting, where after being born children are handed over to 'professional parents'. Some would say that middle-class parents, by using nannies and boarding schools, have been following such a practice for a very long time.

Male domination in the family

The central place that the family has occupied in feminist thought means that it is an area they continuously return to, as the title of the book *What is to be Done about the Family?* (1983) makes obvious. In her introduction to this collection of essays, Lynne Segal makes it clear what contemporary feminists have to say about the anti-family movement of the 1960s: 'Missing from the 1960s critique of the family and sexual repression was any real awareness or analysis of the male domination integral to existing family arrangements, and of a heterosexuality in which women have been seen as sex objects for men.' In considering the capitalism/patriarchy debate, she comments that 'The isolation of housework and the alienation of paid work become conflicts felt not only between different family members, but experienced every day within the life of each working woman. The needs of capitalism itself then interfere with the family ideal, partially undermining male authority and separating family members from each other both physically and emotionally, just as its demands for a mobile workforce have broken up wider family and community networks of support and friendship.' She continues: 'We know that until men's attitudes to domestic work change – and trade unions make the links between work and home, demanding working conditions adjusted to domestic needs to enable men and women each to participate fully in both spheres – then male privilege at home and work remains unchallenged.' Like Barrett and McIntosh, she argues that 'family ideology needs to change, so that "the family" no longer suggests the married heterosexual couple with children, dependent on a male wage, but instead a variety of possible family forms'.

She concludes by arguing that a social structure 'where men and society generally assume responsibility with women for child-care, domestic life and the care of all dependent people, could move towards solving many of our "family" problems'.

The family and ideology

Influenced by **post-modernist** theory, Linda Nicholson (1997) argues that there is a powerful ideology that gives support to certain types of family while devaluing other types. The nuclear family is lauded; single-parent families are demonised and regarded as a threat to the 'traditional' family.

Cheshire Calhoun (1997) takes this idea further by suggesting that sexual orientation can be an important source of oppression and that family ideology contributes to that oppression. In particular, she notes how gays and lesbians have traditionally been regarded as 'family outlaws'. Homosexuals have been oppressed and denied equal status with heterosexuals in many areas, in part because they are seen as a threat to 'family life'. However, Calhoun believes that lesbian marriage and mothering can avoid the exploitation of

Men have responded in a variety of ways to the challenge of feminism.

women and children by men that she sees as typical of the family based on heterosexual marriage. Indeed, lesbian partners may be able to develop forms of marriage and family life that can provide an example of how to create egalitarian domestic relationships.

Questions

1 What does it mean to say that women's oppression is a problem of history and not of biology? Why should feminists find this of interest?

2 What do Marxist-feminists mean when they argue that the family meets the needs of capitalism?

3 What is meant by patriarchy? When did it originate?

4 Why does Segal believe it is necessary to break down the barrier between the domestic sphere and the world of employment?

The family and conflict

In its examination of society, sociology is willing to borrow from other disciplines. Psychology and anthropology (in-depth cultural studies) have both offered explanations of family life which concentrate on its internal workings rather than upon its relationship with the social structure. It is stretching a point to label them 'interactionists' but this is how their views are often presented. Unlike Marxism, which analyses conflict within the family from a structural point of view, these theories explain conflict and tension in the family as a result of psychological tensions between individuals. Rows and fights arise because of warring selves and the stifling emotional atmosphere of 'home bitter home'.

Edmund Leach

The anthropological contribution comes from Edmund Leach, a professor of social anthropology at Cambridge University who argues that 'Far from being the basis of the good society, the family, with its narrow and tawdry secrets, is the source of all our discontents' (Reith Lecture, 1967). Leach was lecturing on the nature of violence in society, and his point was that the family had become a strong, inward-looking unit, which narrowed and restricted individual expression and built up barriers against the world 'outside'. Family life is on the one hand very intimate. Parents and children are forced to spend more time together in modern society because hours of work are shorter, holidays longer and labour-saving devices cut down time spent on housework. Now everyone can sit arguing around the TV, or more likely sit in front of TVs in separate rooms. The parents' class and other prejudices are passed on, and this causes more barriers against society. Leach's comments created a lot of fuss amongst academics, leaders of public opinion and the media. It helped to generate the anti-family thinking which attacked the happy functionalist picture.

The Leach–Fletcher debate

The functionalist Ronald Fletcher (1988) criticises the critics. He is sufficiently angered by Leach's phrase, 'it is the source of all our discontents', to give it as the title of his chapter on Leach. He criticises the lack of **empirical** evidence and says that Leach was being 'provocative' and 'sensational'. Most of Fletcher's criticism is based on the continued existence of the family as proof that it is a good thing. It is a haven, and all the emotional tension exists in the outside world. If it was not a wonderful

institution, people would not keep choosing it. Women particularly yearn for it, and this had proved the feminists wrong as well. Fletcher goes back to the same old functionalist assumptions and ignores the strong hold that the ideology of the monogamous conjugal bond of the family has in society. Leach was pointing out that the family had possibly become too intimate, to the point of suffocation, and that perhaps alternative ways of living could be attempted. In the hippy spirit of the late sixties he advocated some form of commune based perhaps on the kibbutz. However, these alternatives have not been altogether successful perhaps because of the power of prior socialisation. People could not bring themselves to share everything equally because greed and selfishness are passed on as part of the norms and values of society.

Herbert Marcuse (1964) developed an analysis of the family from within the perspective of **critical theory**. He claimed that **alienation** at work leads to a search for fulfilment outside work. Capitalist-controlled family life, associated with products of industry, creates false needs. This myth produces the obedient, motivated worker and the receptive consumer that capitalism requires, making the family man ideal material for exploitation. Marcuse noted that the contradictions of capitalism are becoming apparent in the family: for example, the rising divorce rate and extra-marital infidelity.

Critical theory is also associated with a view of the family that sees it as having authoritarian characteristics exemplified by the patriarchal power of the father figure. Adorno (1950) argued that the family with its authoritarian ideology is designed to teach passivity, not rebellion. The result is that children learn to submit to parental authority and this makes them ready to accept their place in the hierarchy of power and control in capitalist society.

There has been a fusion between the ideas of some neo-Marxists and some radical psychologists. The work of the anti-psychiatrists (so called because they disagree with conventional psychiatry) calls into question the value of the family for the individual. They see the family as providing a constant assault on the 'self'. Their work tends to focus on 'abnormal families' and is particularly concerned with the development of mental illness.

R. D. Laing

In *Sanity, Madness and the Family* (1970) Ronald Laing and a colleague Esterson explain their ideas about the role of the family in causing psychological disturbance and schizophrenia. This is a condition stereotyped by many as 'split-personality' but there is a wide-ranging variety of behaviours which are called 'schizoid'. Nowadays, most psychologists accept the view that it is a biological and genetic disorder, although Laing's ideas on the role of the family in causing it still have some support. He claimed that the reasons for the bizarre behaviour which usually surfaces in the late teens were cultural, and the family and society were to blame. 'The experience and behaviour that gets labelled "schizophrenic", is a special strategy that a person invents in order to live in an unliveable situation.'

> **R. D. LAING (1927–89)**
>
> Psychiatrist and psychoanalyst who became one of the best-known critics of psychiatry in the 1960s. A major theme of his work has been to look at the effect of others on the actions of individuals; this led him to look at the way labels, like mental illness, could be applied to people.

The murdered self

According to Laing, the individual self, present at birth, has to be suppressed and controlled. The child learns to repress its real self and present one that its parents approve of. This then becomes the person, and the real self is 'murdered'. Parents, having killed off the real child, then proceed to subject the model child to an emotional network based on guilt and fear. Parents are not to blame for this, as they are functioning in a sort of zombie trance, their real selves having been murdered years ago. The child may accept the hypocrisy and madness that passes for society, and the functionalists would probably call this a successful internalisation of norms and values. Some, however, cannot keep their real self down, and it begins to emerge and disturb the false harmony. The individual then cannot cope, and schizoid behaviour becomes a release. The more extreme the parental response, the worse things get. In these cases there is often a history of incest, abuse or extreme conflict, and it is these 'environmental stressors' which provoke the so-called breakdown. Laing maintained that it was more of a 'rebirth' of the true self than a breakdown, and critics claimed that he encouraged patients to celebrate their madness and indulge in it as a release.

The family causes 'madness'

The label given to Laing's ideas, 'anti-psychiatry', came about because he was convinced that the usual treatments for schizophrenia – giving schizophrenics electric convulsions, filling them up with drugs, putting them into a strait-jacket – could not help when the problem was in the family relationships. His methods of treatment entailed talking about what was happening. If the walls shrink away when you touch them and the chairs scream when you sit down on them, it may be something to do with the fact that your father has been raping you since you were thirteen. In this case, Laing's patient was encouraged to leave home and learn judo, and not meet her father again until she could defend herself. By placing the blame for schizophrenia and many other illnesses and unhappinesses upon the family, Laing created a social and sociological controversy.

Cooper

David Cooper (1972) takes Laing's theories a step further and uses a more Marxist perspective. The reason for all the tension and guilt is to be found in the contradictions of capitalism. His own studies as a psychiatrist had shown him that the family is an ideological conditioning device. It 'reinforces the effective power of the ruling class in any exploitative society by providing a highly controllable paradigmatic form for every social institution. So we find the family form replicated through the social structures of the factory, the union branch, the school (primary and secondary), the business corporation, the church, political parties and government apparatus, the armed forces and general and mental hospitals.' The abolition of the family will be part of any destruction of capitalist social relations.

The radical nature of these ideas, the underlying Marxist view and the sensation they caused in the 1960s and 1970s have led to much discussion and even a film based on the case studies. They have also attracted much criticism within sociology, particularly from the functionalists. Ronald Fletcher's main criticism as before is: How can you make generalised statements about all families when you have only studied a few, highly abnormal ones?

Criticisms of Cooper and Laing

Fletcher agreed with Cooper and Laing that 1 per cent of the population is likely to be diagnosed as schizophrenic. But Fletcher saw this as a small proportion, and said that the 99 per cent who are not diagnosed must come from 'normal' families. Why have there been no studies of normal families?

Lack of scientific objectivity

Fletcher then criticises the ideological basis which underlies the ideas and leads Cooper and Laing to call for the 'abolition' of the family. The 'mish-mash' of philosophy, psychiatry, religion and revolution, particularly as used by Cooper, makes him the extremest of the extreme in Fletcher's eyes, as this sentence reveals: 'It is hard to believe that anyone could have taken *The Death of the Family* seriously.' There is no science or objectivity in any of Laing, Cooper and Esterson's work, and the jargon of revolutionary ideology does not cover up this weakness. Fletcher rounds off his criticism by sniggering at the dedications in *Sanity, Madness and the Family*, *The Divided Self* and *The Death of the Family*: 'To our parents, children, brothers and sisters'.

Concentrating on such trivialities is amusing and highlights the back-biting that lurks underneath the so-called academic objectivity of the family of sociologists, but Fletcher again fails to give any new criticisms or even to explore old ones. The most telling point is when he discusses Laing's claim that 'normality' is actually insanity, and vice versa. It would seem that Laing advocates madness, yet he has a job whose aim is to cure it. Fletcher misses the point. Curing madness for Laing meant dealing with the ills and inequalities of society. For functionalists, this is a non-starter, because society is a lovely place, and families make it that way!

As the publication of Fletcher's book shows, the 'anti-family' views have now fallen out of fashion, and family psychiatry has moved on from the days of Laing and Cooper. It is still the case that most people experience family life, that the family (single or dual parent) is still seen as the most desirable way to bring up children, and very few, if any, signs are emerging that alternative forms to the family (such as collective child-rearing) are gaining popularity. The family may have changed its form and function but it is as much with us today as it ever has been.

Questions

1 What are the main points of Leach's view of the family?
2 How do the radical psychiatrists argue that the family can produce psychological disturbance?
3 What is the case for abolishing the family?

Industrialisation and the changing structure of the family

For at least the first half of the twentieth century, it was universally assumed that there was a clear pattern in the relationship between industrialisation and the changing structure of the family. This assumed that in a pre-industrial society, the extended family (with three generations) was typical, and under the pressure of the move to the factories and the city, the family shrank to become nuclear (or two generations). Such a belief is explicitly stated in Burgess and Locke's standard text of 1945, *The Family*. Sociologists built theories to explain how the two-generation family came to be typical. Two examples of this are William Goode (1963) and Talcott Parsons (1959a).

The industrialisation debate – Parsons

The essence of Parsons' argument is as follows. In the family, an individual's status is ascribed – the role they play in the family is not of their own choosing, it is given to them. If you are a son or a daughter, there is nothing you can do about it. You will always be a son or daughter. In a pre-industrial society, where **social mobility** was highly restricted, social status was similarly ascribed. If you were born into a serf family, then the probability was that you would die a serf. In all areas of life, your status was ascribed, or given to you.

Role conflict

Industrialisation brought about huge and important changes among which, according to Parsons, the increasing social and geographical mobility of the population was central. Social **status** was no longer ascribed but achieved. Individuals, not through birthright but their own abilities, could move up and down the social structure. (Whether there is any hard evidence for this is considered in chapter 3.) Conflicts began to appear in the extended family structure, where upwardly mobile children began to challenge the **authority** of their parents, especially if they had more influential jobs – what Parsons calls role conflict. The conflict between private and ascribed (**particularistic values**) and publicly achieved status (**universalistic values**) inevitably produces the nuclear family, whose two-generational structure prevents role conflict. Furthermore, the 'isolated nuclear family' (a phrase greatly associated with Parsons' work) continues to specialise as a social agency as it undergoes a process of 'structural differentiation', whereby the traditional roles within the family become taken up by outside agencies such as the workplace, schools, hospitals, social workers, police and so on.

Anderson

The accounts by Parsons and others of the way that the extended family of a pre-industrial society became the nuclear family of a developed industrial society provide a very clear, neat and logical way of demonstrating how functionalist sociology works. This type of account dominated the way that sociologists looked at the family in the middle of the twentieth century. As Michael Anderson (1980) writes: 'We now know, of course, that the fundamental proposition [which sees the] family form and process as a functional consequence of the demands of industrial society ... is hopelessly over-simple ... Indeed, it is a special irony that at least some forms of early industrialisation in Britain actually increase people's dependence on kin (and even their ability to live with them and near them) to a level unknown for hundreds of years (at least) before.' His argument is reinforced by Chris Harris (in Anderson, 1980): 'Industrialisation has no more transformed the family than colonialism disrupted the segmentary kinship system of some peoples. One does not have to be a Marxist, merely historically informed and conceptually competent, to recognise the whole debate about industrialisation decomposing the extended family to be the empirical and philosophical nonsense that it is.' It is empirical nonsense because there is no hard evidence to support this view of the transforming effect of industrialisation on family structure.

Laslett

In a seminal work a group of family historians, organised by Peter Laslett, presented evidence from across the industrial world which argued that: 'The wish to believe in the large and extended household as the ordinary institution of an earlier England and an earlier Europe, or as a standard feature of an earlier non-industrial world, is ... a matter of ideology' (Laslett, 1972). From 1970, he says, 'demographers generally had come to recognise that the nuclear family predominates numerically almost everywhere, even in underdeveloped parts of the world'.

Household sizes

For England, in particular, the evidence of the dominance of pre-industrial nuclear families seems conclusive, whether it is J. C. Russell (1948) finding an average household of 3.5 people in 1517 England, Hallam's (1961) figure of 4.68 per household in the late thirteenth century in South Lincolnshire or Laslett's own figure of 4.75 in the period 1600–1900 from which he concludes: 'In England ... the large joint or extended family seems never to have existed as a common form of the domestic group at any point in time covered by numerical records.' This is not to say that the extended family did not exist, or was insignificant, but that the nuclear family in everyday life is dominant through history and geography.

The British working-class family in the 1950s

Again, to the surprise of many sociologists, it was still possible to find close-knit kinship ties among working-class communities as late as the mid-1950s. Peter Willmott and Michael Young (1960) discovered what they described as 'a village in the middle of London. Established residents claimed to "know everyone". They could do so because most people were connected by kinship ties to a network of other families, and through them to a host of friends and acquaintances. Ties of blood and marriage were local ties.' In their study of East London (1957) they 'were surprised to discover that the wider family, far from having disappeared, was still very much alive in the middle of London.' The extended family survived in this community as a hangover from the industrial revolution. In research into other areas of East London, in the newer estates of Greenleigh and more middle-class Woodford, Willmott and Young found that the pattern of kinship had become looser (see *Table 5.1*).

Willmott and Young (1960) argue that localised 'extended families' – family groups spreading over two or more nearby houses – are the distinctive feature of kinship in the East End. In Woodford they are rare.

The symmetrical family

By the time of their third, and most wide-ranging, study of the family and kinship networks in the

Table 5.1 Proximity of parents – Woodford and Bethnal Green (%)

Parents' residence	Woodford	Bethnal Green
Same dwelling	9	12
Within five minutes' walk	7	29
Elsewhere in the same borough	15	13
Outside the same borough	69	46
Total %	100	100

Number studied: Woodford, 394; Bethnal Green, 369

London area, Willmott and Young (1973) perceived, like many other family sociologists, a pattern to the changing structure of the family before, during and after industrialisation. Synthesising all the available knowledge, they identify four characteristic phases in the development of the family:

Stage 1: the pre-industrial nuclear family (pre-1750)

Marrying late, with their own parents dying early, few families had surviving grandparents. Typically, families constituted their own economic unit of production.

Stage 2: the industrial extended family (1750–1900)

With families living in the city, more children survived, grandparents lived longer and the focus of production became the factory. The central family tie was between mother and daughter with, Willmott and Young claim, the father becoming pushed out of the home and into the public house. Remnants of this lived on in mid-1950s' Bethnal Green.

Stage 3: the modern nuclear family (from 1900)

This is the world of the family beyond Bethnal Green, of two generations per household, father not in the pub but at home (a process sociologists call privatisation) wallpapering or watching the TV and helping enough around the house for Willmott and Young to perceive a movement away from segregated and towards conjugal roles: men are 'more fully home-centred because they are less work-centred. They can more easily leave their work behind them when they leave the premises in which it is done ... Wives have been getting more involved in work, especially when in the kinds of job which have such a hold over men.'

The principle of stratified diffusion

Stage 4: the managing director family

This does not exist yet as a widespread social phenomenon, but is a projection made by the authors, based on trends they identify among the upper middle class. It is their belief – according to what they grandiosely name 'the principle of stratified diffusion' – that the lifestyle of the middle class today will be adopted by the working class tomorrow, as it becomes more affluent. Having become more home-centred in stage 3, the working-class worker will begin to become more work-centred, with work physically intruding into home life. With technology changing the nature of work, and under the impact of feminism, more and more women will be drawn out of the home and into the world of work. 'By the next century,' they write, 'society will have moved from (a) one demanding job for the wife and one for the husband, through (b) two demanding jobs for the wife and one for the husband to (c) two demanding jobs for the wife and two for the husband. The symmetry will be complete. Instead of two jobs there will be four.' It is this final assumption that the family division of labour will become **symmetrical** that feminists, and others, took exception to, though Willmott and Young are careful to say that, in adopting Gorer's (1971) term, they do not mean that there will be egalitarianism, or total equality, within marriage, merely symmetry.

Questions

1 How does Parsons believe that social change has influenced family structure?
2 Do Anderson and Laslett reach the same conclusions about family structure?
3 How similar is Willmott and Young's stage 3 family to the understanding you have of your own and others' family life?
4 Does 'the normal family' exist?

Diversity in family forms

Looking at the state of **kinship** patterns in modern industrial societies, sociologists have questioned whether there is a single type of family that is dominant. They point out that the nuclear family (mother, father and their children) no longer makes up a majority of households or families. Family patterns are now characterised by considerable diversity. Some of the elements in this diversity include:

→ There has been an increase in the number of reconstituted families, where one or both of the parents have remarried.
→ There has been an increase in the number of single-parent families.
→ Marriages in which both partners work, or in which the woman is the main earner, no longer face social stigma.
→ Economic prosperity and demographic change have both played their part in changing the pattern of households. In the UK, under 15 per cent of the elderly lived alone in 1951 but, with the mobility of the modern worker, some 60 per cent of pensioners now live on their own.
→ There continue to be differences between middle- and working-class families in terms of relationships between adults and the way children are socialised.

→ The family of husband, non-working wife and children is found in only 20 per cent of households.
→ There are differences in patterns of family relationships between groups with different ethnic origins and religious beliefs.

Other sociologists have noted that there is also regional diversity in patterns of family life. For example, inner-city areas have comparatively high concentrations of single-parent and ethnic minority families, while traditional rural areas have strong kinship networks.

The significance of family diversity

Rhona and Robert Rapoport (1976, 1989) recognise that there has always been some family diversity. However, they argue that until recently there was a widespread belief in the desirability of the 'conventional' family, i.e. the traditional nuclear family. People who lived in other types of household and family did so more from 'force of circumstances' than free choice. According to the Rapoports, this situation has now changed. The nuclear family is no longer regarded as an ideal that everyone should aspire to and more people are choosing to have different types of

family. They note that families in Britain today are in a transition from coping in a society in which there was a single overriding norm of what family life should be like to a society in which a plurality of norms are recognised as legitimate, indeed desirable.

People in modern societies today seem to be living very different kinds of family lives from each other and the differences seem to be increasing. Indeed, it may seem that the only uniform trend in the overall development of family patterns is the trend toward the recognition of diversity. In Britain in 2001 a wage-earning husband and a non-working wife at home with two dependent children accounted for a mere 8 per cent of all men in paid employment. This means that the traditional nuclear family is a statistical minority.

Janet Finch (1989) insists on the relevance of interactionist theory for understanding the increasing diversity of the family. To understand why people make different choices in family relationships it is necessary to interpret the meanings different individuals bestow on family life. Structural theories (functionalist, Marxist) have difficulty in explaining the diversity in family forms, Finch argues, because they look for a single, overarching explanation of the family.

Is there a typical family form in all societies throughout the world?

In response to these claims about family diversity, Robert Chester (1985) has argued that there is little evidence that people are choosing to live on a long-term basis in alternatives to the nuclear family. He points out that most adults still marry and have children. Moreover, most children are reared by their natural parents and most people live in a household headed by a married couple.

Chester recognises that there has been one major change in the family: women are increasingly taking paid employment and contributing to the family finances. He uses the term 'neo-conventional family' to refer to this new form of family where the wife works outside the home. It differs little from the conventional family, apart from the fact of wives having more involvement in the labour market.

Families and post-modernity

Post-modernists see the growing diversity of the family as evidence to support their view that attempts to provide universal accounts of social phenomena (e.g. Murdock's theory of the family) must be abandoned in favour of recognition of the **pluralism** and difference inherent in the constitution of human identities and in the construction of human knowledge. Judith Stacey (1996) considers that the post-modern family has emerged in contemporary societies such as the USA. She says that like post-modern culture, contemporary Western family arrangements are diverse, fluid, and unresolved. Families today mix together elements from the old and new to produce a wide range of hybrid forms of family life. She suggests that it no longer makes sense to discuss what type of family is dominant in contemporary societies because family forms have become too diverse. Moreover, there can be no assumption that any particular form will become accepted as the main, best, or normal type of family.

Although the New Right and some other commentators protest against the decline of the conventional, heterosexual nuclear family, diversity in family life is more likely to increase than to decrease. Social attitudes and social policies will have to adjust to this diversity if post-modern families are to have a good chance of facilitating fulfilling lives for their members.

Stacey accepts that the post-modern family gives rise to a certain amount of unsettling instability. Nevertheless, she generally welcomes it as an opportunity to develop more **egalitarian**, and more **democratic** family relationships. It is questionable, however, whether diversity and what Stacey terms

the post-modern family have really become that common. It is possible that she exaggerates the extent of change. Research conducted by O'Brien and Jones (1996) into working-class families and kinship in East London in the mid-1990s suggests rather more continuity in the family patterns than that found by Stacey in her studies of American families.

Such findings have led to a questioning of the assumption that conjugal roles are changing among the middle class, let alone the working class. Far from being a present reality, joint conjugal roles and the 'principle of stratified diffusion' are unlikely to be realised in the near future. One reason for Willmott and Young's optimism could be that their own ideas of joint roles did not mean equal roles. They described as 'symmetrical' families where 72 per cent of men studied helped their wife with something other than the washing-up more than once a week. This 'something' could include taking their sons out on a Saturday afternoon.

Power and labour in the family

Patriarchy

A patriarchal society is one where men hold the power – economic, social and political. Women are second-class citizens, discriminated against, dependent upon and dominated by men. These relationships are reflected in the family, and also reinforced and strengthened by what goes on in families. Marxist-feminism places this within the context of a capitalist society. Overthrow this and patriarchal power will disappear along with ruling-class power. There will be an equal division of labour in the home. Radical feminism does not agree, and sees patriarchy as separate from **class**. A radical restructuring of gender roles is necessary. The family structure would be the first to go. Liberal feminists believe that change is possible within capitalist society, and that helping women as individuals and as groups to become aware of their oppression will eventually lead to equality. Power and labour in the home form the basis of this analysis, and it picks up the debate about the changing family structure.

Shared conjugal roles

As we have seen, some sociologists, Willmott and Young in particular, have proposed that the family in modern society is becoming symmetrical, with both parents working inside and outside the home. Housework and childcare in these circumstances may be equally shared. The 'symmetrical family' and also the 'privatised' family of Goldthorpe and Lockwood, *The Affluent Worker* (see chapter 3), are very different to the 1950s family in Bethnal Green where the man was responsible for earning money and the woman for all household tasks.

Ann Oakley, a much quoted feminist, has produced one of the most influential studies of housework (1974a), which traces the role of women in families from pre-industrial times through to industrial societies. Far from leading to equal relationships, marriage and family duties turn women into unpaid slaves, whose productive output is unrewarded by wages and therefore not worthy of being referred to as 'work'.

A gender-neutral society?

The pre-industrial woman took a more active role in society, running parts of the agricultural production unit as well as working in the home. As industrialisation altered this pattern, men 'went out' to work and in latter-day industrialised society women had become almost totally isolated within the home. Society expects women to care for home and children, it is their responsibility. Willmott and Young are being much too optimistic about the growth of joint conjugal roles. They have responded to these criticisms from Oakley and others by saying that roles are more equal but women are still responsible for the home. Oakley is 'anti-family' and insists that a new society, gender-neutral, is needed before new family structures can evolve. She does not go into detail on this new world, which is a weakness in her analysis.

Elizabeth Bott (1957) coined the term 'joint conjugal roles' to share tasks inside it. 'Segregated' roles describes the situation when the man goes out to work and the woman stays at home to work. These are tied in with class, according to Bott. A working-class background gives a tight-knit kin and friendship group. Wife and husband know each other's family and friends, the network is not widely dispersed, all the friends know each other. The couple are forced by the norms of this tight network to conform to traditional ideas about marriage and duties. So the woman does the housework – if she did not, their female relatives and friends would criticise her. If her husband did the ironing, he would be laughed at outside the family. The loosely knit kin and friendship group of a middle-class couple means that there is less influence from any one group. The husband and wife concentrate on each other more, and may have

separate friendships and activities. They are then freer to change roles and share work at home, as there is no rigid value system or peer-group pressure. Joint conjugal roles are more likely here.

Many studies have criticised these ideas, pointing out that in middle-class, so-called 'dual career' families, it is still the woman who takes time off when the children are ill. The debate about power and labour in the home goes on. Some believe that women will attain equality in this area and have equal economic power in the home, taking decisions together with men. There are some indicators that this is already happening and that the rigid roles of the families found in Bethnal Green in the south of England, and in mining and fishing industries in the north of England, are a thing of the past. However, the 'new man' image which pervaded the 1990s may be an over-optimistic assessment of the progress of the women's liberation movement.

The 'new man' – myth or reality?

The sexism of sociology has been challenged, and the male-biased ideas of the likes of Willmott and Young have been much criticised. Women are still largely isolated in the home or in low-paid, often part-time work. Careers mean 'sacrificing' parenthood and family, but only for women. Conjugal role studies abound, and they still show that men's tasks around the home are generally restricted to gardening, maintenance and repairs, doing the dishes after one meal and taking out the rubbish. Everything else is done by women, and they are not paid. As many feminists have pointed out, society could not afford to pay at comparable rates for manual labour.

If the family, the cradle of society, is based upon such blatant exploitation, then it is no wonder that there is conflict, tension and strain within it. Sociologists are still arguing about the various solutions to these conflicts, and their arguments are based on their theoretical differences. The way you look at society influences the explanations you give for its various behaviours. The family is no exception, and the widely varying accounts of what families are all about reflects the theoretical differences involved.

Feminist criticism of the family is based on their understandings of the nature of patriarchal power. These power relationships are rooted in the traditional roles which society insists that men and women take up. Being given power in his own 'castle', the male uses it to dominate and suppress his family, especially the women. In this way, gender roles are reproduced,

HOW MUCH IS THIS JOB WORTH?

Position vacant: Housewife

Applications are invited for the position of manager of a lively team of four demanding individuals of differing needs and personalities. The successful applicant will be required to perform and co-ordinate the following functions: companion, counsellor, financial manager, buying officer, teacher, nurse, chef, nutritionist, decorator, cleaner, driver, child-care supervisor, social secretary and recreation officer.

Qualifications: Applicants must have unlimited drive and the strongest sense of responsibility if they are to succeed in this job. They must be independent, and self-motivated, and be able to work in isolation and without supervision. They must be skilled in the management of people of all ages. They must be able to work under stress, for long periods of time if necessary. They must have flexibility to perform a number of conflicting tasks at the one time without tiring. They must have the adaptability to handle all new developments in the life of the team, including emergencies and serious crises. They must be able to communicate on a range of issues with

people of all ages, including public servants, school teachers, doctors, dentists, tradespeople, business people, teenagers and children. They must be healthy, creative, active and outgoing to encourage the physical and social development of the team members. They must have imagination, sensitivity, warmth, love and understanding, since they are responsible for the mental and emotional well-being of the team.

Hours of work: All waking hours and a 24-hour shift when necessary.

Pay: No salary or wage. Allowances by arrangement, from time to time, with the income-earning member of the team. The successful applicant may be required to hold a second job, in addition to the one advertised here.

Benefits: No guaranteed holidays. No guaranteed sick leave, maternity leave or long service leave. No guaranteed life or accident insurance. No worker's compensation. No superannuation.

and women in homes throughout the land are restricted and repressed in all forms of social expression. There may have been a slight change in labour and power relationships within families in Britain since the Second World War, but the fundamental basis for male power is still intact. In 1991, English and Welsh law changed to make it illegal for a husband to rape his wife, 73 years after women got the vote. Why did it take so long? Women were fully enfranchised citizens, with political power and rights, except at home.

Following the publication of *The Symmetrical Family* in 1973, a number of empirical studies have found Willmott and Young's assumptions about joint conjugal roles lacking. Rapoport and Rapoport (1976), for example, found that in middle-class families where both partners worked, women's careers were still seen as subordinate to their partners', while domestic matters were chiefly seen as her responsibility.

Elston (1980) found that even in households where both partners were full-time doctors, women nevertheless did the great majority of the shopping and cooking, while men undertook most of the household repairs. Interestingly, in 71 per cent of these medical households it was the women who took time off work when their children were ill.

In a study of young mothers and fathers. Elsa Ferri and Kate Smith (1996) found that it was very rare for fathers to take primary responsibility for childcare. This was the case even when the woman had paid employment outside of the home and the man did not. Similar inequality was evident in other areas of housework. For example, two-thirds of working mothers in the survey said they were responsible for cooking and cleaning, and four out of five for laundry.

Carolyn Vogler (1994) studied 1,211 couples and compared their financial arrangements with those of their parents. She found that there had been an increase in the proportion of relationships where control over the finances was broadly shared between the sexes, from about 6 per cent to around 20 per cent. However, this still left a large percentage of relationships where significant inequality remained. Vogler concluded that the increased involvement of women in paid employment had not eradicated inequality in the control of family finances.

These conclusions are known not only to sociologists. In 1993 the market research group Mintel conducted interviews with 1,500 men and women about how domestic labour was shared out. Their conclusions were that 85 per cent of women living with a man said that they did all the laundry and

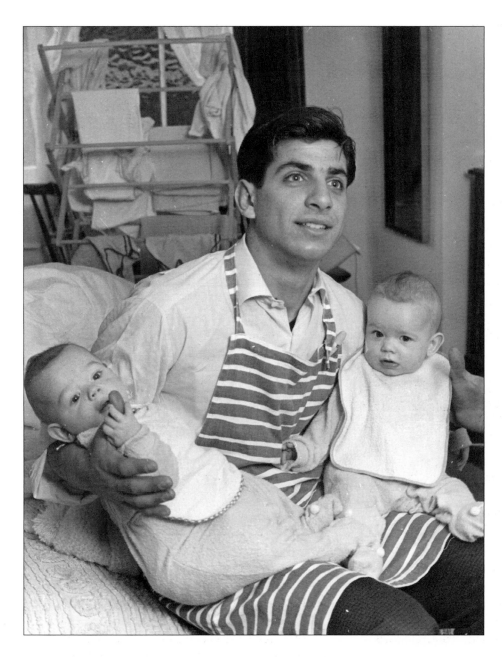

Househusband: myth or reality?

ironing and cooked the main meal. As many as 20 per cent of the women stated that their partner shared only one domestic task, and less than one in ten thought that their partner shared the cooking equally. Only one man in 100 shared domestic tasks equally.

When the wider question of power in the family is examined, a similar picture emerges. Dobash and Dobash (1980) reveal asymmetry in marriage by focusing on domestic violence. Using Scotland for their case study, they found that a quarter of all cases of violence brought to court concerned men assaulting their wives, although the fines they received were frequently lower than the average parking fine.

Questions

1 How does Ann Oakley believe the Industrial Revolution changed the position of women?
2 What does Elizabeth Bott believe is the relationship between social class and conjugal roles?
3 Is the 'new man' a myth?
4 Is the job advert for the housewife accurate?

The family and social policy

There is a tendency to think of the family and the State as two separate entities with little connection between them. The family is concerned with private life and personal relationships, while the State is part of the public domain. However, there is actually quite a close relationship between the two. Government policies in particular can have a major influence on the form of the family. This can be shown with reference to current social policies in Britain.

Payments from the State, such as **family credit**, **child benefit** and maternity allowance, make it easier for people to have children. When the family size in England fell in the 1930s a Royal Commission's findings recommended a family allowance for second children to help encourage a larger family. Soon after the fall in family size in the early 1970s, child benefit became available for each child, replacing the old allowance system. The State also lays down the laws that regulate the forms and conditions under which people marry, and also the procedures for divorce.

One of the reasons why average family size has fallen is that children are required to attend school until they are 16. This means that they are financially dependent on their parents so that many people cannot afford to have a large family. Children in the nineteenth century were more of an economic asset among the working class. State policies also influence whether or not sick and elderly people are looked after within the family. For example, mental health policy in the UK currently encourages people with mental illnesses to be looked after in the community, which in practice often means by family members.

Graham Allan (1985) has argued that some government policies assume that it is normal and desirable for people to adopt the nuclear family as the standard form of family life. Many benefit payments, for example, presuppose that wives are economically dependent on their husbands. The relative lack of government support for crèche and nursery school facilities also indicates the assumption that one family member will be available for children rather than work. Note, too, that schools are organised in such a way that it is difficult for adult members of families to combine full-time work with domestic responsibilities.

Sociological perspectives on the family–State relationship

Functionalists have examined the family–State relationship primarily in terms of whether or not increasing State intervention has led to some loss of functions for the family. MacIver (1955) claims that the State has taken over some non-essential functions that the family used to perform. However, Ronald Fletcher (1962, 1988) says that the State works in harmony with the family to satisfy individual and societal needs more effectively. Functionalists tend to play down the possibility that there might be any conflicts between the family and the State, or that the actions of the State may have different implications for different members of the family.

Marxists point out that in a capitalist system, one of the roles of the State is to ensure that there is sufficient provision for welfare – housing, health care, education, benefits for the needy, etc. – to prevent the build-up of revolutionary consciousness among the working class. However, the State must achieve this without spending so much money that it becomes a crippling burden on the profits of the capitalist class. The family is a useful mechanism that the State can use to deliver welfare provision at low cost. For example, the policy of caring for mentally ill patients in the community means that the State can close large hospitals which were very expensive to run and rely on patients being looked after by family members, who undertake the work with little or no payment from the State.

Marxists also view the family as an agency for ideological conditioning. Louis Althusser (1971) claims that the family, along with schools, the **mass media** and other public institutions, reproduces the attitudes essential for an efficient workforce under capitalism. Within the family, children learn to submit to authority and so emerge as preconditioned to accept the hierarchy of power and control in the capitalist workplace.

Feminists generally view the relationship between the family and the State as being a process of collaboration that directly or indirectly sustains the exploitation of women. Land (1976) has argued that the State upholds the traditional nuclear-based household with its basis in monogamous and heterosexual marriage, and the idea that there is a male wage-earner or head of household. The welfare system in Britain assumes that a woman will be supported by a husband and that she will have her working life interrupted by childbirth. Land concludes that the State, through the welfare system, is operating in the interests of a patriarchal system.

New Right theorists see the family as working best when it has full responsibility for its own affairs. The welfare system provided by the State is criticised for undermining the **autonomy** and self-reliance of the family. It encourages the poorer members of society in particular to become dependent on State benefits rather than pull together as a family in finding solutions to their predicament. There is less incentive for people to be committed to the family and therefore the chances of the family unit staying together are reduced.

As well as arguing for a reduction in the welfare system, New Right theorists believe that measures should be adopted to ensure that parents take full responsibility for their children and that the family becomes the major source of community care for the elderly and infirm. In response to these New Right views, a number of studies have shown that among poor families there is often a lot of support for the values of thrift and self-reliance. The problem is that the poor lack the legitimate means – such as decent jobs – to achieve these values, and so they are forced to depend on State benefits.

The family today

The typical family?

Advertisers love to portray the consumers of their products and services as happy couples with children, gleefully enjoying a new type of breakfast cereal or delighting in the joys of a washing powder that washes whiter than white. Sociologists of the family – particularly Marxists and functionalists – have also been accused of falling into the same trap of building a sociology of the family on the assumption that the typical household or dwelling contains a married couple with children, where the man goes out to work, his wife stays at home to bring up the children and they stay together for life. Statistical evidence gathered over the last 30 years paints an altogether different picture.

Lone-parent families

As *Table 5.2* shows, the long-term trend is towards a decline in the number of households containing married families with children (29 per cent in 2002

compared with 48 per cent in 1961), while the number of people living on their own, or in lone-parent families, is increasing (29 per cent in 2002 compared with 11 per cent in 1961; and 9 per cent in 2002 compared with 6 per cent in 1961, respectively).

When calculated as a percentage of all families with children (rather than by household), lone-parent families rise to 18 per cent in 2002 (compared to 8 per cent in 1971) of whom more than 94 per cent were headed by lone mothers, and less than 6 per cent were headed by lone fathers. The main reason for this increase is the number of women becoming lone mothers either through divorce or without ever marrying. The number of all lone fathers, by comparison, has stayed constant.

The above statistics have been variously interpreted by politicians and sociologists alike. For politicians of the New Right, the breakdown of the nuclear family and the rise of lone-parent families has momentous consequences for the rest of society, particularly as it is claimed that children of lone-mother families, deprived of fatherly help and guidance, are more likely to be brought up in poverty, fail at school, turn to crime and become social problems. With three-quarters of all lone mothers dependent on the State for their income, it has become a political priority for all parents to attempt to restore 'family values' and end a situation where fathers play a minimal and temporary role.

Marriage

Not only does it appear that the nuclear family is breaking down but, it has been claimed, so too is the institution of marriage. *Table 5.3* shows that, while there has not been a significant drop in the total number of marriages, the type of marriage has changed markedly with the declining number of first-time marriages being supplemented by the number of remarriages.

Table 5.2   Households by type, Great Britain (%), 1961–2002

	1961	1971	1981	1991	1993	2002
One-person households	11	18	22	27	27	29
Two or more unrelated adults	5	4	5	3	3	3
One-family households						
Married couple with no children	26	27	26	28	28	29
One to two dependent children	30	26	25	20	20	19
Three or more dependent children	8	9	6	5	5	4
Non-dependent children only	10	8	8	8	7	6
Lone parent with dependent or non-dependent children	6	7	9	10	10	9
Two or more families	3	1	1	1	1	1

Source: *Social Trends* 33, 2003

Table 5.3   Marriages by type, 1961–2000

United Kingdom	1961	1971	1981	1990	2000
			Thousands		
First marriage for both partners	340	369	263	241	180
First marriage for one partner only	36	54	74	75	57
Second marriage for both partners	21	36	61	60	69
Total marriages	397	459	398	376	306

Source: Office of Population Censuses and Surveys; General Register Office (Scotland) and *Social Trends*, 33, 2003

Divorce

Sociologists define divorce as the formal process that achieves the legal dissolution and ending of a marriage, so freeing the partners to marry again if they so desire. There has been a sharp increase in the rate of divorce in most modern industrial societies over the last fifty years or so. In the UK, this can be accounted for by the enforcement of the 1969 Divorce Law Reform Act in 1971 (1977 in Scotland). This made 'irretrievable breakdown' the sole criterion for divorce, and this could be shown if couples had lived apart for five years or more: the empty shell marriages had eventually cracked. For Ronald Fletcher, 'Without any doubt whatever, the Divorce Law Reform Act of 1969 marked a juncture of the greatest significance in the changing and developing nature of the family and marriage in Britain.' The 1984 Matrimonial and Family Proceedings Act further liberalised divorce by allowing couples to file for divorce after their first wedding anniversary. In 1990, almost 10 per cent of all marriages ending in divorce had lasted less than three years, and almost 70 per cent of marriages ended in divorce in less than fifteen years. *Table 5.4* clearly indicates the rising trend in divorce.

Sociologists have offered various interpretations of the rising trend in divorce. Kingsley Davis (1948) has noted that contemporary marriage goals are indefinite. Expectations, too, are often unrealistically romantic compared with the reality. Modern marriage, Davis argues, is mainly a vehicle for sexual gratification and companionship. Outside this sphere, it has no significance that would give it stability. If a marriage does not somehow involve the partners in common activities apart from sexual intercourse, it cannot hope to produce a satisfactory companionship or attain any stability. Davis concludes that the instability of modern marriage clearly shows that it is becoming deficient as a source of emotional security.

William Goode (1963) notes that Western cultures tend to view divorce as a misfortune or a tragedy and thus high divorce rates are taken as evidence that the family system is not working well. Similarly there is a Western bias towards romantic love, and this again leads people to interpret divorce as 'failure'. Goode notes two mechanisms used in other societies to deal with marital strain. Some societies lower expectations concerning what the individual may expect from marriage (e.g. Chinese children are taught not to expect romance or happiness from marriage). Others emphasise the importance of the kinship network to the detriment of the husband/wife relationship.

Goode also maintains that societies vary in what is considered a bearable level of disharmony between husband and wife, as well as in their solutions for a difficult marriage. He suggests that in the last century a degree of disharmony was tolerated which modern couples would not stand. Couples put up with each other for the sake of their children. It could be that such 'empty shell marriages' were a good deal more common then than now.

It should also be noted that the nature of family life changes with industrialisation. As we have seen, extended kinship declines relatively; the family loses some of its functions; it becomes more detached from the community; and it becomes a unit of consumption rather than production. The consequence of these changes is to throw couples together more than they would ever have been in the past. It is claimed by some sociologists that the strains caused by the 'isolation' of modern marriage are considerable and if people do not get what they want from a marriage (i.e. a certain quality and intensity of relationship) they will move on.

Ronald Fletcher (1988) argues that the rise in marital breakdown, as evidenced by the divorce statistics, stems largely from the fact that marriage is increasingly valued. People expect and demand more from marriage than was acceptable in the past. He claims that a relatively high divorce rate may be indicative not of lower but of higher standards of marriage in society. Thus, paradoxically, the higher value placed on marriage may result in increased marital breakdown.

Nicky Hart (1976) provides probably the most thorough sociological analysis of marital breakdown. She argues that any explanation of marital breakdown must consider:

→ factors that affect the value attached to marriage;
→ factors that affect the degree of conflict between the spouses;
→ factors that affect the opportunities for individuals to escape from marriage.

Table 5.4   Divorce, 1961–2001

England and Wales	1961	1971	1981	1990	2001
Petitions filed (thousands)	32	111	170	180	157
Persons divorcing per thousand married people	2.1	6.0	11.9	12.1	11.2

Source: *Social Trends* 33, 2003

In advanced capitalist societies, she suggests, there is a demand for cheap female labour. Families in such societies are bombarded with images of 'the good life'. High material aspirations follow. Women are expected to work and run the home. This conflict of roles and the importance given to materialism can cause serious strains.

Marxist/feminist writers would tend to hold to the view that increasing divorce rates are a reflection of the dissatisfaction of many women with a family system that subordinates them and inhibits their ability to develop their talents and capabilities. Graham Allen (1988) suggests that this is a result of a relaxation of traditional attitudes and legal changes. He sees the family today as a private institution that, lacking substantial contacts with the wider family and society at large, is not integrated into a social network. Family problems cannot easily be shared and in times of trouble there is less pressure to stay together.

Social class is closely related to the incidence of divorce. A marriage where the husband is in an unskilled job is more than four times as likely to end in divorce than one where the husband is a professional. Financial pressures may well be part of the cause as the unemployed are even more likely to divorce than the unskilled group.

Do marriage and family life have a future?

Evidence about the high divorce rate can be interpreted as suggesting that the family and marriage are disappearing institutions. Thus, for Jon Bernades (1990), the variation and diversity of family types leads him to state that 'there is no such thing as "the family" and in reality no such things as "normal families"'. Similarly, Gubrium and Holstein (1990) argue that the continued emphasis on 'the family' is ideological: 'the family is as much idea as thing'. The way forward for the sociology of the family is not by examining the relationship between society and what is thought of as 'the family' (the macro view) but to discover the subjective meaning given to the family by its members.

For social historians, these statistics are nothing new in British life. Peter Laslett (1982) points out that the present situation, where there are more people living outside the nuclear family (solitaries) than in it, is nothing new: 'When Britain was still a pre-industrial society … something like 30 to 35 per cent of all groups were constituted in the same way, and among the solitaries and the few in institutions, a high

proportion were the old and the very old, just as is the case in the 1980s.' Moreover, in the mid nineteenth century, at the height of the Victorian era, the illegitimacy rate reached a three-hundred-year peak, and was at a similar level to that of today.

Other writers have put forward other arguments against any notion that the family and marriage are threatened institutions. Firstly, although the number of divorces is high, it is nevertheless the case that most people who do divorce remarry. The divorce rate does not indicate that people have lost faith in marriage but, in their search for a satisfying relationship, are keen to get out of a bad one. Secondly, although the structure of the family has changed in recent decades, it is not the case that alternatives to the family, such as communes or kibbutz-style arrangements, are taking their place.

DIVORCE

→ Four in 10 marriages are likely to end in divorce

→ Divorce is bad for your health – divorced men aged 25 to 50 are twice as likely as married men to die prematurely

→ Admission rates to mental hospitals are between four and six times greater among the divorced than the married

→ Divorced people smoke more, drink more, and have higher rates of unsafe sex

→ Divorced people are four times more likely to commit suicide

→ Companies lose £200 million a year through absenteeism and impaired work because of marriage breakdown

→ Women are keener than men on divorce – 70 per cent of petitions are filed by wives

→ 51 per cent of divorced men live to regret it, saying they would have preferred to stay married, compared with 29 per cent of women

Source: One Plus One

Questions

1 Is marriage as an institution breaking down?
2 What are the problems of being a lone parent?
3 Does 'the typical family' still exist?

6 Education

It's a sort of a challenge, coming to school thinking 'How can I outwit the teachers today?' The teachers are the establishment, they've done things to you, you don't like what they've done, how can you get back?

'Joey', P. Willis, Learning to Labour, *1977*

Introduction

The chapter begins with a discussion of how the major sociological perspectives view education systems. It then examines the role of the State in promoting the education system in Britain. The new vocationalism and recent educational reforms are then examined. The following section examines data on differential educational achievement and then goes on to look at various sociological explanations. The chapter concludes by looking at the reasons for differential educational opportunities and outcomes for boys, girls and ethnic minorities.

What is education?

If primary **socialisation** begins at home, then the school is the first taste of secondary socialisation the human encounters. It is here that the transition from the particular values of the family to the general values of society is made.

Education selects and categorises the human animal, ensuring that it is well equipped to take its place within society as a useful, functioning member of the productive process. It can be seen as stamping out originality, creativity and imagination and substituting passive, unquestioning **conformity** to social rules and obedience to **authority**. Its purpose may be to instil discipline and respect or to give everyone an equal chance to broaden their intellectual and emotional life. Some people would say it provides a small minority with an intensive, high-quality process of intellectual stimulation until they are 21 years old, and gives the majority a lower quality, basic education until they are 16. Others believe it operates to reproduce the capitalist **class** system, **gender** roles and **patriarchal** relationships. At school pupils learn to read, write, calculate, fight, smoke, and develop social and sexual relationships.

Differential educational achievement

All of this (and more) can be found in education, and as usual the definition you choose depends on your theory. Where you look and what you find, and therefore how you explain it, all depend upon whether you use a **functionalist**, **Marxist**, **feminist** or **interactionist** perspective. The arguments about education all revolve around the question of differential achievement. Why do some groups of people – members of the working class, some **ethnic** minorities and women – tend to 'fail' at school in comparison with whites, males and the middle class? Why do girls and boys do better in different subjects? It is already obvious that there is some complexity here, and there are no 'right' answers, just good or bad arguments. The secondary socialisation process ensures that the general roles of social life are experienced, and there is great stress laid upon the role of the school in training for **citizenship**, i.e. learning your duties and responsibilities as a member of your society. There is a great deal of functionalism in educational policy.

Why do we go to school?

Functionalist explanations

The functions of education

According to functionalists the aims of education are to maintain social stability, keep society running smoothly, and resolve conflict. The magic word of functionalism is **consensus** – the shared agreement about the goals and **values** of the social structure. The individual has to submit to this higher order, which exists outside themselves, which was there before their birth and will continue to exist after their death. The whole is greater than the sum of its parts. The social system is more important than the parts which make it up. Individuals have no importance except as members of society. They must sacrifice a certain level of individuality, and learn to fit in and co-operate with the greater whole. The family provides the first stage in the socialisation process, but in the home the child is a 'special' and particular individual. School provides the next stage, where the child learns that far from being important it is just another person, with new duties and responsibilities.

Meritocracy and consensus

The most important value in **post-industrial** societies is **meritocracy** – success or failure in the education system and position in the system of **stratification** depends on individual merit and achievement. The whole of society is meritocratic and, as Parsons points out, the school is a 'microcosm' of society, a small-scale replica, in the same way that the family is. The school 'bridges' the gap between family and work. Meritocracy is the idea that a system, with its duties, responsibilities and rewards, is based on equality of opportunity. It is fair. If you work hard, you will achieve to the best of your abilities, and will be rewarded on that basis. Ability is to do with talent, and the functionalists are essentially in agreement with Eysenck on the subject of **intelligence**. 'Talent' is innate, and varies from individual to individual. All individuals are given an equal chance to realise their full potential. Those who are most talented and work hardest get the highest rewards. They become head girls and boys, they get the cups and the certificates, the gold stars and lollipops. Those with less talent get less reward, and they accept this inequality as right and proper, knowing that they have all had a fair and equal chance.

This is how functionalism explains 'differential achievement'. White, black, middle or working class,

male or female, it makes no difference. If you have the skills and are prepared to work, then you will succeed. Of course, the harder you work, the more you expect to get for it, and so high-status degrees, leading to high salaries, the so-called 'glittering prizes', are your right. The rest are left to share out the duller prizes, but do so cheerfully, knowing that it is all they are worth and deserve. This view is outlined by the functionalists Davis and Moore in their explanations of social inequality (see chapter 3).

Education as a subsystem

In the 1950s through to the 1970s, mainstream sociology was based on these ideas about education. Talcott Parsons considered education as another subsystem within the social system. In a complex essay published in 1959 he gives his 'structural functionalist' analysis of the school (1959b). He tries to outline the way the structure of a class is related to society. He uses a single class, which is a subsystem within the school, as a model. If schools have functions, this is where they are put into practice. These functions are as an agency of socialisation and to sort people out into their various adult roles – jobs. The school is the 'focal socialising agency' and is based on meritocratic principles. Parsons acknowledges the influence of class, which he calls 'socio-economic status', on achievement.

Parsons the empiricist

He used a sample of 3,348 Boston schoolboys (a good positivist base?). He shows that 80 per cent of boys whose fathers are in 'major white-collar' jobs intend to go to college. Of boys whose fathers are semi- or unskilled only 12 per cent have that intention. So, if you are of high **status** and high ability, the chances are you will get to college; if you are of low status and low ability it is much less likely. He also points out that boys with low ability and high status also go to college – one with 'low academic standards'. He does not say what happens to boys with low status and high ability. High ability here seems to mean a mixture of two things: intellectual skills in the formal curriculum and an acceptance of the 'moral component' of education. The latter, as defined by Parsons, is 'respect for the teacher, consideration and co-operativeness … good work habits'. Achievement is 'living up to the expectations imposed by the teacher as an agent of the adult society'.

Selection

The teacher sorts out those best able to achieve in this sense and differentiates between the children accordingly. This sorting into levels leads to the 'allocation of adult roles'. If you are good at your work, well behaved, and accept that teacher knows best, you will go on to get a good career and salary. The teacher is an extension of the parent, but there are important differences which are necessary if the school is to perform its function. She (and in Parsons' example primary schoolteachers are usually women) is an adult in a superior role to the child. However, the role is occupational, teaching is her job, and her 'family' of children is large. She teaches them **universalistic** or general and society-wide values, and she must respond to their performance of tasks, not their emotional needs.

Teacher and pupil roles

The teacher must be hard: 'She is not entitled to suppress the distinction between high and low achievers just because not being able to be included in the high group would be too hard on little Johnny.' The child must accept the role of the teacher, and respond to that. This is a major step in the socialisation process, and leads the child to accept the value system and therefore their own status in it. Parsons emphasises the importance of family and school sharing the same value system if the child is to succeed. There is a relationship between ability, social status and the process of education. Internalising values and giving a high performance leads to favourable chances in the selection of adult roles.

Criticisms of Parsons

However, critics point out that the 'fairness' of the school system is by no means proven by Parsons, and that he uncritically accepts the status quo. Often, those children who do not succeed come from low-status backgrounds, and Parsons does not address this properly. The education system works to ensure that some groups monopolise success and others are left to fail, and this follows through into the job and career structure. Those who succeed come to school already equipped to do so; they receive good responses from teachers and go on to prepare their own children in the same way. The value system which is such an important part of the school, according to Parsons, comes from one small group in society and benefits them at the expense of others, who are defined as 'low ability' and 'low achievers'.

Questions

1 In what ways can education be regarded as secondary socialisation?
2 What are the key functions of education from the functionalist perspective?
3 How do functionalists regard education as a subsystem?

Marxist explanations

Bourgeois ideology and the reproduction of capitalism

For Marxists, the **economic base**, and the relationship between **capitalists** and workers which is carried on there, shapes the rest of society, the **superstructure**. Control of power in the base is maintained at the level of ideas in the superstructure. This set of ideas, according to Marxism, comes from the **ruling class**. It is an **ideology**. It presents children with a view of society, and their place within it: you should be punctual, polite, respectful of authority; you should work hard to receive rewards; you should be disciplined and do your duty. These are all part of an education system which works to reproduce the capitalist system. Schools must provide the new society with leaders, managers and a great mass of workers for unskilled, semi-skilled and skilled manual labour. This last and largest group must 'fail' in the education system. Those who accept the ideology passed on in school become the 'successes' of the system, and go on to higher education. Capitalist **relations of production** are reproduced and correct ideas and attitudes instilled into individuals. Education is not just about passing on knowledge – in fact a great deal of that commodity is actually withheld from most students.

There was no mass education for the working classes in the early stages of capitalist Britain. There was a fear that an educated workforce might get 'ideas'. At that time any attempts by workers to improve themselves intellectually often led to their imprisonment. As capitalism advanced and needed more literate and numerate workers, educational reform began, leading to the lengthy time spent in school in contemporary capitalism. The ruling class uses the system to reproduce inequalities. The skills and knowledge necessary for individual success in a capitalist society – supposedly fair and meritocratic in the way it gives rewards – have to be passed on in some way to the children of the ruling classes. The pattern of working-class failure and middle-class success is not accidental, but necessary. Marxist analysis tries to point out the processes which help it to come about.

Private education

The existence of a private education system ensures that the highest-status skills and knowledge, which lead to the top positions – ruling-class ones – are passed on to an exclusive group. The major public schools and universities fill the top economic and political positions. (**Elite** groups are examined elsewhere – see chapters 3 and 11.) Private education signals the existence of ruling-class educational privilege in its most obvious form. The ways in which inequalities are reproduced in **State** schools has generated more research. However, one influential Marxist voice on education used no research, putting forward theory instead.

Althusser

Louis Althusser (1971) puts forward a view of ideology which tries to explain how secret and unconscious it is: 'Ideology is a process which takes place behind our backs.' We cannot see it, but before we can think about it we are a part of it. Ideology calls out to us and invites us to see ourselves in certain ways. By going along with it, we become victims. We believe we are that person. Education in modern societies perfects this process. Children are given a set of ideas which they use to understand the world. They are not allowed to examine and discuss these ideas, just accept and believe them. The child is trapped in a position created for them by another group of people – the ruling class. The individual is then controlled and easily controllable, and goes on to conform to the position given to them in the capitalist world of work.

Repressive and ideological State apparatuses

Althusser points out that there are two ways to rule, by force or by consent. The State can use force at any time, and the forces it uses are called repressive State apparatuses (RSAs) by Althusser. The police, used in strikes and riots, and the armed forces are examples of RSAs. Rule by coercion is not easy, it is expensive, and sooner or later must fail. To gain the consent of the masses by constructing their ideas for them is a much better option. RSAs are replaced by **ideological State apparatuses** (ISAs) and their role is to pass on capitalist **norms** and **values**. It is much better to have

workers going more or less willingly to work than having to march behind them with machine guns. People go and stand in smelly, hot, noisy factories for eight hours at a time, performing boring tasks because they want to, or know that they have to. Why don't they all take over the process, kill the bosses, divide up the profits and run the factory between themselves? Not because they think someone will come and shoot them but because they do not see it that way! They see a fair and necessary system. They turn up, do the job, get paid, go home and spend their wages, then come back and they see this as their role in life. Education has become the most influential ISA, replacing the church according to Althusser. Knowledge is passed on in school, but it is 'wrapped up' in ruling-class ideology. Economic history, for example, is presented from a ruling-class viewpoint, where the benefits of capitalism outweigh the disadvantages. Historic working-class resistance is presented from the employer's view. Patriotism and duty are all mixed up with 'facts'. The process which Durkheim applauds as necessary and good is painted in a different light by Althusser. Knowledge is distorted by ideology.

Criticisms of Althusser

His vision of education is of a conveyor belt. The mass of pupils are pushed off the belt at the age of 16 with rule-following, worker attitudes. The next group, ejected at 18 or so, become the managers with leadership values and an order-giving attitude. The smallest group stay on the belt indefinitely, becoming 'ideologues', the 'top' minds of the ruling class. Education passes on ideology in a subtle, complex way. Children are programmed to 'fail' or 'succeed' and this is necessary to reproduce the relations of capitalism.

As stated, the main criticism of Althusser is the lack of supporting and **empirical** research. The essay was a small part of his work, which suggests material for research and thought. Althusser was a philosopher, not a sociologist, but his ideas have influenced modern Marxist sociology.

Bowles and Gintis: correspondence theory

Two American Marxists who could be said to apply Althusser's ideas on education are Samuel Bowles and Herbert Gintis. Their 1976 study explores the relationships within a school and those in the workplace. The whole structure is mirrored, with heads, senior staff and teachers in school; directors, managers and middle managers in the workplace in authority over workers or students. Students learn about hierarchies. Workers do not control their labour. They have no choice over what they produce, no say in its exchange or who has the profits. Students study what the school tells them to, they do not 'own' the end product of their labour. Knowledge is presented as 'compartmentalised'. Students do as they are told, they learn to value time (punctuality), hard work and the reward system: a certificate for a good project, a 'bonus' for working hard, i.e. 'extrinsic rewards'.

Bowles and Gintis found, after studying American secondary schools, that the most original, imaginative individuals were not encouraged, as there was not much room for non-conformity in capitalism. The rule-following, conforming type was most acceptable, and these individuals come mainly from the middle classes. Working-class under-achievement was the pattern they uncovered, even in the functional 'classless' USA. These students were ejected first and became workers, manually skilled and conforming to the role that had been allotted. The next group, mostly middle class, became the new middle classes, and the smallest, most élite group went on to higher education. The system of rewards and punishments, orders and obedience, the lack of pupil control over their own education – the **hidden curriculum** – are all said to correspond to the demands of work. They point out the process whereby knowledge and skills are made exclusive to a few, yet attitudes and opinions are transmitted to all.

Criticisms of Bowles and Gintis

Whilst influential, Bowles and Gintis' book has been subjected to a number of criticisms from Marxists and non-Marxists alike. Both have claimed that it is inadequate to argue that the educational system is shaped solely by the demands of a capitalist economic system. To state this is to posit a **determinism** reminiscent of the crudest functionalism. For some Marxists, such as Henry Giroux (1984), echoing Nicos Poulantzas (see chapter 11), the educational system is 'relatively autonomous' from the rest of society, and is to a large extent able to determine its own direction.

They have been criticised for seeing working-class pupils as passive and for making the assumption that everything that is taught in school is necessarily learnt. Other studies, even from within the Marxist perspective (Willis, 1977), have shown working-class pupils to be anything but passive.

Gender and ethnicity

It has also been claimed that their analysis suffers by ignoring the issues of gender and ethnicity. AnnMarie Wolpe (1988) sees a contradiction in the way that they claim that 'the family's impact on the reproduction of the sexual division of labour is distinctly greater than that of the educational system'. They appear to be arguing that girls are socialised mainly at home and boys at school. 'Girls' ideas', she says, 'have, according to their analysis, been formed in the family. Schooling cannot be as important for women because of the greater power of the family structure and its teaching on sex roles … In one fell swoop they eradicate any importance of education in girls' lives.'

There is also a problem with the claim that school prepares people for a life of work. In the USA, Gloria Joseph (1988) states: 'There exists a significantly large body of Blacks and Latinos who are not in the economic work force at all.' What Bowles and Gintis have to say misses this ethnic dimension. Similarly, it could be said that significant numbers of British school-leavers will experience long periods of unemployment before they eventually find work. How has school prepared them for this? This is the question the theorists of the 'new vocationalism' (see page 150) seek to answer.

Bowles and Gintis reply

Bowles and Gintis (1988), aware of these arguments, have made an effort to reply. Against the key point that **cultures** of resistance exist in schools they argue that 'Such cultural dynamics, far from contradicting the correspondence principle, in fact reinforce it. We would welcome, although there does not appear to exist, a strong argument to the effect that the structure of education is the product of contested class, gender, racial and other relationships.' In other words, it remains the case that education is a key agent of the dominant ideology.

Questions

1 What is an 'ideological State apparatus'?
2 What do Bowles and Gintis mean by the 'correspondence principle'?
3 What would Marxists have to say about a standard national curriculum for all?

The State and education in Britain

Any understanding of the sociology of education demands an examination of how the education system came into existence, the forces that determined its shape, and the assumptions made by various educational reformers in framing their legislation.

For the affluent, a form of education has been in existence for many hundreds of years, including public schools for the nobility, and grammar schools for the merchant classes. For the overwhelming majority of the population there was no systematic attempt at education. This was occasionally justified on the grounds that education for the masses would threaten to disturb the social order – they might start asking too many questions. Prior to 1870, schooling was largely provided by the various denominations of the church, seeking to improve the moral character of the young.

State intervention

Three years after a significant breakthrough was made towards working-class enfranchisement (see chapter 11), the Liberal government under Gladstone, against the prevailing philosophy of *laissez-faire*, began an important intervention in the lives of individuals when Forster put the Elementary Education Act through Parliament. From 1870 the State ensured an elementary education – religion, reading, writing and arithmetic – for all children from five to ten years old. In the next few decades, attendance became compulsory, State schools became free, and by 1918 the school-leaving age had been raised to 14.

There is no single reason why the State became so hugely involved in the lives of its citizens at this time, effectively laying the basis for the modern **Welfare State**. The main factor, however, lay in the need for a literate and numerate population at a time when Britain's main industrial competitors were catching up and threatening to overtake Britain's industrial performance. Further major educational legislation was to follow world wars in which the poor general level of education in Britain was exposed.

Despite being TUC policy since 1890, and also despite intense agitation between the two world wars, secondary education as a right for all children up to the age of 15 was not achieved until, in the closing stages of the Second World War, R. A. Butler passed the Education Act of 1944. This was the first brick laid in the modern Welfare State, taking on the first of Beveridge's 'five evils' – ignorance.

The tripartite system

Up to 1944, only working-class children who 'showed promise' were likely to win a scholarship into a grammar school. After the 1944 Act, all children would attend a type of secondary school, for which they were selected on the basis of an intelligence test: the Eleven Plus examination. Pupils could go in one of three directions after they had taken the test, depending on the kind of aptitude, skills and abilities they had displayed. Children revealed to be logically minded and articulate by the test would receive the academic education offered by grammar schools. Practical and technically minded children would go to technical schools and those who had not shown promise attended secondary modern schools.

Equal value

These three types of secondary school – which made up the 'tripartite system' – were intended to have 'parity of esteem'. In other words, no single part of the tripartite system would be seen to be a more important or valuable form of education than any other. However, private-sector education remained virtually untouched by the biggest restructuring of British education to date. This remains the case today.

Another intention of the Act was to create a genuine educational meritocracy in which naturally intelligent children would be allowed to develop to the maximum of their educational potential, following selection at the age of 11. By the time of the 1963 Robbins report, which stated that: 'a course of Higher Education should be available for all those who are qualified by ability and attainment to pursue one and who wish to do so', it was clear that equality of opportunity and parity of esteem in education had not been achieved. More money was being spent on grammar schools than on the two others, and more children of non-manual workers, with the same IQ (intelligence quotient) as the children of manual workers, were going on to higher education. No one believed the three schools were of equal value. The later findings of the Nuffield Study (Halsey *et al.*, 1980) echoed the observation that the 1944 Act had done little to increase upward **social mobility** for the **working class**.

Instead, it was argued that the tripartite system had a strong tendency to reproduce the wider system of **stratification**, where the children of middle-class professionals attended grammar schools, children of the skilled working class went to technical schools and children of the semi- and unskilled manual working class attended secondary modern schools. As increasing amounts of evidence were gathered to reinforce this argument, the notion of under-achievement was formulated.

There had been a provision in the 1944 Act for local authorities to set up an alternative form of secondary education to the tripartite system, and some LEAs (for example in London, Leicester and Anglesey) set up a form of schooling that dispensed with selection at the age of 11. Instead of sending pupils on to one of three schools, they all attended a single school – a comprehensive.

Comprehensive schooling

The idea of comprehensive schooling had, since 1946, been attractive to the Labour Party, and following its election in 1964 it set about redressing the shortcomings of the tripartite system by introducing comprehensive education on a national basis. By 1988 (with the school-leaving age raised to 16 in 1971–2), State education in the UK had become effectively comprehensive, though the tripartite system still lives on in isolated pockets (see *Table 6.1*).

Comprehensivisation of secondary education was achieved in the face of enormous opposition from many quarters, particularly defenders of grammar schools and those who believed that education must still be able to cater for the 'bright' kids and that the creation of a meritocracy means educational mediocrity. It has been, and continues to be, a political football kicked about between the various political parties. Despite the battle to create equality of opportunity in education, it remained the case that in 1991 7 per cent of all pupils, and 20 per cent of boys and 15 per cent of girls over 16, attended independent or fee-paying public schools.

Table 6.1 Secondary school pupils in the UK, by type of school (thousands)

	1970/ 71	1980/ 81	1990/ 91	1994/ 95	1998/ 99	1999/ 00	2000/ 01
Secondary							
Comprehensive	1313	3730	2843	3093	3207	3266	3340
Grammar	673	149	156	184	203	204	205
Modern	1164	233	94	90	92	108	112
Other	403	434	300	289	291	282	260
All public-sector schools	9507	9806	8453	8996	9276	9341	9367

Source: *Social Trends* 32, 2002

With the passing of the Conservative government's Educational Reform Act in 1988, a major series of changes in the nature of State education was set in train. The Act aimed to enforce the teaching and learning of a national core curriculum; it introduced standard assessment testing at the ages of seven, eleven, fourteen and sixteen; it gave schools the right to 'opt out' of local authority control and be centrally funded; and it gave greater powers to school governors. Also it abolished the Inner London Education Authority. The realisation of these objectives has proved more difficult than the passing of the Act for all concerned.

Questions

1 Why did the State take on responsibility for free and compulsory education?
2 What is meant by the tripartite system?
3 Why were three types of school – grammar, technical and secondary modern – set up after 1944?

The new vocationalism: the future of education?

In a famous speech in 1976, the then Prime Minister, James Callaghan, argued that 'it is vital to Britain's economic recovery and standard of living that the performance of manufacturing industry is improved and that the whole range of government policies, including education, contribute as much as possible to improving industrial performance and thereby the national wealth'. In saying this, Callaghan began the 'Great Debate' about the future of educational provision, which focused specifically on how it serves the demands of industry.

The need for change

In the following year a government Green Paper, *Education in Schools*, targeted three areas where it believed that schools failed industry: a decline in standards with basic skills no longer being adequately taught while 'fringe' subjects were overemphasised; a neglect of the fundamentals of discipline such as good manners and the motivation to work hard; and finally the failure of the education system to provide enough scientists, engineers and technologists.

These themes (without the stress on manufacturing industry) were taken up by the incoming Conservative government in 1979. Part of the solution was seen to lie in giving a greater role in education to

Department of Employment agencies such as the Manpower Services Commission (changed to the Training Agency), the Technical and Vocational Educational Initiative and the Technical and Vocational Educational Extension. By the mid-1980s the Youth Opportunities Programme had become the two-year Youth Training Scheme and a Certificate in Pre-Vocational Education was available in schools and colleges. Later initiatives include the industry-led National Vocational Qualification (NVQ) and the General National Vocational Qualification (GNVQ).

The sceptic's view

The motivation behind this new emphasis on vocational qualifications, on skills and competence, has been viewed sceptically by some sociologists, as is clear in the title of Bates *et al.*'s book *Schooling for the Dole?* (1984). In this searching examination of the new vocationalism, the authors argue that the emphasis on personal and life skills in vocational training may be a euphemism for accepting the social control of the workplace in unquestioning fashion.

Dan Finn, one of the authors, argues that it is not the case that school-leavers are ignorant of the world of work. Most young people, particularly the educational 'failures', have experience of part-time work while at school, as well as unpaid domestic labour and the work disciplines of the school. Another of the authors, Moore, argues that industrial training is in any case the chosen responsibility of industry. In a rapidly changing industrial environment, it is difficult for anyone, let alone educationists, to know what future training needs are: 'the dismal history of manpower forecasting suggests that no-one really knows what industry needs, and the relative isolation of teachers from the world of work as well as the worlds of their pupils suggests that they are in no position to know what their needs are'.

Moreover, it is a false assumption that schools can provide occupationally relevant characteristics in their pupils – all they can do is provide literate and numerate labour. Job allocation happens on the job, through promotion, training and retraining, giving the lie to both functionalist and Marxist arguments concerning the role of schools in placing pupils in the world of work.

Questions

1 What is meant by the new vocationalism?
2 What do the initials NVQ and GNVQ mean?

Differential educational achievement

Differences in educational achievement are usually measured by examination results, sixth form (or post-compulsory education) entry, by those gaining places in higher education, and choice of subject. The three forms of stratification that are evident from these data are social class, gender and ethnicity. It is important to note here that the tables discussed below are numerical, **positivistic** indicators, and the usual anti-positivist arguments about the constructed nature of **social facts** should be borne in mind.

Class

The picture of academic achievement by social class is consistent. The largest survey is that undertaken by Halsey, Heath and Ridge (1980). Using the database generated by the Oxford Mobility Study (see chapter 3), as well as the three-way split of service, intermediate and working classes, they found that boys from the service class (the top strata) had 40 times more chance of attending a public school, and three times more chance of attending a grammar school than a boy from the working class (in a period when the tripartite system was largely still in place). The 1944 Act had, in the 1950s and 1960s, made very little difference to a working-class boy's chances of rising through the academic ranks: he had four times less chance than a service-class boy of still being in school at the age of 16; eight times less chance of being in school at 17; ten times less chance of being in school at 18 and 11 times less chance of being at university.

Higher education

While it was true in 1980 to say that, in absolute terms, more working-class boys were at university (2 per cent), the number of intermediate and service-class boys had also increased, but at faster rates (6 per cent and 19 per cent). In relative terms, then, the number of working-class boys at university, compared to other classes, had shrunk, not expanded. The 1944 Act and post-war university expansion had led to, if anything, a proportionately smaller working-class entry. The observation that the Welfare State has in reality benefited the middle class most is discussed further by Julian Le Grand (see chapter 4).

As *Table 6.2* shows, this pattern showed very little sign of ending throughout the 1990s. While participation rates in higher education increased for all classes, the percentage of students from the higher

Table 6.2 Participation rates in higher education in Britain, by social class (%)

	1991/92	1992/93	1993/94	1994/95	1995/96	1996/97	1997/98	1998/99
Professional	55	71	73	78	79	82	79	72
Intermediate	36	39	42	45	45	47	48	45
Skilled non-manual	22	27	29	31	31	32	31	29
Skilled manual	11	15	17	18	18	18	19	18
Partly skilled	12	14	16	17	17	17	18	17
Unskilled	6	9	11	11	12	13	14	13
All social classes	23	28	30	32	32	33	33	31

Source: *Social Trends* 31, 2001

Figure 6.1 Pupils achieving five or more GCSE grades A* to C or equivalent[1] by parents' socio-economic group, 1989 and 2000

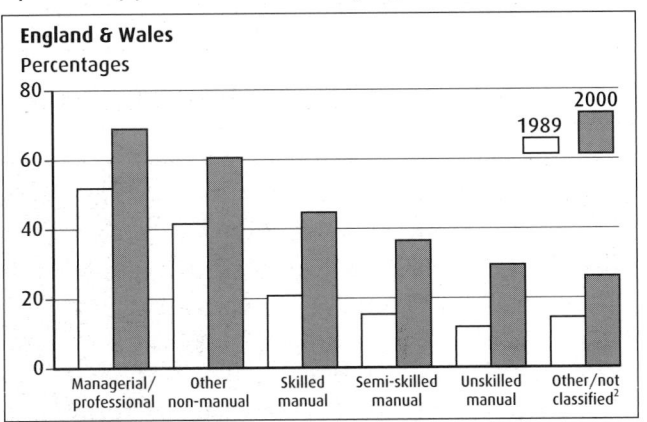

1 Includes equivalent GNVQ qualifications achieved in Year 11.
2 Includes a high percentage of respondents who had neither parent in a full-time job.

Source: *Social Trends* 31, 2001

Figure 6.2 Achievement at GCE A Level[1] or equivalent: by gender[2]

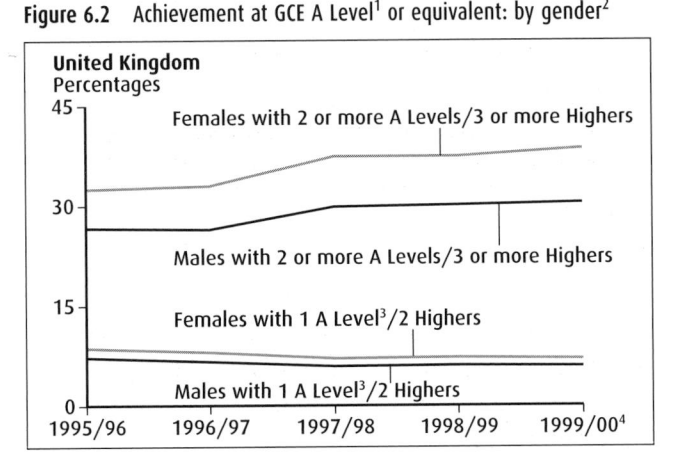

1 2 AS Levels count as 1 A Level pass.
2 Pupils in schools and students in further education institutions aged 16–18 at the start of the academic year in England, Wales and Northern Ireland as a percentage of the 17-year-old population. Pupils in Scotland generally sit Highers one year earlier and the figures tend to relate to the results of pupils in Year S5/S6.
3 Includes those with 1.5 A Level passes.
4 From 1999/00 National Qualifications (NQ) were introduced in Scotland. NQs include Standard Grades, Intermediate 1 & 2 and Higher Grades. The figures for Higher Grades combine the new NQ Higher and the old SCE Higher.

Source: *Social Trends* 32, 2002

social classes still far exceeds the percentage from working-class backgrounds.

Equally, as *Figure 6.1* shows, the pattern of success at GCSE at the end of the twentieth century shows that the gap between the highest and lowest classes remains as high as ever.

Gender

Achievement by gender shows a more complex picture. Where female underachievement was once a prime educational concern, females now outstrip males at all levels in compulsory education, and the gap in achieving two A Levels or more has now been sustained for over a decade (see *Figure 6.2*).

This pattern is now being replicated at the level of higher education, where (as *Table 6.3* shows), at all levels except full-time post-graduate, there are now less men than women, and the focus in education has now moved to the underachievement of men. The curriculum remains genderised, however, with science subjects such as maths and physics continuing to

Table 6.3 Students in higher education by type of course and gender, UK (thousands)

	Undergraduate		Post-graduate		All higher
	Full time	Part time	Full time	Part time	education
Males					
1970/71	241	127	33	15	416
1980/81	277	176	41	32	526
1990/91	345	193	50	50	638
2000/01	511	228	82	118	940
Females					
1970/71	173	19	10	3	205
1980/81	196	71	21	13	301
1990/91	319	148	34	36	537
2000/01	602	320	81	124	1128

Source: *Social Trends* 32, 2002

Figure 6.3   GCE A Level or equivalent entries[1] by selected subject and gender 1999/00

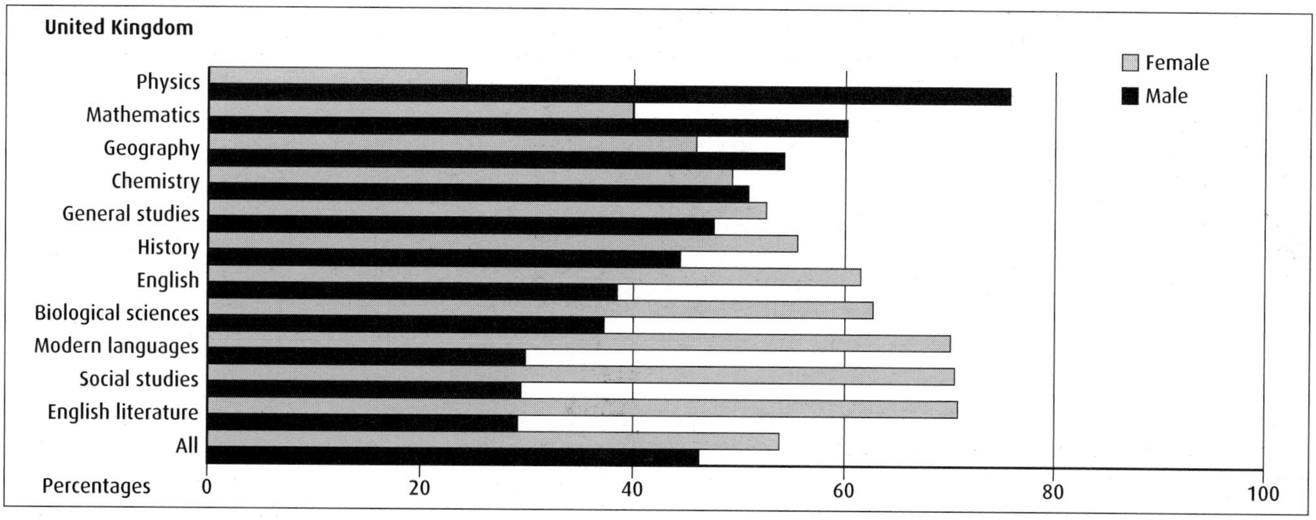

1 SCE H grade in Scotland. For 1999/00 includes the new Scottish qualification framework which contains different subject categories to those previously used. The new Intermediate 1 and 2 qualifications (which overlap with Standard Grades and Highers) are not included in the table.

Source: *Social Trends* 32, 2002

attract more men than women, while languages and social studies are dominated by women, as *Figure 6.3* shows. Boys are also five times more likely to be excluded from school than girls.

Ethnicity

There is a definite pattern of achievement by ethnic group, similar to that for employment and unemployment. As *Table 6.4* shows, whites and Indians have similar profiles, with Pakistanis and

Table 6.5   Permanent exclusion rates, by ethnic group, January 1998, England (%)

	January 1998
White	0.17
Black Caribbean	0.76
Black African	0.29
Black Other	0.57
Indian	0.06
Pakistani	0.13
Bangladeshi	0.09
Chinese	0.05
All	0.18

Source: *Social Trends* 31, 2001

Bangladeshis underachieving in particular, although black students are most likely to be excluded from school (*Table 6.5*).

Questions

1 How does male and female educational achievement compare?

2 In what ways is the pattern of achievement by ethnic group similar to that found in employment?

Table 6.4   Examination achievements of pupils in schools by gender and ethnic origin, 2000, England and Wales (%)

	5 or more GCSEs grades A* to C	1–4 GCSEs grades A* to C	No graded GCSEs
Males			
White	45	26	5
Black	31	31	6
Indian	54	25	0
Pakistani/Bangladeshi	22	34	4
Other groups	40	24	15
All males	44	26	5
Females			
White	55	25	3
Black	46	29	5
Indian	66	21	2
Pakistani/Bangladeshi	37	35	4
Other groups	44	22	14
All females	54	25	4

Source: *Social Trends* 32, 2002

Explanations for differential educational achievement

Intelligence

Genetics

Very many people would attribute their failure to gain qualifications at school to the 'bungalow factor': they haven't got anything upstairs. Other people have –

they were born intelligent, and this is the reason why some do well at school, and others do not. Schools simply separate those who are able from those who are not. There is nothing you can do about it.

Those who think this way agree with a school of psychology that argues that intelligence is innate, a quality that you inherit from your genetically 'intelligent' forebears. Three educational psychologists – Cyril Burt, Hans Eysenck and the American, Arthur Jensen – have all devoted their professional careers to proving this belief. Of these three, Cyril Burt has had the greatest influence on educational policy in Great Britain.

Burt

The world's first educational psychologist, Burt grew up at the beginning of the twentieth century at a time when the 'science' of eugenics was fashionable. According to eugenics, there is a natural hierarchy among humans, based on genetic superiority. Burt (1943) himself argues that 'the higher IQs (intelligence quotients) found among children of the fee-paying (i.e. public school) classes represent inborn differences partly inherited from parents who themselves owe their superior incomes to their superior mental efficiency'. In other words, people are wealthy as a result of their 'natural intelligence', not 'intelligent' as a result of their wealth. A similar argument has been advanced to explain the relatively poor health of the lowest income groups.

Burt's theories, which were based on years of extensive empirical research – in one case involving 40,000 families in a London borough – became the intellectual justification for the formation of the post-war tripartite system, and the process of selection through the Eleven Plus. The Spens Report of 1938 – the basis for the 1944 Act – stated that 'intellectual development during childhood appears to progress as if it were governed by a single central factor usually known as "general intelligence" which may be broadly described as innate all-round intellectual ability. It appears to enter into everything which the child attempts to think or say or do, and seems on the whole to be the most important factor in determining his work in the classroom.'

Burt's disciples

For decades, Burt's ideas dominated thinking in this area. All that schools needed to do was measure an individual's intelligence and educate them appropriately in one of the three types of school where, as Eysenck – Burt's student at University College, London – states, 'What children take out of schools is proportional to what they bring into the schools in terms of IQ.' What Eysenck means here is that, if you are not very intelligent anyway, no matter what kind of school you go to or what kind of teaching techniques were used, you will never get anything out of it.

Even more controversially, another Burt disciple, Arthur Jensen (1967), has argued that there is a racial dimension to genetically determined intelligence: blacks are less intelligent than whites.

Criticisms of Burt

Unfortunately for Burt, Jensen and Eysenck, it came to be generally believed that Burt's research – which largely determined British post-war educational policy – was essentially fraudulent. In the mid-1970s (Burt died in 1971) very big question marks were placed against the status of his research. No one, for example, has ever been able to locate at least five of the research assistants that he claimed to have employed. Nor have they been able to identify the London borough from which the 40,000 families that form the basis of his 1961 study came. His statistical work, particularly in his research on identical but separated (and therefore differently socialised) twins, has been widely criticised for improbability and even impossibility.

One of the most hard-hitting attacks on Burt and those who have claimed evidence for the existence of biologically determined or innate intelligence in humans comes from within natural science. In *The Mismeasure of Man*, Stephen Jay Gould (1981) argues that the idea of intelligence has been reified – that is, what is really an abstraction has become something that is thought to have a demonstrable physical existence, like height or weight. The belief emerges that intelligence is located in the brain and can be measured. From this it follows that people can be ranked according to their measured intelligence.

The fallacy, for Gould, lies in believing that intelligence exists in the first place. This is apparent in the remark made by the inventor of intelligence tests, Alfred Binet, that intelligence can be defined as 'what my tests measure'. Intelligence only exists as a concept because craniologists and psychologists claim it does. Gould reinforces this point by claiming that what has been called objective intelligence testing merely reflects the social prejudices of those who make use of the reified idea of intelligence. In the year the Butler Education Act was passed, Gunnar

Myrdal (1944) argued that it was generally true of biological arguments about human nature (sociobiology) that 'They have been associated ... with conservative and reactionary ideologies. Under their long hegemony, there has been a tendency to assume biological causation without question, and to accept social explanations only under the duress of a siege of irresistible evidence.' The popularity of such arguments reflects the political fashion of the times.

The rehabilitation of Cyril Burt

Having been widely discredited in the 1980s, attempts have been made in recent years to restore Burt's name, and therefore the concept of innate and inherited intelligence. This is mainly due to the publication of two books, the first by Robert Joynson (1989) and the second by Ronald Fletcher (1991). Both these books claim that the attack on Burt was unfair and unjustified. Fletcher in particular seizes on the media's readiness, at the height of comprehensivisation, to accept too readily that Burt was a fraud, and that his evidence was insufficient and lacking vigour.

The publication of these works, coupled with a growing dissatisfaction among teachers concerning mixed-ability teaching, and the persistence of differential rates of achievement among pupils, has led to a growing conviction within organisations such as the British Psychological Society that Burt's work was not based on falsifications and deceptions: the belief is now increasingly widespread that he might have had a point.

Why educationists were so willing to believe Burt at the time, and so unwilling to drop his ideas once they were queried, raises a number of questions about ideology and the sociology of knowledge. What is important for sociology is whether ideas of innate intelligence can continue to have any relevance. The answer must be that they do not. There is no quality that we can isolate and call 'intelligence'. Neither an 'intelligence' gene nor a part of the brain that deals with intelligence have ever been discovered. What we know, we have learnt as the result of socialisation. Our knowledge is culturally constructed – the sociological arguments are surely overwhelming. Cyril Burt and the 'innate intelligence school' are as relevant to the sociology of education as Cesare Lombroso is to the sociology of crime and deviance (see chapter 8).

Explanations of differential achievement, underachievement or underattainment have taken two directions in the sociology of education: those based in the home and what goes on there, and those based in the school and what happens there, between teachers and pupils, pupils and pupils, and teachers and teachers.

Questions

1 What is 'innate intelligence'? How can it be measured? Is it a political or ideological issue?
2 Describe the ideas put forward by Cyril Burt.
3 What is meant by 'reification'?

The home

J. W. B. Douglas

J. W. B. Douglas (1964) carried out a survey of over 5,000 children born in 1946. This longitudinal research followed the children throughout their primary school education until they sat the Eleven Plus and were sent on to different secondary schools in the tripartite system. Overall, he found working-class children do less well in ability tests, and he offers explanations based on the home background, parental attitudes, the parents' hours of work and interest in their children's schooling. In one famous passage he points out that fewer working-class parents visit schools on parents' evenings, and it is usually the mother who shows up, whereas middle-class parents turn up together and assertively demand their sons' and daughters' educational rights in **elaborated code** (see pp. 156–7), seeing the head as well as the teacher. Parental encouragement is seen as a factor in performance, and Douglas seems to suggest that this can be measured by a positivist type of proof. **Social action** theorists would also look at the possible reasons behind these differences: factors in, or affecting, the home, e.g. jobs, hours of work, the need for one parent to look after the children, etc. This study, and another influential but smaller-scale study carried out by Jackson and Marsden in the 1940s and 1950s, formed the backdrop for arguments which suggest that it is home background, and particularly parental participation in education, which explains working-class underattainment.

Criticisms of home-based explanations of underachievement

The implication is that if the State provided spacious homes with quiet places for children to study, a well-stocked library, collages and charts on the wall, classical music, educational outings, educational computer programs, and parents who can spend a lot of time supplementing education, and motivating their children, then everyone would go to university and earn enough to provide those things for their children. Critics of these home-based explanations point out that what is happening here is a culture clash. Speech codes and parents' educational achievements, attitudes towards jobs, careers, ambition, life and death differ according to class. The culture of the working class is at odds with that of schools and society. Their interests and valued skills are ignored or given low status, and there are no explanations given as to the value of university education and all those things taken for granted by the middle classes. Working-class children may rebel, become indifferent, give up and consistently fail to see what the point is – what use is algebra if you believe you are going to work in a supermarket?

There is also the point that behind the statistics there are a number of possible but unexplored interpretations of parental involvement in their children's education such as lack of money for babysitters, shift-working or previous humiliation by teachers in their own schooling, none of which necessarily means that parents are not concerned about or involved in their children's education.

Questions

1 What are the problems of measuring parental involvement?

2 How important is a child's home life to their success in school?

Language codes

Basil Bernstein (1961) is one of the most quoted names in the argument that working-class children and middle-class teachers often communicate ineffectively because of different 'language codes'. He is a British sociologist, often associated with functionalism, although he does not necessarily claim the title for himself. Language codes are a small part of his detailed and complex output, and this argument should be considered in context. The argument revolves around the two types of language in use and the way the education system expects you to express yourself using only one.

Restricted and elaborated codes

Restricted code, he argues, is abbreviated, less grammatical, punctuated by ums, ers, you knows and

BASIL BERNSTEIN (1924–2000)

A British sociologist of education, known especially for his work on the relationship between language, social class and achievement.

body language. Total, explicit detail is unnecessary, as everyone knows what you are talking about. Bernstein's suggestion is that this code is used by middle- and working-class people, particularly children and adolescents. Most youth cultures and each teenage generation have their own slang words, often a code to shut out the older generation. Middle-class children also have access to an elaborated speech code, which is used more by their parents. This is more detailed, 'elaborated' upon, giving references to all things which are needed for a full understanding. The user of elaborated code does not take it for granted that you know what they are talking about, and so they explain in depth. The middle-class parent uses elaborated code when talking to the children, and explains and reasons with them. They are expected to respond in the same way. Working-class parents use restricted code themselves, and their children therefore have no experience of elaborated code, except from their teachers at school.

Abstract ideas

Bernstein's research with children involved showing them cartoon pictures which told a story and asking them to write down what was happening. Children who were used to elaborated code could write the story in full detail, so that the pictures were not needed in order to understand what was happening. Working-class children only wrote the bare bones of the story, and the pictures were vital to get an understanding. He also used interviews to discuss various ideas, so-called 'abstract' concepts, for example religion or truth. Children with restricted code were supposedly unable to express ideas like this in the same way as those using elaborated code.

This ability to deal with abstractions is important in intellectual training, and middle-class children go on to universities to do degree courses which deal with theory – like sociology. The argument, when Bernstein's work was popular in the 1960s and 1970s, seemed to suggest that if you used restricted code, you were unable to cope with so-called 'high status' education. The schools use elaborated codes, because heads and teachers are middle class. Education is geared towards a middle-class definition of what intelligence is. Anyone who comes to school without the accepted speech code will have only limited success.

Labov

What made some sociologists angry was the assumption that the working class could not cope with abstract concepts because of a 'language barrier'. William Labov (1969), one of Bernstein's strongest critics, pointed out that interviewing working-class children in a formal situation, using a middle-class interviewer, was likely to embarrass and restrict them. His own interviews, performed in a more relaxed setting, produced different results. He found that when they felt confident and secure, the children could express their views on abstractions without any problem, often being forceful and articulate. In one interview, for example, he asked an American black boy why he thought God would be white. 'Why?', he replied, 'I'll tell you why! Cause the average whitey out here got everything, you dig. And the nigger ain't got shit, y'know? Y'understan? So-um-for in order for that to happen, you know it ain't no black God that's doing that bullshit.'

This suggests that there is a problem of confidence at the heart of speech and expression, and that the response of teachers to the different ways in which pupils express themselves could be an issue. If middle-class teachers only listen to the ideas articulated by children who are the best users of middle-class speech patterns then the ideas, views and potential of working-class children are undervalued. More recent sociology has addressed the role of the school in constructing 'failure' for some groups of children by ignoring or devaluing their culture, but it was Bernstein's arguments which were among the first to try to explain working-class failure in terms of something being 'wrong' at home.

Questions

1 How does elaborated code differ from restricted code?
2 How does Labov criticise Bernstein?
3 How important is language in interviewing?
4 Which language code is this textbook written in?

Cultural deprivation

In the 1960s the concept of 'cultural deprivation' was put forward to describe and explain what was happening to prevent certain children from doing well in school. According to this, their inability to rise above the basics at school was due to the cultural norms, values and attitudes they brought to the school, evident from their language, life experience, personality, and even their ability to think.

Compensatory education

To compensate for this deficiency, a number of schemes were put forward in both Britain and America, with the aim of making up for this perceived cultural deprivation. In the USA in the mid-1960s the Johnson administration spent billions of dollars on 'Operation Headstart', targeting resources on the 'underprivileged'. In Britain, following the Plowden Report of 1967, four educational priority areas were identified in Liverpool, Birmingham, South-East London and Yorkshire. These were given extra funding, resources and staff in an attempt to enrich the cultural development of the children.

In neither project was any significant improvement discovered. The schemes continued to be defended on the grounds that they had been targeted at children of the wrong age, or for too little time, or – in Britain – with insufficient funding.

Criticisms of the cultural deprivation theory

Others have argued that, as with theories of cultural deprivation in the sociology of crime, health and poverty, those at the bottom of the pile should not be blamed for what appears to be their own inadequacy. Nell Keddie (1973), amongst others, has argued that the concept implies that the culture that the targeted children are part of is in some way deficient. No human can be 'deprived' of culture as it is part of socialisation. What the arguments suggest is that anyone who is deprived of middle-class cultural values is in some way lacking.

According to these critics, the education system, run by the middle class, discriminates against any cultural views which differ from its own. What schools should recognise is 'cultural difference', not deprivation. Working-class culture should be recognised and valued. Those not exposed to middle-class culture in schools would not then underachieve.

Pierre Bourdieu (1973) has criticised the cultural deprivation theory by advancing his own approach, *cultural capital theory*, which is strongly influenced by the Marxist perspective. He argues that the failure of working-class children is the fault of the education system and not working-class culture. Each social class, according to Bourdieu, possesses its own set of meanings or cultural framework, which is internalised through socialisation within the family. Although one culture is not intrinsically superior to another, the power of the dominant class enables them to impose their own framework of meaning on the school as if it were the only legitimate culture. In effect, the dominant class defines what counts as knowledgeable or intelligent activity within the school. Accordingly, working-class children find it difficult to make progress within the education system, while children from the dominant class possess the cultural capital required to achieve academic and eventually occupational success.

Questions

1 What would be included on the timetable of a school which valued and rewarded working-class cultural skills?

2 How does cultural deprivation differ from material deprivation? Could one be the cause of the other?

3 Can you suggest any reasons why schemes of compensatory education fail?

The school and the classroom

As the tripartite system began to merge into comprehensive education, sociologists moved into the classroom, using observation techniques to further their understanding of why some pupils do better at school than others. In these studies, the focus came to be less on the external factors that contribute to differential educational achievement and more on how the organisation of the school, and the teachers within it, contribute to the way the students behave.

Hargreaves and streaming

Three important studies form a complementary sequence of enquiries into secondary modern, grammar and comprehensive schooling. In the first of these, David Hargreaves (1967) used a variety of information-gathering techniques, including teaching, to reach the unsurprising conclusion that students in higher streams have a greater commitment to the values of the school. His main point is that it is the division of the school into streams – student groupings according to levels of academic ability – which creates pupil **subcultures**. These, he says, are of two main types. Those at the top of the streaming system (which went from A to E in the school he examined) form an academic culture which values hard work,

compliance with authority and being well turned-out. At the other end are what he oddly called the 'delinquescents', a subculture which values breaking rules, fighting, smoking, annoying the teachers and bending dress codes.

Hargreaves argues that the school compounds the divisions between the different groups in the way that staff allocation and the structure of the timetable place the two subcultures in separate streams. Like Becker's 'outsiders' (see chapter 8) those in the bottom stream become **deviant** as a common response to the problem of being labelled 'inferior' and 'not worth the effort'.

Lacey

In a similar vein, and also working as a teacher, Colin Lacey (1970) found the same negative effect of streaming prevalent in grammar schools where lower-stream boys were pushed into lives focused outside the school, for example in coffee bars, but not completely into the kind of 'delinquescent' culture described by Hargreaves. In another work Lacey (1975) presents evidence to suggest that when streaming was abandoned in favour of mixed-ability groupings, those academically at the bottom improved their performance in exams, although the most 'able' registered no change.

Ball

These findings were echoed by Stephen Ball's later study (1981) where again he found that grouping students by ability helped form pupil subcultures and that changes away from banding within the school meant that disciplinary and behavioural problems lessened. But it did not necessarily lead to egalitarianism within the school, as teachers continued to make distinctions between 'bright' and 'dull' students, with the 'bright' ones being favoured and encouraged on to better things. Other students were 'cooled out', gently persuaded to drop whatever academic aspirations they may have had on the grounds that they were 'not up to it'. They left school believing that in some way they simply were not intelligent enough, yet this system of stratification within the comprehensive school, Ball says, is actually teacher-defined. Comprehensivisation has not led to equality of opportunity for all up to the leaving age of sixteen.

Rutter and school ethos

Michael Rutter (1979) tried to show, through a six-year longitudinal study and the collection of a mass of statistical information, how objectively similar inner-

London secondary schools could be organised to produce different levels of ability and success: 'Schools do indeed have an effect on children's development and it does matter which school a child attends.'

What matters, Rutter argues, is the quality of the interaction between teacher and pupils, the atmosphere of co-operation, the sense that classes are well planned and prepared. A 'good' school is not necessarily well equipped, but is measured by its overall 'ethos' or value system as determined by indicators such as attendance, academic achievement and behaviour of pupils inside and outside the school. These qualities usually go together, and can be summed up as reflections of the professional organisation and ability of the teaching staff, whether traditional or progressive.

Rutter's work has been heavily criticised, however, mainly for dwelling on what happens in the school, at the expense of variables such as gender, ethnicity, class, what kind of primary school children had attended, or the influence of parents, and what happens to the children when they leave school, once their fifteen thousand hours of compulsory education are up.

Keddie and the teacher's response

The part played by teachers in defining the students' ideas of their own ability is now well documented. Nell Keddie (1971) demonstrated that different types of knowledge are made available to students in different streams, and that questions from different streams are differently treated. Children in the bottom stream are taken less seriously than those in the top streams. As she relates, she asked a teacher whether any pupil had asked in class (as they had in some other classes) 'Why should we do Social Science?' The teacher replied: 'No, but if I were asked by C stream I would try to sidestep it because it would be the same question as "Why do anything? Why work?"' Keddie then asked: 'What if you were asked by an A group?' and the response was: 'Then I'd probably try to answer.'

Yet it is not the case, Keddie argues, that those in the top stream and most favoured by the teachers are necessarily the brightest. They are seen to be succeeding because they match up to the teacher's idea of how an ideal student appears and behaves. 'Good' students do not seek to challenge the fundamentals of what the teacher is presenting, they do not exhibit scepticism about the power structure of the school, the classroom and the knowledge served up within the school. 'Good' students have values and attitudes which match the teacher's values and attitudes.

Although the above studies are based on investigations of how schools can define notions of 'good' or 'bad', 'success' and 'failure', and are couched in the language of interactionism, using concepts of labelling, self-fulfilling prophecies and 'teacher's definitions of the situation', it is a mistake to see them as studies rooted purely in phenomenology. All of them acknowledge the influence of social structure and environmental factors. It is better to see these as studies where sociologists have used whatever methods they feel appropriate to their investigation without being bound by the constraints of one or other perspective. This is a common theme in an area as wide and widely studied as the sociology of education.

Questions

1 What are the main differences between home- and school-based explanations of underachievement?
2 What impact has interactionism had on the sociology of education?
3 What are the main criticisms of concepts of labelling and the self-fulfilling prophecy?

The hidden curriculum

The school curriculum we all know about and understand is the official curriculum, the subjects we see on the timetable. In the early 1970s, sociologists turned their attention to the so-called 'hidden curriculum' – the unwritten, unstudied, tacit, latent, often unnoticed, aspects of school socialisation and learning. Jackson and Marsden (1963) use the term to refer to the unofficial 'three Rs' – Rules, Routines and Regulations – that pupils must cope with in order to fit into a school.

Many of the earlier sociological investigations into the hidden curriculum are indebted to the interactionist sociologist Erving Goffman, whose work on the processes by which individuals adjust and negotiate life in institutions has been very influential in sociology. Goffman did not actually study schools, but his work has been applied to schooling situations, especially his insights on the depersonalising effects of institutions.

Some writers, such as John Holt (1969), imply that the strategy that many pupils have to adopt in order to cope with the institution and the teachers' power is destructive of their love of learning – the curiosity, interest, intelligence and creativity that they naturally have. This is very much in line with the views of Ivan Illich (1976). He sees the hidden curriculum operating to indoctrinate pupils and stifle their imagination. Pupils have very little control over what they learn or how they learn it. He says 'success' is little more than enlightened conformity and adaptation to the demands of authoritarian teaching regimes. Such conformity and obedience are rewarded in schools, not just by a relatively trouble-free passage through the institution, but also by teachers making available, to those pupils who appear to accept the teachers' 'definition of the situation', more highly prized morsels of knowledge, which aid the passing of examination hurdles.

Different perspectives on the hidden curriculum

How a sociologist understands the operation of the hidden curriculum to a great extent depends on the theoretical perspective he or she brings to an analysis. Not all sociologists are critical of the hidden curriculum. For instance, R. Dreeben (1970), in a functionalist interpretation, highlights the contribution that schooling makes to the acquisition of general social norms such as independence and achievement. He sees the hidden curriculum working to act as an important bridge between early socialisation in the home and preparation for adult membership of Western society.

The Marxist view of education as an important aspect of the superstructure of modern capitalist society has for some time stressed the important role of education in passing on attitudes and values which justify the inequalities in the wider society by fostering a view of the status quo as 'natural' and unchangeable. Marxists appear to claim that the details of school subjects are relatively unimportant, whereas the attitudes and values that children internalise via their school experience are most significant. For example, in schools pupils can be encouraged to be competitive rather than co-operative by means of individual work rather than group projects. They can be led to regard the teacher as an authority figure rather than as a friend or an equal. Moreover, sex role divisions can be fostered in various ways and values covertly passed on under the guise of 'objective knowledge'.

The Marxist view thus stresses the 'political' aspect of the education process, maintaining that overall the effect of the hidden curriculum is to foster values that are advantageous to capitalist organisation. The views of Althusser and Bowles and Gintis, which you have already encountered, are in this tradition.

However, it is not necessarily the case that pupils *passively* absorb the hidden curriculum. They may actively attempt to make sense of it, responding in ways that can often be attempts to gain the upper hand and thereby establish the primacy of their own definition of the situation, which may in certain cases conflict strongly with teacher and institutional definitions.

Labelling and self-fulfilling prophecy

Evidence from a number of sociological studies suggests that teachers at all levels may unconsciously discriminate against working-class children. Rosenthal and Jacobson (1968) showed, through a series of experiments, that if teachers are made to believe that certain children have exceptional promise, the children would outperform classmates of equal or even greater talent. Teachers were told that certain children were likely, according to fictitious pre-testing, to spurt ahead, and the children did spurt ahead. The difference between the special children and the ordinary children was only in the mind of the teacher. Incidentally, the performance of the 'ordinary' children in the same classroom tended to improve too, although not as dramatically. The infusion of confidence was contagious.

Palardy (1983) discovered that the brighter a child was assumed to be, the better the results the teacher obtained in class. Groups of boys aged six to seven were matched on ability (based on IQ tests). Teachers then taught them reading in separate classes using the same methods. The only difference was that some of the teachers were told their particular group consisted of boys with above-average ability who should prove faster and more able readers. When the boys were tested at the end of the training period, the teachers' false belief had been transferred into classroom reality – the boys falsely credited with better reading ability could read faster and more fluently.

The combined effect of these researches was to highlight the **self-fulfilling prophecy** and the process of **labelling**. The self-fulfilling prophecy is where a teacher makes an assessment about a pupil. The teacher then predicts progress on the basis of this assessment. This is conveyed to the pupil, who then sees himself/herself in this light. The pupil then begins to live up to the prediction.

Labelling theory is very similar. A pupil does something wrong. The pupil is labelled as a deviant. The pupil then reacts to this label, perhaps feeling he or she is picked on. The behaviour that results may lead to more deviance or behaviour that is seen in that light. To cope, the pupil makes friends with others similarly labelled.

Process and negotiation

Of course, such a sequence, although it does occur, is not inevitable. The pupil may respond to teachers' expectations by ignoring them. Teachers' behaviour will itself have been influenced by pupils' behaviour. An elaborate model of the sequence, therefore, would encompass the idea of process. In interactionist terminology, 'process' implies that human interaction is not fixed but fluid and constantly developing. Each person involved in the interaction process affects the behaviour of all the others concerned, and therefore contributes to the overall nature of the interaction. Thus the nature of the social encounter is not given to the participants but is made by them. Social situations are often said to be 'negotiated' by the participants. In the classroom, both teachers' and pupils' behaviour emerges from a process of negotiation.

However, interactionists have been criticised for failing to explain the mechanisms that lie behind the processes they describe. For example, in her study of a large comprehensive school, Nell Keddie (1973) describes in detail the characteristics of what the teachers considered to be a 'normal' (i.e. 'A' stream) pupil. But she does not explain why the majority of teachers shared more or less the same definition of a normal pupil, nor does she examine the wider structural framework of society that allows this definition to go unchallenged. This wider framework means that some people have more power than others to define situations, and to attach and to resist labels. Likewise, many interactionists note that class differences can influence the forms that interaction takes in the classroom, but they fail to explain how those class differences originate.

Some attempts have been made to combine interactionist studies of schools with sociological perspectives that do take into account the wider context of society. Sharp and Green (1975), for example, studied the way that teachers in an infant school judged the performance of pupils in their classes. But they refused to see these 'judgements' as the product purely of the consciousness of individual teachers. Instead, they showed that a variety of constraints affected teachers' views, including the large size of classes and the pressures even at an early age to classify pupils in the interests of eventual occupational placement. The main theoretical conclusion from Sharp and Green's study is that the meanings held by the individuals concerned do not, on their own, determine what happens within education, and that interactionists need to broaden their concerns to take account of such factors as the educational policies of the State which determine the conditions in which teachers and pupils work.

Knowledge and status

Middle-class knowledge

M. F. D. Young (1971) and others assert that the causes of underachievement are to be found in the interactions between individuals and school. Who controls knowledge? Who defines what is important to learn? Why are some subjects 'high' status, some 'low' status? They argue that the middle classes have a monopoly on knowledge. They succeed in education and are in a position to state what is and what is not important. Literacy and numeracy skills, reading, writing and arithmetic, abstract subjects, classical studies, Latin, Greek, sciences, maths are all considered types of knowledge worthy of the schools. Bricklaying, carpentry and physical development are undervalued, secondary, low-status subjects. This split mirrors the working-class–middle-class culture divide. The things which working-class culture values most are immediate, practical skills, which can be used to help everyday existence. Being 'good with your hands', able to do things, helps you now, whereas months and years of study of abstract maths seems irrelevant.

The children who accept the teacher's idea of what knowledge is will do well. To argue with the teacher about the value and worth of the lesson does not help you. It is not seen as original or challenging thinking, just trouble-making – deviance. The 'brightest' pupils accept the teacher's total control of knowledge, and they live up to this definition in the classroom. The 'failures' rebel and argue along the lines of 'what use is this?' and are seen as unintelligent. They are left to create what meanings they can from their situation, dossing around and bunking off until they can leave school and get a job or go on the dole. Working-class failure is built into the system, and the interactions between teachers and pupils help to make sure that the failures take place. The definition and control of knowledge are maintained by the middle classes for the middle classes, and they go on to secure their hold on education, knowledge, intelligence and success.

Post-modernist perspectives on education

Post-modernists are opposed to any belief that there is a firm foundation of knowledge; they are critical of any attempt to offer totalising and definitive explanations and theories. Post-modernists would therefore view with scepticism the liberal claim that human potential can be achieved through education. They would be equally sceptical about the conservative claim of functionalists that education can produce shared values and social solidarity, and of the Marxist belief that education serves as a tool for the ideological conditioning of the future workforce under capitalism.

Post-modernism also rejects the idea that there is a single best curriculum that should be followed in schools. If there is no one set of truths that can be accepted, then there are no grounds for claiming that one thing should be taught in all schools whereas other things should be excluded. Usher and Edwards (1994) have developed this point by considering how the education system might develop in post-modernity. They recognise that there are many possibilities and reject any attempt to offer a definitive statement about what education should be like in contemporary societies. However, they suggest that education should be sufficiently flexible to cater for different people, including groups that are relatively powerless and currently may be alienated by the education system. This would help to dissolve what Usher and Edwards see as the élitism of modern education with its bias towards serving the interests of dominant groups such as white, wealthy males. They suggest that oppressed groups can fight back against their disadvantages through localised campaigns to shape educational provision so that it reflects their interests and lifestyle aspirations.

Another trend within post-modernism is for knowledge (particularly in the form of qualifications and skills derived through formal education) to become a commodity that can be bought and sold. Knowledge is valued primarily because it can be exchanged for money in the labour market. It may also be valued because it provides a means for disadvantaged and oppressed groups to escape from their situation, i.e. through learning and acquiring qualifications. Usher and Edwards suggest that adult education in particular may be important for these groups, offering an opportunity for empowerment in terms of the increased consumption of desired goods and images.

Post-modernist accounts of education have been criticised for tending to ignore the wider political and economic forces that are shaping education. They therefore tend to neglect the sorts of insights into education offered by Marxists and neo-Marxists. The idea that disadvantaged groups can significantly change their lifestyle opportunities through localised struggles

to transform educational provision may be naive if it is unsupported by an analysis of the wider social and economic forces that constrain and shape the education system. It is also often unclear whether post-modernists are describing changes in the education system or advocating particular changes or both.

Questions

1 What is seen as 'high status' knowledge in school?
2 Is it true to say that the middle and working classes value different types of knowledge?
3 Should manual skills have a higher educational status?

Counter culture

Paul Willis (1977) used a Marxist perspective to inform his research, which was carried out over a two-year period in a manufacturing district near Birmingham ('Hammertown'). He spent time, however, observing, interviewing and participating with a main study group of twelve working-class 'non-conformist' pupils in a tough secondary modern school. Willis was trying to show that there is a strong relationship between factory shop-floor culture and school culture. Responsibility for their actions is allocated to the individuals, or their group, and they are seen as taking an active part in their own failure. The class basis of this is always present in the ways the boys make sense of school. They use ideas which come from their parents, ideas about work. The 'shop-floor counter culture' is the way workers inject some humour and have a laugh at work, while still getting the work done. This humour is sexist, cruel and aggressively 'anti-intellectual'. The boys' fathers revel in the macho aspect of manual labour. They earn good money, work hard, have a laugh at the bosses, whom they see as weaklings, who could not lift a sledgehammer if they tried. They accept their status and are suspicious of authority.

This culture is used and re-created by their sons, who see school as a necessity, a bore unless you spice life up a bit by annoying the staff, fighting, thieving, and avoiding schoolwork. Their rebellion is subtle, obeying the rules but doing so only when necessary, smiling, nudging, playing the innocent. They take the model which teachers offer – 'you listen to me, learn and you will get on' – and turn it upside-down. They are giving their lives some colour and interest by weighing up the teachers, destroying school property, scorning the kids who do accept the teacher's model by calling them 'earoles' or 'lobes'. They call themselves 'the lads'. The lads are aware of their non-conformity. They form a small, extreme group, which creates a cultural space for itself and, from the teachers' point of view, ruins the educational process.

Willis's study is long and overcomplex in its language, but as a piece of ethnographic research it is excellent reading. The creativity of the disruption is a proof of the imagination and humour these boys possess, an originality and wit which is only allowed expression in their working futures when they play practical jokes on their workmates to break up the boredom of another working day.

Cultural style

'Havin' a laff' is the sole reason for being at school. They are rebels, and look down on the 'earoles', although knowing full well what will happen. They accept that the 'earoles' will 'succeed' and go on to get better jobs, but they see that as damnation. They want to embrace their future as manual labourers, because that is where they will be able to continue to express their cultural style – swearing, fighting, sexism, physical labour and easy money. The culture they are embracing – fatalistic, harsh, humorous, manly – is the only way to live. They oppose school values, and this opposition fits in with their class culture. Willis emphasises that their parents may not encourage this, but in the end the culture of their class is available to them. They take this culture, which is the shop-floor response to boredom and alienation, and rework it into their school situation.

The comparative studies Willis carried out, for instance with middle-class anti-school groups in a grammar school, show that they have similar attitudes to 'the lads' in their anti-school activities, but when the middle-class non-conformist gets home he faces a cultural attitude to career and society which mirrors that of the school. This child cannot use the shop-floor counter culture and rework it at school, so the anti-school activities and attitudes are less extreme, unsupported by the class culture.

Cultural space and cultural reproduction

Willis shows how individual and group creation of a cultural space at school, a way to get through the day, having 'a laff' and not working, is related to the class structure of society and the nature of work under capitalism. The lads create their own failure, and do so willingly, rejecting all the middle-class educational values. They are active in ensuring their own 'failure', but they see it as success. The schools and teachers are forced into aiding and abetting this, since there are no methods acceptable in education to try to alter it. These boys are said by staff to deserve their fate. They rebel at school and thus ensure that capitalism continues, as the class structure is reproduced. Working-class kids get working-class jobs because their whole cultural style insists that they must. They do not trust penpushers, but respect honest manual labour. They have actually conformed, willingly participated in reproducing the system, and their conformity is a product of their rebellion.

The Marxist-interactionist aspect of this study makes it an interesting example of the new approach to sociology in the 1970s. One of the main criticisms of Willis is the sexist ignoring of girls' voices in the study – how do *they* see 'the lads', *their* work, and *their* future? The girls are relegated to the role of 'the missus' by the lads, and their mothers say even less. The fact that Willis studied only boys has led some to remark that the subtitle to his work should really read 'How working-class boys get working-class jobs'.

Another problem is that he neglects ethnicity in a school with a substantial number of Asian and Afro-Caribbean students. He has also been criticised for the extent of his 'participation' with the lads, some critics suggesting that he encouraged their behaviour. For example, in one interview he talked to two pupils who told him how they broke into the school. Is this ethical? The most telling criticism is that you cannot generalise from a small, unrepresentative sample. However, this study does provide insights into the two sides of the argument about working-class under-achievement. Class culture, the home and parents' attitudes are important, but the individual social action which reproduces these attitudes, and the interaction between cultures and individuals in school is complex, subtle and loaded with meaning. Willis states that it is most difficult to understand why working-class kids let themselves fail and they leave the middle-class jobs for middle-class kids. His analysis of class, culture and the school goes some way towards answering that, but within a Marxist framework. Education is firmly rooted in the ideological superstructure, and the social processes take care of themselves. Capitalism sits back and lets it happen.

Gender

Girls' experience of school has always been different from that of boys. This is as old as, if not older than, the growth of State intervention in education in the late nineteenth century. In this period, the central motive behind educating girls was that they should become either knowledgeable companions for men if they were middle class (an approach pioneered by Cheltenham Ladies College), or domestically able if they were not. Working-class girls were uniformly taught needlework, cooking and domestic science, in an age where the highest profession any woman could aim for was that of governess. The first women's higher education college, Queen's College, was instituted with the sole aim of training governesses. Women were not allowed to take degrees at the University of London until 1878, at Oxford until 1920, and on equal terms with men at Cambridge until 1948 – although they were allowed to attend some lectures after 1872!

Sexism in education has persisted into the twentieth century and is reflected in numerous government reports. The 1926 Board of Education report – *Education of Adolescents* – advocated an expansion of

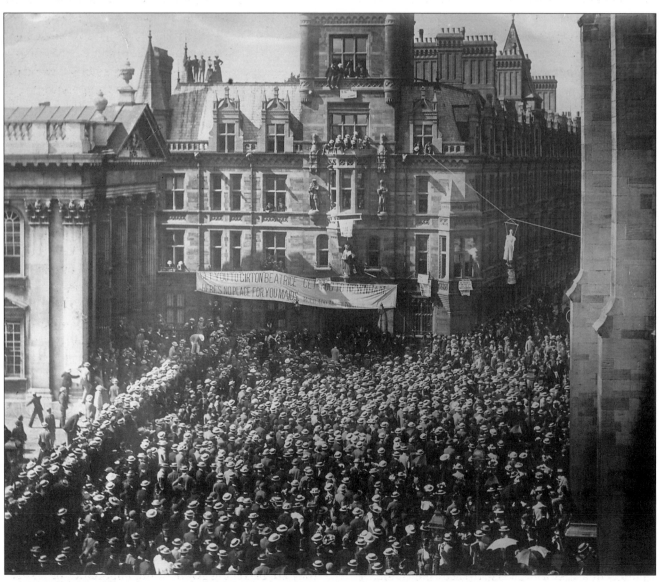

Sexism in education: male students at Cambridge University demonstrate against the admission of women in 1897.

the housecraft syllabus for girls on the grounds that 'Greater efficiency in the housewife would go far to raise her status in the estimation of the community', by which they mean the male community. In the year before the 1944 Act, the Norwood Report accepted the view that the destiny for a boy might be to get a job and be academically successful, while for girls it was to marry and raise children, neither of which require academic success. In the same year as the Robbins Report, the Newsom Report, *Half our Futures* (1963), argued that 'In addition to their needs as individuals, girls should be educated in terms of their main function – which is to make for themselves, their children and their husbands a secure and suitable home and to be mothers.'

The problem of equality

In a different climate, the Sex Discrimination Act of 1975 made it illegal for girls and boys to be treated differently at school, and demanded equal school curricula, with both boys and girls moving out of their traditional subject areas. The Act, however, did not say how this was to happen, and there has been a considerable debate about whether co-educational (mixed) or single-sex schools are more beneficial to girls. The evidence to date – Sandra Harding (1980) and Alison Kelly (1981) – suggests that girls perform better academically when boys are out of the way.

Sexual divisions in education

Girls have long been more successful than boys in the early years of education. However, in the past, boys tended to outperform girls in most areas after the age of 16. This is no longer the case in the UK. In 1981 the proportion of pupils in the UK gaining two or more GCE A Levels (or equivalents) was 30 per cent for boys and 28 per cent for girls. By the early 1990s, however, girls had bridged the achievement gap and since then they have surpassed boys. In 2001 the proportion of pupils gaining two or more GCE A Levels (or equivalents) was 37 per cent for boys and 42 per cent for girls.

The number of females staying on in education or training after the age of 16 has also increased. In 1986, 41 per cent of males but just 33 per cent of females in the UK stayed on in education or training until they were 18. In 1999 there was little difference between the sexes, with 62 per cent of males and 60 per cent of females still in education or training at 18. In terms of access to university places the change is even more dramatic. In 1970 males outnumbered females on university degree courses by 2 to 1. By 1999 females outnumbered males.

In seeking to understand why female achievement in education has improved so markedly in recent years, it is helpful to consider explanations for the underperformance of girls that occurred in earlier decades. It is important to note that some of the processes discussed may still be preventing female pupils from achieving their full potential.

Explanations for female underperformance

In trying to explain female underachievement, the concept of a **stereotype** – a fixed image based on traditional ideas of what someone is or should be like – has been greatly used. The stereotype of girls and boys persists throughout life – not least in education. Girls are domestically inclined, and are centred on the 'internal' world of the home, where they serve men. At school, they opt for subjects that do not challenge their feminine self-concept, making biology their only foray into the scientific domain. Boys, being more outgoing and aggressive, are interested in the 'external' world of discovery and adventure, science and engineering, subjects that confirm their masculinity.

Glenys Lobban (1974) reported on the rigid, stereotyped imagery of gender associated with children's books. The images mirror adult roles. Boys do active things; the girl is at home with mother. The girl is often seen making a cake, washing, sewing, ironing and so on with her mother. Subsequent studies have conducted detailed analysis of reading material, for example Ann Coote (1981) discovered that Ladybird books presented very different role models for boys from those offered for girls. Since this study, there have been major changes in images in reading schemes. It is difficult to assess the impact, however, of sexist imagery, and we cannot state with certainty what the effect is likely to be on children who are constantly exposed to it.

E. Belotti (1975) has shown how girls are expected to conform, more than boys. Bad behaviour by girls is not tolerated as much as it is by boys. Girls are also assumed to be capable of domestic roles, tidying up the classrooms, doing jobs for teacher. AnnMarie Wolpe (1978) refers to evidence of the 'coaching' of little girls by their teachers into appropriate feminine behaviour. She thinks that schooling is especially important in the learning of gender identity, since children are in school for much of the period when they are becoming aware of the importance of sexual relationships, and thus learning the definitions of approved adult masculinity and femininity. She describes schooling for working-class girls as an attempt to produce 'an adaptable, pliable and docile labour source with only marginal skills'.

Jones (1980) found that different types of discipline were administered to girls and boys. Girls received fewer and less severe reprimands. Teachers talked to boys and girls in different ways. Girls were frequently spoken to in a tone of irritated tolerance, for example 'stop the chatter, GIRLS!'. Male teachers verbally encouraged girls, perhaps patting them on the head, but to avoid causing them embarrassment in mixed classes asked them fewer questions and easier ones.

Staffing in secondary education continues to show male dominance. Whilst women hold 60 per cent of the lowest posts in secondary education, only 23 per cent of head teachers are women. The teaching profession is also divided by subject area. Small wonder boys and girls talk of 'boys' and 'girls' subjects. 50–55 per cent of teachers of English are women. Less than 33 per cent of maths teachers are women. Even fewer women teach physics and chemistry.

Confidence

Carol Dweck (1972) suggests that girls in mixed schools have a different profile in the classroom to boys. Boys are more the subject of the teacher's focus than girls, they are disciplined more, while girls are only likely to be picked up for academic mistakes, not their conduct. Girls believe that if they do well, it is because they have worked hard or have been lucky, not because they have more ability; boys attribute their success to their ability but if they fail they blame it on bad luck or lack of effort. Doing well becomes a question of confidence, which teachers fail to bolster in girls. Lacking confidence, girls resist new challenges, learn 'helplessness' and correspondingly lower their aspirations and academic goals. This pattern, Dweck argues, is present for girls even when they become university undergraduates. Males, on the other hand, suffer none of these problems of self-assurance and even entertain wildly exaggerated ideas about what careers lie ahead for them.

This argument can be extended to examine the different types of knowledge and techniques involved in studying arts and science subjects. Subjects such as French, German and Spanish, as well as being once considered 'appropriate' for Victorian middle-class girls as conversational arts, develop by building on an existing knowledge base. Science subjects, such as physics and chemistry, progress through constantly taking on new ideas and concepts, at the same time continuously exposing students to the risk of failure. Biology, however, which does not carry the same masculine identification as other natural sciences, is perceived differently.

The visibility of girls and women

Tessa Blackstone and Helen Weinrich-Haste (1980) suggest that differential educational achievement can be overcome if three areas are tackled. First, positive role models are needed. This involves textbooks where role images are not gender-based, or where girls are seen doing unstereotypical things. This also applies to teachers: women should teach technology and men domestic science and more women should occupy senior positions in schools. Secondly, teachers themselves should raise their expectations of what girls are capable of, as they are a key contributor to reinforcing gender roles. In a series of interviews with seven classes of boy and girl pupils, Michelle Stanworth (1983) collated information that revealed that the students themselves claimed that boys stand out more vividly in classroom interaction, are four times more likely to join in a discussion or make comments in class, twice as likely to demand help or attention from the teacher and to be asked questions, and five times more likely to be the ones to whom teachers pay attention. The third area is pupil motivation. Girls need to be encouraged to develop a sense of independence, self-reliance and belief in their own ability. They suggest that single-sex schools may help girls in their most 'vulnerable' (to losing confidence) years, and science courses should be compulsory up to the age of sixteen. The National Curriculum is a move in this direction.

Sharpe

Sue Sharpe's interviews with Ealing schoolgirls reinforce these ideas (Sharpe, 1976). Although a majority of her respondents expected to stop work for only a few years when their children were small, they nevertheless saw marriage as a career in itself and success in male-dominated areas as abnormal and unattractive. What they have to overcome is the force of their socialisation: 'by the time a girl reaches adolescence,' she says, 'her mind has usually been subjected to an endless stream of ideas and images incorporating sexist values'.

Christine Griffin (1986) found that deviant girls are deviant in a different way from boys. In attempting to replicate Paul Willis's study, *Learning to Labour*, she found that while 'most young men "hung around" in those "gangs of lads" which have provided the foundation for so many studies of youth cultures and subcultures, young women either had one extremely close "best" girlfriend, or spent time with a small group of two, three or four female friends. At the most basic level, there was no clear similarity between the social structures of female and male friendship groups.'

The structure of gender inequality

This is not to say that the position of women in the labour market will necessarily change simply because their schooling has become more genuinely egalitarian. As Carol Buswell (1991) warns: 'Education may occasionally help individuals to change their class but it cannot change their sex, and thus the structural position of women becomes an important aspect of understanding the educational

experiences, achievements and choices of girls.' It is the awareness of inequalities outside of school that will continue to contribute to girls' performance while still in school, no matter how 'gender-free' that experience may be.

It must also be said that, in discussing the relative performance of girls and boys in school and considering the problem of gender-stereotyping, the very notion of 'girls' as a single undifferentiated, homogeneous group is itself a stereotype, as with notions of age, ethnicity or class. Girls can individually and collectively be bright or dull; noisy or quiet; riotously uncontrollable and wild or passive, dutiful and co-operative.

Reasons for the improved achievement of females

A variety of explanations has been offered for the improved achievement of females in education. The

Is the underachievement of boys a new phenomenon?

increased involvement of married women in the labour market, especially since the Second World War, has increased the incentive for women to gain educational qualifications. Sharpe (1994) repeated her 1970s research on teenage girls in the 1990s. She found that they no longer attached primary importance to marriage and having children, and instead emphasised the importance of having a job or career more than their counterparts had in the 1970s.

Eirene Mitsos and Ken Browne (1998) argue that the women's movement and feminist sociologists have highlighted some of the disadvantages faced by girls. As a result, schools are now generally more committed to improving opportunities for girls. They also cite research that shows girls tend to be better organised than boys. Girls' greater motivation and organisational skills may give them an advantage in carrying out coursework tasks, which now count for more in assessments than was the case in the past.

There may also be factors that are causing males to underachieve. The decline in heavy industry has taken away many of the jobs for which working-class boys would traditionally have been expected to train. This may have removed the incentive for working-class boys to try hard at school, as they see little chance of attaining a 'good' job at the end of it. The trend to teach boys and girls together in schools (known as coeducation) may also have contributed to the underperformance of boys. This is because boys are more likely to show off and disrupt the lessons in mixed-sex classes. This partly explains why boys are much more likely to be expelled: some 80 per cent of those permanently excluded from schools in the UK are boys.

Questions

1 Why have girls been treated differently in the education system?
2 What policies have been developed in order to overcome the problem of differential achievement by gender?
3 What have been the main reasons for the improvement in female educational attainment?

Ethnicity

Ethnic minorities in Britain have provided and continue to provide new statistical patterns for sociologists to explain. It is highly misleading – if not racist – to see all non-whites as an undifferentiated mass, lumping them all together as a single ethnic minority. The pattern of educational results shows different levels of achievement between different groups. Broadly speaking, Indians have the same level of attainment as whites, while West Indians and Bangladeshis, by contrast, consistently underachieve. A number of arguments, backed by research, have been put forward to explain this pattern.

The patterns which emerged in the 1960s showed that some children of Asian origin were underachieving, mainly due to language barriers, but that once this is overcome they achieve on a level with white middle-class children. If the categories are further divided there are differences within the Asian group according to caste and class.

Afro-Caribbean British children have also been shown to underachieve, although again this problem is complicated by, for example, gender differences. Why does this group underachieve? Some of the explanations which have been offered are similar to those used to explain social class underachievement. 'Disorganised' families, the lack of encouragement, poor housing and attitudes to white authority have all been blamed.

Ethnocentricity

Experiments in **compensatory education** have attempted to remedy this underachievement, but have had little success. However, explanations which look into the classroom provide more insight. The British government's policy toward education in the 1950s, 1960s and most of the 1970s was to ignore cultural differences and educate all children into a white, British culture. This was reflected in the reading schemes which showed an all-white home and society. Blacks were invisible or in low-status roles such as bus conductors or maids. Enid Blyton's Noddy was mugged by golliwogs; the black witch and the black wood held evil; the white prince and princess were beautiful and good. At a higher level, history gave a glowing account of the wonder and kindness of the British, extending their Empire all over the world and civilising 'savages'. There is a great deal of argument about the effects of these factors, and some argue that a childhood of Noddy and the golliwogs does not make you a racist or a sexist. However, the unconscious internalisation of negative images may leave a stereotype lurking in your head, which makes you racist without you knowing it.

Class

As with other aspects of educational attainment, class is seen as an important dimension of ethnicity, and it has been suggested that Indians and African Asians (most of whom were thrown out of Uganda and Kenya in the 1970s) occupy a higher class position than either West Indians or Bangladeshis. This is a consequence of the differing historical factors behind their immigration into Britain. It then follows that class plays a role in their educational lives in the same ways discussed elsewhere in this chapter. Similarly, it has been asserted that, for historical and cultural reasons, it has been easier for Indians to fit into British culture. Some commentators have also pointed to the disproportionately high number of single-parent Afro-Caribbean families, with insufficient time and money to support their children during their school years.

Gender

Numerous studies have also shown that Afro-Caribbean girls do better than boys while at school. In trying to understand why this happens, Mary Fuller (1980) found that, while black girls are unwilling to show it, they recognise the importance for their futures of getting good qualifications. At the same time they are determined to achieve them without compromising their positive self-image as black and female or showing their teachers, or the boys, that they are too keen. Outwardly, they appear to be uninterested and indifferent to what is happening in the classroom.

It is less clear why Afro-Caribbean boys become unmotivated and develop forms of resistance to school. Racism in the curriculum, from teachers, and in the wider society have all been suggested as contributory factors, but they have not as yet been confirmed by research. These three factors, of course, remain essential to any understanding of the relationship between ethnicity and educational underachievement.

The white middle-class teacher

Unconscious, or covert, racial differentiation can be a part of teaching practice. The teacher is most likely to be white and socialised by a British culture which some anti-racist thinkers claim is riddled with racism. Their outlook and background are white and middle class, steeped in the glories of the British Empire when it was the 'white man's burden' to educate,

Christianise and 'civilise' the blacks. Four hundred years of these attitudes cannot be changed overnight. Teachers may use stereotypes of West Indians as deviant or unintelligent or subnormal. Labelled in this way, meeting racism in reading books, textbooks and from other children, black youths are forced to react and often 'fail'. Stereotypes of being good at sport and music actively work against them: being given time off lessons to practise basketball or to play in the steel band leave gaps in a pupil's education.

Multicultural and anti-racist education

The pattern of underachievement was so marked that it was recognised by Afro-Caribbean parents in the early 1960s, and voluntary Saturday schools, staffed by black parents and teachers, to supplement the basic education have been operational for many years. During the 1970s and 1980s, a policy response to this discrimination was developed – 'multicultural education'. The idea is to provide an education in cultures which exist alongside and within white, middle-class culture. Non-European history, languages and religion were injected into the curriculum in many inner-city, mixed-race schools. However, schools in parts of the country where there were few ethnic minorities (middle-class areas) did not take this up, and the children who needed it most, those whose only meeting with other cultures was in racist texts, never experienced multiculturalism.

The latest direction in education criticises this approach as worthless. Anti-racist educationists say that multiculturalism merely dabbles in cultural differences, and dressing everyone up in saris or listening to calypsos and reggae does not address the real issues of racism, prejudice and discrimination. Leading children to believe that there is racial equality and respect for all cultures in society does not do children any favours. British society is racist, and education should address the issues of discrimination, prejudice and racial hatred.

Questions

1 What is the pattern of educational achievement by ethnic group?
2 What explanations have been offered for differential educational achievement of some ethnic minority groups?

7 Religion

Introduction

The chapter begins by looking at the different ways in which religion can be defined and understood before looking at the values and beliefs held by some of the world's great religions. Functionalist, Marxist and Weberian perspectives on the role of religion in societies, and the key concepts of church, denomination and sect are considered. The question of whether religion continues to play an important role in modern life is considered in the section on secularisation. The chapter ends by looking at contemporary changes in religion, including the emergence of religious fundamentalism and the post-modernist interpretation of these changes.

Problems of definition

Religion is a fundamental feature of any society, and in many cases is central to a definition of that society. Yet defining what is meant by religion is not an easy task. What is seen as religious in one society may not correspond to what is seen as religious in another. Similarly, the role and function of religion in one society may again be different in another. Yet the definition of religion is important: how it is defined will determine how it is perceived, and will inform the debate about the continuing relevance of religion in the twenty-first century (see **secularisation**, pp.181–4).

For Durkheim, what is religious in a society is what is regarded as sacred, as distinct from those aspects of a society that are seen as profane. Religion, then, is 'a unified system of beliefs and practices relative to sacred things, that is to say, things set apart and forbidden – beliefs and practices which unite into one single moral community called a Church – and all those who adhere to them' (Durkheim, 1912). The sociology of religion, according to this definition, should concern itself with examining religious practice towards what is regarded as sacred, and its organisation within a 'church' and the contribution they make to the maintenance and survival of that society. It is the binding and integrative function of the church which distinguishes it from other, similar practices, for example within magic, particularly in its durability.

One problem with looking at religion in this way, as Phillip Hammond (1985) observes, is that not all that is sacred is necessarily religious, and a fully secular society (that is, one without religion) could nevertheless contain things which are sacred, such as the practices that surround nationalism (for example practising allegiance to a flag, or the profane practice of burning it). Others (see, e.g., Robert Coles, 1975) have claimed that even football, with its signs, symbols, ritualistic practices and devoted followers, could be seen as conforming to Durkheim's definition.

From a more Weberian point of view, religion is any set of coherent answers to human existential dilemmas which make the world meaningful. Although it is not a term that Weber believed could be defined, it could be explored through research: 'To define "religion", to say what it is, is not possible at the start ... Definition can be attempted, if at all, only at the conclusion of the study. The definition of religion is not even our concern' (Weber, 1922). This view moves the focus on religion from what religion does to what it is, and how it is experienced by people.

Writing from a **phenomenological** perspective, Peter Berger (1990) defines religion as the 'human enterprise by which the sacred cosmos is established ... By sacred is meant here a quality of mysterious and awesome power, other than man and yet related to him, which is believed to reside in certain objects of experience'. This view of religion, however, is all-inclusive, as all humans face existential dilemmas to which they seek to find answers, though they may not wish to regard these answers as religious, particularly if their sense of awe is towards the scientifically revealed power of the natural world.

Some definitions have attempted to synthesise the notion of what religion is with what religion does. For example, Steve Bruce states that 'Religion consists of beliefs, actions and institutions which assume the existence of supernatural entities with powers of action, or impersonal powers or processes possessed of moral purpose' (Bruce, 1995). Charles Glock and Rodney Stark (1965) argue that however religion is defined, its study should include the different levels of belief that exist at individual and group level, the involvement of individuals in acts of worship and celebration, the sense of the supernatural and spiritual, the breadth and depth of knowledge and understanding of religion, and how all of these aspects affect people's daily lives.

Questions

1 Why is defining religion problematic?

2 In what ways might football be similar to religion?

Religious movements

There is a great deal of crossover between the great religions of the world. In large part, for example, Christianity is derived from the Judaic tradition, while Islam owes much to the rise of Christianity. All these religions see Moses and Abraham as prophets, as do many smaller religions such as the Baha'i faith. Between them they dominate the European landmass, particularly the various forms of Christianity (Roman Catholicism and Eastern Orthodox as well as many forms of Protestantism); Christianity is dominant too in North and South America. Islam dominates much of Africa either side of the Sahara, and the Middle East, as well as significant parts of Central Asia (Pakistan, Afghanistan) and Indonesia. In China the dominant religions are Confucianism and Taoism (if they haven't been suppressed by **communism**) and in the Far East, Buddhism and Shintoism. Hinduism dominates in India, with Sikhism preponderant in the Punjab.

Although exact calculations are impossible, the following list indicates the extent of religious affiliation around the globe (see also *Figure 7.1*).

1 Christianity: 2 billion (or approximately one-third of the world's population)

2 Islam: 1.3 billion (which is predominantly divided into Sunnis and Shi'ites)

3 Hinduism: 900 million

4 Secular/Non-religious/Agnostic/Atheist: 850 million

5 Buddhism: 360 million

Figure 7.1 Religious affiliation

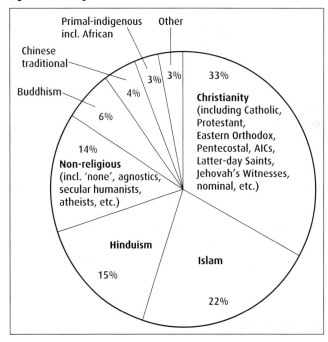

6 Chinese traditional religion: 225 million

7 Primal-indigenous: 150 million

8 African traditional and diasporic: 95 million

9 Sikhism: 23 million

10 Juche: 19 million

11 Spiritism: 14 million

12 Judaism: 14 million

13 Baha'i: 6 million

14 Jainism: 4 million

15 Shinto: 4 million

16 Cao Dai: 3 million

The five great religions of the world are Judaism, Christianity, Islam, Buddhism and Hinduism.

Judaism

Contemporary Western societies are built on Judaism,

itself based on the first five books of the Old Testament or Pentateuch, the word of God through the prophet Moses. The story in Genesis and Exodus tells the story of the flight of the Jews, led by Moses, from Egypt to the Promised Land, now modern-day Israel. A second sacred book, the Torah, contains 613 commandments or Mitzvot. Jews follow Sedarim or orders:

→ Zera'im – contains prayers and agricultural laws

→ Mo'ed – matters concerned with Shabbat (the sabbath) and festivals
→ Nashim – marital and divorce laws
→ Nezikin – civil and criminal law
→ Kodashim – laws of sacrifice and temple ritual
→ Tohorot – laws on personal and religious purity.

Judaism is monotheistic. It believes in only one God, Jehovah, who warns, in the Ten Commandments, not to worship any other gods or images. The Jewish people were dispersed after the fall of the Temple in Jerusalem in AD 70 and did not regroup as a nation until the creation of the state of Israel, following the Nazi programme to exterminate them in the late 1930s and early 1940s, events known as the Holocaust. Jews worship in synagogues. The Jewish calendar is dated from the year they believe the universe was created. (5760 is equivalent to AD 2000. Judaism and Judaic practice are at the core of government practice in Israel.

Christianity

Christianity emerged from Judaism as a **sect** within it, the religion of the followers or disciples of the prophet (or messiah) Jesus Christ. Their calendar is dated from the year of his birth in what is now Israel (Judea), and the word of the Christian God is contained in the Old and New Testaments of the Bible. It is also monotheistic, seeing Jesus as the son of God. Some versions of Christianity are trinitarian, seeing God as made of three people in one: father, son and holy ghost. Responding in faith to the grace of God is seen as the way of overcoming sin and achieving salvation through the Holy Spirit. The fruits of the Holy Spirit are: love, joy, patience, kindness, faithfulness, goodness, humility, self-control and peace.

Christianity has been split into many churches for several centuries, organised in the West as Roman Catholicism and Protestantism, and in Eastern Europe as the various Orthodox churches. The divide between Catholicism and Protestantism originated in the Middle Ages from the disputes initially between Martin Luther and the Pope. Movements to reunite these two wings of Christianity are known as **ecumenism**. Christian worship, in the form of a service or mass, takes place in a church.

Islam

Islam (which means 'submission') originates from the word of the prophet Mohammed, born in Mecca in Saudi Arabia in AD 570. The monotheistic God or Allah gave his words via the angel Gabriel to Mohammed and are now found in the Koran. Followers of Islam, or Muslims, date their Hijri calendar from the year Mohammed migrated from Mecca to Medina (now in Saudi Arabia), which can be calculated on the basis of AH 1420 being equivalent to AD 2000, although Islamic years are eleven days shorter than Christian ones. Islam is built on top of Judaism and Christianity, recognising figures such as Adam, Moses, Abraham and Jesus (Isa) as prophets. Muslims are required to observe five practices in their life – the five pillars of Islam:

1 The recitation of the Islamic creed (Shahadah) that there is no god but Allah, and Mohammed is his prophet.
2 The saying of prayers at five set times of the day (Salat), always facing Mecca.
3 The observance of Ramadan (Sawm), when food and drink may not be consumed during daylight hours.
4 The giving of alms or money to the poor (Zakat), usually at least 2.5 per cent of a person's income.
5 Making at least one pilgrimage (or Haj) to Mecca.

There are a number of groupings within Islam. The great majority of followers are Sunnis. The Shi'a are a smaller group who reject the first three Caliphs or successors to Mohammed and follow Ali, husband of the Prophet's daughter. Shi'ites practise Sharia law, or the literal word of god, as revealed in the Koran, and Sh'ite Islam is the state religion of Iran.

Hinduism

Hinduism (or Sanata Dharma, the eternal way of life) is regarded by many as the world's oldest religion and may be 6,000 years old. Its central figure is Brahman, the one ultimate truth and eternal presence that encompasses all reality, who emerges in millions of manifestations, but most characteristically in the Trimurti (Brahma the creator, Vishnu the preserver and Shiva the destroyer). For many Hindus there are

The height of the Haj: Muslims at the Kaba and Sacred Mosque in Mecca, Saudi Arabia.

four goals (purusharthas) in life: Moksha, the release of the soul from the cycle of rebirth; Dharma, the observation of the code for leading one's life; Artha, the pursuit of material gain by lawful means; and Karma, reincarnation to a higher level through pure acts, knowledge and devotion. Its core beliefs, mainly found in the four Vedas, include reincarnation and the caste system (see also chapter 3). Worship takes place in temples where offerings or Pura are made to the Gods. There are sixteen Samskaras or rites of passage, and four Ashramas or ideal stages of life: Brahmacharin or Student stage, Grihastha or Householder stage, Vanaprastha, the stage of Retiring or Retreating from society and Sannyasin, Holy man who has no ties with society. Hindus, who are mainly located on the Indian sub-continent, do not attempt to convert others to their religion.

Buddhism

Buddhism is based on the teachings of Siddhartha Gautama, or Buddha ('Enlightened' or 'Awakened One'), a sixth-century BC north Indian prince who preached simplicity and asceticism following his spiritual awakening at the age of 29. His teachings, or Dharma, concern the path from reincarnation through the renunciation of desire, and are built around the Four Noble Truths: of suffering (or Dukkha), the origin of suffering (Samudaya), the extinction of suffering (Nirodha) and the path to the extinction of suffering (Marga) containing eight factors (right understanding, right thought, right speech, right action, right livelihood, right effort, right mindfulness and right concentration). To realise these, self-discipline and meditation have to be learned. A state of Nirvana, or the end of suffering, is reached when an individual has overcome the claims of the material world. Buddhists do not worship a God (though Mahayan Buddhists worship Bodhisattvas, or God-like figures who have achieved Nirvana), nor do they aspire to a heaven other than the one revealed through meditation. Praying, meditation and chanting take place in temples. There are a number of schools of Buddhism, including Theravada, Mahayana and Zen.

Although these religions contain diverse beliefs, they have a great deal in common. They are based on beliefs that are many hundreds and usually thousands of years old. They are prescriptive in describing what to think about and believe (usually contained in a sacred text), have ways of marking rites of passage such as birth, marriage and death, and standards concerning how life should be lived and what goals should be aspired to. In this way they describe the path to a stable and ordered society, though they differ in their attitudes to permitting ideas and practices from other faiths. In many societies they either are, or have been, the religion of the State (societies where religious leaders are also secular leaders are described as theocratic). The extent to which the great religions underpin social beliefs and practices is considered below (see Secularisation, pp.181–4).

Questions

1 In what ways are Judaism, Christianity and Islam similar?
2 How does Hinduism differ from Buddhism?
3 To what extent do the great religions conform to the definitions of religion discussed at the beginning of this chapter?

Theoretical perspectives on religion

Functionalism

Answer these questions for yourself before you read this section:

→ What functions does religion perform to help maintain social stability?
→ Does religion impede or encourage social change?
→ Is the role of religion in society changing?

For **functionalists**, religion is an organ in the organism, a sub-system within the system, an interlocking and necessary institution which plays a role in the creation and maintenance of the value consensus. It acts as a conservative force within society, a brake upon social change. The internalisation of a traditional religious belief system and the formal hierarchies which represent it ensures that any social change that occurs is slow, part of social evolution, rather than rapid, with disturbing structural changes which threaten cohesion and stability.

Durkheim

For Emile Durkheim, in *The Elementary Forms of Religious Life* (1912), the importance of religion lay in its division between the sacred and the profane. Through religion, sacred objects were created in society in such a way that society itself became sacred. In his research into the customs and beliefs of aboriginal groups he argues that religion has a role to play in maintaining 'mechanical solidarity', where law is automatic and final. The law of the gods is absolute. How 'organic solidarity' is maintained in larger societies, where rules and values are more flexible, is more complex. The construction of the 'collective conscience' or value system, which underpins law and order, is more problematic.

If you take Christianity as an example, sacred things include the Bible, altar, church, holy water and the cross. The last is a form of execution yet it has acquired religious significance because Christ was put to death on it. As Durkheim says, any object can be invested with a symbolic meaning. It is the belief system which gives it that importance. But what do sacred objects symbolise?

The value system

According to Durkheim, religion is a disguised way for people to worship society itself. The sacred objects come to stand for the value system, the all-powerful, integrating force which has an existence above and beyond the existence of human individuals. The value system is a **social fact**, existing before you were born, continuing to exist after your death, more powerful than you, a vital element which keeps society together and is therefore worthy of worship. Durkheim's view of religion has been criticised as being idealistic – society has been placed upon the altar and deified. Are religious believers really just worshipping society?

Rites of passage

Rather than concentrating on the global social significance of religion, other functionalists have examined religious rituals and ceremonies to see their significance for individuals. Acts of collective worship are supposed to reinforce social **values**, so just by being there you are taking part, consenting to the **consensus**. Why do drunken groups always turn up at church for midnight mass on Christmas Eve? Christenings, weddings and funerals always fill churches with people who are 'just there for the family' but they are nevertheless taking part in a ritual ceremony which serves to integrate them into a community of moral values and beliefs. Funerals help to heal the rift in society and fill the gap left by the deceased. Individuals can mourn and grieve in public, communally, and this reassures them that although their loved one has gone, the community remains. Sooner or later somebody always says 'life goes on' and society goes on with as little disruption as possible. The christening welcomes the new individual to society, the ritual promises they will live life according to the church's (social) values. The worship of society is evident in the fuss made of young babies on these occasions – they are the future of society.

Criticisms

However, like any other organ, the church may lose its power and therefore its functions in society. Does the church really still provide the basis for normative behaviour, the values and morals? Talcott Parsons claims that these are enshrined in the Ten Commandments, but how many people can recall them even if they have had a Christian religious socialisation? The fact that most modern industrial societies are multicultural – there are many forms of religion in Britain and the USA, for example – means that the

Ecumenicalism in action - religious leaders from different faiths pray together in remembrance of the victims of the attacks in Washington and New York, USA, on 11 September 2001.

moral codes may be in conflict. Or have secular values taken over? Is it not a modern value to actually covet your neighbour's possessions and wish you could afford them? Success in financial terms could be said to be the main value of modern industrial societies.

Questions

1 Can societies exist without some form of religion?

2 What does Durkheim mean by saying that when we worship God, we worship society?

3 How may religion be a conservative force in society?

Marxism

Marxist views of religion place it in the **ideological** and legal **superstructure** of society. Religion assists **ruling-class** ideology by helping to keep the workers in a state of **false consciousness**, preventing them from realising that they are being exploited. Religion stops the development of the **proletariat** as a 'class-for-itself'. Revolutionary **class consciousness** is kept at bay by the laws and promises of religion. Although Christianity was a religion which grew out of oppression, which sustained and comforted people whose lives were miserable and hopeless, it also promised eternal salvation to compensate for earthly misery. If you live a 'good' life, without complaining about your conditions and put up with poverty and exploitation, you stand a better chance of getting to heaven. According to the Bible, rich men will have similar difficulties getting through the pearly gates of heaven as camels would have in squeezing through the eye of a needle.

The church and the bourgeoisie

In arguing that 'religion is the sigh of the oppressed creature, the sentiment of a heartless world and the soul of soulless conditions. It is the opium of the people' Marx (1844) tries to show how religion muffles and deadens the harsh experiences of **working-class** life, and makes it slightly more bearable. This has the long-term effect of preventing social change, putting a stop to revolutionary activity. The role of the church as **capitalist** landowner and employer (particularly in the nineteenth century) is further evidence that religion is one more ideological tool used by the ruling classes to control and oppress the workers. The popularity of Methodism with the new manufacturing **middle class** of the 1900s and the attempts to coerce workers into attending services are further evidence. The middle classes were

perturbed by the apparent irreligiosity of the workers. Their promiscuity, gambling and drunkenness were seen as a threat to 'respectability', a key ideological concept at the time. Bible study, so-called 'rational' recreations – educational talks, visits, hobbies – were meant to educate the worker into a decent, sober existence. The pub and the music hall were godless, heathen pursuits.

However, there is evidence to suggest that when it came to opiates and 'spiritual gin' (Lenin), the British working classes preferred the real thing. Horace Mann's 1851 religious census showed that very few working-class people attended church with any great regularity. Perhaps the internal segregation in some churches (middle-class people had their own section) contributed to this. Both Marxist and functionalist theories are forced to see the church as a conservative force, preventing social change from occurring too rapidly. The functionalists note the positive aspects of this, that it maintains stability and keeps society together, and the Marxists point out the negative aspects – religion is seen as a ruling-class ideological prop which offers eventual salvation in return for suffering on earth while the **bourgeoisie** continue to profit.

Questions

1 What does Marx mean by 'the opium of the masses'?

2 Why is religion important to the ruling classes?

Weber

Weber's social action theory allows him to take a more flexible view of the role of religion, particularly in explaining how social change may occur. His argument is that each society has to be looked at as a unique entity, with a history and a social structure which has developed due to a special set of circumstances. In some circumstances, religion may promote and encourage social change rather than oppose it.

As outlined in chapter 1, Weber's perspective on social structure allows him to analyse the rise of capitalism and the influence of the Protestant work ethic upon capitalist ideas and vice versa. The effects of religion on society can be flexible, sometimes acting as a conservative force, holding back change, at other times reinforcing the values which promote and encourage new forms of production in society. Weber's more flexible, interpretive and structural analysis allows him to reflect upon the power of religious thought in everyday life at certain stages of history.

The Protestant Ethic

In *The Protestant Ethic and the Spirit of Capitalism* (1904–5), Weber argues that the regime imposed by Calvinistic puritanism ensured hard work, thrift, sobriety and the **accumulation** of wealth. Societies such as Germany, Britain, and later the USA, were developed through this underlying religious ideology. Capitalism flourished with religious justification, although no causal relationship was put forward by Weber. In other words, he did not claim that Calvinism caused capitalism or the other way around. The similarities between the two systems of belief were so great that they were attracted and flourished together in an 'elective affinity' – a partnership of values and guides to existence. Weber shows that the socio-economic structure of society often coincides with the deeply felt beliefs and meanings which individuals hold about their experiences. The powerful explanations of existence in any society at any time may come together to form a world-embracing ideology that helps transform social structure and sets the scene for new sociological analysis. Weber's ideas contain the seeds of the secularisation debate, as can be seen in his comments upon the change from religious to scientific explanations of reality. This leads to the rationalisation of thought and the so-called 'disenchantment' of the world.

Disenchantment

Disenchantment is a failure of belief in the power of magic in general to explain the world. Religion plays its part, but the eventual rational, scientifically based society is no longer dependent upon bizarre rituals. The laboratory experiment, the ballot box vote, the political conference will replace religious rituals like mass and holy communion. The other founding fathers did not disagree with Weber about the declining importance of religion in advanced industrial societies, but they were certainly divided as to how and why it occurred.

Church, denomination and sect

When people stop believing in God, they don't believe in nothing, they believe in anything.

G. K. Chesterton

It is not only what people believe but the form that belief takes that tells us much about the roles of religion in society. Hence sociologists have constructed typologies of religious forms encompassing all religious organisations, small or large.

Troeltsch

Attempts to classify different forms of religious organisation usually date from Ernst Troeltsch's (1931) church–sect distinction: 'the Church is that type of organisation which is overwhelmingly conservative, which to a certain extent accepts the secular order, and dominates the masses'. At its most developed, the church makes use of the State and the ruling class and becomes an integral part of the social order, represented particularly in the upper classes.

Sects, however, are 'comparatively small groups; they aspire after personal inward perfection, and they aim at a direct personal fellowship between the members of each group … their attitude towards the world, the state and society may be indifferent, tolerant or hostile, since they have no desire to control and incorporate these forms of social life'. They mainly draw their membership from the lower classes, working upwards from below. They are mainly interested in the supernatural and a direct and personal union with God.

Niebuhr

At about the same time as Troeltsch (and also Weber, mining the same seam) was writing, H. Richard Niebuhr (1929) argued that sects should be best understood as split-offs from the church, unable to accept the church's compromising tendencies. Over time, however, this new sect either disappears or takes on church-like features and the same process happens all over again. The life-span of a sect, necessarily, is short-lived. Niebuhr also identified **denominations** (for example, Methodism) as intermediate strata between church and sect. They are larger and more established than sects, but do not yet have the same wide appeal as the church.

Yinger

John Yinger (1957) further redefined this typology and defined six types: the universal church; the ecclesia (less successful than the church in incorporating sect tendencies); the class church or denomination (less successful than the ecclesia and limited by class, racial or regional boundaries); the established sect; the sect (still unsure of its relationship with the world); and the **cult** (at the farthest extreme from the universal church). It is the nature and types of sects and cults that have been of most interest to sociologists.

Wilson

In developing these ideas, Bryan Wilson (1977b) defined sects as ideological movements having as their explicit and declared aim the maintenance and perhaps even the propagation of certain ideological positions. He identified seven types: conversionist (concerned to change the self or gain salvation, as with the early Methodists and the Salvation Army); revolutionist (trying to overthrow the world before Armageddon, as with the Jehovah's Witnesses); introversionist (practising withdrawal from the world, such as the Quakers in the eighteenth century); manipulationist (engaged in a special teaching to enable members to rise above the world); thaumaturgical (which believe that people can experience the supernatural in their lives, as with Spiritualists); reformist (attempting to change the world slowly, for example the Quakers in the twentieth century); and Utopian (attempting to create perfect societies on earth, as the Tolstoyans have attempted).

Wilson accepts that it is the nature of these organisations to undergo change, caused by both internal and external factors. Internal factors can include the recruitment of a second generation or the need to sustain revolutionary zeal. External factors concern how the sect relates to, and is affected by, the outside world. Manipulationist and introversionist sects only emerge at certain stages of social and cultural development, for example as a consequence of the development of metaphysical thought, or when social institutions have developed a certain degree of **autonomy** from each other. They are unlikely to develop in non-Christian societies, where thaumaturgical and revolutionist sects are more characteristic, particularly in societies responding to missionary Christianity. Jamaican Rastafarianism is a good example of this revolutionist response, which is typical of a pre-literate society. Conversionist sects, however, are linked to the rise of individualism. Reformist sects are derived from other religious organisations and Utopian sects are limited to stages of social development in which traditional **cultural** values are being challenged.

Glock and Stark

Charles Glock and Rodney Stark (1965) argue that the church–sect dichotomy ignores many of the different forms religious movements take. In generalising and extending this theory, they build at the same time on Robert Merton's (1949) view that social change arises because of an imbalance between cultural goals and the cultural means to attain them (see also chapter 8). Groups and individuals lacking these cultural means may be described as deprived. Deprivation, then, is 'any or all of the ways that an individual or group may be, or feel, disadvantaged in comparison either to other individuals or groups or to an internalized set of standards'.

Glock and Stark identify five types of deprivation: economic deprivation due to income inequalities; social deprivation due to lower social **status**; organismic deprivation due to physical or mental deformities; ethical deprivation as the result of value conflicts (as in the case of Luther and Wesley, early leaders of the Protestant movement); and psychic deprivation which occurs when people 'find themselves without a meaningful system of values by which to interpret and organize their lives'. The experience of this deprivation leads to change, which may or may not take a religious form. If it does, then the religion may only attempt to compensate for rather than attempt to conquer such deprivation (except organismic and psychic deprivation). The form that new religious movements take, and their chances for survival, depend on the type of deprivation that spurred their formation as shown in *Table 7.1*.

Table 7.1 Deprivation and new religious movements

Type of deprivation	Form of religious group	Success expectations
Economic	Sect	Extinction or transformation
Social	Church	Retain original form
Organismic	Healing movement	Becomes cult-like or is destroyed by medical discoveries
Ethical	Reform movement	Early extinction due to success, opposition or becoming irrelevant
Psychic	Cult	Total success resulting in extinction through transformation or failure due to extreme opposition

Source: Glock and Stark (1965)

Wallis

Roy Wallis (1984) claims that the 1960s and 1970s witnessed a proliferation of new religious movements in the West. They were only new, however, in the sense that they were either reworkings of the dominant indigenous religions based on Judaeo-Christianity such as the Jesus People, or imported from other traditions, as with the International Society for Krishna Consciousness (ISKCON) and the Divine Light Mission. The Unification Church of the Reverend Sun Myung Moon managed to combine both indigenous and exported religions.

These new movements can be categorised into three types: world-rejecting, profoundly rejecting the world around them as corrupt and beyond redemption, as with the Children of God; world-accommodating, neither accepting nor rejecting the surrounding society, such as Neo-Pentecostalists; and world-affirming, accepting most of the goals and values of the wider society. This latter group is typified by psychologically based groups such as Scientologists.

Behind the emergence of these new religions, Wallis believes, is what Weber described as the process of **rationalisation** in industrial societies whereby 'life has become organised in terms of instrumental considerations: the concern for technical efficiency; maximisation of calculability and predictability; and subordination of nature to human purposes'. The disenchantment that results from living in such a routine and predictable world leads many, particularly the young, to search for meaning to an otherwise pointless existence.

Barker and the Moonies

Wallis's general points are backed by Eileen Barker's (1984) study of people who had joined the Moonies. Using in-depth interviews, Barker sought to understand the rationale behind becoming a member of such a group – why would anyone join a church which had, as one of its articles of faith, the belief that its leader, Moon, was ordered to set up his church after experiencing a vision in which Jesus told him he was the Lord of Creation? Moon's mission was therefore nothing less than to be the Second Coming, complete with his own rewritten version of the Bible.

According to Barker, members of the sect are not brainwashed in any conventional sense, although at their first workshop meetings potential new recruits are encouraged to think evocatively about their memories, hopes, fears and even guilt, and the

opportunity of joining a loving and caring community is offered to them.

A certain type of person is attracted to the Unification Church: 'those who have responded have tended to be overwhelmingly between the ages of 18 and 28, predominantly male, disproportionately middle class and usually unmarried', while Home Church or Associate members tend to be older, female, of a slightly lower class (although still disproportionately middle class) and, frequently, married.

Push factors for recruitment

Becoming a Moonie offers an outlet for youth's idealism, its need to experiment and its rebelliousness. They will be expected to give up material aspirations (at a time when they have very few material things to give up). But becoming a Moonie is more than this: it attracts people whose idealism outweighs their materialism because 'it is a religion that offers to change this world, for everyone, so that it is a better world – indeed the best of all possible worlds …. It will be a world in which a loving, caring God has a loving caring relationship with each individual, and in which each individual will also find him or herself as an integral part of a God-centred family' (Barker, 1984). Each individual is given tasks to perform and goals to achieve, such as recruiting new members or fund-raising, in such a way that everyone has a clearly described role and a goal.

Moonies are recruited against a backcloth of general disillusionment and discontent. Many of them see the world as 'a divisive, turbulent, chaotic society, characterised by racial intolerance, injustice, cut-throat competition and lack of direction … everything is relative to the utilitarian interests and desires of a pleasure-seeking, money-grubbing, power-hungry population'. This form of rejection of the material world is only the latest in a series of rejections by middle-class youth dating back to at least the 1960s – indeed, these cults are a result of the failure of the hippy movement of the 1960s to deliver real social and personal change, or to give meaning to a young person's existence. This is what the Unification Church provides. It offers freedom from directionless choices and an opportunity to belong, to do something of value and to be of value. There are therefore, for Barker, more reasons to believe that people join the Moonies as a result of a rational, calculated choice than because of brainwashing.

The importance of sects

As we can see, sects have been of particular interest to those writers concerned with the sociology of religion. As James Beckford (1986) argues, although the actual number of people involved or likely to be involved in sects amounts to a small proportion of the population in Europe and the USA, they are nevertheless important not only to the sociology of religion but to sociology itself. Sects give us insight into future social trends. They represent an 'extreme situation' which, precisely because it is extreme, throws into sharp relief many of the assumptions hidden behind legal, cultural and social structures. They could be described as 'social and cultural laboratories where experiments in ideas, feelings and social relations are carried out. They are a normal aspect of social life and a critical guide to societal problems and prospects.' It could, however, be argued that in focusing on sects and new religious movements, we have learnt a lot about a little, at the expense of ignoring an in-depth understanding of the meaning of religion to the vast majority of the rest of the population.

Questions

1 If sects proliferate, does it indicate that a society is becoming more or less secular?
2 What is the most helpful way to typologise religious organisations?
3 Why do Moonies have a particular appeal to young, middle-class people?

Religion and stratification

Alongside a common sense of place, language, history and culture, a shared religion is one of the key forms of identifier for an **ethnic** group. Most surveys of religious self-identification show members of ethnic minority groups as more likely to relate to a religion than those of the ethnic majority. A number of reasons have been given for this – that an ethnic minority may have originated from an already highly religious society; that religion plays a key role in holding a group together; that group pressures (for example from the family) encourage religious affiliation; and, of course, that religion is one of the key ways that an ethnic group can understand who it is (see *Table 7.2*). When some members loosen their religious affiliation, then a central aspect of what defines that group as an ethnic minority is also loosened.

Gender

Statistics for **gender** and religion show a marked difference in terms of participation, where rates of attendance for women are far higher than for men – for example, two-thirds of church-goers in Britain are women (see *Table 7.3*). This ratio is also consistent across ethnic minority groups. They are also, according to Grace Davie (1994), more likely to engage in private prayer.

At first sight, these findings would seem paradoxical. Most world religions are strongly **patriarchal** in nature, seeing God (or his earthly incarnations and messengers) as male, emphasising a view of the world as male and women as subordinate to men. In the Bible, the temptation of woman (Eve) is seen as responsible for the fall of man (Adam). More generally, in most religions to be born a woman is viewed as a punishment.

From a sociological point of view, women's response to a seemingly opposed ideology makes more sense. From a Weberian view, women's response is precisely because their position in society is a less powerful one than men's. In this 'theodicy of disprivilege', it is no surprise to discover that women have played a central role in the founding of many religious sects such as the Seventh-Day Adventist Church, the Christian Science Movement and the Shakers, where sects reflect the

Table 7.2   Religious affiliation by ethnic group

	White non-Irish	Irish	Caribbean	Indian	African Asian	Pakistani	Bangladeshi	Chinese
None	31	14	28	5	2	2	1	58
Hindu	–	–	1	32	58	–	2	–
Sikh	–	–	–	50	19	–	–	–
Muslim	–	–	1	6	15	96	95	–
Christian	68	85	69	5	3	–	1	23
Other	1	1	3	2	3	2	1	19

Source: Modood and Berthoud, 1997

Table 7.3 Attendance at religious service, Britain (%)[1]

	Males	Females	All
Once a week or more	10	13	12
Less often but at least once in two weeks	1	2	2
Less often but at least once a month	4	6	5
Less often but at least twice a year	8	10	9
Less often but at least once a year	6	7	7
Less often	5	5	5
Never or practically never	53	44	49
Varies too much to say	–	1	1
Not answered	1	2	1
No religion	11	10	10
All	100	100	100

1 Respondents aged 18 and over who said they belonged to a religion or were brought up in a religion were asked how often, apart from special occasions such as weddings, funerals and baptisms, they attended services or meetings connected with their religion.

Source: *Social Trends* 31, 2001

most marginalised groups in society, and their attempts to compensate for their powerlessness.

From a feminist point of view, the oppression of women in a patriarchal society is found again in the oppression of women in religion, in both its ideology and its structures. Religion is part of the ideological superstructure that maintains women in their subordinate position, reflected in the higher rates of female participation in religious activity. Their rejection of patriarchal religion will coincide with their rejection of patriarchal society.

Other explanations have highlighted the fact that women are closer to nature and the facts of birth and death, forcing them more than men to consider these issues and religion's answer to them, and also some argue that the process of secularisation has seen religion become a more personal and home-based concern. It is also connected with age: religiosity is at its lowest among the middle aged and highest among the younger and older sections of the population. As women have a greater life expectancy than men, their religiosity is sustained longer into old age.

There is also a marked gender divide in attitude and belief, men being more likely to see God as powerful and controlling and women tending to see God as loving, comforting and forgiving. This is also true of New Age religions. As Steve Bruce comments: 'the parapsychology and esoteric knowledge side tends to be male. The healing, channelling and spirituality side tends to be female' (1996).

Social class

The pattern of participation by social class is equally paradoxical. The main pattern is that, dividing the main social classes into only two groups, members of the middle class are the most likely to participate in religious activity, whereas they are also the least likely to profess a belief in God. Steve Bruce (1995) expresses this as follows:

The middle classes are much more decisive in their religious behaviour and narrow in their use of terms to describe it. More middle class than working class people are involved with the churches but those who are not are less likely than their working class counterparts to claim religious beliefs or describe themselves as religious.

Questions

1 How are the concepts of religion and ethnicity linked?
2 Why are women more likely to participate in religion than men?

Secularisation

Measuring secularisation

Secularisation is generally thought to be the process of the decline of religious influence upon social life. The problem is: how do we measure that influence? Should we use statistics: **positivistic** indicators like church attendance, marriages, christenings and funerals (see *Table 7.4*)? Or should we rely on more **qualitative** indicators: belief- and meaning-based data on how religion pervades your inner soul and existence – non-positivistic, **interactionist** research. As usual there are some big sociological ideas to look at, with the arguments and problems which run through sociology churning under the surface.

Wilson

Bryan Wilson (1966) defines secularisation as: 'The decline of the influence of religious institutions, thinking and practices upon social life.' He uses hard social data, statistics on all aspects of religious life, to prove his thesis that secularisation is indeed taking place, as earlier writers had predicted. His critics, who analyse religion from an interactionist perspective, point to the fallacy of the 'social facts' of his data, in the same way as Durkheim's critics point to the problems in trusting suicide rates (see chapter 8). The foremost critic is David Martin, who claims that the

Table 7.4 Church membership, 1970–90, UK (thousands)

	1970	1980	1990
Trinitarian churches: Roman Catholic	2,746	2,455	2,198
Trinitarian churches: Anglican	2,987	2,180	1,728
Trinitarian churches: Presbyterian	1,751	1,437	1,214
Trinitarian churches: Other free churches	843	678	776
Trinitarian churches: Methodist	673	540	478
Trinitarian churches: Orthodox	191	203	266
Trinitarian churches: Baptist	272	239	230
All trinitarian churches	*9,272*	*7,529*	*6,890*
Non-trinitarian churches: Mormons	85	114	160
Non-trinitarian churches: Jehovah's Witnesses	62	85	117
Other non-trinitarian churches	138	154	182
All non-trinitarian churches	*285*	*353*	*459*
Other religions: Muslim	130	306	495
Other religions: Sikh	100	150	250
Other religions: Hindu	80	120	140
Other religions: Jewish	120	111	101
Other religions: Others	21	53	87
All other religions	*451*	*740*	*1,073*

Source: *Social Trends* 30, 2000

alleged decline of religion cannot be measured in statistical terms. The figures do not tell us whether people go to church for religious reasons, social reasons or because they have to be seen to be 'respectable', as Martin (1978) says was the case in nineteenth-century England. Studies into the decline or growth of religious belief in people's minds can only be properly carried out using interactionist methods. However, to look back at Wilson's definition – the decline of 'the influence' of religion on 'social life' – perhaps his methods do prove what he is claiming. Attendance at church, the status and number of the clergy, the use of church ritual to signal important points in the life cycle (birth, marriage and death) do show, in however crude a way, that the influence of religious institutions, thinking and practices upon social life is indeed declining. The statistical evidence has all the answers to a positivist's prayers.

Wilson's evidence

Wilson (1977b) himself argues that:

→ in 1950, 67 per cent of the children born alive in Great Britain were baptised in the Church of England; in 1973, this was the case for only 47 per cent.

→ in 1952, about 28 per cent of those aged 15 years in England were confirmed in the Anglican Church;

the proportion was below 20 per cent by the mid-1970s.

→ some 6.5 per cent of the population took Easter communion in the Church of England in 1953; 20 years later, fewer than 4 per cent did so.

→ Methodists had three-quarters of a million members in 1952; their membership had fallen by a third by 1977.

→ in the same period, the number of Baptists fell from 300,000 to 185,000.

→ Congregationalism and Presbyterianism present a similar picture.

→ in the early 1950s, no more than 10 per cent of those polled did not believe in God; by the mid-1970s this had risen to 36 per cent. Less than 40 per cent of people believed in life after death.

Shiner

In a review of the literature on secularisation, Larry Shiner (1971) analyses six different usages and points out their weaknesses:

1 Decline of religion

Symbols, doctrines and institutions lose influence. Research in this area shows that even the members of different faiths may doubt some of the doctrines of their religions: did Christ *really* come back from the dead; did Mohammed *really* speak to an angel; do Catholics *all* avoid using contraceptives? The usual problem with this definition of secularisation is that it assumes a 'golden age of religion' when everyone believed, when the religious authorities were all-powerful and pews were filled. In fact, no such age actually existed. Even the Middle Ages were full of disbelievers.

2 Conformity with this world

A crucial stage in any religious movement is when it turns away from the supernatural and becomes more concerned with this world. Will Herberg (1955) describes the differences between 'conventional' religions in a society, and the 'operative' religions which provide the meaning and value system. Those who belong to the 'conventional' religions (Judaism, Islam, Christianity) actually reflect the values of the 'operative' religion of American society – secular, non-religious values. This has the social effect of bringing the diverse cultural groups in American society together under a value system which may be at odds with the views of each 'conventional' religion.

Again, the difficulties of measuring these shifts of belief away from the scriptures and into everyday life prove impossible to untangle. What could be happening is that people choose to emphasise the aspects of their belief system which are in accord with their lifestyles and the expectations made of them, while ignoring other aspects. Does this mean that they 'believe' any less than their ancestors, who also tailored their beliefs to fit in with 'the world'? Shiner argues that 'increasing secularisation' implies a move away from religious belief, when what in fact is happening is simply a shift in the emphasis of religious belief.

3 Disengagement

According to this definition of secularisation, society is no longer defined and controlled by religion, and so religious belief is 'disengaged' from the social sphere, and becomes a private, inward matter, with no need of corporate institutions. It is confined to the private sphere of life and is no longer an issue of public importance.

There are examples of this in the growth of the State as provider and regulator of public functions, for example education and welfare, which used to be controlled by the church. Another aspect of this definition is the intellectual disengagement of philosophy and thought from supernatural to physical, rational, scientific influences. The problems of deciding whether disengagement actually means that belief is less strong than in the past are obvious. How does the fact that the State has taken over certain social functions, and religion has withdrawn from them, prove that supernatural beliefs have declined? The churches may be as strong as ever but now concentrate more upon specifically spiritual concerns. Parsons (1965) uses a similar idea which he calls differentiation, by which he means that the functions of the church become refined, 'purer', and it is free to concentrate on the sphere of doctrine and creed. Robert Bellah (1964) agrees that this differentiation is a signal of change and that it signifies evolution rather than secularisation. Any rejection of the supernatural and of doctrine are just new ways of using religion, not evidence of a move away from it.

4 Transposition of religious beliefs and institutions

Under this definition of secularisation, aspects of religious belief are 'taken' from religion and given a social, secular nature. Examples are psychoanalysis as a secular form of confession, the spirit of capitalism as a secular 'Protestant work ethic', and the Marxist revolution as a secular Judaeo-Christian Messianic revolution. The 'transposition of beliefs' definition suggests that society steals the most attractive ideas in a religion and strips away their supernatural coverings. This view of secularisation is open to the criticism that it is not clear which came first, the religious or the secular version. Are they really the same thing? And if they are, then does it really matter what form the belief or practice takes if it is performing the same function for society and individuals?

5 Desacrilisation

In this definition of secularisation, everything in the world is described and explained in rational-causal terms. Weber called it 'disenchantment' – the move away from magical explanations toward scientific ones. A prehistoric person kept away from lightning because they knew it was an expression of the anger of the gods, and a modern person keeps away because they know it is a big electric charge. Whatever we think it is, it can still kill you if it hits you. The main problem with this definition is that it is based upon the assumption that religious systems necessarily try to explain these physical events. The Hebraic God has given the world over to men to control and understand; the religion has in effect 'desacrilised' itself in its own beliefs. When the religion itself admits that rational-scientific explanations are valid, how does this prove secularisation?

6 The move from 'sacred' to a 'secular' society

This last definition is much more general. Secularisation here refers to the acceptance of political, legal and social decisions which are based on rational grounds, and the acceptance of change. The concept of social change through stages is considered here, but the problem again is measuring just what was a 'sacred' society and deciding what is a 'secular' society.

These six definitions of secularisation have some overlaps and some obvious differences. They have all been used in **empirical** research, and all have been shown to be occurring. This shows why it is important to understand the definition being used when a sociologist claims that they have evidence for secularisation. Shiner argues that to think of 'religious' versus 'secularised' is to limit the argument to a 'polarised' concept. One problem is that the split between the functions of the church and the functions of the State occurs in Western societies, but not necessarily in other societies. Another is that to polarise secular activity and religious activity, and to claim that when there is a lot of secular activity, religious activity is in decline is also false. In many periods of history, both secular and religious activities were wide-ranging. The final problem in the religious–secular polarity is that it supposes that religion is an 'entity' which can be measured in some way. Bryan Wilson and others define religion in terms of institutional practices and then proceed to measure their decline.

The myth of secularisation

As David Martin (1978) argues, it is impossible to develop criteria to distinguish between the religious and the secular, because the belief systems combined under the name religion are so varied and diverse. Martin suggests that the concept of secularisation has become a 'tool of counter-religious ideologies' which is used to attack religion. Peter Glasner (1977) also has problems with the concept as it has been used, claiming that it has become 'mythicised', no longer related to empirical evidence, and is ideological and confusing. Each social structure needs to be analysed on its own merit, and a specific way of measuring 'religiosity' in that structure needs to be developed before any research can be usefully attempted.

Questions

1 In what ways can secularisation be measured?
2 How can it be argued that secularisation has not taken place in industrial societies?
3 What does the secularisation debate tell us about the positivist/interactionist divide in sociology?

A secular world?

Secularisation and industrialisation

From one point of view then, it can be argued that industrialisation, and the advances in science and technology that it brings in its wake, contributes to a decline in the importance of religious thought and action in society. This position – the secularisation thesis – can be demonstrated statistically through the falling numbers of people attending church, being baptised, taking communion, and so on, while at the same time scientific explanations of phenomena replace religious ones. As Alan Gilbert (1980) argues, 'the enhanced mastery over nature, and the increased material comfort and security that have gone hand-in-hand with modernisation, have guaranteed a human

preoccupation with the present life and temporal world'. It therefore remains the sociologist's task to explain the fit between industrialisation (or modernisation) and secularisation by employing the concepts described above.

The counter-argument

Those sceptical of this argument, however, question the validity of such indexes of secularisation, claiming at the same time that the religiosity of earlier periods of history cannot be taken for granted. In our own age, moreover, new evidence seems to continually point away from the secularisation thesis. In Britain, for example, the organised church does still play a high-profile role in British life. It would be unthinkable if the next monarch were not crowned by the Archbishop of Canterbury in Westminster Cathedral. The 'Lords Spiritual' play an active life in the House of Lords and play an influential role in promoting or combating legislation on a range of issues from Sunday trading to more secular legislation. Religious programming is a marked feature of Sunday television, and comments made by members of the clergy can still provoke national debate and discussion. Other religious organisations and smaller Christian churches (such as the Seventh-Day Adventists) retain strong and even growing memberships. Non-Christian religions such as Hinduism, Islam and Sikhism continue to play important social roles that extend beyond ethnic minority communities. Figures on private and house-based worship are difficult to obtain but may nevertheless indicate thriving activity, while interest in the occult, tarot and astrology – as well as superstition – remains widespread. While the organised church appears to be in decline, it seems also to be the case that cults and sects are proliferating.

Outside Great Britain, organised religion continues to play a major role in shaping post-war world events. In the USA the Baptist church and particularly the Baptist Minister, Dr Martin Luther King, played a central role in the **civil rights** movement in the 1960s. This leadership was itself challenged by the Nation of Islam sect and the figure of Malcolm X. In both examples religion was the main organising force behind social change. In the Reagan era of the 1980s the American New Christian Right sought to gain political power while trying to change social policies on issues such as abortion and how accounts of the Creation were taught in school. Evangelists became both popular and wealthy enough to be able to broadcast from their own television stations.

Religion in decline? Pope John Paul II has attracted massive crowds wherever he has travelled in the Catholic and non-Catholic worlds.

Secularisation has not been synonymous with industrialisation in the Middle East where, Ernest Gellner (1992) remarks, 'Islam is as strong now as it was a century ago. In some ways, it is probably much stronger.' This could not be more clearly demonstrated than by the revolutionary overthrow of the Shah of Iran by the followers of Ayatollah Khomeini at the end of the 1970s. In Latin America Catholics have broken away from papal authority and, calling themselves **liberation theologists**, have backed popular campaigns against autocracy and poverty. In Eastern Europe, both the Catholic and Protestant churches were active in the revolutions of 1989, particularly in East Germany and Poland, where many members of the Solidarity trade union (such as Lech Walesa, who eventually became the President of Poland) were to become members of the new post-communist government with full papal approval.

Wilson

How then can the persistence of religion in an increasingly industrial (and some would say **post-industrial**) world be explained? Bryan Wilson (1982) argues that the new religious movements are profoundly 'anti-cultural'. He sees them as forces making for the destructuring of society and personality rather than playing the traditional role of agencies of **socialisation** and social control. They are unable to channel religious expression into a form that might have significant repercussions for the social and political structures of modern society. In this view, new religions are further evidence of secularisation in society, attempting to compensate for the more demanding features of a secular society.

Other writers have argued that what unites groups such as those of Eastern Europe and others who have turned to religion is that it has been used as a form of cultural defence in defining their nationality and ethnicity against the threat of more powerful forces. It is a feature of the make-up of national or **imperial** organisation that groups at the **periphery** differ ethnically from those at the centre, as with Catholicism and Presbyterianism in Northern Ireland and Scotland. In the case of some **Third World** countries the rise of religion represents the rejection of Western values as the expected modernisation failed to emerge.

The growth of evangelical Protestantism in what has been seen as a traditionally Catholic South America has been seen by writers such as David Martin (1990) as reflecting the aspirations of particular groups in a time of rapid cultural transition, echoing the adoption of Methodism by the working class in England during the Industrial Revolution.

Islam

Ernest Gellner sees no necessary contradiction between the revival of fundamentalist Islam and modernisation. We know from Weber, he says, that modern economies are 'orderly, sensitive to cost-effectiveness, thrifty rather than addicted to display, much given to the division of labour and the use of the free market. It requires those who operate it to be sensitive to the notion of obligation and their fulfilment of contract, to be work-oriented, disciplined, and not too addicted to economically irrelevant political and religious patronage networks, nor to dissipate too much of their energy in festivals or display … Reformist Islam would seem to be custom-made for the needs of the hour.'

For Steve Bruce (1988), the rise of the New Christian Right in the USA is another example of cultural defence, though it is only weakly linked to any notion of ethnicity. It is particularly important in the states of the deep South, which had always been peripheral in American economic, social and cultural life. Bruce explains this phenomenon as the reaction of these states to the permissive era of the 1960s and 1970s at the same time as they became relatively more prosperous and important to the US economy. What is of most importance in understanding this movement, however, is the New Christian Right's lack of political success, only ever being able to influence a handful of senators, and only achieving limited change in general social and moral values – they never did become the 'moral majority'.

Once again, whether contemporary societies are seen as secular or not depends on the perspective adopted and the terms used to define that perspective. For both sides of the argument there is plenty of evidence to suggest that their point of view is the correct one. Empty churches and the separation of church from State certainly do suggest the declining importance of religion, though as many have been quick to observe, this applies only in the case of Western Europe and not in other parts of the world. It could be argued with equal conviction that religion does not die out in importance in society but simply evolves and changes its form.

Questions

1 How can the term 'secularisation' be defined?
2 Are Western societies becoming more or less secular?
3 Can the revival of Islamic fundamentalism be successfully accounted for?

Religion, fundamentalism, modernity and post-modernity

Looking at the views of the founding fathers of sociology, it is clear that they all expected traditional organised religion to fall into decline as society became organised on more rational principles, and that this decline was a feature of modernity. Definite knowledge about religion could be obtained through use of scientific methods, charting, for example, its increasing decline in industrial societies, at either a structural or an individual level.

According to some writers, the problems of defining and measuring religion exist not because these are difficult, but because, in a **post-modern** era, it is no longer possible. The bold claims of modernism are collapsing into the uncertainties of post-modernity. At the most profound level, **metanarratives** or grand attempts to provide all-encompassing answers have now been exposed for what they always were: story-telling. This is as true for social science as it is for religions such as Christianity and Islam, and the evidence is all around us in the way contemporary lives are lived within the post-modern condition.

The hybrid character of new religious movements, where they draw from many religions such as Christianity, Hinduism and Buddhism, bear the hallmarks of post-modernism. Monolithic religious traditions are broken down, and people choose their view of religion from a very wide range of sources on a 'pick and mix' basis: in Britain, 'the proportion of the population prepared to say that they believe in the standard Christian beliefs concerning Heaven and Hell has declined considerably. However, belief in reincarnation (which is not, of course, officially part of the creed of any mainstream Christian Church), has actually been going up. About one-fifth of Britons subscribe to this belief, which is even more marked among the young' (Campbell, 1998).

Increasingly, some commentators argue, religious identity is becoming a matter of individual choice, with religious movements marketing themselves in a manner similar to consumer products in a competitive marketplace. Choosing a religion can be seen as making a statement about lifestyle and identity.

Globalisation and new technologies such as the internet allow widely dispersed memberships for new religious movements and new age movements, without the need for a geographical base. The possibility now exists for virtual religions to exist solely in hyperspace – cybertheology – underlining Baudrillard's observations on the hyperreal (see chapter 10).

The organisation of new religious movements mirrors that of post-modern industrial organisations, where the emphasis on less rigid and authoritarian structures allows greater flexibility and democracy. The focus is away from mass production and consumption and more on niche markets, where technology plays a less dominant and more enabling role. The importance given to self-improvement and self-mastery in new religious movements is similar to the new work ethic of post-modern organisations.

Many writers are sceptical of these claims, as they are of the overall notion that modernity has given way to post-modernity. The selection by individuals of parts of different religions is overstated and applies only to a small section of society. The extent of individual choice is also exaggerated in a world where factors such as **class** and gender continue to be important in determining life chances. Similarly, the depiction of a relativist world where no one knows or cares about the difference between right or wrong is overemphasised. Paul Heelas (1996), for example, found that new age movements work with concepts of absolute truth against which other ideas and beliefs are judged. 'Spirituality' is also taken seriously, and is not seen as part of the throwaway mentality of consumerism, or characteristic of a post-modern era. It is also contradictory to state on the one hand that people are no longer willing to accept authority figures and that they compensate for this by looking to the expert advice offered by new age religions.

Moreover, as Bruce (1996) argues, there is little comfort here for anyone hoping for a revival of traditional religion from the apparent collapse in belief in science, as this had very little to do with the secularisation of the modern world in the first place. The cause of this secularisation can be found more in factors such as increasing cultural diversity, competing religious ideas and greater democracy, which brought about indifference to religion, not disbelief. These trends are likely to continue in what is claimed to be the post-modern era.

Fundamentalism

One feature of the modern, or post-modern, world is the apparent widespread return to first principles and basic values in leading religions such as Christianity and Islam in some parts of the world. This revival, usually described as **fundamentalism**, has as its chief characteristics the call for a return to certainty and tradition (usually immediately and as the result of profound change), the sanctification of politics, and the return of community and strong commitment and engagement from its members. It also locates the cause of many contemporary social problems in the turn away from the observance of religion and its values.

To theorists of post-modernism, fundamentalism is an unsurprising reaction to a post-modern world. Its allure, Zymunt Bauman argues, 'stems from its promise to emancipate the converted from the agonies of choice'. Similarly, its certainties help us 'know where to look when life-decisions are to be made, in matters big and small, and one knows that looking there one does the right thing and is spared the agonies of risk-taking' (Bauman, 1997). Fundamentalist religions in a post-modern world address the need to overcome increasing uncertainty and fear and the loss of identity.

This view is echoed by Davie (1995), who highlights 'the existence of essential truths and their application to twentieth-century realities. Both elements need to be present, for the word fundamentalism should not normally be used to describe the traditional elements of religion that have been left undisturbed by the modern world, nor does it mean the creation of new ideas. It evokes, in contrast, the reaffirmation of essential truths within a situation that has been profoundly disturbed by the pressure of an expanding global economy and the effects that has had on social, political or ideological life.'

In recent decades, particularly since the Iranian revolution in 1979, which saw the eventual replacement of Shah Pahlavi with the Shi'ite Ayatollah Khomeini, the term fundamentalism has usually been linked to Islam. This use has been challenged for a number of reasons. It is a term initially applied to describe a trend within Christian Protestantism during the American Civil War. It reached international notoriety with the Scopes trial in Dayton, Tennessee, in 1925, which resulted in the prohibition of teaching the Darwinian theory of evolution in state schools. More recently it has also been used to describe Christian campaigns against the liberalisation of practices such as abortion and homosexuality, and for giving equal status to the biblical story of the creation and the evolutionary theory of Darwin. Recent scandals involving high-profile evangelical preachers in the USA have made association with these views politically unattractive there.

According to Ilyas Ba-Yunus (1997), no Islamic grouping describes itself as fundamentalist, and the term is not used within Islam. It has become pejorative rather than descriptive or analytical in its use, often deliberatively or carelessly confused with militant political action that is not necessarily linked to advancing the cause of the Islamic faith. This distinction was carefully made around the world after the terrorist attacks in the USA on 11 September 2001, with governments in the West at pains to make it clear that a 'war on terrorism' did not mean a war on the Islamic faith. Nevertheless, 'it seems that whosoever in the Muslim world evokes the name of Islam outside of the mosques is liable to be called an Islamic fundamentalist. Consequently, whenever and wherever a Muslim group is fighting for its survival or its constitutional and basic human rights, whether in Algeria, in Egypt, in Palestine, in Kashmir, in Mindanao or in Bosnia, it has been called Islamic fundamentalist' (Ba-Yunus, 1997). As he concedes, the public image of Islam has nevertheless not been helped by its interpretation by many leaders within Islamic movements, whether political or religious. But it remains the case that others who hold firm principles in other arenas are not described as democratic fundamentalists, capitalist fundamentalists, socialist fundamentalists or secularist fundamentalists. Equally, paramilitary groups which carry out terrorist attacks on either side of the divide in Northern Ireland are not described as Christian, Catholic or Protestant fundamentalists.

Behind this misnomer lies a history of Western antagonism to Islam that is as old as the religion itself, as Shlomo Avineri (1993) writes: 'The underlying assumption has always been that Islam – as a culture and not only a religious creed – was primitive, underdeveloped, retrograde, at best stuck in the memory hole of a medieval splendor out of which it could not disengage itself without a radical transformation; and this could only be based on Western, "rational", "progressive" values.' This antagonism has been exacerbated in recent decades not only by the revival of Islam in a number of countries including the USA, but also because of the collapse of the Soviet Union, and the end of the Cold War, which left the Western military machine looking for a new target.

Some writers view the emergence of Islam in states such as Shi'ite Iran or Sunni Sudan as a temporary phenomenon. For Bruce (2001), clear signs exist in Iran, for example, that the need to establish a social order alongside the religious culture will lead to greater demands for personal freedom and more liberal approaches to issues such as gender, in the same way that the Soviet Union was unable to sustain an equally authoritarian state.

The concept of fundamentalism is therefore unhelpful in understanding the debate between modernists and post-modernists. As Grace Davie (1995) writes, 'It is equally possible to argue that the re-emphasis of this kind of religious life both within and without the mainline churches is an ongoing part of modernity, rather than a post or anti-modern reaction to this … The religious dimensions must therefore be considered an essential part of modernity, though its shapes and forms may be widely diverse.'

Questions

1 What are the characteristics of religion in a post-modern age?
2 Why is the term 'Islamic fundamentalist' problematic?
3 Why might the phenomena of fundamentalism and post-modernism be linked?

Crime and deviance

This chapter starts by examining definitions of crime and deviance. It then goes on to consider the accuracy and usefulness of the official crime statistics. This is followed by a discussion of women and crime, ethnicity and crime, and white-collar crime. Theories that attempt to explain the causes of crime and deviance will be reviewed. These theories include physiological, psychological, functionalist, subcultural and Marxist explanations. The chapter continues with a discussion of the interactionist perspective, focusing on labelling and the concept of the 'self-fulfilling prophecy'. Contemporary explanations for the causes of crime are then examined, with sections on control theory, Left idealism, new administrative criminology, New Right realism, Left realism, and post-modernist theory. The chapter concludes with a review of the debate over suicide and then looks at the sociology of murder.

Defining crime and deviance

Defining crime does, at first, seem an easy matter. Criminal behaviour is that behaviour which violates the criminal law. Basically, it is a legal category. Unfortunately, the term and definition hide more than they reveal. Within such a term are lumped together all violations of the law, although they are markedly different. We plainly see rape and murder as different, qualitatively, from minor traffic and shoplifting offences. Their only similarity is that they infringe the law, and of course the law itself changes over time, so that what is a crime at one point in time is not so at another. For example, homosexual acts conducted in private between consenting male adults over 21 were illegal in the UK until the law was reformed in 1969. Likewise, what is a crime in one society is not necessarily so in another. The consumption of alcohol is subject to very few legal restrictions in most Western societies, for example; yet it is severely curtailed, and in some cases banned altogether, in many Islamic societies.

What constitutes 'crime' and 'criminality' is, therefore, something that is socially defined and highly relative. It depends on the laws in place in a given society at a particular point in time, and the way that those laws are interpreted and enforced. Similarly, social factors play a key part in explaining criminal behaviour. Breaking the law is not something that happens purely as a matter of personal whim or for other individualistic reasons. Rather, such behaviour occurs within a social context and it is influenced by the way the individual sees his or her own act. Indeed, as we shall see later in the chapter, there is a complex interaction between the way society defines crime and responds to criminals and the way that those who are, or may be, involved in illegal activities view themselves.

Deviant acts

Because crime occurs in a social context and is an example of rule-breaking activity, sociologists include it within the wider study of **deviance**. Deviant acts are all acts that are regarded as violating the accepted standards of the community, whether they are legal or illegal. For example, in a society where religious observance is the norm, a person who rejects that pattern of behaviour would be viewed with social disapproval and may be labelled a 'heretic'. Among a group of young people who favour a particular dress code and style of language, a person dressing or speaking in a different way may be treated with suspicion and prevented from joining the group.

The study of deviance is therefore concerned with those acts that incur social disapproval. The problem that faces us is what exactly are the accepted standards? What is normal and acceptable will vary across time and between societies; it may also depend on who commits the act. For instance, rules of dress vary according to time, society, person and place. In many traditional African societies it is normal for women to be naked above the waist. Yet it would be considered deviant in contemporary Western societies for a woman to walk along the streets with her breasts uncovered. However, going topless on the beach is now accepted as legitimate behaviour for women in these societies, whereas it would have been viewed as unacceptable a few years ago. For men to be naked above the waist in a public place, such as a shopping precinct or sports stadium, is far less likely to meet with social disapproval. Hence, it can be seen that it is not the nakedness as such that is deviant, but how other people define it. Deviance is in the 'eye of the beholder'.

Outsiders

The American sociologist Howard Becker (1963) argues that social groups create deviance by making the rules, the infraction of which constitutes deviance. From this point of view, deviance is not a quality of the act the person commits, but rather a consequence of the application by others of rules and sanctions to an offender. The deviant is one to whom that label has successfully been applied; deviant behaviour is behaviour that people so label.

Becker points out that all social groups make rules and attempt at some time and under some circumstances to enforce them. Social rules define situations and the kinds of behaviour appropriate to them, specifying some actions as right and forbidding others as wrong. When a rule is enforced, the person who is supposed to have broken it may be seen as a special kind of person, one who cannot be trusted to live by the rules agreed on by the group. He is viewed as an outsider. Deviance can therefore be regarded as a stigma and a form of rejection and disapproval. Of course, those who are judged to be deviant may reject the idea that their behaviour is in any way abnormal or wrong.

Since deviance is, among other things, a consequence of the responses of others to a person's act, all deviance is not the same. Some people may be labelled deviant who in fact have not broken a rule and some escape apprehension and are not included in the population of deviants. Becker presents a framework to explain different types of deviant behaviour.

	Obedient behaviour	Rule-breaking
Perceived as deviant	Falsely accused	Pure deviant
Not perceived as deviant	Conforming	Secret deviant

In order to understand deviance, Becker says, we must consider the people who make and enforce the rules to which 'outsiders' fail to conform. We will return to this later in the chapter when considering the **interactionist** approach to explaining crime and deviance.

Crime statistics

Crime statistics have to be handled with care. The actual amount of crime committed in society is unknown. In the UK a government department, the Home Office, publishes the official crime statistics annually. However, the statistics refer only to those indictable crimes known to the police. (Indictable crimes correspond roughly to those thought to be more serious.) Less serious offences and those that are not reported to the police are excluded from the figures. Crime statistics are also affected by the fact that the ways of classifying and counting offences change. Moreover, new offences are introduced, such as the offence of kerb crawling (driving slowly in 'red light' districts with the aim of approaching prostitutes for sex) that was introduced in the UK in 1985. Hence, the consideration of the limitations of the statistics becomes almost as important as consideration of the statistics themselves.

Recorded crime is unlikely to mirror actual crime. Some people are fearful of reporting an offence to the police, for example rape. Others may feel that the extent of the offence does not warrant informing the police (for example pilfering of sweets by children) and other measures may be taken. This leads us to the conclusion that there is more actual crime than recorded crime; unfortunately, it does not tell us how much more. The difference between actual and recorded crime is referred to as the 'dark figure'. We do not know if the dark figure is increasing, stable or decreasing. Theoretically, a rise in the crime statistics for a particular offence may only represent more of the actual crime being reported rather than an increase in real crime.

The dark figure is not constant. Research suggests that the dark figure in sexual offences may be as high as 90 per cent, whereas the probability of reporting certain types of property offence (for example theft of motor vehicles) is high and the dark figure is low. The dark figure may also be high in thefts by employees, firms not wanting adverse publicity, perhaps tolerating a small amount of pilfering, and if necessary taking their own disciplinary action without informing the police.

Police recording

Police practices in recording can also have a substantial effect on the nature and extent of the dark figure. For instance, there was a twelvefold increase in the offence of soliciting (seeking clients for sexual activity) between 1994 and 1999 in the Teesside region of the UK. This reflected a new tougher policy of prosecuting rather than a twelvefold increase in such behaviour.

The creation of specialist police squads (for example a drug squad) may lead to an increase in the number of convictions for a particular type of offence. The policy of using special squads and the allocation of police officers to different areas of cities is at the behest of the chief constable. He, in turn, may be influenced in his policy-making by pressures from the media and politicians. The dark figure may also be reduced by the greater efficiency of the police.

There is also evidence that when a crime is reported to the police they use their discretion and they do not always record it. Sometimes it is necessary to decide on which offence(s) to record and multiple offences may be recorded differently by different police officers. Sometimes quite different crimes qualitatively are counted together, for example small and large thefts, because the categories of crime are generalised. There is then often a difference in investigation between offences. A stolen bicycle is likely to be less resourced than a bank robbery. When an offender is caught, the police decide whether to release him/her, or to charge the person and take him/her to court. The court can then find the person either guilty or not guilty.

Media attention

The **mass media** tend to focus attention on particular crimes to the exclusion of others. They may spark off interest and encourage a 'moral crusade' against certain activities. A number of criminologists, Stan Cohen (1972) in particular, have shown how the media play a part in creating 'moral panics', highlighting offences like mugging, football hooliganism, social security frauds, etc. Associated with the moral panics are what Cohen terms the **folk devils** of our time: teddy-boys, mods and rockers, Hell's Angels, skinheads, punk rockers, pornographers, drugtakers, etc.

Administration process

Crime statistics should therefore be used cautiously, because they are produced by a 'process' for administrative, rather than sociological, purposes. A classic study that illustrates this process is Cicourel's *The Social Organisation of Juvenile Justice* (1976).

This study looks at how official files and statistics on juvenile delinquency are assembled in two cities of similar size and socio-economic characteristics. Comparing the two cities, Cicourel found that local police organisation and policy led to different definitions of what constituted delinquency, and subsequently to significant differences in the number of delinquents arrested and charged. He argues that the dominance of **working-class** delinquents in the statistics was the result of interactions between the 'delinquents' and the police and juvenile officers. The **middle-class** boy, if arrested, was more likely to be let off with a caution. Parents were better able to negotiate, promising support in disciplining the boy. In Cicourel's words, 'He is typically counselled, warned and released.'

Cicourel's work shows that the variance in official definitions of delinquency and what police officers consider relevant to their understanding of the problem, and their dealings with those they define as delinquents, should be treated as a basic problem for the researcher.

Crime surveys

Until very recently the estimation of hidden crime was purely a matter of guesswork, but there have been some attempts to measure the dark figure more scientifically. They fall into two categories:

→ Self-report studies, where a population is questioned about delinquent acts they have committed by their own admission and whether these have led to a court appearance. A list of offences is normally provided, the individual being invited to indicate if he/she has committed such an offence, knowing that anonymity can be retained after completion.

→ Victim studies, where a population is questioned as to whether they have been robbed, assaulted, etc.

A national survey of victims in America, *The President's Commission* (1998), found that one in five households had been the victim of a serious crime in 1997. About twice as many major crimes were committed as were known to the police. (In the case of burglary, 71 per cent, and of rape, 78 per cent, were not known to the police.) *The British Crime Survey* (1997) found that rates of reporting crimes varied from 26 per cent for vandalism to 57 per cent for robberies and 97 per cent for the theft of motor vehicles. According to police figures, notifiable offences rose by 67 per cent between 1981 and 1997. Yet the *British Crime Survey* recorded an increase of just 56 per cent over the same period. If the survey was correct then official figures exaggerated the rise in crime over the 1981–97 period.

Self-report and victim studies make possible an estimate of criminal acts and their frequency. They also allow comparison between official and unknown delinquency. Furthermore, a researcher can find out why victims did not report crimes. However, there are drawbacks with self-report and victim surveys. The surveys tend to rely on small unrepresentative populations, for example schoolchildren. Exaggeration occurs, especially when self-report is in a group situation, and some offences are still concealed because of shame. Memory errors may also occur.

The value of crime surveys

Self-report studies, despite their limitations, do challenge established views and show that the dark figure is sufficiently large to cast doubt on statistics based on the number of offences known to the police. While many acts admitted are of a trivial nature, there appears to be a substantial number of people who have committed relatively serious offences that have gone undetected by the police or for which they have not been prosecuted.

The picture that emerges from self-report studies is that sex offences are under-reported; that stealing from shops is an almost normal occurrence as young people grow up; that males commit more crimes than females but only twice as many rather than the five times more suggested by official statistics; and that delinquency is only slightly higher among the working classes than the middle classes although the crime statistics suggest that delinquency is a working-class phenomenon.

Some victim studies have examined closely the influence of factors such as age, **class**, **gender** and race on the nature and extent of crime that people experience. For example, local victimisation studies have underlined the point that where a person lives can affect their chances of becoming a victim of crime. The 1984 Merseyside Crime Survey found that 44 per cent of people on Merseyside had been victimised in the previous year. The Third Islington Crime Survey (1998) reports a burglary rate running at twice the national average, with 8 per cent of women reporting an incident of sexual assault for the previous twelve months. Findings of this kind indicate that in terms of both quantity and the impact of crimes examined, the poor suffer more than the wealthy. Moreover, the study concluded that the cycle of violence and fear confronted by women limits their participation in public places to the extent of virtual curfew.

Assessment of official statistics

Official statistics of crime clearly have many limitations, but even so they are not entirely without use for the sociologist. **Functionalists**, for example, believe that official statistics provide a reliable basis that can be applied to the whole of society by using statistical techniques to take account of the dark figure. The crime statistics at least tell us the nature and extent of the problems facing the courts and the policy-makers. It is also reasonable to assume that they are a fairly accurate indicator of the incidence of some crimes, such as murder and armed robbery. However, we must be careful with the inferences we draw from some of the statistics. Moreover, the validity of some of the sociological and psychological explanations of crime must be doubted where the explanations depend on data drawn from the official statistics.

An increase in crime?

Overall, the number of recorded crimes in the UK rose from 500,000 in the 1950s to one million in the mid-1960s, and two million in the mid-1970s. By 2000 it was 4.3 million. Looking at some of these categories of crime, we find that:

→ Robberies have risen dramatically from less than 1,000 a year, just after the war, to 35,200 (2000). The use of firearms in robberies is also increasing, from 650 cases in 1974 to 2,887 in 2000.
→ Rape offences increased from 1,052 recorded incidents in 1974, to 1,779 in 2000. But the figures for indecent assault have fallen, perhaps indicating a different attitude on charging offenders.
→ Woundings increased from 6,740 in 1974 to 12,538 in 2000.

At face value, these figures suggest that the UK is becoming a more violent and crime-ridden country. The reality is more complex. The Home Office agrees that violence in Britain is increasing but not at the rate suggested by the figures. It suggests that the dark figure is reducing, due to improved police efficiency and computers and that more telephones have led to more crimes being reported.

In the specific cases of rape, domestic violence and child abuse there has been a marked change in the way that these crimes are perceived in recent decades. They are more likely to be reported to the police now, because there is a greater confidence than before that the claims of women and children will be taken seriously and offences against them will be recognised as crimes. Domestic violence is less likely to be accepted as something to be endured. This does not, of course, prevent a male-dominated judiciary from occasionally making comments and advising juries in ways that make it clear that their sympathies are not always with the victims. Each time this happens, confidence in the judiciary is dented, for example when judges decide that women are guilty of 'contributory negligence' if they are raped hitch-hiking home from a party in a short skirt. The suggestion is that women in these situations are in some way 'asking for it' and that when they say 'No' they mean 'Yes'.

We are not suggesting that it is the case that women, children and other victims of violence have perfect trust and confidence in the police and judiciary, but where this confidence and sense of injustice does increase, then it can lead to statistical increases without the actual incidence of crime going up. It may even have gone down, but there may be a much higher rate of reporting.

This is certainly one way that sociologists have explained the apparent increase in the crime rate. Other important contributory factors may be the increase in the number of people who own phones (so they can report to the police with greater ease). Also it is more necessary now to report burglaries to the police in order to make an insurance claim. Another area that has been highlighted is the increased amount of manpower as well as surveillance and information technology now available to the police. The police now routinely use cars, radios, cameras, computers and highly advanced forensic techniques in their battle against crime. There are more police per person. In 1861 the police-to-population ratio was approximately 1:1,000. By 1951 this had risen to 1:694. By the early 2000s this had risen to 1:400. There has also been a considerable increase in the number of civilians (i.e. administrative workers) in the police force. We can therefore say that we are a substantially more policed society than we have ever been before.

It does not necessarily follow, however, that this means that there are more police on the beat, or out looking for criminals. An average force of 2,000 officers might expect to have 100 officers assigned to general patrol at any one time. Studies have shown that as much as 40 per cent of their time can be spent inside police stations, mainly on paperwork. Traffic control also consumes much of their time. It is this side of the police's work that is rarely portrayed by television dramas.

All of this suggests that the world of crime revealed by official statistics needs to be treated with caution.

As many sociologists have argued, what appear to be **social facts** could, on closer examination, be better described as 'social constructions'. It is also the case that factors such as class, race and where they live can have a major bearing on the extent to which a person is at risk of being the victim of a serious crime. If the UK is becoming a more violent and crime-ridden society, the situation is much worse for some (e.g. the poor) than for others (e.g. the wealthy).

Women and crime

Little is known, and even less has been researched, concerning the relationship between women and crime. The main reason for this is because, statistically, women have always been a tiny minority of those engaging in crime.

Before the rise of **feminist** theory in the 1970s, accounts of women's criminality had gone little further than Lombroso and Ferrero's (1895) failure to find a clear correlation between criminal women and their biological characteristics. Furthermore, they argued, although women were less advanced along the evolutionary scale (and therefore more likely to be criminal), the process of natural selection had bred out those women who tended to crime as these 'masculine' women were less likely to find male sexual partners to reproduce with.

Adler

Freda Adler (1975) attempted to discern a correlation between an increase in female criminality and the movement for women's **liberation**, with greater opportunities arising for crime with more women out of the home and in the workplace. Female criminality, she argued, could therefore be seen as an index of the degree of liberation achieved by women.

This initially persuasive theory is the latest in a long line of arguments that have emerged when rises in female crime rates have been detected but, as with so much of the study of criminology, the argument is found wanting because the statistical evidence is thought to be inaccurate. Adler's statistical series, based on figures from the USA between 1960 and 1972, showed rates of increase for juvenile and adult female crime higher than those for male crime. Her data were dogged by the fact that her base for women was very low. A rise in serious crime of 500 per cent can in reality be the difference between one murder by women in one year and five in the next.

A more important question, for writers such as Frances Heidensohn (1985), is: 'Why are there so few female criminals?' There are, at first sight, two possible answers to this question: the statistics are misleading, or women really do not engage in crime at the same rate as men.

Official statistics

Officially, convictions for serious or indictable offences are split approximately 80:20 between men and women, and there are approximately 33 times more men in prison at any one time in Great Britain than women. Even figures for shoplifting, traditionally thought of as a 'female' crime, show that more men are consistently captured and convicted than women.

Social control

Bizarrely, Otto Pollack (1950) explained this pattern by stating that, because women had to hide the fact of menstruation, they are good at hiding things in general, for example their criminality. More modern research, based on self-report studies – such as those of Mawby (1980) – indicate that the proportion of male to female crime corresponds with the reality of people's experience. Nor does it seem to be true that women are dealt with more leniently by the police and courts (the 'chivalry thesis'). If anything they are treated as doubly deviant because they have broken both the stated laws of the land and the unstated laws of feminine behaviour. Moreover, if charged with serious crimes, they are much more likely than men to be seen as suffering from psychological problems than seen to be simply guilty (see Carlen, 1985 and Allen, 1987).

Heidensohn (1985) argues that women's low involvement in crime reflects the constraining nature of the way they are **socialised**, when compared to men. Control over their behaviour is exercised through the family, the school, among peers, by the media and by more formal agents of social control. Girls are more subject to social control in the home. They are socialised to be more law-abiding and expected to be co-operative and docile. These qualities become part of the female's self-image. The socialisation pattern in many homes places less pressure on females to succeed, the emphasis being on marriage and the family.

While differences in socialisation and social control may contribute to an explanation of the relatively low rate of female crime, it does not explain why some women engage in crime. Carlen suggests that this will most readily occur when girls are brought up in care in adolescence, away from the tight gender roles learnt in families where there is a male breadwinner and a female carer.

Women are as capable as men of committing any crime, whether murder, as in the cases of Myra Hindley and Rosemary West in the UK, or child sexual abuse. Indeed, Carol Smart (1989) argues that there are some crimes more commonly committed by women. These include soliciting, infanticide and shoplifting. The 'borstal girls' studied by Anne Campbell (1981) fought in pubs, in streets, and at home, used weapons and broke bones. They were just as aggressive and violent as members of any male gang.

Feminist sociologists argue that sociologists (usually male) have underestimated the problem of women's criminality and more study is required. Carol Smart has suggested that the exclusion of females from studies of those who commit crime is mirrored in the lack of research that has been undertaken into the female victims of crimes. Thus, until recently, there have been very few studies of rape, violence against women, and sexual harassment.

To overcome this bias, feminists have argued that research should be directed towards understanding the effects of male power, or **patriarchy**, on women's lives. Various studies have focused on how inequality in power between the sexes is used to conceal and even normalise male aggression and violence towards females. In their study of domestic violence, Dobash and Dobash (1980) note how actions that might otherwise be regarded as deviant and morally reprehensible, come to be seen as 'normal' and a natural part of life for many women.

Feminist criminologists have also been influential in extending the criminological agenda from the narrower mainstream emphasis on offender-orientation studies to embrace a more focused analysis of victims of crime, particularly the analysis of female victimisation, and more particularly still in the realms of domestic violence and sexual offences. They have drawn attention to the point that women experience far greater levels of victimisation than were previously acknowledged, and that the incidence of sexual offences against women is far higher than both officially recorded data and even national crime surveys suggest. They have also been instrumental in highlighting women's fear of crime and the accompanying constraints on lifestyles and life choices which that generates (for example, going out alone or travelling on public transport at night).

Ethnicity and crime

If the picture of women and crime shows a relative under-representation, an analysis of the criminality of **ethnic** groups in Britain reveals, at first sight, exactly the opposite. There are, proportionately, far more blacks than whites brought to court and sent to prison. They have a higher crime rate. While this can be explained by the fact that black people are concentrated among the working class and, some argue, the **underclass** (see chapter 3), who in turn have higher crime rates, many sociologists have argued that a more profound analysis is needed.

Differential processing

The evidence is that black people have a different experience of justice to white people. According to the Home Office, the prison population in 2001 was classified as being made up of 17.4 per cent black males and 30.3 per cent black females, whereas they make up 6 per cent of the population nationally. They receive longer prison sentences and are more likely to have probation recommendations ignored. Afro-Caribbean youths are more readily remanded in custody and given custodial sentences, even when they have fewer previous convictions than white youths (see Smith, 1994).

As ever, the use of the term 'black' has to be carefully examined. Close analysis shows that groups of Asian descent should be distinguished from Afro-Caribbeans. In 2000, for example, men of West Indian, Guyanese and African origin represented 11.4 per cent of the prison population but only 2.1 per cent of the total population, while Indians, Pakistanis and Bangladeshis represented 3.2 per cent of the prison population and 3.7 per cent of the overall population.

For Daniels (1968), these figures cannot be explained by institutional **racism**, as all minorities suffer equally from such discrimination. The difference lies, he believes, in the patterns and expectations of immigration. Afro-Caribbeans came from islands modelled administratively on Britain, and they spoke English. Believing they were entering the same culture, they were initially outgoing and thus surprised to meet racism and hostility. Asian groups came from cultures already different organisationally and linguistically from Britain and therefore relied on their own resources and communities on arriving in Britain. Afro-Caribbeans therefore placed themselves in situations where they were more likely to encounter racism and discrimination. From 1969 onwards there was also an inflow of well-educated petty bourgeois Asians from East Africa.

As Paul Gilroy (1987) writes, the years between 1972 and 1976 'saw the definition of blacks as a low crime group turned around 180 degrees'. For this writer, their resistance to discrimination and exploitation has politicised them and for this they have in turn been criminalised and subjected to institutional racism by the police and the law enforcement agencies.

Discrimination and racism

Gilroy argues that crimes committed by ethnic minorities are often conscious and deliberate political acts directed against a society that treats them unjustly. At the same time though, Gilroy rejects the idea that ethnic minorities are more prone to being criminal than other sections of the community. Insofar as crime rates are higher for these groups than for the indigenous white population, this is primarily a consequence of racism among the law-enforcement agencies, especially the police. Referring to the UK, Gilroy claims that the police have negative **stereotypes** of Afro-Caribbeans and Asians. Afro-Caribbeans are often seen as 'wild and lawless', or more specifically as 'muggers'. The police frequently regard Asians with suspicion; in particular they are suspected of being illegal immigrants.

Gilroy attempts to explain why racial prejudice and stereotypes exist in terms of the wider structure of society, and the operation of **capitalism** specifically. In a situation of mass unemployment, ethnic minorities can readily be castigated as a 'surplus population'. They are then blamed for a situation that is actually caused by the capitalist system. Moreover, their alleged responsibility for crime helps to justify calls for their 'repatriation' to their countries of origin.

Stuart Hall (1978a) argues that during the 1970s young blacks in the UK were stereotypically associated with the 'mugging problem', which allowed the police to use stop-and-search methods and saturate black areas with police. The belief emerged in schools, courts, police and government agencies that 'immigrants' had difficulty in meeting British demands for the rule of law. The position of the **State** seemed to be that black people should be disciplined and punished if they would not be contained. For many writers, however, the real problem was the entrenched racism of those in power, clearly evident in policing and immigration policy.

If Irish nationalists in the United Kingdom are seen as an ethnic minority, then they present a specific example of this approach, where all aspects of the legal process have been intensified to maintain control, from the way the army has been used to internment without trial and the arbitrary use of the Prevention of Terrorism Act. This view is held by Hillyard (1987). This issue remains an under-developed area of sociological research.

Lea and Young

John Lea and Jock Young (1984) have questioned Gilroy's view that racism among police officers accounts entirely for the high crime rate among ethnic minorities in Britain. As over 90 per cent of crimes known to the police are brought to their attention by the public, they suggest that it is implausible that the preponderance of Afro-Caribbeans in the official figures is solely a consequence of police discrimination. Lea and Young also point out that the recorded rate for crimes committed by whites is consistently slightly higher than that recorded for Asians, so not all ethnic minorities have a high crime rate. They maintain that police racism would have to manifest itself very strongly indeed to be entirely responsible for such rates.

Lea and Young also reject the emphasis that Marxists give to poverty and unemployment being directly responsible for crime. They point out that in the 1930s, unemployment was very high in the UK, yet the crime rate was low compared to the 1980s. Moreover, even though most first-generation black immigrants in the UK had low-paid jobs, they also had low rates of crime.

Lea and Young argue that poverty and unemployment will only lead to crime where a group feels deprived in relation to other similar groups, or its expectations are not met. They point out that the media and advertisers, in particular, have created unrealistic expectations for some groups by suggesting that people should aspire to middle-class lifestyles and patterns of consumption. Groups such as the unemployed and low paid, who are unable to achieve high standards of living, experience pressure which may lead some individuals to commit crime. Many young blacks in particular experience acute **marginalisation**; that is, they feel pushed to the edge of society, doing less well in school, getting badly paid jobs, being likely to be unemployed for long periods, and having few outlets for political expression. At the same time, they also have greater expectations of material success compared to older generations of black people, which are nevertheless thwarted by life

in the UK. Lea and Young argue that part of the difference between Asian and Afro-Caribbean crime rates can be explained by the latter group having internalised materialist values to a greater extent than Asians, whose traditional cultural and religious beliefs have remained stronger.

Much also depends on the particular **subcultural** solution that the individual adopts in response to his or her experience of 'relative deprivation'. Lea and Young stress that it is not inevitable that young people in disadvantaged groups today will develop a set of attitudes and **values** reflecting a criminal mentality. For example, second-generation Afro-Caribbean immigrants' subcultural solutions to their problems include the Rastafarian and Pentacostalist religions as well as 'hustling' for money and street crime.

Questions

1 How does Left realism differ from earlier theories of ethnicity and crime?
2 Are some ethnic minorities more prone to crime than others? If so, why?

White-collar crime

Sutherland

For the first half of this century, most studies of crime focused on what is usually called 'ordinary crime', dealing with criminal activity such as theft, robbery, burglary, vandalism, assault and murder, where there is typically a perpetrator and a victim. The publication of Edwin Sutherland's *White Collar Crime* in 1949 added a new direction to criminology by bringing crimes committed either for or within businesses into the picture.

Since the publication of this book, the study of **white-collar crime** has become more, not less, important, not least because the ratio of white-collar to manual jobs has increased throughout the century, to the point where they now outnumber **blue-collar** jobs in the industrial world. Defining exactly what is meant by white-collar crime, however, has proved more problematic.

Sutherland defined it as 'criminal acts carried out by persons of high social status and respectability in the course of their occupation'. He provided the following examples of white-collar crime: tax or money frauds, bribery, corruption in business or politics, misconduct of professionals (doctors, lawyers, accountants, etc.), and wrongful use of employers' or clients' cash or resources.

White-collar criminal: in 1995 Nick Leeson was sentenced to six and a half years in prison for deceit and cheating. His activities had contributed to the collapse of Barings Investment Bank, where he committed them to liabilities worth $1.3 billion.

Gerry Mars' *Cheats at Work* (1985) expanded the concept of white-collar crime. His studies revealed extensive illegal activities in many jobs and occupations. Mars terms these activities 'fiddling', because the actors themselves may not see their activities as criminal; rather they see them as 'perks' of the job. Fiddling is to be found in both white- and blue-collar occupations.

The importance of white-collar crime and 'fiddling' lies in the way that they are so largely under-reported. This masking of the extent of middle-class and occupational crime renders the crime statistics misleading in the patterns of crime they present.

W. G. Carson (1971) puts forward the following reasons for under-reporting of white-collar crimes:

→ These are crimes without victims – there is no clear individual victim. For example, bribery may be a crime where both participants gain.

→ The victim is the general public. When individuals or firms evade paying taxes, it is the society that suffers the reduction in revenue.

→ Even when occupational crimes are discovered, many firms do not prosecute the wrongdoers. Many firms do not want the publicity that may show up lack of security.

Some writers have distinguished between white-collar crimes carried out by employees against a company (such as fraud or embezzlement) and crimes committed by the companies themselves in pursuit of maintaining or increasing their profit margins. These 'corporate crimes' can cover activities as varied as contravening pollution laws, neglecting health and safety legislation or breaking the Food and Drugs Act.

Corporate crime

The diverse nature of corporate crime means that it is not usually revealed in police statistics, issued by the Home Office or Central Office of Information, but separately in information issued by government bodies such as local government environmental health departments, the Ministry of Agriculture or Customs and Excise. These crimes are therefore not defined and labelled in the same way that ordinary crime is, and continue to escape the attention of many criminologists, attracted to more 'glamorous' forms of crime.

Michael Clarke (1990) argues that ordinary and white-collar crimes differ in that white-collar criminals commit crimes in places where they can normally be expected to be found and the police are unwilling to enter. Furthermore, such crimes are often seen as 'complaintless' and frequently resemble legal behaviour, as in the cases of fraud and confidence tricks, where the presence of the victim appears as voluntary. Organised crime syndicates, such as the Mafia, may choose to resemble legitimate businesses and legitimate businesses may employ corrupt or illegal organisations to secure loan repayments, avoid taxes or to discipline labour. In this way, the distinctions between legal, semi-legal and illegal activity become blurred. How corporate crime in particular can be explained is itself the cause of much debate. Businesses, like conventional bank robbers, are principally concerned to make money but, unlike bank robbers, are already making money in an orthodox and legal way. Why should they then turn to crime?

From a positivist point of view, Clinard and Yeager (1980) argue that variables such as company size, growth rate, diversification, market power and resources mean that some businesses, for example the oil, pharmaceutical and motor vehicle industries, are more likely to offend than others. Passas (1990) attempts to use Mertonian strain theory (see pp. 202–3) to explain corporate crime as an 'innovative' response to the strain of meeting cultural expectations of maintaining profits and surviving in highly competitive markets.

The Marxist view

Marxist-influenced explanations have sought to show white-collar (particularly corporate) crime not as exceptional but as endemic to capitalism. Where legal means are blocked then companies will resort to illegal means. As Frank Pearce (1976) argues, for these companies, 'business is business'. This is at its clearest in the Third World, where unregulated and unscrupulous capitalism thrives. Against this, many writers have argued that the quality of goods and safety records improve as capitalism develops and the goodwill of clients and staff needs to be maintained. A further distinction needs to be made between what is seen as good for capitalism as a whole, such as anti-trust laws, and what only benefits individual capitalist concerns. Poor records on corruption, pollution and safety were also common in **communist** countries. Abuse may therefore be due to the absence of market pressures.

Crime and the State

Attention has also been focused on the way governments appear to have encouraged or allowed corporate crime by being deliberately weak on regulation, by deregulating activities altogether, or (as some have argued with the rapid exploitation of oil from the North Sea) by turning a blind eye to safety issues because of a company's importance to the balance of payments. In such cases, white-collar crime is tolerated because the interests of the State and business coincide.

The issue of political will thus looms large, even at as fundamental a level of consideration as why some activities become criminalised in the first place. However, many, including Nelken (1983), argue for 'coherence without conspiracy' in explaining the low level of white-collar prosecutions, which they say is due to problems of definition, the complexity of the issues and the cost, as well as the need to maintain the goodwill of businesses. Nevertheless, Cook (1989) shows that Social Security fraud is treated differently and more severely to a very similar kind of crime: tax fraud.

Questions
1 What are the differences between white-collar crime and working-class crime?
2 What is meant by the term corporate crime?
3 What is the Marxist explanation for corporate crime?

Theories of crime and deviance

Before sociology: Cesare Lombroso

Cesare Lombroso (1835–1909) was an Italian doctor working for the Italian army. He believed that criminals share common physical characteristics, and to prove this he set about measuring and quantifying certain physical features. He used a number of devices in this task, including a dynamometer (to measure physical strength), a craniograph (to measure the skull) and a pelvimeter (to measure pelvic strength).

In all, he studied over 400 prisoners, whom he compared with an equivalent number of Italian soldiers. Lombroso (1876) then concluded that: criminals have disproportionately long arms; hard expressions; shifty glances; large ears; twisted, upturned or, in the case of thieves, flattened noses and frequently upturned mouths; extra fingers/toes; and upturned nipples. Murderers, he discovered, have bushy eyebrows and beak-like noses.

The fact that they shared these features, he said, was evidence that people who commit serious crimes do so because they are genetically abnormal. They provide evidence of atavism – a throwback to a previous, less civilised age. Their criminal nature has decanted them from society into prison. Crime, he says, 'mingles with all kinds of degeneration: rickets, deafness, monstrosity, hairiness and cretinism, of which crime is only a variation'. The soldiers, by comparison, exhibited none of the characteristics of the criminals.

There are a number of problems with Lombroso's study. He only studied the characteristics of people who had already been caught and sentenced. They may have been arrested because of the way they looked and therefore aroused suspicion. This idea lives on in the folk myth that people with 'their eyes too close together' or eyebrows that meet in the middle cannot be trusted. He does not take into consideration those criminals who were never caught. The prisoners may have had abnormalities because of poverty and malnutrition. These are therefore class and not criminal characteristics. They may well have been rejected by the army for these characteristics, which is why they did not resemble the soldiers.

Women

While Lombroso was keen to differentiate between types of men, his view of women was more general and sweeping, claiming (Lombroso and Ferrero, 1895) that: 'Women have many traits in common with children; … their moral sense is deficient; … they are revengeful, jealous … in ordinary cases these defects are neutralised by piety, maternity, want of passion and sexual coldness, and an underdeveloped intelligence.'

Lombroso's work is a good example of the belief that only some people are predisposed towards deviancy, and their behaviour can be explained through the discovery of characteristics and traits that determine this predisposition towards deviance. Although his work is no longer accepted as valid, the idea of 'deviant natures' has continued into twentieth-century criminology.

The psychological perspective

Psychological theories share certain similarities with biological theories. They see the deviant as different from the population as a whole and it is this 'abnormality' that predisposes him or her to deviance. However, psychological theories differ from biological theories in that they see the deviant's sickness and abnormality as lying in mental processes rather than physical differences.

In the past, some psychological theories about the causes of deviance have led to harsh physical practices supposedly to cure the physical problem. 'Trepanning' (drilling or cutting) involves opening the skull to let out evil spirits. It used to be a great favourite, with most of the bad people in question dying from the operational trauma. This was superseded by attempts to locate the areas of the brain which advances in psychology had decided upon as the site of the impulse to misbehave, where centres of aggression could be isolated by the surgeon's knife. This was trepanning under a clinical guise, and ranged from lobotomies which entailed carving out various parts of the frontal lobe to the more refined leucotomies which pinpointed smaller areas of a malfunctioning, deviant brain. The end result is Jack Nicholson in *One Flew Over the Cuckoo's Nest* – a walking zombie.

Though these ideas have now largely disappeared from medical practice, they still retain some influence on more modern and advanced theories.

Neurology

Other groups of psychologists – neurologists, who are interested in the biology of the brain and the nervous system – are interested in the excitatory and inhibitory substances which are transmitted through the central nervous system, propelled by electrical impulses. The levels of these drug-like chemicals, called neurotransmitters, are said to determine aspects of behaviour. 'Dopamine', large levels of which are found in the brains of deceased schizophrenics, is of particular interest. (For alternative explanations of this complex condition see chapter 5.) Dopamine excess causes 'inappropriate behaviour' – a cultural construct if ever there was one! – where garbled speech and auditory and visual hallucinations are the result. The question is, which came first, the condition or the high level of the neurotransmitter? Psychologists will now point to genetic explanations for this particular form of deviance, but this does not explain entirely why only certain people develop schizophrenia, usually in late adolescence, and why in some cases it is easily controlled and in others it is a continuous and debilitating condition.

At this point, explanations begin to veer towards the cultural, admitting that environmental 'stressors' can be located in the family, peer groups or social class. The best social science renders the nature–nurture debate an artificial one, acknowledging that biological, psychological and cultural factors all play a part. This compartmentalisation is a common situation within social science, as representatives of each discipline tend to stress the importance of their own explanations. Their theoretical spotlight shines only on certain selected 'facts'.

Maternal deprivation

John Bowlby (1971) studied how human beings form attachments, and how they experience grief and loss. He suggested that humans have from infancy a predisposition to form a deep and overwhelmingly important attachment to one person – and that person will probably be the mother. Disruption of the relationship with the mother in childhood by, for example, prolonged separation, will produce anxiety in the child and effects similar to grief for the loss of a loved one. This experience may shape the child's later emotional development and a psychopathic personality could develop. Psychopaths tend to act impulsively, with little regard for the consequences of their actions. Bowlby claimed that criminals, who constantly broke the law and showed little response to punishment or treatment, had suffered from maternal deprivation during their early years. Often they had been raised in orphanages, where they had been deprived of an intimate relationship with a mother figure.

Many sociologists are sceptical about the priority given to childhood experience in Bowlby's work. They reject the view that the individual's early experience, or conditioning, automatically determines his or her behaviour in later life, since this approach ignores a wide range of other social factors that influence the way a person acts during his or her life.

Eysenck and personality

A further psychological perspective is provided by Hans Eysenck (1975; see also chapter 6). Eysenck's Personality Questionnaire (EPQ) is perhaps the most detailed and exhaustive analysis of what makes a 'personality'. Designed from a **positivist** point of view – that the essence of personality can be measured and quantified – Eysenck's questionnaire is cunningly contrived to ask the same question over and over again in a slightly different way, something like a desperate teacher in front of a class intent on improving their powers of non-verbal communication. The EPQ will present a picture of an individual around the concepts of introvert and extrovert personality. The balanced personality comes somewhere between these two extremes, with anyone scoring high on either end of the scale being classed as a deviant, if not psychopathic, personality.

The common thread that runs through these psychological explanations of deviance is that they all concentrate on internal causes of what is deemed to be deviant behaviour. From 'mad' or 'bad' explanations, evil spirits, and excess brain chemicals to the apparently innate criminal behaviour described by Eysenck, the influences and constraints of the wider social and cultural environment are ignored or given a back seat.

The methodology of many psychological theories has also been criticised. For example, there is little agreement among psychologists about what constitutes mental health and how to measure personality characteristics.

Sociological explanations

The essential difference between this type of explanation and sociological ones is that sociologists are interested in the relationship between the individual and **culture**, and how both help to create each other. Some explanations point to the structural, economic backdrop of the social system, others concentrate on the meanings and understandings which are constructed through interaction between individuals, between individuals and groups, and between individuals and those in power. Explanations which look for the causes of deviance solely within the individual lack this broader aspect, and suffer as a result. The concept of deviance is a social construct. If it were not then all societies would have exactly the same laws, with no cultural variation. The way the concept is constructed as a result of interactions has to be an important factor.

Questions

1 How do sociological explanations of deviance differ from the non-sociological?

2 How does Eysenck measure personality?

3 Can deviant characteristics be inherited?

Functionalist theories

Mechanical solidarity

For functionalists it is consensus which is the basis of social stability. It is within this framework that deviance, and the deviant act, must be explained. In exploring the differences between small-scale, pre-literate societies and large industrial social systems, Emile Durkheim noticed that an important aspect of social solidarity was different concepts of law and order. Mechanical solidarity, he observed, existed in smaller groups, where the limits of acceptable behaviour in all social areas are obvious to all. Anyone who breaks the law by sleeping with a parent, commits a murder, steals, is traitorous or breaks any religious taboos will accept or expect punishment – the social sanction which applies to that particular crime or deviant act. Retribution is 'mechanical'.

Organic solidarity

In the more complex organ of industrialised society, there is more choice in all areas of social life, so individuals are free to choose adult roles, religious beliefs, sexual practices and so on. What can possibly keep this society on the straight and narrow? Durkheim's answer is 'organic solidarity', upheld by a 'moral conscience' which ensures that all members of society are instilled with a sense of the importance of the larger social structure, so that their existence within society depends upon the well-being and maintenance of that structure. Collective values, moral codes, ethics, 'a sense of right and wrong' not only influence individual actions but are a central part of the social being. Internalisation, as Parsons says, consists of living and breathing the value system, seeing the world through norm-coloured spectacles. Any transgression has to be explained in terms of the inability of the individual to 'connect' adequately with the collective conscience, that is, poor socialisation.

Suicide and integration

Durkheim's famous study *Suicide* (1897, see pp216–18) highlights integration as an aspect of socialisation where various social attributes lead individuals to volunteer for death. In the societies he studied, if you are young, male, not Catholic, or unmarried you are a high suicide risk. Your degree of integration affects your desire to remain a smaller part of the whole. With family responsibilities, and a caring church, you are much more likely to wish to remain and support your dependants than to end it all. Deviance, then, is the product of the inability to mesh with the greater value system, for whatever reason.

Internalisation and conflict

As usual, the functionalist spotlight has picked out explanations stemming from the need to maintain stability, so transgression of the value system reflects an inability to negotiate it appropriately. Breaking the law goes against the consensus wishes of the majority. Those who engage in these activities are grappling with their own guilt, as they are going against their very personalities, the social being constructed through the socialisation process. Critics (for example Dennis Wrong; see also chapter 1) have pointed out that this conception of individuals overdoes the ease of internalisation, where little or no resistance appears evident. There is a parallel here. The basic assumptions of functionalist theory determinedly play down conflict within the social system; conflict within individuals is likewise ignored.

Changing the law

The internalisation of social **norms** and values is by no means easy, and it is questionable whether it is ever complete, but is rather a continuous process of internal battles which are mirrored in external battles in society. Would laws regarding homosexuality have been changed in Britain if socialisation had been a perfect, one-way process?

Deviance and social change

This aspect of deviant behaviour – the first signs of a new pattern of behaviour – is encompassed within Parsons' ideas concerning social evolution. Change is the product of deviance, from within which new behaviour patterns emerge. Again, the conflict within existing values is not satisfactorily explained, and we are left with the questions: Why do some people deviate and not others? Why do those who indulge in different behaviour tend to come from similar areas of society? Functionalist explanations which are more recent than Durkheim's study attempt to provide answers to these questions, but before we examine them, it would be useful to look at one more theoretical aspect of this argument.

The functions of deviance

Social facts exist in relation to society as a whole. The functions of each aspect of society need to be examined in order to place them within the whole. What are the functions of deviance? How does it contribute to the maintenance of society? Surely behaviour which goes against the grain of social acceptability is destructive, dysfunctional and a disease in the organism? In one sense it is seen in this way by functionalism, and a rapid spread of deviant activity – drug use, non-heterosexual sex, or violence which is not officially sanctioned – are seen as potentially leading to a breakdown of society. However, in another sense, as we have seen, deviant behaviour can lead to social change, as with the scientist who labours against professional opinion and subsequently makes a breakthrough which benefits all humanity. In this sense deviance can be seen as functional.

It can also be seen as functional in so far as it helps to define what is acceptable behaviour. As long as we have violent behaviour, we need laws and sanctions which condemn and prevent it. The variety of sanctions which can be applied here is enormous, and depends on the context. It may be being kept in at playtime for bullying or it may mean ten years in prison for committing grievous bodily harm. Even the level of harm is taken into account, harm that is actual or grievous being defined by law. Now, imagine a society where physical violence was unheard of. How would unacceptable behaviour be signalled? How would we know what we can and cannot do? An eyebrow raised in anger could get you a suspended sentence, a dirty look two years. Swearing might become a capital offence. The point here is that deviance can be functional in that it lets us know where to draw the line. We must then toe the line or be defined as deviant.

Merton and cultural explanations

From a statistical point of view, deviant and criminal behaviour is more apparent in the working classes. The functionalist Robert Merton has evolved an explanation which attempts to deal with this. For Merton (1949) deviance is born out of reaction to the values and norms of society. The major value is success, defined financially. The norm to achieve this goal is hard work. Merton used males for his analysis, reflecting the main

Table 8.1   A typology of modes of individual adaptation

Modes of adaptation	Cultural goals	Institutionalised means
Conformity	+	+
Innovation	+	–
Ritualism	–	+
Retreatism	–	–
Rebellion	±	±

+ = acceptance; – = rejection; ± = rejection of prevailing values and substitution of new values

Source: Merton, 1949

area of concern. Merton does not enter into a debate about sexism, mainly because he and his society at the time – 1940s USA – were sexist. Young working-class males were well aware of the goals of their society, they just lacked the ability to score. Frustrated by lack of qualifications, they are left to devise an alternative means of scoring the goals – the foul. Merton goes on to construct a table which he believes explains why certain people deviate. How many crosses you get against your name determines the causes and nature of your particular brand of deviance. This is known as Mertonian 'strain' theory (see *Table 8.1*).

The gap between goals and means

Inability to achieve the goals of society, due to a problem in engaging in the norms which are beyond an individual's control, which cannot be grasped and used, leaves the individual in a condition of **anomie**, a lack of norms, 'normlessness'. People can suddenly be thrown into this situation for various reasons: the loss of a loved one, marriage breakdown, abrupt financial disaster or success being the most obvious. Disaster leaves you with goals but without the means to achieve them, windfall success leaves you with a lifestyle you can move beyond but without a map to show you how to advance. Hence pools or lottery winners who either say 'It won't stop me going to work' or who decide to 'Spend! Spend! Spend!'

Deviance and the working class

Merton's table attempts to deal with different types of deviance, with type being awarded according to class position. The lower classes are most likely to 'innovate'. Lacking the accepted norms of success, they operate using a new set, which they have adapted in order to realise the goals. In short, they steal, lie and cheat their way to financial success, as they know they would never reach the top through the legitimate route, which for them is manual labour.

The lower middle class

The lower middle class is the most likely to produce the 'ritualist' deviant. This is the person who has long since given up their pretensions to success, and, unable to drop their socialisation, always plays by the rules. They therefore 'go through the motions', no longer expecting success, conforming to failure, and becoming petty, rule-minded sticklers.

By far the most active deviants, and in Merton's words 'the true aliens', are the retreatists, who reject and retreat from the values, refuse to pursue wealth, and live unconventionally. He goes on to characterise these people more distinctly as 'pariahs, outcasts, vagabonds, tramps, chronic drunkards and drug addicts'. Rejection of the norms and values of society and a commitment to replace these with a new order form the response of the 'rebels'.

Criticisms of Merton

Merton's theory is important because it distinguishes between social structure (society's demands) and culture (demands of local subculture). It points out that a number of adaptive responses are possible and so provides a more comprehensive account of crime and deviance. Merton is simply saying that groups will favour certain modes of adaptation, depending upon their structural location within society. However, there are important criticisms of Merton's work that should be noted.

The first criticism is in Merton's wide use of the word 'deviant'. Would the ritualist, with a narrow and conforming lifestyle, be classed as deviant by the rest of society? Some of these forms of deviance carry severe social sanctions, others none at all. This arises from the functionalist concern with consensus and the fixation with the goals of success being financial. It comes back to the same old criticism. Functionalists are obsessed with the mainstream values of society, and use these as the yardstick against which all behaviour is assessed, so conflict must be deviance!

The intrinsic sexism in what Merton says is evident in his failure to see that the one social group which most clearly suffers an imbalance between cultural goals and the cultural means to attain them is that of women. Statistically, though, this is the least criminal group in society.

Another problem area for Merton's theory is that too many people are pushed into too few categories. Merton's famous list of retreatists quoted above shouts this out to the discerning social observer. The 'types' he mentions under the drop-out category are subcultures in their own right, from acid-heads to alcoholics.

Merton's theory has also been criticised for assuming that all people are encouraged by the socialisation process into valuing and pursuing the goal of financial success. Some studies suggest that people from the working class learn from an early age that they have only a very remote chance of rising to the top of the social scale. Hence, they can accept their low status without feeling that it is their own fault and that they have failed to make use of their opportunities.

Albert Cohen and subcultural theories of deviance

Various American sociologists have come up with theories which attempt to refine the broader type of explanation. Albert Cohen (1955) focused on the inabilities of working-class boys (girls are again ignored) to catch up with the 'American Dream', in the same vein as Merton. Cohen's new angle is that individuals do not respond to this frustrating position on an individual basis – they find mates in a similar predicament and, together, reject the dominant system of values, goals and norms.

This, claims Cohen, explains what Merton does not, that is, groups of youths acting out their deviance in uniform patterns, and types of deviance which bring no monetary gain and therefore cannot be classed as 'innovative'. Cohen goes on to elaborate on this subcultural theory, calling inability to achieve success 'status frustration', which leads to the creation of norms and values in direct opposition to those of mainstream society. He locates the cause of failure within the home and environment, a classic case of 'deprivation theory' (see chapter 5). This insists that the cultural values of the working class are in some way deficient. This 'deficiency' leads the boys to fail academically, and so they seek **status** elsewhere – and where else than among their mates!

In subcultural territory, anything goes, anything which in any way threatens those in secure, successful positions – teachers, police, politicians, sociologists and so on – is accepted. The 'toughest kid in the school' may get into trouble with teachers, but it is a hard-won title and his mates will think he is 'well hard'. Cohen's explanation is about taking success where you find it.

There are other, closely related yet slightly differing subcultural explanations. They tend to view deviance from a **structural** stance, attempting to show how patterns of behaviour are related to the wider social group. The constraints of society create the context in which subcultural values are constructed and acted out.

Cloward and Ohlin

Richard Cloward and Lloyd Ohlin (1961) use class subcultures, particularly criminal ones, to explain various types of deviance. They claim to have uncovered yet another aspect of deviance not dealt with by Merton: the existence of groups who engage in stealing to counterbalance their failure to succeed 'legitimately' – criminal subcultures – and those who gain their status by fighting – conflict subcultures. Another group is formed by working-class 'wimps' who cannot succeed. These people fail exams, and cannot steal or fight, so they become junkies, drunks and weirdos – these are retreatist subcultures.

Miller

Walter Miller (1962) has yet another angle, pointing out that working-class subculture is on the whole geared towards 'toughness, smartness and excitement'. This three-pronged concern with life in the fast lane entails being a good fighter and a fast-talking hustler who seeks thrills and pleasure. Miller goes on to point out the predominance of peer-group pressure among the working class. Nowhere else will you find such **conformity**, not to mainstream culture but to their own value systems. Status and security are to be found in the peer group, and any behaviour which helps you attain this status is therefore desirable.

Sociological work

An analysis of the sociological work being done reveals a composite picture. Merton starts the ball rolling with an analysis of the relationship of individuals to the value system. The subcultural thinkers pick the ball up and stagger with it. The point is that Cohen, Miller and others build upon and develop Merton's ideas, in varying directions. Taken as a whole, they do provide a comprehensive explanation for deviant behaviour, each attempting to address issues which others have ignored. Cohen takes Merton a step further by explaining group reactions rather than individual ones. Cloward and Ohlin look at the different reactions of these groups. Miller goes further with his view of working-class values and the importance of peer-group conformity.

Criticisms

Imagine you are born into the lower working class. You live in the inner city. Your culture is 'deficient' in that it leads you to 'fail' educationally. This means that you will not get a high-earning career, but you

are still exposed to the goals of success in financial terms. So you become a thief or a fighter according to your peer-group values. If you cannot thieve or fight you fall into a drop-out subculture. 'Status' is won by adhering to oppositional values, but to be street smart, thrilling and exciting is an overriding necessity. Is this the end of the story?

Sykes and Matza

Sykes and Matza (1962) point out that the entire subcultural argument is too sweeping and too deterministic. Individuals conform or otherwise in various ways. Not everybody tattoos swastikas on their forehead and ACAB on their fingers, and a lot of those who did have saved up their wages to have the marks of subculture removed. Sykes and Matza point out that subcultures are the proverbial 'phase he's going through', and this will be followed by other, possibly more conforming phases, shifts, transitions into the boring stability of adult life.

Miller's three-pronged value system, according to Sykes and Matza, consists of 'subterranean values', which attract all youths, middle- and working-class alike. The difference is that middle-class youth can afford (or rather their parents can afford) to indulge these needs for toughness, smartness and excitement legitimately. For example, whereas Daddy might buy you a Porsche so you can indulge your speed fantasies, less affluent youths will steal somebody else's.

Techniques of neutralisation

The most telling point that Sykes and Matza make is that of 'neutralisation' techniques. When apprehended, how many kids stick to their subcultural values rather than shutting their mouths, nodding meekly and paying the price, accompanying this with various excuses and apologies? Sykes and Matza provide a shrewd criticism of the tendency for sociologists, and particularly those in the structural school, to be too deterministic in the search for a comprehensive explanation. Real life is not so easily confined, and inconsistencies keep spilling over the edge of neat, self-contained explanations.

Questions

1 How can it be argued that deviance is functional for society?

2 What does Merton mean by 'cultural goals' and 'cultural means'? What is the importance of the relationship between the two?

3 Are Merton and the subcultural theorists in agreement?

4 If you are young and live in the inner city, are you doomed to deviate?

Marxism and crime

A non-romantic notion

As with other areas of what we now call sociology, Marx did not write anything that he or Engels might have described as 'a theory of crime and deviance'. What we know of their ideas in this area were formulated while developing what they believed was a scientific analysis of capitalist development and the emerging revolutionary role of the working class. Crime bore no romantic connotations to them, and in some writings they were scathing of criminals, referring to them as 'lumpenproletarians'. These are the peripheral and unproductive working class who find ways of avoiding selling their labour to the **bourgeoisie**, but still earn a living through burglary, theft, black-marketeering and robbery. They are parasitic on the working class, draining their revolutionary power.

It was not until the 1970s that, with the apparent deficiencies of functionalist and interactionist accounts of crime and deviance exposed, new theories emerged from within the Marxist tradition. A good example of this is Richard Quinney (1975).

Quinney and economic determinism

His approach is that of an economic determinist. It is the need to produce that brings people together in society, and it is out of the economy that laws, religious beliefs, family forms, and types of ownership emerge. His position (which has firm roots in Marxism) is that it is the economic arrangements that prevail – the **mode of production** in Marx's term – and from which everything else in society springs. The pattern and nature of crime must therefore originate from the mode of production. Since the breakdown of the **feudal** era in Britain, we have lived under the capitalist mode of production in which the **means of production** are owned by a few (the bourgeoisie) to whom everyone else (the **proletariat**) eventually has to sell their labour power. (This is explained in much greater detail in chapter 3.) The source of crime lies in the unequal distribution of wealth and power, and for this reason it is essentially a material problem, about the struggle for things.

A class State

For Marxists, the State in a capitalist society is not neutral. It does not play the same role as a referee in a football match, but is biased in favour of one side: those who already own all the wealth. The law as we know it, heavily biased towards property rights, emerged with the rise of capitalism and is a central means of enforcing the interests of the dominant capitalist class – those who are already 'winning'. There are any number of examples that Marxist historians have found to illustrate this point, for example the removal of common land and creation of poaching laws in the eighteenth century.

Crimes of control

Although the State under capitalism makes the laws of the land, it is not all-powerful, being subordinate to the capitalist class, and obliges even those who stand to benefit most from its workings, the employers, to abuse it in an attempt to maintain the existing system. What results are crimes of control. These can take many forms, such as police brutality on the streets and in police cells, crimes at governmental level like the Watergate scandal of the 1970s which resulted in Richard Nixon being forced to resign as President of the USA, or crimes of economic domination committed by big business, ranging from deliberate pollution to price-fixing in order to protect or increase profits. What ultimately links these crimes is the fact that capitalism makes a god of money and profit, and the crimes of the rich and powerful emanate from the greed on which the capitalist system feeds and depends.

Working-class crime

Within the working class, it is a different picture. The lumpenproletariat either consciously or unconsciously directs their crimes against the capitalist system, for which they incur the wrath and vigilance of the police, or, as a result of the way that life under capitalism has dehumanised and alienated – 'brutalised' – them, they commit crimes against their own class. Only people without any conception of class consciousness and solidarity would break into another house on the same council estate and raid someone else's gas meter. The 'honest' working class will direct their struggle against exploitation in the workplace through industrial sabotage, deliberately damaging machinery in order to slow down the pace of production. Nearly all crime among the working class is actually a means of survival, an attempt to exist in a society where survival is not assured by collective means. Crime is inevitable under capitalist conditions.

It is Marx's argument that as the capitalist system grows, the cycle of booms and slumps in production will get longer and longer. In slump periods there will be more and more unemployed, the reserve army of labour. Quinney adds that crime will increase, and there will be greater demands for more and more police. When the costs of policing become so great that they are no longer economic, then the State will drop its mask of neutrality and the bourgeoisie will resort to direct political rule through dictatorship. In these new conditions, all crime will become political as the workers realise the true nature of the way they are governed. They will unite against the common enemy – the bourgeoisie – and overthrow them. The result will be a socialist society, run by workers for workers. In this society, as there is no inequality, no system based on greed, no want, no **alienation**, no repression, the problem of crime will disappear along with the need for police and prisons.

Criticisms of Quinney

It is perhaps too easy to see the flaws in Quinney's argument. Does all law protect and advantage only the powerful? Would this explain laws on abortion or homosexuality, traffic laws and child abuse? Can there be an explicitly Marxist account of why mass murderers, such as Dennis Nielsen or the Wests, killed people and hid their bodies under the floorboards? It also seems contradictory to see the working class as one day passive victims of the capitalist system and the next as potentially revolutionary and destroyers of the same system. Quinney is unwilling to acknowledge that the working class has struggled to achieve rights under capitalism that were hard-fought: the right to strike, to form unions, to vote, and so on.

Crimes of the rich and powerful

A similar study to Quinney's, based on fieldwork undertaken in the 1960s, was carried out by William Chambliss (1978). His central argument is that everyone either is, or is potentially, criminal or deviant. The only question is: why do only some get caught? Being captured is not necessarily a question of misfortune or bad luck, it may well be because you are not paying enough backhanders to the local police force, or contributing enough to their charitable funds. The most successful criminals are the ones who can encourage the police to turn a blind eye to their activities. The police, the business community and organised crime work together. Each stand to gain from each other while publicly condemning crime, in order to mask their own corruption. The real criminal class in America is in reality the rich and powerful.

These arguments are reinforced by Frank Pearce (1976). Why is it, he asks, that we give priority to working-class crime when, on financial grounds, the cost of their crime to the community is negligible when compared to the estimated cost of corporate and white-collar crime? Why stop and harass someone in an old Cortina when the real criminals are in the boardroom? It is because of the way the law is enforced that the working class seem to be the main offenders, yet this is simply a reflection of the way resources are concentrated, and that white-collar and corporate crimes provoke less interest because they appear to be **victimless**. Yet for Pearce, they should be the real focus of law enforcement. It cannot be a reflection of the reality of the nature of crime in society that the powerful manage to escape the sanction of the law. They can be involved in insider dealing or price fixing or, through decisions made on the grounds of profit, fail to maintain safety standards in workplaces knowing that inspections are infrequent and fines are minimal. The crimes of the powerful, compared to the relatively powerless, go unpunished because it is not the purpose of the law, as it is enforced, to punish them.

Criticisms of Chambliss and Pearce

Marxists such as Quinney, Chambliss and Pearce opened up new areas of considerations for sociologists, though others have been wary of following in their path. Marx and Engels themselves left the problem of crime well alone, and subsequent Marxist and radical criminologists have been criticised for a **deterministic** view of crime. In other words, they have fallen into the trap of saying that certain conditions will always cause certain consequences. Exploited proletarians will turn to crime because they are alienated by capitalism. The police and the courts will side with the rich because that is the way the system is rigged. The State always favours the interests of the **ruling class**. Formulae such as these are evidence of what has been called 'vulgar' Marxism: simplifying complex social problems by selective reference to evidence that moves towards a picture of an evil, scheming bourgeoisie and a passive, innocent, and intrinsically good working class.

More recent work has tried to move beyond this situation, seeing working-class crime, for example, as more than primitive rebellion, and the State as more than a giant conspiracy in favour of bourgeois interests. The 'New Criminology' attempts to escape vulgar Marxism and portrays criminals as conscious, not passive, actors, and working-class crime as problematic.

Questions

1 What is meant by 'economic determinism' in relation to crime and deviance?
2 What is the role of the State in dealing with crime?
3 What are 'crimes of control'?
4 What reasons do Marxists give for the working class committing crimes?

Interactionism

Interactionists have been responsible for a change in all areas of sociological explanation, and deviance has claimed their attention in particular. They approach the topic from a completely different angle to structural theorists. Most importantly, they do not take the deviant act itself for granted. The interactions between the deviant and society are the focal point. How does society respond to the deviant and vice versa? In their view, deviants are made, not born.

Becker and *Outsiders*

An American sociologist, Howard Becker (1963), is perhaps the best-known of the interactionists. Becker was involved in a 'subculture' – that of a night-club musician. These people live their lives in a way that most people find incomprehensible, sleeping by day and working by night. Their value system develops through their lifestyle, and as such has its own set of meanings and values. This is just one group within a larger one, and this alternative society exists everywhere. The interactionists point out that these lifestyles are a central part of society, and norms are constructed and reconstructed all the time. Everything should be analysed in the sense that it arises out of interactions between individuals, groups and society.

Becker's first point is that there is no such thing as a deviant act. But surely murder and robbery are deviant? The interactionists would say 'only if it is not sanctioned.' Even killing is acceptable if it is sanctioned. 'Terrorists' murder people, but they get 'killed' by the army. If a doctor gives you a shot of morphine, then you are a patient, but if it is administered by someone not medically qualified then you are a junkie. Until 1991, if a man forced

intercourse on his wife, it was sex. If they were not married, it was rape. The law changed and it became rape in both situations. If a man wears a dress in public (or in private) he is a transvestite. If the Archbishop of Canterbury wears one it is a holy vestment. If you appeared in court wearing a long curly horsehair wig, you could possibly be fined for contempt by someone who is wearing exactly the same thing. Now make up your own examples!

Deviance is relative

Becker shows that it is not the act itself which is deviant but it is the response of society that defines it as deviant. It is not only the response of society in general, but the responses of individuals or groups who have power in society. The proof is to be found in a simple analysis of cultures and historical periods. What is deviant in one culture is acceptable (and sometimes even required) in another. The changing attitude towards homosexuality in Britain in the 1960s led to a change in the law. Is homosexuality, which is no longer a crime between (socially defined) adults in private, still considered deviant in Britain in the 2000s? Relating back to our studies of the family (see chapter 5), in Western societies **monogamous** marriage is the only legal form but this is not true in all cultures and religions. It is clear from these examples that deviance is in the eye of the beholder, and the collective meanings which arise out of certain situations lead them to be defined as deviant or otherwise. Which people in society have the power to set up those definitions?

The power to define

Becker is perhaps the best-known proponent of **labelling** theory. The crucial point here is that only those in society who have power can make a label stick. If you steal your sister's pocket money, or if she wears your jacket without permission, you may call each other thief. Will society recognise the label? Will it affect your future career? Will your friends drop you? Unlikely. If you are labelled deviant by those in authority, if you are arrested, charged and convicted of theft, then the police and courts have the power to ensure that this label will stick.

Labelling theory and the self-fulfilling prophecy

Labelling theory works on the basis of the **self-fulfilling prophecy**. If enough people put the label on an individual, eventually they begin to recognise themselves in terms of the label. If people call you a hooligan, you may as well become one. The labelled individual will soon realise that he or she is being watched – 'Look out for that one, he's a right thief.' All behaviour displayed by that individual is interpreted in terms of the label, and any minor transgression is leapt upon with glee. Others may be indulging in similar or worse behaviour, but this goes unnoticed and/or unpunished, because they have not got the label which signals the 'type' of person they are. The prophecy initially made in the light of an isolated incident is fulfilled, proven correct and, the interactionists insist, it is fulfilled because it is made in the first place. To escape fulfilment, to shake off the label, is extremely difficult. In order to do so the labelled individual would need to behave like a saint. This process is also known as **deviancy amplification**.

According to the microsociological approach, concentrating on small-scale interactions between people in society, the individual is more likely to adopt an 'if you can't beat them join them' response. In other words, they start living up to the label, have some fun, and enjoy being a deviant. The media, powerful label makers indeed, used to revile the activities of football fans as 'animal behaviour'. The chant was soon to arise from the terraces to celebrate this new-found bestial status: 'We hate the humans.' The position of the 'animal hooligan', then, is far from one of 'mindless behaviour', but is actually a highly organised, structured existence. The hierarchy on the terraces is well ordered, and fans must progress through a structural pattern, a 'career' of football violence.

The deviant 'career'

Again, Howard Becker has been foremost in defining this idea of 'career', relating to the self-concept of the individuals involved. He considers the problem of becoming a marijuana smoker, an activity that was apparently an important part of the night-club musician's life. The initiate has to learn to smoke the stuff, then learn to perceive the effects, and then go on to enjoy the effects. Then the apprenticeship is completed by learning to hide your habit from the 'straight' world. Being caught, perhaps arrested and so on, could serve to confirm your status, both in your own eyes and in those of society. All other statuses, labels which you own, can be overshadowed by this.

This idea of careers is very important to interactionism, and the progress of an individual through various stages of deviance is well documented. It does not only apply to deviance. Alcohol is a socially accepted form of drug-taking yet acquiring a taste for alcohol is not a one-drink process.

The rewards of following a deviant career clearly do not come from society, but from the feelings of belonging to a group, united in opposition to others, and this helps to form a self-concept which can be lived with. There is an overlap here with ideas on subcultures, where peer-group values can become as, or more, important than mainstream ones. The interactionist approach, however, stresses that it is society's response to deviant acts, and the response of the individual to that social response which leads to a career of deviance. What matters is how individuals come to take on the labels and definitions applied to their behaviour by those they interact with.

The negotiation of deviance

What Becker does is to point out the fragility of such definitions, and reinforce one of the main assumptions of interactionism – that social reality only exists in so far as it is constructed in interactions between individuals. There are no 'true' deviant acts, laid down in tablets of stone, irrefutable and permanent. Rather, there is a process whereby some things come to be defined as deviant, according to the actors involved, the historical period, and the culture. These definitions are open to negotiation; they can and will be changed according to circumstance. They are not fixed immutably in the social structure. This begs a question: 'What about people who indulge in deviant activities, but are not discovered?'

Primary and secondary deviance

Edwin Lemert (1967) addresses this issue by distinguishing between 'primary' and 'secondary' deviance. Primary deviance is when the act is not officially labelled as such, whereas secondary deviance is all out in the open. Did you ever steal from your mum's purse or your dad's wallet? Were you caught? If you were, it is unlikely that they called in the police. Many children go through a phase of shoplifting (a euphemism for stealing) but are not labelled as thieves – unless they are caught and publicly punished. Often the local media have the power here. If it is not reported then it is unlikely to produce a deviant label. Older people have been caught in the same act, and despite their pleas of lack of memory, or too much valium, are prosecuted, as all the shop signs warn. However pitiable their plight, or true their pleas, the stigma attached still makes people wonder. Secondary deviation is the more serious then, in the myopic eyes of society.

Aaron Cicourel

Deviance is to be found in social reactions to an act, not in the act itself. Cicourel (1976), from an **ethnomethodological** perspective, investigates this in relation to the police and their definitions of certain people as delinquents. He found that the police operated using a stereotype of the deviant as a young working-class male who exhibited certain forms of behaviour. If enough traits were exhibited by the youths, then they and their actions were said to be deviant and legal action was taken. These traits concern class when appearance, type of language used, attitude, father's occupation and living in the inner city were taken as indicators. If a youth was arrested then he was more likely to be charged if he had a criminal record. The whole process was built around complex interactions and meanings systems operated by the police, the courts, the probation service and so on. Middle-class youths were much less likely to be classed as deviant, and this applied even when the acts committed were identical.

This has been pointed out by many sociologists in Britain and elsewhere. In Britain, the activities of students in Rag Week, or rugby players after a match, were more likely to be attributed to high spirits, whereas working-class youths indulging in the same acts were labelled as deviants or even criminals. This shows that there are many factors which affect interactions, and that this complexity cannot be ignored when considering what society describes and reclassifies as criminal or deviant.

The relative simplicity of structuralist ideas, in particular functionalist views, has to be mentioned here. In all areas of sociology, the straightforward explanations are initially attractive but, on closer analysis, prove to be much less comprehensive. However, the interactionist perspective is not without its own faults and criticisms.

Criticisms of the interactionists

Some writers have criticised labelling theory for tending to romanticise crime by concentrating on a narrow range of colourful and exotic deviants, producing what Liazos calls 'nuts, sluts and perverts research'. Alvin Gouldner (1970) is especially critical of what he sees as an excessive concern for the 'underdog' in many interactionist studies, and questions whether the deviant is realistically portrayed as a passive nonentity who is rarely responsible for his actions. A further limitation is that labelling theory does not allow for the range of possible responses an individual or group might make to being labelled. Critics suggest that it is not inevitable that a deviant reaction will result once a label is applied.

Another criticism that is frequently aimed at labelling theory and the self-fulfilling prophecy, is: what causes the individual to deviate in the first instance? In other words, how and why do they attract the attention of the labellers? Interactionism is very weak here, and explanations have to be taken from social structure, environment and subculture. Interactionists initially disregarded such causes, preferring to concentrate on the resulting interactions between individuals and those in authority. The theoretical assumptions upon which microsociological approaches rest are most apparent here, and this leads us to the second criticism: interactionist explanations are 'context bound'.

Structuralist critics point out that no interaction takes place in a social vacuum, and that such factors as social class, the economic substructure and the wider social system are the most important factors in determining the outcome of small-scale interactions. This type of criticism is associated with other weaknesses in microanalysis. Is it really little more than descriptive social comment, at best a form of social psychology? What is the point of studying small and marginal groups such as night-club musicians, or hippies and homosexuals?

At the end of a long, expensive research project, the **micro-sociologist** is left with a mere description, albeit rich in quality, reporting meanings and experiences of individuals, from which they cannot generalise or establish universally applicable rules. Here we have the standard positivist criticism of phenomenological schools of thought: what is the point?

Response to criticisms

There are two answers to this type of criticism. The first is that interactionists play down the relevance or importance of **quantitative**, scientific data. They are principally interested in internal meanings and these cannot be explained by tables of figures, graphs and equations. Second, in a response more typical of contemporary sociology, both interactionists and structuralists in fact recognise the importance of each other's analyses and explanations. As we have seen, Cicourel and others recognise the importance of social class, subculture and culture in their explanations. In this way statistical information, 'social facts' gathered from the larger-scale methods of research, can be used alongside the smaller-scale data, providing a richer and more detailed explanation of the wider picture. These are the seeds sown by the Weberian approach which stresses understanding, *verstehen* (see chapter 1), bearing fruit.

Free will

There is further major criticism, related to the interactionists' understanding of social action and social agency. It ignores the autonomy of the individual, their ability to control their own life, and the struggle of **free will** over determinism. Interactionists see the individual as passive not active. Alvin Gouldner complains that Becker's deviants seem to be totally passive accepters of any label which society slaps on them. Gouldner's famous phrase is 'man on his back'. He means that we do not just accept labels or live out the prophecies which others make. We can and do fight back, we reject the stigma and forge our own path. In short, our free will is stronger than this school of thought would have us believe.

This criticism finds support among those who accuse interactionists of being soft, liberal and looking for excuses for the deviant. If you break formal or informal laws, and get caught, you can always blame it on society, parents, police, environment, home life or education. How many people have never said at some time in their lives 'I didn't ask to be born, did I?'

Gouldner's criticisms undoubtedly carry some weight, and have provoked a debate which still continues. Becker points out that interactions are much more complex than the simplistic views stated in the various criticisms. He agrees that not all those who come to be labelled as deviant continue to develop deviant careers. However, he stresses that there are social pressures which make it difficult for those labelled as deviant to avoid their lifestyle, and in cases where they feel their lifestyle is better than that required by society, they willingly adopt deviant attitudes.

It is clear from the above that there are still many arguments and debatable points. As with all advances in sociology, interactionism is full of holes. However, most sociologists would agree that it has uncovered another aspect of deviant and criminal behaviour and the response of society to that behaviour. Sociologists take on board these new ideas, and they have to be considered as additions to existing ideas rather than replacements.

Questions

1 What does it mean to say that deviance is historically and culturally relative?
2 What is meant by a 'self-fulfilling prophecy'? How might such a prophecy be fulfilled, and how might it be refuted?
3 How is deviance negotiated?
4 What are the most important criticisms of interactionist theories of deviance?

Control theory

Hirschi

Alongside subcultural, labelling and many other theories, a theory of deviance exists under the heading of control theory, first put forward by Travis Hirschi (1969). In this work, based on questionnaires given to a random stratified sample of 5,545 children in schools around San Francisco, California, Hirschi critically examines the central sociological concept of socialisation. There is nothing deterministic or automatic about this process of learning how to conform to the dominant norms and values in society. Left to themselves, humans would do anything they pleased. Hirschi, and others such as Stephen Box (1971), are interested in understanding how and why individuals opt into social control, knowing all the time that there are alternatives.

Hirschi identifies four factors: attachment, involvement, commitment and beliefs. By attachment he means the extent to which individuals are sensitive to the thoughts, feelings and expectations of others. The more attached to others you are, the less freedom you have to deviate. Involvement concerns the amount of time individuals have to get up to no good; commitment refers to how much of an investment people have made in things such as education, a career or being socially respected. Delinquent behaviour would jeopardise this investment. Finally, by belief he is referring to the intensity with which people believe they should obey the law, or some laws in particular. So the less socially attached, involved, committed and believing you are, the greater is your freedom to deviate.

The question is not why do most people obey the law but why doesn't everyone break it? An understanding of why people make a social bond with the society in which they live needs to be carefully examined. As Box writes: 'Occurrence of special circumstances is not necessary to bring about the freedom to deviate; freedom is there all the time as a human possibility. It is lost when humans surrender themselves to others' reputations and moralities. It is regained, perhaps only momentarily, when they cease to care about others or perhaps their own social selves, or find segments of conventional morality distasteful.'

Box himself cites five factors that make people likely to deviate: the ease with which they will be able to conceal their deviance; the amount of skill needed to carry out the deviant act; having the necessary resources; the approval of peers; and a belief that status will be gained from carrying out the act. With juvenile delinquency in mind, he adds the question, 'Why would someone who is willing and able want to?'

Criticisms of control theory

The answer is strongly connected to an individual's beliefs that an initial deviant act is the most rewarding line of activity they can pursue, and that they remain unpersuaded by the rest of society's arguments that the risks are not worth taking.

Box himself is aware of the shortcomings of control theory, stating that it relies too much on what he calls 'situational subjective explanations' where there is too much emphasis on the individual and not enough on the role of the social structure. An attachment to school, for example, is important, but the class character of that school will itself play a part in determining the level of attachment. It is for this reason that the methodological approach taken by writers such as Paul Willis (see chapter 6) is to be commended.

Furthermore, while it may succeed in providing the framework in which primary deviance may be explained, it says little or nothing about secondary deviance, when individuals have become habitual criminals and eventually recidivists. Finally, it has nothing to say about the crimes of the powerful, having mostly juvenile delinquents in mind.

Questions

1 What factors does Hirschi identify as important in preventing deviance?
2 What is meant by the phrase 'situational subjective explanations'?
3 What criticisms can be made of control theory?

More recent theories of crime

In recent years, one thing has become clear to criminologists – the theories developed since the Second World War offer at best only partial explanations of the causes of crime. The main evidence for this is the continued increase in the crime rate in industrialised countries. Although various theories have offered suggestions for reform based on their suggested causes, and in some cases these reforms have found their way into social policy, the crime rate as recorded in official statistics rose sharply between 1977 and 1992 and has remained relatively high since then (see *Figure 8.1*). This leaves criminology in a crisis, and has prompted a new set of paradigms to attempt to understand why people commit crimes.

Welfare crime

There has been a psychological response to the failure of the various strands of sociological theory to answer the question 'What causes crime?' The 'social democratic' ideas of the 1950s blamed social conditions and poverty and advocated social reform. This failed and crime rates went up. Marxists offered their analyses, but nobody listened. Crime rates went up. The labelling theorists focused on negotiations between those in control and those who became labelled. Crime rates still went up. All this occurred against the growth of the **Welfare State**, the elimination of **absolute poverty** and a return to full employment. This trend is therefore known as 'welfare crime'. A rapid return to Lombrosian views surfaced: the 'neo-classicist' approach which claimed that people 'prone to crime' at birth and those who were inadequately 'conditioned' were the backbone of

Figure 8.1   Notifiable offences recorded by the police

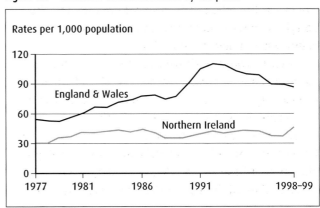

Rates per 1,000 population

the criminal classes. The introduction of ideas of the 'hyperactive' child in the 1970s occasioned some people to advocate sterilisation for some parents, to wipe out the criminal strain in human nature. Sociologists and criminologists had to provide explanations, and four paradigms emerged in the 1980s and 1990s as a response. They claim to solve the crisis of **aetiology**, but do they end up as an apology for 40 years of mistaken or partial theorising?

Four new paradigms of criminology

1 Left idealism

This **paradigm** emerged from labelling theory and Marxist analysis, and is represented in the work of Scraton (1985) and Carr-Hill and Stern (1979) with some of the main ideas drawn from Foucault (1980). Crime, according to this theory, is caused by inequality and greed. The increasing crime rates are just a reflection of police bias against the working classes and black people. The increase is merely a side effect of more police. This increased police presence causes **moral panics**, police stereotypes reinforce this and the police force cries out for more funding and resources to deal with the crime 'problem' they have helped to create. The amount of crime is exaggerated in order to draw attention away from poverty and exploitation. The role of the police is a political one, relating to control and keeping order, putting down illegal pickets and protecting the State. The public are there to be policed, and the only people who can escape police control are the rich and powerful. The crisis is not one of cause – the cause of crime is the system, which is based on greed. The crisis, according to the Left idealists, is that the police are getting out of control. They advocate policies of decriminalisation and closing down prisons.

MICHEL FOUCAULT (1926–84)

French historian specialising in the history of human sciences, penal and medical institutions and sexuality. Foucault is regarded as a structuralist.

2 New administrative criminology

This is not strictly a sociological theory, but one based upon statistical analysis of crime figures carried out by the British Home Office by writers such as Clarke and Mayhew (1980), Clarke and Cornish (1983), and Mayhew and Hough (1983). Points of similarity are to be found with Left idealism in that they both agree

that there is no crisis of aetiology. They are both critical of the social democratic theories of the 1950s and 1960s and both paradigms disagree with the response of the New Right, who call for more police and more prisons.

However, when it comes to the cause of crime, they begin to differ. The new administrative criminology (NAC) argues that most crime is opportunist, that is unplanned and carried out on the spur of the moment: an open window, a handbag on the front seat of a car, the empty shop. The best way to deal with this is to improve security measures. Most crime is 'petty', as opposed to 'serious' crime, and the increasing crime rate is caused by people being more willing to report petty crime. The fear of crime is much greater than the reality of crime, and really, statistically speaking, people have little need to worry, if they take the correct security measures.

The most likely victim of crime bears an amazing resemblance to the 'typical criminal' – young, male, single and a heavy drinker. The police play a small role in the detection of crime and arresting criminals, because 90 per cent is reported and solved by the public. The fictional images offered by TV serials, with the police solving crimes by detection, clues and violence mislead us. A realistic police programme would show us images of police dealing with lost property, giving advice, directions and telling people the time but that does not make for exciting viewing. The public play a vital role, and should co-operate with the police in 'Neighbourhood Watch' and other schemes. There is no aetiological crisis as crime is only being reported more. There is no real increase, it just seems as if there is.

The final two paradigms disagree on this, as they both take a 'realist' approach, which accepts that there is a real increase in crime, and also accept that there is no real, overriding explanation as to why this is.

3 New Right realism

James Wilson is the main theorist here, and the title of one of his books *Crime and Human Nature* (1985) gives a heavy clue to the basic assumptions. Crime is caused by a number of factors. Some people are born with a 'proneness to crime', it is a part of their innate physical constitution. There are echoes of Lombroso, Sheldon and Glueck and Hans Eysenck here, and Eysenck's ideas provide another possible causal factor: the importance of social conditioning in the family. The child is socialised inadequately, fails to develop a conscience, and does not know right from wrong. This is compounded by the weak punishments and attractive rewards of crime – crime really can pay. The crime rate has increased, and will continue to rise. This is partly due to the increase in the proportions of young people in the population, who are said to be more impulsive and prone to criminal behaviour. The changes in culture and socialisation in agencies like the family, media, schools and churches mean that people are not being taught respect.

Wilson, being a realist, offers no sure-fire solutions, but points out the difficulties: you cannot change people's physical constitution, and you cannot change the demographic structure. It is both difficult and slow to address the problems of family conditioning, and the culture of American society, and possibly British society, is based upon a grasping, individualistic culture in which everyone is encouraged to grab what they can for themselves. This can lead people to use illegal methods of attaining success.

The New Right advocates a 'trial and error' approach to tackle the crime problem: try various things and see what works. The police are effective if they maintain a high profile, keep order by moving people along and disperse groups. Wilson is adamant that this is the best job that the police do, and the public feel more secure if the police are there to prevent disorder. It is the thought of chaos, 'no-go areas' that frightens the public, so increasing patrols

might eventually slow down the crime rate. However, the police are restricted by rules and regulations, and need to be given a free hand. Rather than decriminalise, the New Right approach is to clamp down, give the police powers to control legal deviance, arresting people for being 'suspicious looking', or behaving oddly. Persistent, 'recidivist' criminals should be given massive sentences regardless of their crime, in order to protect the public. The main critic of all these paradigms is Jock Young (1994).

4 Left realist critique

Although there are many points of disagreement between Left and Right realism, there are a number of comparisons. They agree that there is a real problem and people are right to be worried. Both hold that the police–public relationship is vital. Both paradigms agree that little is known, very little can be done and that there is a need for more criminological research. Both paradigms agree that earlier criminological views were partial, and only focused on specific aspects of the problem.

Relative deprivation

New Left realism argues that the main cause of crime is **relative deprivation**: some people in the social structure feel deprived in relation to the majority of people. The most marginalised groups are the lower

Table 8.2 New criminological paradigms

Paradigm	Cause of crime	Explanation of crime rate	Effect of crime	Role of police	Role of public	Crisis of aetiology
Left idealism	Inequality, poverty, greed	Reflects police bias, side effect of more police	Police stereotypes, moral panics, more police funding	Political order and control, e.g. strike-breaking	To be policed, unless they are members of powerful groups	Does not exist, no rise in crime just moral panics, only crisis is that police are out of control
New administrative criminology	Opportunist, therefore more security needed	Serious crime is a small part of all crime, petty crime reported more, more opportunities	Typical victim: young/male single/drunk. Fear of crime is greater than reality	90% crime is reported by public. Other demands more time-consuming	Co-operation with police, more Neighbourhood Watch schemes, more home security	Does not exist, crime is not caused, crime rate is result of increased public reporting
New Right realism	Conditioning, physiology, rewards and punishments of crime	More opportunity, more young impulsive people, no reason not to commit crime	Difficult to change conditioning, part of culture, policing not effective	Police presence encourages informal control to keep 'order'	Good parents, Neighbourhood Watch schemes, help police	Causes are physical constitution, conditioning and the rewards and punishments of crime
New Left realism	Relative deprivation of working-class and black people	Increase in criminal behaviour plus a lower tolerance of deviance	Some areas and some groups are at high risk. Victims those most vulnerable	Should be seen to act justly and fairly	Informal control but not initiated by police, sense of community	Solved – new causation theory of 'relative deprivation'

working class and certain ethnic minorities. These people feel deprived, and therefore the push towards crime among them is greater. This is much more likely to happen when changes in the economy, such as unemployment and de-industrialisation, exacerbate the disadvantages experienced by deprived and marginalised groups.

Young stresses that these things only cause crime in certain conditions, in other words, determinism is mistaken. Crime is not inevitable under these conditions, just more likely to occur. The increase in the crime rate is partly explained by the bias amongst those in authority when labelling criminals, but labelling theory does not explain everything. Some behaviour is classed as criminal by all sections of society, so criminal deviance is not merely a product of negotiations. Another factor is the increased sensitivity to crime, which leads to more crime being reported. However, this only gives half of the story, as crime really is increasing, and it is a combination of more crime, less tolerance of crime and more labelling which leads to higher crime rates.

The square of crime

The main thrust of Left realism, therefore, has been to emphasise that crime and deviance are the products of a complex process of interaction involving many elements in society. This means rejecting mono-causal explanations as too simplistic. Left realists argue that crime and deviance are never the product of a single cause, such as unemployment, deprivation, drug abuse, police response, status frustration, labelling, etc. Rather, in order to understand these socially constructed phenomena it is necessary to adopt a more comprehensive approach.

Young and Matthews (1992) have developed this idea by using the term 'the square of crime' to depict the processes through which 'crime' is constructed (see *Figure 8.2*). They argue that crime is the product of relationships between four key elements – victims, offenders, the State and the public. In order to understand crime, each element has to be studied both in itself and through its complex relationships with each of the other elements.

Young and Matthews suggest that each particular form of crime will have a different set of determinants within the square. Thus white-collar crime and street crime involve different types of victim–offender relation and are regulated by a different combination of formal and informal controls. It is this mixture of elements, and the ways in which they combine, which give different crimes their own particular characteristics. Understanding the dynamics of the construction of particular types of crime and their constituent elements is crucial to the development of more effective crime control policies, Young and Matthews argue.

Left realists criticise the view that the fear of crime is greater than the reality, as there is an undoubted, real risk of crime, particularly for vulnerable groups: the elderly, women and children on inner- and outer-city estates. The police play an important role, but if they are seen to be acting unfairly, using brutality, false arrest and so on, then this will lead to more disorder. Social order depends upon a sense of justice and fairness, in the courts, and by the police. This point was amply demonstrated by the events in Los Angeles in 1992, when four white policemen were acquitted of assaulting a black man, after the world had seen them committing it on video. The acquittal led to two nights of riots.

When James Wilson advocates more police and longer sentences, he is encouraging this sort of injustice, which could trigger off more social problems. It is the groups who are marginalised that the police need to co-operate with, and it is just these people who become alienated by blatant injustice. The informal communal controls, which have broken down, are much more effective than 'artificial' systems, like Neighbourhood Watch, which have been imposed by the police.

Reconstructing informal community control means reconstructing the communities, and the Left realist solution is a political one. The crisis of aetiology has been solved, and relative deprivation is the cause of crime. Getting rid of this deprivation means changing

Figure 8.2   The square of crime

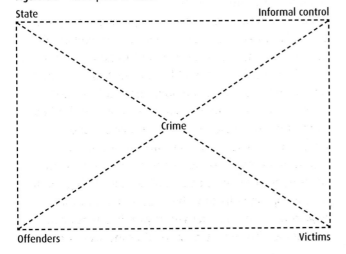

society, so getting rid of crime means a new social and political ethos, based upon socialist ideas. The industrial countries with the highest crime rates are those countries with no real socialist parties.

Criticisms of Left realism

Critics point out that Left realists have failed to gather their own data on the motives of offenders. Accordingly, they are unable to explain the causes of street crime in terms of the subjective states of the offenders. They can only speculate about the motives for such crimes. Another limitation is that Left realism fails to explain why some people who experience relative deprivation turn to crime, while others do not. It has also been suggested that the theory serves better as a theory of property crime than of violent crime. It is easy to understand why the sufferers from relative deprivation might turn to theft or burglary to solve their material problems; it is less easy to see what they might gain from violence. Moreover, corporate and organised crime cannot be readily understood within the framework of Left realist theory. Finally, Left realists have concentrated on conventionally defined crime, ignoring the issues raised by labelling theory and Marxism about how certain types of activity come to be defined as 'crime'. They have therefore been accused of overlooking some of the supposed advances in criminological theory of recent times.

Questions

1 How does Left idealism differ from Left realism?
2 What are the political and ideological assumptions underlying each perspective?

Post-modernist perspective

Post-modernists reject the theories of crime we have just examined on the grounds that they are **metanarratives** or 'totalising discourses'. In other words, they are large-scale theoretical interpretations that claim to have universal application and offer a complete account of the causes of crime. Post-modernists argue that such overarching, unifying grand narratives and claims to truth are no longer credible. Rather, in post-modern society there are multiple claims to truth – a 'plurality of discourses' – competing with each other but having no absolute basis for claiming privileged access to truth.

Carol Smart (1995) argues that the post-modernist critique applies particularly well to criminology because both traditional and realist criminological thinking are especially wedded to what she terms 'the positivist paradigm' of modernism. That is, they embrace a belief in establishing verifiable knowledge of truth about crime and its causes and in constructing explanations that will provide a basis for solutions and/or strategies of intervention.

Because crime takes diverse forms and occurs in widely varying social circumstances, Smart suggests that it is inappropriate for criminologists to assume that any single grand theory can explain such disparate and wide-ranging phenomena. Post-modernists advocate studying particular categories of crime (such as theft, murder, rape, etc.) and exploring different types of discourse. Smart argues that because criminology is focused on the study of crime as a single problem, it categorises a vast range of activities and treats them as if they were all subject to the same causal factors. The thing that criminology cannot do is to deconstruct crime. It cannot locate rape or child abuse in the domain of sexuality, for example, or theft in the domain of economic activity or drug use in the domain of health. To do so, Smart claims, would involve abandoning the idea of a unified problem that requires a unified response – at least at the theoretical level.

Post-modernists also reject the determinism that they see as inherent in traditional theories of crime. These theories make it seem that certain people are propelled into acting illegally by factors that are wholly or largely beyond their control. By contrast, post-modernists tend to see crime as something that results from the individuals exercising choice and active free will in creating an identity and lifestyle. Individuals may choose an identity as a bank robber or a heroin addict, for example. From this perspective, crime is simply a product of 'the general condition of freedom itself'. Each criminal act is, in effect, to be regarded as a unique event.

Post-modernists are possibly right in pointing out that it is unlikely that one theory could explain all crime. The claim that there is no fundamental essence that distinguishes criminal behaviour from all other behaviour also seems valuable, though it is hardly original as essentially the same point lies at the heart of the interactionist perspective on crime and deviance. Attacking the determinism in many traditional theories of deviance has merit, though post-modernists have been criticised for going too far in the opposite direction by making it seem that engaging in criminal activity is purely a matter of individual choice and lifestyle. If crime were entirely a 'process of free self-creation' it would be impossible to explain, for example, why certain groups are likely to resort to certain types of crime rather than others.

Suicide

Suicide is a form of deviance. It is so because most people do not do it and because of religious and cultural taboos. The study of suicide also contains in a nutshell the essence of sociological theories and methods.

Suicide is dramatic. It is individualistic and personal. Often it is tragic not only for the person who has committed suicide but for those who are left behind. It might seem that sociology would have nothing to say on this sad subject; surely individual pathology, biology or psychology is more relevant here.

Durkheim's analysis

In attempting to get his positivist version of sociology accepted as the way to investigate society, Durkheim (1897) produced a major comparative analysis of the suicide rates among European countries (see *Table 8.3*). The statistical base of the comparison gives the study its positivist, scientific aspect. It has been influential, if only for its large-scale and detailed analysis of what makes people kill themselves. According to Durkheim, personal reasons are irrelevant. Psychological explanations lack scientific validity. A macroanalysis, comparing the only real, social facts about suicide – the national suicide rates between various countries – is needed in order to get at the 'real' reasons for suicide: social reasons. You do not kill yourself; society kills you. This type of explanation works well with positivist and functionalist theory. Functionalists look at external social realities, which are above and beyond individual actions. Positivism relies on measurable, quantifiable details in order to maintain objectivity. In the suicide rates, Durkheim finds both external realities which can be measured and compared between countries, and general laws that can be predicted. The general law on suicide is, he says, that: 'Each society is predisposed to contribute a certain number of voluntary deaths.' In every society, some people 'volunteer' for death. The only thing that varies is the rate from country to country.

Firstly he gathered together secondary data on the number of suicides in various countries. He then examined them in terms of patterns or similarities that may be observed. Next he went on to put forward theories on the social causes of this patterned behaviour. There must be social causes, he argued, because the suicide rates were similar in terms of different countries, different religions and different marital statuses. Individual pathology, psychology or biology did not explain this pattern; sociology did. Suicide was not an act of individual will, it had a social cause. The cause of suicide lay outside the individual. Society causes suicide.

Types of suicide

Durkheim argued that social order is possible because society controls or at least severely limits people's behaviour by integration: the process by which we share the values and expectations of others in our society. We are also regulated: society establishes a legitimate set of goals for us and provides some means to achieve these goals. He argued that suicide was the result of too much or too little social regulation. Further, he argued that the form of suicide was determined by an imbalance between these two aspects of social regulation. He cites four different forms of suicide: egoistic, altruistic, anomic and fatalistic. Egoistic suicide occurs when a society is characterised by a lack of integration. Durkheim observed that Catholic societies have a lower rate of suicide than Protestant societies. This is due, he argued, to the individual being integrated into religion and the church which is in turn integrated into the State and civil society. In Catholic societies individuals are encouraged to take their problems to the church and the priest plays a major (some would say intrusive) part in social life. Problems are more likely

Table 8.3 Rate of suicides per million inhabitants in the different European countries

| | Period | | | Numerical position in the | | |
	1866–70	1871–75	1874–78	1st period	2nd period	3rd period
Italy	30	35	38	1	1	1
Belgium	66	69	78	2	3	4
England	67	66	69	3	2	2
Norway	76	73	71	4	4	3
Austria	78	94	130	5	7	7
Sweden	85	81	91	6	5	5
Bavaria	90	91	100	7	6	6
France	135	150	160	8	9	9
Prussia	142	134	152	9	8	8
Denmark	277	258	255	10	10	10
Saxony	293	267	334	11	11	11

Source: Emile Durkheim, *Suicide*, 1897

to be resolved and sins can be forgiven in the confessional. Once forgiven the sinner is reintegrated into the body of the church and by extension, therefore, the wider society. Italy is a strongly Catholic society and has a low suicide rate; Saxony in Germany is strongly Protestant and has a high suicide rate.

Durkheim also observed that married people and especially couples with children were much less likely to commit suicide than single, divorced or widowed people. The family integrates its members and the family is integrated into the wider society. (For a contrary view to this see chapter 5.) Egoistic suicide occurs when an individual lacks or loses group support. They are not part of society; they do not fit in; they are not integrated.

Egoistic suicide

Durkheim considered that egoistic suicide would increase as societies were transformed from traditional (pre-industrial) to modern societies. This is because in traditional societies people are bound together by shared beliefs and values and by ascribed status. This he called mechanical solidarity. In industrial societies the basis of social integration is very different and is based on people needing each other indirectly. The increased division of labour increases differences, creates mutual interdependence and causes organic solidarity which is less strong a force than mechanical solidarity. People are less integrated in modern society, and so egoistic suicide increases.

Altruistic suicide

Altruistic suicide may be regarded as the opposite of egoistic suicide. It occurs when an individual is over-integrated into society. The individual places a greater value on society, the social group or 'the cause' than they do on themselves. They are willing to give up their life for the greater good or glory. Durkheim thought that this form of suicide was greater in traditional societies than in modern societies which place a greater value on the importance of the individual. Some examples of this form of suicide include: soldiers, particularly the élite corps who are trained to place a very high value on the corps, the regiment, the monarch, country or president. It is not just élite soldiers though. In the Battle of the Somme in 1916 60,000 soldiers died in one day, 1.5 million in five months, many of them dying in an appallingly gruesome manner.

In Hindu culture it still occurs that on the death of her husband a woman will throw herself onto his funeral pyre, thus committing 'suttee'. She is nothing without him. The deaths of some 'terrorists' are altruistic, as is the practice of hara-kiri and kamikaze missions. Altruistic suicide is not confined to other cultures nor is it a thing of the past.

Anomic suicide

Anomic suicide is more typical of modern industrial society, argued Durkheim. We can think of anomie as a state in which our old norms and values have become irrelevant in a particular situation or context. This is often due to sudden social change which may result in downward or upward mobility. We can envisage the 'loss', in every sense of the word, for those, once rich, thrown upon hard times. Those who suffer this experience find that their social world and their friends often change. What they experience is being transported into another world full of alien people with alien values and behaviour. What is worse is that there is only one way back home and they cannot afford it.

An example of this form of suicide was provided in the 1929 Wall Street Crash when a number of stockbrokers allegedly threw themselves from high office windows. A less dramatic form of anomie occurs to 'skidders' – those who experience downward social mobility. The 1980s and early 1990s has been a period of economic restructuring which has resulted in fortunes being made and lost. It is likely that anomie may be a useful concept to explain much suicide in this period. In any event modern society tends to encourage high expectations of material rewards which are not easy for everyone to achieve. The gap between hopes and reality may result in some people becoming very unhappy with their lot in life.

Perhaps less easy to imagine is a situation in which we suddenly gain a vast amount of money. How would you know who your friends were? Does your lover really love you or just your money? What would you do if you did not work? Do you really want to spend your time with new 'friends'? Such 'problems' may occur for people who win the pools, the National Lottery or inherit a fortune.

Fatalistic suicide

Fatalistic suicide may be regarded as the opposite of anomic suicide. This form of suicide is caused by there being no change. There is no prospect of improvement, no hope. The individual is over-controlled. Perhaps due to misguided optimism Durkheim thought that this form of suicide was of very little importance in contemporary society. He thought that it might be the cause of suicide for slaves or for some long-term prisoners. Fatalism has long been regarded as one characteristic of traditional working-class culture. We might also postulate that 'fatalism' may be a characteristic of the new 'underclass' of the 2000s.

The interactionist critique

A very different way of examining suicide has come from that branch of sociology known as interactionism. Two theorists are particularly relevant here: Jack Douglas (1967), a **symbolic interactionist**, and J. Maxwell Atkinson (1978), viewing suicide from an ethnomethodological stance. These theorists put forward a general critique of positivism, arguing that the social world cannot be studied in the same way as the natural world because human beings have consciousness, their actions are influenced by the meanings or interpretations that individuals put on social forces or external stimuli. What matters is not what goes on outside of the individual (objective reality) but what goes on inside their heads (subjective reality). There are therefore no social facts. Suicide is not an unambiguous social fact to be innocently compiled, tabulated and correlated ready for a scientist to look for explanations or causes (hence the rejection of causality). On the contrary, suicide is a label that is attached to a particular phenomenon after a social process of interpretation, negotiation and decision-making. Suicide is socially defined; it is a social construct.

Interactionists criticise Durkheim for an uncritical acceptance and use of statistics for the above reasons and because these statistics have been compiled by people other than sociologists, often for very different reasons. The quantity and quality of such statistics are open to manipulation and misuse.

Douglas

Suicide does not have a single meaning for everyone within a society or between societies. Thus Douglas argues that we cannot assume that in Catholic societies people do actually commit less suicide than in Protestant societies. In Catholic societies suicide is a mortal sin which results in eternal damnation. Relatives will be severely distressed if it is thought that their loved one committed suicide. The deceased and their family will suffer stigmatisation in the community if such a label is attached. There is therefore a social pressure not to attach this label. A process of

negotiation may take place which results in a particular death being interpreted as, say, accidental death.

It may not be the case that single people commit more suicide than married people with families. It is possible that the husband or wife of a deceased person would, being the first on the scene of the death, be predisposed to destroying some of the evidence that a suicide had taken place, for example they may destroy a suicide note, their objective being to avoid social shame or distress to other members of the family. Police and coroners in some senses have to negotiate with those who are left behind. For single people there is no one to cover up their actions, the first person on the scene of the death is more likely to be a stranger with less vested interest in 'bending' the assessment of the cause of death. There is no family to upset and police and coroners are freer to reach their own conclusion.

Atkinson

Maxwell Atkinson is particularly interested in this process of negotiation and definition. The suicide note is often a major cue which influences this decision positively. Yet, as we have seen, notes can be destroyed by loved ones and murderers may forge suicide notes. Relatively few suicide notes are found at the scene of a death which later becomes diagnosed as suicide.

Evidence shows that the mode of death is given great significance by coroners. Road deaths are usually labelled as accidental. Though a gruesome form of death, this is regarded as a common form of suicide despite it not being labelled as such. Perhaps the thinking here is that because there are a great number of road accidents, it is possible that the death was accidental, and therefore it is acceptable to attach the accidental death label in this circumstance. Hanging, on the other hand, is fairly difficult to do accidentally yourself, therefore it is usually labelled as suicide. This tends to sidestep the fact that it is not particularly difficult to be hanged by someone else, in which case the verdict could be murder.

Death by drug or alcohol overdose presents more difficulties for coroners. The line between getting 'out of it' temporarily and for ever is often a fine one. Coroners tend to use the quantity of drugs taken as a guideline in their decision-making as to whether the death was intentional or not. It seems to be more accepted that the elderly who die from an overdose did so accidentally because they were likely to be confused than a young person who, it is thought, has more awareness and intent as to what they are doing.

Another cue that is often used by coroners is that a person who dies through drowning at sea is more likely to have committed suicide if their clothes were left neatly folded than if they were not. The folding of the clothes implies premeditation and intent or, of course, it could be the usual behaviour of a very tidy person. In the 1970s, the Labour MP John Stonehouse was at first thought to have committed suicide when his clothes were found on the beach neatly folded after he had disappeared. It was later discovered that he had disappeared due to his involvement in fraud.

The 'amplification' of suicide

Atkinson also refers to cultural or social influences which may amplify the real or perceived incidence of suicide. He refers to the widespread view in our society that students are prone to commit suicide due to exam, parental and social pressure. The more students hold this view the more likely they are to contemplate suicide as a solution to their problems. The more coroners share this view the more likely they are to label a student death as suicide. The more suicide verdicts there are on student deaths, the more the media will highlight this. The more the media highlights this, the more students are likely to contemplate it, and so on. Thus society amplifies the incidence of suicide.

Interactionists have argued that suicide is best understood as a form of secondary deviance. They see it as a reaction to stigmatisation, to the application of a label to them. Such labels may include failure, being terminally ill or poor. It is important to know who attaches these labels and how the process works. Coroners are likely to be influenced by the past personal, medical and psychological biography of an individual, particularly if they were prone to being depressed or psychotic.

Interactionists reject the reliance on statistics and instead focus their study on individual cases of suicide and attempt to discover the meaning of the act for the individual suicidee, their family and friends. They then are in a position to discover if there are any patterns to these individual meanings. Such patterned meaning may include revenge, repentance, escape and a cry for help. We may then be able to link these patterns to wider social and cultural influences.

Parasuicides

We can see that in the study of suicide the theoretical perspectives are sharply exposed and opposed. We can say that, even from within the empiricist tradition, strong criticisms have been made of Durkheim's reliance on official statistics of actual suicide rates. Ettlinger and Flordah (1955) found that out of 500 cases of self-injury almost 90 per cent were 'gambles with fate'. These were situations in which there was a very serious risk of death. The individual had made no plans that would ensure their discovery in time. These are not fake suicides, they are not mere attempts to draw attention to oneself; on the other hand they are not suicides because they were not successful. They are known as parasuicides. Most people in this situation are not sure whether they want to live or die. They undertake a 'trial by ordeal' in which the outcome is left up to fate. There are approximately 100,000 admissions to hospitals in England and Wales every year under this category. What is important to note here is that Durkheim and those who have followed in his footsteps did not count these parasuicides. If he had done so he may have come up with very different theories.

It is also necessary to point out that the simple dichotomy of positivism on the one hand and phenomenology (or interpretivism) on the other, is perhaps a false one – or at least not a simple one. Douglas does not escape the positivist trap entirely. He rejects the use of suicide statistics because they are the result of a process of negotiation and are unreliable. He argues that we should focus on meanings. The way to get to these meanings is to carefully study case histories and documentary evidence. Yet these, too, are the result of a process of negotiation. If it is possible to get an accurate description of suicide cases then it is possible to get accurate statistics.

Feminists have also criticised Durkheim for what they see as his **sexism**. This is evident in his discussion of differential rates of suicide for widows and widowers. A widow is less likely to commit suicide, firstly because 'her sensibility is rudimentary rather than highly developed' and secondly because, being less a part of society, she does not have the same need for social support systems: 'With a few devotional practices and some animals to care for, the old unmarried woman's life is very full. Very simple social forms satisfy all her needs.' Women are less complex and also more the product of nature than society. With women, it is argued, his social analysis breaks down because he fails to see them as fully socially determined as he does men.

A new synthesis

In a recent study of suicide, and in an attempt to escape the problems that have dogged the study of suicide in particular, Steve Taylor (1990) uses a realist scientific approach (see chapter 1) to investigate this phenomenon. In doing so, he believes he is following Durkheim, whose search for the 'structural switches' that influence behaviour has been overemphasised, allowing him to be too readily characterised as a positivist theorist. Unlike Durkheim, however, he stresses not the degree of integration into the social structure but the individual's thoughts and feelings about themselves and the people closest to them.

Taylor categorises suicide in four ways, under two main headings: ectopic and symphysic. Ectopic suicides are inner-directed, demonstrating what a person thinks of themselves. They can be either submissive, when a person is certain they no longer want to live, or thanatative, resulting from someone's decision to gamble with their life (e.g. Russian roulette). Symphysic or other-directed suicides are mainly attempts to let others know how desperate someone is feeling. People commit sacrifice suicides to let others know how much they have been hurt and disappointed. Appeal suicides can often be dramatic attempts to show other people how they feel about others close to them.

In terms of deviance the study of suicide brings to the fore many classic arguments. Does society cause the act? Is it the result of too little or too much constraint, too much or too little integration, too much or too little regulation? These are arguments over the validity of statistics and causal explanations based on them. Suicide can be seen as secondary deviance, the result of a deviancy amplification spiral and a social construct.

Questions

1 What are social facts?
2 What are social constructs?
3 What are the main criticisms of Durkheim's approach to the study of suicide?
4 What is the importance of the study of suicide to the theory and methods of sociology?

Murder

Having looked at the important section on suicide, what issues would you expect to be involved in a sociology of murder? What aspects would the dominant perspectives focus on? Could there, for example, be an interactionist approach? Would the methodological problems raised by the study of suicide re-emerge?

One of the best-known studies of murder has been undertaken by the American M. E. Wolfgang (1958). He looked at the class background of those convicted of homicide, and found that the vast majority, between 90 and 95 per cent, were from the manual working class, although the victims came from a wider class background. Other studies have argued that the motives for homicide differ according to the class of the murderer – middle-class killers are much more likely to have financial motives, and to hire someone to do their killing for them, while working-class murders are far more likely to originate from small arguments about nothing. Katz (1988) found that of 56 upper-class people who had been involved in the killing of their husband or wife, 11 had hired someone to do it for them.

British statistics are revealing. In 1988 there were 592 homicides in England and Wales (Scotland and Northern Ireland have different judicial systems), of which 356 were murders of men and 236 involved female victims. This distinction between male and female is important. 45 per cent of female victims were killed by their partner as opposed to only 7 per cent of male victims being killed by their partner. 13 per cent of female victims were killed by someone unknown to them; 37 per cent of male victims were killed by an unknown attacker.

Of the total of 592 people murdered, 22 per cent were killed by their partners or ex-partners, 51 per cent by someone, such as a relative, who was known to them, and only 27 per cent by a stranger. More than 80 per cent of the homicides of women were of a 'domestic' character. Most murders occur at the weekend. A similar picture emerges from Katz's study, where only 3 per cent of murders were carried out by women killing other women, and in his study only 6 per cent of the victims of female murders were unknown to their killers.

From a positivist point of view, the sociology of murder is substantially about working-class men killing people close to them in their leisure time. Land et al. (1990) have taken this a step further and argued, with clear echoes of Durkheim, that the probability of homicide increases the more economically deprived an area is; it increases as population density increases; and it correlates with high divorce rates among males.

Katz has been particularly concerned to understand the normative framework in which murderers exist at the time of the killing. In the case of 'domestic' murders he focuses on ideas of righteousness and sensuousness, or what he calls 'distinctive sensual dynamics'. Usually, killers do not care about the legality of what they are doing, which makes the concept of deterrence problematic. By righteousness he means the killer's belief that what they are doing is morally correct, a defence of respectability (for example marriage vows) or property rights. In some cases the killer's own sense of self-worth has been challenged and humiliated, leading to escalating righteous indignation, often resulting from small arguments that get out of hand.

Marxists see murder in a much broader way, moving away from individuals and recognising that many people may die as a consequence of preventable economic deprivation. In the mid-nineteenth century, Friedrich Engels (1845) wrote: 'Murder has been committed if thousands of workers have been deprived of the necessities of life or if they have been forced into a situation in which it is impossible for them to survive. Murder has been committed if society knows perfectly well that thousands of workers cannot avoid being sacrificed so long as these conditions are allowed to continue. Murder of this sort is just as culpable as the murder committed by an individual. At first sight it does not seem murder at all because responsibility for the death of the victim cannot be pinned on any individual assailant ... But it is murder all the same.'

Questions

1 What would an interactionist view of murder focus on?
2 How reliable are the statistics of murder?
3 How does the sociology of murder compare with its media portrayal?

9 Work, organisations and leisure

> There is no greater modern illusion, even fraud, than the use of the single term work to cover what for some is ... dreary and painful and for others is socially reputable and economically rewarding.
> *J. K. Galbraith,* The Culture of Contentment, *1992*

Introduction

This chapter looks at the different ways work and leisure can be defined before examining aspects of the world of work in detail. The changing composition of the workforce and the role of women and ethnic minorities are investigated before looking at the management and organisation of work. Key concepts such as Fordism and post-Fordism are discussed, as are the importance of technological change and sociological research into work satisfaction and industrial conflict. The extent, causes and effects of unemployment are also considered. The chapter ends by looking at the changing nature of leisure and its relationship to work.

Problems of definition

Everyone knows what work is, yet it is a difficult concept to define. There is a similar problem with leisure. It is easy to understand work as paid labour, something you travel to and from – 'going to work' – and leisure as activities undertaken outside of work. The distinction seems clear, but grey areas abound. Is a car worker or plumber at work if they spend a weekend mending their own car or installing the central heating? Do full-time volunteers or burglars work? Do housewives work? If you are unemployed and go to a library for something to do, is it leisure time you are using? Do professional, multi-millionaire golfers play golf as a leisure pursuit, or – even if they give the money away – are they still nevertheless working? Are we at leisure when not working, or is there another area of non-work?

For Gershuny and Pahl (1980), economic activity exists under two main headings: the formal and the informal. The formal is the world of paid and taxed labour. The informal is more complex, made up of the hidden or 'black' economy, the household economy and the communal economy. The hidden economy is work undeclared to the Inland Revenue or Welfare Benefit Office. The household economy consists of unpaid labour we do for ourselves and others within a household – in the house, garden or car, for example. Although it is not officially quantified, estimates of the value of this economy see it as the largest of all. The communal economy concerns voluntary work for community or neighbourhood organisations.

In attempting definitions of these terms, many writers suggest that the distinction between work, non-work and leisure will be blurred, as old certainties, such as lifetime employment with only one employer, using one set of skills, disappear. Work is frequently thought of as meaning the same as labour and employment, although only the concept of employment implies a social relationship between employer and employee. For this reason, it is more accurate to describe people as unemployed rather than out of work. Both 'work' and 'labour' carry wider connotations, and are thought of as activities necessary for survival.

The term 'leisure' presents similar difficulties. One of the main writers in this area, Stanley Parker (1983), identifies three broad groups of definitions: the 'residual' type of definition that sees leisure as existing when people are not working, a wider definition that sees leisure as a positive activity, and what he calls the traditional or classical view which emphasises contemplation, enjoyment of self in search of knowledge, debate, politics and cultural enlightenment. Leisure is not necessarily free time. If work is 'time that is not your own' because it is time bought by an employer, client or customer, then time that is your own, non-work time, becomes leisure when it is used positively or creatively. This is still an unsatisfactory definition. What needs to be examined is the quality of the use of work time and leisure time, and the way the two concepts are related.

To heighten these distinctions, Parker describes a continuum where work – 'sold time' – stands at one end, and leisure – 'choosing time' – at the other. In-between are three categories: work-related time or work obligations (such as getting ready for or travelling to work), existence time spent doing things like eating and washing, and the category of non-work obligations or semi-leisure such as gardening or taking the dog for a walk. Even then, these activities are not carried out in isolation or separately: while engaging in primary activities (like eating) we can also listen to the radio as a secondary activity. There are also many people for whom these distinctions are hardly perceivable. Do mothers at home (or, less frequently, fathers), the retired or unemployed, experience work, work obligations, physiological needs, non-work obligations and leisure separately?

Since the early days of the industrial revolution, what has been thought of as work has been transformed as workers transferred from fields, cottages and villages to factories, terraced houses and urban areas. Much of what sociologists have thought of as work, inspired by questions posed by the founding fathers, has been an attempt to understand the impact and dynamic of the industrial era. Specific **paradigms** were created to do this, including the concept of **Fordism**, following Henry Ford's creation of a mass-production car plant in Detroit in the early twentieth century.

Much of the recent debate in this area concerns the extent to which the growth of the service sector means that 'Fordist' or even 'industrial' paradigms still hold, with many sociologists now claiming that industrial societies have been superseded by **post-industrial** societies, Fordism by **post-Fordism** and modern organisations by post-modern organisations. Much speculation also exists over the future of work and the impact of new technologies such as information and communications technology, and the increased emphasis on functional flexibility at work as

well as the emergence of new work patterns such as homeworking and increased part-time work.

Questions

1 Why are work and leisure difficult terms to define?

2 What kinds of work constitute the 'informal' economy?

The founding fathers and industrialisation

Durkheim

To understand the importance sociologists give to the role of work in society we need first to look at how the founding fathers viewed the changing nature of their own societies. From a **functionalist** point of view, industrialisation is part of social evolution. The most stable society copes with change yet still holds together. Durkheim characterises these changes as the movement from mechanical solidarity, where there is very little difference between people and the roles they play, to organic solidarity where roles become more specialised and differentiated (see also chapter 1).

As societies grow larger and more complex, the way in which order is kept – the means of social control – must change to handle the complexities of a highly differentiated **division of labour**. Industrial society is a web of interdependent relationships, where individuals can only exist through co-operation with others. That this concept of order is tied up with the structure of society reflects the main concerns of functionalism – the generation and maintenance of stability and **consensus**. Both Durkheim and Herbert Spencer were fascinated by the process of an increasing division of labour, the splitting and fragmentation of work tasks into many smaller ones, and the creation of new tasks and roles in the interests of greater productivity.

Durkheim (1893) was aware, however, that this increasing specialisation brought problems, where some individuals became 'no longer anything but an inert piece of machinery, only an external force set going which always moves in the same direction and in the same way'. The resulting **anomie** or normlessness was a product of a rapidly changing society. The pace of early industrialisation was rapid, the vast changes brought about by new technology and a new system of social relationships were difficult to keep up with and left individuals feeling lost and helpless in the maze of new social conditions. There were no rules to recognise or follow; order had not yet been created from the chaos. When order did emerge, the social inequalities which had seemed so sharp and brutal, so unfair and cruel, would disappear. Moral regulation would be restored on the lines being established by professional associations. Social inequality would nevertheless remain as 'social inequalities exactly express natural inequalities'.

HERBERT SPENCER (1820–1903)

Victorian sociologist and an important figure in evolutionism and social Darwinism. His functionalism influenced structural-functional sociology via Durkheim and Malinowski.

Marx

For Marx, work, production and creativity should be at the centre of life. A fulfilled, satisfying existence involves producing artefacts, food and materials which would be owned and shared by all. The worker would be a fully active part of the productive process, exercising creative powers and feeling ennobled by the work they do.

In his lifetime, though, industrial societies were **capitalist** societies based on **class** conflict, exploitation and **bourgeois** control. One group is oppressed and forced into a life of meaningless activity which has as its end result nothing more than high profits and a luxurious life not for themselves but for the capitalist class. Labour produces marvels, palaces, beauty, technology and skill, but only for the **ruling class**. The worker shares in none of these but is left with only the world of animal functions to give meaning to existence, concentrating on personal adornment, eating, drinking and sex. Marx welcomed the technological innovations associated with the capitalist **mode of production** when it overthrew the **feudal** mode of production, but these technological innovations were misused as a tool of oppression and misery, when they could have been used for the greater benefit of all. The capitalist mode of production produces selfishness and **alienation**.

Alienation

By alienation Marx meant more than the consequences of the division of labour. He was referring to the way capitalist social relations alienate workers from their creative nature, their 'species-being', whereby the full fruits of their labour are expropriated – effectively stolen – from them, leaving them as wage slaves, less than human, with the capitalist machine crushing the life out of them, allowing no control over what they make or the speed and technique with which they make it. Selfishness and alienation are a product of the capitalist mode of production, not innate human qualities: 'The mode of production of material life determines the general character of the social, political and spiritual processes of life. It is not the consciousness of men that determines their being, but on the contrary, their social being determines their consciousness' (Marx, 1859). The only resolution to this situation was for the workers to take control of the means of production for themselves.

Although Marx and Durkheim considered the same social structures, they reached very different conclusions about how these large and mysterious systems worked. This reflects the power of theoretical concepts in determining the nature of social exploration. The two theorists began from a different set of assumptions about the basis of society, social order and social change.

Criticisms

If developments in capitalist social relations may not have proved Marx correct, many Marxists, amongst others, would argue that Durkheim's idealistic and optimistic version of industrial society based on a consensus over morals and natural inequality has not materialised either. The functionalist view of social change is of a slow, steady progress towards a system based on co-operation and shared values, the collective conscience which binds all together. This assertion has been extensively discussed in the debate about **embourgeoisement** (see chapter 3).

Questions

1 What does Marx mean by the term 'alienation'?
2 What is meant by the 'division of labour'?

The occupational structure

Occupations and the labour market

The labour market identifies all those people who are either in, or wish to be in, paid employment. The occupations found within this market are sometimes divided into two large categories. Manual, or **blue-**

collar workers work in occupations that involve physical labour, often wearing protective clothes, working with material objects. These workers are often subdivided into three further categories of worker: unskilled (such as packers), semi-skilled (such as shop workers) and skilled (such as electricians, plumbers). Those engaged in work that is usually office-based are described as non-manual labourers, or **white-collar workers**. Again, these are categorised at different levels, from clerical workers through to managers and professionals. Each level is defined by the amount of training and qualifications necessary to take on employment. Where the dividing line falls between and within each category has been the source of much debate in sociology, informing the work of writers such as John Goldthorpe, Dave Lockwood and Harry Braverman, for example around the concepts of embourgeoisement and proletarianisation (see also chapter 3).

Another way of conceptualising the labour market is not by level of skill and physicality, but by its internal structure. For some analysts (for example Giddens, 1973; Barron and Norris, 1976; and Rex and Tomlinson,

1979), there is not one labour market but two. There is a **primary** or core **labour market**, and a secondary or **peripheral** market. The former is characterised by high wages, job security, in-service training and some form of career structure, while workers in the secondary are less secure in their employment, and less likely to enjoy perks and privileges. This **dual labour market** exists mainly because it suits employers to have loyal workers on the one hand, and more disposable workers on the other. This argument has been used to understand the relatively privileged position occupied by white men in the **primary sector** on the one hand, and women and ethnic minorities in the **secondary sector** on the other.

There is disagreement about whether a dual labour market can be said to exist. Mann (1992) questions whether the distinctions between the two are clear enough, when some employment can attract high wages (a characteristic of the primary market) and low job security (characteristic of the secondary market) and vice versa. The role of **trade unions** in being able to achieve high wages or job security is underestimated or ignored, as well as their role in excluding or including women and ethnic minorities

Casual labour – the temporary employment of children on very low wages is a common feature in some developing countries.

within the workforce. Although these theories show that particular groups are located in either of these sectors, they fail to show the processes that have placed them there.

Marx, and many Marxists since, argued that the capitalist labour market contains a labour force and a **reserve army of labour**. The reserve army exists because of the booms and slumps in production, pulling them into employment in periods of high profitability and rejecting them during downturns. With employers knowing there is a pool of cheap and available workers, the reserve army mitigates against those in employment taking industrial action to improve their conditions of work. Marx had an unsympathetic attitude to this group, seeing them as unlikely to develop a revolutionary **class consciousness**. As Mann argues, 'When he asserts that certain sections of the reserve army of labour breed more rapidly, and "succumb to their incapacity for adaptation", while others are part of some criminal class, Marx reproduces the prejudices of the Victorian middle classes.' This prejudice also prevents him from defining the reserve army in objective and economic terms, seeing them as in part responsible for their own situation, particularly those he describes as paupers or lumpenproletarians.

Other writers (such as Reich *et al.*, 1973), also looking from a Marxist perspective, have argued that the contemporary labour market consists of more than two sectors, and should be seen as segmented, as the result of a management divide-and-rule policy over workers, creating artificial divisions to overcome the tendency of **monopoly capitalism** to create a homogeneous (or uniform) **working class** able to recognise itself as a 'class for itself', as well as a 'class in itself'. Trade unions and professional associations have only helped reinforce this process of segmentation.

The argument that the workforce has become more flexible is at the heart of the debate about Fordism and post-Fordist work organisations. Atkinson (1985) distinguishes between two forms of flexibility, both of which, he says, are management led. Functional flexibility concerns the way employers are able to move core workers between tasks, while numerical flexibility describes the expansion and contraction of the number of workers within the periphery, which itself is composed of two sectors. These are full-time workers with low job security on the one hand, and part-time and temporary workers on the other. Firms may also pull in subcontracted and agency and self-employed workers to work on specific tasks and

projects. As Dex and McCullough (1997) observe, fixed-term contracts, teleworking. homeworking, zero-hours contract employment, seasonal and shift work can also be added to this list.

The flexible nature of such an organisation is of greatest benefit to employers and core workers, according to Atkinson. Peripheral workers have less opportunity to broaden their skills base, and are less likely to be involved in decision-making processes, although neither group of workers is likely to become less skilled as a result of increasing flexibility.

Theories of flexibility have attracted much discussion. Pollert (1988) sees it as presenting a simplified account of complex processes, assuming that a flexible work organisation is a new development. There is little evidence to support the view that temporary work is increasing markedly, while the number of part-time workers in manufacturing is decreasing, and is often a response to short-term economic trends rather than longer-term restructuring of the workforce. The deep recession in the 1990s also showed that very few jobs can ever be described as secure, whether part time or full time, whether at the core or the periphery of the labour market, although many surveys show that employers do not distinguish between part-time and full-time workers when considering their viability and status.

Questions

1 What is a 'dual labour market'?

2 In what ways have work practices become more flexible?

Patterns and trends in the occupational structure

The changing relative size of the manual and non-manual sectors of the economy has been of great interest to sociologists. In the course of the twentieth century, manufacturing and extractive industries, where most manual workers were located, shrunk dramatically in developed market economies, while the service sector, where most non-manual workers were located, has increased rapidly.

The industrial revolution, beginning in the United Kingdom in the mid-eighteenth century, was led by the development of the coal, iron and steel, shipbuilding, engineering and textile industries – the 'Victorian staples'. As industry grew, agriculture declined sharply so that by the beginning of the twentieth century, less than 10 per cent of the workforce in the UK were employed on the land, and half that number, or a million workers, immediately after the Second World War. During this period, manufacturing grew, and accounted for almost 40 per cent or 8.5 million workers by 1951, with strong growth in the chemical and metal industries. Looked at in terms of occupational classification rather than sector, manual workers constituted 75 per cent of all jobs in 1911, only falling to just under two-thirds by 1951.

The second half of the twentieth century then saw a progressive decline in manufacturing and extractive industries in the West. The numbers employed in the coal industry had been falling continuously throughout the century, from 1,333,000 workers in 1921 to 679,000 by 1951 and less than 10,000 by the turn of the century. All sectors of manufacturing also witnessed a decline, such that by the end of 1991 only 21 per cent of the total workforce was in manufacturing employment, as *Table 9.1* shows.

As manufacturing declined, the service sector rose sharply, accounting for over half of the workforce by the late 1960s. more than two-thirds by 1991. Part of this is due to the growth of the **Welfare State** (particularly in health and education services), but also by business and leisure services, especially in the

financial sector, where employment grew from just over one million to almost three million in the twenty-five year period from 1966 to 1991. All of these trends are likely to continue to well into the twenty-first century.

What these changes spell out is a long-term shift away from blue-collar (manufacturing and extractive sectors) work to white-collar (service) work. This shift carries profound implications not only for the social structure, but also for people's self-identity and orientation to work, in very simple daily issues like whether they work with objects or with people, and what skills therefore make up their work tasks. As Duncan Gallie writes of his 1998 survey, 'Only 22 per cent of those employed in the extractive industries mentioned that dealing with people constituted at least half of their working time and in none of the manufacturing industries was the proportion higher than 30 per cent. In contrast, this answer was given by 52.6 per cent of those in banking, finance and insurance, by 59 per cent of those in national or local government and by over 80 per cent of those in the welfare and in the leisure industries' (Gallie *et al.*, 1998).

Over the same period, the occupational structure of the British workforce has also been transformed (see *Table 9.2*). There has been an increasingly specialised division of labour: the census of 1851 identified approximately 7,000 occupations, that of 1881, 12,000, and this had grown to 23,000 by 1980. One area of white-collar work – clerical – grew from less than a million (4.5 per cent of the working population) in 1911 to almost two and a half million (or 10.4 per cent) by 1951. During this period, women also began to form the majority of workers in this classification, 59 per cent by 1951.

Table 9.1 Industrial change in Great Britain, 1966–91, employees (thousands)

	1966	1971	1981	1991	1991 as % of 1966
Agriculture	753	635	515	456	61
Energy and water	968	764	709	448	46
Metal manufacture/ chemicals	1,478	1,407	941	655	44
Mechanical engineering	3,725	3,669	2,839	2,148	58
Other manufacture	3,258	3,049	2,413	2,025	62
Construction	1,880	1,669	1,606	1,731	92
Distribution, hotels and catering	4,396	4,206	4,405	4,808	109
Transport and communications	1,614	1,564	1,496	1,492	92
Financial industries	1,193	1,348	1,796	2,821	236
Public administration	1,400	1,572	1,638	1,567	112
Education	1,094	1,370	1,434	1,459	133
Medical services	900	988	1,247	1,439	160
Recreational services	268	260	438	540	201
Other services	1,173	1,056	1,245	1,659	141
All industries	24,169	23,733	22,916	23,452	
All manufacturing	8,460	8,125	6,194	4,828	57
All services	12,039	12,362	13,699	15,784	131

Source: Halsey and Webb, 2000

Table 9.2 Changing occupational class structure in Great Britain, 1911–91

	1911		1951		1991	
	No. (000s)	Percentage of total workforce	No. (000s)	Percentage	No. (000s)	Percentage
Total in employment	18,347		22,514		25,406	
Manual workers	13,685	74.6	14,448	64.2	9,322	37.7
Skilled manual	5,608	30.6	5,616	24.9	3,566	14.4
Semi-skilled manual	6,310	34.4	6,123	27.2	4,354	17.6
Unskilled manual	1,767	9.6	2,709	12.0	1,402	5.7

Source: Halsey and Webb, 2000

The workplace is becoming increasingly white collar in nature, with new technology prevalent.

The general pattern of change in the twentieth century is from a labour force dominated by manual work at the beginning of the century to one where by the end there was a fairly even spread between professionals and managerial (33 per cent in 1991), intermediary occupations (29 per cent) and manual labour. Part of the reason for this is that the growth areas of employment, in service sectors such as education and health, contained a high proportion (up to two-thirds) of professionals and managers.

Questions

1 How did the occupational structure change in the twentieth century?

2 How does blue-collar work differ from white-collar work?

Women and work

Women have always occupied a disadvantaged position in the labour market, having been increasingly excluded from it throughout the nineteenth century, to a point where, as Ann Oakley (1974a) shows, it was seen as natural that a woman's place was in the home. The law backed the rights of employers not to employ women or to pay them less money than men for the same work. Indeed, the 1842 Mines Act, which bans women from underground work in mines, is still in force. In both world wars, women were sucked into the labour force and immediately thrown out again when men returned to reclaim 'their' jobs when the wars ended. This situation persisted in the UK until two pieces of legislation were passed in the 1970s. These are the 1970 Equal Pay Act (enforcing the same pay for the same job regardless of sex) and the 1975 Sex Discrimination Act, which banned discrimination in employment on the grounds of sex alone.

From being a minority confined to specific areas at the turn of the twentieth century, women had become a significant and generalised component at its close, although sex segregation nevertheless remained discernible. Thus, as *Table 9.3* shows, in 1911, 35 per cent of women were part of the workforce, growing to over half by 1998. During the same period, men's participation rates fell from 94 per cent to 71 per cent. Overall, the percentage of women in the workforce grew from 30 per cent in 1911 to 44 per cent in 1998. Most of this increase can be accounted for by the changing employment role of married women, particularly those aged between 35 and 44, whose

Table 9.3   Labour force participation rates, Great Britain, 1911–98

	Males	Females	All	Women as a percentage of the labour force
1911	93.5	35.3	63.0	29.3
1931	90.5	34.2	60.7	29.0
1961	86.3	37.5	62.8	31.3
1998	71.3	53.8	62.3	44.3

Source: Gallie in Halsey and Webb, 2000

participation rate grew from 10 per cent in 1911 to 72 per cent in 1998, while the number of single women at work remained almost constant at around two-thirds.

The pattern of women's employment is very different from men's, however, with only a small majority being employed full time, while over 90 per cent of men are employed full time (see *Table 9.4*).

Table 9.4   Full-time and part-time employment by sex in the UK, 1984–99 (millions)

	Males		Females	
	Full time	**Part time**	**Full time**	**Part time**
1984	13.41	0.61	5.54	4.36
1987	13.49	0.8	5.95	4.65
1990	14.39	0.92	6.64	4.97
1993	12.99	1.04	6.38	5.09
1996	13.2	1.25	6.47	5.31
1999	13.64	1.38	6.77	5.44

Figure 9.1   Full-time and part-time employment by sex in the UK, 1984–99

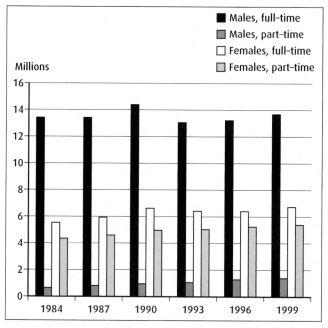

Source: *Social Trends* 30, 2000

Table 9.5   Occupational segregation, Great Britain, 1901–91

	Percentage of men working in occupations with				Percentage of women working in occupations with			
	100%	90%	70%	50%	100%	90%	70%	50%
		male workers				female workers		
1901	47	74	89	95	11	52	71	82
1931	35	69	84	94	0.1	41	62	73
1961	22	62	77	85	0	21	53	79
1991	0	38	68	83	0	23	63	76

Source: Gallie in Halsey and Webb, 2000

Sex segregation at work also broke down in the course of the century, though this was always more pronounced in traditionally male areas of work. At the turn of the twentieth century nearly half of all male workers were in occupations in which only men worked and almost 90 per cent were in occupations where at least 70 per cent of workers were male. The position for women was less pronounced, with 11 per cent working in entirely female occupations and 90 per cent in occupations where at least 50 per cent were female. By the end of the century feminisation of the workplace had spread across all sectors, with no occupations, being entirely dominated entirely by men or women, as *Table 9.5* shows.

Women's pay is also gaining steadily on men's, as *Figure 9.2* shows, though it has not yet reached parity.

These statistics can be explained by an examination of the location of women in the workforce. It remains the case that the top positions in most workplaces are dominated by men. In 1992, women still constituted less than 1 per cent of chief executives and members of boards of directors, less than 2 per cent of chief

Figure 9.2   Ratio between men's and women's pay

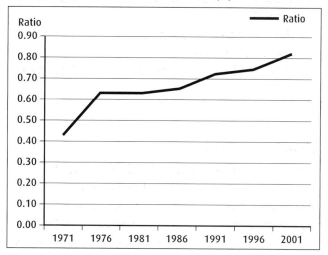

Source: *New Earnings Survey*, Office for National Statistics, 2001

executives in local authorities, less than 3 per cent of permanent secretaries in the Civil Service and 4 per cent of all judges. In trade unions, less than 3 per cent of general secretaries were female. The virtual absence of women in these top positions is frequently described as 'vertical segregation', or the **glass ceiling** that women encounter as they progress in their careers but beyond which very few go.

Horizontal segregation

Secondly, women are also segregated within the labour market by the work that they do. While men dominate professional and managerial posts in general, as well as jobs in science, engineering, technology, security services, construction, transport, mining and transport, women form the vast majority of workers in lower grades in education, health, clerical and office work, catering, cleaning and other personal services. This is known as the horizontal segregation of work.

One consequence of this is that women not only earn less than men on average but that they dominate the worst-paid jobs. Using the Council of Europe's decency threshold, in 1991 79 per cent of all women working part-time in the United Kingdom were classed as low paid. Of the total of all workers, part-time and full-time, classed as low paid, 65 per cent were women.

To explain the location of women in the labour force, Barron and Norris (1976) argue that the labour market is made up of two sectors: a core or primary sector of highly paid secure employment with promotion possibilities, and a peripheral or secondary sector of low-paid, insecure employment with low promotion prospects often involving unskilled work. Women occupy the secondary sector of this dual labour market. This analysis draws attention to the belief that women are only seen as temporarily in employment, on loan from their main roles as wives and mothers, developing less of an industrial consciousness, and are less likely to join trade unions and to demand as much pay as men. This largely stereotypical view has been challenged by a number of writers (for example Dex, 1985) for its simplistic division of the labour market into only two sectors, and its assumption that women 'accept' lower wages. The role of male trade unions in alienating and excluding women is not examined and it is unable to explain why women in the same jobs as men do not get promoted when the men do, and why some women in the primary sector continue to be relatively less well paid.

A reserve army of labour?

From a more **Marxist** point of view, women are an industrial 'reserve army' of labour, sucked into and expelled from the world of work with the ebb and flow of capitalist and economic fortunes. According to this theory, women will be the last to be taken on in times of expansion, and the first to be thrown out with recession. Evidence for this theory, however, is slim. As we have seen, in the 1980s the number of women in work increased, while the number of men fell. As women earn on average less than men, the cost to the capitalist of employing them is also less. To explain why women are located in specific sectors (horizontal segregation) some writers (Walby, 1986) have highlighted the role of trade unions in preventing women from entering traditionally male areas of employment.

Unpaid labour

Behind the world of paid labour lies an unquantified level of unpaid labour undertaken by women. This is as carers, for children, relatives and partners, where it is argued they are the slaves of wage slaves. In Ann Oakley's (1974a) study of housewives, women did at least 48 hours, at most 105 hours and on average 77 hours of domestic labour, whether in full-time employment or not. It is the low status accorded, culturally, to this work that may be the key to women's poor standing in the formal labour market where, for some writers, the work women do can be seen as an extension of their domestic role, providing for and cleaning up after men.

One view of the structural location of women that has aroused great controversy is that advanced by Catherine Hakim (1995). This is because she seeks to attack what she sees as a new **feminist** orthodoxy, where a form of political correctness among sociologists has prevented them looking dispassionately at women's orientations to work. For Hakim, there are five myths about women's employment. These are:

1 *Women's participation in the labour market has increased markedly in recent decades.* In fact, the real difference is in the number of women who have moved from part-time to full-time employment.
2 *Women working part-time are as committed to their work as men working full-time.* Hakim's research showed that, instead, many women working part-time have their family as their prime commitment and orientation. When asked if they would still work if they didn't need the money, 75 per cent of men

said yes, compared to only 66 per cent of women. The main difference in attitude is found in women working part-time.

3 *Mothers are prevented from taking up employment because of a lack of childcare places.* For Hakim, women who have consciously chosen to have a child will then dedicate themselves to rearing that child, and won't look to return to or take up employment during that period.

4 *Part-time workers are exploited.* This is contradicted by the substantial amount of legislation and rights at work supporting these workers.

5 *Women working part-time will have the same absentee and turnover rates as full-time workers.* In fact, the statistics show that women working part-time are relatively more unreliable and unstable workers.

Hakim is particularly concerned to show women as conscious authors of their actions. Some women, who have not chosen an employment career path, are happy with their choice of motherhood as their prime identity, and are not passive victims of a **patriarchal** culture. They 'give priority to the marriage career, do not invest in what economists call "human capital", transfer quickly and permanently to part-time work as soon as a breadwinner husband permits it, choose undemanding jobs with no worries and responsibilities when they do work, and are hence found concentrated in lower grade and lower paid jobs which offer convenient working hours with which they are permanently happy'. In this way, her analysis echoes the view of the 'lads' presented by Willis.

Her arguments have been attacked by many of the people she targeted, for example in Ginn *et al.* (1996). These writers are mainly concerned to dispute the validity of her data, and her interpretation of it, as well as the question of whether feminism has indeed been disseminating myths about women's employment. The coherence of her view that women who express a strong commitment to their family are therefore less committed to their part-time job is also questioned, as is her division between work and motherhood as orientations, when many women switch between both. As Dex says (in Ginn *et al.*, 1996), 'Most women want to enjoy both work and home life to the full'. Her argument about childcare will also be tested in coming years with the Labour Government's policy objective of increasing the number of childcare places for children under five. Finally, as Crompton (1997) argues, in portraying women as choosers and as actors, Hakim appears to present their choices as made without structural constraint: 'Women – and men – can choose but are also constrained, a fact which lies at the root of sociological explanations of human behaviour. The tension between "structural" and "action" explanations is a long-standing one in sociological theory and research, and has not yet been satisfactorily resolved' yet Hakim's work 'might focus the argument on the sterile dichotomies of choice or constraint, structure or action'.

Questions

1 Why do women earn less than men?
2 How can Hakim's argument be seen as an attack on 'feminist orthodoxy'?

Ethnicity and work

The most comprehensive and detailed account of the relationship between ethnicity and work can be found in Modood *et al.*'s 1997 study. As with any study of ethnicity, it is important to distinguish between different groups to understand the full complexity of the picture. As *Table 9.6* shows, Caribbean, Pakistani and Bangladeshi men are overrepresented in the workforce among manual workers, and underrepresented in senior white-collar positions. This

Table 9.6 Job levels of full-time male employees, 1994 (%)

	White	Caribbean	Indian	African Asian	Pakistani	Bangladeshi	Chinese
Professional/managerial/employers	30	11	19	26	14	7	41
Other non-manual	21	20	28	31	18	22	26
Skilled manual and foremen	31	37	23	22	36	2	5
Semi-skilled manual	14	26	22	17	28	65	20
Unskilled manual	4	6	7	3	4	4	8
Non-manual	42	31	47	47	32	29	67
Manual	58	69	52	52	68	71	33

Source: Modood *et al.*, 1997

Table 9.7   Job levels of full-time female employees, 1994 (%)

	White	Caribbean	Indian	African Asian	Pakistani	Chinese
Professional/managerial/employers	21	4	3	14	7	38
Other non-manual	58	76	61	66	60	55
Skilled manual and foremen	3	2	2	3	3	–
Semi-skilled manual	17	18	32	17	29	7
Unskilled manual	1	1	3	–	–	–
Non-manual	62	80	64	80	67	93
Manual	37	21	37	20	32	7

Source: Modood *et al.*, 1997

picture is not reproduced for women from ethnic minorities, with a more even spread across all groups and sectors. Only one in five Caribbean women, for example, works in manual work (see *Table 9.7*).

Overall rates of pay are equally revealing, with white and Chinese men earning most, while Caribbean, African Asian and Chinese are the highest earning women (see *Table 9.8*). As in education, women from all backgrounds are now beginning to make marked changes in their overall social profile. Breugel (1986), however, claims that these figures do not show the full picture of how these wages are earned, with many women from minority ethnic groups having to work above average hours, living in urban areas where housing costs are high. Arguments attempting to explain the position of ethnic minorities in the labour market are also to be found in chapter 3.

Table 9.8   Average gross weekly earnings of full-time employees by ethnic group, 1994

	White	Caribbean	African Asian	Pakistani	Chinese
Men	£331	£287	£335	£227	£336
Women	£224	£267	£254	£181	£287

Source: Modood *et al.*, 1997

Most of the self-employed are men (73 per cent of a total of three million), with the desire to be independent given as the main reason for taking this course, though it is built into many occupations. The picture of self-employment (not included in the tables above) in *Figure 9.3* shows very high levels of participation in Pakistani, Bangladeshi and Chinese groups, with the lowest activity found in the black community. Two-thirds of all self-employed Chinese people and over half of all Indian self-employed work in the distribution, hotels and restaurants sector, as do two-fifths of the Pakistanis and Bangladeshis who describe themselves as self-employed.

Questions

1 How is the employment situation of ethnic minorities similar to that of women?

2 How does the employment pattern of ethnic minorities differ from the pattern of educational achievement?

Figure 9.3   Self-employment (%)[1] by ethnic group, 2000–01[2]

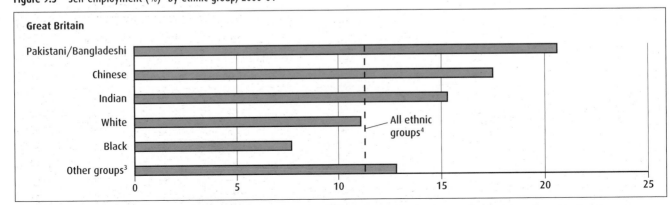

1 Percentage of all in employment who were self-employed.
3 Includes those of mixed origin.

2 Combined quarters: Spring 2000 to Winter 2000–01.
4 Includes those who did not state their ethnic group.

Source: *Social Trends* 32, 2002

Age

The pattern of employment participation by age shows that the lowest rates are recorded between the ages of 16 and 24, and over the age of 45, across all ages and genders (see *Table 9.9*). The percentage for older groups is declining under the combined impact of early retirement schemes and redundancy packages, although the retirement age for both male and female workers is now 65. The experience of work and age is therefore strongly cross-cut by the fact of class.

A closer examination of the data shows that:

→ The UK's unemployment and economic inactivity rates for older workers is currently 37.8 per cent, whilst the rate for the rest of the working population is 26.1 per cent.

→ Nearly a third of those over 45 are without work (some 2.8 millions).

→ Older workers in the UK are 25 per cent more likely to be unemployed, or economically inactive than younger workers.

→ Over two and a half million workers – more than a third of those between the ages of 45 and 65 – are officially classed as unemployed and economically inactive.

→ There are eight times as many older workers out of work for more than twelve months than younger workers.

For groups such as the Campaign Against Age Discrimination (CAADE), this profile is due to **ageism** and age discrimination against senior workers. This discrimination takes place particularly in recruitment (where employers are able to specify the age bracket of the employees they are looking for), in training and promotion, both of which decline as workers get older, and through practices such as early retirement and redundancy, both of which are designed to remove expensive older employees who are thought to be 'set in their ways', in favour of cheaper and more 'flexible' employees. Much of this discrimination, however, is now set to come to an end, with the approval of the Economic and Social Policy Council of the European Union's directive of October 2000 which obliges all European governments to have legislation against age discrimination in the workplace in place by 2006.

Question

What forms of age discrimination exist in employment?

The management and organisation of work

The post-industrial society thesis

The argument that industrial societies have now become post-industrial is mainly associated with Daniel Bell in *The Coming of Post-Industrial Society* (1973), in which he argues that the primacy of manufacturing has been replaced by the service sector, which in turn creates a new increasingly important class of professionals and technocrats. This class, whose main commodity is knowledge, become decision-makers in all spheres of society, particularly politics and economics. He argued that the increasingly

Table 9.9 Economic activity rates by ethnic group, gender and age, 1999–2000, UK (%)

	Males				Females			
	16–24	25–44	45–64	All aged 16–64	16–24	25–44	45–59	All aged 16–59
White	78	94	78	85	70	78	71	74
Black Caribbean	77	89	65	80	63	78	72	75
Black African	50	84	77	76	40	65	71	61
Other black groups	78	83	..	81	59	72	..	67
Indian	62	95	74	82	56	69	56	63
Pakistani	56	89	62	74	35	31	21	30
Bangladeshi	55	81	40	65	36	..	..	22
Chinese	..	83	73	63	..	63	64	57
None of the above	55	86	79	76	50	56	65	57
All ethnic groups	76	93	77	85	68	76	70	73

Source: *Social Trends* 31, 2001

scientific and rational basis for production would at the same time end class conflict and see 'the end of ideology' (Bell, 1961) as work became less arduous and more rewarding. The predominance of white-collar work would lead to a challenge in attitudes and **values**, with more workers able to pursue their interests inside and out of work, while the most unpalatable aspects of market forces would be ameliorated by planning and increased social welfare. A similar argument was advanced at the same time by John Galbraith (1967), who advanced the view that power was becoming increasingly located in the 'technostructure' of large **corporations**, rather than with owners and shareholders.

Although this line of argument has inspired many writers to construct similar views of the future, it has also been criticised from a number of angles. Many have seen the rate of decline of manufacturing as overstated, with production simply moved from the metropolitan **core** out to the **newly industrialised countries**, while the global number of industrial workers and products increases. The manufacturing sector has never contributed the majority of the workforce, with the combined number of jobs in agriculture and services always exceeding those in manufacturing since the Industrial Revolution. Blue-collar work has never been the characteristic form of work of what has been termed 'industrial' societies.

Not all jobs within the service sector are non-manual or white-collar. As Gershuny(1978) observes, many of the activities involved in distributing goods and services, such as working at a petrol pump, are in fact manual in character. Bell's assumption that the newly created white-collar jobs would be more satisfying or attractive has also been questioned, with the realisation that work in this sector includes such work as restaurant and retail work, both of which are characterised by low pay and casual labour. Furthermore, for Marxists, while modern societies may be post-industrial in the sense that manufacturing has become relatively less important, they are as much characterised by the capitalist labour process in its monopoly phase as they ever were (see Callinicos, 1990).

The post-industrial thesis is based on an assumption that economic, and particularly technological, forces are the main drivers in determining change in society. Many writers within sociology are willing to accept that profound changes are taking place, but the profusion of terms used to describe them (such as post-Fordism, post-modernism and post-structuralism) indicate an unwillingness to confine this analysis

solely to the apparent dominance of the service sector at the expense of manufacturing.

Questions

1 What is the post-industrial society thesis?
2 What is meant by technological determinism?

The labour process and the control of labour

Two models of the management and organisation of work in particular have been hugely influential since their development in the early decades of the twentieth century. The first model emerged with the publication in 1911 of F. W. Taylor's *Principles of Scientific Management*. The second model is the human relations school.

Taylorism

The adoption of ideas from the *Principles of Scientific Management* led to new methods of work organisation which were eventually to spread across the world. As a management consultant in the USA, Taylor was interested in the question of maximising worker output and efficiency, and overcoming the phenomenon of 'goldbricking' or 'soldiering', where workers conspire to slow down the rate of production in order to keep their rates of pay high.

His answer to this was to remove control from the workers and transfer it instead to a management layer. This could be achieved by, firstly, greater division of labour whereby each work task would be reduced to its simplest form. This would remove any notion of skill from the tasks the workers would be required to do and allow individual work tasks to be carried out more quickly. Secondly, managers would control the pace of production and control the production process. Thirdly, time and motion studies would allow cost accounting and individual targets to be set. In advocating the adoption of these principles,

---

F. W. TAYLOR (1856–1915)

'Taylorism' is often used as another term for scientific management. Taylor was a consultant at the Bethlehem steel works in the USA where he conducted his experiments into improving productivity of workers. He believed that management should organise the production process to make it efficient and that workers should be given the incentive of wages paid in relation to the level of their productive output.

Taylor took a monetary view of worker motivation, believing that they will trade interest and satisfaction in their work for the higher economic rewards that would result from greater productivity, not only from higher wages but also possibly from profit sharing.

Taylor's ideas were taken up and developed most widely by the car manufacturer Henry Ford, who between 1908 and 1914 introduced mechanised mass production and the assembly line, with each worker being asked to undertake a specific simple and repetitive work task for the then (1914) high wage of $5 per day. This was brought in, however, partly to combat absenteeism. The spread of this work organisation around the world, creating a new level of management responsibility, is known as 'global Fordism', characterised by mass production of a few types of commodity. It has also meant that the car industry has been the subject of considerable interest to sociologists throughout the twentieth century, particularly theorists of the 'labour process approach'.

The human relations model

The second model also emerged out of attempts to increase productivity. This was the Hawthorne studies carried out by an American sociologist, Professor George Elton Mayo, between 1927 and 1932. He wanted to find out why there was so much grumbling and dissatisfaction among the 30,000 employees at the Hawthorne Works of the Western Electric Company in Chicago. His original idea was to attempt to increase productivity by playing with the light switches. He took one group and increased the intensity of illumination, measuring the expected increase in their productivity levels. However, the group who had been left in the dark had been working harder as well. They then reduced the illumination for the group who had a taste of the bright lights, and found that this made them work even harder. So the lighting was not the

important factor, but something was encouraging these employees to get their noses to the grindstone.

Further research involved a five-year programme with a selected group of female workers, whose output was recorded, and who were involved in all the details of the observation. They were put through a complex series of shift and work changes: one break, two breaks, a break plus free meal, early finishing times, all of which produced changes in output, which mostly increased. For example, when they left at 4.30 p.m. instead of 5 p.m. output went up, but when this was changed to 4 p.m. output stayed the same. The largest increase was recorded when the women were put back on normal working conditions: no breaks, Saturday work and no free meals or early leaving. When the women had been working under these conditions before the research they had produced 24,000 relays (an electronic part) per week. When they were returned to exactly the same conditions after all the research, this had gone up to 30,000 a week, the highest ever recorded.

It seems difficult to believe that during the five years that this went on for, the researchers were not aware that the main factor affecting output was *their presence*, and this has become the standard criticism of observation as a research method – the 'reactivity' of the subjects, i.e. their response to being observed. Could the involvement of the workers in both pieces of research have heightened their sense of importance, their interest in work and their job satisfaction? It could be claimed that it was this new sense of actually being involved with something meaningful that decreased the workers' sense of alienation. It certainly shows how problematic this kind of research can be.

The importance of the Hawthorne studies for sociologists and theorists of industrial relations is that they showed a different dimension to worker motivation, particularly that productivity is as much affected by the amount of interest shown in the work done as any other factor, and that informal interactions between workers are important to production norms. The findings of what became the human relations school point to significant other factors than financial motivation, such as psychological needs, in understanding worker motivation.

ELTON MAYO (1880–1949)

Australian-American social anthropologist who greatly influenced managerial practices world-wide. Mayo tried to counter the ethics of the school of scientific management. He argued that workers needed more than economic incentives to make them work hard. It is the task of management to apply sociological principles to the study of work to understand how to overcome the alienation of workers from the co-operative work processes.

Braverman

The American Marxist, Harry Braverman (1974), describes what he believes are the consequences of an ever-increasing division of labour under developed capitalism. Capitalism is geared towards the pursuit of profit, not towards the attainment of consensus or social solidarity, as functionalism proposes. A consequence of this need to maximise profits is the general and progressive deskilling of jobs. As we have already seen, capitalists have been aware of the advantages of an ever-increasing division of labour for centuries, particularly because fragmentation can lead to huge increases in productivity– output per person. The logical result is total **automation** of everything – factories, petrol stations, railway lines, food and drink dispensers and hotels. This necessarily involves a devaluing and downgrading of human skills, often ending in redundancy. Humans are a by-product, so much so that job-loss is referred to as 'natural wastage'.

According to Braverman, the resulting increase of routine mechanical work, simple and monotonous, will cut down the barriers within the working class. Crafts which in the past enjoyed **status** and respectability, through skill and high wages, have gradually disappeared with mechanisation and automation, as in the printing industry. The high hopes held out for the morale-boosting team work in the process industries are unfounded. The working class melts into one big, semi-skilled, homogeneous group, with similar pay and boredom levels. Braverman challenges the view that skill levels have increased. The end result of this **deskilling** would see an end to distinctions between manual and non-manual work, between the traditional and new working class, because some skills would disappear and technology would mean a levelling of skills. This not only increases profits, but it also increases control. Capital cannot rely on its workers, due to the conflict of interests, so control is vital.

Control of labour

Theories of management, as in Taylor's 'scientific management', recognise the need for managers to monopolise 'brain work'. They conceive of and plan the ideas, while workers, under strict control, execute them. The more separate these two areas, the more efficient. New machine technology will incorporate this control, as the machine decides on time and motion. Control of labour is therefore more easily achieved given this technology, but it is always a vital part of capitalism, and as such, control of labour is independent of technology.

Criticisms of Braverman

Braverman's thesis has been criticised on a number of points. The first is that he gives us a picture of an inert, passive workforce, which does not fight back against management control. He neglects trade-unionist class consciousness and worker resistance to management. He also assumes that all managers will adopt scientific management techniques. This is not always the case, and some management strategies are designed to give workers some autonomy in their work situation. In making these sweeping assumptions, Braverman depicts a homogeneous, lifeless working class, rendered helpless through deskilling. There is no reference to differences within the working class, except a somewhat romantic view of the skilled artisan of the past. There is no historical analysis of the social conditions of craftworkers and therefore no comparison between their lives and those of deskilled workers in late capitalism. Braverman has uncritically adopted the myth of the 'golden age' of craftworkers, living in cosy, productive family units. He is also accused of using an individualistic, task-centred idea of skill and the labour process, thinking in terms of the individual manager's 'conceptions' and individual worker's 'executions'. Labour is reorganised, as a result not of class struggle, the key Marxist assumption, but of managerial design. An important point here is that although **Taylorism** takes capitalist control to its logical conclusion, management has always had control in its hands. The control brought about by deskilling and Taylorist methods is simply a new and stricter form of capitalist control. Other factors which play a part in the production process are the size and availability of labour markets – workers have more power when they are in scarce supply. Trade-unionism and politics are also important, but again, ignored by Braverman. Furthermore, he has also been criticised for over-estimating the extent to which Taylorism has been taken up, and not appreciating that many new jobs require as much or more skill than the jobs which have disappeared.

Questions

1 What is 'Taylorism'?
2 What is 'the Hawthorne Effect'?
3 Why is Braverman critical of scientific management?

Fordism and post-Fordism

Braverman's ideas have certainly been influential and his work remains controversial. More recent writers have analysed work and the labour process in a similar way, for example Harley Shaiken (1986) and David Noble (1984) who both argue that Taylorism (or Fordism as it is sometimes called) lives on.

Other writers are less sure, believing that the 'Fordist' age is being superseded by 'post-Fordism'. Fordism means mass production techniques using machines and labour trained to undertake only one task where the workforce works with relative job security in a hierarchically structured organisation, collectively negotiating their wages and producing goods for a mass market. The epitome of this was the assembly-line method of car production pioneered by Henry Ford, symbolised by his statement on consumer choice: 'You can have any colour you like, as long as it's black.'

Post-Fordism, sometimes called 'flexible accumulation' or neo-Fordism, is the pattern for the future, based on projecting currently observable trends. Here, there is less job security for those outside the 'core' of the employment market as many companies will sub-contract others to undertake specific tasks for specific markets (batch production and niche marketing), using micro-electronically controlled multi-purpose machines. Cheap mass-produced products will be less popular, as higher quality products appeal to more discerning consumers. Workers will increasingly work in groups or on their own, possessing more skills than before, and being paid on their individual performance. The four areas of change are therefore the labour process, workers' contracts, the goods produced and the technology involved in producing them. The key concept is flexibility, and these trends are the most observable in the most advanced capitalist economies.

Factories are not only becoming smaller, but the number of people working in them is also shrinking, with only 300 factories employing more than 1,000 people. British manufacturing produced approximately the same amount of goods in the late 1980s as it did in the early 1970s – with about two million less workers. In the 1980s, for the first time in British industrial history, the number of workers employed in non-manual work overtook those doing manual work, rising from 37.5 per cent in 1961 to 52 per cent in 1984.

FORDISM AND POST-FORDISM

Fordism	Post-Fordism
Economy, competition and production process	
Protected national markets	Global competition
Mass production of standardised products	Flexible production systems/small batch/niche markets
Bureaucratic hierarchical organisations	Flatter and flexible organisational structures
Compete by full capacity utilisation and cost-cutting	Compete by innovation, diversification, sub-contracting
Labour	
Fragmented and standardised work tasks	Flexible specialisation/multi-skilled workers
Low trust/low discretion, majority employed in manufacturing sector/blue-collar jobs	High trust/high discretion, majority employed in service sector/white-collar jobs
Little on-the-job training, little formal training required for most jobs	Regular on-the-job training, greater demand for knowledgeable workers
Small managerial and professional élite	Growing managerial and professional service class
Fairly predictable labour-market histories	Unpredictable labour-market histories due to technological change and increased economic uncertainty
Politics and ideology	
Trade-union solidarity	Decline in trade-union solidarity
Class-based political affiliation	Declining significance of class-based politics
Importance of locality/class/gender-based lifestyles	Fragmentation and pluralism, global village
Mass consumption of consumer durables	Individualised consumer choice

Whether Fordism is no longer a dominant influence in the world of work depends on views of how far it was considered to have spread in the first place and how successfully it has been superseded by other practices. Alain Lipietz (1993) sees the New Right policies of British and North American political and industrial leaders in the 1980s as intensifying rather than replacing Fordism, failing to successfully transplant Far-Eastern ideas of work organisation such as 'just in time', 'continuous improvement' and 'total quality management'. The resistance to this new culture, he argues, has contributed to the West's economic decline.

One key indicator of the demise of Taylorist thinking would be the disappearance of the idea of work-task design based on a separation of thinking from doing. It is argued, however, that the emergence of practices such as 'multi-skilling' do not overcome this duality as they mean only that the number of tasks a worker can be expected to undertake has increased, not that the work tasks themselves have become enlarged.

Many writers now argue that the traditional focus on manual work is now out of date, and that the focus for sociologists of work should move to the service sector, where diverse forms such as job-splitting, job-sharing, self-employment, part-time working, temping, agency work, flexi-working, contract working, home-working and telecommuting need to be examined.

Questions

1 How does Fordism differ from post-Fordism?
2 How relevant is the concept of Fordism today?

Skill and deskilling

The extent to which skills at work are changing has been examined in four areas: enskilling (gaining skills), multi-skilling (combining skills), reskilling (replacing old skills with new ones), as well as deskilling (loss of skills). Both Zimbalist (1979) and Shaiken (1986) support Braverman's case for deskilling, with new technology primarily introduced to increase managerial control. The description of a job or work task as skilled or unskilled is seen by many as ideological, with many feminists, for example Beechey (1983), arguing that much of the work undertaken by women is incorrectly described as unskilled, although it is in the interests of both male managers and trade unionists to continue to see it in this way.

Other studies, for example Straussman (1985), see new technology as demanding reskilling and enskilling, although Winch (1983) does not identify a trend to either deskilling or reskilling, arguing that changes in the workplace owe as much to the need to compete with other firms as they do to maintaining workplace control. Ainley (1993) argues 'Enskilling, multi-skilling, reskilling and deskilling can all happen simultaneously to individuals within one employment and to the workforce as a whole as technology changes.' This range of effects is particularly true of the impact of new technology in the workplace. Like the debates concerning embourgeoisement and proletarianisation, the extent to which workplace skill levels are increasing and decreasing seems to depend on the way they are defined, as well as the sociological perspective of the author.

Question

Is work becoming deskilled?

Bureaucracy and changing organisational cultures

Influenced by the work of Weber, the sociology of work has become increasingly interested in the wider environment in which work happens – the organisation – and the increased role of management and white-collar staff within it. For Parsons (1960), organisations are 'social units (or human groupings) deliberately constructed and reconstructed to seek specific goals'. Thus a school exists to educate its pupils, a hospital to cure the sick, a manufacturing firm to make products and profits. **Bureaucracies**, originally associated with government departments, are now features of all large work-based organisations. It was the increasing role played by this form of organisation that particularly concerned Weber.

The concepts of **authority**, organisation and bureaucracy are central to Weberian theory. By authority, Weber means legitimate power, where the co-operation of people is on the basis of their consent. This authority can be of three types: traditional (following established custom and practice), charismatic (based on the personality of an individual or group of people), and rational-legal, based on the following of rules which are seen as fair, impartial and based on reason. Of these Weber sees modern societies as increasingly based on rational-legal authority, and bureaucracies as the characteristic form in which rational-legal authority is exercised.

For Weber (1922), a bureaucracy is the most appropriate administrative form for pursuing goals rationally and efficiently. An 'ideal type' of bureaucracy has a number of key elements: a high degree of specialisation and a clear division of labour; a hierarchical structure with a clear line of command; a formal body of rules governing the organisation; impersonal relationships between members of the organisation and its clients; and staff who are recruited long-term on the basis of knowledge and ability and whose salary is separate from any private income. Organisations conforming to these characteristics would not only be effective because they were rationally organised, they would also be predictable and capable of implementing sophisticated plans. They would also, however, stifle imagination and creativity, where the logic of rational organisation would ultimately create its own 'iron cage', stifling many human freedoms, including democratic activity. Bureaucratic organisations therefore represented two-edged swords to Weber, increasing technical effectiveness on one side, and limiting creativity and spontaneity on the other.

This ambivalence towards bureaucratic organisation has informed much of the subsequent work in this area. Writing at the same time as Weber, Robert Michels (1911) was pessimistic about the possibility of any organisation being controlled and regulated through democratic processes, even political parties formed with the purpose of widening democratic power. His analysis of the German Social Democratic Party before the First World War showed that the combination of size and the need for efficiency were in constant tension with control by the membership and accountability. As the organisation grew, paid officials became increasingly distant, more powerful and more conservative in their ambition. Ultimately, their prime goal became to protect themselves and their own position, as the membership became more apathetic. This process is what Michels describes as the 'Iron Law of Oligarchy', where it is in the nature of all organisations that **power** ultimately gravitates into the hands of a few.

After the Second World War, new studies of organisations emerged. In the main, these studies were critical of Weber's ideal type of bureaucracy. The work of sociologists like Merton, Blau, Selznick and Gouldner borrows from and develops the Weberian view of organisations as efficient institutions. This microanalysis revealed weaknesses within organisations, flaws which are a direct result of bureaucracy. There was a gap between the model of bureaucracy, the **ideal type**, and the reality. Bureaucracies spawned 'bureaucratic personalities', 'bureaucratic inertia' and, last but not least, 'red tape'. Merton (1949a) and Blau (1955) highlight the costs of bureaucratic organisation. The inefficiencies of the system lead to the necessary breaking of the rules, in order to get the job done. This analysis of the informal aspect of organisations – the 'social action' within bureaucracies – is the main strength of the 1950s debate. It is perhaps fair to say that Weber himself was more concerned with large, public, **State** bureaucracies than with the workplace, although he knew about and was a supporter of Taylorism. Using Weber's model as a yardstick, the realities of different types of organisation emerge on closer analysis, as Merton and Blau show.

Merton

Merton saw that the very elements which lead to efficiency in general produce inefficiency in specific instances. He draws attention to the following possible bureaucratic dysfunctions:

→ *Impersonality:* Clients of various State organisations may expect staff to be sympathetic and interested in them as people. Bureaucratic procedures emphasise the importance of objective, impersonal treatment.

→ *'Red tape':* The rule systems so beloved of bureaucracies can become the be-all and end-all of the organisation. The maze of regulations may cause staff to lose sight of the original goals for which the rules were made. These rules could make the organisation less effective.

→ *Inflexibility:* Training staff to follow rules rigidly can produce inflexibility. A situation may arise where the organisation's goals could be achieved by bending the rules or ignoring them for a while but the bureaucrat has not been trained to be adaptable or innovative. They will stick to the very letter of the law, and efficiency will be reduced.

Blau

Blau's work is concerned with case studies which highlight the existence of informal structures within the larger organisations. These can and do help efficiency, and go some way towards putting right the various inefficiencies caused by the rules of bureaucracy. Blau's original research followed the working life of employees of a federal agency in Washington DC. They worked on individual cases which involved complicated tax laws. They were officially forbidden from discussing cases with each other, but were reluctant to consult their bosses. So they broke the rules, discussed details and asked each other for advice on a regular basis. The outcome of this rule-breaking was more efficiency on the job. The agents learned from each other and pooled their experiences. This gives them an insight which would not have been available had they played it by the book. So informal structures can promote efficiency.

Mechanistic and organic types

Burns and Stalker (1961) distinguish between two types of organisation: mechanistic and organic. Mechanistic organisations are largely unchanging and best suited to stable external conditions. Organic institutions are more dynamic and best suited to changing external conditions such as the emergence of a new commodity market.

The characteristics of 'mechanistic' forms are:

→ the overall task is broken down into specialised tasks – the division of labour
→ the specialised tasks are 'abstract' in that they are pursued separately from the end concern. (People try to improve the machine which glues the sugar bag, forgetting the end product – a bag of gluey sugar.)
→ superiors reconcile these tasks by joining them together
→ each role has defined rights, obligations and technical methods
→ these rights, obligations and methods are transferred into responsibilities in a functional position
→ a hierarchic control, authority and communication structure – the 'pecking order', 'chain of command', 'procedures'
→ this hierarchy is confirmed by the controllers at the top, who reconcile all the tasks and ensure the end product
→ communication between superior and subordinate – 'up and down' the pecking order
→ operations and working behaviour are governed by superiors
→ staff are loyal and obedient
→ knowledge of tasks within are more important than general, external knowledge – you could be a brilliant sociologist but you know nothing about packing sugar

The 'organic' model is less rigid, more flexible, adaptable to change, problems and new conditions. These are the organic characteristics:

→ specialist knowledge and experience contribute to the overall task of the concern
→ individual tasks must be seen 'realistically', as part of the overall concern, not as separate
→ interaction will lead to redefinition of individual tasks
→ 'responsibilities' are the province of everyone, and should not be passed up the line – 'the buck stops here' syndrome must go
→ commitment is more than a technical term – it should be spread to the whole concern
→ control, authority and communication should be a network of interactions, and people work in their roles because of community and co-operative interests rather than being forced to by impersonal contracts
→ everyone may have knowledge which can be used in the control network – the all-knowing boss would not exist
→ communication and information should travel in all directions not just up and down
→ emphasis is on information and advice rather than instructions and decisions
→ loyalty and obedience are replaced by commitment to the task
→ externally recognised knowledge and experience are valid, not just internal know-how

Human relations

It is clear that, for Burns and Stalker, the organic system (with its multidirectional communications, its recognition of the ideas and knowledge of individuals, its emphasis on less formal controls and its ethos of listening and advising rather than rigid order structures) is the preferred and more efficient system. The two forms neatly outline the differences between 'scientific management' (mechanistic) models and 'human relations' (organic) models. In the latter, individual commitment is strongly emphasised, as if all this informality will buy the heart and mind of the worker more effectively than a mere contract to the cold face of mechanistic organisation. There is recognition of seniority and expertise, but it is not used for control. The workers' co-operation is ensured by commitment to the goals and values of the organisation. The workers are important and feel important, so they are less likely to develop self-interest. Most organisations are to be found somewhere between these two poles.

Writing from a Marxist perspective, Burawoy (1979), sees the Weberian emphasis on examining the role of efficiency and rationalisation within organisations, and the functionalist focus on harmony and consensus, as forgetting the real reason they exist: to make a profit for owners and shareholders. These studies also overemphasise the harmony and consensus that exist within organisations, when much of their actual practice is geared to promoting and maintaining social control. Conflict is usually seen as a problem to be designed out when in fact, according to Burawoy, it is inherent in any work organisation within capitalism, a point underestimated by Braverman in his analysis of the capitalist labour process.

Modernism and post-modernism

Stewart Clegg (1979) argues that contemporary Japanese industries have developed a new style of organisation since the Second World War. He distinguishes between 'modernist' – those based upon the Weberian model which was also called 'Fordist' because Ford was the first industry to use the authoritarian, bureaucratic form – and 'post-modernist' or post-Fordist organisations which are based on the flexible 'organic' model used by Burns and Stalker and supported by the human relations approach.

Japan

The Japanese version of this emerged as a response to the economic crisis of the 1970s, which continues to dog the world economy. The modernist structure was struggling to survive, for all the usual reasons, mainly that the need for surveillance in hierarchies became too expensive and efficiency was falling. Clegg suggests that the modernist organisation will be an outdated system in the future, relegated to underdeveloped countries. The centralisation behind all this decentralisation continues to exist, but the way Japan has responded is perhaps unique, due to post-war social conditions.

The post-modern organisation

The stress in the post-modern organisation is upon all the factors mentioned in discussion of previous models – flexibility, less authoritarianism, collective decision-making and less supervision. Workers are committed to the company, not their occupation, and they are seen as contributing towards 'core-competencies' (Prahalad and Hamal, 1990). All expertise is used to help further the organisation's interests through a system of cross-unit relationships; 'contracts' and workers are 'multi-skilled'. As Clegg shows, this applies to about a third of the Japanese workforce – those who are on the inside, part of the company for life, with all the benefits and lifestyle options which this brings. These lucky few enjoy the advantages of post-modernism, becoming committed through the attraction of this security and a process of organisational indoctrination.

Core and periphery

Singing the company song was mentioned above, but 'spiritual training' goes deeper. Workers are subjected to a Moonie-like programming into social co-operation, responsibility, reality-acceptance and perseverance in tasks. Encouraging commitment by a process as blatant as this would, to a Marxist, be a straightforward construction of **false consciousness**, without even the subtlety of ideology. Spiritual training is a process which takes place in front of your eyes. These 'core-workers' tend to be mostly male, with women very heavily marginalised. Indeed, two-thirds of the workforce, those employed externally to the companies, are in seasonal jobs and do not enjoy the benefits of the post-modernist organisation. This could be the organisational type of the future. The picture of a society characterised by a secure, well-paid minority and a hard-pressed, marginalised majority echoes the existence of a 'dual labour market'. Lifestyle options are restricted to the few, who enjoy private pensions, health schemes, education, all aided by the company, whilst the rest struggle on. Perhaps the future will see an 'immiserated' proletariat. The post-modernist organisation has substituted authoritarian control with commitment and a high degree of connection between worker, task, leaders and goals. As control has improved, so has efficiency. The dated, modernist bureaucratic structure is being thrown out and old methods of worker–management relations are becoming redundant and fossilised.

Questions

1 What are the characteristics of bureaucracies?
2 What are mechanical and organic organisations?

Technological change and work

Bell's *The Coming of Post-Industrial Society* and Braverman's *Labor and Monopoly Capitalism*, published within a year of each other, set a research agenda that has not yet been completed over a quarter of a century later. Their views of change within the workplace were radically different from each other, and were opposed on many points. As Harris and Hannah (1993) write, 'where Bell forecast a significant reorganization of the workplace in the new "game between persons", Braverman saw only further centralization and management authoritarianism. Where Bell projected a workforce that would be considerably "upskilled", Braverman insisted that the workers would be further "deskilled". Where Bell glimpsed only more rewarding and fulfilling work, Braverman noticed intensifying worker alienation and the steady "degradation" of work.' Given these opposing views, sociologists are now in a position to identify which view is best borne out by what has happened in the intervening period.

For Braverman, the emerging post-industrial society that Bell believed he had identified looked very similar to the existing industrial one, in particular the central role played by the profit motive in any form of work organisation. What is now known as information technology was as much part of the struggle between capital and labour as any other part of the labour process. As Perrolle (1991) notes, 'If information itself is seen as a commodity produced for profit by the rational organization and mechanization of intellectual labor, then information can be produced by the computer in the same way that products were made by the factory machinery of the first industrial revolution through the alienation of laborers from the production process.' According to Aronowitz and DiFazio (1994), a handful of 'superprogrammers' will produce intelligent software that in turn will produce the low-level routine software produced by programmers today: 'each generation of technological change makes some work more complex and interesting and raises the level of training or qualification required by a (diminishing) fraction of intellectual and manual labour; for the overwhelming majority of workers, this process simplifies tasks or eliminates them, and thus eliminates the worker.'

Other writers have found evidence to support aspects of both Bell's and Braverman's positions. This is partly due to the lack in both works of operational definitions, for example of the concept of skill. Several studies have nevertheless attempted to gauge the impact of information technology, for example Zuboff (1988), who argues that the increased efficiencies promised by information technology will eventually force managers to utilise its potential to the full. This

will oblige managers to end hierarchical work structures and adopt more participatory forms of workplace organisation, realising a 'historic opportunity to more fully develop the economic and human potential of our work organizations'. For Pinchot and Pinchot (1993), this means the end of bureaucracy: 'Bureaucracy is dying because it produces organizations that lack the systems for assembling a collective intelligence to think both globally and in local detail, both near-term and long-term, and in terms of both freedom and community.'

There is, nevertheless, resistance to using new technology in this way, mainly because management groups have a personal vested interest in maintaining the status quo, also because of the deep-seated changes this would require in the cultural and technical organisation of work. According to Sproull and Kiesler (1991), this requires 'a flexible, internally motivated, continuously learning work force; a strong internal culture to support information sharing and participation in problem solving; delegation or shared responsibility in recognition that dispersed activity requires local action and flexibility and creation of dynamic procedures, structures and groupings to amplify expertise and technology'.

The price of not restructuring work has been expensively learnt in the motor industry. In the 1980s, General Motors spent $40 billion on introducing automotive technology into its factories, at the time a sum larger than the combined total value of Honda and Nissan. At the same time it made no changes in its work structures, while both Honda and Nissan changed their work organisation without automating, achieving 45 per cent reductions in assembly time and quality defects. As McKersie and Walton (1991) observe: 'The upshot is that advanced technology by itself fails to achieve performance gains. Only when innovation in work organization accompanies technological innovation do we see significant performance advantages.' When General Motors adopted Japanese management practices (by working collaboratively with Toyota), investing in people rather than technology, there were significant gains in productivity and worker satisfaction. In other words, technology does not play the determining role in work organisation it was once thought to, and the way it is implemented is as important as the technology itself, as Osterman (1991) claims: 'high-technology strategies, in the absence of significant changes in human resource practices produce no significant productivity or quality improvements'.

Questions

1 What are the implications of new technology for (a) employees and (b) bureaucracies?
2 How important is technological innovation to work efficiency?

Industrial relations and conflict

Strike statistics

Official strike statistics provide some basic data on industrial conflict. As with all statistics, interpreting what they mean involves an understanding of how they are collected. The figures are collected by the Department of Employment, and include only strikes which lasted more than one day and involved more than ten workers. Calculations of how many workers are involved in the strike may be misleading because of the difficulties of knowing who actively supports the strike and who has been laid off as a consequence of the strike. The statistics similarly do not reveal how many workers in other industries have been made idle as a result of a strike elsewhere. Nor is it possible to know how many days were lost per striker, because some workers may make up the time afterwards, or may return to work during the strike. One strike may cause massive distortion to the statistics, for example the 27,135,000 days lost in 1984 which were largely due to the year-long conflict between the National Union of Mineworkers and the National Coal Board (British Coal) (see *Figure 9.4*).

Strikes as a social problem

Moreoever, focusing on strikes reveals only one aspect of industrial conflict: some industries may be strike-free but have high rates of absenteeism or labour turnover. A strike involves conscious, collective action, it is 'a temporary stoppage of work by a group of employees in order to express a grievance or enforce a demand' (Griffin, 1939). Losses of production because people either do not turn up to work or walk out on the job because they hate the way they are dehumanised by work are less-discussed forms of grievance, but no less a problem for management. It may be the case that more days are lost through workers having bad backs than being on strike.

Similarly, some writers, such as Hyman (1972), see strikes as only one side of a structural problem. Focusing on strikes avoids looking at how employers use their power. For 'as well as the lock-out, conflict with the employee can take the form of plant closure, sackings, victimization, blacklisting, speed-up, safety hazards, arbitrary discipline, and so on. The routine practices of employers do not count as "industrial conflict"; they are part of the normal, repressive reality of work.' The main area of industrial conflict studied by sociologists is nevertheless the strike.

Two questions need to be asked: Why do strikes happen at all? Why are some industries more prone to strikes than others? In many ways, some sociologists see these as the same question, arguing that strikes are a product of the wider social structure and the conflict between labour and capital in general, and the

Figure 9.4 UK working days lost in labour disputes, 1952–98 (millions)

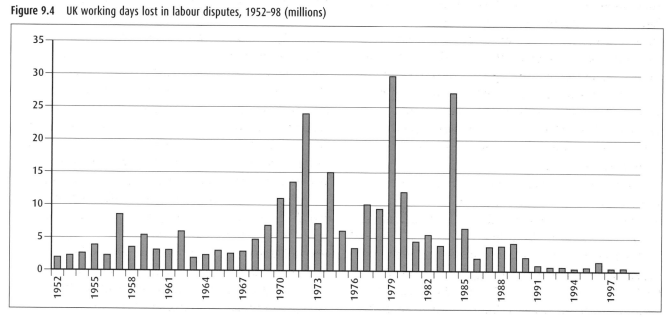

Source: *Social Trends* 30, 2000

organisation of the labour process in particular. A number of causes of strikes have been suggested, and the parts played by 'agitators', communications, community integration, technology and the system of industrial relations have all been examined.

Agitation

Management and the media frequently refer to shop stewards as 'agitators' but this has been given little credence by social scientists, largely because shop stewards are elected officials, and represent the opinion of the members who elected them, and also because they cannot agitate successfully without there being widespread grievances in the first place. It is also observed that trade-union officials, including shop stewards, are just as often involved in preventing strikes as they are in fomenting them.

Communication

Poor communication between management and workforce has received more critical attention, particularly from those writers working within the human relations tradition. Scott and Homans (1947), looking at wartime Detroit, then centre of the American car industry, and W. H. Whyte (1951) see strikes as caused by the fact that workers and management simply do not talk to each other enough: 'In the long run a number of strikes seemed to stem from faulty communication' (Scott and Homans, 1947). The key problem of this approach is that it does not adequately explain why some industries appear to be more strike-prone than others. It could also be the case that more information, for example concerning planned redundancies, management salaries or profit margins, could lead to more strikes, not less.

Integration

The industries that have been most strike-prone in the industrial West in the twentieth century have been those that are at the heart of industrial development, particularly mining, shipbuilding, dock-work, iron and steel and motor-vehicle manufacture. Kerr (1964) argues that strikes in these industries reflect the employees' high degree of integration as workers with 'their own codes, myths, heroes, and social standards', with a relatively low level of integration into the wider community. Concomitantly, workers who are less likely to strike will be more closely integrated into the wider community.

Technology

Technology is also believed to play a major role in determining the character of industrial relations. This point is argued by three writers: Woodward (1958), Kuhn (1961) and Sayles (1958). For Kuhn the key point is the extent to which the organisation of technology allows what he calls 'fractional bargaining', that is, *ad hoc* bargaining outside institutional structures such as trade unions. New technology, he says, gives rise to 'regular changes in work methods, standards or materials; the opportunity for considerable interaction between workers; the grouping of the labour force into a number of roughly equal departments; and the sequential processing of materials into a single end product.'

Criticisms

The problem with such explanations, as many of the authors are aware, is that they veer towards monocausality and technological determinism, and do not take into account wider influences on behaviour. To broaden the picture, Dunlop (1958) describes an 'industrial relations system' of workers and their organisations, managers and their organisations and governmental agencies all concerned with the workplace and work community. Further variables on behaviour are technology, market and budgetary constraints, and wider power relations. Collectively, he says, these factors create 'an ideology or a commonly shared body of ideas and beliefs regarding the interaction and roles of the actors which helps to bind the system'. It is the culture of such a system that encourages or discourages the development of strikes.

Such explanations clearly have their roots in structuralist explanations informed by a positivist philosophy. For Eldridge (1968), any analysis of industrial conflict must examine 'the interaction of cultural, economic and organisational factors'. Within this interaction, it is necessary to perceive how the situation is seen and defined by the actors, as well as understanding the goals and motives they bring to the situation.

This point is neatly made in an influential British study by Goldthorpe *et al.* (1968): 'The attempt to provide explanations from the point of view of the "system" entails the neglect of the point of view of the actors involved … The orientation which workers have to employment and the manner, thus, in which they define their work situation can be regarded as mediating between features of the work situation objectively considered and the nature of the workers' response.' This study reveals, for example, different attitudes to absenteeism in mining and the steel industry. Amongst miners it was seen as acceptable to take a day off; however, this was frowned upon by steel workers.

Similarly, there may be differing definitions of how to use the strike – as a weapon of the first or last resort, for example, partly depending on how seriously management will take threats of strike action. For Hyman (1972), 'the meanings attributed to a strike will vary so much between situations where stoppages are routine and those where they are unprecedented that it is unhelpful to define it as the same action in both cases. Where the significance of their action is so differently regarded by the strikers themselves, the precipitating causes are likely to be similarly distinctive.' Once again, the interplay between social structure and social action is central to the understanding of social phenomena.

Two developments in the United Kingdom in recent decades have also been cited as instrumental in explaining the apparent decline in industrial conflict. The first is the rapid decline in the last quarter of the twentieth century of the areas of the manufacturing base traditionally associated with industrial action, for example dock work, mining and steel, to the point where mass action is either impossible or meaningless, against a background of rising mass unemployment. The defeat of the miners' strike in the mid-1980s also signalled the determination of the government not to yield to any trade-union demand.

The second is the legislation passed by the Conservative government, and unrepealed by the Labour government since its accession to power in 1997. Arguing that trade unions are a brake on the workings of a free market economy, the New Right within the Conservatives secured the passing of eight Acts between 1980 and 1993 which substantially changed and weakened the circumstances within which trade unions were able to act. These included the end of 'secondary picketing', secret ballots prior to strike action, and a series of changes designed to end the 'closed shop', a workplace where all employees are obliged to join a trade union.

The responses of trade unions to these changes is generally known as 'the New Realism', where some trade unions argued for new ways of defending members. These included an increased emphasis on single union workplaces, negotiation rather than strike action and 'no strike' deals, where employers and trade-union members are bound by the findings of arbitration.

Millward (1994), commenting on a series of workplace surveys, observes that the marginal role played by trade unions is a feature of newly created workplaces, and that, in general, unions are being increasingly emasculated: 'The decline in union representation between 1984 and 1990 was not generally a weakening of the role of unions from one of full negotiation and representation to a partial role... Rather, it involved a wholesale reduction of the trade unions', with these organisations failing to respond quickly enough to the growth in part-time work, mainly undertaken by women. The earlier pattern of multi-union workplaces was also changing, with most workplaces either without union representation (49 per cent) or represented by a single union (23 per cent). No-strike agreements, part of the 'New Realism' being prompted by trade-union leaders, however, were rare.

Although strikes are the most documented form of industrial conflict, they are not the most representative. Others include overtime bans, go-slows and working to rule, all of which are less dramatic and harder to quantify than strikes. Whether strike action is in terminal decline is inconclusive. The election in 1997 of the Labour Party, heavily sponsored by the trade-union movement, raised expectations of a new era of co-operation rather than conflict, centred around investment in the public sector. The strike action taken by firefighters over pay in 2002 and 2003, however, was seen by many as a return to the 1970s and 'Old Labour', whose 'winter of discontent' in 1978–9 was a central cause of its exile from power for the next twenty years. As Hyman (1972; 4th edition 1991) argues, 'There is always the inevitability of industrial conflict in a society in which the main purpose of industry is profit, and in which the relationship between employers and workers is dominated by the drive to extract surplus value from the labour of men and women.'

Questions

1 What forms of industrial action can be taken?
2 How do structuralist and interactionist views of industrial conflict differ?
3 Why are some workplaces more prone to strikes than others?

Strikes in the public sector: firefighters in 2002.

The experience of work

Work satisfaction and orientation

Why people work, what they think of work, and the factors that determine these attitudes to work have been the subject of considerable research in sociology, particularly since the Second World War. The great majority of these studies have been focused on the paid employment of men working in manual labour, but more recently the focus has moved more into non-manual labour and non-traditional definitions of work. **Technologically determinist** arguments see the type of technology used in the workplace as the main reason why people may or may not derive satisfaction from their jobs. Socially determinist arguments see the nature and type of relationships at work as being the main contributor to attitudes to work, which in turn govern the way technology is used. The theories described below exist towards one or other end of the continuum between social and technological determinism.

Blauner

Blauner's (1964) study is famous for attempting an operational or working model of the alienation concept. However, he annoys Marxists by rejecting the Marxist viewpoint, as Blauner claims that alienation is not a product of class position in capitalism. For him, it is the nature of the work and the type of technology which are important. He provides a watered-down version of the concept of alienation, reducing it to a variety of work satisfaction as measured by workers' attitudes.

Alienation exists, he says, 'when workers are unable to control their immediate work processes, to develop a sense of purpose and function which connects their jobs to the overall organisation of production, to belong to integrated industrial communities, and when they fail to become involved in the activity of work as a mode of personal self-expression'.

He first split the concept into four separate, measurable segments, taken from M. Seeman (1959):

1 *Powerlessness:* Do workers feel that they have any control over their work? Do they feel that they have some power in the work situation, that they contribute to decisions? Or are they powerless, unable to contribute anything other than labour?

2 *Meaninglessness:* Does work mean anything to those involved in it? Do they approach the factory gates in eager anticipation of tasks which give them a sense of purpose? Or is work meaningless, boring, repetitive, with no point at all other than earning money?

3 *Isolation:* Do workers feel an accepted part of society? Does the job have high or low social status? Do they have the respect of others? Another aspect of this is whether workers are socially integrated at work or isolated individuals, restricted in communication with their fellow workers by the disciplines of the shop floor and working process. A high degree of isolation would encourage alienation.

4 *Self-estrangement:* Are the workers involved in their work, or do they cut themselves off, dream of other things, divorcing themselves from their actions, becoming like robots, automatic and unthinking, concentrating on the next tea-break, smoke-break and so on?

Measuring alienation

If all of the above are present to a high degree, then Blauner would claim that alienation exists. As mentioned above, the cause of alienation lies not in capitalist class relations but in the level of technology. Attitudes to work and job satisfaction depend upon how highly skilled the job is. Does it take skill or is it a matter of pulling levers and pushing buttons? To test out these ideas, Blauner looked at work methods in different types of industry and tried to measure and compare levels of alienation. Each industry is an example of a different technological method (see *Figure 9.5*).

Printing

The printing industry was used as an example of 'craft industry' – this was in the days of typesetting by hand, which is now being rapidly replaced by electronic publishing. Skill, judgement and initiative were an integral part of the job. The division of labour was low, as the job was not split up into smaller tasks using specialised skills. Each worker was highly skilled and worked on their own initiative. There was a high demand for this work, leading to job security, a strong union and high wages. Their sense of powerlessness was low because they had a high degree of control over the work process and conditions. The meaninglessness levels were also low, as the workers had knowledge of the whole process and each product was unique and individual. Their sense of isolation was similarly low, printing being a well-respected skilled trade. The social community provided in the mainly small, decentralised workshops meant high integration within the workplace too, unlike the case of the Ford workers quoted above. All this obviously means that their self-estrangement is low, as the traditional, highly skilled work brings with it a sense of identification and intrinsic satisfaction. The questionnaires Blauner used show that this particular craft had the highest level of job satisfaction. Automation has brought a deskilling of printing, and levels of satisfaction may have changed.

Mass production

The second area of industry examined by Blauner was 'mass production'. This means the mechanisation of crafts such as weaving and textiles, with a high division of labour where tasks are reduced to simplicity, e.g. machine-minding. Such industries are characterised by labour intensiveness, poor job security, and the use of a lot of employees at the lowest-paid end of the labour market such as ethnic minorities and women. The tasks are routine, paced by machines and strictly supervised. The powerlessness is high, with control out of the workers' hands entirely – the machine has the power; you have to stand in the same place all day and cater to its every whim. The textile worker and others who experience similar working conditions should feel the meaninglessness and isolation at its highest pitch, but, he found, they do not. Their lives are given meaning by their community, a traditional tight-knit social group. The boring jobs and low pay are overridden by loyalty to the company and social network. Self-estrangement is high though, as there is little involvement with the actual work. For the large numbers of women in the industry there may have been social pressures and 'role-strain', with conflicting ideas created by sexist ideologies concerning childcare and housework. For these women, the social integration within the factory must have provided relief from the boredom and arduousness of being a housewife, but it did not mean they loved the actual work involved. In this case, influences outside, from the traditional community, counteract the alienating consequences of technology and the boring, meaningless activity which occupies most waking hours.

Assembly work

The 'assembly line' has the highest levels of alienation, with no community life as a substitute. There is no control, as the line determines the speed of work entirely. The worker does not have to move, and the supervision is absolute. The work is routine, standardised and social isolation is high. Workers are not integrated at work, nor do they have a high standing in the eyes of society – no tradition or skill, just high wages and a media-led reputation for laziness. Powerlessness, meaninglessness and isolation are at an all-time high then, and the self-estrangement scaled similar heights. Workers were hostile to the work, and only put themselves through it for the pay – a purely instrumental attitude. The shifting communities of workers, moving to where the work was, with high lay-off rates and low job security meant that there was social alienation and no traditional occupational community. This is Goldthorpe's privatised worker and Willmott and Young's symmetrical family, drawing the curtains and shutting out the dull reality of their lives, taking comfort from all the things advertised on the TV which they can afford, replacing their estrangement from themselves with a commitment to consumerism.

Continuous process technology

However, the U-curve in job alienation, low in pre-mechanisation and at its highest with assembly-line

Figure 9.5   Technology and alienation

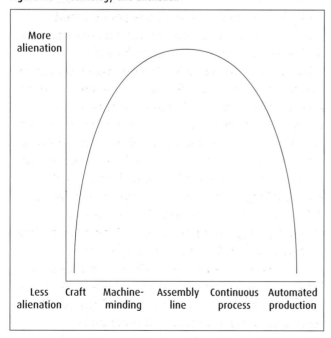

Source: adapted from R. Blauner, *Alienation and Freedom* (1964)

technology, turns back down when the results of the automation–continuous process technology are examined. Blauner's examples of this are the oil and chemical industries. The trend towards alienation is reversed, and control, integration and involvement are restored to the worker. The division of labour is low as each worker is a highly skilled, responsible team member. Powerlessness and meaninglessness are low, as operators have control, monitoring dials, gauges, using initiative and working with others. They have a knowledge of the whole process, and can re-train in other jobs within the plant. The social integration is high within the workplace populated by highly satisfied workers with good promotion chances. This compensates for the lack of traditional status, and self-estrangement is also low, as the work is found satisfying.

Consensus

In examining these areas, Blauner has identified important variables relating to job satisfaction: the division of labour, the social organisation of the industry and the economic structure within which they operate. However, the overriding factor for Blauner is the type of technology employed. His conclusions were that automation in industry will bring alienation at work to an end. There will be consensus, consultation and co-operation between management andworker, instead of conflict and control. Loyalty to the firm will mean that the worker in automated industry will be middle class in outlook and status. Blauner's optimistic conclusion has been criticised in a number of ways. Research carried out by other sociologists does not support Blauner, particularly that of Goldthorpe and Lockwood, who found that attitudes and behaviour relating to work were little influenced by technology.

Blauner is aware of the shortcomings of his methodology, which is mainly based not on his own work but on a study by Elmo Roper in 1947, carried out over twenty years before the publication of Blauner's book. This was a questionnaire given to 118 printing workers, 419 textile workers, 180 automobile workers and 78 chemical workers, chosen as a quota sample. Blauner's own research was based on interviews with 21 randomly chosen chemical plant workers, as well as a limited amount of observation in the same industry. He is well aware of the problems of generalising these data in order to reach any meaningful conclusions about alienation at work, commenting that the industries he investigated cover only three million of the US workforce, and that it would be impossible to characterise industries such as iron and steel as based on craft, machine-tending, assembly-line or continuous process technology.

Goldthorpe and Lockwood

Goldthorpe and Lockwood (see also chapter 3) used a social action approach to investigate 'affluent' workers. They found the same pattern of job satisfaction as Blauner, with skilled maintenance workers enjoying their jobs more than machinists and assemblers. Their findings show that workers had very similar attitudes to work, irrespective of the technology used. They all had 'instrumental' attitudes to work: work is only performed for pay – extrinsic as opposed to intrinsic motivation. As all workers had this attitude, Goldthorpe and Lockwood claim that this orientation to work was brought to work, not created there. Loyalty to the firm can be found anywhere, as long as pay is high. A decrease in wages leads to a downturn in loyalty. Goldthorpe and Lockwood claimed that the process workers, whom Blauner claimed would be highly satisfied, were the most likely to be critical and hostile. Goldthorpe and Lockwood conclude that this is due to the fact that their pay was lower than that of assembly-line workers. Work companionship was also much less likely amongst the process workers.

Critics of Goldthorpe and Lockwood have pointed out that their sample was not representative: it consisted of married men between the ages of 21 and 46, 86 per cent of whom had dependent children, in a town of migrant workers, whose high geographical mobility was caused by moving specifically for the high wages. A high percentage of these affluent workers were downwardly mobile in social terms, possibly from skilled manual workers. In Goldthorpe and Lockwood's study then, there was no support for Blauner's argument that automation will lead to a decrease in alienation.

Mallet

Integration and conflict

Serge Mallet (1963), a French Marxist, does agree with Blauner on this point, believing that greater integration of workers will be a result of increased automation. However, as a Marxist he sees this increased integration amongst workers as helping them develop a political consciousness and realising their common position of conflict with management

and owners. Automation will encourage the proletariat to become a 'class-in-itself'. The workers in automated industry will become the leaders of class struggle. However, the main criticism of Mallet's ideas is that he does not give details of any research to support them.

Gallie

Blauner revisited

Duncan Gallie (1978) has studied the effects of automation in four automated oil refineries, two in France and two in Britain. One of his reasons for carrying out this work was his questioning of the methodology of both Blauner and Mallet. Studying the same industry in two different countries enabled him to assess the effects of technology independent of national or regional factors. Different **cultural** attitudes should not interfere with the findings.

This research found little support for either Blauner or Mallet. Gallie concludes that automation on its own has no effects. There were many differences in attitude between French and British workers, and these could be traced back to historical and cultural differences. A theory which claims that technology on its own can affect job satisfaction ignores the cultural context in which the industry exists. This cultural context is much more influential than the method of production. The most common attitude to work was indifference and this existed in both countries. Workers received similarly high wages, but the British were satisfied with this whilst the French were not. Gallie found a higher level of co-operation and consensus between British workers and management, with antagonism and conflict marking that relationship in the French refineries. Gallie concludes that these differences in job satisfaction are due to the French working class being more committed to socialist values than the British. French management was more autocratic and paternalistic than the British, which led to conflict with the workforce. The role of trade unions was also different, with the French unions taking a left-wing, ideological role, while the British unions were concerned with pay and conditions rather than overthrowing capitalist society.

From these studies, it becomes apparent that attempting to measure job satisfaction and alienation is full of methodological problems. To concentrate on a single factor, such as technology, and ignore the social and cultural context, and other non-technological factors like age, gender, pay and job security may lead to a distorted picture of workers' attitudes to work.

However, there are some factors within the workplace which affect these attitudes:

→ where work is controlled by machines
→ where the task is fragmented
→ where the task is repetitive
→ where the work is unskilled and needs little training
→ where the workers are isolated

There also seems to be a trend towards higher levels of satisfaction in manual jobs as they become automated, while those in the professions may become more dissatisfied as their jobs become automated and bureaucratised.

Beynon

Working for Ford

Huw Beynon's (1973) research argues that informal social groups can create a sense of identity and purpose even in situations where there is a detailed division of labour. In the Ford factory where Beynon's study was carried out, workers were well aware of management's attitudes, and much bitter, shop-floor humour deals with the role of being 'another machine'. In one factory, the standing joke was a tale of a worker who had dropped dead on the line, and the first thing the foreman did was to 'clock him out', ensuring that he would not be paid for any minutes after he had died. Beynon points out that the fact that 'the line never stops' becomes something to be challenged, beaten in various ways. They have to keep up with it, or better still, get ahead of it and have a laugh or half a fag. The line determines pace, and the worker who cannot keep up with it is sacked. Beynon's research shows the attitude of workers to the 'timings':

They decide on their measured day how fast we will work. They seem to forget that we're not machines, you know. The standards they work to are excessive anyway. They expect you to work the 480 minutes of the eight hours you're on the clock. They've agreed to a built-in allowance of six minutes for going to the toilet, blowing your nose and that. It takes you six minutes to get your trousers down.

The speed-up process

Beynon found that the main enemy of the workers was the 'speed-up' process. This means a systematic increase in the pace of work demanded by the line.

Speed up the line, and the workers adjust their pace, working faster, sometimes without being aware of it. 'Making time' – getting a few sections ahead then taking a break – becomes more difficult, and the worker is suspicious. When he started work, the line speed was 30 cars per hour, he left with it moving at 35 cars per hour. So, the workers devise strategies to deal with this, again showing the importance of informal group norms in the workplace. The most effective response is walking out.

The lads said 'sod you', we're not doing it. It worked as good as anything else you know. We just said no, and if they pushed it, we just went home.

Forms of resistance

Walk-outs did not always happen, there were other methods available: sabotage of machinery, pulling the safety wire and stopping the line, deliberately doing a bad job so the work was sent back. Beynon sees this as workers defending the last remaining part of their autonomy to control. These methods are used in other jobs. Ditton's (1977) research into bread delivery drivers shows that they resort to 'fiddling' the books, adding extra on to people's bills. Informal **norms** control the fiddling, ensuring that it does not go too far (for example, it was not fair to 'do' old people). Crusting up stale loaves so they feel fresh through the wrapper and selling them as fresh improves the delivery driver's income and avoids boredom – it's a laugh!

Braverman accuses social science studies of bias towards management, seeing workers as a 'problem' if they use these methods of resistance. Deskilling, speeding up the line and strict supervision all threaten workers' dignity, pride, independence and privacy. These are valuable things, and protecting them is a rational act.

The human relations response

Volvo

The human relations model tries to take account of these ideas. Poor industrial relations are said to be the result of poor communication between management, poor group cohesion and overall weak management. In the human relations model, there is less attention paid to conflicts of interest, and more stress upon harmony and equilibrium. An example of this model in practice is the Volvo car assembly plant at Kalmar, Sweden. In the mid-1970s Volvo attempted to change the nature of assembly-line production from the workers' viewpoint. Jobs would be meaningful and interesting. Technology would not be allowed to set the pace or influence discipline. Volvo turned to the new methods because they had to – workers were definitely not attracted to the car plants, with high absenteeism and people quitting their jobs.

Attitudes to work have changed because people are more informed, more likely to ask questions, and need to understand the reasons behind what they are doing. More rights have been given to unions, there is more control over factors such as lighting, heating, ventilation, and the right to call a halt if there is potential danger. Rules regarding sickness leave and pay are more relaxed. Work has to be made as rewarding as possible with team work, job rotation, talking on the job, in short the 'small workshop atmosphere'. The belt, with all of its connotations of pace-setting and technological control, has been replaced by computer-controlled trolleys, which carry parts around the plant. The workers have been given rest rooms, fridges and saunas, toilets, showers, fitted carpets in the coffee rooms. The human relations model seems to be flourishing there, but the fact that absenteeism is still high (around 12 per cent) shows that workers are not all that keen to get involved in this way. Critics say that it is the nature of Swedish society which forced these changes. From a Marxist viewpoint, the workers are still there to make profits for the employer and are exploited because the full value of their labour is not paid for. The 'softer' management methods are just a new facet of ruling-class ideology.

Zuboff's work (1988) seeks to understand the impact of computers on the experience of work. Looking primarily at eight workplaces that were introducing or extending the use of information technology, she relates the impact of these changes by employment type. For workers whose experience had been mainly in manual labour, physical skills were being replaced by what she calls 'intellective' ones, requiring them to deal with a greater amount of information on a screen in directing the production process. For white-collar workers at an insurance company, computers reduced both the physical aspects of their work (for example, standing up to file a piece of paper) as well as the need for face-to-face interaction with others and opportunities to use their initiative. It meant that 'jobs which had once allowed them to use their bodily presence in the service of interpersonal exchange and collaboration now required their bodily presence in the service of a machine. Jobs that had once required their voices now insisted that they be mute.' Many also began to feel overqualified for the tasks they were now being asked to complete.

Computers, according to Zuboff, have also greatly increased the ability of management to control, survey and monitor their workers' output. In a telecommunications company, and with clear echoes of Taylorism, computers were used to give out work tasks, as well as work out how long it should take to do them, as well as estimate how efficiently the job had been done. In other workplaces computers were also used to identify which work was at fault when something went wrong. Surveillance also took place hierarchically, with computers being used to analyse the performance of employees through all layers of the company's management structure.

In other places of work, computers were having an opposite effect on hierarchies within companies, for example using computer conferencing to enable the sharing of ideas and information across a pharmaceuticals company, although this facility was withdrawn by senior management during the course of her research.

Computers at work can therefore be used to promote and share information (to 'informate') or to increase control over workers (to 'automate'). The direction taken by an organisation is dependent on how people use computers, rather than how computers use them – smart people using the machine or smart machines using people. In her own view, the choices that need to be made will ultimately have to be used primarily to 'informate'. Kling (1996), however, argues that, while computers can have a major impact on work, the extent of this impact depends entirely on how they are used within the workplace. In some instances, they can enhance the image of an enterprise as modern and efficient without making any tangible efficiency gains at all, as in the case of an urban management information system in the USA. The role they play in enskilling or deskilling (see p. 238) will vary from job to job, and work organisation has only been dramatically changed in very specific sectors such as banking and copy-typing.

The study of work satisfaction has not been confined to the workplace. Many studies of housework now exist, following Oakley's 1974 study. Calculating women's domestic tasks as consuming an average 77 hours per week, Oakley also found that attitudes to housework were similar to those found in factory work, it being seen as tedious, repetitious and routine. Young mothers in particular expressed resentment and dissatisfaction at the role they were now playing, regardless of how valuable they knew their contribution to be. Significantly, Schwartz Cowan (1983) found that technology in the home has made housework no easier, more satisfying or less time consuming.

The wide range of research into work satisfaction and orientations to work shows us that the attempt to isolate out single factors, such as the use of technology, as determinant is unlikely to bear fruit. A sense of satisfaction or alienation at work depends on a number of aspects including the technology used, the involvement of staff, the pay and conditions of employment, the strength of union organisation and worker resistance as well as factors external to the labour process, such as the pre-existing attitudes that people bring to work. Orientations to work – whether it is seen merely as a means to an end such as a wage (instrumentalism) or is seen as intrinsically useful and beneficial – are equally complex. Devine's (1992) research into 'affluent workers' at the same car plant studied by Goldthorpe and Lockwood three decades earlier showed that job security had become as pressing a concern as securing the highest pay possible, while overall attitudes to work were influenced by a wide range of external factors such as stage in the life cycle, the state of the housing market and the national political environment. The experience of work, then, is also part of the experience of **stratification**, particularly class, and the issues analysed under the headings of embourgeoisement and proletarianisation.

Trade unions and professional associations

The interests of most of those in the world of employment are organisationally divided into three sectors: trade unions, representing manual and white-collar workers, professional associations representing more senior and higher status employees and employers' organisations representing employers, such as the Confederation of British Industry and the Institute of Directors. At the same time, many employers and employees are unrepresented by any organisation. All three types of organisation have long histories, paralleling the growth of industrial societies. It is since the Second World War, and the growth of corporatism, that they have been of particular interest to sociologists.

Corporatism

Corporatism is a term used to describe the phenomenon of the State co-operating with employers' organisations and trade unions to formulate an industrial policy, principally aimed at smoothing the process of bargaining over wages and conditions of service without undue industrial strife. In Britain, this 'voluntary corporatism' was exemplified at a national level by the creation of the National Economic Development Council in 1962, made up of members of trade unions, employers' organisations and representatives of the Conservative government, and taken further with the creation of a National Enterprise Board under Labour in 1975. At a local level it involved a move to **industrial democracy** through the increasing involvement of trade union shop stewards in processes of negotiation and consultation.

Richard Hyman (1989) offers a number of reasons for the emergence of corporatism in Britain: first, the State desired to intervene in wage settlements in order to control inflation; secondly the State itself had become increasingly involved as a major employer as more and more industries and services became nationalised; and thirdly the co-operation of the other two sides of this tripartite agreement could be useful in solving wider social and economic problems.

Trade-union power

Over time, however, the perception grew that trade unions had become too powerful, out of control and were overstepping the line between industrial relations policy and wider political concerns. This had become apparent as early as 1968, when the government-commissioned Donovan Report remarked that 'Britain has two systems of industrial relations. The one is the formal system embodied in the official institutions. The other is the informal system created by the actual behaviour of trade unions and employers' associations.' In other words, the national system was failing to work. Hyman himself claims that this was because the status of national union leaders was deliberately overstated in order to gain the co-operation of their membership.

Fear of trade-union militancy grew throughout the 1970s, with miners' strikes bringing down the Heath government in 1974, culminating in the Labour government's inability to prevent the 1978/9 'winter of discontent' when many unions, in both the private and the public sector, refused to obey government-imposed limits to wage rises. Ostracised by the hostile Conservative governments from 1979, they left the NEDC in 1982 and the era of corporatism had effectively come to an end, to be replaced by the discipline of more anonymous 'market forces' and a series of measures designed to deregulate the labour market by the Conservative government.

Trade unions

Trade unions became effective when they were made legal in the nineteenth century, following the repeal of the Combinations Acts in the 1820s, allowing workers to collectively represent themselves and protect their interests in the workplace through their union and eventually at a national level through the Trades Union Congress, dating from 1868. Having first embraced skilled workers, union membership filtered down to semi-skilled and unskilled workers by the end of the nineteenth century. Membership continued to grow throughout the twentieth century up to the early 1980s. At its maximum in 1980 more than 50 per cent of the registered workforce were members of unions (see *Figure 9.6*).

European trade unions

The main purpose of trade unions is to collectively protect the interests of their members, particularly with regard to their pay, conditions of service and employment rights. British trade unions can be distinguished from many others in the industrial world in a number of ways. First, because they organise not by plant or employer, as for example in Germany ('industrial unionism'), but by trade. In a place of work there may therefore be a number of different unions which may co-operate through joint shop stewards' committees. A second difference is their relatively high density of membership, i.e. the

percentage of unionised members of the workforce compared with the overall workforce.

As we know from the work of Duncan Gallie, trade unions in France and Britain, for example, interpret their role differently, with French trade unions being more willing to see themselves as **ideological** leaders, trying to raise the political consciousness of their members, and entering into wage negotiations at a national level, removing most workers from the decision-making process. This means, Gallie argues, that French and British workers have different attitudes to their work and their employers.

During the twentieth century, as unions became part of the apparatus of industrial relations, they also became increasingly organised and bureaucratised, employing full-time officials and a hierarchical power structure, mirroring the structure of the firms their members work for. For many writers, the existence of legitimate, organised unionism has reduced the potential for conflict, easing their transition into becoming conduits of the dominant value system.

Functionalism

This observation informs much of the functionalist view of unionism. For writers such as Parsons and Davis and Moore (see chapter 3) the value consensus in society implies that a consensus similarly exists between employers and employees, where benefits are made from working co-operatively, with each having their own particular role. Strikes are explained as minor problems of communication and adjustment or as necessary breaks from the monotony of work. In stable democracies, union officials provide a line of communication to the workforce for the management, preventing unofficial (or 'wildcat') strikes, not sanctioned by the union. They are not seen as agents of class conflict.

Pluralist theorists are more willing to recognise differences of interest between employers, seeking to keep costs down, and employees, seeking to use their union to maximise wages. These differences are not so great, however, that they prevent co-operation and coexistence. Conflict, where it exists, can be minimalised through institutionalised annual pay rounds, agencies such as ACAS and industrial tribunals. The emphasis here is on trade unions as incorporated rather than marginalised organisations, participators in the process of creating an industrial and social democracy. This vision, put forward by writers such as Ralf Dahrendorf (1959) in Britain, and Lipset (1964) in America, seems less plausible now,

Figure 9.6 Trade-union membership in the UK (millions)

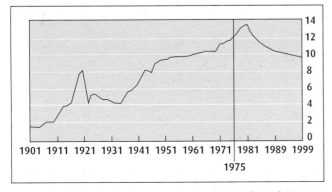

Source: *Social Trends* 30, 2000

given the developments of the last two decades, as well as the high level of strikes throughout the 1970s.

Feminist writers have been sharply critical of the role played by unions throughout industrialisation, seeing them as patriarchal organisations formed partly to keep women out of paid labour. Writers such as Rubery (1980) and Walby (1986) claim that they contribute to the genderisation of labour by preventing the claims of women as skilled workers being recognised, while seeking to maintain the definition of some men's work as skilled, for example in clerical, textile and engineering work. Even in unions with a largely female membership, it remains the case that the majority of full-time officials are male.

Marxism

Marxism views trade unions with ambivalence. At one level, they are evidence of the existence of a separate working-class consciousness, formed to resist exploitation at the hands of the bourgeoisie. At another level there is the belief that trade unions can only ever develop an 'economistic' level of consciousness, concerned more with improving the lot of workers under capitalism than struggling for a new social formation or tackling the issue of control over the labour process. Only a revolutionary party can unite the trade-union movement towards this end. More than a hundred years after the death of Marx, unions show very little sign of wanting to negotiate more than the terms of their obedience to employers. For some writers they have failed even in this limited ambition, being unable to prevent mass unemployment, the collapse of the manufacturing sector in the early 1980s or a substantial decline in union membership.

In the last twenty-five years, unions have undergone a series of changes to their legal and political powers. The Employment Acts passed by the Conservative government in 1980, 1982, 1988 and 1990, as well as the Trade Union Acts of 1984 and 1993 (which Hyman describes as a campaign of 'coercive pacification') restricted and weakened trade-union activity and the return of mass unemployment meant that membership began to fall steadily to the present day, both in absolute terms and as a percentage of the civilian workforce in employment. Between 1978 and 1987, for example, membership fell from 13.1 million to 10.2 million, while registered unemployment rose from 5.7 per cent to 10.7 per cent, reaching 13.5 per cent in 1985. By 1999, only 33 per cent of the labour force belonged to a trade

union. This picture, however, is complicated by a number of factors, particularly the changing composition of the workforce, shifting away from men working full time in manual jobs. At the same time, the number of strikes, measured in days lost per worker, has also fallen to an all-time low. In 1993, Wage Councils, setting a minimum wage in some industries, were abolished.

The debate on trade unions

For some writers (for example Purcell, 1982 and Bassett, 1987) the power and influence of trade unions has been fatally damaged, particularly because of the changing composition of the workforce and the changing nature of employment terms and conditions. Thus the 'traditional' blue-collar male trade unionist, working full-time as part of a close-knit industrial community, is disappearing, being superseded by more part-time, white-collar and female workers, none of whom are usually associated with the class consciousness necessary for solidaristic action. The introduction of compulsory competitive tendering in the public sector has also allowed some public-sector employees to favour non-unionised companies. At the same time, there has been a growth in individually, rather than collectively negotiated contracts, performance-related pay and the implementation of the practice of human resource management and total quality management, emphasising the importance of individual commitment to enterprises. All of these have worked against the existing trade-union philosophy of collective action.

Other writers (such as Kelly, 1988 and Grint, 1991), however, argue that the diminution of trade-union power has been overstated, and that it is more realistic to see a pattern of stability and continuity. Union organisation and collective bargaining remain intact, and many national agreements continue to exist. The number of union convenors and shop stewards has not markedly fallen, and in areas such as public-sector employment union membership has actually increased. The cause of the decline in overall membership can be found not in the changes listed above but in the fact of the downturn in the business cycle. Union membership and strength will therefore be restored with an upturn in the business cycle. It remains the case that wages have continued to exceed the rate of inflation, and significant victories have been won in areas such as the railways and motor vehicle industries. New industrial relations practices, such as the introduction of no-strike agreements, have received a lot of publicity but have not become widespread. They are confined to new companies, particularly those from the Far East, that have set up in Britain. Similarly, new legislation has not been widely used by employers. Compulsory ballots on union and political affiliation have shown overwhelming support for Labour Party membership. Finally, doubts have been expressed about the allegedly low level of class consciousness and the existence of a golden age of class solidarity. Trade unions have survived hostile conditions before, particularly in the inter-war years, and they will successfully survive them again.

Trade unions in the future

Trade unions are undoubtedly under pressure to change. Those most willing to change are characterised as modernists or realists and those wishing to resist change are seen as traditionalists or dinosaurs. Some have earned the wrath of other trade unionists by being willing to enter into single-union and no-strike agreements and other unions have had to merge or consider merging, leading to the phenomenon of 'conglomerate unionism'. Many hope for improved fortunes with economic upturn and the election of a Labour government, though they will not necessarily benefit from either.

Professional associations

Higher and lower professions

Professionals differ from manual and routine non-manual workers in that they specialise in the development and dissemination of technical knowledge. Following the Registrar-General's classification (see also chapter 3) they can be split into two levels – the higher professions, including lawyers, architects and doctors, and the lower professions (sometimes also described as semi-professionals) made up of occupations such as teachers, nurses and social workers. What distinguishes these two levels is the extent of training and qualifications needed to take up these posts.

It is the task of professional associations in particular to define and preserve the standards and ethics necessary to each profession. Thus it is the relative success of organisations such as the British Medical Association, founded in 1832, in defining the standards and ethics required of medical practitioners that has allowed this group to be accepted as being of professional status.

Professional associations are normally thought to represent the interests of the higher professions, the Law Society in the case of the legal profession and the British Medical Association in the case of doctors. The status of groups representing the lower professions is less clear. In some ways they clearly have the character of the higher professions in terms of status and tradition, in others they more closely resemble trade unions, being increasingly more inclined to engage in the kind of collective actions typical of traditional unions. This is particularly true of teaching unions and, increasingly, nursing.

In the 1980s almost all professional groups came under fire from a Conservative government which perceived their existence as a restriction on the free market for labour. Traditionally autonomous groups such as lawyers and doctors found themselves targeted for professional restrictive practices, as with the control of house conveyancing by solicitors, or barristers' claims to sole representation (or 'right of audience') of clients before the upper courts. Significantly, however, lawyers, through their professional associations, have been one of the few groups to resist such attacks successfully and their monopoly remains, in practice if not in law.

Functionalism

The discussion in chapter 4 on sociological perspectives of the medical profession is also relevant to this discussion of professional associations. Thus, from a functionalist point of view, the professions, through their associations, are a microcosm of a cohesive moral community, the ethics of which will, according to Barber (1963) and Halmos (1970), following Durkheim, spread out into the whole of society, particularly industry, setting a model of consumer relations (see also Parsons, 1951). They also integrate professionals into an occupational group, providing ethical standards and a code of practice. Because they serve the community, as well as their clients, professionals are consequently highly rewarded for playing their roles and given high status.

Other writers (for example Johnson, 1972) have argued that professions have gained their status not through altruism but self-interest, by preventing competition to keep their market value high and by encouraging the public to believe their services are necessary rather than optional. In the words of the Parrys (1976), this amounts to a 'strategy for controlling an occupation in which colleagues set up a system of self-government' in which the professional associations play a central role. This forms the core of the neo-Weberian view, emphasising occupational closure, through the control of training, supply and entry, and the claim that their behaviour is exemplary and necessarily self-regulating, preventing others from performing the same tasks, as doctors achieved with the Medical Registration Act of 1858, following the formation of the BMA in 1832. Teachers professionalised later and therefore failed to gain such a strong hold on their profession, failing, for example, to control entry to it.

Marxism

Marxists believe that this emphasis on autonomy is overstated, seeing the professions instead as agents of capital, with the higher professions in particular occupying an intermediary position between the bourgeoisie and the proletariat. They are increasingly losing their independence and are becoming directly employed by the bourgeoisie in large companies. Following Braverman, this perspective sees the end of this process as an accelerating division of labour and the proletarianisation of the lower professions in particular (see also chapter 3).

From a neo-Marxist perspective, Ehrenreich and Ehrenreich (1979) break with the orthodox two-class Marxist analysis in claiming that a professional-managerial class, not owning the means of production but 'whose major function may broadly be described as the reproduction of capitalist culture and capitalist class relations', exists between the bourgeoisie and the proletariat. This class exists like any other, empirically distinct through its own reproduction, but paid out of the surplus produced by the proletariat, although the professional-managerial class are also wage labourers. Professional associations serve to maintain the independence of this class from the ruling class, although ultimately their interest is in maintaining the capitalist system.

The perhaps obvious criticism from within Marxism of this theory is that it does not take into account the proletarianising tendencies that exist within the professions that other Marxists such as Braverman claim, even though as fellow Americans they are all aware that the professions in the USA are better organised than they are in Europe. In both continents it is the case that professionals are increasingly becoming directly employed by large organisations as in-house workers. Other neo-Marxists such as Erik Olin Wright (1985) deny the existence of a separate

class of professionals but see them instead as occupying a **contradictory class location**, possessing some of the characteristics of the other two classes.

These organisations may therefore be seen as serving a primarily integrative role; as largely autonomous organisations self-interestedly defining their own role; or as agents of capital subject to the control and direction of the bourgeoisie. Since the Second World War, they have come under the increasing scrutiny of the State, initially with the aim of co-ordinating industrial policy. More recently they have struggled to sustain their identity and position in an increasingly deregulated and insecure labour market.

Questions

1 How do Weberians view the professions?
2 How has the position of trade unions changed since the Second World War?
3 How important are political factors in determining the role of these organisations?

Work and non-work
Unemployment

Unemployment and the sociological imagination

When, in a city of 100,000, only one man is unemployed, that is his personal trouble, and for its relief we properly look to the character of the man, his skills, and his immediate opportunities. But when in a nation of 50 million employees, 15 million men are unemployed, that is an issue, and we may not hope to find its solution within the range of opportunities open to any one individual. The very structure of opportunities has collapsed. Both the correct statement of the problem and the range of possible solutions require us to consider the economic and political institutions of the society, and not merely the personal situation of a scatter of individuals.

C. Wright Mills, 1959

Measurement of unemployment

Unemployment statistics are among the most controversial statistics issued by governments. Until 1913, for example, the figures were collected not by the State but by the trade unions operating unemployment benefit schemes. The Department of Employment, from whom unemployment statistics now originate, considers that only statistics collected since 1923 are truly accurate, particularly in showing fluctuations in unemployment. There are six different estimates of the level for 1921, for example. In the inter-war period, the changing status of some workers as insured confuses the picture because unemployment insurance schemes were the main way of gauging unemployment levels.

Since the National Assistance and National Insurance Acts of the late 1940s, the unemployment figure is believed to be more reliable and consistent. This figure included anyone drawing **unemployment benefit** and those, such as school leavers, newly arrived immigrants and married women, who were registered at the Department of Employment as seeking work but not entitled to draw benefit.

Statistical massaging?

Following the election of the Conservative government in 1979, and the rapid rise in unemployment in the early 1980s, the official measurement of unemployment was changed nineteen times up to 1987. For example, those on youth training schemes who would otherwise be unemployed, those seeking part-time work only, and those seeking work but not registered unemployed were all excluded. At the same time, the number of people in the labour force was increased by adding the self-employed. The number of people unemployed as a percentage of the labour force therefore automatically decreased. As unemployment is a highly political issue, the way in which the number of

unemployed is calculated has become the subject of debate not only between sociologists, but politicians as well. Arguments persist as to what the 'real' rate of unemployment is, with those on the Right suggesting that some of those registered as unemployed are not genuinely seeking work (as they may, for example, be already working in the **hidden economy**), and those on the Left arguing that many more people are in fact unemployed than the official statistics show. Given these reservations, it is nevertheless possible to construct a picture of unemployment in the United Kingdom in the twentieth century (see *Figure 9.7*).

Region

An analysis of unemployment by region shows that, traditionally, the hardest-hit areas tend to be those furthest from the metropolitan centre. Hence, the areas worst hit by unemployment in the twentieth century have been Northern Ireland, Scotland (particularly Strathclyde), South Wales, the North-East and North-West regions of England, as well as the West Midlands. Within these areas, it has been in the industries most closely associated with the Industrial Revolution – coal, steel, shipbuilding, textiles and mechanical engineering – that the highest rates have been recorded.

Figure 9.7   Numbers unemployed, UK, 1900–96

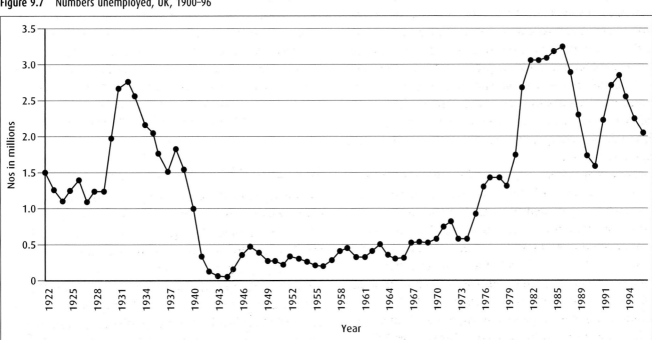

Source: Halsey and Webb, 2000

Figure 9.8   Rates of unemployment by region

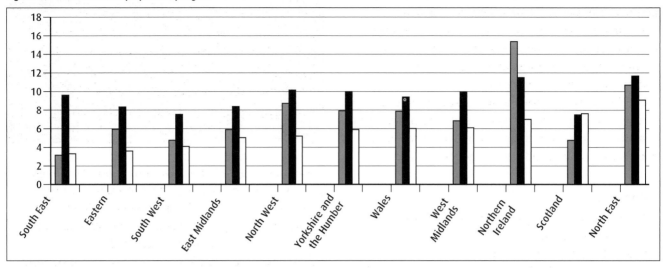

Source: *Social Trends* 25, 1995 and 32, 2002

Changing geography of unemployment

In the 1990s, however, the geography of unemployment has altered radically, with falls in Northern Ireland and substantial increases in the traditionally high employment areas of the South East, the South West and East Anglia. This is because of the 'white-collar' character of the early 1990s recession, with substantial job losses being suffered in financial services, as well as in construction, mining, and the manufacture of cars and computers. It is therefore becoming simplistic and inaccurate to say that unemployment is a particular problem for the North rather than the South, inner-city rather than suburban areas, and industrial rather than urban areas. Post-war unemployment is no longer confined to areas where heavy industry was the main source of jobs. Towards the end of the 1990s, however, a more familiar pattern of regional unemployment was restored, as *Figure 9.8* shows.

Age

By age, the highest percentage of those unemployed are men over 50 and both sexes under 30 (see *Table 9.10*). In absolute terms it is men and women in their twenties who have been hardest hit. The likelihood of experiencing long-term unemployment (more than twelve months of continuous unemployment) increases with age, though older people may also see themselves

Table 9.10   Unemployment rates: by gender and age, UK (%)

	1992	1993	1994	1995	1996	1997	1998	1999	2000	2001
Males										
16–17	17.7	18.5	18.8	19.2	21.3	19.6	18.1	21.5	20.1	17.7
18–24	19.0	21.1	19.3	17.7	17.2	14.8	13.1	12.6	11.8	10.9
25–44	10.5	10.9	10.2	8.9	8.7	6.9	5.7	5.6	4.8	4.3
45–54	8.4	9.4	8.6	7.6	6.4	6.1	4.7	4.9	4.8	3.5
55–59	11.2	12.3	11.6	10.3	9.8	8.0	6.7	6.4	5.4	3.9
60–64	10.2	14.2	11.6	9.9	8.9	7.6	6.9	6.4	5.8	5.2
65 and over	4.9	4.6	3.7..	4.0	4.1	..	..	..	..	
All aged 16 and over	*11.5*	*12.4*	*11.4*	*10.1*	*9.6*	*8.1*	*6.8*	*6.7*	*6.1*	*5.3*
Females										
16–17	14.0	15.1	16.9	15.5	15.3	16.0	15.3	14.0	16.9	12.5
18–24	11.0	12.9	11.8	11.6	10.2	9.8	9.4	9.3	8.5	7.8
25–44	7.3	7.3	7.0	6.7	6.3	5.4	5.1	4.8	4.5	4.1
45–54	5.0	5.0	5.0	4.5	4.1	3.7	3.1	3.2	2.9	2.4
55–59	4.5	6.0	6.5	4.7	4.3	4.8	3.5	3.5	3.1	2.0
60 and over	3.1	3.9	2.9	..	..	2.1	2.0	1.9	..	..
All aged 16 and over	*7.3*	*7.6*	*7.3*	*6.8*	*6.3*	*5.7*	*5.3*	*5.1*	*4.8*	*4.2*

Source: *Labour Force Survey*, Office for National Statistics

as 'prematurely retired', which is how unemployed men over the age of 60 are officially classified.

As *Table 9.11* shows, all ethnic minorities endure higher rates of unemployment than whites, with the highest rates recorded among blacks and Pakistanis/Bangladeshis. The pattern of unemployment therefore shows that rates are highest for the young, particularly men, and particularly those from ethnic minorities. As such, this picture closely mirrors that of educational achievement.

Questions

1 Why might sociologists be wary of official statistics on unemployment?
2 Is full employment possible?

Causes of unemployment

The only sovereign remedy yet discovered by democracies for unemployment is total war.

W. Beveridge, 1944

Unemployment, a term first coined in the 1880s, has been a persistent but periodic problem in modern British socio-economic life. Its most severe periods have been in the inter-war period, and at the start of the 1980s and 1990s, though some writers believe that the experiences of pre- and post-Second World War unemployment are not comparable. This is because of the relative lack of post-war protest against unemployment, compared with the continuous campaigns of inter-war organisations such as the National Unemployed Workers Movement (see Croucher, 1987), changes in attitudes to work, leisure, and the existence of universal benefits. Nevertheless, the causes of unemployment remain hotly debated within the world of politics, sociology and economics.

Table 9.11 Unemployment rates by ethnic group and age, 2000–01, UK (%)

	16–24	25–34	35–44	45–59/64	All aged 16–59/64
White	11	5	4	4	5
Black	32	14	11	10	15
Indian	13	5	7	6	7
Pakistani/ Bangladeshi	28	14	12	..	17
Other groups	24	9	11	7	12
All ethnic groups	12	5	4	4	6

Source: *Social Trends* 32, 2002

W. BEVERIDGE (1879–1963)

British social reformer, politician and architect of the Welfare State. Early in his life Beveridge campaigned for old age pensions, free school meals and government action to help the unemployed. As a civil servant he produced the Beveridge Report, which became the blueprint for the modern welfare state in Britain.

Common-sense ideas about unemployment might point to idleness, people getting too much on the dole, too many people living in Great Britain, or new technology taking away people's jobs. Very few of these ideas are academically accepted. The unemployment of the last twenty years cannot easily be explained by sudden mass outbreaks of laziness or increases in unemployment benefit.

Different types of unemployment are identifiable. *Frictional unemployment* refers to the unemployment of workers temporarily between jobs, or in the process of being matched to a job. This type of unemployment can exist in times of full employment.

Structural unemployment exists when the occupational and industrial structure of the economy changes. Unemployed workers need to be retrained or relocated into new jobs, if there are any.

Seasonal unemployment affects workers whose jobs only exist during certain periods of the year. It is expected that, for example, unemployment rates will rise in agriculture, construction and tourism in the winter months, and seasonal adjustments are made to unemployment statistics to reveal the underlying rate.

For Marx (1867), unemployment is an intrinsic part of capitalism, which would worsen as capitalism develops. This development would be cyclical, with periods of boom followed by periods of bust, although the boom periods would become shorter and shorter, while downturns would become progressively longer and more frequent. Each expansion and contraction of the economy creates a reserve army of labour who are employed as profits rise and laid off again as they fall. Increasing unemployment allows wage rates to fall and profit levels to be restored as workers are forced to accept whatever employment and wage rates they can find. For a wide range of reasons (detailed in *Capital*), rates of profit become increasingly difficult to maintain and workers are squeezed harder and harder, as the slumps in production become longer and longer, and unemployment rises relentlessly. A class-conscious proletariat realises it has no option but to take control of the means of production to end the economic chaos that is capitalism. Unemployment is therefore both part of the misery that capitalism creates, and a central cause of its downfall.

Keynes's *General Theory*

For many writers, the long period of more-or-less full employment following the end of the Second World War can be explained by the adoption, at governmental level, of the economic ideas of John Maynard Keynes (1883–1946). Put briefly (though explained fully by Keynes, 1936), Keynes believed that the State could intervene in the workings of the market economy, stimulate demand, and keep unemployment low. The belief that Keynes had solved the problem of unemployment is clearly put by Michael Stewart (1972): 'the basic fact is that, with the acceptance of the General Theory, the days of uncontrollable mass unemployment in advanced industrial countries are over. Other economic problems may threaten; this one, at least, has passed into history.'

The New Right

Such certainties dissolved in the 1970s with the breeching of full employment levels, and the appearance of simultaneous rising inflation and economic stagnation: 'stagflation'. It was the persistence of stagflation, and Keynesianism's apparent inability to deal with it, that led to the revival of monetarist theory in economics, and the New Right in politics. From this point of view, unemployment occurs because of impediments to the smooth workings of the labour market. As Patrick Minford (1982) argues: 'the proximate cause of unemployment is excessive high wage costs, produced either by high wages or by low productivity'. There are, he says, two major distortions in the UK labour market which prevent real wages and productivity from adjusting naturally to shifts in technology, demand and industrial structure, and from relocating

J.M. KEYNES (1883–1946)

A Cambridge economist who produced a major work called *The General Theory of Employment, Interest and Money* (1936). He believed that governments could have a major role to play in introducing economic policies to reduce or eliminate unemployment.

those freed from one sector into other sectors. These are the operation of the unemployment benefit system and the power of trade unions to raise wages relative to non-union wages.

New technology

One of the most popular beliefs concerning unemployment is the role played by new automation taking the place of human labour. There are two arguments here. On one side, the labour-replacing nature of automation is uncritically accepted. However, others point out that automation and robotisation will increase productivity (and therefore economic growth) and free labour to undertake other productive tasks. For Marx, if machinery ultimately comes to take the place of labour, then the creation of surplus value cannot occur.

Those who see new technology as unimportant point out that the introduction of technology is a constant feature of the process of industrialisation, and cannot therefore account for rises and falls in unemployment. This is disputed by Jones (1986) who argues that information technology is having consequences not witnessed since the earlier days of the Industrial Revolution. This is because, unlike other new technologies, microelectronics allows output in industry to be increased while inputs such as capital and energy, and particularly labour, can continually be reduced. The service sector, he says, will suffer job losses most dramatically, leading to a social choice between the possibility of leisure for all, involving the restructuring of work commitments, or unemployment for a growing number.

If automation does lead to unemployment, then it leads to severe consequences for the economy at a macro or national level. In the first place, it means the State takes on a heavier burden in paying unemployment benefits, and secondly, those still working are taxed more heavily (directly or indirectly) to meet this cost.

Equilibrium

The return to mass unemployment since the mid-1970s has provided the opportunity to test the accuracy of two theories of unemployment: the equilibrium theory and the saturation of labour markets theory. In the first, which is closely allied to classical or New Right thinking on unemployment, areas of high unemployment will produce low wages, while areas of full employment witness wage rises.

Equilibrium will result as workers move from low to high wage regions (the thinking behind the former Conservative MP Norman Tebbit's famous 'Get on your bike' speech) and employers relocate from high wage to low wage regions. There is little evidence that this did in fact happen in the 1980s.

Saturation

In the second theory, new jobs will be created not in areas of high unemployment, but in areas of low unemployment and economic buoyancy. This is because the workers in these areas already possess the skills that new industries need and other services are also available, whereas workers in high unemployment areas have only the skills of outmoded industries, and need to be retrained, an expensive option for many growth industries. The saturation theory best explains the pattern of unemployment in the 1980s, although it should also be noted that some of the new businesses of the late 1980s and early 1990s also encountered severe problems.

The full employment Beveridge wrote of was defined by him as less than 3 per cent of the workforce unemployed. Britain has therefore experienced continuous mass unemployment since 1975, though during the 1990s this rate began to fall to a point where it was one of the lowest in the industrial world (see *Table 9.12*).

A number of reasons have been given for this change, including the possibility that the statistics do not accurately reflect the full extent of unemployment in the United Kingdom (see p. 257). For Jackman (1998), this could simply be due to Britain experiencing its cyclical upturn before other countries, though, he argues, other factors are discernible. Alongside persistently low inflation, the reduction in trade union power and lower benefit levels have both increased the demand for labour, while the introduction of the Jobseeker's Allowance in 1996 may have had the effect of obliging more claimants to take up paid labour, though insufficient research exists to confirm or deny this last claim.

The Labour government, coming to power in 1997, is keen to claim the credit for the reduction of unemployment, citing such policies as the 'New Deal', employment zones and the institution of a minimum wage as major contributors. Critics of this claim, however, are quick to point out that unemployment was falling before the Labour Party was elected, just as many other economic indicators were improving. The real test of the government's policies will be their ability to withstand other factors such as a downturn in global production.

Questions

1 What factors can cause unemployment?
2 How can governments help increase or reduce unemployment?

The effects of unemployment

How unemployment has been experienced is of great interest to sociologists. The main findings are that it is experienced differently according to social group, the amount of time employed prior to unemployment and the amount of social support, though whether you are young or old, male or female, black or white, working class or middle class is also seen as important.

Social class

Social class is seen as important by sociologists because unemployment may affect different areas of life for different social classes. Ashton (1986) argues that 'if you are a doctor for whom work is a central life-interest and you lose your job, the experience is likely to be different from that of an assembly-line worker for whom work is boring, monotonous and physically demanding'. The main impact is felt in three areas: work identity, financial situation and identity within the family. For the doctor, he says, the main problem will be that his social identity through work will be threatened. This will not be the same for the assembly-line worker, where the main problems are that on losing their job they will have only short-term financial security, while their family identity (as breadwinner) will be threatened by unemployment, in a way that their work identity will not. These three areas are least problematic for females seeking part-time work, mainly housewives returning to the job market.

Table 9.12 Unemployment as a percentage of the labour force in selected countries, 1992–2002

Year	United Kingdom	EU average	France	Germany	G7 nations
1992	10.2	9.1	10.0	6.4	7.0
1996	8.2	10.2	11.9	8.7	6.8
1998	6.3	9.4	11.4	9.1	6.4
2002	5.2	7.5	8.7	8.2	6.4

Source: *Labour Market Trends*, Office for National Statistics, 2002

Youth unemployment

For youths, the problem is mainly that the possibility of having a work identity is threatened, while access to adult status is delayed and dependence on the family is enhanced. Social class is also a factor here, with work and success seen as of central significance to the attainment of young people's self-identity. This will be undermined by long-term unemployment. Lower working-class youths, who do not expect much from work, have in any case developed ways of 'doing nothing' and what frustrates them is lack of money. For them, unemployment is 'just part of the everyday experience of the labour market' (Ashton, 1986) mitigated by membership of peer groups.

The growth of government youth training schemes since the late 1970s has attracted the critical attention of many sociologists. The number of schemes points to the depth and extent of youth unemployment, which in turn has been seen as a reflection of the fact that the number of unskilled jobs has declined, that part-time service sector jobs are taken by married women, and that traditional 'school-leaver' jobs in clerical work are being replaced because of new office technology.

Paul Thompson (1983) argues that, first, these training schemes are evidence that schools, contrary to Bowles and Gintis (1976), do not train youths directly for work, and secondly, that such schemes are mainly designed to produce a pool of semi-skilled workers prepared to receive low wages in a newly restructured youth labour market.

Gender

The picture for young women is different (as Griffin argues, 1985). Young females rely more on work as a means of breaking out of the parental home and domestic isolation. If they cannot do this, they are likely to be obliged to take on additional domestic responsibilities. For women who have left home but cohabit with a partner, being without work means any financial independence they may have is threatened. Several sociologists, however, have argued that, as women's main source of identity is as mother and housewife, and work will be fitted in with domestic responsibilities, their identity is unthreatened by unemployment. For women working full time, this does not apply to the same extent.

Ethnicity

For people from ethnic minorities, the problem of unemployment is compounded by **racism** in employment practices, despite the fact that this is illegal. According to Roberts (1984), unemployment among Afro-Caribbean school-leavers was 40 per cent above that for whites even where they had left school with superior qualifications. They have more difficulty in finding work, and will be out of work for longer if they lose their jobs. Once they are convinced that this is happening because they are black they may then retreat into ethnic subcultures such as Rastafarianism, refusing to work for whites and do their 'trash' jobs.

Unemployment and health

Given that different groups experience unemployment differently, there is general agreement that unemployment usually has deleterious effects on mental and physical health: 'it is not in serious dispute that research shows that unemployment can impair psychological health in many people' (Haworth and Evans, 1987).

Sinfield (1981) suggests that the psychological pattern following redundancy is firstly to feel shocked or surprised, then optimistic, then pessimistic and finally fatalistic as the adjustment to the idea that unemployment will not be short-lived is made. The initial feeling that an unexpected holiday has been gained, giving opportunities to undertake jobs around the house and to use time as they please becomes a meaningless, unremitting series of unremarkable, uneventful days with nothing to look forward to, as this quotation from Binns and Mars (1984) shows: 'I'll tell you about daily life. I sit in this chair peeking out of a wee slit in the window looking at the world. Not that it changes much from day to day, though somebody did take away the railings this morning. That was interesting.'

In general, then, unemployment has a wide range of effects on the unemployed, challenging their ability to structure time, maintain a sense of identity, to survive a severe decline in income and cutbacks in expenditure, and maintain the relationships they had with family and friends while employed. As Sinfield (1981) notes, unemployment also affects those in employment in making them feel less secure and less able to bargain for higher wages. It also restricts their ability to leave jobs where they feel unhappy and allows some groups to **scape-goat** others for causing unemployment or taking jobs. The imperative on employers to promote equal opportunities is also weakened as the pool to recruit from expands. The combined effect of these factors, Sinfield says, means unemployment 'devalues or debases the standard or quality of life in society'.

HOW THE UK FILLS ITS DAY

Mostly sleeping, eating, watching TV

The Time Use Survey, conducted in 2000, showed that eating, working, sleeping and watching TV are what people in the UK do most. These activities take up more than half the day. A third of the day is spent sleeping.

On weekdays, 77 per cent of adults are awake and up by 8 am. Forty five per cent then work or study until at least 4 pm. Afterwards, people do housework, eat or do some form of leisure activity. Main meal times fall between 8 am and 9.30 am, at 1 pm, and from 5 pm to 9 pm. By midnight, 81 per cent of adults are asleep, 12 per cent are still enjoying some free time and 4 per cent are working or travelling.

At the weekend, people tend to get up later (69 per cent by 9 am), work less but do more housework, travelling and leisure activities. Peak meal times don't vary greatly from weekdays, but people spend longer eating and on personal care at other times of the day. On average, adults go to bed an hour later – 89 per cent are in bed by 1 am.

The survey also shows that four in five people did some type of physical activity in the four weeks before the survey and that they spend more time taking part in sports and other physical activities than watching it on TV (16 minutes a day compared with 4 minutes a day).

Household income is an important indicator of activity levels, with the less affluent much less likely to take part in sport or cultural activity. There also appears to be something of a general participation effect, with participation in one increasing the likelihood that people also take part in another. So it is often both or neither, rather than one or the other.

Source: 2000 Time Use Survey, *Office for National Statistics, published on 30 July 2002*

Questions

1 Why are social characteristics such as age, gender, ethnicity and class important when studying unemployment?
2 How has the geography of unemployment changed in recent decades? What reasons might there be for this?

Leisure

Perspectives on leisure

The emergence of two distinct concepts of 'work' and 'leisure' as industrialisation advances has been differently viewed by the main perspectives in sociology.

Functionalism

The functionalist view sees work and leisure as interlocking parts of the social system. As Dumazedier (1974) argues, leisure is necessary to help people adjust to their social situation and for the maintenance of social order. Leisure helps people to rest between work periods, and those who engage in leisure pursuits during work-time are seen as deviant. The three main aspects of leisure are relaxation, entertainment and personal development.

Weber

In the Weberian view what were originally loosely organised and uncoordinated activities have become increasingly rationalised, systematised and rule-bound. The same forces that have changed the nature of work (see above) have also changed leisure pursuits. The underlying forces that come to control leisure pursuits are the same as for work. A good example of this is the way football and rugby football have developed since the middle ages into highly rule-bound activities (Dunning and Sheard, 1969).

Marxism

For Marxists, work in a socialist society will not lead to alienation but will be fulfilling in itself. The need for leisure will be transformed. Under capitalism, the key issue is the battle for the workers to wrest free time from the employing class and to develop their own distinctive culture, sometimes called 'popular culture'. The most significant use of the time gained from the reductions in the working week as a consequence of the Ten Hours Act in the nineteenth century onwards, was for political and trade-union meetings. There is also the emphasis, as in the study of youth cultures, on the concept of gaining 'cultural space' from the dominant ideology (see, for example, Clarke, Critcher and Johnson, 1979 or Clarke and Critcher, 1985).

Feminism

Whether women experience anything that can be called 'leisure' in the same way that men do is of particular interest to feminists. Rosemary Deem (1986) argues that women's opportunities for leisure are different from those of men in the private world of the home, as well as in the outside, public world. As interest in the sociology of women's leisure has grown, a number of studies have argued that women's opportunities for leisure are limited by men, partly because of their control over women's sexuality. This can prevent or constrain journeys out at night, or they may be prevented from going to pubs and discos by their partners. Writers, such as Deem, argue that as women, generally, do not riot, kick each other in the vicinity of football grounds and create public disorder, public provision for their leisure needs is relatively neglected, as placating their needs is seen as less urgent or necessary.

In general women in full-time employment have less leisure time than men. Moreover, as Deem (1988) points out: 'men's leisure is often out of the home and may revolve around sport … and informal group activities like going for a drink. Women tend to spend more leisure time at home (sometimes through necessity rather than choice), whether alone or with friends … Once out of their teens, they are seldom involved in sport.' Within the home, the only place that is seen as a woman's exclusive place is the kitchen. Among women, those with least leisure time are mothers of children under five. Generally, according to Deem, leisure for women is a reward extended grudgingly for good behaviour and well-executed housework.

Questions

1 Define work and leisure. What other time uses can be identified?
2 How do functionalist and Weberian views of leisure differ?

The changing pattern of leisure activities

The impact of industrialisation

Early industrialisation is associated with a loss of free time, and the introduction of new time disciplines and orientations by employers. This is an aspect of the 'Protestant work ethic' described by Weber (see chapter 7). Marrus (1974) estimates that, in the Middle Ages, one third of the year was devoted to leisure. According to Wilensky (1963) the typical working day of 12 hours, with a two-hour rest, in 1700, became a working day of between 14 and 18

hours a century later. During the course of the nineteenth century, the reduction of the working day became the focus of intense industrial and political agitation, and led to the Ten Hours Act of 1847 though, as with much industrial legislation, this was only achieved for certain workers in certain industries. As *Table 9.13* shows, time spent at work has shrunk ever since.

As *Table 9.14* shows, workers in the United Kingdom work the longest hours in Europe. When overtime hours are included, overall hours of work in the United Kingdom are no shorter than the 44–48-hour working week characteristic of the period before the Second World War. Working hours everywhere in Europe remain far in excess of Gorz's (1984) estimation that a working life will eventually involve only 20,000 hours of labour.

One of the main ways in which leisure time has been gained is through paid holidays. As *Figure 9.9* shows, while the number of people having at least one holiday has remained constant since the 1970s, the number having two or more holidays a year is slowly increasing. The frequency of holidays is directly proportional to social class, with unskilled workers taking least (see *Figure 9.10*).

Many left-wing writers are critical of the way leisure time is used, arguing that the free time that does exist is nevertheless absorbed and reclaimed by the dominant culture of capitalism. Leisure and money are inseparable. To participate in some sports it may be socially necessary to wear the appropriate kit bearing the right brand names. Advertising may have a powerful influence on the choices people make when spending their money in their free time. Jeremy Seabrook (1984) argues that, far from being an escape from work, many leisure activities are nostalgic attempts to return to the industrial past. Model railways can be seen as nostalgia for the days of steam and sailing is a sublimation of centuries of naval history. The interest in crafts, pottery, embroidery, sewing, weaving, and the creation of working

Table 9.13   Changes in the working week, 1870–1965

Date	Working hours	Working days
1870	70	7
1900	60	6
1950	44	5
1965	40	5

Source: Wilensky in Smigel, *Work and Leisure*, 1963

Table 9.14 Average hours usually worked[1] per week by full-time employees: by gender, EU comparison, 1999

	Hours	
	Males	Females
United Kingdom	45.2	40.7
Greece	41.7	39.3
Portugal	41.5	39.4
Irish Republic	41.3	38.0
Spain	41.1	39.6
Germany	40.5	39.4
Luxembourg	40.5	38.0
Austria	40.3	39.9
Sweden	40.2	39.9
France	40.2	38.6
Finland	40.1	38.3
Italy	39.7	36.3
Denmark	39.6	37.9
Netherlands	39.2	38.3
Belgium	39.1	36.9
EU average	*41.2*	*39.0*

1 In main job; excludes meal breaks but includes regularly worked paid and unpaid overtime.

Source: *Social Trends* 31, 2001

Figure 9.10 Number of holidays per year: by social class in Great Britain

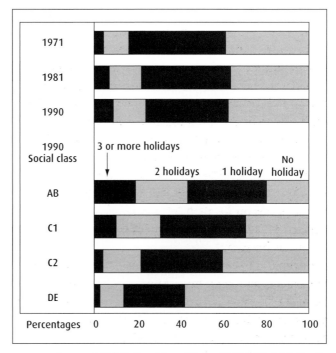

Source: *British National Travel Survey*, British Tourist Authority

museums suggest a powerful impulse to escape the modern world to a time when there was a personal input into work. The needs which leisure activities are called upon to answer are perhaps far more profound than the words themselves suggest.

Deem (1988) sums up these issues: 'it is easier to see fundamental changes taking place over long periods of time, so that there is clearly a vast difference between a factory worker's experience of leisure in the mid nineteenth century and the same worker's experience of leisure in the late twentieth century. But the differences may be less great than we suppose; certainly fewer hours of employment are involved and for many in full-time employment there is more paid holiday entitlement. But activities such as drinking are just as prevalent now as then even though new leisure activities like TV, videos and home computer games have appeared.'

Figure 9.9 Holidays taken by Great Britain residents: by number taken per year

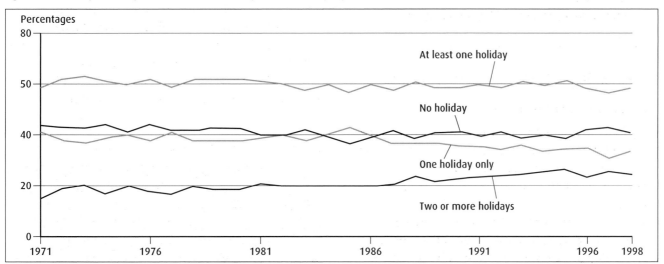

Source: *Social Trends* 21, 2001

The relationship between work and leisure

The idea that what people do in their spare time is directly or indirectly related to what they do in their work hours is disputed. Bacon (1975) finds no strong evidence: 'To a considerable extent, the things that people choose to do in their free time are unrelated to the nature of their employment.' Roberts (1974) argues that 'at the levels of individuals' life-styles, leisure interests are often only weakly related to characteristics of people's jobs, though types of work do have some bearing upon leisure interests'.

Patterns of work and leisure

Stanley Parker (1983) argues that three patterns are perceivable. Some people extend their working life into their leisure hours – their leisure time is clearly identified with their working life; others have leisure patterns that are deliberately opposed to their work, where the content of the two worlds contrasts; the third group display a neutrality about the type of leisure they choose – the content of work and leisure is separate, but not deliberately so.

The relationship between work and leisure, Parker believes, is determined by the nature of the work. Highly autonomous or self-directing work, where people's abilities are used intensively, produces an extension into leisure. This is true, he says, of the social workers he studied, and also of successful businessmen, doctors, teachers and self-employed workers. Neutrality includes minor professionals other than social workers, and the oppositional pattern is characteristic of unskilled manual workers, assembly-line and oil-rig workers and tunnellers. Another significant variable is the type of education the workers have had.

Unemployment and leisure

The return of mass unemployment from the mid-1970s onwards has, for many writers, falsified the claim that a leisured future lay beyond the work ethic of a post-industrial society. When unemployed, people watch more television, do more housework and reading, but go out less. They do not necessarily increase or decrease the amount of sporting, religious, community, creative and outdoor activities. If anything, studies (for example Kelvin *et al.* 1984; Miles, 1984) have shown that people reduce their leisure activities when they become unemployed. This is true even where local authorities have provided low-cost or free leisure facilities.

The implication is that the work ethic is still strong, and that unemployed people have difficulty in seeing leisure as an end in itself, or as a viable alternative to employment. However, the problem seems to be mainly financial, though there is also difficulty in learning how to structure free time. This is also a problem for retired people.

Neither leisure, nor unemployment, it seems, can meet the five characteristics of employment outlined by Jahoda, Lazarsfeld and Zeisel (1933): time-structuring, shared experiences outside the family/household, goals and purposes additional to their own personal ones, personal status and identity, and enforced activity.

Questions

1 How has leisure-time changed in the past 300 years?
2 How are class and gender related to leisure-time?

---

10 Mass media

Introduction

This chapter begins by looking at what is meant by the term 'mass media' and continues by looking at the different patterns of usage of the many forms of media. The question of who determines the content of the mass media is discussed, and three perspectives are examined in detail: the pluralist, Marxist and post-modernist. The same perspectives are also used to investigate the reporting of politics and current affairs, and the way different social groups such as women and ethnic minorities are represented. The extent to which the mass media are able to influence social attitudes and behaviour is also considered in detail, with a discussion of the leading theories and models in this area. There is also a specific focus on the role of the mass media in reporting and promoting social violence. The chapter ends by considering the particular problems that are posed for researchers in the mass media.

Anything which transmits a message from person or group to another person or group is a medium. Any medium which transmits a message to a large group of people is a mass medium. Television, radio, films, advertisements, newspapers, magazines, video and the internet are all examples of mass media, though many more examples could be found, and their number is growing all the time. The main aspects of the mass media that sociologists are concerned with are the question of who determines what messages the main media send – theories of content – and what effect, if any, these messages have on people's social behaviour and attitudes – theories of effect.

Social patterns in listening, viewing and reading

In the developed world, the relative importance of different forms of the mass media changed rapidly in the course of the twentieth century. In the earliest decades, radio, cinema and the printed medi dominated. In the UK, in 1947, for example, almost 90 per cent of all households possessed a radio, at a time when television ownership was almost unknown; listening to it remains the third most popular home-based leisure activity. Independent local radio stations are the most listened to, accounting for over 40 per cent of all listeners, and as many as 67 per cent of listeners under 15.

As *Table 10.1* shows, there has been a rapid decline in the number of cinemas in the last sixty years, from a pre-war peak of almost 5 000 to just under 500 by the close of the century. Attendance, however, has fluctuated, with a low of 67 million admissions by 1987, though this figure began to rise again in the 1990s. Attendance is highest in the 15–24 age group, with adults over 35 being the lowest participating group.

The proportion of people reading a national daily newspaper has fallen steadily since the 1980s, to only 53 per cent of the population by the turn of the

Table 10.1 Cinemas and admissions in the twentieth century

	1939	1949	1959	1964	1969	1979	1983	1989	1994	1996
Number of cinemas	4,901	4,659	3,414	2,057	1,581	1,564	1,432	481	505	495
	1950	1960	1965	1970	1980	1987	1990	1995	1996	
Admissions (millions)	1,396	510	327	193	96	67	78.6	97	112	

Source: Gershuny in Halsey and Webb, 2000

Table 10.2 Readership of daily newspapers (%)

	Sun	Mirror	Mail	Express	Star	Telegraph	Times	Guardian	Independent	FT	Any
Market share of daily newspaper readership 2000/01	20	12	12	4	3	5	3	2	1	1	
Readership by sex (99/00)											
Males	24	14	13	6	5	6	5	3	2	2	59
Females	17	12	12	5	2	4	3	2	1	1	50
All over 16	*21*	*13*	*12*	*5*	*3*	*5*	*4*	*2*	*1*	*1*	*54*
Readership by social class (1994)											
AB	7	7	14	9	1	6	8	8	6	5	
C1	18	13	13	10	4	6	3	3	3	2	
C2	29	22	8	8	7	2	1	1	1	–	
DE	30	20	6	5	7	1	1	1	1	–	

Source: *Social Trends* 25, 1995; 31, 2001; 32, 2002

twenty-first century. The *Sun* remains the most popular paper in the UK, as well as the most widely read by all social classes, though its main readership is drawn from the manual working class (*see Table 10.2*).

Men are more likely than women to read a newspaper, though women are more likely than men to read a magazine. The four most popular periodicals are all television listings magazines.

Watching television is the most popular home-based leisure activity, and has been for several decades, across all ages, classes and sexes. The average amount of time per week spent watching television is 26 hours (compared with 19 hours listening to the radio), with viewing hours increasing with age. The propensity to watch news and current affairs programmes also increases with age, although drama (particularly soap operas) and light entertainment programmes are the most popular with all age groups.

As *Table 10.3* shows, BBC1 and ITV are the most popular stations, accounting for more than 50 per cent of market share, although in recent years cable and satellite stations have increased their profile.

In the last four years of the last century, subscriptions to cable television increased by almost 100 per cent, with satellite subscriptions increasing by 50 per cent in the same period. Managerial, technical and skilled manual workers are the heaviest subscribers, along with the retired and unoccupied.

Ownership of a personal computer has increased from 13 per cent of households in 1985 to over 40 per cent in 2001, with professional workers being most likely to own one. As *Figure 10.1* shows, there is a strong correlation between age and use of the internet, with use declining with age, and men being heavier users than women. The most frequently cited reason for not using the internet in 2001 was lack of interest (42 per cent of non-users), with lack of access to a PC second (26 per cent).

The transformation of the forms taken by the mass media in recent decades and the potential of the digital revolution (which will allow televisions to

Table 10.3 Percentage share of TV viewing figures

	BBC1	BBC2	ITV	Channel 4	Five	Other
1997	30.8	11.6	32.9	10.6	2.3	11.8
1998	29.5	11.3	31.7	10.3	4.3	12.9
1999	28.4	10.8	31.2	10.3	5.4	14.0
2000	27.2	10.8	29.3	10.5	5.7	16.6
2001	26.9	11.1	26.7	10.0	5.8	19.6
2002	26.2	11.4	24.1	10.0	6.3	22.1

Source: Broadcasters Audience Research Board (BARB), *www.barb.co.uk*

Figure 10.1 Use of internet (percentage)

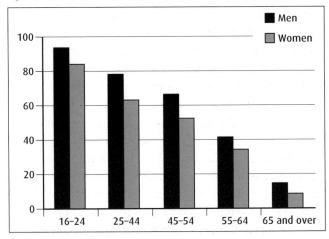

Source: *Social Trends* 32, 2002

become more like PCs and vice versa) have prompted two views of the future for the mass media and society, for the way people live and work, and the way they use their leisure time.

According to one view (sometimes called the 'digital liberation' hypothesis), changes in media forms and use will be benign and permit a form of social liberation (Negroponte, 1995). Interactive media will increase on-line activities such as shopping, saving personal time and reducing pollution as home deliveries are made. More opportunities will exist to work and study from home. Television will become more interactive and programmes (for example, films) will be available for viewing on demand. 'Surfing' will become the characteristic viewing mode, for both television and internet usage, with the tradition of following the plot of a television series being abandoned. The distinction between user/consumer and producer will break down as more people become empowered to create their own websites and use and transmit video technology. The vast increase in the sources and types of information will make forms of social control such as censorship and copyright impossible. Participation in the global media village will take place regardless of the participant's class, sex or ethnic identity. It is easy to see how this view of the future would gain favour from **pluralists** and **post-modernists**.

A more pessimistic view, expressed by, for example, Clifford Stoll (1995), more akin to the **Marxist** approach, sees the information revolution being led by the established forces of **capitalism**, and used for the same ends. New opportunities to reach into households means more opportunities for junk mail: in websites, by email, mobile phone, answerphone and any means possible. In this advertising wasteland it will be difficult to find anything of use or value. Large technology-based corporations such as Microsoft will be unable to resist the temptation to charge for software and support that is currently free (such as use of browsers), and many small groups will be priced out of the internet market, as it becomes as dominated by the **conglomerates** as any other media. All material that challenges the values of capitalism will then be censored or removed. The prevalence of media technology in the home will mean that social contact outside it becomes minimal, and the main form of community interaction will be between those portrayed in television soap operas and the isolated individuals watching them on the other side of the screen.

Questions

1 In what ways might the mass media become more interactive?
2 What are the advantages and disadvantages of the information revolution?
3 Which forms of the mass media are most likely to survive the twenty-first century?

Pluralist, Marxist and post-modernist theories of the nature and role of the mass media

The study of the mass media is a relatively new phenomenon in sociology, and approaches to it are changing as fast as the mass media itself. Broadly speaking, two perspectives have come to dominate its study. These are the pluralist and Marxist approaches, whose application to the study of the mass media parallels their use in the study of **power** and politics (see chapter 11). More recently, post-modern approaches to the mass media have come to play an increasingly important role, as they have in others areas of sociology. Much of the debate about the ownership and control of the mass media, the role of the **State** and political processes, the content of the mass media, particularly news production, the representation of different groups in the mass media and the effects of the mass media on audiences are largely informed by the debates between these viewpoints.

The pluralist perspective

The pluralist perspective (sometimes also called the 'market model') does not see the mass media as representing any one point of view in society but instead focuses on the diversity of views, opinions and representations to be found in the mass media, the multiplicity of forms they take, and the range of opportunities the public has to influence their content. The mass media are therefore seen mainly as a vehicle for public opinion. In this way, the media are similar to any other commodity in a market-led society, where the consumer is sovereign, and the products on sale reflect the laws of supply and demand. In a market-led society, all media forms have to respond to consumer need and follow the laws of supply and demand.

This approach does not discount the influence of owners, journalists, advertisers, the State or the law, but the most important force is the public. In the words of John Whale (1977): 'The strongest influence has undoubtedly remained the reader, listener and viewer. This reader, in particular, has again and again been shown to wield more power over the content and survival of newspapers than proceeds from any other single quarter. Listeners and viewers are less directly influential….But audience sizes are carefully computed, and nothing else is so important in determining a programme's place in the schedules.'

The content of the mass media will therefore show the full range of views, opinions and interests present in society and portray all sections of the community. It will reflect the world as it is merely a mirror held up to it. Any bias or prejudice in the media merely reflects the bias and prejudice found in society. All questions about the content of the mass media can be answered by the observation that this is what the public want, no matter how trivial, sensationalist, ephemeral or irrelevant it may appear. No-one is forcing readers to buy tabloid newspapers, or to watch television, any more than they can be made to buy any other product.

The public also has a considerable number of opportunities to directly influence the content of the mass media, by making programmes for 'community slots' on television, writing letters to editors, complaining on feedback programmes, contributing to phone-ins, quizzing politicians on panel programmes, producing their own websites and so on. In these ways the public gets the mass media it both wants and deserves. The media may have biases but there are many biases, and the public can choose which bias it desires. New technologies such as the internet, satellite and digital broadcasting can only increase the opportunities for greater diversity. In any case, research shows that, at best, the mass media only ever reinforce already existing public attitudes, and have little effect in telling people what to think and how to behave, as the interpretive model (see p. 285) shows.

The evidence for this is to be found everywhere in the mass media, where media forms and accessibilities (broadcast, cable and satellite television, a variety of national and local radio stations, multiplex cinemas, video and DVD shops, the internet, thousands of different types of magazines and newspapers) cater for all political and social persuasions. Consumer sovereignty is evident from newspapers that have closed because of low circulation, television series that have been abandoned because of poor ratings, or radio programmes that have been sustained through public support. That the very notion of 'mass' (rather than fragmented or diverse) media is increasingly questioned is even more evidence of the truth of the pluralist case.

Criticisms of the pluralist perspective

There are many flaws in the pluralist's portrayal of a free, diverse and responsive media. They underestimate the role of the State in regulating what is said and how it is said. Broadcasting by radio or television in the UK depends on obtaining a government licence, the distribution of which is tightly controlled. The content of a television station's output is determined by the content of its licence, which is in turn regulated by the State. The time of evening news programmes, for example, is determined through negotiation with the government of the day. Access to news sources such as government ministers and documents is similarly controlled (see 'Media content and news' below). There are laws against incitement to racial hatred (though not all other forms of discrimination), as well as libel laws, that can be used to prevent the publication or broadcasting of anything that might defame someone's character.

Many commentators have argued that it is not consumer choice but advertising revenue that determines the overall structure and content of the mass media. Almost all forms of the mass media depend on advertising to keep them afloat, and it is the ratings of a television programme, or the circulation of a newspaper, as well as their consumer profiles, that will attract advertisers. Commercial forms of the mass media that fail to reach target markets, offend their advertising sponsors, or seek to reach an audience that does not interest advertisers, are unlikely to survive in highly competitive markets. Similarly, as with its perspective on power and politics (see chapter 11), the pluralist view of the mass media can be criticised for seeing the mass media one-dimensionally, looking only at what is included, and not at what is excluded (**gate-keeping**), or the process by which the mass media and their contents are made attractive (shaping desires). Finally, while the pluralist view has some similarities with the post-modernist approach, many of its criticisms are contained in the Marxist perspective.

Marxist perspectives

For Marxists, the part of any society in which ideas are disseminated is its ideological **superstructure**. In Marx's own time (the nineteenth century) this consisted mainly of the legal, political and religious systems. The mass media as we know it did not exist. Marx was clear about where the control of such ideas lay: 'in any age the ruling ideas are the ideas of the ruling class: thus their ideas are the ruling ideas of the epoch' and 'the class which has the means of production at its disposal, has control at the same time over the means of mental production' and can 'regulate the production and distribution of the ideas of their age' (Marx, 1845–6). Taking these statements as their starting point many Marxists have seen the modern mass media as being at the heart of contemporary **ruling-class** ideology, taking on many of the functions of religion, and acting as one of the main ways in which **bourgeois** control over the **proletariat** is maintained.

This notion has been refined and adapted into two neo-Marxist models, usually known as the mass-manipulative and hegemonic views.

The mass-manipulative model

This model is usually associated with the Frankfurt School of the 1930s, 1940s and 1950s and with the work of Herbert Marcuse in particular. Their starting point is the phenomenon of the mass which by the twentieth century existed at all levels: in production, consumption, culture and society. The mass media became a tool of the ruling class to consciously and deliberately manipulate and control the minds of the masses, effectively removing the possibility of critical thought from them and thus perpetuating their subservience. As Marcuse says: 'The hypnotic power of the mass media deprive us of the capacity for critical thought, which is essential if we are to change the world'. Not only is the content of the mass media safe and unchallenging, it also exists to market or sell capitalist commodities, whether directly through advertising, or indirectly through programmes such as home and garden improvement, holiday programmes, chat shows where guests promote books, films or compact discs, or quiz shows where the lucky winner is rewarded with cash or goods. Its content is specific to the demands of capitalism, and the creation and shaping of desire for its products.

In most advanced capitalist societies the mass media is owned and controlled by a few large conglomerates, whose media output does much to support – and little to undermine – the ruling values of those societies. Equally, many of the leading figures in these organisations have made statements that show that they view their media channels as a means of

transmitting their own pro-capitalist views, as Lord Northcliffe (when owner of the *Daily Mail*, *Daily Mirror* and *The Times*) made clear when he stated: 'God made people read so that I could fill their brains with facts – and later tell them who to love, whom to hate, and what to think.' Many journalists and editors have also reported that media owners such as the late Robert Maxwell, when owner of the *Daily Mirror*, or Rupert Murdoch (see 'Ownership and control', pp. 273–5) directly interfered with editorial decisions.

There is equally little to support the pluralist argument concerning choice. In the same way that ownership and control is in the hands of a few, so too is the distribution and delivery of mass media products, minimising the widespread distribution of any new media offering views that challenge the dominant ideology. The same is true of content. Despite the apparent plethora of films, TV channels, newspapers and magazines, they nevertheless all come from the same few media stables and are built around the same concept of safe and soporific content. A multiplex cinema, for example, may be showing dozens of films, but they will have come from the same few Hollywood studios, themselves owned by massive global conglomerates, built around a handful of predictable and formulaic themes, with none of them being ever likely to contain a single idea that may threaten bourgeois control.

The content of the mass media is as much determined by owners and advertisers as it is by the consumer. Selling is at the heart of the mass media, and has been since its inception. To help it win a sales war with Unilever's Oxidol washing powder, and to help promote their own Rinso, in 1933 Procter and Gamble subsidised the American radio programme *Ma Perkins*, thus ensuring that a guaranteed targeted audience would always be available to hear adverts for Rinso, as well as frequent mentions of it in the script. In this way, the modern phenomenon of soap operas was born, while the practice of 'product placement', where companies pay for their products to be either displayed or mentioned in mass media such as films and television programmes, has become commonplace.

The nature of ownership and the narrowness of distribution and content thus make the mass media more akin to powerful tools for transmitting capitalist propaganda, ensuring that only its message is heard and enabling it to ensure that its goods will continue to be bought by a compliant and docile proletariat. In taking this view, the mass-manipulative model is also aligning itself with the hypodermic syringe' view of media effects (see 'Effects', pp. 283–7) in its assumption that a message is received with the same intent with which it is sent. The view of the media as mass manipulative can also be found in some aspects of **feminism**, where it is seen as a tool for transmitting the propaganda of the ruling **patriarchy**.

The hegemonic model

The concept of **hegemony** is usually associated with the Italian Marxist Antonio Gramsci (1891–1937). He used it to describe the **ideological** leadership that is achieved through winning consent, rather than through brute force and coercion. How this was achieved was a particularly important question to him in the 1920s after he had witnessed the failure of the Italian left and the triumph of Mussolini's Fascists, who had imprisoned him. For Gramsci, the lesson had been that the focus within Marxism on control of the **means of production** neglected the question of how people's 'hearts and minds' were won. It made him consider what needed to be done to win over people's sympathies, and to reach a point where it was accepted that socialist ideas were 'common sense'. It does not automatically follow that control of the means of production leads to the control of ideas – ideological leadership is there to be won. The mass media therefore plays a central role in this battle.

Unlike the mass-manipulative model, from this viewpoint there is nothing conscious, necessary or conspiratorial about what becomes the content of the mass media. If it reflects the values of the ruling class it is not because of the intervention of its owners but because this is the class from which most of the editors and journalists are broadly drawn, and where their class lie. The view of the world portrayed by the mass media is one of white, middle-aged and middle-class men. New journalists become socialised into the culture created by these values, which become seen as the natural and common-sense values of the society in which they live. There is nothing automatic about this, however, and with a shift in the balance of class forces, other views may also come to hold sway.

The values of this class become translated into the new values of the editors and journalists, for example in the way that some news stories are prioritised (**agenda-setting**) and some are deliberately ignored or ridiculed (gate-keeping). It is also evident in the way that certain groups are effectively guaranteed immediate access to newsrooms and journalists, such as politicians, members of the royal family or captains or industry, while others, such as **trade unionists**, pressure groups, or the wider general public, struggle to be heard. This phenomenon is known as structured access.

Criticisms of the Marxist perspective

In addition to the criticisms made from pluralist and post-modern perspectives, the Marxist view of the mass media is also criticised from within Marxism. One main concern is that, in looking at the mass media largely in isolation from society, and as part of its ideological superstructure, the mass-manipulative and hegemonic views underestimate the importance of the economic substructure as the basis of power in society, and understate the real control that lies with ownership of the means of production. This view, which among others, has been articulated by Abercrombie, Turner and Hill (Abercrombie *et al.*, 1980) applies to other Marxist-influenced studies of the superstructure, such as education and religion. They argue that the very concept of a single and 'dominant ideology' is misconceived.

The attribution of unlimited power to the owners of the mass media is also unrepresentative. Governments do not always accede to the will of the conglomerates. Rupert Murdoch's News Corporation, for example, has been unable to gain or extend new franchises either locally in the United Kingdom, or internationally, where his Star satellite television has been banned in China and Malaysia. Similarly, the failure to take local cultural factors into account has seen the failure of global ventures in some locations, where the output of satellite television has either overestimated the desire for American-centred material and the wish to embrace Western values, or has been seen as offensive to locally held beliefs and traditions.

The capitalist goal of short-term profit maximisation can also mean that its media may be prepared to carry any content that sells, regardless of whether that content underpins capitalist values. This content can be as varied as stories exposing fraud and corruption within large financial organisations to cartoons series aimed at adult markets, where, for example, *The Simpsons* is seen as containing subversive content. The notion of a single culture within journalism is also seen as problematic, where many critics have argued that it is not a united grouping but made up of competing factions, in the same way that the dominant **élite** is. Many journalists do not believe they are working to support the status quo, particularly investigative journalists such as Bernstein and Woodward (who played a large part in the downfall of US President Richard Nixon in the Watergate affair of the 1970s which was depicted in the film *All The President's Men*. They used their positions in the *Washington Post* to do so.) Others work for publications such as the *Guardian* which is owned in trust, not by a media conglomerate, and frequently carries content that is critical of the dominant ideology's values.

Post-modernism

The role played by new media technologies is central to the overall post-modernist case (as articulated by, for example Jean Baudrillard), where the digital age is seen as transforming all aspects of society, from the way it is structured to the values that are held within it. The distinction between élite and mass culture has collapsed as the new media have thrown open access to unlimited sources of information, to the extent that the concept of a 'mass' medium is no longer helpful or appropriate. Individuals are now enjoying a rich diversity of image sources, none of which gain any detailed attention as surfers hop from channel to channel and website to website, and any notion of a mass audience disappears within a huge range of options, fragmented identities, lifestyle choices, disconnected images and ephemeral experiences.

Meanings and values become lost as individuals choose their own interpretations of media messages, and are unwilling to accept the all-embracing accounts of the world given by science (**metanarratives**). These are progressively undermined by a chaotic and confusing information overload. Without any fixed or permanent standards to be judged against, concepts such as 'truth' and 'knowledge' cease to be absolutes. Everything becomes as worthy or irrelevant as everything else, as the distinction between the everyday world of the 'real' (and the media-based world of the 'hyperreal') becomes increasingly blurred.

Criticisms of the post-modernist perspective

Most criticisms of the post-modernist view focus on the vagueness of their argument, which is usually made impressionistically and without reference to any systematic research, although an engagement with any such research would oblige these theorists to acknowledge a scientific method they no longer believe in. Post-modernism's refusal to recognise structures and power relationships in society masks the real and tangible inequalities that exist. There are

times when a society engages with the media as a mass, as viewing figures for soap operas and some sporting events show; this is particularly evident during events such as the football World Cup and royal family rites of passage which themselves mark traditions that have been embedded within the culture for many centuries. Finally, the extent and prevalence of technology in people's lives has been overstated, with data on ownership and use of new technologies and viewing and readership patterns being less diverse, chaotic and widespread as the post-modernists might suppose; there is nothing in the post-modern world that couldn't be discovered in the modern.

Questions

1 What are the similarities between the pluralist and post-modern perspectives?
2 How does the mass manipulative approach differ from the hegemonic?
3 What evidence is there that a mass culture persists?

Ownership and control of the mass media

By the turn of the twentieth century, educational reforms had created a newly literate mass market. The demand for new reading materials was met by the publication of most of the newspaper titles that are on the newsstands today, with many of their owners and publishers (such as Lord Beaverbrook at the *Daily Express* and Lord Rothermere at the *Daily Mail*) dominating the market for news in the United Kingdom throughout that century. With his successful purchase of the *Sun* in 1968, the Australian (now naturalised American) Rupert Murdoch gained his first foothold in the British media, joining the ranks of of the 'press barons' controlling the printed media, before extending this hold across the globe.

Murdoch's media career has been of particular interest to sociologists and journalists alike. This is partly because of the speed with which he has gained such a large stake in the global media market, and partly because of his outspoken views and daring interventions in all dimensions of the media. Having inherited the *Australian* newspaper from his father, Murdoch went on to own the *Sun*, *Times*, *Sunday Times* and the *News of the World* in the United Kingdom. In the USA he gained control of a series of publications before moving into broadcasting and satellite television stations (see box). These moves to global media control

THE MURDOCH GLOBAL MEDIA OPERATION IS CONTROLLED BY THE NEWS CORPORATION.

Its holdings can be summarised as follows:

Filmed Entertainment (10 companies including Twentieth Century Fox, including Fox Studios and Fox TV)

Television (8 companies including BSkyB and Star TV)

Cable (11 companies including Fox Movies, National Geographic and Los Angeles Dodgers)

Magazines and inserts (6 companies including Gemstar – TV Guide International)

Newspapers (22 newspapers in Australia, the *New York Post* in the USA, and 8 publications in the UK, including the *Sun*, *News of the World*, *Times*, *Sunday Times* and *Times Educational Supplement*)

Books (3 publishers including HarperCollins) as well as other assets.

were mirrored by other companies such as Time Warner so that large parts of the global media are now in the hands of a very few conglomerates.

Looking at the USA as a whole, in the 1980s, according to Bagdikian (1997) there were 50 dominant media corporations. By 1990 this had shrunk to 23, and only 10 by 1997, with every likelihood that this number will decrease again, to the point where a communications cartel can be described. The character as well as size of these organisations is also changing; it is now more common for companies not previously involved in the media to buy media organisations (general rather than communications conglomerates), such as the General Electric Company's purchase of NBC, one of the three largest coast-to-coast broadcasters in the USA.

The global trend towards increasing ownership and control of the mass media by a few very large companies is important to the mass-manipulative approach, and makes the concept of a 'free press' in a democratic society problematic. As others have argued, however, it is far from a decisive point in the debates between these leading perspectives on the mass media. The BBC, for example, is not owned by any conglomerate but is part of the State in the United Kingdom – a parastatal organisation run by a government-appointed governing body, guardians of a State-determined charter and licence. These documents enshrine the BBC's commitment to report

events objectively and impartially as a public service to its citizens. Whether they succeed in this aim is explored below.

Pluralist perspectives

Pluralists focus on the dispersed and fragmented nature of mass media ownership, mirroring their view of power in society. As recently as 1983, Tunstall could identify as many as twenty-five companies in competition for the British media market, with no one company dominant. Moreover, it is no longer the case that ownership of a company is the same as (or involves the same individuals in) control of a company. This is yet another dimension of the diverse and widespread nature of power within companies. Although these owners may have profit as their primary motive for involvement in the mass media, and must answer in the first instance to their own organisation and its shareholders, their influence, as Whale remarks 'where it survives at all must still defer to the influence of readers' (1977). In determining the content of the mass media, it remains the case that the consumer, rather than the owner, remains sovereign. In any case, television is the most popular medium, and the BBC – which is owned by no-one – is the most frequently accessed outlet. The influence of the 'media barons' therefore cannot be as great as is supposed (Congdon, 1995).

Marxist perspectives

For Marxists, that there is a tendency towards monopoly in ownership and control of the mass media is unsurprising, as this tendency is part of the development of any capitalist society. The main debate within Marxism concerns the importance of the role of owners of the mass media in influencing its content. For **structuralist** Marxists, it follows axiomatically that in a capitalist society the dominant ideology will be that of the ruling class, with the mass media as a central means of transmitting these ideas. The phenomenon of the separation of ownership from control, or the role played by specific media entrepreneurs, is unimportant: since 'proprietors and other capitalists do not need to intervene in newspaper production since the logic of the prevailing market structure ensures that by and large the output endorses rather than opposes their general interests' (Murdoch, 1980). No matter who owns the mass media, in a capitalist society the output of the mass media will reflect the ideology of the ruling class, with the implication that only a fundamental revolutionising of the ownership of the means of production can bring about a change in the ideological superstructure of which the mass media form a core part.

A more instrumentalist approach, similar to the mass-manipulative view, argues that the class background of media owners and their editorial interventions in their publications are important. It is because they are also members of the bourgeoisie that they use their media outlets to defend their class, and play an important part in shaping the desires for consumer products, 'legitimating' capitalism. This view of the mass media, which echoes much of the debate between Marxists concerning the role of the State (see chapter 11), sees possibilities in challenging for alternative control of the media, in the belief that some small partial change is possible, albeit temporarily. From the point of view of the hegemonic approach, ownership of the mass media is less important than the class character of the journalists and editors who produce its content.

Post-modernist perspectives

The issue of who owns or has financial control of the mass media is unimportant in understanding its impact. Attempts to look at the wider picture of the mass media's structural location in society constitute a move towards constructing the very metanarratives that post-modernists are critical of, attempting, for example, to find causal links between ownership and content. The only real issue is to identify the part played by the media, and media technology in particular, in creating the 'post-modern condition'.

Questions

1 How might ownership differ from control of the mass media?
2 Why is the question of ownership important to the mass-manipulative view?

The mass media, the State and the political process

The issue of how the mass media cover politics, and their relation with politicians and the State, has become increasingly important as political parties and pressure groups have become more conscious of the way they are presented. This has changed markedly since the end of the Second World War, when no reporting was allowed at all in the weeks immediately

before a General Election, and it was assumed that the voting public could learn all they wanted about each political party from reading manifestos and by attending rallies and hustings. Any television coverage ran the risk of presenting a biased view of one or other political party and either boosting or damaging their chances of election.

Televised reporting of politics has been almost completely transformed: elections are largely fought on television, sittings of the Houses of Parliament are broadcast daily, politicians are interviewed by reporters and the public, and the Prime Minister's Press Secretary has become a household name in successive governments. Real concerns have been raised that the use of the media by governments to present and discuss issues is undermining parliament and the democratic process. Announcements (such as the content of a Budget speech) may be 'leaked' to the press before they are announced to the House of Commons, for example. Attempts by politicians to present themselves and their parties in the best light has given rise to the phenomenon of 'spin doctors' – political aides employed by their party to put the most favourable interpretation (or 'spin') on events of the day to the media.

The debates concerning the role of the mass media and the political process in recent decades have crystallised around the concept of 'news'. This is of particular interest to sociologists as it contrasts a media view of the world to the one they themselves wish to portray in their own research. With an almost infinite number of events to be reported on, journalists' 'news values', and the reasons why particular media adopt particular values, have become a specific focus.

The pluralist view

The claim that, in a democratic society, all citizens have an equal chance to be elected, form a government as part of a political party, and understand and contribute to all sides of political debate, lies at the heart of the pluralist case. As there is no monopoly of power or control, in the State or the mass media, all political points of view, differing political ideologies, minority views and pressure groups will be represented within the mass media, which plays a central role in the dissemination of these ideas.

There are a number of reasons to believe this. If it was the case that the mass media only represent the interests of the ruling class then parties critical of

Public servant or 'spin doctor'? Alistair Campbell, British Prime Minister Tony Blair's Director of Communications and Strategy until his resignation in the summer of 2003.

entrenched power and interest would never get elected, yet in the era of the mass media, there have been regular changes of government, with the Labour Party in power for half of the period between 1945 and 1979, and twice elected from 1997. For pluralists, the ability of newspapers to influence voters has been overstated. Early studies, such as Blumler and McQuail (1968), who investigated the 1964 General Election campaign (won by the Labour Party and ending thirteen years of Conservative rule) claimed that it is audiences and not the media who naturally occupy the middle ground in politics. If anything, the mass media helps push them further in this direction, even if a wide range of the political spectrum is represented by the media.

In the long era of Conservative rule from 1979 to 1997, many opinion polls showed that the readership of overtly right-wing papers such as the *Sun* was as likely to vote Labour as it was Conservative. In the 1987 election (the third successive election won by the Conservative Party), for example, 63 per cent of the *Sun*'s readers believed it supported the Conservative Party, though only 41 per cent of its readers voted Conservative, with 31 per cent voting Labour. Similarly, in the same election, 68 per cent of the *Daily Mirror*'s readership saw it as a pro-Labour newspaper, but 45 per cent of its readers nevertheless voted for parties other than Labour (Beynon, 1987). One conclusion from this could be that their own or the newspaper's political persuasion is not the main reason why readers prefer one newspaper over another.

Media campaigns against politicians can nevertheless be powerful and frequently lead to their resignation, as, for example, in the final years of John Major's Conservative government. It was the mass media, including 'The Tory Press', who reported the 'Tory Sleaze' that played a significant factor in their ultimate demise in the mid-1990s.

The pluralist position is one that many journalists working in the media themselves take. This is particularly true of those working within 'parastatal' organisations such as the BBC, who have a legal responsibility to present news and current affairs in a balanced, objective and unbiased way. Nicholas Jones (1986), a BBC radio reporter during the year-long dispute between the National Union of Mineworkers and the National Coal Board in the mid-1980s, has argued that if one side in a strike appears to be more favourably depicted by the media, it is because they are better at courting publicity and 'playing the media' not because of any innate bias in the media towards them. Furthermore, as Gunter *et al.* argue (1994), the majority of the public do not perceive political bias in the broadcast media, and there is an even split between supporters of the two main parties among the minority who do believe there is bias.

For pluralists, news values are determined by the journalist's knowledge of what the public want, their duty to report on affairs of state, and practical considerations such as the presence of cameras and reporters at the site of the news story. There is no conscious or deliberate attempt to give a distorted or partial view of the world, merely a desire to meet the public's demand for the public's priorities – typically, for stories concerning sport, celebrities and personalities, bizarre, tragic or spectacular crime and (least of all) public and current affairs. Most of the main criticisms of the pluralist view are contained within the mass-manipulative and hegemonic approaches.

The mass-manipulative view

The mass-manipulative model argues that the content of the mass media is largely controlled and determined by members of the ruling class, rather than journalists or the public, with the object of using the mass media to maintain their control over the proletariat. They do this either by diverting them from seeing the **class** relations of a capitalist society for what they are, or by portraying any groups who challenge bourgeois control as sinister, dangerous and misguided.

Newspaper owners in particular (for example, Lords Northcliffe, Rothermere and Beaverbrook) have actively used their publications to influence political or industrial events (such as elections and strikes) to articulate the ruling-class view.

From this perspective, the State is seen as merely the executive arm of the ruling class, with governments maintaining good relations with the media barons, offering knighthoods and peerages in return for sympathetic treatment in the press. In the 1980s, for example, Rupert Murdoch's influence with Mrs Thatcher was such that he was described by one of his own editors as 'Mr Prime Minister, except that it's no longer much of a joke. In many respects he is the phantom Prime Minister of the country' (*Times* editor Charles Douglas-Home, quoted in Belfield and Hird, 1991). When the media magnate Silvio Berlusconi was successfully elected Prime Minister of Italy (first briefly in 1994, and again in 2001), all of these forces were rolled into one.

The possibility of any critical reporting of affairs of State in the UK is hampered by a number of problems, particularly the application of the 1911 Official Secrets Act which forbids the unauthorised disclosure of any information by any servant of the Crown whether that information is classified or not. Reporting events at the heart of government (such as the twice weekly Cabinet meetings) is therefore in breach of the Official Secrets Act. To circumvent this, senior civil servants, such as the Prime Minister's Press Secretary, give 'confidential and unattributable' briefings to selected lobby journalists, who then refer to them in the media as 'sources close to the Prime Minister' or 'senior figures in Whitehall'. This means that these journalists can only legally report what they are told, and are under pressure to write the article or broadcast the item in a way sympathetic to the government to maintain their privileged access. As Cockerell *et al.* (1985) remark: it is 'a formal and intimidating apparatus within which governments may practise an anti-democratic technique to their hearts' content. The technique is news management.' As already noted, this technique has become more refined and specialised in recent decades, with politicians surrounding themselves with an increasing number of media aides or 'spin doctors'.

Restrictions on matters relating to defence and war are equally troubling, with many commentators arguing that the main purpose of censorship and other controls in these situations is not for security purposes but to present the government, who may be using the conflict as a smokescreen to distract from pressing domestic problems, in a more favourable light. During the conflict with Argentina in 1982 over the Falklands, for example, Cockerell *et al.* write: 'For ten weeks the government and the military engaged in a campaign of news management that had not been equalled since the Second World War. In part the campaign involved military censorship and suppression of sensitive information that could endanger men's lives. But the other part involved disinformation for military purposes and the projection of "good news" for political ends.' Unlike the war in Vietnam, no live pictures were sent back from the South Atlantic, and journalists' reports were heavily censored and delayed. Official accounts of events sometimes bore little resemblance to reality, including announcing the capture of Goose Green a day before it had actually happened.

The portrayal and treatment of enemies, or potential enemies, of the State in the build-up to war conforms to the process of prediction, exaggeration and symbolisation described in accounts of deviance amplification (see below). These are summed up by Phillip Knightley as follows: stage one, the crisis; stage two, the demonisation of the enemy's leader; stage three, the demonisation of the enemy as individuals; and stage four, atrocities (Knightley, 2002). This would exactly describe the process of 'demonisation' of Saddam Hussein from a position in the 1980s, where Iraq gained support from the West in their war with Iran, to one where he came to be seen as an intolerable and evil presence on the world stage. The role of the media as the propaganda arm of the State is also examined in relation to the 'troubles' in Northern Ireland by Liz Curtis (1984).

Despite the seriousness of the issues presented by parts of the media, there is still a sense that the social construction of the news as a product implies that its contents should be viewed superficially. As Postman claims 'We are urged by the newscasters to "join them tomorrow". But what for? One would think that several minutes of murder and mayhem would suffice as material for a month of sleepless nights. We accept the newscasters' invitation because we know that the "news" is not to be taken seriously, that it is all in good fun…Everything about a news show tells us this…the good looks and amiability of the cast, their pleasant banter, the exciting music that opens and closes the show' (1984). The 'News' is a show to be viewed, not part of a political process that should be engaged in through informed debate.

The hegemonic view

Where the mass-manipulative view sees external agents as having the greatest influence in political reporting, the hegemonic approach argues that the bias that is evident in political reporting emerges as a result of the class culture of journalists and the news values which emerge from it. This is the main argument of the Glasgow University Media Group (GUMG) to be found in a series of books that have emerged since the publication of *Bad News* in 1976 (GUMG, 1976).

Using **content analysis** (see chapter 2), the GUMG argues that the reporting of industrial relations, for example, favours the employers over the employed. This can be found in the way journalists are willing to use information supplied by the employer's side in a dispute uncritically; the use of language that describes employers in a strike as making 'offers' and 'pleas' while strikers make 'demands' and 'threats'; interviews with employers in the calm of their office while strikers are shown shouting from the picket lines, and the continuous re-editing of footage that comes to only focus on one aspect of what actors in the dispute (such as politicians) have said about its consequences. In this way, it is the actions of the strikers, rather than the employers, which are seen as disruptive and unnecessary.

The news becomes, in Stuart Hall's view (Hall *et al.*, 1980), an open rather than a closed text (see 'Media effects' below), with events presented narrowly as facts and a true picture, rather than as what they are: a selective and partial account, revealing as much about the news values of the journalists as the story itself. In this way, 'the news' comes to articulate what Hall calls the 'dominant-hegemonic position': 'News values appear as a set of neutral practices, but we also need to see formal news values as an ideological structure – to examine these rules as the formalisation and operationalisation of an ideology of news' (Hall quoted in GUMG 1976). These news values are central to the process of cultural reproduction as they in turn help shape the dominant ideology and maintain the status quo.

The GUMG's view of broadcast television news has been criticised in detail by Martin Harrison (1985). Writing from a largely pluralist viewpoint, he argues that the same accusations of bias that the GUMG makes can be made of their own research in that their own method of content analysis was used selectively and unrepresentatively over short periods of time that do not fully reflect the overall presentation of news stories. (This point is then countered by the GUMG which points out that Harrison himself was helped and partly financed by ITN in his research.) Moreover, many of the GUMG's findings contain generalisations that are not based on the evidence they collected, that this evidence is not in any case factual, and their own claim to objectivity is in fact a bias towards trade unions. The GUMG, he says, is unwilling to admit that management often feels itself to be unfairly portrayed in industrial disputes, and there is nothing in journalists' news values that necessarily favours management over trade unionists. He also argues that there is nothing wrong in emphasising the effects of industrial action on the public, claiming that 'Television is more productively considered not as essentially one dimensional but as conveying a range of contradictory contentions and explanations – the site of ideological conflict, rather than simply fostering a "climate of conformity".'

There are a number of criticisms of both the mass-manipulative and hegemonic views of political reporting, given that both see the media's role as maintaining and reinforcing the status quo in society. In those countries where there is a State monopoly of the mass media and freedom of the press is suppressed (such as the former Soviet Union), the evidence is that news stories focus on 'good news' stories such as increases in industrial production or the opening up of new public facilities, rather than the focus on crime, violence or industrial unrest that characterise news output in Western democracies. The public, who have a sophisticated ability to decode and comprehend media conventions, do not see news output in the West as propaganda, and would stop watching and reading if they did.

The role of the State in a mixed economy remains problematic for Marxist-inspired views of the mass media, as it is for wider views of politics and power (see chapter 11). Many commentators are unwilling to accept the view that parastatal organisations such as the BBC are mouthpieces of the ruling class, particularly when a number of BBC documentaries and drama serials (such as *Panorama* and the plays of Alan Bleasdale) have earned criticism from the political right for their alleged left-wing content. It is also a strong accusation to make of journalistic professionalism and intregrity to portray their output as biased and monolithic in this way, when many of them see their own output as either balanced or often critical of big business or the government of the day.

The post-modernist view

In three articles, called 'The Gulf War will not take place'. 'The Gulf War: is it really taking place?' and 'The Gulf War did not take place', Jean Baudrillard (1995) gives a good illustration of the post-modern view of the relationship between the media and political reporting. Baudrillard highlights the virtual nature of the war between Iraq and the Western Allies in the Gulf in 1991. Thus, many of the actors in the war and its reporting saw the conflict through screens – in the pilot's cockpit as they dropped bombs, for the war reporters there watching the images through cameras and televisions rather than live with their own eyes, through to the viewers at home watching their televisions.

This mediated view of the war becomes more real – or hyperreal – than the war on the ground experienced by the combatants suffering from Allied attacks. The experience of the war for everyone on the Allied side was by simulation of what was happening, or what he calls a simulacrum. The conflict becomes no more real than a video game or Hollywood film, with footage presented from the nose-cameras of missiles and relatively few images of the casualties and real horror and confusion of war. Our understanding of the world in a post-modern age is therefore limited to superficial access to televised news, which is read as a text of subjectively interpreted images and signs. These have become as much part of our reality as the world beyond that they can never portray.

Christopher Norris (1992) has been particularly critical of this view, arguing that Baudrillard and post-modernism are contributing to the Allies' aim of hiding the real nature of the war (when the American public is still having difficulty coming to terms with losses in Vietnam), where real people are killed by real munitions, as well as aiding the belief that it is no longer possible to say that, in absolute terms, an act is right or wrong. Baudrillard's views are at best controversy for its own sake, and at worst destructive of the possibility of peace or understanding.

Questions

1 What is meant by the term 'news values'?
2 Why does Baudrillard maintain that the Gulf War did not happen?
3 How can television news be seen as entertainment or propaganda?

Representations of gender, disability, age and ethnicity

The pluralist claim that the media is a mirror held up to society, and that all aspects and dimensions of human life can be found there comes under close scrutiny when questions about the representation of **gender**, age, class, **ethnicity** and disability in the mass media are asked. Given the assertion from both the mass-manipulative and hegemonic camps that the mass media is used, consciously or unconsciously, by a white, male and middle-aged ruling élite to maintain social control, we can expect the mass media to be responsible for the creation, maintenance and reinforcement of negative stereotypes of non-white, female, working-class groups who are either young or old. The evidence and counter-evidence for these claims is examined below.

The various categories of **stratification** do not stand in isolation from each other. The classification 'woman', for example, is cross-cut with class, ethnicity, age and physical ability in the makeup of their social identity. We could therefore look to examine portrayals of disabled, elderly, middle-class, white women, or able-bodied young black men, and any other permutation of these categories. Taken to its extreme, this approach would throw up an almost infinite combination of identities which would make the examination of the media's portrayal of stratification impossible.

This is, of course, an observation that post-modernists would enthusiastically endorse, highlighting the fluid nature of social identity, the diverse and fractured nature of media content, and the interactive nature of modern media technology which has created the post-modern phenomenon of the hyperreal, where the real and imagined become indistinguishable. One example of this would be the sense that characters in soap operas are real people whose daily lives impact on our own. An extreme example of this would be public campaigns against the wrongful imprisonment of these characters, or the funeral wreaths that are sent to television studios when they die. In this way, televisual portrayals have ceased to be representations but real, or as Baudrillard remarks, 'It is no longer a question of a false representation of reality but of concealing the fact that the real is no longer real, thus saving the reality principle' (Baudrillard, 1983).

Women

It starts when you sink into his arms and ends with your arms in his sink.

Much of the printed and broadcast media targeted at women focuses on them as lovers, mothers and potential housewives, as essentially feminine. An intrinsic part of this femininity is the depiction of women whose lives revolve around the possibility of romance. Why this image of femininity is projected at women, who projects it, and whose interests it serves is the subject of much debate. Do women become involved in romance as part of a great lie that men construct to trap them in domestic roles, or should more men become sensitive to the emotional and expressive issues discussed in romantic fiction and women's magazines? Is the whole notion of romantic love simply a smokescreen through which women cannot recognise their oppression? Do the media shape women's sexuality into one of heterosexuality, passivity and subservience? Do women have any control over the way they are presented in the media?

Teenage magazines

There is much agreement over the nature and intent of magazines aimed at teenage girls, whose sales can reach as many as half a million copies. These magazines rely on a formula of written stories, photo stories and problem pages. Certain characteristic features emerge: relationships are heterosexual and **monogamous**; love and sex go together and are both mystical and magical; the male is dominant while the female is passive and ideally virginal; the male 'takes' the female and she adapts to his needs; and friendships are secondary or unimportant. For Angela McRobbie (in McRobbie and McCabe, 1981) they describe the world of teenage girls in a way that is both limited and limiting. The central message of *Jackie* is that girls' lives should be oriented to capturing and thinking about boys. In doing this, *Jackie* is 'a friendly text book, a manual which works on the assumption that there are no real alternatives to this prescribed goal'.

A similar argument, expressed in a much more virulent tone, is put by the journalist and feminist Polly Toynbee (1978) in her examination of the girls' magazines published by IPC, like *My guy* and its genre. 'All that matters in the world,' she says 'is to get an attractive "fella", hold on to him and love him to distraction.' Problem pages encourage the idea that there is something wrong with a girl, if she 'hasn't got a "fella", doesn't want a "fella", feels she's not pretty/developed enough to get a "fella", is passionately interested in playing the violin, hockey, chess, reading books, solving maths problems or mending bikes'. In analysing the function of girls' magazines, Toynbee takes a mass-manipulative view, seeing them as little more than a 'shower of propaganda to those who are most vulnerable'. Against the argument that such publications are not meant to be taken seriously and that even the girls who read them see them as a joke, Toynbee replies 'What's funny? Where's the joke? The joke is that after all these years of battering on for a new deal for women, struggling with Equal Opportunities, Equal Pay, anti-sex discrimination, equal schools curricula, striving to release young girls from the stultifying role stereotypes of the past, magazines like these are actually travelling fast in the opposite direction.'

McRobbie, however, is far less willing to concede such a powerful role to these magazines: '*Jackie* cannot be held solely responsible for the narrow and restricted lives many girls are forced to lead. Ultimately, the girl's "career" at home and in the workplace is determined by her social class, her sex and her race.'

Both McRobbie's and Toynbee's articles were written in the 1970s when teenage girls' magazines were at the height of their popularity. In more recent decades the image of women in the media has changed. Women's romantic fiction in general is more likely to project their heroines as successful with exciting jobs, though they are nevertheless likely to be read by women doing semi-skilled and unskilled jobs.

The cult of femininity

An altogether different view of women's magazines is given by Marjorie Ferguson (1983). Unlike publications for men, these magazines track women's biographies – there are magazines for very young girls, teenage girls (*Just 17*), young women, pregnant women, brides-to-be, mothers and housewives (*Good Housekeeping*) not paralleled by magazines for men. These provide a **normative** direction for the course of women's lives. Ferguson argues that these publications can be best understood through adapting Durkheim's interpretation of the role of religion (see chapter 7). Women's magazines are the organising focus for the **cult** of femininity. The parallels are that 'the women's magazines; the high priestesses who select and shape the cult's interdictions and benedictions are women's magazine editors; the rites,

rituals, sacrifices and obligations (offerings) that they exhort are to be performed periodically by the cult's adherents'. What 'every women knows' is sacred knowledge, where the rituals are beautification. child-rearing, housework and cooking. The totemic object is not men, however, but women. The house equates to the church, with the kitchen as its inner sanctum.

Paraphrasing Durkheim, Ferguson claims that when women read *Woman* magazine, they are worshipping women. Women's magazines socialise women into femininity in a way that men are never socialised into masculinity. The real mystery to be addressed is therefore 'How are men socialised into their male roles?' The issue of masculinity, however, is only just beginning to be addressed by sociologists.

Unlike McRobbie and Toynbee, Ferguson argues that women's magazines play a benign role in improving the collective lives of women: 'For some women, there may be nowhere outside the pages of these journals where they are consistently valued so highly, or accorded such high status. It may be that only within the pages of *Good Housekeeping* or *Women's Realm* do some women find an easy, accessible and regular source of positive self-esteem and social support' as women.

In a similar vein, John Fiske (1990) manages to see good in television programmes targeted chiefly as women – soap operas and game shows such as *The Price is Right* which, he argues, have a liberatory dimension for women. Consumer-based quiz shows with mainly women contestants, he says, celebrate women's knowledge, in this case the price of household commodities: 'Two main forms of liberation are expressed in the game show audience's enthusiasm: the first is to give public, noisy acclaim to skills that are ordinarily silenced; the second is simply to be "noisy" in public, to escape from demure respectability, from the confines of good sense that patriarchy has constructed as necessary qualities for "the feminine".' Money is replaced by knowledge, symbolically liberating women from men's economic power. In these ways, Fiske claims, women cannot be seen as the 'cultural dopes' identified by Garfinkel. They are not complicit, and find no pleasure, in their subordination. These game shows can therefore be seen as an example of women using popular culture for their own, more subversive, ends.

The mass media targeted at women can therefore be seen in at least two ways: either, as McRobbie and Toynbee argue, as vehicles for transmitting a limiting and reactionary patriarchal ideology, or, as with

Ferguson and Fiske, as an organising force for women, and as one of the few instances in which women are the sole object of their own attention, albeit within a patriarchal culture.

Disability

Anne Karpf (1988) argues that two dominant media images of the physically disabled exist: as the subject of miracle cures or as objects of pity and charity who need to be helped on televised fund-raising events. They are only portrayed because of their disability, with the wheelchair as the often exclusive icon of disability. 'What is more,' Karpf says, 'the media often cast able-bodied actors as disabled characters, producing unconvincing portrayals which the disability movement likens to those of blacked-up actors of the past.' Endorsing this view, Cumberbatch and Negrine (1992) also highlight the stereotypical images of the disabled as evil or monsters (the 'villains' in James Bond films, for example, are often shown as having a disability), maladjusted, dependent and incapable, or courageous and heroic in living with or overcoming their disability. What is absent in both of these media accounts are portrayals of disabled people going about their everyday life or engaging in celebration (for example the Paralympics) in spite of their disability, as people who have claims to rights rather than charity, and do not need others to speak on their behalf.

In the field of mental health, the Glasgow University Media Group argues (GUMG, 1995) that mental illness is frequently equated with schizophrenia by the mass media, with the assumption that people with a mental illness are usually violent – 'psychopathic lunatics'. Against this unfortunate stereotype is the real world of complex levels and types of mental illness (such as depression) where the overwhelming majority of people diagnosed in this way are not violent, including those labelled 'schizophrenic'.

Age

Two age groups in particular have been the object of close scrutiny. Though it is generally accepted that childhood is now portrayed in a less patronising manner, and more from the child's point of view, the representation of young adults and the elderly continue to be the subject of debate.

That there is a social group identified as 'adolescents' at all is partly attributed to the influence of the media by some commentators. Alongside factors such as the raising of the school leaving age and the full employment that allowed the emergence of a new consumer market, mediated images around the birth of rock and roll in the 1950s, according to Davis (1990), were responsible for the creation of teenagers in the image and myth-making surrounding figures such as James Dean and Elvis Presley.

The study of adolescence has largely focused on **working-class** men. In general, the media have depicted this group as dangerous and a new threat to social order. The media's role in portraying this group as modern **folk devils** is examined in detail below (see 'The amplification of deviance' below), although, as Hebdige (1979) claims, it also plays a central role in reclaiming and defusing youth **subcultures**. The reincorporation of this group happens in two ways. First, their rebellion is shown as a temporary deviation. Second, a subculture's distinctive signs and symbols become commodified as objects of mass production. An example here would be the way that punk music, in Malcolm McLaren's phrase (manager of the Sex Pistols), became part of 'the great rock and roll swindle', with only the band failing to recognise that those around them saw them as a source of fast money.

Images of the elderly have generated less interest, although they have become a more visible social group as their spending power has increased. Lambert *et al*.'s (1984) content analysis of people over 60 on television, conducted over a two-week period, found that most images of the elderly on television were of men in positions such as politicians, businessmen and experts, as well as quiz masters and news readers. They are seen as positive images, men with gravitas, with no corresponding images of women of this age. Elsewhere, research has shown no clear or single picture of the elderly, with overtly **stereotypical** portrayals of the elderly as mean and resentful (such as Harry Enfield and Paul Whitehouse's 'Old Gits'), or as on 'an extended plateau of active middle age' (Featherstone and Hepworth, 1995), and in magazines such as *Retirement Choice* where the final stages of ageing are largely ignored.

Ethnicity

The media's treatment of issues concerning ethnicity, particularly ethnic minorities, has received considerable attention from sociologists, and clear views of this issue from the leading perspectives are discernible.

The pluralist view acknowledges that the historically negative and marginal portrayal of ethnic minorities in the media is a reflection of the relatively weak and powerless role these groups have played in society. It is also concerned to point out, though, that this portrayal is changing, with increasing representation from ethnic minorities in the media as journalists and editors, and more programmes and publications being produced for ethnic minority groups. This has occurred as a result of positive discrimination policies and successful lobbying by pressure groups, as well as the increasing consumer power of minority groups. That such changes can occur is evidence of the pluralist argument that the media reacts to, but does not create or cause, social change.

Where minority ethnic groups are portrayed negatively it is as a result of journalistic news values that emphasise conflict and play on public fears (for example of asylum seekers). As Paul Hartman and Charles Husband argue (1974) 'good news' stories, or issues such as housing, employment or education, are seen as less worthy of inclusion. The mass media also cannot be held responsible for reflecting the negative views that are held in the wider society, although the media helps to sustain this: 'The way the media define the situation is seen as resulting from the definitions prevailing in the general culture and from institutional factors that stem from the media themselves' (Hartmann and Husband, 1976).

Stuart Hall's (1978a) analysis of the moral panic around mugging illustrates the hegemonic view of the reporting of 'race' issues in the mass media, particularly in the press. In the 1970s, he argues, the term 'mugging' had been hardly used by the British press to refer to street robbery with violence and was a term only used with reference to this phenomenon in the USA, with the suggestion that it could one day become a problem in the United Kingdom. It made its first appearance with reference to a British crime in 1972. Throughout this year the issue of mugging became a central question in the British press, featuring all the characteristics of a **moral panic**, with the most tenuous links made in order to keep this issue alive. There was a clear pattern of prediction, exaggeration and symbolisation, where by 1975 young West Indians in urban areas were principally identified as 'muggers'.

For Hall, this portrayal was far from the facts. It is difficult for statistics on mugging to rise when there is no such category of crime recorded by the police: there could therefore be no 'problem of mugging'. Figures for the nearest equivalent 'robbery or assault with intent to rob' were actually in decline in this period. The 'problem' of mugging was being created and used by the control culture, in concert with the media, to instead assert and intensify its own power

and control over the working class, at the same time using **racism** to divide it, in a period of heightening class struggle. In this way, the dominant class not only ruled but played the leading role in the ideological struggle taking place in the decline of the long period of post-war expansion.

Teun Van Dijk (1991) argues that it is the close relationship of media workers and the ruling elite that allows choices to be made about what is seen or not seen as newsworthy. There is basically very little difference in the way in which both groups see the world. Moreover, the press in particular contributes to this negative image in the language it uses, where the two words most often connected to the word 'race' in the period of his study were 'police' and 'riot'. In addition, he says, 'ethnic minorities are consistently less quoted than majority group members and institutions, even on subjects, such as experiences of racial attacks or prejudice, on which minorities are the experts'.

For more orthodox Marxists, the real distinction in society is based on class and not ethnic divisions. According to Castles and Kosack (1973), any focus on questions of race is a diversion from the class struggle, and intended to divide the working class. For example, attempts by the mass media, as agents of the ruling class, to portray immigration as a cause of unemployment, where members of ethnic minorities are shown as 'lazy' and as 'scroungers', scape-goats for problems that are in fact caused by capitalism and can only be overcome by united working-class action, regardless of ethnic identity.

Questions

1 What problems might be faced in undertaking a content analysis of women in the mass media?
2 In what ways could the mass media celebrate disability?
3 Why might the term 'mugging' be unhelpful and inaccurate?

The effects and uses of the mass media

Most of the theories of the mass media examined so far have been concerned with its content, only implicitly looking at the question of the extent to which readers, viewers and listeners of the media are influenced. In this section we consider research into attitude formation and reinforcement, looking historically at how theories have developed as new forms of the mass media have emerged.

The hypodermic syringe model

The earliest model of the effects of the mass media on audiences is known as the 'hypodermic syringe' model, so called because it assumes that the media has the power to inject its message into the audience with the force of a hypodermic syringe. If someone is exposed to a mass media message, it will be so powerful that it will cause them to behave in the way the mass media dictates, effectively controlling their behaviour. In the 1930s, the Nazis' use of cinema and radio, orchestrated by the Propaganda Minister Josef Goebbels, was widely thought to be responsible for Hitler's hold over the German people. In this same decade, Orson Welles's *The War of the Worlds* radio broadcast fooled panic-stricken Americans into thinking that Martians had invaded, giving further credence to the hypodermic syringe model.

A similar view can also be found in a number of studies of film and television violence conducted by a range of researchers. Bandura's well-known work with children and filmed violence on 'Bobo' dolls claimed that children would imitate the violence they had witnessed through mediated images (Bandura *et al.*, 1961). William Belson's study of 1565 boys in London (1978) found that 'high exposure to television violence increases the degree to which boys engage in serious violence', and recommended that 'steps should be taken as soon as possible to achieve a substantial reduction in the total amount of violence being presented on television'.

The assumption that the media are able to determine attitudes and decisively affect behaviour is also implicit in the practice of censorship, advertising (where the promotion of items such as tobacco and alcohol are tightly controlled), as well as areas of politics such as voting behaviours, where the political directives of newspapers have been seen as decisive to the result of general elections. It is also strongly implicit in the mass-manipulative model, where it is suggested that the ruling class not only intends to control the minds and behaviour of the proletariat, it also succeeds.

All subsequent theories of media effects are to some extent critiques of the hypodermic syringe model, but criticisms specific to this model have also been made. Much of the work of researchers such as Bandura and Belson has been seen as methodologically suspect, particularly the use of experimental and laboratory methods. The assumption that people's minds are a blank sheet (or 'tabula rasa') until the media come to write indelibly on it has also been seen as simplistic.

Prior socialisation is not taken into account. The hypodermic syringe model assumes that people will interpret the same message in the same way, as an undifferentiated mass. In claiming a direct causal relationship with subsequent behaviour, it is also claiming that people will respond immediately to external stimuli, discounting the possibility of longer-term media effects.

Nevertheless, recent research has been unwilling to dismiss this model entirely. Writing about his research into the miners' strike of 1984, for example, Greg Philo writes 'The earliest mass communication researchers...saw media power as akin to a hypodermic needle injecting society with ideologies and propaganda. Later it became apparent that audiences bring much of their own culture and history to their understanding of media messages...our own research shows that at least some of the information which is used when these audiences think about the world is itself provided by television and the press. It is also clear that it can be very difficult to criticise a dominant media account if there is little access to alternative sources of information. In these circumstances we should not underestimate the power of the media' (Philo, (1990). In other words, in certain circumstances some credence must be given to the claims of the hypodermic syringe model when people have very little opportunity to consider another point of view.

The normative or two-step flow model

The normative model, also known as the two-step flow model, chronologically followed the hypodermic syringe model, though its conclusions are very different. It is mostly associated with the work of Robert Merton (1946), Elihu Katz and Paul Lazarsfeld (1955), and became influential enough to hold sway in the three decades following the Second World War.

Lazarsfeld's research (1944) into the US Presidential election of 1940 found that the mass media's impact on voting behaviour was minimal, with half of all voters making up their minds about who to vote for many months before polling day. Those who did change their minds did so because of the influence of the people in their immediate social circle. His subsequent work with Katz (Katz and Lazarsfeld, 1955) argued that an individual's personal beliefs and attitudes are mainly formed within social groups – families, friends and colleagues, in other words by the agents of primary and secondary **socialisation**. If the mass media has a role at all, it is to influence the opinion leaders within these groups. The two steps of the two-step flow model are therefore 'from radio and print to opinion leaders and from them to the less active sections of the populations', though the opinion leaders cited many more sources than the mass media as influencing their decisions. It was nevertheless the case that the opinion leaders identified exposed themselves more to the media than the people they influenced, though they still saw the media as only one of a range of influences on them.

Although the two-step flow model was useful in redirecting research into media effects away from a too simplistic hypodermic syringe model, it has also been seen as lacking sophistication, for example by dividing the audience into two categories of 'active' and 'passive', as well as failing to state why there are only two steps to the flow model, when there is no reason why there could not be many more. It also assumes that power and influence only exist between individuals and groups, ignoring the power of large social institutions such as the State and big business.

Uses and gratifications model

The uses and gratifications model reverses the question about the effects of the mass media on people and instead asks how people use the mass media. Looked at in this way, the 'gratifications' given by the mass media are less obvious than simply providing information or entertainment. For Lull (1990), the mass media are used for a wide variety of purposes. They may be used for companionship or background noise, to regulate time, to denote status and provide role models, to allow people to join in with group conversation, to facilitate 'family occasions' or help create or maintain relationships as well as to promote social learning, for example through the transmission of values.

To this list, according to McQuail (1972), can be added uses such as escaping from routine, or joining in imaginary communities, such as those of soap operas like *EastEnders* and *Coronation Street*. They can also give a sense of personal identity if we see ourselves, for example, as 'the kind of person who reads *The Times*', or listens to Radio 1. It also has a major use in allowing people to understand what is happening in the world around them, satisfying the need to keep abreast of events.

That the list of other possible uses and gratifications found in the mass media could potentially be very long, and would show different uses by different groups (such as men and women) is testimony to the value of this approach in examining the impact of the mass media. However, research in this field has overemphasised the extent to which activities such as watching television are planned or structured, and the extent to which individuals, rather than groups, engage with the mass media. The fundamental assumption that people use the mass media to meet needs fails to answer the question of why those needs exist in the first place, or what the mass media's role may have been in creating needs and shaping desires. It also has little to say about the dysfunctional nature of the media, for example in the way that a desire to discover what is happening in society through the media may lead to the view that there are high crime levels and this could discourage people from leaving the house. Similarly, the post-modernist view expressed by Baudrillard (1983b) argues that, although the audience may interact with the media, they are now so caught up in its world (the simulacra) that they are unable or uninterested in acting in their own 'real' world.

Interpretive model

The interpretive model, which complements the pluralist model in the same way that the hypodermic syringe model complements the mass-manipulative model, focuses on the way audiences choose to interpret media messages. There are three main dimensions to this: selective exposure, whereby the audience choose what they want to watch, read or hear and avoid what they don't; selective perception, where they choose to interpret a media message in a way with which they are comfortable; and selective retention, where they choose to retain or forget aspects of a media message. This model therefore focuses on the way that audiences seek media messages that will reinforce what they already think (congruent change) rather than search out programmes and articles that will challenge deep-seated attitudes.

This process of interpretation will exist at different levels, according to the media literacy of the audiences. At the higher levels of literacy lie the ability to understand the media conventions that surround different genres (such as drama or light entertainment), the intentions of the people who made the programme, for example being able to understand which people we are being asked to sympathise with, and the different narrative structures that exist (the different ways in which a story is told, for example through one character, or through flashbacks and fantasy sequences). The clear implication here is that a greater ability to read the media will allow a more critical and active interpretation of its message.

The interpretive model is therefore most successfully applied to those with high levels of media literacy and discretion. It has little to say about those who are less selective in their engagement with the media, and are less wary of its potential influence. Nor does it take into account the 'slow drip' of media messages over time and different media formats. It sees the audience mainly as individuals, playing down the collective way the mass media is consumed.

Structured interpretation model

The structured interpretation model attempts to redress some of these problems. Stuart Hall (1980), writing from a broadly hegemonic perspective, argues that media messages (the 'text') contain the values of the dominant ideology, as transmitted by the journalists. This intended (or 'encoded') message is described as the preferred reading, the way in which a message is implicitly intended to be understood by its authors. How the message is decoded, however, will depend on the cultural knowledge and context of the audience, leading to a wide range and variety of audience interpretations. The mass media is polysemic – it can be read as containing many messages.

Texts can be read in three main ways: a preferred reading is where the audience interprets a media message in the way intended by its authors, or according to its construction; a negotiated reading occurs where the audience accept the media message but still do not see it as relevant to their own lives or situations. This can be a contradictory position to occupy. An oppositional reading occurs when the viewer or reader effectively rewrites the media message in a way that opposes the dominant-hegemonic position being articulated, for example a pacifist refusing to accept a media account of why a war may be necessary. Those texts that encourage a very narrow range of readings or interpretations are described as closed texts, and those that can be very widely interpreted are open texts. In theory, television news is an open text; in practice, according to the hegemonic view, it is a closed text.

Hall's arguments have been put to classic effect by David Morley in his research into the 1970s television news magazine programme *Nationwide* (1980). This study investigated the views of 26 groups of people of similar stratified characteristics, where they were invited to watch editions of *Nationwide* collectively,

with Morley investigating their perceptions of the programme through group interviews. His findings allowed him to relate the different audiences' perceptions to Hall's typology of readings, finding, for example, that apprentices and bank managers saw *Nationwide* as commonsensical (the dominant reading or decoding, corresponding to Hall's preferred reading). Full-time trade unionists took a negotiated reading while shop stewards offered an oppositional reading, seeing the programme as presenting a consensus view of society and ignoring the conflicts they knew to exist. A group of black further education students simply saw the programme as irrelevant to their own concerns and experiences, instead seeing it as portraying a view of the world more relevant to middle-class shoppers and businessmen, itself a form of oppositional reading.

Although Morley's work has been influential both in terms of his findings and his methodology, it is not without its critics. Morley himself has argued that as most television viewing takes place within the family his research should have been based within a family context rather than in groups he identified. He also pays little attention to why there appeared to be a connection between groupings such as class and ethnicity and the types of readings discussed, and why other factors, which may have been equally important, were ignored.

Morley's work, however, is important because of the balanced consideration it gave to the active role of the audience and the intentions of the producers. As he says: 'audiences produce meanings, but have to work on material which has been pre-selected and organized in particular ways by producers'.

Cultural effects model

Where most attempts to study media effects have looked at the short-term effects of the mass media, attempting to gauge attitudes 'before and after' exposure, the cultural effects model attempts to investigate the longer-term 'slow drip' effects of the mass media. It also seeks to take into account the social situation of the audience, and how their own cultural beliefs and understandings may incorporate and respond to media messages.

An early attempt to do this can be found in Hadley Cantril's *The Invasion from Mars* (1940). In this study, Cantril attempts to look at the cultural context within which Orson Welles's famous 1938 radio broadcast was received, where it appeared that Welles had managed to fool a large number of American radio listeners into thinking that Martians were invading the Earth and landing in the New York area. The belief that many people had been profoundly panicked by this broadcast led to changes in the rules governing radio broadcasting to prevent any similar reoccurrence, as well as reinforcing many people's belief in the hypodermic springe model.

By interviewing 135 people who had heard the broadcast, as well as using the findings of two large national surveys. Cantril argues that understanding its effects on the audience is more complex. First, the surveys showed that although six million had heard the broadcast, only one million believed a real invasion to have been taking place. Most of these, it seemed, had turned on their radio after the programme had started, expecting to hear the scheduled news broadcast. Instead, they heard a radio play attempting to reproduce a live news bulletin, in an era where radio news was seen as the most honest and reliable form of news reporting.

At a more profound level, Hadley takes into consideration the point in history when the broadcast was made. It went out on the evening of 30 October 1938. This was almost a decade after the Wall Street crash of 1929, which quickly led to the depression years of the 1930s, when belief in the 'American dream' and confidence in the future had been shattered. The fear of war was increasing, especially with the intensive talks between the British Prime Minister Neville Chamberlain and German Chancellor Adolf Hitler throughout September 1938, culminating in the Munich Agreement. Attack by a foreign power was not unexpected and interruptions of radio programmes with news flashes were also increasing in frequency. In these circumstances, people's credulity was ready to be stretched even further in this mix of the medium used, the message sent, and the cultural and historical circumstances in which it was received.

In a similar vein, but several decades later, Stan Cohen's *Folk Devils and Moral Panics*, also tries to locate responses to the apparent seaside violence between mods and rockers in England in the 1960s to the wider cultural circumstances in which they took place, in this case the breakdown of post-war austerity. These events were part of 'a whole pattern in which pregnant schoolgirls, CND marches, beatniks, long hair, contraceptives in slot machines, purple hearts and smashing up telephone boxes were all inextricably intertwined'.

Cultural effects theory therefore argues that the mass media do have an effect, but the size and shape of this impact are dependent on a number of factors. Some of these, such as the slow-drip effect of media messages over time, are almost impossible to quantify and measure.

Given the amount of variants identified – the medium used, the message sent and the historical and social location of the audience who receive it – it is also very difficult to identify any causal links, or determine whether one variant is more important than another. So many factors can come into play that the concept of an effect being dependent on a culture's interpretation of a message (rather than the many individuals who make up that culture) may be lost.

There are, then, a great many perspectives on the effects of the mass media, from theories that attribute great powers of effect to the mass media, to those that give them very little. The variables involved in comprehending any possible effects are numerous and varied, taking into account timespans and cultures as well as individuals. It could be said that this research is no more conclusive than Professor Berelson's statement from the 1940s that 'some kinds of communication on some kinds of issues, brought to the attention of some kinds of people under some kinds of conditions, have some kinds of effects' (in Diamond and Bates, 1992).

Questions

1 What are the two steps of the two-step flow model?
2 In what ways do people use the mass media?
3 What is a preferred reading?

The mass media, violence and the amplification of deviance

As we have seen, the hypodermic syringe model claims that exposure to the mass media can directly influence or even determine the behaviour of individuals in society. From this point of view, one specific concern has always been the portrayal of **deviance**, and violence in particular, with the assumption that the portrayal of violence in the media can lead to violence in society. Following incidents of mass killing, such as those at Hungerford and Dunblane in the United Kingdom and Columbine in the USA, a search usually begins to look for the cause of these incidents by finding out about viewing habits of the perpetrators. The murder of two-year-old James Bulger in 1993 is also strongly linked to the similarity between his young murderers' acts and those depicted in the film *Child's Play 3*. This had been rented by one of the boy murderers in the weeks prior to the murder, and the judge in the subsequent trial made reference to his suspicion that 'exposure to violent films may in part be an explanation'. The film director Stanley Kukbrick withdrew copies of the film *A Clockwork Orange* after repeated claims that the film was causing incidents of 'copycat' violence.

Many attempts have been made to show a causal link between the media and social violence, often by use of the experimental method. Among the best known of these is that carried out by Bandura (1961), in an experiment where children were shown three clips of televised images of inflated dolls being attacked. In the first case the attackers were punished, and in the second they were rewarded and in the third nothing happened. When encouraged to play with dolls themselves, it was the children who had seen the attackers punished who were least likely to imitate what they had seen on television, while children from the other groups were more likely to attack the dolls. Similarly, Liebert and Baron (1972) found that children exposed to television violence were more likely to hurt other children than those who hadn't been exposed.

Such studies will always be vulnerable to the criticisms made of experiments: that they are artificial and at best can only demonstrate short-term effects. Belson's research on 1,565 boys (1978) attempted to look at the long-term effects of exposure to television violence. In doing this, he differentiated between different contexts and portrayals of violence, for example gratuitous and non-gratuitous violence in television drama, or that in cartoons and comedy. Where violence does have an effect, he found, it is where boys have a high exposure to violence, particularly portrayals in film and drama, although cartoons were seen as having little effect: 'high exposure to television violence increases the degree to which boys engage in serious violence...steps should be taken as soon as possible to achieve a substantial reduction in the total amount of violence being presented on television'.

Belson's work has also been widely criticised, for example in his assertion that heavy exposure to any form of television, violent or not, increases the propensity to violence in children. Similarly, those boys with the highest propensity to violence were not the heaviest television watchers, but only moderate viewers. The heaviest viewers were not the most likely to be the most violent. His research was also based on

asking the boys to remember television programmes they might have seen up to twelve years before, when they were in their infancy. As Murdock and McCron argue (1979), his use of adults to judge the level of violence in television programmes did not allow an exploration of the boys' perception of violence on television. He also looked at the boys individually, and not as members of gangs and subcultures, ignoring their social experience and background.

In attempting to understand the effects of mediated violence, the concepts of disinhibition and desensitisation have been developed. Disinhibition refers to the consequences of becoming increasingly familiar with televised violence such that it becomes commonplace and even acceptable in society. Desensitisation refers to the way that continuous exposure to mediated violence ceases to have a shock effect on viewers, leaving programme makers looking for ever more graphic and gruesome portrayals. Critics such as Martin Barker (1984), however, are highly sceptical of this argument, observing that firefighters and medical staff become desensitised after attending traffic accidents over a number of years, but retain a sensitivity and desire to help the victims.

It may also be the case that the opposite happens: that the mass media sensitise people to violence, and help prevent its occurrence in society. Certainly, live pictures of the war in Vietnam beamed into people's homes in the USA contributed to the anti-war movement there, and the reporting of war has been carefully considered by governments and the media ever since. Similarly, news stories concerning violent crime, particularly against children, encourages the public to contact television programmes such as *Crimewatch* and report information to the police. Mediated violence, according to Gunter and McAleer (1990), may have a cathartic effect, allowing the potentially violent to release those emotions when watching violence rather than carrying it out in their own lives.

As with research into the general effects of the mass media, studies of the relationship between television and violence are inconclusive, incurring similar methodological problems. Looking specifically at young people, Hagell and Newburn (1994) argue that 'those who blame the mass media for crime are on a doomed mission in search of a simple solution to a complex problem. No informed person can simply say that TV is bad or that it is good for children. For some children, under some conditions, or for the same children under other conditions, it may be beneficial. For most children, under most conditions, most TV is probably neither particularly harmful nor particularly beneficial'.

Other writers studying violence and the media have identified other roles played by the mass media. One frequently observed discovery is that the mass media can increase the focus on, or amplify, the extent of deviance in society to a point where the public's fear of crime is greater than the reality of the crime itself. In creating an awareness of particular crimes and types of deviance, the mass media can also promote and extend deviance (an 'amplification spiral'), as well as play an organising role for the containment of such behaviour.

One of the best-known sociological analyses of this effect can be found in Stan Cohen's *Folk Devils and Moral Panics* (1972). A moral panic occurs when 'a condition, episode, person or group of persons emerges to become defined as a threat to societal values and interests' when 'the moral barricades are manned by editors, bishops, politicians and other right-thinking people; socially accredited experts pronounce their diagnoses and solutions; ways of coping are evolved or (more often) resorted to.' A moral panic can occur at any time, and can even involve the re-emergence of a forgotten issue. It begins with the identification of a social problem or deviant group, and follows a predictable pattern, in which the mass media plays a central part.

The 'folk devils' of his title are the mods and rockers of the 1960s. Cohen points out that small seaside town disturbances which became associated with these groups had been common since the late 1950s. Why, then, did a few isolated scuffles between gangs of youths at that point turn into a widescale moral panic, spreading new fashions, music and the images of gang warfare into the living rooms and school playgrounds of Britain?

Easter 1964 was cold and wet, and groups of youths in Clacton were bored. They rode up and down the streets on their scooters and bikes, wrecked a few beach huts and broke some windows. There were fights and crowds in the streets. The Monday papers, starved of news after the holiday period, seized upon the events as news, and the following headlines appeared: 'Day of terror by scooter groups' (*Daily Telegraph*), 'Youngsters beat up town – 97 leather jacket arrests' (*Daily Express*), 'Wild ones invade seaside – 97 arrests' (*Daily Mirror*). Old people and respectable families of holidaymakers were often reported as being intimidated by the fighting youths. According to Cohen's research into local press and eyewitness reports, this intimidation rarely took place.

'Deserted beaches' were empty, not because of the fear of violence, but because of the bad weather. In fact, those holidaymakers who did turn out did so to watch the fighting.

By making predictions about what might happen next, through the symbolisation of the youth cultures as dangerous and deviant, and by exaggerating the scale of the problem, the mass media, Cohen argues, contributed to the **labelling** of a deviant group and the creation of a **self-fulfilling prophecy**. They helped sustain a moral panic they had helped to create, with the clear implication that the 'problem' would be insignificant and would probably disappear without saturation media coverage.

The prospect of further violence on public holidays became the subject of continuous media speculation, with reporters and journalists sent to seaside towns to cover any possible 'events'. Any activity was seized on as newsworthy, and it became the ambition of some young people to see their own photos in the papers the next day. More police were sent to cover the next public holiday, and there were more mods, rockers and 'innocent bystanders', leading to more arrests and more media coverage. As Cohen remarks, 'If one is in a group of twenty, being stared at by hundreds of adults and being pointed at by two or three cameras, the temptation to do something – even if only to shout an obscenity, make a rude gesture or throw a stone – is very great and made greater by the knowledge that one's actions will be recorded for others to see.'

In contributing to the amplification spiral in this way, the mass media also help articulate the formation of a 'control culture' whose role is to encourage politicians, judges and other agencies to punish the newly identified folk devils, in much the same way that vigilante groups would hunt out witches. In this way, the forces of discipline and surveillance become strengthened, and gain new resources with which to fight a distorted and enlarged enemy: 'an adequate medium of communication must be present for spreading the hostile belief and mobilizing potential participants'.

The study of moral panics (a phrase initiated by Cohen, though the phrase **deviancy amplification** is taken from Wilkins (1964)) is now well researched and there is a considerable literature concerning the process of deviancy amplification, for example Hall (1978) and Atkinson (1978) to the extent that a periodisation of their study has been proposed by Muncie (1987). Thus, those of the 1950s and early

1960s are described as 'discrete', the later 1960s are 'diffuse' and the 1970s and 1980s 'generalised'.

Cohen's important study clearly owes much to the **interactionist** tradition, and should be examined alongside the sociology of deviance generated by this perspective. His emphasis on the process of labelling and the self-fulfilling prophecy clearly owes much to Becker, and Lemert's claim that 'social control leads to deviance' forms one of the central premises of the book. One of Cohen's main contributions to this tradition has been to incorporate and highlight the role of the mass media in these processes: 'The student of moral enterprise cannot but pay particular attention to the role of the mass media in defining and shaping social problems.'

Critics of Cohen's work (for example McRobbie, 1994) point out that the role of the audience is assumed rather than evidenced, as Cohen carried out minimal research in this area, looking at letters to the press, parliamentary debates and conducting interviews with some members of the public. As Cohen acknowledges, the media may have little influence in creating primary deviance, and they cannot cause it to happen. It is still unclear how far they contribute to the creation of secondary deviance, and from this point of view, his work is subject to the criticisms made in general of the interactionist view of crime and deviance.

Questions

1 What is meant by the amplification of deviance?
2 In what ways could the media portrayal of violence encourage less violence in society?

Issues in researching the mass media

Researching the mass media has posed particular problems for sociologists. The mass media constitute a very large area of study, covering types of media as diverse as film, television, the press and the internet. They are also constantly changing with new technologies such as video games or satellite television emerging all the time, with a global impact. This makes the concept of mass media hard to define, and even harder to measure, where hugely different audiences have to be taken into account. The very notion of a mass medium is in any case fundamentally challenged by theories such as post-modernism and, to a lesser extent, pluralism.

In the field of media effects, the time span across which they are measured will produce different results, with long-term effects being particularly difficult to discern and verify. The method used will also yield specific types of results, with questions of **validity** and **reliability** attached. Laboratory experiments may show certain effects, but they can never replicate the circumstances under which the mass media are actually consumed. A television programme, for example, may be intensively watched in one household while serving as background noise in another. There has also been a reluctance to employ a range of methods simultaneously, as Gunter (1995) notes: 'The limitations of much of the research done so far are really to be found in the methods used. Most studies have been uni-dimensional, approaching the subject from one angle, employing one kind of measure and drawing conclusions which their measures do not entitle them to make.'

Where the mass media rather than the consumer become the object of study, there has been a tendency to use other key concepts in sociology in a limited and undefined way when, in fact, they demand as careful a use as some of the terms studied in the sociology of the mass media. This includes concepts such as class or gender, which are often examined in isolation from each other, or terms like violence and deviance. The result can be the stereotypical use of complex terms. Equally, some issues can be approached in a narrow way, leading to the exclusion of other dimensions to the topic. The issue of television violence has been largely dominated by the possibility that it may cause or be related to violence in society, when other issues could also be looked at. These include the role of other agencies around violence, such as the willingness of witnesses to report or prevent violence, or the police to deal with it. Concentrating on an issue in one way can crowd out equally relevant concerns.

The extent to which media researchers remain distant from their subject of study should also be highlighted. Much of the existing research into the mass media has suffered from the lack of objectivity with which it has been studied, damaging the credibility of other research in this field. This issue, for example, is at the heart of the debate concerning television news, with both Harrison and the GUMG accusing each other of bias and a lack of objectivity, and of representing vested interests. Similarly, ethnographic methods (which may, for example, involve researchers watching television with people in their homes) can be intrusive and even voyeuristic, running the risk of alienating the group under study in the interests of generating qualitative data. There is also a problem of reflexivity in the study of the mass media in that research into it can become a news story in itself, with mass media personnel able to influence the way the public views research into itself.

Question

What particular problems are involved in researching the mass media?

11 Politics and power

*The State is a group of humans who have successfully monopolised
the legitimate use of violence in a given territory.*
Max Weber

Introduction

This chapter begins by focusing on notions of power, authority and ideology. Functionalist, Marxist, élitist and pluralist theories of power are then examined in some detail. You will then go on to look at the role of the State in Britain, which is followed by a discussion of political parties and their respective political ideologies. The chapter closes with an examination of changing sociological explanations for voting behaviour, with a discussion of class (partisan alignment), dealignment, issue voting and rational-choice models.

Power and authority

Power relationships exist everywhere in society, whether between domestic partners, parents and children, teachers and students, police and citizens, priest and congregation, editor and readers or newspaper magnate and editor. According to the roles we play, we are all relatively more or less powerful. Many sociologists have argued that people seek power over others to compensate for the lack of power they possess in other situations, for example at work between employer and employed – or more frequently, between workers and their immediate bosses. So what do we mean by this term power?

Weber

The clearest explanation comes from Max Weber. According to Weber, power exists where one individual or group is able to get their way over another group – to oblige them to act or behave in a certain way – whether the others resist or not. As he puts it, power is 'the probability that one actor within a social relationship will be in a position to carry out his own will'. The power that some possess over others may be recognised by the passive group as legitimate – legally acceptable – in which case it will be seen as **authority**. Power not recognised as legitimate is coercion or force.

Three dimensions of power

Steven Lukes (1974) has argued that three views of power have been articulated. The difference between them is the number of dimensions to power that is perceived.

The *one-dimensional view* focuses on the behaviour of decision makers, the decisions they make, the central issues that are decided on, and the forms of conflict that are openly observable. This view of power is most appropriate to **élitist** and **pluralist** views.

The *two-dimensional view* looks at power in terms of decisions that are made, as well as decisions that are not made – it looks at what are potential as well as actual issues. As Bachrach and Baratz (1963) argue, the two-dimensional view questions who it is who sets the agenda concerning the decisions to be decided on, and what other issues they are able to block from becoming areas for public discussion.

The *three-dimensional view* is similar to the two-dimensional view in questioning who sets the agenda for decision making, but goes further by arguing that some fundamental issues never emerge because, under the hold of propaganda or ideological control, no other possible alternative is imagined or considered.

Other views of power have sought to move the term away from the idea that it is something to be possessed or not – you either have power or not.

Power can also be seen as a potential and something that can be generated. Societies, and organisations within them, can become more or less powerful according to the degree to which the potential power is organised. For Michael Mann (1986), power can be mobilised in ideological, political, military and economic forms. None of these forms of organisation automatically possesses power. It only becomes – or ceases to be – effective when its organisational form allows it. Thus, if the modern State has power, it is due to the immense amount of organisational ability that it now possesses.

The term authority is not synonymous with the term power. Authority is the exercise of legitimate power. The two do not always co-exist. People may have the authority to carry out an action, but be unable to carry it through because they lack the power (such as a teacher trying to keep a class quiet). On the other hand, people may be able to succeed in their actions without the legitimacy to do so, as with one country invading the territory of another. In this case, they would have power without authority. They would then seek to make this power legitimate.

Weber distinguished between three different types of authority in society: traditional, charismatic and rational-legal. In the first, order is maintained on the basis of established custom and procedure – 'we've always done it this way'. The authority once possessed by the aristocracy is a good example of this. In the second, individuals or groups maintain authority because of the particular qualities they possess, particularly leadership, that make people want to follow them. Mahatma Gandhi is a good example here. The third refers to authority that is maintained because of the importance given to formal rules which are followed regardless of the individuals enforcing them. Respect is given to the position someone holds, not to the person holding the position. **Bureaucratic** authority is what Weber had at the front of his mind here, where norms have a semi-legal status.

Questions
1 How do the one-, two- and three-dimensional views of power differ?
2 How does power differ from authority?
3 What is Weber's view of power and authority?

Theories of power
Functionalism
There is very little writing of any substance that has appeared – especially in the last twenty years – that articulates the concept of power from a **functionalist** point of view. The paucity of such material points to the conclusion that this is one of the weakest and least elaborated areas of functionalist theory.

Parsons
As ever, it is with Talcott Parsons that we will find the most comprehensive attempt to theorise power from a structuralist perspective (for example in *Politics and Social Structure*, 1969). His argument proceeds in a manner that closely resembles his ideas on **stratification**. Power, like social inequality, originates from the collective needs of the whole society. The amount of power in society can be measured by the degree to which collective goals are being realised. There is a difference between what a society wants – for example an increasing standard of living – and its ability to attain that goal. Power, for Parsons, exists as 'a facility for the performance of functions in and on behalf of the society as a system'. A society is at its most powerful and efficient when these goals are being effectively realised – what Parsons calls a 'variable-sum' notion of power. In the same way that stratification is necessary, so too is it vital for some to have more power than others. These powerful individuals or groups will exercise power on behalf of the wider society.

In a Western **democracy**, some are powerful because that power has been entrusted or 'deposited' with them, in much the same way that money is placed in a bank by creditors. And in the same way, that trust can be withdrawn through elections when the electorate feels it needs to withdraw it. The possibility of sectional interests of the **State** holding on to power for its own sake is therefore unconsidered.

Criticisms of the functionalist view
The shortcomings of functionalist – or Parsonian – theory here are glaring, and it is no surprise that little work has been done recently on its application. Parsons is effectively limited to describing Western democracies, and there is a strong sense that he is really only thinking of democracy in the USA. He makes what many see as a naive assumption about the efficient working of a democratic system and

citizens' ability to express their will through it – this is perhaps a result of the **consensual** nature of American politics, where the differences between Republicans and Democrats are not as great as they have traditionally been between, for example, Conservatives and Labour in Britain.

Questions

1 Define what Parsons meant by a variable-sum concept of power.

2 What are the shortcomings of the functionalist viewpoint of power?

Marxism

The State in Marx's lifetime

From Marx's point of view, an understanding of the nature of the State is simple. It is, he said, 'but a committee for managing the whole affairs of the bourgeoisie'. By this he meant that the State existed to referee Victorian **capitalism** and act on behalf of the **bourgeoisie** to maintain their **class** control over the **proletariat**. And at first sight, this point of view seems persuasive. In his lifetime, 1818–83, the great debates within the State took place between a fading aristocracy and a rising bourgeoisie. Only those who owned or possessed a certain amount of property could vote, and some with enough property could vote twice. The claims of the **working class** for political participation through organisations such as the Chartist movement were ignored or suppressed. The State represented the interests of one class in society, which enabled it to control and direct key parts of the **superstructure** such as the police and the army. The State was the political expression of **ruling-class** power. In a Communist society, Engels predicted, the State would become obsolete and 'wither away'.

After Marx died, and as the proletariat gained the right to participate at a political level through voting, a debate developed between **Marxists**: would the working class, through its own political organisations, be able to take control of the State and use it for its own ends, or did the State itself need to be transformed out of all recognition in order to truly represent the working class? This debate raged in the early decades of this century, mainly between German Social Democrats and Russian Bolsheviks, with anarchists on the fringe making their own unique contribution.

Bolshevism

With the establishment of Soviet government by 1922, following the Russian Revolution of 1917, the Bolsheviks put their own ideas into practice, at first by spreading the idea of government by local councils of workers, soldiers and peasants. Yet, while arguing that the State in the capitalist West represented the 'monopoly of violence', the Soviet State in the 1930s under Stalin was to unleash State violence on a scale that paralleled Hitler's, giving rise to the term **totalitarian** to describe the similarities between the two State-centred systems of Nazism and **communism**.

For Western Marxists, the State outside totalitarian countries continued to be seen as a system of social control run either by or for the owners of the **means of production**. Important differences emerged as to how the ruling class maintained their control, particularly in Marxist debates of the late 1960s and early 1970s between Ralph Miliband and Nikos Poulantzas, who represented what have come to be seen as the 'instrumentalist' and 'structuralist' wings of Marxist theories of the State.

Miliband

Ralph Miliband's (1969) view is a basic restatement of Marxism in order to counter more conventional ideas of the State prevailing at the time, such as pluralism. For Miliband, a clearly visible capitalist ruling class exists, in both the élite positions of industry and the élite positions of the State. The State is simply an instrument of the capitalist ruling class, the individual members of whom are closely linked to the leading positions in the State through ties of family, religion, education and culture. In finance, in industry and the State, there is a single homogeneous class.

There is an abundance of evidence to support this view. For example, the Conservative Prime Minister, Alec Douglas-Home's Cabinet of 1963 contained 21 members who had attended private schools – one of the key agencies of ruling-class reproduction. Mrs Thatcher's first Cabinet of 1979 contained seven ministers who had, at some time or other, attended Eton. In 1983, the heads of both the Civil and Foreign Service, the Chief of Defence Staff, the editor of The Times, the chairman of the BBC, the governor of the Bank of England and four of its directors had all attended Eton. In the 1992 general election one-third of the Conservative MPs who were elected described themselves as company directors. Of all Conservative

MPs, 47 per cent had been educated at a private school. Exactly the same proportion had attended Oxford and Cambridge universities, as had 22 per cent of Labour MPs. In the same year, *The Whitehall Companion* showed that the eight largest government departments are run by permanent secretaries who went to fee-paying private schools, of whom only one did not attend Oxbridge. Of all the graduates in the highest grades of the Civil Service, more than half had attended these same two universities (see also chapter 3).

Poulantzas

Yet for the Marxist Nikos Poulantzas this focus on the profile of individuals is mistaken. He argues against Miliband (1969). It does not matter who it is who runs the State, whether they are from Eton or a south London comprehensive, whether their father was a merchant banker, an unemployed gnome maker or even if they are a grocer's daughter from Lincolnshire. The point is that the structure of society is capitalist. There is therefore a structural guarantee that the State will serve the needs of the leading capitalists, even if those running the State are not actually of the capitalist class themselves. It cannot be any other way, because the structure of a capitalist society demands this of the State. The State may, according to Poulantzas, be 'relatively autonomous' or self-directing, where an institutional separation can exist between the political power existing in the State and economic power in society's base. At this level, the professionals who run the State will be able to overcome what divisions may exist within the capitalist class and make any necessary concessions to the working class.

Structural super-determinism

In putting forward this view of the State, Poulantzas has provoked a great deal of criticism. One strand of it comes from Miliband, who asserts that Poulantzas is guilty of 'structural super-determinism', by which he means Poulantzas simplistically accepts the literalness and automatic nature of the **economic base** necessarily determining the superstructure, or that because a society is capitalist it necessarily follows – simply by assertion – that the State serves the interests of the capitalist class. A second objection is the almost structural-functionalist nature of Poulantzas' argument. He appears to argue that, simply by existing, the State must be functional to the needs of capital.

Gramsci and hegemony

Somewhere between Miliband's instrumentalism and Poulantzas' (and Althusser's) structuralism lies the analysis of Antonio Gramsci (1891–1937). He was an Italian Communist who, having spent many years fighting for communism, spent many more years in jail under Mussolini in Italy. Much of his best-known work – for example the Prison Notebooks – became popular in Europe in the 1970s and 1980s. One of his most important ideas is the concept of **hegemony**, by which groups in society gain intellectual leadership (see also chapter 1). Whoever holds hegemony in society holds the dominance of ideas. By making a division between political society or the formal institutions of the State (particularly the police and the army) and civil society (which may be the family, the church, trade unions, the media, education system and so on), Gramsci is able to highlight the difference between capitalist control through the State and, more importantly, their ideological control and domination of civil society. It is the wrong approach, Gramsci argues, for the working class to target its struggle solely on the State. What they must first do is establish their own ideological supremacy in civil society through the permeation of a revolutionary **class consciousness**. At all levels, he says, they must win the battle for ideas to gain hegemony. The division between **ideological State apparatuses** and repressive State apparatuses also re-emerges in the work of Louis Althusser.

Neo-Marxism and the State

In *The Context of British Politics* David Coates attempts to construct a neo-Marxist model of the British State (Coates, 1984). Employing Gramscian concepts and seeing the State as more fluid than Miliband and Poulantzas, Coates argues that the main pressures on the State derive from the demands of international and domestic capital, in the form of banks, finance houses and large businesses. Industrial capitalism, by comparison, is much weaker. The power and influence of the ruling class is divided rather than monolithic, made up as it is of many constituent parts. At the same time, its ideological control over the working class is far from total. The proletariat, as individuals, possesses 'dual consciousness'. At times they are under the sway of hegemonic control, at others, in the grind of their daily lives, they realise the serious deficiencies of capitalism and grope towards class consciousness.

To maintain control, the State is occasionally prepared to make real concessions in its power, for example to **trade unions** or in the form of public ownership. This is true for the long period of economic expansion in the decades following the Second World War. Economic contraction creates crisis in which ideological dominance, in the harsher form of Thatcherism, is far harder for the ruling class to maintain.

Questions

1 How do modern Marxist views of the State all differ from that of Marx in the nineteenth century?
2 How does Poulantzas' view of the State differ from Miliband's? What does he mean by relative autonomy?

Elitism

Classical and modern élite theories

The theories which are gathered together under the heading of 'élitist' are wide and varied. It is necessary to distinguish between 'classical' élitist theories (so called because they came first and are the oldest, classical models) and modern élite theories. One of the most important things to do is to distinguish between Marxism as an élite theory (in which the ruling class can be seen as an élite group) and the rest. The most famous names in classical élitism, Vilfredo Pareto (1978; first published in 1902), Gaetano Mosca (1896) and Robert Michels (1911), were spurred to write in reaction to Marx's theories.

Pareto's work is considered to be the classic refutation of Marxist economics and sociology. It is said that of all anti-Marxist writing, this book caused Lenin the most concern.

Lions and foxes

Pareto was a **positivist** and followed Durkheim's lead in criticising Marxism for having no scientific validity. However, he did have time for some of Marx's thinking: 'There is in Marx a sociological part, which is superior to other parts and is often in accord with reality. Marx has one very clear idea – that of class conflict.' However, Marx's Capital was criticised as vague and obscure. Pareto was willing to admit that class conflict was real, but it was caused by more than just the economic base. He believed that some individuals were innately superior. According to Pareto these superior individuals wanted power, whereas the mass of mankind was politically inactive. For him

political movements could only ever be the work of active minorities; the élites. Most people in society are passive instruments in the power struggle. The élite fall into two categories – 'lions' and 'foxes'. Lions are strong, brave and rule forcefully and with little fear of the outcome. Their leadership is direct and open, with little political cunning or trickery. Foxes on the other hand are cunning manipulators, manoeuvring politically behind the scenes. They rule through manipulation and deceit, and overcome their political enemies by stealth rather than direct, forceful action.

These élites sometimes hold power and are sometimes in opposition throughout history. Changes in political fortunes are a consequence of the inevitable tendency for the ruling group to become decadent, soft and ineffective leaders. When this happens, that power structure gives way to the next, foxes step down and lions take over or vice versa. This 'theory of circulating élites' is said by Pareto to be reflected in the past two thousand years of human society. Critics of Pareto usually criticise the simplicity of his basic ideas. Although the characteristics of 'lions' and 'foxes' can be found in certain leaders, the theory relies on the psychological make-up of individuals, and is therefore considered to be weak when applied to social structure, where many other factors intervene.

VILFREDO PARETO (1848–1923)

Italian economist and sociologist. He is well known as an élite theorist believing in the inevitability of élite circulation to regenerate élites in power. The advent of new social élites to power maintains the social equilibrium.

Mosca

Gaetano Mosca had a similar aristocratic approach when it came to talking about 'natural' superiority in some social groups. Mosca believed that the masses were unfit to rule, and at best they could be allowed no more than to participate as voters in a **representative democracy**. Mosca believed in the right of the **upper classes** to rule by birth. Only those from old established families could possibly have the intellectual and leadership abilities necessary to carry the burden of power. He gradually came around to accepting that representative democracies could work, but he believed that this was true only when the élites formed the leadership of political parties, and therefore ensured that power only changed hands between one élite group and another. Any attempts to allow the masses a share of power would be disastrous. Democracy was only acceptable in that it keeps the majority politically inactive for most of the time. As long as real decisions are taken by those with the correct family backgrounds, then democracy poses no threat to the stability of the élite leadership.

> ### GAETANO MOSCA (1858–1941)
>
> An Italian political theorist and one of the founding fathers of élite theory. He is best known for his work *The Ruling Class* (1896) in which he argued that a political class, monopolising power and the advantages it provides, is a universal feature of all societies.

Michels and oligarchy

Robert Michels was a friend of Mosca, and his work can be considered as belonging to the classical élite explanations of power. He saw bureaucracy as an enemy of individual liberty, and claimed that democratic organisations are based upon the bureaucracy which is needed to organise them. This necessity for a rigid hierarchy comes about because of the sheer size and complexity of democracies, and also because the masses need leadership from above. According to Michels, the leadership in any organisation tends to separate from the masses because of their knowledge and ability to work the dense bureaucratic system. Matters of process, points of order, minutes, agendas, sub-committees, reports, complex voting systems, arcane language and ritualised events all help to mystify the role of the leadership. Keeping power becomes the goal of bureaucracies, and the wants and needs of the masses are secondary. Capitalist and communist societies are ruled by these élites, the **oligarchies** whose main interest is to maintain their own power. The masses are content to leave it to the experts.

Michels, Mosca and Pareto see no benevolence in democracies such as those that have developed in the West or in any possible communist state. Elite groups rule, and the main difference when compared with Marx's ideas is that none of these thinkers sees any chance of the masses ever taking power from the hands of the élite. For Pareto and Mosca the masses lack the psychological and intellectual skills which seem to be a natural property of the upper classes. For Michels that section of the masses which led any

revolution would seize power for itself and become another élite, oligarchical group based on bureaucratic organisation and which would work hard to maintain its own privileged position and prevent the masses from taking part in the power structure.

Testing for democracy

Critics of Soviet communism point out that this was the case there following the 1917 Revolution despite its claims to represent the highest form of democracy. Others argue that democracy still works, even though élite groups dominate the process. For them the real test is to look at how well or badly the needs and interests of the masses are being served. Even if the majority of politicians, leading industrialists, bankers and the leadership of the armed forces come from the same backgrounds – private schools and the 'best' universities – if the systems they control can be shown to serve the needs of the people, then democracy still works. Examinations of power-sharing in modern societies do not always reflect this. C. Wright Mills (1956), an American sociologist, developed a theory which has come to be known as 'modern' élite theory. The main difference between this and the 'classical' élite theory of Pareto, Mosca and Michels is that Mills takes a critical view of élite groups in the USA.

C. Wright Mills: the military-industrial State

Mills distinguishes three groups: the military, economic and political élites. He claims that they effectively form a closed group, barring people from other parts of society from any real political participation. Membership of the three groups is often interchangeable, for example powerful military figures, who may have business interests, may go from military to political service. It is considered normal for politicians to have business interests, and business is active in politics, not least through financing political parties and individuals. This interlocking, self-serving group of élites has a monopoly of power, and therefore runs society not by bending to the collective will of the people, but by maintaining and increasing its own power. Representative democracy just serves to disguise the existence of the élite leadership.

Although at times his ideas seem to take on a Marxist tone, Mills is analysing American society from an élitist perspective, and there is no suggestion that power exists solely within the economic base or that communist societies would be any better. Mills does seem to argue that there should be a way to share power so that the needs and interests of the majority, rather than a select minority, should be served. However, the pluralist view of power in Western democracies claims that this is exactly what happens – the minority élite only exists so that they can use their political expertise to answer the demands of the mass. The pluralists argue that the proof of the political pudding is in the decision-making process. If you analyse the decisions which are made and work out in whose interests they are made, you will find that all groups in society are receiving equal benefit from the role of the élite groups. If not, the people would throw out one élite and vote in another.

Questions

1 How do the views of the classical élite theorists differ from those of C. Wright Mills?
2 What evidence is there to suggest that power is in the hands of a few?

Pluralism

A plurality of views

'Pluralist' is a label which describes the view of power adopted by social theorists who envisage a plurality of many different groups competing for some say in the political process. The State, far from being the capitalist-controlled and directed committee described by Marxism, is a neutral body, open to influences from all groups in society, not serving the interests of an élite minority.

Political parties are seen as an important part of this process, as are **pressure groups**. The various combinations which arise in democracies to fulfil the needs of groups of people are in competition, and the State bends to the will of those best able to get their voices heard.

State neutrality

Requests for State action are put forward by pressure groups and political parties and the State must process these demands and take decisions which represent the majority interest. If the State consistently took decisions in favour of any one group at the expense of the others, then at elections there would be a shift of power, another government would be elected, and their policies would be formulated to best serve the demands of the majority groups in society. The whole thing depends upon the neutrality of the State in processing the demands made upon it. The plurality of interests ensures that the élite groups do not manipulate the power they hold to serve their own interests.

The State maintains a balance in society, making sure that all is fair. Pluralist evidence is usually to be found in the analysis of decision-making processes in democratic societies. Robert Dahl (1961), Polsby (1963) and others claim that an examination of key decisions taken should show an overall balance of interests being met by those holding political power, at both national and local government levels.

A frequent criticism of this argument is that it does not go deeply enough into political processes or the real nature of power. To get at the real issues, it is necessary to examine the processes by which issues emerge in the political arena in the first place. This argument insists that élite groups control this process by making sure that demands which could pose a real threat to the élite power base never surface as public issues – this is the power of non-decision making. For Marxists, a clear example would be the issue of private ownership of the means of production or the massively unequal distribution of **wealth** in the hands of a few. These are issues that no interest group or political party raises at general elections or any other time, because to do so would fundamentally challenge the power of the bourgeoisie and encourage the formation of working-class consciousness. According to Marxists, the issue the pluralists miss is that effective power does not reside in the State but in the private ownership of the means of production.

Elite pluralism

To take account of the unequal distribution of power, and to over-come some of the weaknesses of classical pluralism, more recent pluralist theorists acknowledge that in a great many cases decisions are made by organised groups without direct – and sometimes even indirect – reference to the mass of the population. Furthermore, some groups are more powerful than others, according to whether they are seen as insiders in the political system whose voices are frequently heard, such as the Confederation of British Industry, or outsiders, such as the Campaign for Nuclear Disarmament. It can also be the case that some pressure groups have no effective access to the ear of government, though this may mean they have to find new ways of exerting pressure. A good example of this would be the way that environmental groups have moved from being seen as 'cranks' to serious and influential organisations.

This view, put forward by writers such as Richardson and Jordan (1979) and Budge (1983), has been described as 'élite pluralism' or 'neo-pluralism'. It propounds the view that difficult and unpopular issues can be forced onto the political agenda through the democratic process, against the will of some élite groups, while accepting that there is not a 'level playing field' of power. In such a situation governments cannot rule by force, and cannot manipulate affairs simply to suit themselves.

Questions

1 How many of the 'dimensions of power' are expressed in the pluralist view?
2 How many interest groups would want to be involved in trying to enable or prevent the sale of tobacco?
3 What is meant by non-decision making?

What is the State?

Powers of the State

Just about everywhere we turn in modern life we encounter the State. The State in some form is present when we post letters, use money to buy stamps, watch television, travel abroad bearing passports, go to school, or attend further or higher education. The State obliges birth, marriage and death to be registered. It takes a cut from the money you earn. The roads you walk and drive on belong to the State. The State can declare you insane and institutionalise you. It can kick your door down at five in the morning and arrest you under laws against terrorism. It can conscript you and send you to war. The State can remove all your belongings if you do not pay your taxes. Clearly, the State is a powerful and diverse organisation. It is easiest to think of it in three parts: **legislature**, **executive** and **judiciary**.

At the heart of the State is its ability to draw up and pass laws. These are then enforced by the executive – the agents who carry out or execute the will of the legislature. In a democracy, the legislature is the representative or delegated body partly or wholly elected by the people in periodic elections. In the United Kingdom this is the House of Commons and the House of Lords. The House of Commons is the more important and powerful of the two. The House of Lords is not elected by the people.

The executive carries out the orders of the legislature. In Britain, once an Act of Parliament is passed it is the job of civil servants to make sure that these new laws are enforced. The executive is divided into ministries, headed by ministers who meet together in twice-weekly cabinet meetings. Between them, these people head executive power in the modern British State.

The third arm of the State is the judiciary. This is primarily responsible for interpreting laws once they have been passed, and enforcing them in the courts. The judiciary includes untrained magistrates and highly trained and experienced High Court judges in the Old Bailey in London.

The growth of the State

In the past 150 years, the State has grown in size to play a role in people's lives in a way unthinkable in early Victorian Britain. In the era of *laissez-faire* or free-market economics of the nineteenth century, the guiding belief was that the State should play as little part as possible in the lives of its citizens (the vast majority of whom were unable to vote). This principle was slowly eroded as the century progressed, as the working class gained the right to vote and as local government spread (municipalism). At the same time that the Liberal Party came under serious threat from the rise of the Labour Party, it found itself using the

---

THE STORY OF THE VOTE IN BRITAIN

Although the UK boasts the 'Mother of Parliaments', full adult suffrage is a relatively recent achievement. These are the key dates in its development:

1832 The electorate rose from 478,000 to 813,000 in a population of 24m (or one in every seven adult males).

1867 The electorate rose from 1,430,000 to 2,500,000, in a population of 30m (or one in three adult males).

1884 The electorate rose from 3,000,000 to 4,900,000 (or two in three adult males).

1918 All adult males over 21 and, after a long and intense struggle, women over thirty were able to vote.

It is important to note that, before 1918, entitlement to vote was based on a property qualification, not a simple matter of right or citizenship.

1928 All women over 21 were enfranchised.

1970 All adults over 18 allowed to vote.

power of State, in the First World War, to conscript workers into the army and send them off to fight and possibly to die. This was the very opposite of the principle of minimising government intervention in the lives of citizens.

After the Second World War, when the State again conscripted its citizens, it maintained the central role it had come to play in the war (through, for example, rationing) with the creation of the Welfare State by the Labour government of 1945–51 (see chapter 4). The broad commitment of all the major political parties to the maintenance of the Welfare State meant that there was a long period of what has been described as consensus politics. The divide between Labour and Conservative politics had become very narrow, best expressed in the term 'Butskellism', where the budgets of one Chancellor of the Exchequer – Butler, for the Conservatives – were very similar to those of the Labour Chancellor – Gaitskell. Both Labour and Conservative parties in this period were strongly influenced by the economic ideas of John Maynard Keynes who advocated government intervention in market economies to keep unemployment rates low.

The end of consensus

This long period of consensus came to an end in the turbulent last years of the 1974–79 Labour government and any notion of political consensus disappeared entirely in the years of the Thatcher Conservative government (1979–90). According to Thatcherist **ideology** the State should again play a minimal role in people's lives, yet where it did intervene it should be forceful and strong. In the 1980s, the theme was 'rolling back the frontiers of the State', in the field of taxation and by privatising industries and services such as gas, water and electricity. It is a fiercely debated point whether, as Prime Minister, Mrs Thatcher succeeded in contracting State power in favour of individual freedom, or merely centralised the State more than it already had been.

Questions

1 What is consensus politics?
2 How has the role of the State changed in the twentieth century?

Who controls the State?

The official view of who controls the State in the United Kingdom is that it is ultimately controlled by its **citizens**. Any citizen has the freedom to form a political **party**, or to vote for a political party which may then in turn take control of the machinery of State. In reality, in the United Kingdom only one of two political parties is likely to take power, the Labour or Conservative Party, although smaller parties such as the Liberal Democrats or an Ulster Unionist party may come to hold the balance of power if no party has an overall majority in an election.

First past the post

Voting in general elections, held at least every five years, is done on the basis of the 'first past the post' system. The United Kingdom is divided up into 659 roughly equal electoral areas called constituencies, containing approximately 85,000 electors each. Electors elect one Member of Parliament (MP) for each constituency on the basis of a simple majority. The political party that gains 330 MPs or more in this way is guaranteed an overall majority in the House of Commons, and the ability to turn their policies into law.

It does not at all follow, however, that the party forming a government does so by virtue of a simple majority of votes. Mrs Thatcher's Conservative governments of the 1980s, for example, won power with between 42 per cent and 43 per cent of votes cast. This does not include those registered to vote who did not do so (which takes the figure down to around a third of the electorate) or even those eligible to register to vote who did not even do so, for whatever reason. In 1979, for example, the Conservative Party won 339 seats, 70 seats more than the Labour Party, with the votes of less than a third of all adults over the age of eighteen (see *Table 11.1*).

Table 11.1   Mrs Thatcher's government 1979

		Tory votes as percentage of:	
Votes cast for Tories	13 697 690		
Total votes cast in election	31 220 010	Total votes cast	43.9
Electorate	41 093 264	Electorate	33.3
Total adults over 18	42 100 000	Total adults over 18	32.5
Total population	55 822 000	Total population	24.5

Source: compiled from Butler and Butler (1994)

Table 11.2 Voting in general elections – 1951 and 1974

	Labour	Conservative	Liberal
(a) 1951 (Total seats = 625)			
Votes	13 949 105	13 718 069	730 552
Seats	296	320	6
(b) 1974 (Feb) (Total seats = 635)			
Votes	11 661 488	11 928 677	6 056 713
Seats	301	296	14

Source: compiled from Butler and Butler (1994)

Similarly, it does not follow that the party gaining power even wins more votes than other single parties. The winning party only needs to win majorities in half plus one of all constituencies. How it performs in the remaining constituencies then becomes unimportant. This can lead to anomalous situations as shown in *Table 11.2*.

As we can see, this system of electing a government contains many strange quirks and anomalies. For example, the Liberal Party gained more than six million votes in February 1974 and yet won only 14 seats, while the party that came to form the government received less than twice as many votes as the Liberals and yet gained twenty times as many seats.

Critics of this system, particularly Liberal Democrats, argue that the only fair form of electoral system would be proportional representation, where the number of seats gained reflects the overall number of votes cast. Parties that do form governments under the existing system, however, are unlikely to want to change the system that brings them to power, and it is improbable that they will do so unless forced to in a power-sharing agreement with the Liberal Democrats. The Labour Party does at least seem willing to consider this possibility, though it has done little to take it forward since its election in 1997. It is unlikely ever to be taken up or even considered by the Conservative Party.

Turnout

Defenders of the system, however, can point to the fact that, although the party that gains power rarely does so with a majority of the electorate's votes, it is nevertheless the case that the vast majority both of those who have registered to vote, and of those entitled to vote, do so in a general election. In 1979, for example, when the electorate totalled more than 41 million people, over 31 million (or 76 per cent) turned out to vote. At the same time, the adult population over eighteen numbered 42,100,000, meaning that 74 per cent, or almost three-quarters of those over eighteen, voted in the 1979 general election. These figures are representative: since 1935 the highest turnout has been 82.5 per cent (1951), with the lowest only 71.2 per cent (1935). In this way, it can be said, the electorate legitimates the electoral system itself every time it turns out and votes in a general election.

Once a party is elected into government, even with an overall majority, they do not have a free hand to govern as they wish. Opposition parties and dissenters within the government's own ranks can try to influence the course of legislation as it passes through the Houses of Parliament (the Commons and the Lords), through debates in the Chambers, in committees and in votes on amendments to the three readings of Bills.

Pressure groups

Outside of the Houses of Parliament, pressure groups exist to influence the course of legislation at all its stages, as well as to encourage political parties to adopt new policies. Two types of politically oriented pressure groups can be discerned – interest or sectional pressure groups who protect the interest of their members, of whom trade unions and professional associations such as the British Medical Association (see also chapter 9) are among the largest. Promotional pressure groups exist to draw attention to specific issues and causes, whether it is the environment (in the case of Greenpeace and Friends of the Earth) or poverty, as with the Child Poverty Action Group and Save the Children. A wide range of methods is used to draw their campaigns and interests to the attention of Members of Parliament and the general public, from demonstrations and boycotts to media campaigns and lobbying MPs in the House of Commons. Some groups are able to claim success in meeting short-term objectives (such as the Anti-Poll Tax Campaign of the late 1980s) while others have longer-term objectives and need to maintain continuous pressure, as with campaigns to make roads safer.

If pressure groups and the wider public are unable to influence the course of legislation, then three courses of action remain possible: to disobey the law, for example by withholding payments or mass trespasses; to challenge it in the courts, in the United Kingdom or in Europe; or by voting out the government in a general election and replacing it with a government which will adopt that particular cause.

Pluralism

It is the existence of all these courses of action, persuasion and protest that persuades many people, particularly those at the heart of the system, of the truth of the pluralist case that the electorate gets the government it deserves. In various ways it is continually able to let its elected representatives know of the depth of feeling concerning the way they are being governed, and that the epicentre of power is therefore always shifting to reflect the public's mood.

This is, of course, only one view of what the State is and how it is controlled, focusing on how decisions are made and seeing the State as a referee between different groups, with no interests of its own. As we have seen above, from a functionalist point of view, the State can also be seen as an instrument responding to the majority will, enabling society as a whole to focus its energy. The Marxist approach, on the other hand, begins from the assertion that the State is a committee for managing the affairs of the bourgeoisie, an instrument of class rule that will itself wither away when class divisions disappear. Elite theorists see the State as a vehicle for élite opinion and interests.

The autonomous State

An entirely different point of view (though hinted at by some Marxists) is to see the State as a self-interested organisation, an independent force with its own rules of action. This is echoed in Skocpol's (1979) claim that the State is a 'structure with a logic and interests of its own not necessarily equivalent to, or fused with the interests of the dominant class in society, or the full set of member groups in the polity'.

In the same vein, other writers have observed that the ideological persuasion of the political parties when in government makes very little difference to the way Britain is governed. As Rose (1984) argues, necessity, rather than ideological consensus, has usually held sway: many policies would have come into being regardless of who was in power, with only slight shifts of emphasis in practice. All parties have sought to increase economic growth and sustain the basic provisions of the **Welfare State** – education, health and social security. Even the Thatcherite campaign of privatisation was part of a global phenomenon in industrial societies and is unlikely to be immediately reversed by any incoming Labour government. In matters of foreign policy, there have been barely perceptible differences in the conduct of each party's foreign ministers.

This phenomenon has been explained in three ways. First, convergence theorists have argued that industrial societies have a developmental logic of their own, posing the same choices at particular stages of development; second, there is the claim that government ministers are unable to outwit and outmanoeuvre the vested interests of their civil servants who have political priorities of their own, as well as a large say in how ministers are advised and what information they receive; third, the innate **conservatism** of the British electorate prevents any government or party from straying too far away from the political centre.

The Thatcher governments

Many commentators are willing to accept that the years of 'consensus politics' from 1945 to the mid-1970s can be characterised in this way. The extent to which the Thatcher governments (from 1979 to 1990) changed the role of the State in British political life has been more keenly debated. Part of the reason for this is the contradictory nature of the Thatcher government's record, and the difference between its rhetoric and what really happened. It was certainly Mrs Thatcher's stated intention to break with the past when she remarked that 'For me, consensus seems to be the process of abandoning all beliefs, principles, values and policies' (Kavanagh, 1985).

In attempting to release the population from the grips of the State, more people nevertheless became dependent on it as recipients of welfare benefits, particularly **unemployment benefit**. The rate of crime rose and prisons became fuller. Private housing and farming continued to be subsidised. Controls were exercised over the ability of local government to run its own services and some (particularly in education) were taken into central control, although many others were put out to tender. New and unelected quangos (quasi-autonomous non-governmental organisations) were created in many areas including the privatised public utilities. The power and influence of trade unions and public sector professionals were markedly reduced while the business and finance community were given a greater say in government decisions, although the manufacturing sector was substantially reduced in size.

None of this suggests that power became more pluralised, unless the élite pluralist model is followed, although the interests of what is frequently described as the 'establishment' (the Church of England, BBC, the universities, and higher civil service) were also challenged. On the other hand, the importance given to the ethics of capitalism in this period would support the Marxists' model.

The sovereign State?

Many sociologists have argued that the focus on the State, or the nation State as a sovereign body, exaggerates its importance in an increasingly interdependent and **globalised** world where trans-national political organisations such as the European Union and the United Nations are becoming increasingly important, although they are still relatively ignored by sociologists. At the same time, issues of **ethnicity**, national identity and small-scale **nationalism** remain as strong as ever, as developments in the new nations of the former Soviet bloc and the former Yugoslavia show. Sociologists need to examine international and local developments as much as national developments in their search for the epicentres of political power in society.

Questions

1 What evidence is there for a pluralist view of power?
2 In what ways is the United Kingdom a democracy?
3 How can pressure groups exert influence on the course of legislation?

Political parties and ideology

Marxism and ideology

As with many other terms in sociology, the word ideology carries different meanings according to the context in which it is being used. In its broadest usage it refers to any belief system holding a particular group together (see also chapter 1). In other senses, particularly those given by Marxist sociologists, it refers to a belief system that, while claiming to represent the truth, is in reality a set of distorted ideas. To Marxists, the concept of bourgeois ideology not only denotes the value system of the capitalist class, derived from their position as owners of the means of production, but also the view that this belief system constitutes a **false consciousness**, a false view of reality. Furthermore, only a classless society and the application of scientific Marxism can show the world as it is and break away from this world of illusion. The term ideology therefore carries great importance within Marxism and consequently has been much debated within Marxist thought, particularly by writers such as Louis Althusser and Antonio Gramsci.

Outside of the Marxist perspective, the term ideology is used to refer to the ideas, values and beliefs of discrete power groups in society. In Bill Jones's (1991) formulation, it can be described as 'a comprehensive and systematic perspective whereby human society can be understood together with a framework of principles to guide future action'. According to Jones, an ideology has four components: a perspective or set of assumptions about human nature and the world; a critique of why that perspective is better than any other; a set of objectives concerning political goals and a set of prescriptions of how these objectives should be realised in practice. Political objectives are described in ideological terms, for example as fascism, communism, socialism, liberalism and conservatism. In the 1960s, the American sociologist Daniel Bell had this sense in mind when he declared *The End of Ideology* (1961), indicating that real differences between political parties no longer existed, having been replaced by a consensus on political values. It is in this sense that it is explored in this section.

It is through political parties that political ideologies eventually become policies and legislation. The concept of party was of particular interest to Weber (1922–3) who defined it as any group seeking to pursue 'communal action no matter what its content may be'. Sociologically, Weber says, they represent interests 'determined through "class situation" or "status situation", and they may recruit their following from one or the other respectively. But they need be neither purely "class" nor purely status parties. In most cases they are partly class parties and partly status parties, but sometimes they are neither.'

Forming the ideology is a complex process drawing on a range of ideas of thinkers, from Marx on the left to F.A. Hayek on the right. More immediately, policy 'think tanks', such as the Adam Smith Institute or the Policy Studies Institute, also exist to contribute ideas, arguments and research to this process. Within political parties, particular figures may play the role of ideological leaders, seeking to develop their party's policy in a particular direction. This would be the case with the former Conservative MP Sir Keith Joseph or one of the founder members of the short-lived Social Democratic Party, Roy Jenkins. Through books, pamphlets, speeches, newspapers and even videos, their ideas will be disseminated to elected representatives, party officials and activists, the politically interested and eventually, at election time, the electorate. The battle to try to make these ideas seem 'common sense', the only political possibility, is described as a hegemonic struggle. The way the New Right, under Margaret Thatcher, won the ideological battle in the late 1970s, ending the era of consensus politics, can be described as a 'hegemonic shift'. It amounted to, in Stuart Hall's (1978) phrase, 'the great moving Right show', and highlighted the way that traditional left-wing and centrist policies and solutions were falling out of favour in all areas of political life. The New Right attempted to redefine the way people thought about themselves in relation to the State.

Numerous attempts have been made to understand the relationship between political parties and the ideologies they expound. It often appears in the form of a continuum with 'left-wing' ideas, such as equality, the redistribution of wealth and common ownership, at one end, and 'right-wing' ideas, encompassing individual freedom and free enterprise, at the other. Applying this to the political spectrum in the United Kingdom it can be shown as in *Figure 11.1*.

This type of model does not always work – it is difficult, for example, to include Ulster Unionist parties such as the Democratic Unionist Party or nationalist parties such as Plaid Cymru on such a scale because of the importance given by them to nationalist causes. Nor does it easily describe the Green Party who, unlike the parties named above, reject the idea of economic growth as a fundamental objective. No model exists to solve this problem.

Figure 11.1

Left wing		Centre		Right wing
SWP	Labour	Lib Dems	Tories	BNP

Figure 11.2

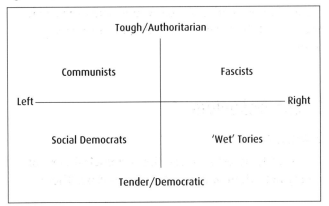

Some writers have suggested that a more realistic or representative way of seeing all this is as vertical and horizontal axes as in *Figure 11.2*.

The Conservative Party

The modern Conservative Party emerged from the Tory party of the eighteenth and nineteenth centuries, seeking to protect the power of the landed gentry against the claims of the rising bourgeois class and its doctrine of anti-protectionism and *laissez-faire* economics. In the late nineteenth century it redefined itself under Benjamin Disraeli to appeal to a new generation of working-class voters, in the process becoming a 'popular' party and surviving the threat of the rise of the Labour Party and the decline of the Liberals. Following the end of the Second World War it committed itself to the broad aims of the Beveridge Report (see chapter 4) until sections of the party became convinced that the organisation of the Welfare State was hastening Britain's decline.

The election of Margaret Thatcher as leader of the party in 1975 and as Prime Minister in 1979 began a radical change of direction, ushering in the politics of the New Right. 'Thatcherism' had five major objectives: to promote free trade and minimise State intervention in the economy; to squeeze out inflation through tight control of the money supply; to promote individual choice by breaking the power of State monopolies; to curb the power of trade unions and reduce the role played by corporate bodies in government decision-making; and to enforce strict obedience to the rule of law and those in authority. The strong emphasis on free market economics aligned the party more closely to the values of nineteenth-century liberalism: it was these values that Thatcher had in mind when she championed the 'Victorian values' of thrift and hard work.

Some writers (such as Stuart Hall, 1978) have doubted whether Thatcherism amounted to a coherent ideological position as such, withdrawing the role of the State in some areas, particularly the industrial sphere, while increasing it in others such as law and order. For this reason it has been described as 'authoritarian populism', carried on after her fall in 1990 in a more diluted form by John Major.

The confusion and disagreement over major issues such as Europe has led to a spectacular collapse in the party's fortunes since the election of 'new' Labour in 1997, though the replacement, as leader, of Iain Duncan Smith with Michael Howard in the autumn of 2003 may lead to a reversal of their fortunes.

The Labour Party

The Labour Party is effectively as old as the twentieth century, defining itself as a democratic socialist party, seeing the State as instrumental in achieving its aims of increased social justice and equality. For much of its life it has committed itself to Clause 4 of its 1918 constitution, seeking to bring about 'common ownership of the means of production, distribution and exchange'. After 1945, when it won a landslide victory in the general election, it took large sections of the economic infrastructure such as the mines and railway network into public ownership by nationalising them. At the same time, it consolidated the Welfare State, for example through the creation of the National Health Service and a universal scheme of National Insurance. In 1995, under the leadership of Tony Blair, the Labour Party agreed to alter Clause 4 as part of a programme of modernisation.

The immediate post-war Labour government was perhaps the most radical and reforming of the twentieth century (though many would argue that it nevertheless failed to create anything resembling a democratic socialist society). In the long periods since then that it has been out of power – in the 1950s, 1980s and 1990s – it has sought to redefine itself as the party of the affluent (particularly those living in 'middle England') as well as the disadvantaged.

In 1994, following fifteen years out of power, the election of Tony Blair as leader of the party provided Labour with the opportunity to provide a new statement of its values and drop its central commitment to nationalisation. It did this in 1995 by changing its party constitution and describing itself as a party seeking to create 'a society in which power, wealth and opportunity are in the hands of the many, not the few', achieved through a 'dynamic economy, serving the public interest, in which the enterprise of the market and the rigour of competition are joined with the forces of partnership and co-operation to produce the wealth the nation needs and the opportunity for all to work and prosper, with a thriving private sector and high quality public services, where those undertakings essential to the common good are owned either by the public or are accountable to them'.

Critics of this move say this makes it harder than ever to distinguish much of the Labour Party's ideology and stance from other parties. It has also been frequently observed that, in changing Clause 4, the long battle begun by the breakaway 'Gang of Four' in 1981, founding the Social Democratic Party, has now been won as the Labour Party under Blair is now, in effect, the party that Williams, Rodgers, Jenkins and Owen sought to fashion all along. It was the promotion of these values (often described as 'Blairism') that finally saw its election in 1997 and re-election in 2001.

The Liberal Democrats

The present Liberal Democrat Party exists as the result of a merger between the Social Democratic Party (which itself split away from the Labour Party in the early 1980s) and the Liberal Party of the nineteenth century. The Liberal Party itself emerged from the Whig Party, playing an important part in laying the foundations of the Welfare State (see chapter 4) before being eclipsed by the Labour Party in the second quarter of the twentieth century. It has been out of power ever since, although it briefly shared power with the Labour Party in the 'Lib–Lab Pact' of the late 1970s. As the third party in British politics, it does not expect to form a government in its own right (although it is a major player in local government), with its only hope being a hung parliament, where no single party has overall control through a simple majority. In these circumstances it would join any coalition government that may be formed on the condition that it introduced a form of proportional representation.

In terms of values, the Liberal Democrats stand for a mixed economy, supporting the aim of improved funding for public services such as health and education, but sharing some of the Conservative Party's hostility to trade unionism and the organised labour movement. The Liberal Democratic Party struggles to maintain a policy of political 'equidistance' from the main parties, at the same time as co-operating with sections of the Labour Party at local government level. Increasingly, under the leadership of Charles Kennedy, it is being seen as to the 'left' of the Labour Party on a number of key issues.

Voting behaviour

Partisan alignment

In the early post-war years, the sociological view of voting behaviour was based on social class. There

Table 11.3   Voting patterns, 1945–59 (%)

Class	AB	C1	C2	DE
Conservative	85	70	35	30
Labour	10	25	60	65

Source: Tapper and Bowles, 1981

Table 11.4   Labour and Conservative share of votes cast, 1945–59 (%)

	Conservative	Labour	Conservative and Labour
1945	39.6	48.0	87.6
1950	43.4	46.1	89.5
1951	48.0	48.8	96.8
1955	49.7	46.4	96.1
1959	49.4	43.8	93.2

Source: *The Guardian Guide to the House of Commons 1992*,
Fourth Estate Ltd, 1992

were two main classes: the working class, who consistently saw themselves as such, identified themselves with the Labour Party, and would always vote for it; and the middle class who saw themselves as middle class and identified themselves with the Conservative Party, consistently voting for that party. This pattern of class loyalty was deemed regular and predictable enough for writers such as David Butler and Donald Stokes (1974) to describe it as one of 'partisan alignment'(see *Table 11.3*).

This was also clear from an analysis of the way the two leading parties dominated the overall share of the votes cast (*see Table 11.4*). Moreover, there were relatively small margins of change in the parties' share of the vote from one general election to another. Between 1950 and 1970, for example, the Conservative share of the vote ranged from 49.7% (1955) to 43.4% (1950) and Labour from 48.8% (1951) to 43.8% (1959). Stability was the order of the day and it was difficult to envisage a change in the party system.

Allegiance to one of the two main parties on the basis of class came about through a process of political **socialisation**. These values were learnt from others in much the same way as any other key aspect of socialisation. They came from people met with in everyday life, particularly at home and in schools. People voted according to their class image of the society they lived in.

Deviant voters

As the case for **partisan alignment** seemed clear, attention turned to the problems of why a minority of

people voted against their class – 'deviant voters' – while others changed their allegiance from one election to another – 'floating voters'. Why, for example, did 10 per cent of AB class voters vote Labour and 30 per cent of DE class vote Conservative on average in the period 1945–59?

The phenomenon of the working-class Tory was explained by the tendency to deference that exists in part of the working class. By 'deference', writers such as McKenzie and Silver (1968) meant the willingness on the part of workers to believe that an individual would make a good politician simply because they already possessed a high, and often ascribed, status. This pattern, however, was dying out as working-class voters became increasingly interested in the specific policies each party was offering. In identifying this new phenomenon of 'secular' voting, McKenzie and Silver anticipated the direction of later theories of voting behaviour, or psephology.

Middle-class Labour voting, Frank Parkin (1971) argued, could be understood in a similar way. Public sector professionals, such as teachers and social workers, did not perceive their work in an instrumental way, but identified with the wider altruism of the Labour Party and its commitment to the public sector.

Butler and Stokes (1974) themselves believed that deviant voting could be understood within the concept of partisan alignment. As the skilled working class became more affluent and underwent a process of **embourgeoisement**, they argued (see chapter 3), they would be more likely to vote Tory as an expression of their new values because the lines of class division had shifted. As we know from *The Affluent Worker* studies of the 1960s (Goldthorpe *et al.*), however, as well as from the work of Eric Nordlinger (1967), the opposite was closer to the truth. **Psephological** trends and patterns were still best explained by the nature of an individual's political socialisation within their class.

Partisan dealignment

The early 1970s were the watershed years for both political parties, especially the Labour Party, and for political sociologists. The Labour and Conservative parties' combined share of 90 per cent of the vote in general elections between 1945 and 1970 fell to around 75 per cent in the elections of 1974 and has remained around that level since then. Electoral stability has been replaced by fluidity and the two-party, two-class model by three-party, less-class-based voting (see *Table 11.5*).

Table 11.5 The Conservative and Labour vote (%), 1974–2001

	Conservative	Labour	Conservative and Labour
Feb 1974	37.8	37.1	74.9
1979	43.9	37.0	80.9
1987	42.3	30.8	73.1
1992	41.9	34.4	76.3
1997	31.7	43.2	74.9
2001	31.7	40.7	72.4

Source: Bill Jones *et al.*, *Politics UK*, Longman, 2001

Many commentators argue that it is now more accurate to talk of partisan dealignment than of partisan alignment. They cite the 1987 general election in particular, when the Conservatives gained a clear majority of the skilled workers' vote, with 40 per cent compared to Labour's 32 per cent. Likewise, in the 1997 election there was a massive swing to Labour among the C1s, or lower middle class, a pattern sustained in their election victory in 2001. Labour gained 41 per cent of the vote among the C1s compared to just 26 per cent for the Conservatives. In the previous general election in 1992, the Conservatives had won 48 per cent of the C1 vote compared to 28 per cent for Labour. This seemed to confirm that people were now much more likely to switch party allegiance between elections.

Class decomposition

Political sociologists such as Sarlvik and Crewe (1983) argue that this dealignment can best be explained by divisions that are present in both the working and middle classes and the motives behind voting choices. In voting terms, there are now two perceivable working classes: the traditional and the new. Where workers live, whether they are home-owners or not, whether they belong to trade unions and whether they work in the public or private sector as well as their occupations all have to be taken into account. Belonging to a trade union and not owning a house increases a propensity to vote Labour. It is also important to realise that voters make 'rational' decisions about how they vote, based on experience, knowledge and policy preference rather than on the grounds of simple class identification and loyalty. If a political party is not offering what voters want, no matter which class they appear to represent, they will not vote for them.

A similar pattern was discernible among the middle classes where there was also division between private sector workers, two-thirds of whom voted Conservative, and public sector workers, less than half of whom voted Conservative. This figure had declined since 1983. The process of class dealignment seemed to be gathering pace.

Rational-choice voting

In a **longitudinal** study of a group of voters from 1959 to October 1974, Himmelweit, Humphreys and Jaeger (1981) dispense with concepts of political socialisation and develop the concept of rational choice by voters. Voters, they say, behave in the same way as any other consumers faced with important financial choices. 'Brand loyalty' (which would correspond with partisan alignment) does not necessarily exist. The voter–consumer will make their choice according to the policies which are on offer at the time, and if they are unhappy with their choice they may well change it at the next opportunity. Some critics have claimed that it is difficult to draw valid conclusions from this study as it is based on an ultimate **sample** of only 178 men living in the greater London area, the majority of whom were non-manual workers. Nor are we able to discover the basis on which these voters made their choices in the first place.

A new model of class

Other writers are less convinced that class can be so quickly discounted. Heath, Jowell and Curtice (1985) argue that a more sophisticated model of class than those previously employed needs to be considered. Their own model, used to examine the 1983 election, sees five classes, which are defined in terms of labour-market position, and incorporate both men and women:
→ *the salariat* are managers and professionals who wield power in the workplace and over their own working lives – vote Conservative (54 per cent) or Alliance;
→ *routine non-manual workers* on low wages with little control over the labour process – vote Conservative (51 per cent) or sometimes Alliance (31 per cent);
→ *the petty-bourgeoisie* and self-employed who neither employ workers nor are employed by others – strong Conservative vote (71 per cent);
→ *foremen and technicians* who supervise others – vote Conservative, but not in the majority (48 per cent);
→ *all forms of manual workers* who are most likely to vote Labour (49 per cent in 1983).

As their results from viewing class in this way proved inconclusive, they then devised an 'odds ratio' which compared the way that class strata voted in elections with the way they ought to vote in terms of class alignment. This revealed, far from conclusively, that the working class and salariat vote was not significantly less partisan in 1983 than at other elections in the previous 20 years.

Other factors also needed to be taken into account, not least of which was the fact that, while the manual working class has shrunk as a proportion of the labour force, the number of people in non-manual jobs has increased. Yet it seems clear that people do not vote on the basis of issues, as the Labour Party was thought by voters to have the best policies on the most important issues. The Labour Party failed because of its overall image in the eyes of the voters and it did not manage to match this to the individual policies it campaigned for.

Gender and voting behaviour

Although the main debate in voting behaviour centres around the concept of **class**, age and **gender** are also important factors. Women have always formed a significant constituency for the Conservatives.

It has generally been thought that men are more aligned to the Labour Party than women because they are more likely to be engaged in the organised labour movement, to belong to a trade union, and have a sense of solidarity as industrial workers. Women, at home, are more likely to be concerned with family values and issues and will vote for the party that campaigns hardest on these issues, usually the Conservative Party. Some writers have argued that it was because women were seen as a bloc against the rise of the Labour Party that they were enfranchised in 1918.

In the 1980s, however, the 'gender gap' in voting was temporarily reversed, with more men than women voting Conservative. One reason for this appears to be that younger women, attracted by Labour's image as a 'caring' party on issues such as health and education, were more likely to vote Labour than older women, while younger men were attracted by Mrs Thatcher's 'macho' image and voted for her. The gender gap was restored in 1992, with John Major as the Conservative leader (see *Table 11.6*).

Age and voting behaviour

Analysis of voting behaviour by age alone shows that support for the Conservative Party increases as people grow older, while it decreases for the Labour Party. Two forces are thought to be at work here: on the one

Table 11.6   Sex and party choice in general elections 1964–2001

		Conservative	Labour	Lib/SDP (Alliance)
1964	Men	40	48	11
	Women	46	42	12
1970	Men	44	49	8
	Women	51	41	8
1983	Men	46	30	24
	Women	43	28	28
1992	Men	38	36	19
	Women	44	34	16
1997	Men	31	44	17
	Women	32	44	17
2001	Men	31	41	17
	Women	32	40	17

Sources: Nuffield Studies, 1964–70; *Guardian*, 13.6.83; *Daily Telegraph*, 14.4.92; BBC/NEP exit polls, 1997, 2001

hand, each new political generation of first-time voters forms a loyalty to a political party that stays with them for many years. In the late 1940s this would have been the Labour Party, in the 1980s, the Conservative Party. However, as people get older they become wealthier and more prosperous. They therefore become less dependent on the Welfare State, and are less concerned about those who are. In this way, they become more likely to vote Conservative, thus class and age combine as factors in voting behaviour.

Opinion polls

Finally, it is important to realise that most of the statistics presented above are only accurate in the sense that they are computed from the replies given to opinion pollsters at the time of each election. In other words, they are figures gathered by polling organisations such as MORI, Harris and Gallup, not official statistics or even primary data gathered by sociologists. It is frequently the case that different commentators will cite different figures in their account of an election, because of the number of polling organisations. These data are generated by taking a stratified sample of the electorate across a random selection of constituencies and asking them a series of questions about how they would vote in a general election. This is what sociologists would call a closed-ended structured **interview**.

In the 1992 general election, opinion polls became an issue in themselves. Prior to election day, very few of the 57 polls conducted showed a Conservative lead, and if they did it was by a margin of 1 per cent or less.

Even when polling had been completed, exit polls (where voters are asked how they voted as they leave polling booths) predicted a Conservative victory of only between 4 and 5 per cent. In the end, the Conservatives won by a clear margin of 7.6 per cent (42.8 per cent to Labour's 35.2 per cent). The polls conducted before the 1997 and 2001 elections were much more accurate in correctly predicting Labour victories by large margins.

This underestimation of the strength of support for the Conservatives raises questions about interviewers' ability ever to get the truth out of their respondents. It may be, for example, that the interviewee does not yet know what they think. After the election, many polling organisations argued that a significant number of people had either made up or changed their minds in the days and hours before voting. It may also have been the case that a disproportionately high number of people who answered 'Don't know' then went on to vote Conservative and could not be accounted for by statistical margins of error. Another argument is that, because of what is seen as the selfishness associated with voting Conservative – putting yourself and your family first – enough people hide this fact from the pollsters as to seriously underestimate the real Conservative vote. It was also suggested that a substantial number of respondents who said they would vote Labour did not do so as they had not paid their poll tax and were therefore not eligible. It could also be that respondents do not take opinion polls as seriously as they take entering a ballot box, and use the interview as a way of venting short-term grievances, before reluctantly voting Conservative anyway.

Questions

1 What is meant by partisan alignment and dealignment? Which best explains trends in voting behaviour?
2 How does the voting behaviour of women differ from men?
3 How reliable are opinion polls?

Past examination questions

In preparing to sit the examinations, it is a good idea to familiarise yourself with the layout and style of the papers. You may also find it helpful to sit a mock examination based on past papers. You should certainly aim to study some past examination questions in order to understand the level at which the questions are set and the requirements for success at AS and A Level.

The structure of the examination papers is summarised below. Some sample examination papers are also provided.

The examination papers

Advanced Subsidiary (AS) Level
→ There are two AS Level papers.
→ They may be taken half way through an A Level course and then re-sat, if required, at the end of the A Level course, **or**
→ They may be taken at the end of an A Level course during the same examination session as the two A Level papers.
→ Paper 1 is worth 50% of the AS qualification (25% of the full A Level).
→ Paper 2 is worth 50% of the AS qualification (25% of the full A Level).
→ The two papers contain different types of questions.

→ Paper 1 has six essay questions, divided into three sections that have two questions each – candidates must answer two questions from different sections.
→ Paper 2 has three data response questions – candidates must choose two of these.
→ AS Level papers form part of the full A Level examination.

Advanced (A) Level
→ There is one A Level paper.
→ It is taken at the end of your A Level course.
→ Paper 3 is worth 50% of the A Level qualification.
→ The paper contains twelve essay questions, and each question is in two parts.

Paper 1 Principles and Methods 1

Answer **two** questions, each from a different section.

Section A

1   'Social order may be the product of consensus or coercion, depending on which sociological perspective is adopted.' Explain and discuss.   [25]

(9699/1 May/June 2002)

2   Assess the usefulness of the concept of subcultures in understanding the social identities of young people   [25]

(8699/1 May/June 2001)

Section B

3 Assess the factors that influence the sociologist's choice of research method(s). [25]

(8699/1 Oct/Nov2001)

4 Using examples from relevant studies, discuss the value of the different types of interview used in sociological research. [25]

(8699/1 May/June 2001)

Section C

5 'Gender segregation in employment takes many forms, and not all female workers are affected by it to the same extent.' Explain and discuss. [25]

(8699/1 May/June 2001)

6 Assess different sociological explanations of the causes of poverty. [25]

(9699/1 Oct/Nov2002)

Paper 2 Principles and Methods 2

Answer any **two** questions.

Section A

1 Read the passage below and, drawing on this and your own knowledge of sociology, answer the questions which follow.

Socialisation is the process by which individuals learn to become members of society, both by internalising the norms and values of society and also by learning to perform social roles. The primary agents of socialisation are the family and the school. Socialisation is not confined to childhood, however, and it continues throughout the life-course.

There is an ongoing dispute about the relative importance of nature versus nurture (or heredity and environment) in human development. Sociology is generally associated with the view that social factors (nurture rather than nature) are the main influence on human behaviour.

There is also a debate about the extent to which socialisation produces conformity in society. The functionalist perspective sees socialisation as the process through which people internalise values and learn to follow the norms of society. However, this view has been criticised for implying an allegedly 'over-socialised' concept of the relationship between the individual and society. For example, interactionists argue that socialisation is not simply a one-way process, in which individuals learn to fit into society, since people may also negotiate their social roles and obligations and choose alternative courses of action.

(a) Explain what is meant by the term 'social roles' and give an example. [2]

(b) Identify and explain **two** sources of evidence that sociologists use to support the claim that social factors are the main influence on human behaviour. [5]

(c) Explain how children come to internalise the norms and values of society. [8]

(d) Assess the extent to which socialisation produces conformity in society. [10]

(8699/2 Oct/Nov2001)

2 Sociology has had to fight to establish itself as a social science. Using the principles of the scientific method established by the natural sciences, sociologists have developed methods of data collection that enable them to claim that sociological knowledge is as reliable as that found in any other sphere of the social sciences. This does not mean that Sociology can produce universal laws of society (laws that are true for all times and places). However, it can endeavour to follow the rules of the scientific method to establish verifiable data and valid correlations that may be used to confirm or deny an *hypothesis* (or create a new one). In essence, this involves testing theoretical statements against evidence that is gathered by the most logical method in an objective manner and interpreted in an impartial way.

(a) What is meant by the term *hypothesis*?   [2]

(b) Describe **two** methods of data collection used by sociologists.   [4]

(c) Explain the principles and rules of the scientific method established
     by the natural sciences.   [8]

(d) Assess the view that sociological research should be based on the
     methods and principles of the natural sciences.   [11]

(9699/2 May/June 2002)

3   Read the passage below and, drawing on this and your own knowledge of sociology, answer the questions which follow.

Social mobility research measures the movement – usually of individuals but sometimes of whole groups – between different positions within the system of stratification in any society. It is conventional to distinguish between 'upward' and 'downward' mobility (that is, movement up or down a hierarchy of privilege).

Evidence of high rates of social mobility may be used to argue that the society in question is characterised by achievement rather than ascription, that individuals reap their rewards according to their personal qualities, rather than on the basis of 'unfair' advantages such as inherited wealth, or personal connections – in short that a true meritocracy is in operation.

However, it is questionable whether the extent of social mobility is an accurate measure of the 'openness' of industrial societies. High rates of upward mobility, for example, are not necessarily an indication that equality of opportunity exists in society. Indeed, many sociologists have questioned the extent to which modern industrial societies are characterised by achievement rather than ascription.

(a) What is meant by the term 'meritocracy'?   [2]

(b) Identify and explain **two** factors that affect the amount of social
     mobility in modern industrial societies.   [5]

(c) Explain why high rates of social mobility are not necessarily an
     indication that equality of opportunity exists within a society.   [8]

(d) Assess the claim that modern industrial societies are characterised
     by achievement rather than ascription.   [10]

(8699/2 May/June 2001)

Paper 3 Social Change and Differentiation

Section A: Families and Households

1   (a) Describe the functions of the family.   [9]

    (b) Evaluate the view that the family in modern industrial societies has
         lost some of its functions.[16]

(9699/3 Oct/Nov 2002)

2   (a) Describe, with examples, the types of conjugal relationships that
         may be found in societies.   [9]

    (b) Assess the claim that conjugal roles have become more equal in
         recent years.   [16]

(9699/3 May/June 2002)

Section B: Education

3 **(a)** Explain, with examples, the meaning of *meritocracy*. [9]

   (b) Assess the extent to which education is linked to social mobility. [16]

   (9699/3 May/June 2002)

4 **(a)** Describe, with examples, the types of pupil *subcultures* that can
            be found in schools. [9]

   (b) 'Factors within schools are the main influence on educational
            achievement.' Assess this view. [16]

   (9699/3 Oct/Nov 2002)

Section C: Religion

5 **(a)** Describe sociological explanations of how religion may legitimise
            social order.[9]

   (b) Evaluate the view that religion is the means by which the poor
            are controlled in society. [16]

   (9699/3 Oct/Nov 2002)

6 **(a)** Describe, with examples, the process whereby a sect may
            become a denomination. [9]

   (b) 'Religion is the belief of the marginalised'. Evaluate this view. [16]

   (9699/3 May/June 2002)

Section D: Crime and Deviance

7 **(a)** Explain how the level of official crime statistics may be affected
            by the activities of law enforcement agencies. [9]

   (b) Assess the view that crime is an activity largely undertaken by
            young working class males. [16]

   (9699/3 May/June 2002)

8 **(a)** Explain, with examples, the meaning of *anomie*. [9]

   (b) Evaluate the usefulness of the 'New Criminology' in explaining
            why people commit crime. [16]

   (9699/3 Oct/Nov2002)

Section E: Work and Leisure

9 **(a)** Describe, with examples, the main features of *bureaucracy*. [9]

   (b) Evaluate the claim made by some sociologists that organisations
            are inevitably undemocratic. [16]

   (9699/3 Oct/Nov2002)

10 **(a)** Explain, with examples, the meaning of *alienation*. [9]

   (b) Evaluate sociological research which argues that worker satisfaction
            can be improved. [16]

   (9699/3 May/June 2002)

Section F: Mass Media

11 **(a)** Describe how the mass media may influence the outcome of
            elections. [9]

   (b) Assess the view that the mass media only serve the interests of
            the ruling classes. [16]

   (9699/3 Oct/Nov2002)

12 **(a)** Describe, with examples, the process of *deviance amplification*. [9]

   (b) Assess the view that the mass media are a major source of
            stereotypes of young people. [16]

   (9699/3 May/June 2002)

Further reading

1 The sociological perspective

P. Abbott and C. Wallace, *An Introduction to Sociology: Feminist Perspectives*, Routledge, 1997

S. Ahmed, J. Kilby, C. Lury, M. McNeil and B. Skeggs, *Transformations. Thinking Through Feminism*, Routledge, 2000

E. Cuff, W. Sharrock and D. Francis, *Perspectives in Sociology: Classical and Contemporary*, Routledge, 1998

J. Donald, *'Race', Culture and Difference*, Open University, 1992

K. Gelder and S. Thornton (eds), *The Subcultures Reader*, Routledge, 1997

N. Mouzelis, *Sociological Theory: What Went Wrong*, Routledge, 1995

D. Owen (ed.). *Sociology after Postmodernism*, Sage, 1997

J. Scott, *Sociological Theory: Contemporary Debates*, Edward Elgar, 1995

R. Stones (ed.), *Key Sociological Thinkers*, Palgrave Macmillan, 1998

2 Sociological methods

H. Coombes, *Research Using IT*, Palgrave Study Guides, 2001

N. Denzin, *Interpretive Ethnography: Ethnographic Practices for the 21st Century*, Sage, 1997

F. Devine and S. Heath, *Sociological Research Methods in Context*, Palgrave Macmillan, 1999

P. Kendall and P. Langley, *Writing Your Sociology Coursework*, Connect Publications, 1998

R. Levitas and W. Guy, *Interpreting Official Statistics*, Routledge, 1996

P. McNeil, *Research Methods*, Routledge, 1990

J. Scheurich, *Research Methods in the Postmodern*, Falmer Press, 1997

M. Walsh, *Research Made Real*, Nelson Thornes, 2001

3 Social stratification and differentiation

A. Adonis and S. Pollard, *A Class Act: The Myth of Britain's Classless Society*, Hamish Hamilton, 1997

C. Barnes, G. Mercer and T. Shakespeare, *Exploring Disability: A Sociological Introduction*, Polity Press, 1999

A. Blaikie, *Ageing and Popular Culture*, Cambridge University Press, 1999

H. Brown, H. Gilkes and A. Kaloski-Naylor (eds), *White Women: Critical Perspectives on Race and Gender*, Raw Nerve Books, 1999

D. Byrne, *Social Exclusion*, Open University Press, 1999

F. Devine, *Social Class in America and Britain*, Edinburgh University Press, 1997

D. Mason, *Race and Ethnicity in Modern Britain*, Oxford University Press, 2000

S. Miles, *Youth Lifestyles in a Changing World*, Open University Press, 2000

T. Modood, R. Berthoud et al., *Ethnic Minorities in Britain: Diversity and Disadvantage*, Policy Studies Institute, 1997

B. Parekh, *The Future of Multi-Ethnic Britain*, Profile Books, 2000

T. Skelton and G. Valentine (eds), *Cool Places: Geographies of Youth Cultures*, 1998

K. Woodward (ed.), *Questioning identity: Gender, Class, Nation*, Routledge, 2000

4 Health, welfare and poverty

C. Barnes and G. Mercer (eds), *Exploring the Divide: Illness and Disability*, The Disability Press, 1996

D. Marsland, *Welfare or Welfare State?*, Macmillan, 1996

R. Levitas, *The Inclusive Society?: Social Inclusion and New Labour*, Macmillan, 1999

D. Pilgrim and A. Rodgers, *A Sociology of Mental Illness*, Oxford University Press, 1999

P. Townsend, *The International Analysis of Poverty*, Harvester Wheatsheaf, 1993

R. Walker (ed.), *Ending Child Poverty*, Policy, 1999

M. Whitehead, *Health Inequalities*, HMSO, 1997

5 The family

G. Allan (ed.), *The Sociology of the Family: A Reader*, Blackwell, 1999

G. Allan and A. Crow, *Families, Households and Society*, Palgrave, 2001

A. Carling, S. Duncan and R. Edwards (eds), *Analysing Families: Morality and Rationality in Policy and Practice*, Routledge, 2002

D. **Cheal,** *Sociology of Family Life,* Palgrave, 2002

S. **Dex,** *Families and the Labour Market,* Joseph Rowntree Foundation, 1999

D. **Gittins,** *The Family in Question,* Macmillan, 1993

J. **Haskey, K. Kiernan and P. Morgan,** *The Fragmenting Family: Does it Matter?,* IEA, 1998

G. **Jagger and C. Wright (eds),** *Changing Family Values,* Routledge, 1999

K. **Kiernan, H. Land and J. Lewis,** *Lone Motherhood in the 20th Century,* Clarendon Press, 1999

J. **Lewis,** *The End of Marriage? Individualism and Intimate Relations,* Edward Elgar, 2001

S. **McRae (ed.),** *Changing Britain: Families and Households in the 1990s,* Oxford University Press, 1999

D. **Morgan,** *Family Connections,* Polity, 1996

E. **Silva and C. Smart (eds),** *The New Family?,* Sage, 1999

J. **Stacey,** *In the Name of the Family: Rethinking Family Values in the Postmodern Age,* Beacon Press, 1996

6 Education

M. **Arnot, M. David and G. Weiner,** *Closing the Gender Gap: Postwar Education and Social Change,* Polity Press, 1999

J. **Demaine,** *Education Policy and Contemporary Politics,* Macmillan Press, 1999

D. **Epstein, V. Elwood, V. Hey and J. Maw,** *Failing Boys? Issues in Gender and Achievement,* Open University Press, 1998

D. **Gilborn,** *'Race', Ethnicity and Education: Teaching and Learning in Multi-Ethnic Schools,* Unwin Hyman, 1990

A. **Halsey, H. Lauder, P. Brown, A. Wells (eds),** *Education, Culture, Economy and Society,* Oxford University Press, 1997

M. **Hammersley and P. Woods,** *Life in School,* Open University Press, 1993

T. **Heaton and T. Lawson,** *Education and Training,* Macmillan, 1996

R. **Lowe,** *Schooling and Social Change,* Routledge, 1997

J. **Thompson,** *Women, Class and Education,* Routledge, 2000

R. **Usher and R. Edwards,** *Postmodernism and Education,* Routledge, 1994

G. **Weiner,** *Feminisms in Education: An Introduction,* Open University Press, 1994

7 Religion

J. **Bird,** *Investigating Religion,* Harper Collins, 1999

C. **Brown,** *The Death of Christian Britain,* 2001

S. **Bruce,** *Fundamentalism,* Polity Press, 2001

G. **Chryssides,** *Exploring New Religions,* Continuum, 1999

G. **Davie, L. Woodhead and P. Heelas,** *Predicting Religion: Christian, Secular and Alternative Futures,* Ashgate, 2003

P. **Heelas,** *The New Age Movement: The Celebration of the Self and the Sacralization of Modernity,* Blackwell, 1996

K. **Flanagan and P. Jupp,** *Postmodernity, Sociology and Religion,* Palgrave Macmillan, 1999

R. **Stark and W. Bainbridge,** *The Future of Religion,* University of California Press, 1985

S. **Sutcliffe and M. Bowman (eds),** *Beyond New Age: Exploring Alternative Spirituality,* Edinburgh University Press, 2000

B. **Wilson and J. Cresswell (eds),** *New Religious Movements: Challenge and Response,* Routledge, 1999

8 Crime and deviance

H. **Becker,** *Outsiders,* The Free Press, 1973

R. **Collier,** *Masculinities, Crime and Criminology,* Sage, 1998

H. **Croall,** *Crime and Society in Britain,* Addison Longman, 1998

R. **Dobash, P. Dobash and L. Noaks,** *Gender and Crime,* University of Wales Press, 1995

S. **Holdaway and P. Rock (eds),** *Thinking About Criminology,* UCL Press, 1998

J. **Muncie,** *Youth and Crime: A Critical Introduction,* Sage, 1999

R. **Sparks,** *Television and the Drama of Crime,* Open University Press, 1992

K. **Thompson,** *Moral Panics,* Routledge, 1998

P. **Walton and J. Young (eds),** *The New Criminology Revisited,* Macmillan, 1998

E. **Wincup and J. Lewis,** *Crime, Deviance and Social Control,* Hodder and Stoughton, 1999

9 Work, organisations and leisure

U. **Beck,** *The Brave New World of Work,* Polity Press, 2000

C. **Critcher, P. Bramham and A. Tomlinson (eds),** *Sociology of Leisure: A Reader,* E. and F.N. Spon, 1995

D. **Gallie,** *Social Change and the Experience of Unemployment,* Oxford University Press, 1994

P. **Gregg and J. Wadsworth (eds),** *The State of Working Britain,* Manchester University Press, 1999

S **Franks,** *Having None of It: Women, Men and the Future of Work,* Granta, 1998

K. **Grint,** *Work,* Polity Press, 2002

G. **Morgan,** *Images of Organization,* Sage, 1997

K. **Thompson (ed.),** *Work, Employment and Unemployment,* OUP, 1994

P. **Thompson and C. Warhurst (eds),** *Workplaces of the Future,* Macmillan, 1998

S. **Walby (ed.),** *New Agendas for Women,* Macmillan, 1999

T. **Watson,** *Sociology of Work and Industry,* Routledge, 1995

10 Mass media

N. **Abercrombie,** *Television and Society,* Polity, 1996

A. **Briggs and P. Cobley,** *The Media: An Introduction,* Longman, 2002

S. **Craig (ed.),** *Men, Masculinity and the Media,* Sage, 2002

G. **Dines and J. Humez (eds),** *Gender, Race and Class in the Media,* Sage, 1995

J. **Eldridge et al.,** *Mass Media and Power in Modern Britain,* Oxford, 1997

J. Gabriel, *Whitewash: Racialised Politics and the Media,* Routledge, 1998

I. Law, *Race in the News,* Palgrave, 2002

R. McChesney, *Rich Media, Poor Democracy,* The New Press, 2000

G. Philo (ed.), *Message Received,* Longman, 1999

A. Ruddock, *Understanding Audiences: Theory and Method,* Sage, 2000

P. Scannell, *Radio, Television and Modern Life: A Phenomenological Approach,* Blackwell, 1996

11   Politics and power

T. Bottomore, *Political Sociology,* Pluto Press, 1993

I. Budge, I. Crewe, D. McKay and K. Newton, *The New British Politics,* Pearson, 2000

D. Clarke, D. Sanders, M. Stewart and P. Whitely, *Britain (not) at the Polls,* University of Essex, 2001

D. Coates and P. Lawler (eds), *New Labour in Power,* Manchester University Press, 2000

G. Evans and P. Norris (eds), *Critical Elections: British Parties and Voters in Long-Term Perspective,* Sage, 1999

A. Giddens, *The Third Way and its Critics,* Polity Press, 2000

A. Heywood, *Key Concepts in Politics,* Palgrave, 2000

P. Hirst, *From Statism to Pluralism,* UCL, 1997

B. Jones *et al.*, *Politics UK,* Longman, 2001

S. Lukes, *Power: A Radical View,* Blackwell, 1986

S. Saggar (ed.), *Race and British Electoral Politics,* UCL Press, 1998

Bibliography

Note: In order to place these texts in their appropriate historical context, dates of first editions have been given where possible.

Abbott, P. and Sapsford R., 1987, *Women and Social Class,* Tavistock

Abbott, P. and Wallace, C., 1997, *An Introduction to Sociology: Feminist Perspectives,* Routledge

Abel-Smith, B. and Townsend, P., 1965, *The Poor and the Poorest,* G. Bell and Sons

Abercrombie, N., Hill, S. and Turner, B., 1980, *The Dominant Ideology Thesis,* Allen and Unwin

Abrahamson, P., 1998, 'Combating poverty and social exclusion in Europe' in W. Beck, L. Van der Maesen and A. Walker (eds.), *The Social Quality of Europe,* Policy Press

Abrams, M., 1959, *The Teenage Consumer,* Routledge and Kegan Paul

Abrams, M. *et al.,* 1960, *Must Labour Lose?,* Penguin

Acker, J., 1973, 'Women and social stratification: a case of intellectual sexism', *American Journal of Sociology,* 78

Adam Smith Institute, 1994, *The End of the Welfare State*

Adler, F., 1975, *Sisters in Crime,* McGraw Hill

Adorno, T. W. et al., 1950, *The Authoritarian Personality,* Harper

Ainley, P., 1993, *Class and Skill: Changing Divisions of Knowledge and Labour,* Cassell

Allan, G., 1985, *Family Life,* Blackwell

Allen, Hilary, 1987, *Justice Unbalanced,* Open University Press

Althusser, L., 1969, *For Marx,* Allen Lane

Althusser, L., 1971, *Essays on Ideology,* New Left Books

Anderson, M., 1971, 'The relevance of family history' in M. Anderson, *Sociology of the Family,* Penguin, 2nd edition, 1980

Anderson, M., 1972, 'Household structure and the industrial revolution' in P. Laslett (ed.), *Household and Family in Time Past,* Cambridge University Press

Ariès, Philippe, 1962, *Centuries of Childhood,* Jonathan Cape

Armstrong, W. A., 1972, 'A note of the household structure of mid-nineteenth-century York in comparative perspective' in Laslett

Aronowitz, S. and DiFazio, W., 1994, *The Jobless Future: Sci-Tech and the Dogma of Work,* University of Minnesota Press

Ashton, D., 1986, *Unemployment under Capitalism,* Wheatsheaf

Atkinson, A. B., 1983, *The Economics of Equality,* Oxford University Press

Atkinson, J. M., 1978, *Discovering Suicide,* Macmillan

Atkinson, J., 1985, 'The changing corporation', in D. Clutterbuck (ed.), *New Patterns of Work,* Gower

Atterhead, Sven, 1985, 'Intrapreneurship: the way forward?' in Clutterbuck

Avila, Manuel, 1969, *Tradition and Growth,* University of Chicago Press

Avineri, S., 1993, 'The return to Islam', *Dissent,* Fall

Bachrach, P. and Baratz, M., 1963, 'Decisions and non-decisions: an analytical framework', *American Political Science Review,* vol. 57

Bacon, A. W., 1975, 'Leisure and the alienated worker', *Journal of Leisure Research,* vol. 7, no. 3

Bagdikian, B., 1997, *The Media Monopoly,* Beacon Press

Bagehot, Walter, 1867, *The English Constitution* (Fontana, 1963)

Ball, Stephen, 1981, *Beachside Comprehensive: A Case Study of Secondary Schooling,* Cambridge University Press

Bandura, A. *et al.,* 1961, 'The imitation of film-mediated aggressive models' *Journal of Abnormal Psychology,* 66

Banton, M., 1987, *Racial Theories,* CUP

Baran, B., 1988, 'Office automation and women's work' in R. Pahl (ed.), *On Work,* Blackwell

Barber, B., 1963, 'Some problems in the sociology of professions', *Daedelus,* vol. 92, no. 4

Barker, E., 1984, *The Making of a Moonie: Choice or Brainwashing?,* Basil Blackwell

Barker, M., 1984, 'Nasty politics or video nasties?' in M. Barker (ed.), 1984, *The Video Nasties: Freedom and Censorship in the Media,* Pluto Press

Barrett, Michele and McIntosh, Mary, 1982, *The Anti-Social Family,* Verso

Barrett, Michele and McIntosh, Mary, 1985, 'Ethnocentrism and socialist-feminist theory', *Feminist Review,* 20

Barron, R. D. and Norris E. M., 1976, 'Sexual divisions and the dual labour market' in D. Barker and S. Allen (eds.), *Dependence and Exploitation in Work and Marriage,* Longman

Bassett, P., 1987, *Strike Free,* Macmillan

Bates, I. *et al.,* 1984, *Schooling for the Dole?,* Macmillan

Baudrillard, J., 1983, *In the Shadow of the Silent Majorities … Or the End of the Social and Other Essays,* Semiotext(e)

Baudrillard, J., 1983b, *Simulations,* Semiotext(e)

Baudrillard, J., 1988, in M. Poster (ed.), *Jean Baudrillard: Selected Works,* Polity Press

Baudrillard, J., 1995, *The Gulf War Did Not Take Place,* Power Publications

Bauer, Peter, 1976, *Dissent on Development,* Weidenfeld and Nicolson

Bauer, Peter, 1981, *Equality, the Third World and Economic Delusion,* Weidenfeld and Nicolson

Bauman, Zygmunt, 1988, *Legislators and Interpreters,* Polity Press

Bauman, Z., 1997, *Postmodernity and its Discontents,* Polity Press

Ba-Yunus, Ilyas, 1997, 'The myth of Islamic fundamentalism',
http://www.geocities.com/CollegePart/6453/myth.html

Beck, U., 1992, *The Risk Society,* Sage

Becker, H. S., 1963, *Outsiders: Studies in the Sociology of Deviance* (The Free Press, 1973)

Becker, H. S., 1967, 'Whose side are we on?' *Social Problems,* 14

Beckford, J., 1986, *New Religious Movements and Rapid Social Change,* Sage/UNESCO

Beechey, V., 1983, 'The sexual division of labour and the labour process: a critic assessment of Braverman, in S. Wood (ed.), *The Degradation of Work Skill. Deskilling and the Labour Process,* Hutchinson

Belfield, R. and Hird, C, 1991, *Murdoch: The Great Escape,* Time Warner

Bell, D., 1961, *The End of Ideology,* Collier-Macmillan

Bell, D., 1973, *The Coming of Post-Industrial Society,* Basic Books

Bellah, R. N., 1964, 'Religious evolution', *American Sociological Review,* 29

Belotti, E., 1975, *Little Girls,* Writers and Readers Publishing Cooperative

Belson, William, 1978, *TV Violence and the Adolescent Boy,* Saxon House

Bendix, R. and Lipset, S. (eds.), 1966, *Class, Status and Power,* The Free Press

Benedict, R., 1982, *Race, Science and Politics,* Greenwood Press

Berger, Bennett, 1960, *Working-Class Suburbs: A Study of Auto Workers in Suburbia,* University of California Press

Berger, B. and Berger, P., 1983, *The War Over the Family,* Hutchinson

Berger, P., 1966, *Invitation to Sociology,* Penguin

Berger, P., 1990, *The Sacred Canopy: Elements of a Sociological Theory of Religion,* Anchor Books

Berle, A. A. and Means, G. C., 1932, *The Modern Corporation and Private Property,* Macmillan

Bernades, Jon, 1990, 'The family in question', *Social Studies Review,* September

Bernstein, Basil, 1961, 'Social class and linguistic development: a theory of social development' in A. H. Halsey *et al., Education, Economy and Society,* The Free Press

Berry, B., 1978, *Race and Ethnic Relations,* Houghton

Beveridge, William, 1942, *Social Insurance and Allied Services* (The Beveridge Report), Cmd 6404, HMSO

Beveridge, William, 1944, *Full Employment in a Free Society,* Allen and Unwin

Beynon, Huw, 1973, *Working for Ford,* Allen Lane

Beynon, J., 1987, 'General election 1987: the electoral impact of the partisan press', *Social Studies Review,* vol. 3, no. 2

Binns, D. and Mars, G., 1984, 'Family, community and unemployment: a study in change', *The Sociological Review,* vol. 32, no. 4

Birke, L., 1986, *Women, Feminism, and Biology,* Wheatsheaf

Blackstone, Tessa and Weinrich-Haste, Helen, 1980, 'Why are there so few women scientists and engineers?', *New Society,* 21.2.80

Blau, P. M., 1955, *The Dynamics of Bureaucracy,* University of Chicago Press

Blauner, R., 1964, *Alienation and Freedom,* University of Chicago Press

Blumer, H., 1969, *Symbolic Interactionism,* Prentice Hall

Blumer, H., 1975, 'Exchange on Turner', *Sociological Inquiry,* vol. 45

Blumler, J. G. and McQuail, D., 1968, *Television in Politics: Its Uses and Influence,* Faber and Faber

Booth, C., 1889–1903, *Life and Labour of the People of London,* Macmillan

Bott, Elizabeth, 1957, *Family and Social Network,* Tavistock

Bottomore, T. and Rubel, M., 1976, *Karl Marx: Selected Writings in Sociology and Social Philosophy,* Pelican

Bourdieu, P., 1973, 'Cultural reproduction and social reproduction', in R. Brown (ed.), *Knowledge, Education and Cultural Change,* Tavistock

Bourne, Richard, 1979, 'The snakes and ladders of the British class system', *New Society,* 8.2.79

Bowlby, J., 1946, *Forty Four Juvenile Thieves,* Tindall and Cox

Bowlby, J., 1971, *,Childcare and the Growth of Love,* Penguin

Bowles, S. and Gintis, H., 1976, *Schooling in Capitalist America,* Routledge and Kegan Paul

Bowles, S. and Gintis, H., 1988, 'Schooling in Capitalist America: reply to our critics', in M. Cole (ed.), *Bowles and Gintis Revisited,* Falmer Press

Box, Stephen, 1971, *Deviance, Reality and Society,* Holt, Rinehart and Winston

Bradshaw, J. and Holmes, H., 1989, *Living on the Edge,* Tyneside CPAG

Brake, M., 1985, *Comparative Youth Culture,* Routledge

Braverman, Harry, 1974, *Labor and Monopoly Capitalism: The Degradation of Work in the Twentieth Century,* Monthly Review Press

Brewer, R. M., 1993, 'Theorising race, class and gender' in S. James and A. Busia (eds), *Theorising Black Feminisms,* Routledge

Britten, N. and Heath, A., 1983, 'Women, men and social class' in E. Gamarnikow *et al., Gender, Class and Work,* Heinemann

Bruce, Steve, 1988, *Rise and Fall of the New Christian Right: Protestant Politics in America 1978–88,* Clarendon Press

Bruce, Steve, 1990, *A House Divided: Protestantism, Schism and Secularisation,* Routledge

Bruce, Steve (ed.), 1992, *Religion and Modernisation: Sociologists and Historians Debate the Secularisation Thesis,* Clarendon Press

Bruce, S., 1995, *Religion in Modern Britain,* Oxford University Press

Bruce, S., 1996, *Religion in the Modern World: From Cathedrals to Cults,* Oxford University Press

Bruce, S., 2001, *Fundamentalism,* Polity Press

Bruegel, I., 1979, 'Women as a reserve army of labour: a note on recent British experience', *Feminist Review,* 3

Bruegel, I., 1986, 'Sex and race in the labour market', *Feminist Review,* 32

Budge, I., 1983, *The New British Political System,* Longman

Burawoy, M., 1979, *Manufacturing Consent,* University of Chicago Press

Burgess, E. and Locke, H., 1945, *The Family,* American Book Company

Burnham, J., 1943, *The Managerial Revolution,* Putnam and Co.

Burns, T. and Stalker, G., 1961, *The Management of Innovation,* Tavistock

Burt, C., 1943, 'Ability and income', *British Journal of Educational Psychology,* 13

Burt, C., 1961, 'Intelligence and social mobility', *British Journal of Statistical Psychology,* vol. 14

Buswell, Carol, 1991, 'The gendering of school and work', *Social Studies Review,* January

Butler, D. and Butler, G., 1994, *British Political Facts 1900–1994,* Macmillan

Butler, D. and Rose, R., 1960, *The British General Election of 1959,* Frank Cass

Butler, D. and Stokes, D., 1974, *Political Change in Modern Britain,* Macmillan

Butler, Robert, 1975, *Why Survive? Being Old in America,* Harper Row

Calhoun, C, 1997, 'Family outlaws' in H. L. Nelson (ed.), *Feminism and Families,* Routledge

Callinicos, Alex, 1990, *Against Postmodernism: A Marxist Critique,* Polity Press

Calnan, M. and Johnson, B., 1985, 'Health, health risks and inequalities: an exploratory study of women's perceptions', *Sociology of Health and Illness,* 7

Campbell, Anne, 1981, *Girl Delinquents,* Basil Blackwell

Campbell, C., 1998, 'The easternisation of the West', in B. Wilson and J. Creswell (eds), *New Religious Movements: Challenge and Response,* Routledge

Cantril, Hadley, 1940, *The Invasion from Mars: A Study in the Psychology of Panic,* Princeton University Press

Carlen, P. (ed.), 1985, *Criminal Women,* Polity Press

Carr-Hill, R. and Stern, N., 1979, *Crime: The Political and Criminal Statistics,* Academic Press

Carson W. G., 1971, 'White-collar crime and the enforcement of factory legislation' in W. G. Carson and P. Wiles (eds), *Crime and Delinquency in Britain,* Martin Robertson

Castells, Manuel, 1977, *The Urban Question,* Edward Arnold

Castells, Manuel, 1983, *The City and the Grassroots: A Cross-Cultural Theory of Urban Social Movements,* Edward Arnold

Castles, S. and Kosack, G., 1973, *Immigrant Workers and Class Structure in Western Europe,* Oxford University Press

Chambliss, William, 1978, *On the Take: From Petty Crooks to Presidents,* Indiana University Press

Chapman, A. D., 1984, 'Patterns of mobility among men and women in Scotland, 1930–1970', Ph.D. thesis, Plymouth Polytechnic

Chester, R., 1985, 'The rise of the neo-conventional family', *New Society,* 9 May

Cicourel, Aaron, 1976, *The Social Organisation of Juvenile Justice,* Heinemann

Clarke, C. *et al.,* 1979, *Working-Class Culture,* Hutchinson

Clarke, J. and Critcher, C., 1985, *The Devil Makes Work: Leisure in Capitalist Britain,* Macmillan

Clarke, M., 1990, *Business Crime: Its Nature and Control,* Polity Press

Clarke, R. and Cornish, D. (eds.), 1983, *Crime Control in Britain,* SUNY Press

Clarke, R. and Mayhew, P. (eds.), 1980, *Designing out Crime,* HMSO

Clegg, H. A., 1979, *The Changing Structure of Industrial Relations in Great Britain,* Blackwell

Clegg, H. and Adams, R., 1957, *The Employers' Challenge,* Basil Blackwell

Clegg, Stewart, 1979, *The Theory of Power and Organisation,* Routledge

Clinard, M. and Yeager, P., 1980, *Corporate Crime,* The Free Press

Cloward, R. and Ohlin, L., 1961, *Delinquency and Opportunity,* The Free Press

Clutterbuck, D. (ed.), 1985, *New Patterns of Work,* Gower

Coates, D., 1984, *The Context of British Politics,* Hutchinson

Coates, K. and Silburn, R., 1970, *Poverty: The Forgotten Englishmen,* Penguin

Coates, K. and Topham, T., 1986, *Trade Unions and Politics,* Blackwell

Cockerell, M., Hennessy, P. and Walker, D., 1985, *Sources Close to the Prime Minister,* Papermac

Cohen, A., 1955, *Delinquent Boys: The Culture of the Gang,* Glencoe Free Press

Cohen, A., 1985, *The Symbolic Construction of Community,* Tavistock

Cohen, Stanley, 1972, *Folk Devils and Moral Panics: The Creation of Mods and Rockers,* MacGibbon and Kee

Cole, M. (ed.), 1988, *Bowles and Gintis Revisited,* The Falmer Press

Coleman, James, 1979, 'Sociological analysis and social policy' in T. Bottomore and R. Nisbet, *A History of Sociological Analysis,* Heinemann

Coles, R., 1975, 'Football as surrogate religion', in M. Hills (ed.), *A Sociological Yearbook of Religion,* SCM Press

Commission on the Poor Law and Relief of Distress, 1909, *The Poor Law Report of 1909,* Macmillan

Congdon, T. *et al.*, 1995, *The Cross Media Revolution*, John Libbey

Cook, J. and Watt, S., 1987, 'Racism, women and poverty' in C. Glendinning and J. Miller (eds.), *Women and Poverty in Britain*, Wheatsheaf

Cook, S., 1989, *Rich Law, Poor Law*, Open University Press

Cooke, P. (ed.), 1989, *The Changing Face of Urban Britain: Localities*, Unwin Hyman

Cooper, David, 1972, *The Death of the Family*, Penguin

Coote, A., 1981, *Positive Action for Women*, National Council for Civil Liberties

Coronary Prevention Group, 1986, *Coronary Heart Disease and Asians in Britain*, Coronary Prevention Group/Confederation of Indian Organisations

Coward, Ros, 1987, 'Violent Screen Play', *Marxism Today*, December

Coyle, Angela, 1984, *Redundant Women*, The Women's Press

Crewe, I., 1992, 'Why did labour lose?' *Politics Review*, vol. 2, no. 2

Crompton, R., 1980, 'Class mobility in modern Britain', *Sociology*, vol. 14

Crompton, R., 1991, 'Women and work in the 1990s', *Social Studies Review*, May

Crompton, R., 1997, 'Gender and employment: current debates', *Social Science Teacher*, vol. 26, no. 2

Crompton, R. and Jones, G. (eds.), 1984, *White Collar Proletariat: Deskilling and Gender in Clerical Work*, Macmillan

Crosland, C. A. R., 1956, *The Future of Socialism*, Cape

Croucher, R., 1987, *We Refuse to Starve in Silence*, Lawrence and Wishart

Cumberbatch, G. and Negrine, R., 1992, *Images of Disability on Television*, Routledge

Curtis, L., 1984, *Ireland: The Propaganda War*, Pluto

Dahl, R., 1961, *Who Governs? Democracy and Power in an American City*, Yale University Press

Dahrendorf, R., 1959, *Class and Class Conflict in an Industrial Society*, Routledge and Kegan Paul

Daniels, W., 1968, *Racial Discrimination in England*, Penguin

Darwin, C., 1859, *The Origin of Species* (J. M. Dent, 1971)

Davie, G., 1994, *Religion in Britain Since 1945*, Blackwell

Davies, G., 1995, 'Competing fundamentalisms', *Sociology Review*, vol, 4, no. 4

Davis, J., 1990, *Youth and the Condition of Modern Britain: Images of Adolescent Conflict*, Athlone Press

Davis, K., 1948, *Human Society*, Macmillan

Davis, K. and Moore, W. E., 1945, 'Some principles of stratification', *American Sociological Review*, vol. 10

Deem, Rosemary, 1986, *All Work and No Play: The Sociology of Women and Leisure*, Open University Press

Deem, Rosemary, 1988, *Work, Unemployment and Leisure*, Routledge

Delmar, Rosalind, 1976, 'Looking again at Engels' *Origin of the Family, Private Property and the State*' in Juliet Mitchell and Ann Oakley, *The Rights and Wrongs of Women*, Penguin

Delphy, C., 1981, 'Women in stratification studies' in H. Roberts (ed.) *Doing Feminist Research*, Routledge

Dennis, N., Henriques, F. and Slaughter, C., 1956, *Coal is Our Life*, Eyre and Spottiswood

Denzin, N., 1970, *The Research Act*, Aldine

Department of Health and Social Security, 1980, *Inequalities in Health*, Report of Working Group chaired by Sir Douglas Black. Reprinted as *Inequalities in Health: The Black Report*, ed. Peter Townsend and Nick Davidson, 1988

Devine, F., 1992, *Affluent Workers Revisited*, Edinburgh University Press

Dex, S., 1985, *The Sexual Division of Work*, Wheatsheaf

Dex, S. and McCullough, A., 1997, *Flexible Employment: The Future of Britain's Jobs*, Macmillan

Diamond, F. and Bates, S., 1992,*The Spot*, MIT Press

Ditton, J., 1977, *Part-time Crime*, Macmillan

Dobash, P. and R., 1980, *Violence against Wives: A Case against Patriarchy*, Open Books

Douglas, J. W. B., 1964, *The Home and the School*, MacGibbon and Lee

Douglas, Jack D., 1967, *The Social Meaning of Suicide*, Princeton

Downing, J., 1975, 'The balanced white view' in C. Husband (ed.), *White Media and Black Britain*, Arrow Books

Dreeban, R., 1970, *The Contribution of Schooling to the Learning of Norms*, Glenview

Duffy, K., 1995, *Social Exclusion and Human Dignity in Europe*, Council of Europe

Dumazedier, J., 1974, *The Sociology of Leisure*, Elsevier

Dunleavy, Patrick, 1979, 'The urban bases of political alignment', *British Journal of Political Science*, vol. 9

Dunlop, J., 1958, *Industrial Relations Systems*, Holt

Dunning, E. and Sheard, K., 1969, *Barbarians, Gentlemen and Players*, Oxford University Press

Dunning, E. *et al.*, 1988, *The Roots of Football Violence*, Routledge

Durkheim, E., 1893, *The Division of Labour in Society*, first translated by George Simpson (Macmillan, 1933)

Durkheim, E., 1895, *The Rules of Sociological Method*, first translated by Sarah Solovay and John Mueller (University of Chicago Press, 1938)

Durkheim, E., 1897, *Suicide: A Study in Sociology*, first translated by John Spaulding and George Simpson (The Free Press, 1951)

Durkheim, E., 1902–6, *Moral Education* (The Free Press, 1961)

Durkheim, E., 1912, *The Elementary Forms of Religious Life*, first translated by Joseph Ward Swain (Allen and Unwin, 1915)

Dweck, Carol, 1972, 'Learned helplessness and negative evaluation', *Educator*, vol. 19, no. 2

Dyson, S., 1987, *Mental Handicap: Dilemmas of Parent–Professional Relationships*, Croom-Helm

Edwards, M., 1989, 'The irrelevance of development studies', *Third World Quarterly*, vol. 11, no.1

Ehrenreich, B. and J., 1979, 'The professional-managerial class' in P. Walker (ed.), *Between Labour and Capital*, Harvester Press

Eisenstadt, S., 1956, *From Generation to Generation*, The Free Press

Eisenstadt, S., 1966, *Modernisation: Protest and Change*, Prentice Hall

Eldridge, J., 1968, *Industrial Disputes*, Routledge and Kegan Paul

Elston, M., 1980, 'Medicine: half our future doctors?' in R. Silverstone and A. Ward (eds.), *Careers of Professional Women*, Croom Helm

Engels, Friedrich, 1845, *The Condition of the Working Class in England* (Penguin, 1988)

Engels, Friedrich, 1884, *The Origin of the Family, Private Property and the State* (Penguin, 1986)

Esterson, A., 1972, *The Leaves of Spring*, Penguin

Ettlinger, R. and Flordah, G., 1955, 'Attempted suicide', *Act Psychiatrica*

Etzioni, Amitai, 1964, *Modern Organisations*, Prentice Hall

Eysenck, H. J., 1971, *Race, Intelligence and Education*, Temple-Smith

Eysenck, H. J. and Eysenck, S. B. G., 1975, *The Manual of the Eysenck Personality Questionnaire*, Hodder and Stoughton

Featherstone, M. and Hepworth, M., 1995, 'Images of positive ageing', in M. Featherstone and A. Wernick, (eds), *Images of Ageing*, Routledge

Ferguson, Marjorie, 1983, *Forever Feminine: Women's Magazines and the Cult of Femininity*, Heinemann

Ferri, E. and Smith, K., 1996, *Parenting in the 1990s*, Family Policy Studies

Feyerabend, P., 1998, *Against Method*, Verso

Field, Frank, 1989, *Losing Out: The Emergence of Britain's Underclass*, Blackwell

Finch, J., 1989, *Family Obligations and Social Change*, Polity Press

Firestone, Shulamith, 1970, *The Dialectic of Sex*, Paladin

Fiske, John, 1990, 'Women and quiz shows: consumerism, patriarchy and resisting pleasures' in M. E. Brown (ed.), *Television and Women's Culture*, Sage

Fletcher, R., 1962, *Family and Marriage in Britain*, Penguin

Fletcher, R., 1988, *The Abolitionists: The Family and Marriage under Attack*, Routledge

Fletcher, R., 1991, *Science, Ideology and the Media: The Cyril Burt Scandal*, Transaction

Foucault, M., 1980, *Power and Knowledge: Selected Interviews and Other Writings 1972–77*, Harvester Press

Frank, A. G., 1967, *Capitalism and Underdevelopment in Latin America*, Monthly Review Press

Frank, A. G., 1969, *Latin America: Underdevelopment or Revolution*, Monthly Review Press

Frank, A. G., 1981, *Crisis in the Third World*, Heinemann

Frankenburg, R., 1957, *Communities in Britain*, Routledge

Freeman, D., 1983, *Margaret Mead and Samoa: The Making and Unmaking of an Anthropological Myth*, Australian National University Press

Freire, Paolo, 1972, *Pedagogy of the Oppressed*, Penguin

Freire, Paolo, 1976, *Education: The Practice of Freedom*, Writers and Readers Cooperative

Friedson, E., 1975, *Profession of Medicine*, Dodd, Mead and Co.

Fuller, Mary, 1980, 'Black girls in a London comprehensive school' in R. Deem (ed.), *Schooling for Women's Work*, Routledge and Kegan Paul

Galbraith, J. K., 1967, *The New Industrial State*, Hamish Hamilton

Galbraith, J. K., 1992, *The Culture of Contentment*, Sinclair Stevenson

Gallie, Duncan, 1978, *In Search of the New Working Class*, Cambridge University Press

Gallie, D., White, M., Cheng, Y. and Tomlinson, M., 1998, *Restructuring the Employment Relationship*, Clarendon Press

Gans, Howard, 1962, 'Urbanism and suburbanism as ways of life' in A. M. Rose, *Human Behaviour and Social Processes*, Routledge

Gans, Howard, 1967, *The Levittowners*, Allen Lane

Gans, Howard, 1973, 'The positive functions of poverty', *American Journal of Sociology*, vol. 78, no. 2

Garfinkel, H., 1967, *Studies in Ethnomethodology*, Prentice Hall

Gellner, E., 1992, *Postmodernism, Reason and Religion*, Routledge

George, V. and Miller, S., 1994, *Social Policy Towards 2000: Squaring the Welfare Circle*, Routledge

Gershuny, J., 1978, *After Industrial Society*, Macmillan

Gershuny, J. and Pahl, R., 1980, 'Britain in the decade of the three economies: the implications and future of the informal economy, *New Society*, 3 January

Gerth, H. and Mills, C. Wright, 1954, *Character and Social Structure*, Routledge and Kegan Paul

Giddens, Anthony, 1973, *The Class Structure of the Advanced Societies*, Hutchinson

Giddens, Anthony, 1980, *The Making of Post-Christian Britain*, Longman

Giddens, Anthony, 1984, *The Constitution of Society*, Polity Press

Giddens, Anthony, 1990, *The Consequences of Modernity*, Polity Press

Gilbert, A., 1980, *The Making of Post-Christian Britain*, Longman

Gilroy, P., 1987, *There Ain't no Black in the Union Jack*, Hutchinson

Giner, S., 1976, *Mass Society*, Martin Robertson

Ginn, J., Arber, S., Brannen, J., Dale, A., Dex, S, Elias, P., Moss, P., Pahl, J., Roberts, C and Rubery, J., 1996, 'Feminist fallacies: a reply to Hakim on women's employment', *British Journal Sociology*, vol. 47, no. 1

Giroux, H., 1984, 'Ideology, agency and the process of schooling' in L. Barton and S. Walker (eds.), *Social Crisis and Educational Research*, Croom Helm

Glasgow, D., 1981, *The Black Underclass*, Vintage Books

Glasgow University Media Group (GUMG), 1976, *Bad News*, Routledge and Kegan Paul

GUMG, 1980, *More Bad News*, Routledge and Kegan Paul

GUMG, 1982, *Really Bad News*, Routledge and Kegan Paul

GUMG, 1985, *War and Peace News,* Open University Press

GUMG, 1995, *Mass Representations of Mental Health/Illness,* GUMG

Glasner, Peter, 1977, *The Concept of Secularisation,* Routledge and Kegan Paul

Glass, David (ed.), 1954, *Social Mobility in Britain,* Routledge and Kegan Paul

Glock, C. and Stark, R., 1965, *Religion and Society in Tension,* Rand McNally

Goffman, Erving, 1959, *The Presentation of Self in Everyday Life,* Doubleday Anchor

Goffman, Erving, 1961, *Asylums: Essays on the Social Situation of Mental Patients and Other Inmates,* Anchor Books

Goffman, Erving, 1971, *Relations in Public,* Basic Books

Goldthorpe, John, 1966, 'Social stratification in industrial society' in R. Bendix and S. Lipset (eds.), *Class, Status and Power,* The Free Press

Goldthorpe, John *et al.,* 1968, *The Industrial Worker: Industrial Attitudes and Behaviour,* Cambridge University Press

Goldthorpe, John *et al.,* 1969, *The Affluent Worker in the Class Structure,* Cambridge University Press

Goldthorpe, John, 1980, *Social Mobility and Class Structure in Modern Britain,* Clarendon Press

Goldthorpe, J., 1983, 'Women and class analysis: a defence of the conventional view', *Sociology,* 17

Goldthorpe, J. and Payne, C., 1986, 'On the class mobility of women', *Sociology,* 20

Gomm, R., 1982, 'Science and values' in R. Gomm and P. McNeill, *Handbook for Sociology Teachers,* Heinemann

Goode, William, 1963, *World Revolution and Family Patterns,* The Free Press

Gorer, G., 1971, *Sex and Marriage in Britain Today,* Nelson

Gorz, A., 1984, *Pathways to Paradise,* Pluto

Gough, E., 1959, 'Is the family universal?', in N. W. Bell and E. F. Vogel (eds), *A Modern Introduction to the Family,* Collier MacMillan

Gould, S. J., 1981, *The Mismeasure of Man,* W. W. Norton and Co.

Gouldner, A., 1968, 'The sociologist as partisan: sociology and the welfare state', *The American Sociologist,* 3

Gouldner, A., 1970, *The Coming Crisis of Western Sociology,* Basic Books

Graham, Hilary, 1984, *Women, Health and the Family,* Wheatsheaf

Gramsci, Antonio, 1971, *Selections from the Prison Notebooks,* New Left Books

Grieco, M., 1987, *Keeping it in the Family: Social Networks and Employment Change,* Tavistock Publications

Griffin, C., 1985, *Typical Girls?,* Routledge and Kegan Paul

Griffin, C., 1986, 'It's different for girls', *Social Studies Review,* November

Griffin, J., 1939, *Strikes: A Study in Quantitative Economics,* Columbia University Press

Grint, K., 1991, *The Sociology of Work: An Introduction,* Polity Press

Gubrium, J. and Holstein, J., 1990, *What is Family?,* Mayfield Publishing

Gunter, B., 1995, *Television and Gender Representation,* John Libbey

Gunter, B. and McAleer, J., 1990, *Children and Television: The One-Eyed Monster,* Routledge

Gunter, B. *et al.,* 1994, *Television: The Public's View,* John Libbey

Gurevitch, M. and Blumler, J., 1977, 'Linkages between the mass media and politics' in J. Curran *et al.* (eds.), *Mass Communication and Mass Society,* Edward Arnold

Habermas, J., 1976, *Legitimation Crisis,* Heinemann

Hagell, A. and Newburn, T., 1994, *Young Offenders and the Media,* Policy Studies Institute

Hagen, E., 1962, *On the Theory of Social Change,* Dorsey

Hakim, C., 1995, 'Five feminist myths about women's employment', *British Journal of Sociology,* vol. 46, no. 39

Hall, S., 1978, 'The great moving right show', *Marxism Today,* December, reprinted in S. Hall, *The Hard Road to Renewal,* Verso

Hall, S. 1978a, 'Mugging, the State and the law' in S. Hall *et al., Policing the Crisis,* Macmillan

Hall, S., 1980, 'Encoding/decoding', in S. Hall, D. Hobson, A. Lowe and P. Willis (eds), *Culture, Media and Language,* Hutchinson

Hall, S., 1987, 'Urban unrest in Britain' in John Benyon and John Solomos, *The Roots of Urban Unrest,* Pergamon

Hall, S., 1990, 'Cultural identity and diaspora' in J. Rutherford (ed.), *Identity,* Lawrence and Wishart

Hall, S. and Jefferson, T. (eds.), 1976, *Resistance through Rituals,* Hutchinson

Hall, S., Hobson, D. and Willis, P. (eds) 1980, *Culture, Media and Language,* Hutchinson

Hallam, H. E., 1961, 'Population density in medieval Fenland', *Economic History Review,* 14

Halmos, P., 1970, *The Personal Service Society,* Constable

Halsey, A. H. and Webb, J., 2000, *Twentieth Century British Social Trends,* Macmillan

Halsey, A. H., Heath, A. F. and Ridge, J. M., 1980, *Origins and Destinations,* Clarendon Press

Hammersley, M. (ed.), 1993, 'Introduction' in *Social Research: Philosophy, Politics and Practice,* Sage Publications

Hammond, P., 1985, *The Sacred in a Secular Age: Toward Revision in the Scientific Study of Religion,* University of California

Harding, J., 1980, 'Sex differences in performance in science examinations' in R. Deem (ed.), *Schooling for Women's Work,* Routledge and Kegan Paul

Harding, S. (ed.), 1987, *Feminism and Methodology,* Open University Press

Hargreaves, D., 1967, *Social Relations in a Secondary School,* Routledge and Kegan Paul

Harris, C. C. *et al.,* 1987, *Redundancy and Recession,* Basil Blackwell

Harris, M. and Hannay, S., 1993, *Into the Future: The Foundations of Library and Information Services in the Post-industrial Era,* Ablex

Harrison, M., 1985, *T.V. News: Whose Bias? A Casebook Analysis of Strikes*, Television and Media Studies, Hermitage

Hart, N., 1976, *When Marriage Ends*, Tavistock

Hartmann, P. and Husband, C, 1974, Racism and the Mass Media. *A Study of the Role of the Mass Media in the Formation of While Beliefs and Attitudes in Britain* Davis Poynter

Hartmann, P. and Husband, C., 1976, 'The mass media and racial conflict', in S. Cohen and J. Young (eds), *The Manufacture of News: Deviance, Social Problems and the Mass Media*, Constable

Harvey, David, 1989, *The Condition of Postmodernity*, Blackwell

Haste, H., 1993, *The Sexual Metaphor*, Harvester Wheatsheaf

Haworth, J. and Evans, S., 1987, 'Meaningful activity and unemployment' in D. Fryer and P. Ullah (eds.), *Unemployed People*, Open University Press

Hayter, Teresa, 1971, *Aid as Imperialism*, Penguin

Hayter, Teresa, 1981, *The Creation of World Poverty*, Pluto

Heath, A., 1981, *Social Mobility*, Fontana

Heath, A. and Britten, N., 1984, 'Women's jobs do make a difference'. *Sociology*, vol. 18, no. 4

Heath, A. *et al.,* 1985, *How Britain Votes*, Pergamon

Hebdige, D., 1979, *Subculture: The Meaning of Style*, Methuen

Heelas, P., 1996, *The New Age Movement*, Blackwell

Heidensohn, Frances, 1985, *Women and Crime*, Macmillan

Herberg, Will, 1955, *Protestant, Catholic, Jew*, Doubleday

Hillery, G. A. Jnr, 1955, 'Definitions of community: areas of agreement', *Rural Sociology*, 20

Hills, J., 1998, *Income and Wealth: The Latest Evidence*, Joseph Rowntree Foundation

Hillyard, P., 1987, 'The normalization of special powers: from Northern Ireland to Britain' in P. Scraton (ed.), *Law, Order and the Authoritarian State*, Open University Press

Himmelweit, H., 1958, *Television and the Child*, Oxford University Press

Himmelweit, H. *et al.,* 1981, *How Voters Decide*, Academic Press

Hirschi, Travis, 1969, *The Causes of Delinquency*, University of California Press

Hodge, B. and Tripp, D., 1985, *Children and Television*, 1985

Holt, J., 1969, *How Children Fail*, Penguin

Hood-Williams, J., 1990, 'Patriarchy for children: on the stability of power relations in children's lives' in L. Chisholm *et al., Childhood, Youth and Social Change*, Falmer Press

Hooks, B., 1990, *Yearning: Race, Gender and Cultural Politics*, South End Press

Howarth, C., Kenway, P., Palmer, G. and Street, C., 2000, *Monitoring Poverty and Social Exclusion: Labour's Inheritance*, New Policy Institute and Joseph Rowntree Foundation

Howitt, Dennis, 1982, *Mass Media and Social Problems*, Pergamon Press

Hudson, B., 1989, 'Discrimination and disparity: the influence of race on sentencing', *New Community*, vol. 16, no.1

Humphreys, L., 1970, *Tearoom Trade: A Study of Homosexual Encounters in Public Places*, Aldine Publishing Company

Hyman, R., 1972, *Strikes*, Fontana (4th edition, 1991)

Hyman, R., 1989, 'What's happening to the unions?', *Social Studies Review*, March

Illich, Ivan, 1975, *Limits to Medicine: Medical Nemesis – The Expropriation of Health*, Marion Boyars

Illich, Ivan, 1976, *Deschooling Society*, Pelican

Illsley, R., 1955, 'Social class selection and class differences in relation to stillbirths', *British Medical Journal*, 2

Illsley, R., 1986, 'Occupational class, selection and the production of inequalities in health', *Quarterly Journal of Health Affairs*, 2

Jackman, R., 1998, 'Unemployment and labour market policy', *Economic Review*, February

Jackson, B. and Marsden, D., 1963, *Education and the Working Class*, Routledge

Jahoda, M. *et al.,* 1933, *Marienthal: A Study of an Unemployed Community*, Aldine/Atherton

Jameson, Frederic, 1991, *Postmodernism or the Cultural Logic of Late Capitalism*, Verso

Jeffcoate, R., 1984, *Ethnic Minorities and Education*, Harper and Row

Jencks, C. and Peterson, P. (eds.), 1991, *The Urban Underclass*, Brookings Institution

Jenkins, R., 1991, 'Disability and social stratification', *British Journal of Sociology*, vol. 42, no. 4

Jensen, A., 1967, 'How much can we boost IQ and scholastic achievement?', *Harvard Educational Review*, 29

Johnson, T., 1972, *Professions and Power*, Macmillan

Jones, B., 1991, *Politics UK*, Philip Allen

Jones, C., 1980, *Fostering Femininity in Middle School Girls*, Routledge

Jones, I. and Cameron, D., 1984, 'Social class: an embarrassment for epidemiology?', *Community Medicine*, 6

Jones, N., 1986, *Strikes and the Media: Communication and Conflict*, Basil Blackwell

Jordan, B., 1973, *Paupers: The Making of the Claiming Class*, Routledge

Jordan, B., 1989, 'Universal welfare provision creates a dependent population. The case against'. *Social Studies Review*, November

Joseph, G., 1981, 'The incompatible ménage à trois: Marxism, feminism and racism' in Lydia Sargent (ed.), *Women and Revolution: A Discussion of the Unhappy Marriage of Marxism and Feminism*, Pluto Press

Joseph, G., 1988, 'Black feminist pedagogy and schooling in white capitalist America' in M. Cole (ed.), *Bowles and Gintis Revisited*, Falmer Press

Joynson, R., 1989, *The Burt Affair*, Routledge

Karpf, A., 1988, *Doctoring the Media: The Reporting of Health and Medicine*, Routledge

Katz, E. and Lazarsfeld, P., 1955, *Personal Influence; The Part Played by People in the Flow of Mass Communications*, The Free Press

Katz, J., 1988, *Seductions of Crime: Moral and Sensual Attraction in Doing Evil*, Basic Books

Kavanagh, D., 1985, 'Whatever happened to consensus politics?', *Political Studies*, vol. 33

Keddie, Nell, 1971, 'Classroom knowledge' in M. F. D. Young (ed.), *Knowledge and Control*, Collier-Macmillan

Keddie, Nell (ed.), 1973, *Tinker, Tailor ... The Myth of Cultural Deprivation*, Penguin

Kelly, A. (ed.), 1981, *The Missing Half: Girls and Science Education*, Manchester University Press

Kelly, John, 1988, *Trade Unions and Socialist Politics*, Verso

Kelvin, P. et al., 1984, *Unemployment and Leisure*, Sports Council

Kerr, C., 1964, *Labor and Management in Industrial Society*, Doubleday

Kerr, C. et al., 1960, *Industrialism and Industrial Man: The Problems of Labor and Management in Economic Growth*, Harvard University Press

Kessler, S. J. and McKenna, W., 1978, *Gender: An Ethnomethodological Approach*, John Wiley

Keynes, J. M., 1936, *The General Theory of Employment, Interest and Money* (Macmillan, 1973)

Kincaid, J., 1973, *Poverty and Equality in England: A Study of Social Security and Taxation*, Penguin

Kitching, Gavin, 1982, *Development and Underdevelopment in Historical Perspective*, Methuen

Kling, R., 1991, 'Computerisation and transformation', *Science, Technology and Human Values*, vol. 16, no. 4

Kling, R., 1996, *Computerization and Controversy: Value Conflicts and Social Choices*, Academic Press

Knightley, P., 2002, *The First Casualty: The War Correspondent as Hero and Myth-Maker From the Crimea to Kosovo*, John Hopkins University Press

Kollontai, A., 1977, *Selected Writings of Alexandra Kollontai*, Norton and Co.

Kuhn, J., 1961, *Bargaining in Grievance Settlement*, Columbia University Press

Kuhn, T., 1962, *The Structure of Scientific Revolutions*, University of Chicago Press

Labov, W., 1969, 'The logic of non-standard English' in Keddie, 1973

Lacey, C., 1970, *Hightown Grammar*, Manchester University Press

Lacey, C., 1975, 'Destreaming in a "pressurised" academic environment', in S. Eggleston (ed.), *Contemporary Research in the Sociology of Education*, Methuen

Laing, R. D. and Esterson, A., 1970, *Sanity, Madness and the Family*, Penguin

Lakey, J., 1997, 'Neighbourhoods and housing' in T. Modood et al. (eds), *Ethnic Minorities in Britain*, Policy Studies Institute

Lal, Deepak, 1983, *The Poverty of Development Economics*, Institute of Economic Affairs

Lambert et al., 1984, *The Image of Elderly on T.V.*, University of the Third Age

Land, H., 1976, 'Women: supported or supporters?' in D.L. Barker and S. Allen, *Sexual Divisions and Society*, Tavistock

Land, K. et al., 1990, 'Structural covariates of homicide rates', *American Journal of Sociology*, 95

Larner, R., 1966, 'Ownership and control in the 200 largest non-financial corporations – 1929 and 1963', *American Economic Review*, Sept 1966

Laslett, P. (ed.), 1972, *Household and Family in Past Time*, Cambridge University Press

Laslett, P., 1982, 'Foreword' in R. Rapoport et al. (eds.), *Families in Britain*, Routledge and Kegan Paul

Lather, P., 1991, *Getting Smart: Feminist Research and Pedagogy with/in the Postmodern*, Routledge

Lazarsfeld, P., Berelson, B. and Gaudet, H., 1944, *The People's Choice*, Columbia University Press

Lea, J. and Young, J., 1984, *What is to be Done About Law and Order?*, Penguin

Leach, E., 1967, *A Runaway World?*, BBC Publications

Leavis, Q. D., 1932, *Fiction and the Reading Public*, Chatto and Windus

Leech, K. and Amin, K., 1988, *A New Underclass? Race, Poverty and the Inner City*, Child Poverty Action Group

Lees, S., 1986, *Losing Out: Sexuality and Adolescent Girls*, Hutchinson

Leeson, J. and Gray, J., 1978, *Women and Medicine*, Tavistock

Le Grand, Julian, 1982, *Strategy of Equality: Redistribution and the Social Services*, Allen and Unwin

Lemert, Edwin, 1967, *Human Deviance, Social Problems and Social Control*, Prentice Hall

Lerner, D., 1964, *The Passing of Traditional Society*, The Free Press

Lewis, Oscar, 1958, *La Vida: A Puerto Rican Family in the Culture of Poverty*, Panther

Lewis, Oscar, 1961, *The Children of Sanchez*, Random House

Lewis, W. A., 1954, *Economic Development with Unlimited Supplies of Labour*, Manchester School

Liebert, R. and Baron, R., 1972, 'Short term effects of television aggression on children's aggressive behavior', in J. P. Murray, E. A. Rubinstein and G. A. Comstock (eds), *Television and Social Behavior*, vol. 2, *Television and. Social Learning*, United States Government Printing Office

Liebow, E., 1967, *Tally's Corner*, Little Boston

Lipietz, A., 1993, *Towards a New Economic Order: Postfordism, Ecology and Democracy*, Polity Press

Lipset, Seymour, 1963, *Political Man*, Mercury Books

Lipset, Seymour, 1964, 'The changing class structure of contemporary European politics', *Daedalus*, vol. 93

Lipset, Seymour et al., 1956, *Union Democracy*, The Free Press

Lloyd-Warner, W., 1953, *American Life* MacGraw-Hill

Lockwood, D., 1958, *The Black-Coated Worker*, Allen and Unwin

Lombroso, Cesare, 1876, *L'Uomo Delinquente*, Fratelli-Bocca

Lombroso, C. and Ferrero, W., 1895, *The Female Offender*, Fisher Unwin

Lukes, S., 1991, *Moral Conflict and Politics*, Clarendon

Lukes, Steven, 1974, *Power: A Radical View*, Macmillan

Lull, J, 1990, *Inside Family Viewing: Ethnographic Research on Television's Audiences*, Routledge

Lynch. M., 1993, *Art and Artefact in Laboratory Science*, Routledge

Lynd, R. S., 1939, *Knowledge for What? The Place of Social Science in American Culture*, Princeton University Press

Lyotard, Jean-François, 1984, *The Postmodern Condition: A Report on Knowledge*, Manchester University Press

MacInnes, J., 1987, *Thatcherism at Work*, Open University Press

MacIver, I., 1955, *The Idea of Society*, Routledge Kegan Paul

MacIver, R. M., 1931, *Society. A Textbook of Sociology*, Macmillan

Mack, J. and Lansley, S., 1985, *Poor Britain*, Allen and Unwin

Maguire, M. and Pointing, V. (eds.), 1988, *Victims of Crime: A New Deal?*, Open University Press

Mallet, S., 1963, *The New Working Class*, Spokesman

Mann, K., 1992, *The Making of an English Underclass*, Open University Press

Mann, Michael, 1973, *Consciousness and Action Among the Western Working Class*, Macmillan

Mann, Michael, 1986 and 1993, *The Sources of Social Power*, 2 vols., Cambridge University Press

Marcuse, H., 1964, *One Dimensional Man: Studies in the Ideology of Advanced Industrial Society*, Routledge and Kegan Paul

Mares, P. *et al.,* 1987, *Training in Multiracial Health Care*, National Extension College

Marmot, M. *et al.,* 1983, 'Immigrant mortality in England and Wales', *Population Trends*, 33

Marrus, M., 1974, *The Emergence of Leisure*, Meckler

Mars, G., 1985, *Cheats at Work*, Routledge

Marshall, G. *et al.,* 1988, *Social Class in Modern Britain*, Hutchinson

Marshall, T. H., 1970, 'Review of *The Affluent Worker in the Class Structure*', *Economic Journal*, 80

Marsland, D., 1989, 'Universal welfare provision creates a dependent population. The case for'. *Social Studies Review*, November

Martin, David, 1969, *The Religious and the Secular*, Routledge and Kegan Paul

Martin, David, 1978, *A General Theory of Secularisation*, Blackwell

Martin, David, 1990, *Tongues of Fire: The Explosion of Protestantism in Latin America*, Blackwell

Martin, David *et al.,* 1988, *The Prevalence of Disability Among Adults*, HMSO

Marx, K., 1844, 'Contributions to the critique of Hegel's *Philosophy of Right*', in T. Bottomore and M. Rubel, *Karl Marx: Selected Writings in Sociology and Social Philosophy* (Pelican, 1976)

Marx, Karl, 1845, 'Theses on Feurbach' from T. Bottomore and M. Rubel, *Karl Marx: Selected Writings in Sociology and Social Philosophy* (Pelican, 1976)

Marx, Karl, 1845–6, *The German Ideology* (Lawrence and Wishart, 1965)

Marx, Karl, 1857/8, *The Grundrisse*, translated by Martin Nicolaus (Pelican, 1973)

Marx, Karl, 1859, 'Preface to a contribution to a critique of political economy' in Bottomore and Rubel, 1976

Marx, Karl, 1867, *Capital*, translated by S. Moore and E. Aveling (Penguin, 1976)

Marx, Karl and Engels, Friedrich, 1848, *The Communist Manifesto*, translated by S. Moore and edited by A. J. P. Taylor (Penguin, 1967)

Massey, D., 1984, *Spatial Divisions of Labour*, Macmillan

Matza, D., 1964, *Delinquence and Drift*, John Wiley and Sons

Mawby, R., 1980, 'Sex and crime: the results of a sef-report study', *British Journal of Sociology*, vol. 31, no. 52

Mayhew, P. and Hough, M., 1983 and 1985, *The British Crime Survey*, HMSO

Mayhew, P. *et al.,* 1989, *The 1988 British Crime Survey*, HMSO

Mayo, Elton, 1933, *The Human Problems of an Industrial Civilisation*, Macmillan

McClelland, D., 1961, *The Achieving Society*, Princeton University Press

McIlroy, J., 1988, *Trade Unions in Britain Today*, Manchester University Press

McKenzie, R. and Silver, A., 1968, *Angels in Marble*, Heinemann

McKeown, T., 1976, *The Modern Rise of the Population*, Edward Arnold

McKersie, R. and Walton, R., 1991, 'Organizational change', in M. Morton (ed.), *The Corporation of the 1990s. Information Technology and Organizational Transformation*, Oxford University Press

McLuhan, M. and Fiore, Q., 1967, *The Medium is the Message*, Penguin

McNaught, A., 1987, *Race and Health Policy*, Croom Helm

McQuail, D., 1972, *The Sociology of Mass Communications*, Penguin

McRobbie, A., 1994, *Postmodernism and Popular Culture*, Routledge

McRobbie, A. and Garber, J., 1976, 'Girls and subcultures: and exploration' in S. Hall and T. Jefferson (eds), *Resistance through Rituals*, Hutchinson

McRobbie, A. and McCabe, T., 1981, *Feminism for Girls: An Adventure Story*, Routledge and Kegan Paul

Mead, Margaret, 1928, *Coming of Age in Samoa: A Study of Adolescence and Sex in Primitive Societies* (Penguin,1961)

Medawar, P., 1985, *The Limits of Science*, Oxford University Press

Merton, R., 1946, *Mass Persuasion*, The Free Press

Merton, R., 1949, *Social Theory and Social Structure*, The Free Press

Merton, R., 1949a, *Bureaucratic Structure and Personality*, The Free Press

Michels, Robert, 1911, *Political Parties: A Sociological Study of the Oligarchical Tendencies of Modern Democracy*, The Free Press

Miles, I., 1984, *Unemployment, Time Use and the Context of Experience*, University of Sussex

Miles, I. and Irvine, J., 1979, 'The critique of official statistics', in J. Irvine et al. (eds), *Demystifying Social Statistics*, Pluto Press

Miles, R., 1982, *Racism and Migrant Labour*, Routledge and Kegan Paul

Milgram, S., 1992, *The Individual in the Social World*, MacGraw-Hill

Miliband, Ralph, 1969, *The State in Capitalist Society* , Weidenfeld and Nicolson

Millar, J. and Glendinning, C., 1989, 'Gender and Poverty', *Journal of Social Policy*, vol. 18, no. 3

Miller, Walter, 1962, 'Lower-class culture as a generating milieu of gang delinquency' in M. Wolfgang *et al.*, *The Sociology of Crime and Delinquency*, John Wiley and Sons

Millett, K, 1970, *Sexual Politics*, Doubleday

Mills, C. Wright, 1956, *The Power Elite*, Oxford University Press

Mills, C. Wright, 1959, *The Sociological Imagination*, Oxford University Press

Millward, N., 1994, *The New Industrial Relations*, PSI

Minford, Patrick, 1982, *Unemployment: Cause and Cure*, Basil Blackwell

Ministry of Education, 1963, *Half Our Future: A Report of the Central Advisory Council for Education*, HMSO

Mitsos, E. and Browne, K. (1998) 'Gender differences in education', *Sociology Review*, vol. 8, no. 1

Modood, T. and Berthoud, R. (eds), 1997, *Ethnic Minorities in Britain*, Policy Studies Institute

Mogey, J. M., 1956, *Family and Neighbourhood: Two Studies in Oxford*, Oxford University Press

Moores, Mike and Breslin, Tony, 1991, 'So what is good sociology? The view from the chief examiners', *Social Science Teacher*, vol. 20, no. 3

Morley, D., 1980, *The 'Nationwide' Audience*, British Film Institute

Morley, D. and Silverstone, R., 1990, 'Domestic communication: technologies and meanings', *Media, Culture and Society*, 12

Mosca, G., 1896, *The Ruling Class* (McGraw Hill, 1939)

Muncie, J., 1987, 'Deviancy amplification', *Social Studies Review*, November

Mungham, G. and Pearson, G. (eds), 1976, *Working Class Youth Culture*, Routledge and Kegan Paul

Murdock, G. P., 1949, *Social Structure*, Macmillan

Murdock, G., 1980, 'Class, power and the press: problems of conceptualisation and evidence' in H. Christian (ed.), *The Sociology of Journalism and the Press*, University of Keele

Murdock, G. and Golding, P., 1977, 'Capitalism, communications and class relations' in J. Curran *et al.*, *Mass Communication and Society*, Edward Arnold

Murdock, G. and McCron, R., 1979, 'The broadcasting and delinquency debate', *Screen Education*, 30, Spring

Myrdal, G., 1944, *An American Dilemma: The Negro Problem and American Democracy*, Harper and Brothers

Navarro, V., 1976, *Medicine under Capitalism*, Croom Helm

Negroponte, N., 1995, *Being Digital*, Hodder and Stoughton

Nelken, D., 1983, *The Limits of Legal Process: A Study of Landlords, Law and Crime*, Academic Press

Newby, H., 1979, *Green and Pleasant Land: Social Change in Rural Britain*, Hutchinson

Newby, H., 1985, *Restructuring Capital: Recession and Reorganisation in Industrial Society*, Macmillan

Newby, H. and Bell, C., 1971, *Community Studies*, George Allen and Unwin

Newson, J. and E., 1974, *Patterns of Infant Care in an Urban Community*, Penguin

Nicolson, L., 1997, 'The myth of the traditional family' in H. L. Nelson (ed.), *Feminism and Families*, Routledge

Niebuhr, H., 1929, *The Social Sources of Denominationalism*, Holt, Rinehart and Wilson

Nisbet, R., 1966, *The Sociological Tradition*, Heinemann

Nkrumah, Kwame, 1965, *Neo-colonialism: The Last Stage of Imperialism*, Nelson

Noble, David, 1984, *Forces of Production*, Knopf

Nordlinger, E., 1967, *The Working-Class Tories: Authority, Deference and Stable Democracy*, MacGibbon

Norris, C., 1992, *Uncritical Theory: Postmodernism, Intellectuals and the Gulf War*, Lawrence and Wishart

Nyerere, Julius, 1973, *Freedom and Development*, Oxford University Press

Oakley, A., 1972, *Sex, Gender and Society*, Temple Smith

Oakley, A., 1974a, *Housewife*, Allen Lane

Oakley, A., 1974b, *The Sociology of Housework*, Martin Robertson

Oakley, A., 1981, *Subject Women*, Martin Robertson

O'Brien, M. and Jones, D., 1996, 'Revisiting family and kinship' *Sociology Review*, February

O'Connor, J., 1973, *The Fiscal Crisis of the State*, St Martin's Press

Office for National Statistics, 2000, *Social Inequalities*, The Stationery Office

Opie, Peter and Iona, 1967, *The Lore and Language of Schoolchildren*, Clarendon Press

Ortner, S. B., 1974, 'Is female to male as natural as nature is to culture?', in M. Z. Rosaldo and L. Lamphere (eds), Women, Culture and Society, Stanford University Press

Orwell, George, 1945, *Animal Farm*, Martin Secker and Warburg

Osterman, P., 1991, 'The impact of IT on jobs and skills', in M. Morton (ed.), *The Corporation of the 1990s. Information Technology and Organizational Transformation*, Oxford University Press

Pahl, Ray, 1965a, *Urbs in Rure*, Weidenfeld and Nicolson

Pahl, Ray, 1965b, 'Urbs in rure: the metropolitan fringe in Hertfordshire', *Geographical Papers*, LSE

Pahl, Ray, 1965c, 'Class and community in English commuter villages', *Sociological Review*, 6

Pahl, Ray, 1968, *Readings in Urban Sociology*, Pergamon Press

Pahl, Ray, 1975, *Whose City?*, Penguin

Pahl, Ray, 1984, *Divisions of Labour*, Basil Blackwell

Pakulski, J. and Waters, M., 1996, *The Death of Class*, Sage

Palardy, J., 1983, *Elementary Education*, Lanham

Pareto, Vilfredo, 1978, *Socialist Systems*, first published in 1902, Librairie Droz

Park, R. E. and Burgess, E., 1921, *Introduction to the Science of Sociology*, University of Chicago Press

Park, R. E. and Burgess, E., 1925, *The City*, University of Chicago Press

Parker, H., 1974, *View from the Boys*, David and Charles

Parker, Stanley, 1983, 'Work and Leisure' in E. Butterworth and D. Weir (eds.), *The Sociology of Leisure*, George Allen and Unwin

Parkin, Frank, 1971, *Class Inequality and Political Order*, MacGibbon and Kee

Parry, N. and J., 1976, *The Rise of the Medical Profession*, Croom Helm

Parsons, Talcott, 1951, *The Social System*, The Free Press

Parsons, Talcott, 1952, 'The superego and the theory of social systems', *Psychiatry*, 15

Parsons, Talcott, 1953, 'A revised analytical approach to the theory of stratification' in R. Bendix and S. Lipset (eds.), *Class, Status and Power*, The Free Press

Parsons, Talcott, 1959a, 'The social structure of the family' in R. Anshen (ed.), *The Family: Its Functions and Destiny*, Harper and Row

Parsons, Talcott, 1959b, 'The school class as a social system', *Harvard Educational Review*, Fall

Parsons, Talcott, 1959c, 'The principal structure of community' in Carl J. Friedrich (ed.), *Community*, Liberal Arts Press

Parsons, Talcott, 1960, *Structure and Process in Modern Societies*, The Free Press

Parsons, Talcott, 1965, 'Religious perspectives in sociology and social psychology' in Lessa, W. and Vogt, E., *Reader in Comparative Religion*, Harper and Row

Parsons, Talcott, 1969, *Politics and Social Structure*, The Free Press

Parsons, Talcott, 1969a, *Structure and Process in Modern Societies*, The Free Press

Parsons, Talcott and Bales, R., 1955, *Family, Socialisation and Interaction Process*, The Free Press

Parsons, Talcott and Shils, E., 1951, *Towards a General Theory of Action*, Harvard University Press

Parsons, Talcott *et al.*, 1953, *Working Papers in the Theory of Action*, The Free Press

Passas, N., 1990, 'Anomie and corporate deviance', *Contemporary Crises*, 14

Patrick, J., 1973, *A Glasgow Gang Observed*, Eyre Methuen

Payer, Cheryl, 1974, *The Debt Trap*, Harmondsworth

Payne, G., 1990, *The Social Mobility of Women: Beyond Male Models*, Falmer Press

Pearce, Frank, 1976, *Crimes of the Powerful*, Pluto Press

Pearson, G., 1983, *Hooligans: A History of Respectable Fears*, Macmillan

Pen, J., 1971, *Income Distribution*, Allen Lane

Perrolle, J., 1991, 'Intellectual assembly lines: the rationalisation of managerial, professional and technical work', in C. Dunlop and R. Kling (eds), *Computerization and Controversy: Value Conflicts and Social Choice*, Academic Press

Phillips, A., 1987, *Divided Loyalties*, Virago

Philo, Greg, 1990, *Seeing and Believing*, Routledge

Philo, Greg, 1991, 'Seeing is believing', *Social Studies Review*, May

Piaget, Jean, 1954, *The Construction of Reality in the Child*, Basic Books

Pinchot, G. and Pinchot, E., 1993, *The End of Bureaucracy and the Rise of Intelligent Organisation*, Berrett-Koenler

Pollack, O., 1950, *The Criminality of Women*, University of Pennsylvania Press

Pollert, A., 1988, 'Dismantling flexibility', *Capital and Class*, 34

Pollock, Linda, 1983, *Forgotten Children*, Cambridge University Press

Polsby, N., 1963, *Community Power and Political Theory*, Yale University Press

Polsky, N., 1969, *Hustlers, Beats and Others*, Penguin

Popper, Karl, 1963, *Conjectures and Refutations: The Growth of Scientific Knowledge*, Routledge and Kegan Paul

Postman, N., 1984, *Amusing Ourselves to Death*, Methuen

Postman, Neil, 1985, *The Disappearance of Childhood*, Comet

Poulantzas, Nikos, 1969, 'The problem of the capitalist state', *New Left Review*, vol. 58

Prahalad, G. and Hamal, G., 1990, 'The core competence of the corporation', *Harvard Business Review*, 90

Pryce, Ken, 1979, *Endless Pressure*, Bristol Classical Press

Purcell, J., 1982, 'Macho managers and the new industrial relations', *Employee Relations*, vol. 4, no. 1

Quinney, Richard, 1975, 'Crime control in capitalist society: a critical philosophy of legal order' in I. Tayor *et al.* (eds.), *Critical Criminology*, Routledge and Kegan Paul

Radcliffe-Brown, A. R., 1952, *Structure and Function in Primitive Society*, Cohen and West

Rapoport, R. and R., 1976, *Dual Career Families Re-examined*, Martin Robertson

Rapoport, R. and Rapoport, R. N., 1989, 'Ideologies about family forms – towards diversity' in K. Boh *et al.* (eds) *Changing Patterns of European Family Life*, Routledge

Rathwell, T. and Phillips, D., 1986, *Race, Disease and Health*, Croom Helm

Redfield, Robert, 1941, *The Folk Culture of Yucatan*, University of Chicago Press

Redfield, Robert, 1947, 'Folk society', *American Journal of Sociology*, 52

Reich, M., Gordon, D. M. and Edwards, R. C., 1973, 'A theory of labour market segmentation', *American Economic Review*, vol. 63

Rex, John, 1968, 'The sociology of a zone of transition' in R. E. Pahl (ed.), *Readings in Urban Sociology*, Pergamon Press

Rex, John and Moore, Robert, 1967, *Race, Community and Conflict*, Oxford University Press

Rex, J. and Tomlinson, S., 1979, *Colonial Immigrants in a British City*, Routledge and Kegan Paul

Richardson, J. and Jordan, G., 1979, *Governing under Pressure*, Martin Robertson

Robbins, D., 1963, *Higher Education* – report of the committee appointed by the prime minister under the chairmanship of Lord Robbins, 1961–3, HMSO

Roberts, H. (ed.), 1981, *Doing Feminist Research*, Routledge

Roberts, H., 1987, *Women and Social Classification*, Wheatsheaf

Roberts, K., 1974, 'The changing relationship between work and leisure' in I. Appleton (ed.), *Leisure Research and Policy*, Scottish Academic Press

Roberts, K., 1984, *School Leavers and their Prospects: Youth and the Labour Market in the 1980s*, Open University Press

Roberts, Ken *et al.*, 1977, *The Fragmentary Class Structure*, Heinemann

Rodney, Walter, 1972, *How Europe Underdeveloped Africa*, Tanzania Publishing House

Room, G., 1995, *Beyond the Threshold*, The Policy Press

Rose, H., 1982, 'Making science feminist' in E. Whitelegg *et al.*, (eds.), *The Changing Experience of Women*, Martin Robertson

Rose, R., 1984, *Do Parties Make a Difference?*, Macmillan

Rosenhan, D., 1994, *Abnormal Psychology*, Norton

Rosenthal, R. and Jacobson, L., 1968, *Pygmalion in the Classroom*, Holt, Rinehart and Winston

Rossi, P. and Blum, A., 1968, in D. P. Moynihan (ed.), *On Understanding Poverty*, Basic Books

Rostow, W. W., 1960, *The Stages of Economic Growth: A Non-Communist Manifesto*, Cambridge University Press

Roth, J. (ed.), 1979, *Approaches to Psychology*, Oxford University Press

Rowntree, B. S., 1901, *Poverty: A Study of Town Life*, Macmillan

Rowntree, B. S. and Lavers, G. R., 1951, *Poverty and The Welfare State*, Longman

Royal Commission on Trade Unions and Employers' Associations (the Donovan commission), 1968, *Report*, Cmd 3623, HMSO

Rubery, J., 1980, 'Structured labour markets, worker organisation and low pay' in A. H. Amsden (ed.), *The Economics of Women and Work*, Penguin

Russell, J. C., 1948, *British Medieval Population*, Melbourne University Press

Rutter, M. and Madge, N., 1976, *Cycles of Deprivation*, Heinemann

Rutter, Michael *et al.*, 1979, *Fifteen Thousand Hours*, Open Books

Sarlvik, B. and Crewe, I., 1983, *Decade of Dealignment: The Conservative Victory of 1979 and Electoral Trends in the 1970s*, Cambridge University Press

Sayers, Janet *et al.*, (eds.), 1987, *Engels Revisited*, Tavistock

Sayles, L., 1958, *The Behaviour of Industrial Work Groups*, Wiley

Scarman, Lord, 1981, *The Scarman Report: The Brixton disorders 10–12 April 1981*, Cmd 8247, HMSO

Scheff, T. J,, 1982, *Being Mentally Ill. A Sociological Theory*, Aldine

Schumacher, E. F., 1973, *Small is Beautiful*, Harper and Row

Schwartz Cowan, R., 1983, *More Work for Mother*, Basic Books

Scott, John, 1979, *Corporations, Classes and Capitalism*, Hutchinson

Scott, John, 1986, 'The debate on ownership and control', *Social Studies Review*, January

Scott, John, 1991, *Who Rules Britain?*, Polity Press

Scott, J. and Homans, G., 1947, 'Reflections on the wildcat strikes', *American Sociological Review*, January

Scraton, Phil, 1985, *The State of the Police*, Pluto Press

Seabrook, Jeremy, 1984, *The Leisure Society*, Basil Blackwell

Seeley, J. *et al.* 1963, *Crestwood Heights*, Basic Books

Seeman, M., 1959, 'On the meaning of alienation', *American Sociological Review*, 24

Segal, L., 1983, *What is to be Done about the Family?*, Penguin

Selznick, P., 1949, *The TVA and the Grassroots: A Study in the Sociology of Formal Organisation*, California University Press

Shaiken, Harley, 1986, *Work Transformed: Automation and Labor in the Computer Age*, Lexington Books

Sharp, R. and Green, A., 1975, *Education and Social Control*, Routledge

Sharpe, Sue, 1976, *Just Like a Girl: How Girls Learn to be Women*, Penguin (2nd edition 1994)

Shaw, C. and McKay, H., 1942, *Juvenile Delinquency and Urban Areas*, University of Chicago Press

Shelton, B. A., 1992, *Women, Men and Time*, Greenwood

Shils, E., 1971, 'Mass society and its culture' in B. Rosenberg and D. M. White (eds.), *Mass Culture Revisited*, Van Nostrand

Shiner, Larry, 1971, 'The concept of secularisation in empirical research' in K. Thompson and J. Tunstall, *Sociological Perspectives*, Penguin

Shipman, M., 1981, *The Limitations of Social Research*, Longman

Silverman, David, 1970, *The Theory of Organisations*, Heinemann

Simmel, Georg, 1903, 'The metropolis and mental life' in K. Wolff (ed.), *The Sociology of Georg Simmel*, The Free Press

Sinfield, A., 1981, *What Unemployment Means*, Martin Robertson

Sklair, L., 1973, *Organised Knowledge*, MacGibbon and Kee

Sklair, L., 1991, *Sociology of the Global System*, Harvester and Johns Hopkins University Press

Skocpol, T., 1979, *States and Social Revolutions*, Cambridge University Press

Smart, C., 1989, *Feminism and the Power of Law*, Routledge

Smart, C., 1995, *Law, Crime and Sexuality*, Sage

Smith, Adam, 1776, *The Wealth of Nations* (Everyman, 1991)

Smith, D., 1994, 'Race, crime and criminal justice' in M. Maguire *et al.*, *The Oxford Handbook of Criminology*, Clarendon Press

Spelman, Elizabeth, 1988, *Inessential Woman*, The Women's Press

Sproull, L. and Kiesler, S., 1991, *Connections. New Ways of Working in the Networked Organisation*, MIT Press

Stacey, J., 1996, *In the Name of the Family*, Beacon Press

Stanworth, M., 1983, *Gender and Schooling: A Study of Sexual Divisions in the Classroom*, Hutchinson

Stanworth, M., 1984, 'Women and class analysis: a reply to Goldthorpe', *Sociology*, 18

Stern, J., 1983, 'Social mobility and the interpretation of social class mortality differentials', *Journal of Social Policy*, vol. 12, no. 1

Stewart, Michael, 1972, *Keynes and After*, Pelican

Stoll, C., 1995, *Silicon Snakeoil: Second Thoughts on the Jnformation Highway*, Macmillan

Straussman, P., 1985, *Information Payoff: The Transformation of Work in the Electronic Age*, Basic Books

Strinati, Dominic, 1992, 'Postmodernism and popular culture', *Sociology Review*, April

Sutherland, Edwin, 1949, *White Collar Crime*, Holt, Rinehart and Wilson

Sykes, G. and Matza, D., 1962, 'Techniques of neutralisation: a theory of delinquency' in M. Wolfgang *et al.* (eds.), *The Sociology of Crime and Delinquency*, John Wiley and Sons

Szasz, T. S., 1992, *Insanity, The Idea and Its Consequences*, John Wiley

Tapper, T. and Bowles, N., 1981, 'Working-class Tories: the search for theory', *Teaching Politics*, vol. 10, no. 2

Taylor, F. W., 1911, *The Principles of Scientific Management*, Harper

Taylor, John, 1979, *From Modernisation to Modes of Production*, Macmillan

Taylor, Steve, 1990, 'Beyond Durkheim: sociology and suicide', *Social Studies Review*, November

Thompson, P., 1983, *The Nature of Work: An Introduction to Debates on the Labour Process*, Macmillan

Thompson, P. and McHugh, D., 1990, *Work Organisations*, Macmillan

Thorns, D., 1973, *Suburbia*, Granada Publishing Limited

Tiger, L. and Fox, R., 1972, *The Imperial Animal*, Seeker and Warburg

Tönnies, Ferdinand, 1887, *Community and Society*, Harper Row

Townsend, Peter, 1979, *Poverty in the United Kingdom*, Penguin

Townsend, P., 1985, *The Family Life of Old People*, Penguin

Townsend, P. *et al.,* 1986, *Inequalities in Health in the Northern Region: An Interim Report*, Northern Region Health Authority

Townsend, Peter *et al.,* 1987, *Poverty and Labour in London*, Low Pay Unit

Toynbee, P., 1978, *The Guardian*, 30.10.78

Troeltsch, E., 1931, *The Social Teaching of the Christian Churches*, Allen and Unwin

Trow, M., 1957, 'Participant observation and interviewing: a comparison', *Human Organisation*, vol. 16

Tudor-Hart, Julian, 1971, 'The inverse care law', *The Lancet*, 1

Tumin, M., 1953, 'Some principles of stratification: a critical analysis', *American Sociological Review*, 18

Tunstall, J., 1983, *The Media in Britain*, Constable

Tylor, E., 1871, *Primitive Culture*, Murray

Usher, R., and Edwards, R., 1994, *Postmodernism and Education*, Routledge

Van Dijk, T., 1991, *Racism and the Press*, Routledge

Veit-Wilson, John, 1986, 'Paradigms of poverty: a rehabilitation of B. S. Rowntree', *Journal of Social Policy*, vol. 15, no. 1

Vogler, C., 1994, 'Money in the household', in M. Anderson *et al.* (eds), *The Social and Political Economy of the Household*, Oxford University Press

Wadsworth, M., 1986, 'Serious illness in childhood and its association with later life achievement' in R. G. Wilkinson, *Class and Health: Research and Longitudinal Data*, Tavistock

Walby, S., 1986, *Patriarchy at Work: Patriarchal and Capitalist Relations in Employment*, Polity Press

Waldron, I., 1976, 'Why do women live longer than men?', *Social Science and Medicine*, 10

Walker, A., 1990, 'Blaming the victims', in C. Murray, *The Emerging British Underclass*, Institute of Economic Affairs

Walker, A. and Townsend, P. (eds.), 1981, *Disability in Britain*, Martin Robertson

Wallerstein, Immanuel, 1974, 1980 and 1989, *The Modern World System*, 3 vols., Academic Press

Wallerstein, Immanuel, 1979, *The Capitalist World Economy*, Cambridge University Press

Wallerstein, Immanuel, 1984, *The Politics of the World Economy*, Cambridge University Press

Wallis, R., 1984, *The Elementary Forms of the New Religious Life*, Routledge and Kegan Paul

Warren, Bill, 1980, *Imperialism, Pioneer of Capitalism*, Verso

Warwick, D. P., 1983, 'On methodological integration in social research' in M. Bulmer and D. P. Warwick (eds.), *Social Research in Developing Countries*, Macmillan

Watson, Catherine and Hayter, Theresa, 1985, *Aid: Rhetoric and Reality*, Pluto Press

Weber, Max, 1904, 'Objectivity' in *On the Methodology of the Social Sciences*, translated by Edward Shils and Henry Finch, The Free Press, 1949

Weber, Max, 1904–5, *The Protestant Ethic and the Spirit of Capitalism*, translated by Talcott Parsons (George Allen and Unwin, 1930)

Weber, Max, 1922, *Economy and Society* (Bedminster Press, 1968)

Weber, Max, 1922–3, 'Class, status, party' in H. Gerth and C. Wright Mills, *From Max Weber: Essays in Sociology*, Oxford University Press, 1946

Weber, Max, 1958, *The City*, translated by Don Martindale and Gertrud Neuwirth, The Free Press

Westergaard, J., 1996, 'Class in Britain since 1979' in D. Lee and B. Turner (eds), *Conflicts about Class*, Longman

Westergaard, J. and Resler, H., 1976, *Class in a Capitalist Society*, Penguin

Whale, J., 1977, *The Politics of the Media*, Fontana

Whitehead, Margaret, 1987, *The Health Divide: Inequalities in Health in the 1980s*, Health Education Council

Whitely, P., 1983, *The Labour Party in Crisis*, Methuen

Whyte, W. H., 1951, *Pattern for Industrial Peace*, Harper and Row

Whyte, W. H., 1956, *The Organisation Man*, Doubleday Anchor Books

Wilding, P. (ed.), 1986, *In Defence of the Welfare State*, Manchester University Press

Wilensky, H., 1963, 'The uneven distribution of leisure: the impact of economic growth on free time' in E. Smigel (ed.), *Work and Leisure*, College and University Press

Wilkins, L., 1964, *Social Deviance: Social Policy, Action and Research*, Tavistock

Willis, P., 1977, *Learning to Labour: How Working Class Kids Get Working Class Jobs*, Saxon House

Willis, P., 1990, *Common Culture: Symbolic Work at Play in the Everyday Culture of the Young*, Open University Press

Willmott, P. and Young, M., 1960, *Family and Class in a London Suburb*, Routledge and Kegan Paul

Willmott, P. and Young, M., 1973, *The Symmetrical Family*, Routledge and Kegan Paul

Wilson, B., 1966, *Religion in Secular Society*, Watts

Wilson, B., 1977a, 'How religious are we?', *New Society*, 27.10.77

Wilson, B., 1977b, *Religion in Secular Society*, Watts

Wilson, B., 1982, *Religion in Sociological Perspective*, Oxford University Press

Wilson, James and Herrnstein, R., 1985, *Crime and Human Nature*, Simon Schuster

Wilson, W. J., 1987, *The Truly Disadvantaged*, University of Chicago Press

Winch, G., 1983, *Information Technology in Manufacturing Processes: Case Studies In Technological Change*, Rossendale

Wirth, Louis, 1938, 'Urbanism as a way of life', *American Journal of Sociology*, 44

Wolfgang, M. E., 1958, *Patterns of Homicide*, Wiley

Wolpe, AnnMarie, 1988, *Within School Walls: The Role of Discipline, Sexuality and the Curriculum*, Routledge

Wolpe, M., 1978, *Some Processes in Sexist Education*, Women's Research and Resources Centre Publications

Woodward, J., 1958, *Management and Technology*, HMSO

Wootton, B., 1959, *Social Science and Social Pathology*, Allen and Unwin

Wright, E. O., 1985, *Classes*, Verso

Wrong, Dennis, 1961, 'The oversocialised conception of man in modern sociology', *American Sociological Review*, vol. 26

Yinger, M., 1957, *Religion, Society and the Individual*, Macmillan

Yinger, M., 1981, 'Toward a theory of assimilation and dissimilation', *Ethnic and Racial Studies*, vol. 4, no. 3

Young, J., 1971, 'The role of the police as amplifiers of deviance, negotiators of reality and translators of fantasy' in S. Cohen (ed.), *Images of Deviance*, Penguin

Young, Jock, 1988a, 'The tasks of a realist criminologist', *Contemporary Criminology*, 2

Young, Jock, 1988b, *Realist Criminology*, Sage

Young, Jock, 1994, 'Incessant chatter: recent paradigms in criminology' in M. Maguire *et al.*, *The Oxford Handbook of Criminology*, Clarendon Press

Young, J. and Matthews, R., 1992, *Rethinking Criminology: the Realist Debate*, Sage

Young, M. F. D. (ed.), 1971, *Knowledge and Control*, Collier-Macmillan

Young, M. and Wilmott, P., 1957, *Family and Kinship in East London*, RKP

Zeitlin, Maurice, 1974, 'Corporate ownership and control: the large corporation and the capitalist class', *American Journal of Sociology*, vol. 79, no. 5

Zeitlin, Maurice, 1989, *The Large Corporation and Contemporary Classes*, Polity Press

Zelizer, V., 1985, *Pricing the Priceless Child*, Basic Books

Zimbalist, A., 1979, 'Case studies on the labor process', *Monthly Review Press*

Zuboff, S., 1988, *In the Age of the Smart Machine*, Basic Books

Zweig, F., 1952, *The British Worker*, Pelican

Glossary

absolute poverty   state of poverty in which a person lacks the minimum needs to keep them alive and healthy (*contrast* relative poverty)

accumulation   term used within Marx's theory to describe the process by which the capitalist class gain profit which accumulates and so forms the basis of their wealth and therefore their power

aetiology   the study of the causes of an event or phenomenon (e.g. crime or illness)

ageism   prejudice or discrimination against an individual on the basis of age, on the assumption that particular age-groups are superior or inferior

agenda setters   people who decide what subjects the mass media will report or bring to the public's attention

agrarian society (culture)   society (or culture) based on agriculture (*contrast* urban society)

alienation   often used to describe the sense of meaninglessness, powerlessness, isolation and self-estrangement many individuals feel at work or at home. Used by Marx to describe the way that capitalism dehumanises people as a result of their abilities, and the products of their abilities, being taken over by the bourgeoisie

anomie   term used by Durkheim to mean a situation where the norms and values of a society are unclear and people feel unsure about the rules that should guide their behaviour. People are in effect without norms

authority   power in a society or social group which is accepted as legitimate (fair or just)

automation   production of industrial goods by self-controlling machines, with minimal human supervision

autonomy   power to act with free will, to govern your own actions

blue-collar worker   manual worker, whether skilled, semi-skilled, or unskilled (*contrast* white-collar worker)

bourgeoisie   owners of the means of production in capitalism (the capitalists) (*contrast* proletariat)

bureaucracy   type of organisation that is based on agreed and established rules and procedures. It is organised hierarchically and staffed by full-time, salaried officials (bureaucrats)

capitalism   organisation of society in such a way that the wealth and means of production are privately owned by capitalists, commodities are produced for profit through a market mechanism, and workers are free to sell their labour to the highest bidder (*contrast* feudalism)

case-study method   a type of research that takes as its subject a single case or a few selected examples of a social phenomenon, such as work groups, families or communities. A variety of methods may be used in case-study research, but quantitative analysis is less common than in survey reports

caste system   hierarchical, stratified system, ranking individuals in society according to prestige, often on religious grounds. The status of individuals is ascribed at birth, not achieved, and social mobility is highly limited, with no intermarriage between castes

causation   occurs when one variable factor (the cause) – an event or state of affairs – is thought to produce another (the effect) (*see also* aetiology)

child benefit   in the UK, a benefit paid by the State to mothers (and occasionally fathers). The amount a mother receives is related to the number of children. This is a universal benefit and is not based on need

citizen   member of a nation-state, or political community, with rights and duties resulting from that membership

civil rights   freedoms and rights, guaranteed by law to all citizens of a given nation-state or political community

class   no clear agreement in sociology, but most definitions refer to a group of people in the same or similar socio-economic circumstances, usually defined by occupation or relationship to the means of production. The socio-economic differences between social groups result in differences in wealth, power and life chances

class consciousness   degree of awareness by a class of a class system, of their common economic interests, and of their capacity for collective political or industrial action

coercion   rule exercised by force or the threat of force

communism   political theory, associated with Marx and Engels, relating to a society where the means of production are held in common and separate classes do not exist, creating an egalitarian society without class conflict. Up to 1989–91, used to refer to Eastern Europe and the Soviet Union; today, to China, Vietnam, Cuba and other similar states

compensatory education   additional educational help given to socially disadvantaged groups to enable them to have equal educational opportunities

conformity   behaviour that follows the established norms and values of society, often as a result of group pressure to accept these norms (*contrast* deviance)

conglomerate   business corporation which consists of different companies producing or trading in a range of products or services

consensus   agreement that exists in society concerning the values by which people live their lives and by which society is organised, leading to social stability

conservatives   people who desire slow, evolutionary change in society or, in some instances, no change, in order to conserve traditional institutions, relationships and behaviour

content analysis   a research technique for the objective, systematic and quantitative analysis of various forms of communication produced by the media

contradictory class locations   positions in the class structure which combine characteristics of class positions immediately above and below them; mostly applied to routine white-collar, lower professional and managerial workers

core   countries which have a central position in the world economy, mostly the highly industrialised countries (e.g. the USA, Western Europe and Japan) (*contrast* periphery)

corporations   larger business companies

corporatism   originally associated with the ideas of Mussolini and fascism in Italy in the 1920s, but more often now a view of business organisation, prevalent in the 1970s, based on a partnership between leaders of employers' organisations, trade union leaders and government

correlation   the degree of a regular, statistical relationship between at least two variables, which can be measured; the correlation can be either positive or negative

critical theory   approach to the social sciences developed by the Frankfurt Institute in the 1930s and 1940s. It is an interdisciplinary theory drawing on the early work of Marx and the late work of Freud. It aims to criticise, as well as understand, society and is therefore opposed to positivism

cult   small religious grouping similar to a sect, emphasising private, individual experience rather than group fellowship, with individuals only loosely affiliated, and lacking any permanent structure

culture   mainly used in sociology to describe the shared norms and values, as well as the shared language, knowledge and material goods, of a society. As noted in chapter 1, however, it has many other meanings

democracy   political system in which citizens are able to choose their government through elections. It is characterised by freedom of movement, freedom of speech and freedom of the media, and the separation of the judiciary from the legislature and executive (*see also* representative democracy; *contrast* oligarchy, totalitarianism)

denomination   institutionalised religious body, with a significant number of members, but with less influence than the established church

deskilling   process described by the Marxist, Braverman, whereby a job loses its skill and becomes more simplified and routinised (e.g. a chef becomes a fast-food worker as a result of the introduction of new technology)

determinism   theory that people have no choice in their behaviour, as their behaviour is caused by social forces beyond their control (*contrast* free will)

deviance   behaviour which departs from social norms and values held by the majority in a social group; its definition varies across time and cultures (*contrast* conformity)

deviancy amplification   process by which mass media coverage and exaggeration creates more crime or deviance

division of labour   the way that roles in society (e.g. at work and in the home) are divided so that they become far more differentiated and specialised, creating economic interdependence. It is more complex in industrial societies, and there is now a global or new international division of labour (NIDL), where parts of a commodity are made across the globe before final assembly

dual labour market   labour market which is split into primary (or core) and secondary (or peripheral) sectors

economic base   the economy and economic institutions which produce goods and services. Often characterised as the 'engine' of any society, it is of key importance, usually influencing many other aspects of social life. Marxists argue that class relations are determined here (*contrast* superstructure)

ecumenical movement   movement attempting to achieve greater unity between various Christian denominations

egalitarian society   society in which everyone is treated as being equal (*contrast* meritocracy)

elaborated code   pattern of speech thought to characterise the complex structure of middle-class language. The term is mainly associated with the work of Basil Bernstein (*contrast* restricted code)

élite   minority group at the apex of society or a social group who have power and influence over others

embourgeoisement   theory that, as capitalism expands, the working class adopt the norms and values of the middle class as their wages and living standards improve

empiricism   empirical investigation is based on evidence collected in the physical or social world; empiricism claims that all knowledge is based on such evidence

entrepreneur   someone who takes risks in developing a new market in a capitalist economy

ethnicity   the properties of people who share a similar culture, particularly language, customs, religion and history, that is distinct from that of other groups in society. The existence of different ethnic groups is often associated with variations in power, wealth and life-chances (*contrast* race)

ethnography   the case-study method applied to the study of groups or communities, examining the rules by which social reality is constructed

ethnomethodology   sociological perspective that investigates the rules concerning how people create and sustain meanings in everyday life

executive   those people, such as civil servants, charged with the administration of laws (*contrast* judiciary, legislature)

extended family   a family is vertically extended if it contains at least three generations (e.g. grandparents, parents, children), usually living under the same roof. Cousins, uncles, aunts form a horizontally extended family. The nuclear family is at the core of any extended family (*see also* nuclear family)

false consciousness   Marxist term meaning that the workers fail to see the true nature of their exploitation, or their real interests, owing to the power of bourgeois ideology

family credit   in the UK, a benefit paid by the State to those families deemed to be on low pay. The idea is to encourage people to work by supplementing low incomes

feminism   theory, dating from the late eighteenth century, based on the observation that women are systematically disadvantaged in society, and that women have the right to equality with men in all spheres of life

feudalism   system of production based on the ownership of land. The key relationship is that between landlord and serf, who is effectively owned by the landlord and has no rights. Feudalism preceded capitalism in Western Europe (*contrast* capitalism)

folk devils   concept developed by the interactionist sociologist Stan Cohen. It refers to groups in society who are identified as being different from the mainstream and then demonised as deviant and as posing an imagined or exaggerated threat to society

Fordism   system of mass production on assembly lines, developed by Henry Ford, undertaken in large factories, with work-tasks increasingly simplified

free will   theory that people have choice over their behaviour and are able to resist external influences (*contrast* determinism)

functionalism   sociological perspective which emphasises the functional importance of institutions in society, and their role in maintaining a value consensus which leads to continuity in that society

fundamentalism   belief in the need to keep to, or return to, the original meaning of religious texts, particularly associated today with interpretations of Christianity and Islam

gate-keeping   process by which the mass media refuse to cover those issues and values seen to be outside the mainstream consensus

gender   culturally learnt aspect of a person's sexual identity. People are biologically female or male, but their behaviour is either feminine or masculine as defined by the social expectations of their society. In this way, behavioural differences between men and women are culturally created

generalised other   social group within which we are socialised, where the individual takes in the values of a given group or society; associated with G. H. Mead

glass ceiling   invisible barrier which prevents people from breaking through to top jobs, frequently used in sociology in relation to female inequalities

globalisation   theory that the development of social, cultural and economic relationships on a world scale has created a single social order or world system, in which many aspects of an individual's social life are affected by organisations and developments located thousands of miles away (e.g. investment decisions, pollution, the mass media, production and cultural patterns)

hegemony   intellectual leadership, and ideological and political dominance. Concept used by Antonio Gramsci to explain the continued rule of the ruling class with the support of the working class. He believed that this leadership can and should be challenged, both politically and through the institutions of civil society

hidden curriculum   the 'unstated agenda' involved in school organisation and teachers' attitudes which develops behaviour and beliefs that are not part of the formal timetable (e.g. beliefs about gender, ethnic or class differences), and which some sociologists argue forms the main way that schools socialise their pupils

hidden economy   informal economy where people do jobs for others and may get paid 'cash in hand'. Such people do not pay income tax or national insurance contributions and will not show up on government statistics as employed. Indeed, they may show up on the unemployment register as without work

historical materialism   theory that historical change is determined by material and economic factors, particularly changes in modes of production. This concept was applied by Marx to envisage social change being brought about in a scientific and informed way

homogeneous group   group that is uniform, rather than mixed, in composition

hypothesis   idea or guess about an event or phenomenon, which then has to be tested by conducting empirical research and collecting evidence to prove or disprove the original idea

hypothetico-deductive method   an approach to scientific investigation that involves testing general theoretical assumptions about what should occur through the use of prediction and observations. Also referred to as scientific method

ideal type   Weber's notion that abstract models (such as perfect competition or bureaucracy) could be used to make comparisons with the real world

ideological State apparatus   term used by the French Marxist Louis Althusser to describe those parts of the superstructure (such as religion, the media, the family or education) which maintain class control through consent rather than coercion

ideology   first used by Destutt de Tracey in the eighteenth century, the term meant the science of ideas. It has also come to be used in a pejorative sense to mean false or mistaken ideas imposed by one group on another to maintain their advantaged position in society, for example bourgeois, racial or patriarchal ideologies. These shared beliefs, seeming to justify the interests of dominant groups, are to be found in all societies where systematic inequalities exist between social groups, and are thus closely related to power. The term is now used with both meanings

imperialism   policy of making or maintaining an empire under the control of one country, formally or informally, particularly associated with the period of European colonisation of Africa and Asia in the nineteenth century and with economic and political control by great powers in the twentieth century

induction   process of drawing general conclusions from the collection of particular facts or observations

industrial democracy   a way of organising a firm or industry whereby the employees have some participation or representation in some of the decision-making processes of that firm or industry (*contrast* workers' control)

intelligence   a particularly controversial term in sociology. Hans Eysenck defined intelligence as abstract reasoning ability, measurable through intelligence tests. It is often thought to be innate

intergenerational mobility   social mobility from one generation to the next; it can be vertical (up or down) or lateral within a social stratification hierarchy, and can be short-range or long-range (*contrast* intragenerational mobility)

interpretive sociology   another term for phenomenology, which emphasises the role played by actors in interpreting their social situation

interviews   a technique for collecting information based on social interaction between the interviewer and the interviewee. Interviews vary in style and format, from the structured interviews based on a questionnaire, to the unstructured interview based on a list of topics to be covered

intragenerational mobility   social mobility during an individual's working life; it can be vertical (up or down) or lateral within a social stratification hierarchy, and can be short-range or long-range (*contrast* intergenerational mobility)

judiciary   collective noun for judges and magistrates (*contrast* executive, legislature)

kinship   central to the study of anthropology, the study of kinship examines the relationship of biological connections, such as blood ties, marriage or adoption, to other forms of rights and obligations in society. In modern societies kinship involves few social obligations, but it plays a vital role in the social life of more traditional societies

labelling   the way that people place labels on others, often based on stereotypes. It is particularly associated with the study of education and deviance, with individuals becoming failures or deviants because of the label attached to their behaviour by those in authority

latent function   unintended action of a social institution (e.g. the way a religious ceremony can unite a group), a term used by functionalists (*contrast* manifest function)

legislature   body which makes formal laws in a society (e.g. parliament) (*contrast* executive, judiciary)

legitimacy   term used to describe the sanctioning by society of institutions, actions and ideas, and the belief that a particular political, social or economic order is just and valid. Social and political changes can produce legitimacy crises

liberation   setting free or releasing of a group from social injustice, subordination, prejudice or abuse

liberation theology   Christian doctrine, mixing elements of Marxism and Catholicism, which supports the poor in their struggles for equality and freedom; particularly associated with Latin America. It is disowned by the official Catholic Church

longitudinal research   research which is replicated over a period of time to find out how much change is taking place in a society or smaller group

macro-sociology   study of social systems, large social groups or organisations; usually associated with functionalist or conflict theory sociologists (*contrast* micro-sociology)

manifest function   intended action of a social institution (e.g. a religious ceremony as an act of collective worship), a term used by functionalists (*contrast* latent function)

marginalised group   group that is pushed onto the periphery, or edge, of society

Marxism   sociological perspective based on the writings of Karl Marx, in particular his division of society into economic base and superstructure, and the analysis of class conflict as the main source of social change

mass media   forms of communication designed for the consumption of mass audiences (e.g. newspapers, magazines, radio, television, cinema)

means of production   means by which material production is organised in a society. It includes the key resources for providing society's goods (e.g. land, factories), the technological aspects (e.g. tools, techniques) *and* the social relations between the producers

meritocracy   society in which individuals achieve educational qualifications, and their consequent position in the stratification system, on the basis of merit, talent, skills, ability and achievement (*contrast* egalitarian society)

metanarrative   this term is used by post-modernist writers to refer to the way that language may be manipulated to provide accounts of social phenomena that are more logical and persuasive than they would be were the subject to be viewed in a more critical and reflective way

methodological pluralism   rejection of the idea that any one theoretical stance or approach to research is superior, and acceptance that sociological studies may be enhanced by the use of different techniques for analysing and collecting information

micro-sociology   study of small-scale aspects of human behaviour, often of one-to-one interactions; usually associated with interpretivist sociologists (*contrast* macro-sociology)

middle class   non-manual workers, from professionals to routine clerical staff, often referred to as white-collar workers

mode of production   specific forces and relations of production that determine the character of a historical period (e.g. feudalism, capitalism)

monogamy   situation in which a man and woman have only one partner at any one time. Serial monogamy describes a succession of monogamous relationships

monopoly capitalism   Marxist term to describe the situation that occurs in mature capitalism where firms become larger due to take-over and can control the market, for example through cartels

moral panic   wave of public concern about a social activity or group, which becomes seen as a threat to the common values or interests of society as a result of exaggerated, stereotypical and sensationalised coverage by the mass media or politicians

morbidity rate   degree or incidence of illness and disease in a society or social group

mortality rate   degree or incidence of death in a society or social group

nation-state   particular type of state, especially associated with modern societies, in which a government has sovereign power over a specific territory, and where the population (or citizens) think of themselves as belonging to that nation; closely associated with the rise of nationalism

nationalism   set of political and cultural beliefs and symbols expressing a sense of identity for a particular national community, a community that does not necessarily conform to the boundaries of an existing nation-state. Taken to extremes, it results in aggression towards other nations and in hatred of foreigners

newly industrialising country (NIC)   a less developed country which, in recent times, has undergone extensive and rapid industrial expansion (e.g. South Korea, Hong Kong, Singapore)

norms   expected patterns of rules and social behaviour which specify appropriate conduct in different social contexts, either prescribing or forbidding this conduct; enforced by sanctions, either positive (rewards) or negative (punishment)

nuclear family   family group consisting of two generations (parents and at least one child) living in the same household. A tendency in modern societies is for the nuclear family to become privatised, i.e. becoming isolated and separated from wider kin and society, with members spending time together in home-centred activities (*see also* extended family)

objectivity   investigation of behaviour free from the personal opinion or prejudice of the investigator, associated with the natural sciences. Sociologists attempt to achieve objectivity by trying to reduce or eliminate bias in their interpretation of data, and making their findings open to critical assessment (*contrast* subjectivity)

oligarchy   rule by a small group of people (*contrast* democracy, dictatorship, totalitarianism)

paradigm   conceptual framework against which other theories are compared

participant observation   research method whereby the researcher joins and takes part in the activities of the group they are observing. Their identity may be disclosed to the other members of the group (overt) or may be undisclosed (covert); this is often referred to as fieldwork

particularistic values   values which judge people on the basis of ascribed status (e.g. parents thinking that their own children are unique and special) (*contrast* universalistic values)

partisan alignment   voting according to self-identification as a member of a class; where this identification begins to weaken, the term 'partisan realignment' is used

party   according to Weber, the political aspect of stratification, the other two aspects being economic (class) and social (status); operating via organised political parties

patriarchy   domination by men over women in all aspects of society – economic, social, political and cultural. Most societies are patriarchal, though there are some exceptions. The women's movement has attempted to alter the existing patriarchal institutions in society

peer group   friendship group, composed of individuals sharing similar age and social status, with whom an individual mixes socially

periphery   countries which play only a marginal role in the world economy, for example less-developed countries that are dependent on the developed, or core, industrial economies (*contrast* core)

perspective   set of ideas, or viewpoint, which helps you to explain the world

phenomenology   *see* interpretive sociology

pluralism   ownership, power and influence diffused between a multiplicity of competing groups, for example in politics or the media. Pluralist theories of democracy are based on this view of a plural society containing many different groups

positivism   view that the methods of natural science can be used with equal effect in social science, as they share a common logical framework

post-Fordism   argument that the era of mass production has ended as a consequence of deregulated capitalism, which now prefers flexible production of small, specialised batches of items by small groups of unorganised, often temporary, employees

post-industrialism   theory that suggests modern society is in transition, no longer being primarily based on manufacturing but moving into a phase of development beyond the industrial production era, where, for instance, knowledge, information and services will be of prime importance

post-modernism   theory that modern social development is more than just the end of the era of industrialism, but rather a complete break with the concept of 'modernity' (institutions and modes of life based on the ideas of a shape to history, the concept of continuing progress etc.). Post-modernity instead sees the 'end of history' (with no overall concepts of history making any sense), rejects the idea of 'progress' (whether in history, science or society as a whole), and sees the creation of a highly pluralistic society with individuals possessing a multiplicity of identities

post-structuralism   theory that rejects the idea of a unified sociological paradigm, and is critical of all theories because they all contain the subjective element of the observer. Consequently, sociology (and other sciences) must accept a wide variety of perspectives as inevitable

power   ability of individuals or social groups to exert their will over others, and to ensure decisions taken reflect their own interests; hence societies often contain conflicts over power, and unequal access to resources

pressure groups   groups formed to put pressure on powerful organisations and those in power to implement the policies they favour. They may be sectional, promoting a sector (e.g. the elderly), or promotional, representing a cause (e.g. the abolition of smoking). Pressure groups have been increasingly studied with the development of pluralist theory

primary labour market   area of the economy with secure, well-paid, usually full-time, jobs

primary sector   part of a modern society's economy based on the gathering or extraction of natural or raw materials (e.g. farming, mining, fishing) (*contrast* secondary sector)

private health care   health-care services which are only available to those who are able to pay the full cost of them

professionalisation   the techniques and strategies used by professional occupational groups to achieve effective control over their market position and conditions of existence as an interest group, and thereby to achieve power in society

proletariat   subject class in capitalism. This group (the industrial working class) are exploited by the bourgeoisie and are defined as having only their labour power to sell to the highest bidder (*contrast* bourgeoisie; *see also* working class)

psephology   sociological and statistical study of voting behaviour and trends

qualitative research   research methods that replace data, such as statistics, with a depth study of people's meanings and understandings that is non-statistical and therefore not capable of generalisation (*contrast* quantitative research)

quantitative research   use of methods that generate statistical data that can be compared and contrasted (*contrast* qualitative research)

questionnaires   a technique for collecting information based on a document that contains a list of questions relating to the research topic. The questions may be closed or open-ended

race   category which includes a large number of individuals having physical or biological characteristics different from other human groups or categories; now felt to be a scientifically dubious and politically dangerous concept (*contrast* ethnicity)

racism   belief and/or behaviour based on the assumption that a social group is inferior/superior on the grounds of racial or ethnic origin (defined by reference to certain inherited physical or biological characteristics). Often used to justify political and material inequalities

rational thinking   way of thought based on scientific thinking and logic

rationalisation   according to Weber, the process by which all parts of society become increasingly subject to precise calculation, measurement, organisation and control

relations of production   social relationships that characterise a particular mode of production and involve ownership/non-ownership of the means of production (e.g. between peasants and landlords in feudalism, or bourgeoisie and proletariat in capitalism)

relative poverty   poverty that is seen in relation to the standard of living of the majority of people in any one society at any one time (*contrast* absolute poverty)

reliability   the extent to which a technique for collecting or analysing information may be used repeatedly and produce the same results

representative democracy   system of democracy in which all members of a social group participate indirectly and individually in the decision-making processes by electing political leaders to represent their views and interests

representativeness   the extent to which a research study provides an accurate portrayal of the typical characteristics and known diversity of the population from which the sample was selected

reserve army of labour   workers that can be moved in and out of the labour force. In the case of women, they may be encouraged or coerced to become carers and housewives at home, where they form a reserve army of labour until required for paid employment. Also used in relation to ethnic minorities and immigrants

restricted code   according to Bernstein, the language spoken by working-class people, in which meaning is dependent on context, is often implicit, and in which sentence structure is not developed (*contrast* elaborated code)

ruling class   Marxist term describing the group who own the means of production and exploit the subordinate classes. In a capitalist society this is the bourgeoisie

sampling   selection, in a scientific and systematic way, of a representative group of individuals or cases from a larger survey population; in sociology, the sample is often given a questionnaire, or is interviewed

scape-goating   blaming an individual or social group for a problem or situation which they are not responsible for

secondary sector   the part of a modern society's economy based on the production of manufactured goods (*contrast* primary sector)

sect   religious group or movement which has broken away from a more orthodox mainstream religious denomination, or represents an entirely new religious formation

secularisation   term generally used to describe the process by which a society loses its religious orientation and values, with religion thus losing its social significance and influence. This is thought to be true of modern societies, but it is difficult to quantify

self-fulfilling prophecy   situation in which people act in accordance with predictions made by people in authority about their likely behaviour or performance; associated with labelling theory in the study of education and deviance

semiotics　study of how non-verbal phenomena can have important cultural meanings (e.g. styles of clothing)

sexism　belief and/or behaviour based on the assumption that a gender group as a whole is inferior/superior on the grounds of differences in capacities and abilities. As with racism, often used to justify inequalities in society

social action　interaction of people, or actors, with each other in social situations

social construction　term derived from action theory describing the process by which social roles are produced through interaction and negotiation between actors

social facts　term used by Emile Durkheim to describe the external phenomena constraining an individual's behaviour, for example formal laws

social mobility　movement of individuals or groups in a social hierarchy of stratification. Movement between social positions can be vertical (up or down) or horizontal (lateral) (*see also* intergenerational mobility, intragenerational mobility)

social self　combination of the inner self with the reflected self, emerging through interaction with others. According to G. H. Mead, this combination is the basis of self-consciousness in human individuals, the individual achieving self-consciousness by becoming aware of their social identity

social surveys　research projects that collect standardised data about large numbers of people. The data is usually in a statistical form and various methods may be used for collecting the data, although the most usual would be a questionnaire

socialisation　social process by which people learn norms and values and a distinct sense of self; mainly takes place during childhood, but continues throughout life via various agencies of society (e.g. educational system, mass media)

sovereignty　undisputed, or claimed, political rule of a state over a given territory

State　political apparatus of any society (including the legislature, judiciary, executive, police and armed forces) ruling over a given territory, and with authority backed by law and force. Virtually absent in traditional hunting and food-gathering societies

status　refers to the prestige or 'social honour' that the community attaches to a particular individual or role. Achieved status means any social position held by an individual as a result of his or her personal accomplishments in open competition with others. Ascribed status refers to the allocation of roles on the basis of characteristics that are predetermined for the individuals concerned, e.g. kinship, age, sex and ethnicity

stereotype　fixed, general, over-simplified image of what an individual or group is like, allowing for few differences between members of the same group, and often stated in an over-simplified or even erroneous way

stratification　division of society into a hierarchy of unequal social groups who have differential access to material goods and power (e.g. groups defined by class, gender, age and ethnicity)

structuralism　theoretical approach, originating in the study of language (Ferdinand de Saussure), which concentrates on attempting to identify and analyse structures in social and cultural systems

subculture　culture within a culture, with some norms and values exclusive to it and distinct from those of the majority in a society. Though a subgroup's culture will be different in many ways from the main culture, there will also be some aspects of culture that they share

subjectivity　investigation of behaviour which involves the researcher allowing their own experiences and opinions to affect their research (*contrast* objectivity)

subordination　the keeping of an individual or group in an exploited or disadvantaged situation

superstructure　system of structures and ideas that are formed to fit in with the needs of the economy, and to ensure the continuity of a given society (*contrast* economic base)

surplus value　in Marxist theory, the value of an individual's labour power which is 'left over' when an employer has repaid the costs involved in employing the worker, i.e. the profit that is made by paying an individual for fewer hours than the economic value of the hours actually worked

symbolic interactionism　theoretical approach and sociological perspective, developed by G.H. Mead, that emphasises motives and meaning for individuals. It focuses on the importance of symbols for people, particularly language, as the core elements of all human interaction

symmetrical family　family in which the conjugal roles of husband and wife have become more alike and equal

Taylorism　practice of the ideas of F.W. Taylor and his theory of scientific management, whereby the labour process is broken up into its simplest parts (involving simple co-ordination operations in industry), and management controls the pace of work

technological determinism　idea that technological developments direct, in a causal way, developments in industry, the economy and the wider society

Third World   former colonial countries of Africa, Asia, Central and South America and Australasia, based mainly in the southern hemisphere. They are characterised as being less developed than countries of the First World or Second World, with industrial production either virtually non-existent, or only developed to a limited degree. Usually referred to now as developing, or less-developed countries (LDCs); the majority of the world's population live in such countries

time–space convergence   process by which distances become 'shortened' as a result of improvements in transport and communication systems, especially as an aspect of globalisation

totalitarianism   form of government in which everything is under the political control of the State, and opposition is not tolerated; ordinary people lack any control over the decisions of government, which is in the hands of a small group of people, or even an individual (*contrast* democracy, oligarchy)

totemism   system of religious belief which ascribes special and holy significance to particular objects, animals or plants

trade union   employees' organisation formed to protect pay, conditions and rights at work

triangulation   the combined use of quantitative and qualitative research techniques to complement and verify one another, in order to achieve robust research results

underclass   lowest social class, beneath and detached from the working class. This term is rejected by many Marxists, who see this group as merely the most exploited section of the working class. Usually used in relation to ethnic minorities, immigrants, the long-term poor and unemployed, and female single parents

unemployment benefit   in the UK, benefit paid by the State to people who are out of work and qualify for payment of the benefit

universalistic values   values which base the judgement of individuals on meritocratic criteria (e.g. you get a job on the basis of qualifications and suitability) (*contrast* particularistic values)

upper class   social class based on inherited wealth and/or the ownership of large businesses and/or holdings of stocks and shares

urbanisation   development of towns and cities to become major centres of population as people move from rural to urban areas. De-urbanisation is the movement of populations from urban to rural areas

validity   this means the degree to which a research strategy measures what the researcher intends it to measure

values   beliefs and goals held to be important in a society

victimless crime   activity which is defined as criminal, but which only involves an individual (e.g. drug-taking) or has no obvious victim (e.g. bribery, illegal gambling)

wealth   money, and/or property and other fixed assets, held by an individual or social group, which can be sold for the benefit of the owner(s)

Welfare State   arm of the State that deals with the welfare of people through providing education, health care, housing, and support in times of want (such as unemployment). It has been described as the commitment by the State to care for its citizens 'from the cradle to the grave'

white-collar crime   criminal activity committed by those in white-collar or professional jobs, often while performing their job

white-collar worker   non-manual worker, though this term is increasingly used to describe those whose work is non-professional and non-managerial (e.g. clerical or other office work) (*contrast* blue-collar worker)

work   activity by which humans produce from the natural world in order to survive. In traditional societies, money payments for such activities are rare, but in modern societies, such production of goods or services usually receives a wage or salary; however, that performed (mostly by women) in the home (housework) remains unpaid

workers' control   a way of organising a firm whereby the employees make all the major business decisions affecting that firm (*contrast* industrial democracy)

working class   social class comprising those workers who earn their income through manual labour, often referred to as blue-collar workers. In Marxist theory, comprises all people who sell their labour (the proletariat), predominantly blue-collar workers in Marx's lifetime (*see also* proletariat)

Index